THE DYNAMICS
OF ENGLISH
INSTRUCTION

George Hillocks UNIVERSITY OF CHICAGO

Bernard J. McCabe EDUCATIONAL RESEARCH COUNCIL OF AMERICA

James F. McCampbell UNIVERSITY OF CHICAGO

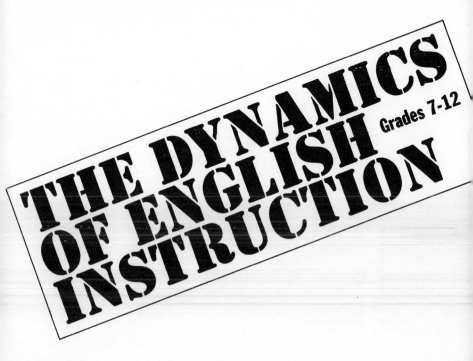

THE DYNAMICS OF ENGLISH INSTRUCTION
Grades 7-12

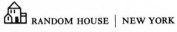

RANDOM HOUSE | NEW YORK

CONSULTING EDITOR **Paul Nash** BOSTON UNIVERSITY

ISBN: 0-394-30208-7

Library of Congress Catalog Card Number: 70-121345

Manufactured in the United States of America by H. Wolff Book Mfg. Co., Inc., New York, N.Y.

First Edition

987654321

to Our Students

CONTENTS

PART TWO
Teaching Literature 135

INTRODUCTION

In the past, secondary school administrators, supervisors of English in the schools, and even some university instructors of English teachers seem to have viewed the English teacher as one who conveys what is in English textbooks. The efforts of administrators and supervisors in in-service training programs have been directed at familiarizing teachers with the content of the literature anthology and grammar book used at each grade level. The methods course has aimed at how to teach "a poem," "a novel," or *Macbeth*. Everyone involved has assumed that the English teacher's chore is that of a middleman who is supposed to convey knowledge from textbook to student. As a result, the English teacher has frequently been no more than a cafeteria attendant dumping equal amounts of the same food on each student's tray, regardless of the student's appetite or inclination.

Fortunately, this stultifying view of the English teacher's role is changing. In the more exciting schools at least, curriculum work is no longer consigned to a small committee that meets one hour a week during the course of a semester in order to choose one or two texts to be used by all students. The more imaginative administrators encourage their teachers to use a wide variety of materials and activities appropriate to a wide range of student needs. Even the unimaginative administrators give lip service to the concept. In many schools department chairman and supervisors involve their teachers in planning new curricula. A few school systems encourage that effort by providing blocks of time each week to be spent on planning in addition to the teacher's traditional "prep" period. The old order changes, even in the public schools.

This book is concerned with the new order, slow though it may be in coming. The book's basic principle is that an English teacher must *plan* his curricula and not simply and arbitrarily assign a story, a composition, or a book report. There is much more to teaching English than making assignments. Assigning tasks is appropriate only when the students already know how to do those tasks. And if the students already know how to do them, what is the point in requiring the performance for its own sake? The real question is how can we teach so that the students learn *how* to do the tasks they cannot already do. How can the English teacher create an environment and a sequence of experiences in which the student becomes increasingly sophisticated as reader, writer, listener, speaker, and, above all, thinker? In other words, how can he create a curriculum that will enable the student to write forcefully and clearly without the aid of his English teacher's red pencil and to comprehend a poem without the benefit of the teacher's interpretation?

This question subsumes several other important questions. First, how can a teacher know where to begin with the particular students in his classes? The fact that students have been labeled twelfth graders is no reason to believe that the twelfth-grade literature anthology represents the most appropriate curriculum for them. Second, once the teacher knows what his students can do when they enter his class, how does he decide what to teach them next? The textbook is not likely to provide a useful answer. Yet the answer is crucial. Since any given class will represent a wide range of skill and background, the teacher must answer a third question: How can he organize his teaching so that it is appropriate to each of his students? Finally, how can he evaluate the effectiveness of his instruction? Most teachers concern themselves only with evaluating the students—that is, assigning them grades—as though the teachers themselves and what they do in the classroom were above evaluation. Clearly, the difference between evaluating students and determining the effectiveness of instruction is significant.

These questions and related ones are the province of this book. They must be answered if English instruction is to be dynamic rather than static. If we (prospective and experienced teachers) face the questions squarely and attempt to answer them, perhaps the old order will pass entirely. Perhaps the image of the English teacher as a cafeteria attendant will disappear.

Arriving at Answers

One can derive answers to the questions cited above through intuition, the experimental trial of alternatives, various kinds of theories, or through some combination of these approaches.

Intuition

Intuition might be defined as knowing something without knowing how we came to learn it. It is governed, in part, by the workings of the unconscious mind and, in part, by experience. Everyone possesses intuition. For some it is a very powerful tool, for others it only seems powerful. What is intuitively obvious to some is often obscure to others. Some people get good results by following their intuition. But for others, following intuition may result in catastrophe.

If a teacher likes Poe and feels his class will like Poe, he might teach a unit on Poe in an unstructured way and have great success, doing things mainly by feel. But because he is unable to pass on his personal insights, his experience is not generally useful to his colleagues.

On the other hand, faulty intuition has led many a teacher astray. A teacher who notices that his students make many mistakes in their use of pronouns may, intuitively, reach for the school grammar and teach a series of lessons on pronouns. Some individual teachers may have met with some success using this intuitive procedure, but many more have not. Their sad experiences are documented extensively in educational research.

Intuition cannot be disregarded. Many aspects of experimental design are intuitive—for example, determining what to experiment on in the first place. The selection of elements in a theory rests on intuition about what is central and important in experience. A large part of philosophical thought deals with how to make intuitions objective—in the basic area of formulating definitions, for example. The problem is that although intuition may be reliable for some, it is not generally reliable for most. Still, good intuitions are to be cherished rather than scorned.

Experiment

Intuitions are subjective and internal whereas experiments are objective and external. Ideally, experiment should produce the best curricula. In a carefully worked out experimental design, there will be no guesswork. Empirical investigation relies upon a critical appraisal of evidence of the senses in which the results are derived by only such thinking as the mathematical kind. Such methods minimize the chance of failure from "human" causes: subjective, qualitative judgments and the like. Unfortunately, empirical methods don't eliminate failure.

Although systematic experiment may be the soundest way to develop curricula, few curricula are based on experimental findings to any significant degree. The trouble is that with any teaching-learning problem beyond the level of teaching pigeons to open doors or peck at circles the variables involved are impossible to control. Think of the difficulties involved in experimenting to determine the most efficient method of teaching students to write a relatively simple verse form like the limerick. First, is it more efficient to lecture on the characteristics of the form or to have the students discover them inductively for themselves? The experimenter will need two matched groups of students to control that condition. Second, should the students examine a model limerick or not? To control for that condition, the number of matched groups must be increased to three: one lecture with a model, one lecture without a model, and one inductive group with a model. (By definition, an inductive group without a model is impossible.) A third important question is whether the students should learn about rhyme in the same lesson or in a previous lesson. To introduce that condition doubles the number of matched groups to six. There are many other necessary learnings to consider: scansion, the humorous effects, and so on. Every condition introduced doubles the number of matched groups, so that two more conditions would require a total of twenty-four matched groups.

There are many reasons to explain why curricula are rarely, if ever, developed through rigorous empirical methods:

1. Many of the learnings that might constitute the curriculum content are extremely complex, unlike the limerick, which is relatively trivial and easy to describe. As the task increases in complexity, it becomes extremely difficult to describe the desired learning in a rigorous way.

2. As the learning task increases in complexity, the number of alternative conditions increases. Matching the required groups in a rigorous way is extremely difficult. With even a small number of alternative conditions, many schools or school systems would not find enough groups available. In situations where *homogeneous groupings* are used, another condition is added to the problem. Which conditions pertain directly to groups of different types?

3. Introducing such variables as alternative texts used as central materials complicates things tremendously. In dealing with learning to write any prose form, for example, consider the number of available models alone, not to speak of the critical texts that discuss the models.

4. It takes a great deal of time to prepare and evaluate experiments. Meanwhile, school does not stop. It is necessary to have some kind of program going while the experiments are being designed, carried out, and evaluated.

5. Finally, the teacher variable must be considered. Operationally, teacher comfort in the use of any methods or materials can make a great difference in results. Thus, it is necessary to match not only students but teachers.

Of course, all this is not to say that the English teacher should ignore research in general. When adequate research is available, he should make use of it in his formulation of curricula—for example, the research on the teaching of vocabulary and on the relationship between knowledge of grammar and ability to write. The point here is that the experimental trial of alternatives as a means of developing curricula is almost hopelessly complex and time-consuming.

Theory

The third general method of curriculum development is to base curriculum practice on one or more theories. The term "theory" is used here in its technical sense. It does not mean nebulous thinking or guesswork. Rather, it means rigorously developed and stated formulations that begin in experience

—that is, in the careful, often experimental, examination of experiences, which are treated as data in a scientific way.

These data are then analyzed, and a hypothesis is formed. The statement of the hypothesis is a rather general and abstract one about the fundamental characteristics of the data and the relationships that exist among them. Furthermore, if the hypothesis is applied to new data, it should predict the characteristics of the new data and the kinds of relationships existing among them.

When the hypothesis has been repeatedly tested against new observations and is found to predict accurately the characteristics and relationships, it is at last promoted to the rank of theory. If later observations are made that seem to contradict the theory, *they* are at first thought to be suspect, not the theory. Theory is not a euphemism for guesswork.

Today, when the English teacher faces a number of competing theories on English curricula he may select for his guidance the one that he finds to be the most satisfactory. In making the selection, a model for theory evaluation is useful:

1. Any educational theory must have comprehensive explanatory power. For example, since much of learning is internal, the theory must deal with internalizations in some way. If the theory states that internalizations are unimportant or only hypothetical—or even nonexistent—this qualification has been fulfilled. If the theory ignores internalizations, it lacks explanatory power, by definition. In addition to discussing internalizations in some way, it must discuss empirically observable behaviors and the results of such behaviors (such as finished compositions).

2. A theory must be applicable to every observation of any datum. A theory of reading, for example, must discuss all kinds of reading: looking up numbers in a telephone book as well as reading E. E. Cummings' poetry, James Joyce's prose, and stock market reports.

3. The theory must be able to predict the character of data as yet undiscovered. A theory of spelling, for example, must state how words not yet in the language will be spelled when they are introduced into the language. Ideally, the theory will predict what cannot occur as well as what may occur.

4. The structure of the theory is important. If it is constructed in terms of levels, all the elements at a given level must be conceptual parallels. For a capricious but clear example, imagine a theory of "house architecture": Windows and doors could occur on the same level because they are conceptual parallels: wallpaper and roof timbers, not being conceptual parallels, could not occur on the same level.

5. When a number of theories appear to satisfy the foregoing criteria equally well and when the teacher must make a priority decision, he should choose the simplest one for his guidance. At one point in history, astronomers were faced with such a choice in dealing with "cosmological" theories presented by the Ptolemaic and Copernican schools of astronomy. Reliance on the simplicity criterion would have resulted in the better choice—the

Copernican theory—as it was by far the simpler; ultimately, as better observational and analytical techniques were developed, the theory was shown to be better in other respects. A further lesson from history in this regard: as even more observations and analyses were developed, the Copernican theory was supplanted by theories with more comprehensive explanatory power.

The value of theory for curriculum development resides in the saving of time and energy. If curriculum development is not theoretically based, one recourse is to develop it along empirical lines, an almost impossible task. Should both these approaches be ignored, and the curriculum be developed intuitively, the best result that one can legitimately hope for is a curriculum that will satisfy the biases of those whose intuitions are used as a basis for the curriculum. Intuitive curriculum makers must hope for sound intuitions.

Although a teacher's thinking may be controlled by theories of course content and instruction (both are necessary), his curriculum work may be weak, either in the stage of its formulation or its actual operation. The weakness can stem from any or all of three reasons: (1) a misunderstanding of the formulation of the theory, (2) an intellectual or operational misapplication of the theory, or (3) a fundamental lack of power of the theory itself.

It would be nice if a person could sit quietly and, in a contemplative way, carefully construct all the necessary theoretic paraphernalia that he needs. It would be nicer still if good theories were developed through quick and special insights of the kind that we have been led to believe Newton enjoyed. The apple falls on the head: Gravity! The ruler falls on the floor: Instruction! Sad to say, most of us are gifted neither with special contemplative power nor with the ability to receive special revelations. We must rely, instead, on careful observations of phenomena and careful analysis of our observations. This may be a laborious process.

Certainly, in most cases, a sound theory will require, at the least, years in its formulation. Observations of new phenomena and development of new analytic techniques will result in the continuous reassessment of the theoretic formulations. Although theoretic work is tiresome and a certain amount of trial-and-error is inescapable, reliance on trial-and-error alone does a disservice to both teacher and student. The error constituent of trial-and-error, if not irreversible in learning, is almost certainly ineradicable.

Although the teacher can mentally cross off error-producing situations and structures in his teaching as they affect his future work and chalk them up to "experience," the student will be burdened by the error. Although it could result merely in his failure to integrate into the patterns of his school, it could have profoundly pernicious consequences throughout his life.

As Homer Macauley's mother said in *The Human Comedy,* "Schools are only to keep children off the street, but sooner or later they've got to go out into the streets, whether they like to or not." It seems to us that teachers should send their students into the streets in the best shape possible.

The Organization of This Book

For the reasons suggested above, this book moves from theory to practice. The chapters in the first section present aspects of a theory of instruction as well as a number of specific lessons, units of instruction, and specific teaching procedures. These chapters discuss various aspects of planning and classroom operation from an examination of English as a subject of study to the underlying concepts that should guide the teacher in deciding what to teach, and, finally, to the ways in which the teacher can evaluate his instruction.

Sections II, III, and IV on teaching literature, language, and composition, respectively, proceed from a consideration of the traditions in each area to a discussion of the philosophical and theoretical ideas that underlie the specific suggestions about instruction. The theoretical chapters are an important aspect of the book because, without a theoretical base, a teacher will be unable to generate systematic instructional plans for the variety of students he is likely to encounter. Instead, he will have to rely on guesswork or on some commercial source of lessons that may or may not be appropriate to the students in his classes.

Several fully developed units of instruction have been included. Their inclusion should not suggest, however, that they can be used widely without adaptation, although some teachers may be able to use them in their classrooms with only minor revisions. They are intended as models for the creation of other units. Most of them indicate a grade level at which they might be used, but all but two of them can be used at any one of several grade levels, depending on the students. The "Animals in Literature" unit in Chapter 4 is probably only appropriate for seventh or eighth grades. The "Black Protest" unit in Chapter 15 should probably be limited to the eleventh or twelfth grade in most schools, although it has been used successfully with advanced ninth graders. Other units such as "Satire" can be adapted for use at several grade levels by adjusting the objectives and materials, as explained in Chapter 12. In addition to full instructional units, the text contains a large number of detailed lessons and suggestions for lessons.

The book as a whole may be approached through the specific instructional materials or through the theoretical chapters. But eventually, the theory and practice sections must be examined in relationship to each other.

Acknowledgments

We are grateful to Dr. Henry C. Meckel of San Jose State College in California for his initial suggestion and encouragement to write this book and to Dr. James R. Squire, then Executive Secretary of NCTE, for his encouragement as we undertook the project. Dr. Bernard O'Donnell's close reading of the manuscript and his extremely perceptive comments have been invaluable. He has saved us from many grievous blunders. Any that remain should be attributed to the authors.

In addition to their patient listening to long discussions about the teaching of English, their typing and proofreading, and their comments on the manuscript, our wives have played a special role in the production of this book. They have been patient when we were grouchy, understanding when we were discouraged, and nagging when we were lazy. What can we say but thanks?

We owe special thanks to the many teachers who worked with us over the years as the theories and materials that constitute this book were developed and evaluated and to the great number around the country who adapted the ideas and materials for use in their classrooms and reported the results to us. One group must be singled out: the teachers who helped in developing materials used at the Project English Demonstration Center at Euclid Central School in Euclid, Ohio, and Case-Western Reserve University, especially Miss Jane Barber, Mr. Michael C. Flanigan, Mr. Jack L. Granfield, Mr. John C. Ingersoll, and Mrs. Betty Lou Miller; and Mr. Gary Elliot of Newton, Massachusetts.

In a very real sense, however, this book does not belong to us. It belongs to our students at every level from whom we have learned a great deal, sometimes at their expense, about the dynamics of English instruction.

THE DYNAMICS
OF ENGLISH
INSTRUCTION

Elements of Instruction

In order to do his most effective classroom teaching, a teacher must plan his work carefully. Before he can begin planning, he must have given thought to the character of the discipline of English as a field of study, and he must have precise information about his students.

The first chapter of this section begins by examining the discipline of English in terms of traditional teaching styles and the instructional viewpoint implied by each style, and then sets limits to the field of English studies.

The second chapter discusses the methods that the teacher uses in getting information about his students' attitudes, skills and knowledge. The most useful method of getting this information is through employing inventories that he develops.

When he characterizes his students in terms of individual attitudes, skills, and knowledge, he will find that there are many differences among them. The third chapter presents a number of techniques that may be used in differentiating instruction.

The fourth chapter analyzes the components of the formal planning of individual lessons and longer units of instruction, specifying the distinctions between the teacher's purposes, subject matter concepts, and the students' objectives in learning.

Chapter 5 describes inductive teaching, demonstrating techniques of questioning, leading discussions, and encouraging interaction among students and teachers.

The final chapter of the section considers the many kinds of evaluation the teacher must make including test development, the assessment of affective responses to the instruction, and the broader appraisal of the course content.

1 English As a Subject: Structure and Process

Before an English teacher can determine what his students are like in relation to his subject, and before he can decide how to teach them, he must answer an important question. What is the subject of English? Many teachers never answer the question in an explicit, coherent fashion. Many simply accept the dictates of tradition, a fad of the moment, or a particular personal bias. But the question should be answered for the benefit of both teacher and student. The school principals of the world will not obtain materials for teachers without at least a superficial answer. And if a faculty has not answered the question, the students in their school may have an English program with almost no continuity at all. If you were to spend your professional leave day visiting Point Tipia High School, you would be likely to see a number of approaches to English teaching, each based upon a different philosophy of English. The word "philosophy" is used loosely. The bases for many approaches are more appropriately described as a set of beliefs collected from a variety of sources.

Begin at one end of the English corridor in Point Tipia High School and observe some of the teachers. First in line is Miss Soma, who teaches ninth graders and believes that nothing is more important than that the youngsters enjoy their work. Reading, she believes, should be fun. Her students recently studied *Treasure Island,* and Miss Soma feels they enjoyed it very much. Before they had even read the book, she told them that *Treasure Island* was about a hidden treasure and asked what they knew about pirates. A brief dialogue ensued in which the students talked freely of the films they had seen. Next, Miss Soma announced that the class would have a treasure hunt. The students elected a pirate committee to hide the treasure (candy bars) and make maps providing clues. Highly motivated, the committee spent a good deal of time in these activities, and after they were completed, the rest of the class spent three periods seeking the treasure.

4

According to Miss Soma, the whole activity was very successful. Then the class began reading *Treasure Island.* As they read, they periodically answered such questions as the following: What do you think of Long John Silver? What was the black spot? Why were the pirates so superstitious? When they had completed their reading, they worked on various projects, such as making elaborate treasure maps, writing out a ship's log for the voyage, and building model ships and stockades.

Miss Soma is presently planning a unit on mythology in which the students will collect words and trade names in current use that come from mythological sources. They will also make posters of the gods and scenes of Olympus. At the end of the unit they will have a party, with each student dressing as some mythical figure.

Mrs. Baugh, who teaches tenth graders, believes that literature is of little value if it is not relevant to the lives of the students. *Treasure Island* she would not touch with a ten-foot pole. She begins the year by getting students to list and then to examine their problems, a process that takes anywhere from one to four weeks. The students then decide which problems they would most like to investigate. The favorites have always been grades, dope addiction, dating, sex, juvenile delinquency, segregation, and, most recently, psychedelics. Once the students have chosen their first topic, they go to the library and begin doing research with the *Reader's Guide* and other research tools. Meantime, Mrs. Baugh seeks out relevant stories, poem, novels, and biographical materials. The topic of delinquency, for example, turns up such perennial favorites as *Hot Rod, Road Rocket,* and *West Side Story.* For dating she finds plenty of adolescent books, especially for girls. Sex offers certain problems as a topic for study.

The students enjoy the approach, and once they get going, they talk volubly about their own experiences and those of their friends. Each unit is capped off by group reports, panels, and so on.

Mr. Roper is a tenth- and twelfth-grade teacher. It has been his belief for years that students need to be exposed to the great literary works of our culture. He believes that if they don't get them in high school, they may never have another opportunity. Therefore, in the tenth grade he teaches *Ivanhoe* and *Julius Caesar* and in the twelfth grade *The Return of the Native* and *Macbeth,* and he includes as many other great works as possible. Although a few students—those who are the best all-around students in school—seem to appreciate the materials, there are times when most of them do not. Mr. Roper is convinced, however, that someday all will thank him. Someday they will recall the great moments of literature and that knowledge may give them strength in moments of crisis. If they do not like Shakespeare now, they will later.

Because the students frequently do not read their assignments, Mr. Roper makes a practice of giving weekly quizzes—sometimes even two or three in one week. They are usually short-answer quizzes, which are intended to keep students on their toes. To be absolutely sure that students read the assignments, Mr. Roper covers them in class after each quiz, sometimes with each student reading a paragraph aloud until the end of the hour.

At the twelfth-grade level; the emphasis is on English literature. Mr. Roper explains each author's life and times, and the students read three or four selections from that author. They receive what he believes to be a thorough coverage of English literature from *Beowulf* (of which they read a brief passage) to World War I. By the end of the year, he expects them to know who Chaucer, Wordsworth, Keats, and the other authors were, what they wrote, and when they lived. He also expects them to be able to recall, in full, certain passages that he has assigned for memorization. This approach, he believes, prepares students not only for college but for life.

Miss Grimis, who has taught the tenth and twelfth grades for years, emphatically believes that students need to learn to use their language, not simply adequately, but forcefully and gracefully. Yet she has a fear that she is failing despite her long and strenuous labor. She notes with dismay that each day radio announcers, TV personalities, newspaper and magazine writers, not to mention the common workingman, continue to degrade the language. She is determined, however, that her students will learn better. Even if they fail to carry what they have learned beyond the walls of the classroom, at least her classroom itself will remain a sanctuary for the language as it should be. So her tenth graders labor for half the school year over such niceties as the correct past tense form of "lie," the split infinitive, and the agreement of pronouns with such antecedents as "everyone" and "somebody." They fill page after page of notebook paper with sentence diagrams in order to rid their compositions of the despised pair: run-on sentences and fragments of sentences.

One of Miss Grimis' special pleasures is watching her students improve in this respect. Though not many eliminate run-ons and fragments completely, at least such atrocities become somewhat rarer during the course of the school year. However, she does not ordinarily recognize the corresponding change that comes in reduced sentence length and complexity. But if she did, she would argue that students should not be allowed to write long sentences unless they can write them correctly. It is quite obvious to her that one cannot really communicate without the fundamental skills she teaches in tenth-grade grammar.

Despite what the research says, Miss Grimis is confident that she is using the right approach. What she finds rather frustrating, however, is having to teach so much grammar all over again to the same students in the twelfth grade. She has a rather strong suspicion that certain of the other tenth-grade teachers do not know grammar themselves—or at least they don't use it correctly. But she knows, in fact, that Mr. Slide and Mr. Goodrich have admitted quite publicly in the teacher's lounge that they teach no grammar at all.

Although Miss Grimis is quite right about Mr. Goodrich, she has misunderstood Mr. Slide's position. He believes heartily in what he calls "practical English" or sometimes "everyday English." He knows from experience that students abhor grammar of the diagram and fill-in-the-blank-with-the-correct-form varieties. He knows too that they are bored by most American literature in the anthology as well as by *The Scarlet Letter* and other "nineteenth-century stuff" that most eleventh graders are expected to read. He admits that there are a few who can handle it, but they are exceptional, indeed. He argues the importance of English in everyday life and builds his course to teach his students the essentials of reading and writing. They learn to fill out job applications and to write business letters and letters to the editors of nonexistent newspapers. They write short reports on hobbies and mechanical processes—in short, they do writing that is calculated to be useful in everyday situations.

Mr. Slide's treatment of grammar is essentially practical. When his students make a certain kind of error, he selects several compositions that illustrate the error, makes transparencies for projection, and throws them upon the screen for the students to examine. To Mr. Slide it seems to be a perfectly logical technique. Show the students the error in their own work so that they won't make it anymore. He finds it frustrating, however, that students apparently don't pay attention, that some who didn't make the error before make it afterward and that those whose papers were the actual subjects of criticism continue to make the same errors.

The class's reading comes largely from magazines and newspapers. As for fiction, Mr. Slide feels that boys far prefer *The Bridge over the River Kwai* to *The Scarlet Letter.* He devotes little time to poetry, although when he can find them, he uses poems about sports and adventure. Mr. Slide contends that poetry is not practical for these students who will later work a forty-hour week and spend their leisure at the corner tavern or in front of the TV set.

Mr. Goodrich, who teaches tenth and eleventh grade English, although he agrees with Mr. Slide on some issues, disagrees rather strongly on others. One of his favorite remarks is that human beings are more important than the aesthetic structure of a poem or grammatical formalities. He holds that literature, because of what it reveals about the human condition, must be the heart of an English program. His concern is with people—both his students and the people in the books they read. He feels, for instance, that his students need to understand the problems of American society. Therefore, he builds his units of instruction around such motifs or themes as the black power movement. Feeling that there are certain values that his students ought to have, he presents them through the medium of literature. Of course, it is always difficult to tell whether student values and attitudes actually change, but Mr. Goodrich assumes that they should be changed and hopes that his teaching will help to accomplish this.

The compositions that Mr. Goodrich's students write grow out of the problems they have been reading about. The assignment he regards as most successful is the one that the students write in response to the question, What would happen if a Negro family moved into your neighborhood? In telling colleagues about this topic, he notes that the students always have something to say about it, and what they have to say, of course, is his primary concern. He ignores errors in grammar and spelling, for he has found that marking the errors frequently results in far less sophisticated expression. As he takes a certain pleasure in observing in front of Miss Grimis, "There is really no point in emphasizing grammar in the eleventh grade. Kids who write grammatically correct papers, usually have nothing to say, and their expression is weak. Besides, if they haven't learned it by the end of the tenth grade, how can I teach it to them in a single year?"

Perhaps this profile of an English faculty is a bit exaggerated. Perhaps not each of the stereotypes would exist in a single school. But within many a school system, we can find them all and more. The group obviously has little in common, except that each member calls himself an English teacher. Although each teacher's instruction has some clearly admirable characteristics, the differences are so fundamental that no one of them can be considered completely adequate.

Miss Soma's desire to have all the students enjoy their work is clearly commendable, but whether her students do, in fact, enjoy the games they play or the materials they read is not so clear. Further, her objective is to have the students read individual works and know their content rather than to structure the lessons in such a way that the students learn more about how to read literature.

Mrs. Baugh is also concerned that her students be interested in what they read—that the materials be directly relevant to their personal lives—and for many students this is very important. But she ignores one important aspect of literature, its ability to take the reader out of his immediate confines and expand and intensify his sensitivity to the human situation. Again, as with Miss Soma, there is a question as to whether her choice and arrangement of materials enable the students to learn how to read literature. Although her students read *Hot Rod* and *Seventeenth Summer* with interest, many had read them or similar books years before with the same interest and understanding. In mathematics a similar technique would be patently absurd—that is, no arithmetic teacher would continue to give his students a type of multiplication problem that they had already learned to do adequately. Instead, he would take them on to a more difficult kind of multiplication or to division. It would be possible to ask some sophisticated questions about the rhetoric, structure, or aesthetic value of *Seventeenth Summer,* but Mrs. Baugh does not appear to have considered that possibility.

Mr. Roper, on the other hand, has very little concern for student interest. His motivating devices are tests and grades. Although he is aware of the humanistic values of literature, his arbitrary ordering of materials has little to do with the human beings in his classes. If he were asked to define his curriculum, he would list the authors or works he requires his students to read and explain that the arrangement is designed to reflect what he calls the "development of English literature," an arrangement that places some of the most difficult material (John Donne, for example) early in the year and the easier material (Somerset Maugham) later in the year. He realizes that many of his students have difficulty in getting even the literal meanings of the works he assigns; they get low grades. Many others are not capable of interpreting what they read. "Still," he says confidently, "if they pay attention to class discussion and to what I say, they will pass the exams." If anyone asked, Mr. Roper would certainly say he wanted his students to read and interpret literature without his help, but his methods and his exams suggest his real concern: that his students display an understanding of the works he assigns and discusses. If and when he accomplishes this, he believes his duty to preserve the students' cultural heritage is complete. When he fails, as he does with many students, he attributes it to their stupidity.

No English teacher would argue with Miss Grimis' stated goal for her students: to use the language forcefully and gracefully. But what she means by the words "forcefully" and "gracefully" is certainly open to question. Whatever she may mean ideally, her practice reveals that, for her, language can be neither graceful nor forceful if it is not first "correct," correct in the sense that it uses the forms prescribed by the grammar book. Yet we cannot escape the fact that the language of a nonstandard dialect can be forceful in inciting to riot, that the dialect of an illiterate can be poignant and graceful in lamenting the death of a child. But even if her premises were right, her methodology cannot change dialect patterns in oral language. And if it brings the prescribed forms to written language, a concomitant effect is a change to oversimplicity in the effort to be "correct."

Mr. Slide's goal—meeting the vocational needs of his students—is certainly important. Unfortunately, because it is his only goal, English becomes merely another job-training class and loses its traditional liberalizing function. The reading of books becomes perfunctory, the writing of compositions simply utilitarian. The students read what they enjoy reading—what they can probably already read with little effort—and no real instruction takes place. The "practical" goal that Mr. Slide has established embodies a widespread belief that a certain breed of student is capable of, and interested in, little else than vocational training. But what can we expect of those students when the alternatives they most frequently encounter are those offered by Mr. Roper and Miss Grimis?

Mr. Goodrich's course is based on his conviction that literature has a liberalizing value and that it therefore should be used to develop values and change attitudes. Unquestionably, literature does have the power to develop and change attitudes, to give insight into aspects of the human condition, and to help us know how it feels to be someone else. In making use of this power, however, Mr. Goodrich assumes that his students have the facility to gain from a book or poem whatever is there to be gained. If they do not, he assumes they can get it from class discussion, an assumption that both he and Mr. Roper hold. Further, he ignores the necessity for a critical and aesthetic evaluation of what his students read. The particular works that they read were chosen because he believes that they should approve the underlying ideologies. In short, Mr. Goodrich, like many other teachers, is not vitally and specifically concerned with helping his students to become sophisticated, independent readers who are capable of making their own judgments about the values reflected in what they read.

Many teachers assume either that their students are already competent readers or that they simply need to read books, poems, and other works in some order—chronological, interest-oriented, theme-oriented, and so on—in order to become competent. Very seldom is the order of the assigned reading related directly to either the ability of the students or a careful analysis of how literature has meaning.

The same is true of composition. Too many teachers assume that learning to write is simply a function of learning grammar of one kind or another and writing compositions every week or two. The only instruction in these cases consists of assigning, collecting, and correcting. Ordinarily, the teacher has made no analysis of the composing process as a whole, from the urge to write to the final product. Without an analysis of what composition is, Miss Grimis ignores the voluminous research that demonstrates the negligible effect a knowledge of traditional school grammar has on writing ability. Although the overhead projector can be a very effective tool for teaching, the projection of errors is better suited to teaching the error than eliminating it.

Clearly, a list of works or authors with composition assignments is an inadequate description of what English teaching is all about. Nor is a list comprised of work-attack skills, dictionary skills, usage items, and writing conventions an adequate basis for instruction. If we are to construct a curriculum for English, and every English teacher must do so for each of his classes, we must ask and attempt to answer a very basic question: What should our instruction attempt to do for each student?

Even though our six teachers are so much at variance in their approaches to teaching English, they would probably say they were concerned with the apprehension and interpretation of values as conveyed in language. Certainly each examines with his classes the values and ideas reflected in what they read, and occasionally in what they hear. Ultimately, this may be what the teaching of English is all about.

In the context of solar history, perhaps our moment is even more brief than Shakespeare supposed it to be. But our lives are real. We do endure for a measurable space of time, and most of us must believe that we have some significance, at least in terms of our relationships with others. Our values and ideas shape our lives out of animal existences, influence our attitudes toward ourselves and our perceptions of the world, and determine the happiness, integrity, and even the humanity of others. To English teachers, the problem of values has a special significance. They are the experts on language in our culture; and language is the subtle shaper and inescapable vehicle of value systems.

History affords ample instances of how well-chosen language can program the values of the few into the many—the many who cannot control the language and who are unable to determine its effects. In a technological society, which is closer to *1984* than we might wish to believe, the necessity for a clear understanding of language is amplified a thousandfold.

To a certain degree, each man unavoidably sees himself as the center of existence. His language is a primary means of gaining perspective on his egocentricity and insight into the existence of others. Accordingly, language develops and shifts values.

From before the time of the cave paintings and petroglyphs, man has communicated through nonverbal means. In this century electronic media have made much of nonverbal aspects of communication. Still, it remains for language to translate and interpret the meanings conveyed by nonverbal means. Language is still our most significant means of understanding, of thinking, of organizing our perceptions, of being and becoming men.

The Structure of the Subject

It is not the responsibility of the English teacher to impose ideas and values but to help his students understand how language works, cognitively, affectively, and aesthetically so that they can examine the values that are conveyed and shaped by language and can use language to formulate, synthesize, and evaluate their own values.

The first step in planning to reach this goal is to consider how people use language. Each normal person is both a receiver and an originator of language. In order to perform either function well, he must also be an interpreter of language meanings. As a receiver, he is both listener and reader; as an originator, he is both speaker and writer. All four of these functions are concerned with language that is external. The fifth function, that of interpretation or analysis, is primarily internal, working with language that has been received and designing language that will be expressed.

Obviously, neither the reception nor the production of language is simply a mechanical process. Philip Wylie once defined the American school as an "organism which teaches reading and writing . . . so that the pupil can communicate." To this he added the admonition that "these accomplishments should also be taught so that the pupil can think. . . ."[1] Whatever else we might think about Wylie, we must applaud this distinction, though we might prefer a different phrasing: Reading, writing, listening, and speaking *must* be taught in conjunction with thinking. We cannot afford the mechanical production or reception of ideas. This internal function of language—the thinking process—should be of pressing concern to the English teacher. In our culture, thinking cannot be divorced from language except momentarily and in minor ways. Thus, the English teacher, as an expert on language, cannot confine himself to the traditional quadrivium of language arts skills (reading, writing, listening, and speaking); he must be dynamically concerned with the thinking processes that lie beneath them, with the identification and validation of ideas and value systems. At the same time these internal processes present the greatest difficulty and frustration, for *there is absolutely no way to observe the processes themselves.* The best we can do is to examine the external language that the student receives or produces. From this evidence and the evidence of our own experience, we can infer the internal processes of thinking.

Our examination of this evidence must attempt to answer two important questions: (1) *How does language convey meaning, cognitively, affectively, and aesthetically to the reader or listener?* and (2) *What aspects of the composing process and product must the writer or speaker be aware of and make use of? The answers to these questions lend structure to the subject matter.* Without them we cannot define, except vaguely, the goals of English instruction and must confine our teaching to random reading and writing assignments that are ordered by the seasons of the year, chronology, what the teacher hopes are the students' interests, or perhaps by nothing at all. Moreover, we cannot make instruction appropriate to both subject and student, for we have no way of determining what he already knows of the subject and no basis for deciding what to teach him next. But once we have determined the structure of the subject, we can help the student to understand how the language works and how to use it.

Thinking signifies conscious processes, and one clear reason for studying English in a formal setting is to bring external language under conscious control. In a democratic society we cannot justify teaching students to react to language unconsciously or to produce it unconsciously. This does *not* mean, however, that we must eliminate subconsciously derived reactions to, or expressions of, language but rather that we must help students to examine their reactions and ideas consciously. Readers often badly misinterpret what they read or hear because of some subconscious reaction that they assume is adequate. For example, it is common to hear adults dismiss movies or books with a pejorative comment or two that, too frequently, are the result of automatic, unexamined reactions. On the other hand, readers frequently have brilliant insights into the meaning or structure of a poem through a process that can only be called intuition. Certainly, such an intuition is worthy of conscious analysis and examination. A poet may have a compulsion to write a line, a stanza, or a whole poem, but, once written, he typically does not leave it unexamined and unrevised. The compulsive and intuitive, those understandings that emerge mysteriously from the subconscious, cannot and should not be disregarded.

The challenge for the English teacher is to give his students a solid understanding of the structure and meaning of language and, at the same time, to enable them to make the most sophisticated use of their intuitions by examining and evaluating them against that background. The intuition of a student who has the background to approach a language experience at all its levels of significance will be far more relevant, meaningful, and extensive than that of one who is unaware of all but the most obvious aspects of his language experience.

Students, Goals, and Process

One immense stumbling block in teaching English is the conflict between liberal and vocational goals, the conflict existing between the philosophy of a Mr. Roper who forces the same literature upon everyone and that of a Mr. Slide who uses literature to train his students in vocational skills. To some extent the conflict exists in every English teacher. On the one hand, he wants his students to have the skills necessary for survival and advancement in the workaday world; on the other, he wants them to enjoy literature and benefit from its liberalizing capabilities. The conflict, however, exists more in the mind of the teacher than it does in the needs of the students. It arises ordinarily because a teacher views the study of literature as distinct from the more basic skills of simple literacy, when, in fact, they are both part of the same process.

Although a degree of literacy may not be essential for physical survival in our culture, most nonliterates tend to live at a subsistence level compared to what we have come to believe is an acceptable standard. Their families disintegrate, their life expectancy is short, their children can have little hope for the future. Think of their limitations. They cannot read the labels of food packages and therefore cannot spend money on food intelligently. They are unable to pass driving tests in most states. They cannot read legal contracts or the conditions of credit under which they make purchases. In short, although they may survive, they can have no real integration with the culture.

Learning to read and write will not cure all the problems of poverty, but it at least helps to disintegrate the barriers that otherwise confine nonliterates. This basic literacy should be regarded as a minimal goal by the schools: enough skill at reading and writing to pass a driver's test, to read package labels, to enter into simple contracts, to fill out forms, to follow simple directions, and so on. Subsistence level skills such as these at least permit the person to operate intelligently and flexibly within the economic spheres of the culture.

Yet because these minimal skills are oriented toward subsistence in the world of jobs and money, teachers often regard them as essentially foreign to English as a subject. But if we realize that a student cannot proceed to sophisticated listening, speaking, reading, and writing without the most basic language skills, it becomes clear that they are integral to the highest goals for the study of English.

It is not so easy, however, to define the highest goals. In one sense, defining a maximum suggests setting an arbitrary limit, and our ultimate goal should be infinite. For our purposes, it is enough to say that the highest goal should involve an understanding of the structure of the subject in the fullest sense of its cognitive, affective, and aesthetic dimensions and an ability to use those understandings.

Knowing the structure of the subject enables us to determine increasingly sophisticated student goals, beginning with those aspects of understanding closest to the students' current ability and leading ideally to the most advanced understanding of which they are capable. With appropriate instruction, the student should move as far as possible along the continuum, through the subsistence level skills to the humanistic study of language, literature, and composition.

This process by which the student learns to cope with the structure of English as listener, speaker, reader, and writer will necessarily involve a special emphasis on the study of written language. Yet the experience of oral language is also extremely important, for two reasons. First, the more limited a student's oral language the more difficult a time he will have with written language. Second, many of the learnings about written language will be developed and evaluated orally, so that *considerable time will be devoted to oral activities.* The reciprocal relationship of understanding oral language to understanding the written is obvious. Learnings in the one support learnings in the other.

Too often the English teacher is the only person in the class who expresses himself with any frequency. But if a teacher wishes his students to become more sophisticated in their dealings with language, he must create an environment that includes materials, problems, situations, and even seating arrangements in which each student can express his ideas and react freely to the ideas of others. Such an environment, of course, requires careful planning.

The Materials of English

If the teacher's goal is to have his students understand and use language at increasing levels of sophistication, he must be concerned with the materials and concepts he will use to achieve it. As mentioned earlier, the content of an English curriculum is frequently viewed simply as a list of titles, authors, or concepts. To Mr. Roper, for example, it was the list of works his students were required to read. In such an approach, the student's recall of the contents of the works is of primary importance. Mr. Roper, like many of the other teachers discussed, does not design his instruction so that his students will learn to handle new problems independently. Nor are the problems of student ability, skills development, and appropriate goals and materials ever considered.

In selecting materials, therefore, the teacher should avoid the use of arbitrary lists. Instead, he must consider (1) the ultimate goal of helping his students to understand how language works cognitively, affectively, and aesthetically and to use that knowledge; and (2) the current level of the students' sophistication. In other words, the teacher should set appropriate goals in light of the students' current abilities and select the materials that will help them to meet those goals. If he chooses either concepts or materials for which the students have not had adequate preparation, they will benefit very little from the instruction. For instance, if a class has difficulty making simple inferences about characters, they obviously will be unable to make the inferences required by a symbolic poem. On the other hand, if the teacher chooses a relatively simple book for a group of fairly bright students—say, *Hot Rod* for above-average tenth graders—they may read and enjoy the book, but they are unlikely to learn anything that they could not have learned without a teacher. In either case, the teacher fails to fulfill his instructional function.

In short, there must be a dynamic relationship between the abilities of the students, the goals in teaching the subject, and the materials and concepts students study to reach those goals.

This concept of relating the materials to the teaching goals clarifies some problems about what to exclude from the curriculum. Some teachers still believe that one special function of the English teacher is instruction in courtesy—how to act on a date, for example. Others feel that using the telephone is appropriate subject matter for all eighth graders in English. But the English teacher is no more responsible for teaching in these areas than is the science or math teacher. The only feasible excuse for teaching how to answer the telephone and ask for a date at the superficial level that appears in most texts is to develop oral language skills of students whose oral language has been retarded by severe physical or psychological damage, or for practice by nonnative or nonstandard speakers.

Approached from a different angle, however, role-playing of dates and telephone conversations can teach students a good deal about point of view, connotative language, audience analysis, and the like. But the emphasis should be on how language conveys meaning, not on superficial forms. Similarly, TV programs, movies, comic strips, and pictures of various sorts are all appropriate for study *if their study contributes to an increased understanding of language and how it works.* Frequently, in fact, such materials can be extremely useful not only in introducing and reinforcing abstract ideas in concrete terms but in arousing the interest of the students. But the teacher who uses such material without relating it to the use of language is simply failing to fulfill his obligation as a teacher of English. "Enjoyment" alone is not enough. Students can enjoy watching commercial TV with no help from a teacher. On the other hand, enjoyment quite obviously contributes to the alacrity with which students learn things. The trick is to make it possible for them to enjoy what they are learning. Nonliterary materials, even nonverbal materials, are important not solely because they can arouse interest but because they can provide considerable opportunity for insight into abstract concepts about language.

Structure, process, and materials must all be considered if the concept of subject matter is to be dynamic rather than static. The study of English is a process through which students at various ability levels confront appropriate materials in various situations to derive an understanding of the structure of the subject.

*   *   *

How would teachers who had reached this definition of English as a subject matter respond to concrete problems in curriculum? Listen in for a moment to an English department meeting at Utopiaville High. One teacher is describing a class that she has called "a real problem":

"They're functional and all that. But their inventory responses were just minimal. They just don't seem interested. I think they all wound up in my class because the boys are taking two shop courses, and all of them take business math. None of them is planning on college. And some were frank about leaving school when they turn sixteen. I've got to find a beginning unit that will really interest them. Wake 'em up a little."

Thomas Green, a new teacher, makes a suggestion, "If they're taking math and shop courses, couldn't they study about machinery, visit some factories, interview their fathers on their work and give oral reports to the class? Maybe that would interest them."

The chairman comments, "Tom, maybe it would interest them. But Betty said that these kids are *functional* now. They read and write adequately. They're reluctant but able. The problem isn't one of finding something, anything for them to read and write about. Betty's class now has enough skills to study English. Your suggestion might be O.K. for work with a remedial group. But with functional kids we have to limit our work to English studies."

Green clears his throat. "But they'd be reading and writing. They'd be speaking formally. They'd be doing research. Isn't *that* English?"

"Sure. It's English in a sense. People read and write and speak and listen in English class—the language arts. But they do the same things in social studies, and science, and math, and phys. ed., and everywhere else in school, almost. If language arts were the only criteria we used to limit our field of teaching, it really wouldn't be limited at all, would it?"

He pauses. "Betty needs a unit that's going to deal directly with English studies. That's what she's trying to interest the kids in. It will have to be more than routinely interesting; but it can't be a substitute for literature or language or composition. Hopefully, it will contain all these elements. And it ought to begin with something that will really get interest quickly."

Such a unit is the one on humor that follows. It maintains high interest throughout and provides an environment of appropriate materials and situations in which the students can extend, in specific ways, their language capabilities. The unit emphasizes student involvement from the inductive lessons at the beginning to small-group discussions, whole-class, student-led discussions, and the production of part of the play. It provides for a great deal of oral participation, which is important in maintaining interest.

*   *   *

AN INTRODUCTION TO HUMOR
Outline of a Unit on Language, Literature, and Composition*

The aspects of *language study* involved in the unit are connected with the humor-producing devices. These are both semantic and structural in character: for example, misplaced modifiers may be regarded as structural defects that lead to semantic ambiguity or confusion.

The forms of *literature* encountered are jokes and anecdotes, parodies, satirical sketches, burlesques, and a full-length play. Besides these whole-class experiences, each student chooses a book for independent reading. In addition, a number of current teleplays are reviewed.

The criticism involves both analysis and evaluation. The works studied are classified on the basis of criteria developed through student analysis: type of humor-producing device(s) employed; apparent intent or purpose of the author; presumed audience. The evaluations are essayed on the basis of subjective reactions to the works rather than on the basis of the exposed criteria. Although the students pursue their criticism with awareness of the various patterns, they are not brought to direct recognition that they are engaged in critical processes.

The *compositions* are of two general types: criticism of the type suggested in the preceding paragraph and parodies. In working with both types, the students follow different kinds of models. The first parody is a direct imitation of a specific literary model; the student approaches it somewhat intuitively after some classroom analysis and discussion. The second parody allows the student to select his own model and his own subject from a corpus of literary experience; in addition, he reads and discusses models of the writing of other students at his approximate level of development, the models repre-

---

* This is not a complete unit of instruction. Study guides and model compositions have been omitted.

senting successful attempts at the same kind of problem. The third parody is written without the benefit of a model; and additional difficulty lies in the student's selection of subject—he must draw his subject from direct life experience.

Revision is an important aspect of the composition experience of the unit. Styling is the key element in producing successful parodies. Students who show initial success at imitating a style act as mentors to their groups. Each group is composed of persons who attempted the same style with less success. Workshop-like periods for this revision are implicit in the appropriate lessons.

OBJECTIVES FOR THE UNIT

To analyze various humorous works

To name, characterize, and identify various humor-producing devices and various forms of humor

To apply certain techniques of expository writing in completing written analyses and criticism

To write parodies

To criticize certain television programs

MATERIALS

Outline of study sequences	Teacher-prepared sheet of jokes
Sheet of fables	Sheet of excerpts from "Tribune
Student-made models of stylized	Primer" by Eugene Field
parodies	Book list of supplementary titles

Study guide for *A Midsummer Night's Dream* by Shakespeare

E. A. Poe, "The Cask of Amontillado," "The Tell-Tale Heart"

Recording of "The Tell-Tale Heart" read by Basil Rathbone (National Council of Teachers of English, Stock No. 86828)

Appropriate television programs

Student-written models of each composition assignment

Student-written unit examination

EVALUATIONS

The final unit evaluation is in two parts:

A. The development by the students of a comprehensive examination of the unit content. Is it comprehensive?

B. The answers to the questions on this examination. Are they precise?

(The expository writing in the unit serves the purposes of evaluation also.)

Other evaluation devices and techniques are discussed in connection with specific lessons.

PROCEDURES

PRELIMINARY About two weeks before the beginning of instruction in the unit a book list of various titles classified as "humor" in the school library is distributed. Students are instructed to read one of the books on the list or any other book purportedly humorous.

Lesson 1

The unit outline is distributed and discussed. The objectives of the unit are explained. A general plan for study is suggested.

Joke sheet is distributed and read silently. Teacher directs attention to particular joke and asks, "What makes it funny?" (Example: Seven days in a jeep make one week. Seven days in a week; the rough ride in a jeep would make you weak.) When the source of humor is identified, the device is named, either as drawn from the class or, if the students are unfamiliar with the term, supplied by the teacher.

Other jokes using the same device are then identified by the class. This procedure continues until all the devices have been dealt with. A distinction is drawn between joke and anecdote.

HOMEWORK Each person is to write an exposition analyzing a joke that is familiar to him. The analysis is in terms of the humor-producing device(s) used.

EVALUATION Is a suitable exposition developed? Is the humor-producing device named accurately? Is a suitable definition provided for this?

VOCABULARY Joke, anecdote, device, pun, misplaced modifier, incongruity, mixed metaphor, spoonerism, malapropism, Freudian slip.

Lesson 2

A sheet of parodies is distributed, selections from "The Tribune Primer" by Eugene Field. The items are read silently with the preparation: "Does the author use any of the humor-producing devices we learned about yesterday?" These items are noted in the discussion that follows. Next point: "What was the intent of the author in writing these?" (He was imitating children's books or primers. He was poking fun at the style in which primers are written. Unacceptable response: "He was ridiculing primers.") If the appropriate response is not forthcoming, the teacher introduces the idea with a question. The desired insight is that Field did not want his readers to laugh at primers themselves, or at children who use them, but only at the style. The students then list the elements of style that Field imitates: sentence construction, vocabulary choice, tone, and so on. The class is divided into committees to draw up lists of items that a contemporary writer might include in such a parody: paper clips, newspaper, rubber bands, ball-point pens, and the like. These topics are listed on the chalkboard.

HOMEWORK Using two items on the list, one developed in your committee and one suggested by another, write an entry for a primer as Field might. (Optional, extra credit: Write a third using an item not mentioned in class.)

EVALUATION Are the imitations successful?

VOCABULARY Primer, parody, parodies, ridicule, imitate.

OPTIONAL PROJECT Using items written by the class, publish "The Utopia-ville Primer."

Lesson 3

Distribute prepared sheets of fables, which are read silently with the preparation: "What elements do you find that these fables have in common?" (Subsequent discussion develops: All contain animals; animals talk, animals represent types of people; all have morals.) See Chapter 4 for a detailed expansion of this lesson.

VOCABULARY Fable, moral.

Lesson 4

Students read "The Shrike and the Chipmunks" with the preparation: "Considering our analysis of fables, can this be characterized as a parody?" and "Does Thurber go beyond mere imitation here?" (The discussion develops: This is a parody; Thurber's contains the same elements and humor; Thurber does not ridicule fables nor those who read them, only their style.) Next must be developed insight into some wives' treatment of their husbands. The teacher points out that when humor has a serious purpose, a specific target, and an implicit "hope" of effecting changes in the target, it may be labeled satire.

Lesson 5

Students read "The Great French Duel." Questions: "What is Twain's apparent purpose?" "Does he seem to want to effect a change in dueling practices in France? Or is he ridiculing the whole tradition?" "What is the principal device he uses to produce humor?" As these are answered in discussion, the form is identified: burlesque. Short discussion of the semantic shift associated with the word.

Lesson 6

Preparation for the analysis of style. Students read Poe's "The Tell-Tale Heart" as they listen to a recording of it. They discuss the effect of the story and the main character. Then the teacher focuses his questioning on style and elicits the elements peculiar to the style of the story. As the discussion develops, he makes a list on the chalkboard of aspects of style to examine in any piece of writing: point of view taken by the writer, sentence structure, diction, kind of details used, figurative language, and so on. When the list is complete, the teacher divides the class into heterogeneous groups and assigns Poe's "The Cask of Amontillado." The groups read the story and make a stylistic analysis of it in terms of the elements of style listed on the board. Class discussion of the story and its style follows.

Lesson 7

Library reading of highly stylized materials. A variety of such material is required—*True Romance* short stories, *The New Yorker, Time,* Jimmy Breslin, the Bible, Poe, Grimm, and so on. The students choose the material they wish to study. Reading not completed during this period must be completed during the remainder of a two-week period as outside reading. When the reading has been completed, the students must take a well-known story or type of one style and restylize it. For example, *Time* reports on Snow White. The writing assignment is given after the analysis of *Midsummer Night's Dream.* On the day the assignment is made, the students read and discuss models of such work taken from the work of previous students. But the writing assignment is announced before the library period begins.

Lesson 8

About seven days devoted to explication and analysis of *Midsummer Night's Dream.* One act is covered on each of the first five days. The pattern of each day's work is as follows:

1. A guidesheet for the act is distributed and read. The teacher prefaces the act with a brief synopsis of the action.
2. The teacher provides appropriate glosses for a scene. Silent reading of the scene. Roles are assigned. Players read lines from their seats. The same procedure is used for the next scene, and so on.
3. Material in the act not completed in class is completed at home.
4. The next day's class begins with committee discussion of questions on guidesheet for previous day's reading.
5. Student-led, whole-class discussion of same.
6. Continue with next act as in (1) above, and so on.

Lesson 9 (Optional)

Students produce the Pyramus and Thisbe interlude, the play within the play. Class elects director and assistant director who in combination with the teacher cast the play and set up costume, prop, and general arrangement committees. Student directors block play and encourage actors with stage business. Once rehearsals are under way, the teacher stays in the background except for occasional suggestions. The actors may carry lines if necessary. The more ludicrous the casting, costumes, and acting, the better. The class might present its production to other English classes meeting that hour or to students in study halls. The teacher should not strive for a finished performance. Students' errors usually contribute to the humor of the production. (See a student teacher's description of such productions in Chapter 14.)

Lesson 10

Students watch a number of TV comedy dramas. By comparing two or more in written exposition, they are asked to answer either A or B:

A. Which type (satire, parody, burlesque) is each of them? Which verbal devices are used, and what nonverbal devices, if any, contribute to the intensification of humor?
B. Which of two or more programs of the same format is the more successful development of the type?

EVALUATION Is the paper a satisfactory expository form? Does the student show command of the various technical terms he uses? Does he demonstrate his thesis: that one program is a different type from another or that one is better than another in exemplifying a type?

VOCABULARY Format, sight gag, slapstick, mug, take, double take.

Lesson 11   An Original Satire

Ask students to write on some topical event in a satirical vein using the technique of literary parody. For example, Edgar Allen Poe writes a math exam, Mother Goose teaches a gym class, political campaign promises written in Biblical style.

Lesson 12   Examination

Preparatory homework: Students are asked to develop a series of questions that would make a good comprehensive examination of the unit. Questions should deal with vocabulary, analysis of form, and the production of original work. Also some questions on reading content.

Classwork: When students bring their questions to class, committees are formed; questions are compared, and each committee makes a trial exam. The trial exams are compared, and from these is developed the true exam. On the subsequent day, students write this exam. On the next day, each student scores his own paper on the basis of class discussion. The entire procedure described here is not revealed beforehand.

NOTE

1. Philip Wylie, *Generation of Vipers* (New York: Pocket Books, 1964), p. 77.

SUGGESTIONS FOR FURTHER READING

1. HAROLD C. MARTIN, *et al.,* The Commission on English, *Freedom and Discipline in English* (New York: College Entrance Examination Board, 1965). An examination of the content of English as a subject.
2. JOHN DIXON, *Growth Through English* (Reading, England: National Association of the Teaching of English, 1967). Suggestions for fulfilling some of the more general purposes of English.
3. HERBERT J. MULLER, *The Uses of English* (New York: Holt, Rinehart and Winston, 1967). An examination of the content, structure, and purpose of English.
4. DWIGHT L. BURTON, Chairman, Committee on the Check List, Commission on the Curriculum, National Council of Teachers of English, "A Check List for Evaluating the English Program in the Junior and Senior High School," *English Journal,* LI (April 1962). Available as a reprint from the National Council of Teachers of English, 508 South Sixth Street, Champaign, Illinois, 61829. A useful guide for planning improvement as well as evaluating the status of the English program in a school; covers all aspects of the program.
5. GEORGE HENRY, "Style of Teaching and Teacher Evaluation," *English Journal,* 59 (October 1970), pp. 921–927.

2 | Inventories: Assessing Student Abilities and Interests

Before realistic curriculum planning begins, the teacher should make a careful assessment of the interests, attitudes, and abilities of his class. Thus, the beginning of the school year is the inventory period, a time when the teacher takes stock.

Although the teacher's impressions of the "quality" of the class may suffice for making general judgments about the types of things to avoid, he should not plan specific work without concrete information about individual performance. To do otherwise is certainly risky and may be disastrous. He should not plan a unit of work around one of Shakespeare's plays, for example, unless he has clear indications that the class members will be able to understand the relationships expressed in the reading matter and to write a sequence of at least three paragraphs that displays some rational ordering. Without these skills as bare minimums, either the class will flounder, or the project will be of such superficial quality that it had better be avoided.

Sources of Information

There are three sources of information about the students that are available at the beginning of the year: (1) the informal history of the students; (2) their scores on standardized tests; and (3) an operational inventory of their established learnings. The last-named source is the most useful, but let us briefly examine the first two.

1. INFORMAL HISTORY The school's general cumulative records, the English department cumulative folders, and the memories of their previous teachers are all valuable sources of information about the students. At the beginning of the year, however, the usefulness of this information is limited.

First of all, the teacher must assimilate all the available data and select from it what is pertinent, at a time when he knows his students only as names on a class roster.

Similarly, in weighing the impressions of previous teachers, he will find it difficult to associate those impressions with the unknown students and to dissociate the personal biases of the teachers from objective reporting. Finally, the teacher will have difficulty in finding the time to do the work because the administrative details connected with opening the school year will consume major portions of his time and energy.

2. STANDARDIZED TESTS Although the standardized test score has some advantages over the informal history as an information source, it has its drawbacks.

The test scores will save the teacher time and energy in collecting data, for in a relatively short time he can collect a set of test scores for the entire class. Moreover, the data are relatively objective. Since a standardized test is developed painstakingly by experts in carefully controlled situations, the scores are free from the personal biases that influence school personnel in day-to-day, face-to-face contacts with pupils. In addition, standardized test scores are highly specific in reporting. A score in reading comprehension, for example, will report a student's proficiency at certain reading skills without being colored by such considerations as his reactions in class discussion and his desire to make up missed work.

The credibility of the test scores may, however, depend upon the administrative practices used in recording them. If the recording has been done by hand, there is always the danger of clerical error. (If the tests were originally *hand-scored,* this danger is multiplied.)

Aside from possible clerical error, the recording of scores is often incomplete. Many standardized tests are developed as series of subtests. A reading test, for example is divided into parts that test vocabulary and comprehension. Some tests further subdivide these areas and have other major parts (such as reference skills tests). The scoring allows for reports on the subtests and then a final, cumulative overall score. If a wide imbalance exists between the scores on the subtests, the resulting overall score, taken alone, will give a distorted picture. As an extreme example, if a pupil scores sixth grade in *vocabulary* and tenth grade in *comprehension,* his resulting overall score, say eighth grade, will not reflect his ability to handle ninth-grade reading materials. Unfortunately, many schools record only overall scores.

Another drawback may be the teacher's inability to interpret the scores adequately. Usually, standardized tests report three scores: the raw score, the percentile, and the grade score, but some sophistication is needed to interpret them. In addition to scores on tests dealing with subject matter, there are intelligence test scores. As well as the reported IQ, it is desirable to know the type of test that was administered, the scores on the subtests, and such information as mental age, percentiles, and chronological age in order to make a reasonably sound interpretation. Added to all this is the need for knowledge about expected correlations of intelligence measures with scores on subject-matter tests. Therefore, it follows that if a teacher doesn't understand all these things, he will be wasting his time collecting the scores because he cannot make intelligent use of the information he has collected.

The final caveat on using standardized test scores is on the validity of the test in reflecting the kinds of skills that are required of a student in daily routines. A standardized test in reading, for example, typically presents a short passage of measured difficulty. The subject responds by selecting a "best" answer from a series of multiples that are presented to him. Compare this relatively simple response in a closely controlled situation with a comparable classroom task:

After finishing *Hamlet* (which has been read slowly and with much discussion and comparison of interpretations), the class is asked to choose from a selection of writing problems (such as "In view of all the evidence, to what extent is Hamlet's experience with the Ghost hallucinatory?") and develop a response in essay form. The material used, the variety and complexity of responses expected, and the time involved in these experiences in actual class situations are simply not reflected in standardized testing procedures.

In addition to the weaknesses cited in using informal histories and standardized tests as primary sources for data on student performance, there is a more pertinent objection. The development of adolescents is not regular and paced. They often grow in spurts. It is frequently the case that the person who leaves school in June is barely recognizable when he returns in September. In addition to maturation, he may have had some special training to overcome deficiencies. There is no way to predict the extent of change that can occur even over so short a period as three months. Hence, historical information of any sort may present a badly distorted view.

The better use for both informal histories of pupils and standardized test scores is in supporting (or disestablishing) opinions developed in more immediate ways.

Operational Inventories

Before he can start planning his course, the teacher needs the answers to a series of questions about his students. The answers must be obtained on a student-by-student basis.

1. What attitudes and interests do they have that may affect their work in English?
2. How well do they read and write?
3. To what extent can they work independently, without immediate teacher supervision?

As the year goes on and the teacher designs specific units of work, he adds two other questions to the list:

4. How much of the content of the unit I am planning do they already know?
5. Were my presumptions about their previous learning correct?

Very often, a teacher's inadequacies in instruction and in class control can be traced to his failure to ask these questions or to obtain good answers to them. He obtains the best answers most efficiently if he designs his own instruments for obtaining them. These instruments are called *inventories*. He uses them in actual teaching situations using real instructional materials; hence, they are *operational inventories*. They inventory learnings that students bring to him from previous years; as such, they are *operational inventories of established learnings*.

The questions listed above lead to the development of four types of inventories:

Interest inventories on student attitudes and interests that may affect their work in English.
Skills inventories to reveal how well they read and write.
Independent study skills inventories to determine the extent to which they can work independently.
Information inventories on the amount and kind of content they recall.

Many advantages result from the teacher's designing his own instruments. For example, he can use actual classroom materials, the kinds of questions that he asks in daily lessons, and the instructional methods he prefers. Thus, he knows how the students respond to *his* teaching, rather than to previous teachers' work or professional testmakers' efforts. Since the inventories are a part of his instruction, he learns concrete information about his students: their names and faces, their reactions to various types of instruction, and their classroom personalities. Thus, the results of the inventories are highly valid from his point of view.

In addition to this gain in personal validity, there are advantages that relate to the efficient use of time. Many teachers find the two or three opening weeks of school to be the least productive period of their teaching. Using the opening days in a systematic way and in a way that is of such great value in determining subsequent practices mitigates the September doldrums.

The major objection to this procedure is that there may possibly be a loss of objectivity resulting from the fact that all aspects of data collection and interpretation are under the teacher's control. This loss is offset, however, by the concomitant condition that any other evaluative technique is in some measure subjective—and a teacher's judgments in his classes are the *critical* judgments in most circumstances anyway. Then, too, as noted above, there are other sources of information that can supplement the teacher's findings and judgments: the informal histories and standardized test scores.

Interest Inventories

One of the teacher's most important concerns at the beginning of the year is to establish rapport with his class. Therefore, it is essential that he avoid experiences that may tend to weaken it. For example, if many students have a strong distaste for oral reports, it is a strategic error to schedule work so that the opening unit involves oral reporting. On the other hand, if many students enjoy drama, a unit involving plays undertaken early in the year should help establish rapport.

Interest inventories help pinpoint such biases toward English class activities. These inventories take two forms, questionnaires and compositions, both of which will supply information that the teacher needs. When he wants specific reactions to activities and procedures he plans to use (for example, reading poems, writing stories, giving oral talks, arranging for small-group discussions) or when he wants specific information about the students (Do you have a library card? Do you type?), he uses a questionnaire. Making the questionnaire is a simple matter. The teacher simply lists the types of activities that he plans to use (oral talks, and so on) and asks the class to rate each on a general scale, 1 to 5, 1 indicating *preference for,* 5 indicating *dislike of.* At the end of his list, he leaves some blank spaces and asks the class to fill in items of their own choosing and rate them.

When the teacher wants unprompted and open-ended responses, he asks the students to write a brief composition in class: "What I Like and What I Hate in English Class." The writing is preceded by a short discussion that elicits types of activities they have previously experienced in English class. As an activity is named, it is written on the chalkboard. Then, with the admonition that everything has not been named and perhaps a person could think of other things to write about, students are asked to write. When the papers are read, both positive and negative responses are listed and tallied.

It is important in using either type of inventory to obtain frankness in responses. Some students might use the opportunity to curry favor with the teacher by indicating that their preferences are what they assume the teacher's to be. Therefore, greater candor is obtained if the papers are submitted anonymously.

An advantage to the composition is that it gives the teacher an opportunity to be. Therefore, greater candor is obtained if the papers are submitted skills, such things as spelling and punctuation ability. These insights should be regarded as tentative, however, until the teacher obtains more detailed inventories of composition skills (see Chapter 21).

Either inventory technique allows for interesting follow-up procedures. Committees of students can tabulate the results and submit a report of their findings to the class. (In addition to the interest value for the students, this procedure saves the teacher's time and energy.) The teacher might read the compositions to the class, perhaps a few a day. This procedure affords the hostile and the weak some legitimate recognition, for it is rare that the compositions of weaker writers are shared with the class. (One suspects that such students will draw the inference that here is an understanding teacher.) Minimally, the practice of revealing responses communicates the differences in attitudes held by different persons. Some students "love" spelling, for example, whereas others simply "hate" it.

Another type of interest inventory that provides useful information is an inventory of interests of a more personal and general kind, interests not specifically related to English studies. Knowing beforehand which pupils are talented in art, music, woodworking, and so on, helps the teacher in planning special projects and reports that tie in with the units of study. For example, in a study of animal imagery in literature, a class artist might draw pictures of the animals encountered in the literature, a musician might play and discuss music containing animal imagery, a student interested in biology might report on his scientific experiences with animals as contrasted with his literary experiences. In addition, the guidance and motivation of reluctant readers and writers are aided by the teacher's knowledge of their interests. Many otherwise reluctant students are stimulated to read and write when topics are chosen with an eye to their interest power.

Once again, the teacher uses a questionnaire and a composition. Since the information gained on this inventory relates to specific students rather than to the students as a class, there is no anonymity in responding.

In designing the questionnaire, the teacher anticipates pertinent items and constructs the instrument to include such items as:

Do you have a library card?
Magazines your family gets regularly:
Newspapers in your home:
Musical instruments:
Special skills:
Hobbies:

Again, some space is left for other items that may occur to students. Presenting the questionnaire on larger index cards facilitates filing for quick reference.

One type of composition inventory begins with interviews developed as a class activity. This is especially useful in larger schools when members of a new class do not know one another at the beginning of the school year. In smaller schools a teacher can use the ploy "I want to get to know you" to support the activity.

The teacher initiates a discussion about different kinds of interviews, asking the students what kinds of interviews they are familiar with and what sorts of questions are asked in interviews. As pertinent items are mentioned (such as name, age, occupation), the teacher lists them on the chalkboard. Indicating that each class member will be interviewing someone in the class whom he doesn't know, he then asks for additional items that should be structured into the interviews (interests, hobbies, likes and dislikes). If important areas are overlooked, the teacher adds them to the list developed on the chalkboard. Students are paired off and carry out interviews along the lines discussed. When the interviews are completed, each interviewer presents the student he interviewed to the class. As the students are presented to the class, probably a few each day, the teacher notes pertinent information that is revealed on index cards, one for each pupil, and keeps the cards on file for future reference.

Follow-up activities to this inventory are developed around composition work. One composition is "The Person I Interviewed."* Another one, which is written after the series of presentations, can be developed as a "superlative" ("The Most Interesting Person in This Class," "The Most Widely-Traveled," "The Best Athlete," and so on), the title being suggested by the content of the presentations. The subject is not identified by name, only described. If these compositions are read to the class, they may try to guess the identity of the subject. (The guessing activity is most appropriate for junior high classes.)

Interest is a potent motivator, and the canny teacher is at pains to exploit every advantage that his insight into class interests offers him.

Skills Inventories

Even more important to the teacher than the students' interests are their skills, for if he knows the types of skills they have acquired and the level of proficiency they have attained, he can immediately determine the specific kinds of work the class can do. Moveover, if he has this knowledge before he starts an instructional sequence, he will be able to evaluate the skills the students have acquired by the time the unit is concluded.

Our essential concern is with the skills involved in *reading* and *writing*. This concern in no way intends to deprecate the importance of *listening* and *speaking* skills, the other members of the language arts quadrivium. In most classes, listening and speaking are the primary skills on which instruction in reading and writing is based. Generally, however, by the time a person reaches the secondary grades, his speaking and listening skills have reached a far more sophisticated stage of development than his reading and writing skills. Moreover, the teacher is at hand when these skills are employed, and an assessment is virtually automatic and inescapable. On the other hand, reading and writing are carried on by a student independently, and much of the reading and writing that is required of him is done when he is not under the immediate supervision of his teacher.

---

* This composition is discussed below in connection with writing inventories. See Chapter 22.

Listening Skills

Of chief interest in the inventory period are the listening skills required to take directions, especially for outside assignments, and to take notes from oral reports and class discussions. The former is treated in the section on study skills (see pp. 34–37). Concern with the latter is largely determined by the importance of informational content in the curriculum. If the curriculum is heavily information-oriented, note-taking is an essential skill. The students' note-taking habits can be simply observed by the teacher. If they are not in the habit, then lessons in note-taking should be developed, and frequent reminders will probably be needed during the early part of the year. Notes may be collected from time to time and evaluated. Needless to say, all oral presentations must be structured to facilitate note-taking.

Speaking Skills

Oral reporting, dramatic interpretation, and class discussions of various types are the focuses of speaking experiences in class. The students' attitudes toward these activities are elicited as part of the interest inventories. Interpretive reading skills and the like are best dealt with as appropriate curriculum experiences are encountered during the year. The rules for class decorum control many aspects of class discussion. Analysis of small-group discussion is considered elsewhere (see Chapter 3). Panel discussions and oral reports are controlled by the immediate purposes and objectives of the activities as specified in the curriculum; thus, these items are dealt with as they arise, rather than in a general way. Finally, there is the problem of students with such speech defects as stuttering and lisping. The classroom teacher should seek the guidance of a trained specialist in dealing with such students.

Reading and Writing Skills

Because instruction in literature and composition is directly dependent on the extent to which the students have developed their reading and writing skills, the discussion of reading and writing inventories has been deferred to the literature and composition sections of this book (see Chapter 11 for the reading inventory and Chapter 21 for the writing inventories).

Much language instruction is instruction in informational content. Therefore, inventories dealing with language instruction per se are developed in connection with specific units as the teacher plans them throughout the year. The planning of content inventories is discussed below (p. 39).

Study Skills

In the secondary grades much of the students' work is done outside of class, when his teacher's help is unavailable to him. The purpose of the study skills inventories, then, is to help the teacher to avoid making bad assignments. If the routine homework time period is about thirty minutes in length, the student spends about one-third of his learning time without the benefit of supervision by the teacher. Imagine the consequences for the year's learning, if, when the children entered the English classroom just after Labor Day, they were not to have the direction of any teacher at all until just before Christmas.

The alert teacher will at once question the efficacy of the homework arrangement. The bulk of published articles along this line have concerned themselves with homework in the elementary grades.[1] The lack of teacher supervision in study has its obvious drawbacks. If a student has misunderstood a concept or a technique developed in class and does homework practice predicated on the assumption that he has understood, and if he practices according to some inappropriate principle, he systematically learns error.

Many teachers have seen the results of such learning. Typically, they are manifest in the areas of usage and grammatical analysis. For example, if a student has misunderstood the rules and conventions governing the use of subject and object case forms with pronouns, his errors may haunt both the teacher and the student all through the year (in the student's case, perhaps all through his life).[2]

There is no way to "unlearn" anything. The best a person can do is to master some competing set of learnings and hope to achieve this in such a way that his behavior and attitudes are controlled by the more appropriate set of learnings. However, the neural mechanisms (and whatever related mechanisms) involved in these competing learning patterns are far from being fully understood. Animal experiments dealing with competing learnings often succeed in reducing the animals to states resembling such human emotional disturbances as "nervous breakdowns," catatonia, and other variations of schizophrenia.[3]

There are other dimensions to the homework problem. One of the terminal objectives of the school curriculum, taken as a whole, is to develop the student's ability to study on his own. Such study involves research, the use of reference materials, techniques for recording, and finally the preparation of the ends of the study (usually data) in a way that facilitates communication, much of which are English-class-oriented skills. The English teacher, therefore, plays a key role in seeing that students attain this important educational objective. Since homework is one of the essential elements in the program, homework in the English class is the most important of all the student's independent study responsibilities.

The effects of homework assignments on classroom discipline must also be considered. The student who must handle poorly conceived assignments may experience frustration, anxiety, and resultant hostility toward the assignment, subject, teacher, school, and all that these images symbolize. In fact, he may become so frustrated that he does no work at all.

The classroom consequence can spell disaster for the teacher. A consistent failure to turn in homework may be interpreted by both teacher and student as a successful challenge to authority. If the student's hostility is carried into the classroom, the teacher may lose control over the class and successful learning experiences may thus be impeded. Making no assignments is better than making bad ones.

Outside study can be classified into two general types: homework that is contingent upon reference skills and research techniques, and homework that derives from routine classwork without corollary research.

REFERENCE SKILLS AND RESEARCH

The learning of reference and research skills is cumulative and remains a part of a person's curriculum as long as he continues his education—through graduate study and beyond. Consequently, in designing an inventory of these skills, a teacher should not try to run the entire gamut of possible skills. Rather, he should select only those that his students will be called upon to use. In each inventory, the results will indicate quite clearly the content of subsequent instruction: the mastery of those skills that the inventory reveals as being deficient or defective.

The first inventory should be of the reference skills needed to handle the books that are routinely used in class, the anthology and the grammar. This inventory fits naturally into lessons introducing these books to the class. The items should be cued by the structure of the books and should test the use of the table of contents, index, glossary, and any other such helps. Typical inventory questions are as follows:

"What is the longest story in this book?" (use of table of contents)

"Who wrote 'The Highwayman'?" (table of contents or title index)

"On what page does it begin?"

"What form of literature is 'Ulalume'?" (type index)

"On what pages is information about nouns?" (index and cross reference)

"What is ellipsis?" (glossary)

The next focus of attack should be dictionary. The items should be cued by the content of the dictionaries that will be used. Students in earlier grades should respond to items involving alphabetizing, guide words, diacritical helps at the foot of the page, and choosing appropriate definitions. Most grammars contain useful materials related to using the dictionary. If the teacher opts to use the grammar for this purpose, he must be sure that grammar examples match the class dictionaries. If matching is not close, he should develop his own materials, although he can be guided by the grammar.

As part of inventories, more advanced students should be introduced to the wealth of information on the many aspects of language that is available in the front matter of the better desk dictionaries, to interpreting etymologies, and to evaluating definitions.

LIBRARY RESEARCH

If the classroom contains no reference works beyond the dictionary, the student will have to work in the library to use such other reference works as the thesaurus, encyclopedia, *Readers' Guide,* the various biographical reference books, and almanacs. A series of class visits to the library will be necessary to inventory the skills needed in using these sources. Thus, in addition to the inventories of reference skills, there should be an inventory of the use of the library itself.

Each library has its own rules of decorum and procedures. The mechanical organization of libraries differs (such things as where reference tools, card catalogs, periodicals and nonfiction are kept). Obviously, a class new to a building will be unaware of the structure and functions of the library, so an inventory will be superfluous, and the teacher, working with the library staff, should develop lessons to familiarize the students with the library routines. If the class is not new to the building, an inventory of library procedures is in order. This inventory should be jointly developed by the librarian and the teacher.

After the student becomes familiar with the physical plant of the library and the library rules, inventories of his skill in using research facilities should be made. Since many students do not know how to alphabetize beyond the first letter of the word, the inventory should begin with alphabetizing and move to using the card catalog and should continue through the reference aids that will be needed during the year.

A list of relatively simple research problems keyed to the nature and number of the reference tools should be developed and presented in duplicated form so that each student receives a copy. If only a limited number of reference tools are available, alternative questions can be employed. For example, if the library contains only two sets of encyclopedias, a question with alternative parts can be developed as follows:

In which volume (number) will information on the following authors be found? What is the page reference for each?

1. Henry Adams
2. Washington Irving
3. Edgar Allan Poe
4. Henry James
5. Ralph Waldo Emerson

Thus, students need find the information for only one author. Because seeking out only one of these will demonstrate facility in locating any of them, each student should be assigned only one item on the list.

The starting points on the inventory should be staggered. Some students begin with the card catalog problem; some, the encyclopedia; some, the unabridged dictionary; some, the thesaurus, and so on. This practice prevents mad scrambles of great numbers of students to any one source.

More advanced students receive more advanced problems involving the use of more than one source or alternative sources and requiring related value judgments. An example of a library skills inventory developed for high school students is shown on page 36.

Needless to say, outside research assignments must be delayed until the students have demonstrated appropriate facility in research skills.

ROUTINE HOMEWORK

The first step in developing the homework inventories is to list the types of home study assignments that are anticipated. This type of classification should be made by referring to the precise kind of skill that will be employed in doing the assignment. For example, writing assignments may be subclassified as follows in terms of the precise skills employed: assignments that are essentially copying; the making of lists; brief responses to questions; longer original writing; prestructured writing, and so on. Before an outside assignment is given, the teacher should have some evidence from classroom observation that the skills required are within the power of the students. A good practice is to reserve a large part of the class period so that students can make a start on assignments that constitute part of the inventory system.

The second aspect of home assignments that must be considered carefully is their timing. Again, classroom observation of behaviors is necessary in order to match the performance of study tasks with preconceived ideas of the time that should be needed to accomplish them. Of course, much of this information will have been obtained in the course of the reading and writing inventories. But it may be augmented by observing the students in the actual performance of an assignment—that is, by starting the home assignment in class, allowing fifteen or twenty minutes for the work, and then checking to see if it has been about half completed, Thus, assignment length and timing should be adjusted experimentally.

The final dimension is an inventory of the general approach to problems of home study: budgeting time, forming good habits, the arrangement of the study corner, and so on. Chapter 16 on reading offers suggestions about how students should approach homework that involves reading assignments (see pp. 390–393). A simple questionnaire should be devised to obtain insight into the students' general study patterns. The responses will indicate the direction of subsequent instruction.

Although they are not specifically in the nature of inventories, we must at this juncture consider the responses made by the class at the point in the lesson when the assignment is made. Part of the student's general approach toward study should be to write down assignments and all directions clearly and carefully. He should have with him at all times a special assignment

Library References and Research Skills Inventory

1. Answer either A. or B., but not both.

   a. The author of the article "Sociology" in the Encyclopaedia Britannica speaks with authority on trends in U.S. population. What experience of his (with the U.S. Government) enables him to do this?

      Answer _____
      Source(s) _____

   b. At which university did the author of the article "Painting" in the World Book Encyclopedia earn his degrees? (A.B., M.A.)

      Answer _____
      Source(s) _____

2. In what magazine (title and date) found in this library was the movie "Dr. Strangelove" reviewed?

   Answer _____
   Source(s) _____
   Optional. Was the review favorable or unfavorable?

3. Who wrote the famous line: "The world is too much with us"?

   Answer _____
   Source(s) _____

4. What is the title of another book by the author of Mrs. 'Arris Goes to Paris?

   Answer _____
   Source(s) _____
   Optional. Under what classification are these titles catalogued?

5. Name the first publication in which work by O. Henry appeared in print. What was his real name?

   Answer _____
   Source(s) _____

6. Which are the two most widely circulated magazines in the United States?

   Answer _____
   Source(s) _____

notebook that is kept separate from his notebook for class notes. The assignment notebook should be arranged to receive assignments for at least one week in advance and to allow space for assignments given daily. In addition to space for page references, he will need space to take down specific instructions for the outside work, and space for some sort of statement of the assignment's objectives. A simple visual check by the teacher will ascertain whether students are habituated to this practice. If they are not, a careful discussion of the practice and the rationale behind it should be mandatory. One of the more easily remediable causes of inadequate preparation of outside work is a breakdown in communications at the point at which the assignment is made.

In addition to the oral assignment, assignment sheets prepared in advance and chalkboard reminders should be used. All of this means that a considerable part of classroom time should be spent in making assignments. If the student is to spend upwards of a third of his learning time without teacher supervision, he must be as adequately prepared as possible so that he can use his time in a meaningful way. Therefore, the practice of making assignments at the end of the class period (or as sometimes happens, even after the bell has rung) is pedagogically poor in all respects. If the assignment has meaning, and for some reason cannot be presented well because there is not enough time to present it well, it had better be delayed.

In summary, the development of outside assignments is specially contingent upon the following:

1. The teacher must have sure knowledge that the skills involved in completing any assignment are within the power of the students. He must determine this by observation of classroom behavior, not by observation of the results of outside study.
2. The teacher must set outside assignments with an eye to the time required to complete them. He should determine the students' time requirements by classroom observation.
3. The teacher should clearly state the objectives of each assignment.
4. Specific directions for each assignment should be made clear to the students in an unhurried way and through a number of avenues.
5. Outside assignments must be a meaningful part of the instructional program.

The final point carries a number of implications. Outside work should not simply be done and turned in. It must be organically and sequentially related to all the work. This means that a certain amount of class time subsequent to the completion of outside work should be devoted to doing something in class that is contingent upon the completion of the outside work. This, in turn, means that the making of an assignment for some such purpose as "seeing what they will do with it" is *not* a legitimate practice. In any assignment the teacher will "see what they have done with it."

Interpreting the Inventory Results

As the individual inventories are marked, the results should be charted in the grade book as are the results of any of the student's work.

The systematic procedures outlined up to this point will give the teacher a good idea of the character of his class and of the characteristics of the class members. Further, he will have strong notions about what will be appropriate directions for some of the year's work. These notions can be clarified further.

After developing the various records and analyzing the accumulated data from several approaches, the teacher will be able to specify the relative strengths and weaknesses of his pupils. One type of pattern he may find is that of the student who appears to be weak at all of the skills examined. The teacher's central problem, then, is where to start remedial work. As indicated earlier, the central concerns of English teaching are reading and writing. Between them, the place to begin, without any question at all, is with reading.

Reading must have priority because our culture demands that people read easily and well. Such cultural items as telephone directories, billboard advertising, cooking directions on packaged foods, and traffic signs attest to the fact that reading skill is considered as a universal norm in our culture. Not only is the person who does not read easily hamstrung in the simplest pursuits of daily life, but when his lack of reading skill becomes manifest to others, he is likely to become the target of scorn, contempt, and even worse. So strong are attitudes about literacy that persons without reading skill are in continual torment, much of it self-inflicted. Imagine the feelings of shame and self-contempt suffered by the adult who cannot do what "every schoolboy" can.

Within the framework of the school as a social institution, the reading requirement is even more pronounced. Few are the classes, including those in manual training and physical education, where reading ability is not at least peripherally important. Although some teachers recognize reading disability, others—especially in secondary school—are unaware of the phenomenon. Moreover, most secondary school teachers are entirely unequipped to deal with very weak readers.

A person can get along with minimal writing skills in most life situations in the general culture, including vocational ones. Simple listings of a limited number of vocabulary items will suffice for a large number of persons. Even in the schools, the popularity of the "objective" tests, with their multiple-choice responses, attests to the general diminution of the significance of writing skills. Consequently, if individuals, groups, or classes show dysfunction in both reading and writing, reading has clear priority, and attention to writing can be delayed.

As for those who are functional—or better—at reading, attention must be given to developing their skills so that they will become sophisticated in dealing with the more literary as opposed to the more "mechanical" aspects of reading comprehension. With them, such instructional thinking and practice should be routine and more careful attention should be given to their writing.

Information Inventories

Up to this point, we have considered what the teacher must know about his students in order to plan a meaningful curriculum. When he has this information in hand, he can design his units of work.

Information forms a large part of any study unit—for example, items of fact, the superficial content of specific stories, poems, and plays, definitions, and concepts. As the teacher prepares a specific unit of study, he may need therefore, to design an inventory that will reveal how much of the unit's information the students already know. Let us assume, for example, that a school system has adopted a curriculum that features drama study, and the eleventh-grade teacher's responsibility is Arthur Miller's *The Crucible.* The students had studied *The Lark* by Jean Anouilh when they were in the tenth grade. To make efficient use of the time allocated to *The Crucible,* the teacher must know which learnings from the tenth grade have pertinence for eleventh-grade work and which of these have carried over. Obviously, there is little point in repeating experiences that are familiar to students. Consequently, the purpose of the inventory is to assess the pertinent carry-over, the pertinence having been arbitrarily determined previously by the curriculum makers.

The inventory can check the students' knowledge of specific data like places, names, and dates, and such specific terms as "simile," and "alliteration," and "allegory." For example, depending upon the kind of learnings from the study of *The Lark* that are regarded as pertinent to the study of *The Crucible,* an inventory of concepts of varying degrees of complexity could be made to test the students' familiarity with the names of the concepts. In other words, the students could be asked to identify such terms as dramatic unities, character, protagonist, tragedy, depending upon which concepts receive emphasis in the curriculum. Failure to identify key terms would indicate that direct instruction in the terms or concepts may have to be repeated, whereas a high frequency of appropriate identifications would suggest that instructional time related to *The Crucible* should be used otherwise.

Inventories in Summary

The preparation, administration and scoring of inventories is an arduous task. Although the preparation of an inventory battery is initially time-consuming, carefully prepared inventories will be useful year after year with only moderate revision, because they relate mainly to general behaviors and skills rather than to discrete elements of content. The information inventory can become an integral part of a curriculum, which focuses on learning specific content. If a number of teachers are involved in preparing inventories, the initial work can be cut down.

Such is not the case with the scoring and evaluation of results. Without doubt the heaviest paper load of the year occurs during the inventory period, yet stretching the inventory period to accommodate the workload tends to defeat the purpose of the inventory procedure. In school systems in which lay readers are employed, the burden of scoring papers can be eased, but even in this case, the delicate and time-consuming job of evaluation must be done by the teacher.

A sound practice is to return the inventories to the class and go over the rationale and the results with the students, offering them insights into their own strengths and weaknesses. Student-kept records of the results of inventories should prove useful here, especially if the inventories indicate that much class attention will have to be devoted to remedial instruction.

Should the teacher use inventory results to help determine students' course marks? His basic purpose in making inventories is to assess the levels of performance of various kinds to help him in his instructional planning. Yet, to the extent that marking is related to the students' actual performance of tasks as measured against their presumed ability, it is obvious that inventories will play a part in judgments concerning course grades. Even beyond this consideration, work done in the course of the inventories can be "counted" toward grades simply because it is real work, and as such, it is a direct measure of achievement.

Of course, the inventories will have little value unless the students really do work at them. For this reason, before the teacher undertakes the inventories, he should carefully discuss their purpose with the class. The students will be sure to ask if the inventories "count." The teacher must not hedge in his answer and must answer directly and frankly. If he answers, "Yes," he motivates workmanlike attitudes. Hedging, on the other hand, may result in a lack of honest effort and defeat the purpose of the inventories.

Although inventories mean a lot of work for everyone involved, a good inventory program will predict a good course. Without such a program, the teacher is forced to proceed by guesswork.

The sample inventories presented in this book are not intended as models to be imitated in a mechanical and unthinking way. Rather, they are intended as guides to the kind of thinking that teachers must do in making and using inventories in connection with their own work and in meeting their own needs. However, all the models presented and suggested here have been repeatedly tested in the classroom. They have been found to have considerable utility and may be used with some confidence as they are, or with appropriate modifications, by any teacher. Whether the teacher uses the specific inventories presented in this book or develops his own, he will need concrete information about individual performance. Proceeding without it is certainly risky and may be disastrous. Inventories provide concrete information.

NOTES

1. Avram Goldstein, "Does Homework Help? A Review of Research," *Elementary School Journal,* 60 (January 1960), pp. 217–224.
2. Amelia Diebel and Isabel Sears, "A Study of Common Mistakes in Pupils' Oral English," *Elementary School Journal,* 17 (September 1916), pp. 44–45.
3. I. P. Pavlov, *Conditioned Reflexes* (Oxford: Oxford University Press, 1927).

3 | Differentiating Instruction

When the teacher completes his inventories, he will find that his class shows a wide diversity in interests, attitudes, and abilities. No matter what course content he plans, if he does not make some provision for differentiating instruction, his procedures will misfire with a number of his students.

This diversity exists even in schools in which the administration provides for some homogeneous grouping through scheduling. How can this be so if the classes are scheduled homogeneously? Let us briefly examine some administrative scheduling practices and what such scheduling implies for planning instruction.

Administrative Grouping

Probably, the most frequently encountered kind of secondary school scheduling is tracking. Ordinarily, there are three or four tracks, ranked from high to low in general ability, but classes within each track are put together on the basis of chance.

Studies have questioned both the desirability of such grouping[1] and the reality of the results of the grouping.[2] One of the reasons for this is that most schools are not large enough to accommodate truly homogeneous classes at the ends of the distribution curve. For example, suppose that a school administration decides to make an honors track for students having high IQs, say 130 and above. Suppose further that the school population reflects the normal distribution curve as far as its IQ is concerned. In order to have a tenth-grade honors class of only 20 students there would have to be 1,000 tenth graders in that school. There are very few schools large enough to accommodate such groupings.

Some administrative grouping is essential, however, in providing a sound, workable English program because some differences in ability simply cannot be handled in a heterogeneous class. For example, the needs of students seriously deficient in reading and writing skills cannot be met if such students are scheduled into "normal" classes. Usually, because of a lack of special training and appropriate materials and his feeling of responsibility toward his other students, the teacher has to let these students stumble along as best they can.

All work in all English classes depends on the degree of skills development, especially in reading and writing, that students have attained. A student's skills determine how well he functions. Thus, students may be classified according to the way they function.

The first broad grouping made in terms of function is the grouping "nonfunctioning/functioning." Students classified as "nonfunctioning" in English studies are those very few who cannot read or write at all. For example, blind students are nonfunctioning at reading. Recent immigrants who cannot read, nor write, nor understand English are nonfunctioning. Severely retarded students or those with neurological or physical handicaps that prevent them from reading and writing are also nonfunctioning. In most schools there are relatively few such students. Their chronic and desperate needs dictate special classes for them, so their instruction must be in the hands of trained specialists.

By far, most students in secondary schools are *functioning*. These functioning students can be classified by another dichotomy, "dysfunctional/functional." "Dysfunctional" students are those whose skills are so weak that they interfere with the *intended* function of the skills. Dysfunctional readers can do some reading—that is, they can go through the motions, call a considerable number of words accurately, and understand the simplest sentences. But they often do not comprehend even the main ideas of what they read; or worse, completely misinterpret the main ideas. They cannot go far beyond reading for key details with any material and will score far below grade level on any standardized reading test.

Dysfunctional writers go through the motions of writing. But whoever reads their writing must actually analyze it to get any meaning whatever out of it. Even the simplest words are misspelled; many words are omitted; punctuation is erratic; and often, the handwriting is itself undecipherable. The mechanical errors are so numerous and overpowering that a teacher doesn't even consider commenting on the content of the message.

Figure 3.1 is an example of the first paper of the year, answers to a reading inventory, submitted by a dysfunctional ninth grader.

Often, a student shows both reading and writing dysfunction. In such cases reading instruction must receive priority because of the demands of the culture. The needs of dysfunctional students demand special programs.

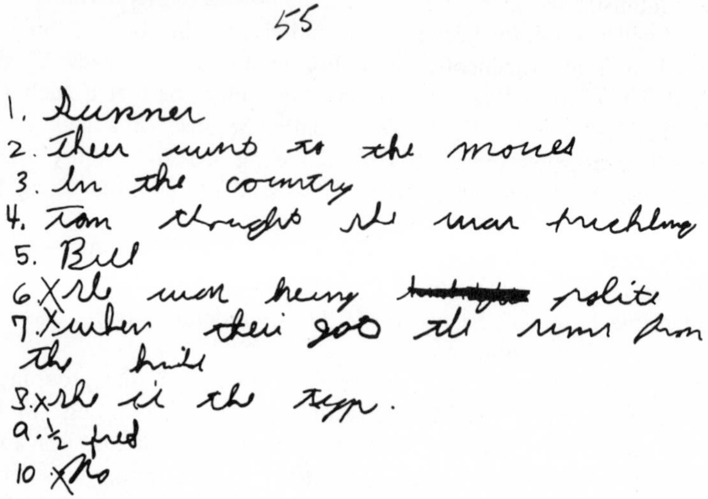

FIGURE 3.1 First paper of the year submitted by a dysfunctional ninth grader.

Administrative grouping practices ought to allow for classes of such students; but in too many schools there are none. It is obvious that even with the most sophisticated in-class grouping techniques, teachers cannot deal with a small group of students in such areas as phonics and word attack while their classmates are working at grade-level tasks. The program difference is just too humiliating. When the whole class needs such instruction, the embarrassment to individuals is greatly reduced.

The functional group contains a subgroup that needs a special program. This subgroup contains students who are "fluent" in skills. The fluent reader scores well above normal on standardized tests. He adapts his reading techniques, including rate, to his reading purposes and the material. He deals readily with such comprehension problems as author's viewpoint, relating reading materials to one another in many ways, evaluating reading in terms of life experience, and making evaluations in terms of various literary traditions. The fluent writer exhibits similar skill in his writing, having a deft touch with nuances that elude his less gifted peers. He produces compositions that are stylized appropriately to his purpose and that are generally free from mechanical errors.

The special needs and abilities of these students are ignored even in many honors classes. Too often their instructional program in all its aspects is identical with that of other students. Of course, because of their superior endowments, these students perform any curriculum task very well. Their achievement at a given task will be obviously so much better than that of members of "ordinary" classes that teachers are convinced that their curriculum content is appropriate. In such cases, the corollary evaluation is not made: that the curriculum content for the "ordinary" classes is inappropriate.

Let us consider, for example, two twelfth-grade classes studying *The Admirable Crichton*: the first an honors group; the second a group of college-bound students who are functional at reading and writing. The focus of the study is the satirical commentary on social class structure that Barrie makes throughout the play. The honors group reads and writes with greater skill and insight than the other group. If the play and approach are "right" for the honors group, can it be "right" for the less gifted group? If the material and approach is appropriate to both groups, what is the rationale for having two groups?

In terms of skills, then, there are four recognizable groups that might serve as the basis for tracking: the nonfunctioning, the dysfunctional, the functional, and the fluent. In some schools the administration helps to differentiate instruction by assigning students to appropriate tracks. In others pupils are grouped heterogeneously. Whichever grouping practices the administration of a school may follow, the teacher will face a spread in ability, interest, and attitude in any class. Consequently, he needs techniques for differentiating instruction.

Differentiated Questions

Let us first consider some of these techniques that do not require the physical movement of students. Even if the reading inventories indicate that the reading material the teacher plans to use will not frustrate any students, there will still be an ability range among them in terms of handling different sorts of comprehension questions. (See Reading Inventory, pp. 239–246.) In introducing a reading assignment, the teacher should prepare a list of questions that range in difficulty. Not all students should be assigned to answer all questions. Instead, the teacher should name a group of students and indicate which questions they are to answer. Another group should deal with another set, and still another group with a third set ("John, Bill, Paul, Mary, and Edith answer questions 1, 3, 7, and 8. Peter, Howard, Louise, Cathy, and Phil, answer 2, 4, 7, and 9.") All students should answer the one or two key questions in the lesson. The groups and the questions should be matched on the basis of inventory results, a group being assigned the most difficult question type it handled adequately on the inventory and the next most difficult type. There will be much overlapping. The final touch is structuring the list in mixed order in terms of difficulty so that invidious student judgments about one another and themselves will not follow from assignments of questions obviously arranged from easy to hard.

For a concrete example, let us assume that a tenth-grade teacher is beginning a unit on character analysis and has decided to focus on "the inner man."

The first few lessons are to deal with various mechanisms of compensation and how authors relate these to the behavior of their characters. The class has finished reading "That's What Happened to Me" by Michael Fessier, a story about a boy who daydreams. The next lesson is built around "The Secret Life of Walter Mitty" by James Thurber. The central concept developed in this lesson is that daydreaming is a typical compensation mechanism for people of all ages. Two key questions in the lesson are as follows:

1. About how old is Walter Mitty?
2. Compare the daydreams of Walter Mitty and Bottles Barton in "That's What Happened to Me." What are their similarities and differences? What triggers the daydreams of each character?

Since both of these questions bear on the central concept of this lesson, both are assigned to the whole class, regardless of the relative implicit difficulty of the questions.

A number of other questions are developed that range in difficulty from relationships stated in the reading to a question dealing with the structural elements of the story:

3. Who was usually kept waiting?
4. Why did Mitty hurry to the hotel?
5. Explain how Mitty's daydreams are specifically connected to reality.
6. What attitudes do Mitty and his wife have toward each other?
7. At what point are you first aware that Mitty is a *habitual* daydreamer? Explain.

The reading inventory has indicated that all students in the class could read for main ideas and key details, therefore no questions of this type are presented. The best readers in the class had difficulty in perceiving the author's point of view; and no one could handle the more difficult types at all. Consequently, the more difficult question types are not used.

The weakest readers then will be assigned questions 1, 2, 3, and 4. Another group questions 1, 2, 4, and 5. Another group 1, 2, 5, and 6, and so on—specific assignments being determined by the results of the reading inventory.

Before the questions are presented to the class, the order of questions 3–7 is scrambled, and the questions renumbered. Thus, the order of questions does not cue their relative difficulty nor the relative reading skill of the class members. This technique permits grouping of students for differentiated instruction in reading without rearranging the furniture for committee work.

Another technique that provides for some differentiation and does not involve committee work is to adjust the seating plan. Obviously, when a teacher begins the year, one of his major problems is learning the names and faces of his students. Additionally, there are many administrative details to deal with: distributing books, keeping records, taking attendance, and so on. To help with these tasks, he arranges his classroom seating plan alphabetically. But when he has learned the names and faces and when the September administrative trivia are out of the way, there is no longer any purpose in his alphabetical seating arrangement.

Occasionally, in every class, some changes are made: to bring a student with vision or hearing difficulty closer to the front; to break up undesirable conversational groups; to bring inattentive or mischievous students closer to the teacher. Otherwise, the seating usually stays fixed alphabetically, an arrangement that helps neither student nor teacher, whereas a change in the seating plan could be working for both.

An important consideration in teacher-led discussions is obtaining maximum response, having many students volunteer, seeing many hands raised. Let us consider some typical responding patterns in students. First, there is the very fast responder: The minute a question is asked (even rhetorically) his hand goes up; his answer may not be appropriate, but his response is quick. Another type is the student who never volunteers: Sometimes, even very able students never contribute; perhaps they are too shy, but their voluntary responses are nil. These are the extremes. Another group responds only when they are certain their response will be "correct." Another type —the most numerous—will respond, but they are rather more deliberate in their reactions than those with the quick hands.

What sometimes happens in daily routine is that the teacher falls into the habit of recognizing those with the quick hands in order to get on with the lesson. Meanwhile the class develops the habit of letting the few quick responders carry the burden during teacher-led discussion. If these roles become fixed, even the technique of waiting a few moments until other hands go up may not prove fruitful. Those who might have responded earlier in the year—given a little time—have learned the habit of letting the students with the quick hands carry the ball.

A change in the seating plan can help keep bad response patterns from developing. When the students are known by name to the teacher, alphabetical seating has outlived its usefulness. The first seating change should be to move the students with the quick hands to the rear of the classroom. Then when the teacher asks a question and their hands go up, only the teacher sees them. Those who react somewhat more slowly can have a few more moments to formulate responses without being distracted or intimidated by the hands of their faster-reacting peers. The teacher, then, can simply wait a bit before calling on anyone.

Frequently, there are two or three students of another type in a class who can be accommodated by changes in the seating plan. Some students seem to have difficulty in following any directions, even the simplest. These students should be seated close together in some location where the teacher can get to them easily whenever he gives directions of any kind—usually, this means in the front of the class. Then, when directions are given, the teacher can check these students visually, and if necessary, he can give them immediate help. In this way he can prevent them from learning error as a result of doing things wrong because of misunderstood directions.

Another important technique in conducting teacher-led discussions depends on group classifications that the teacher keeps in mind. As a teacher learns his class, he finds that many students may be classified according to the types of answers they usually give to questions. Many useful questions do not have answers that can be characterized as "right" or "wrong." Some questions invite purely subjective responses; for example, "Which is your favorite Dickens character?" Another type of question invites responses that are not personal but that are also not amenable to the right/wrong dichotomy: "Which of Poe's short stories shows the greatest concern for justice?"

Although answers to such a question cannot be classed as right or wrong, they may be classed by a type of frequency count. Let us assume that most students would respond to this question by naming one of two stories, either "A Cask of Amontillado" or "The Black Cat." Since these are the most typical answers, they may be thought of as "convergent." Another possible answer, though one not given very frequently, might be "The Tell-Tale Heart." Although this is capable of being reasonably supported, it may be considered "divergent" as it does not occur with great frequency.

Many students may be classified in terms of the convergence/divergence dichotomy on the basis of responses they habitually make. Moreover, there is yet another type to consider here, the summarizer. The summarizer, in this case, would name all three stories with amplifying comments and then select one as being *most* concerned with justice.

In leading discussions, the teacher should recognize students of each type according to his purpose in the discussion. If the purpose is a quick review of a small amount of material from the previous day's work in order to go forward, he should recognize the summarizer. If he intends a review lesson over a longer range of previous lessons, he should concentrate on students who make convergent responses. If he wishes to illustrate that some issue is complex, he should call on students who give divergent responses, especially at the beginning of a discussion. At the close of the discussion, he should recognize a summarizer who will tie all the elements together. Calling on a summarizer *first* in this situation would exclude many from the discussion and might suggest that the issue is not complex after all, since only one student had to speak to it. Thus, some differentiating of instruction can be done without ever moving furniture in the classroom.

Differentiation Through Group Work

Some teaching situations do demand in-class grouping. One of these is discussed in Chapter 13. The use of groups is an essential part of the technique in teaching concepts; as teacher support is withdrawn, students find intellectual support in small peer groups. As discussed in Chapter 24, "A Theory of Teaching Composition," small groups of students are invaluable in criticizing one another's composition work. Whenever the class is studying drama, the practice of in-class grouping gives all students an opportunity to read roles in plays. Often it is necessary to have students engage in small-group discussion for various other reasons. Grouping techniques are therefore essential in the teacher's repertoire.

Many teachers are afraid of in-class grouping on three counts. They feel that any teaching pattern other than teacher-led discussions, oral reporting, or independent study threatens a loss of control. They feel that when students are in committees, many of them are not working, and hence time is being wasted. They are afraid of noise of any kind in a classroom. Yet if all the phases of the work are carefully structured, the teacher will be able to retain control, the students will be attentive, and the noise will be kept at a minimum. Although the students will be making some noise—that is, talking—as they work in groups, it will be *good* noise, not suggesting loss of control, lack of discipline, or any other negative element in the classroom atmosphere.

Many teachers are unaware of the simple and reasonable techniques required for successful group work. First of all, the teacher should plan his grouping and structure his groups carefully (specific suggestions for group structuring are detailed below). When group membership has been planned, the names of the members of the different groups should be written together on the chalkboard. Each student will know then, without asking, which group he belongs to, and one of the major causes for confusion in committee work will thus be eliminated. Keeping group size to five and below will help with the noise problem. When groups are larger, a student has to talk across several others and so must raise his voice. Students in other groups will have the same problem, and soon the voices get into competition with one another in an upward-spiraling escalation.

The next step is planning group placement. The groups should be placed as far apart as physically possible, and each group should be bunched together as close as is physically possible. Keeping the groups distant from one another provides insulation against voices traveling from group to group and thus reduces intergroup competition, helping to keep the general noise level down.

The next problem is moving students into their groups. One of the sources of noise in grouping is caused by the movement of furniture, sliding it across the floor, and bumping it into other furniture. It is not necessary for a student to use "his own" furniture. The first step in getting a class grouped is to have the furniture for only one group set into place. For example, suppose the teacher has decided to place one group in the front, left-hand corner of the room. The furniture that is closest to that corner should be moved there while the rest of the class stays in place. Unless everyone in the group will be writing, it is not necessary to move five desks. Almost invariably, however, one person will be writing, so one desk and five chairs should be moved into the appropriate space. Next, the teacher should indicate that the students who are to occupy that space should move into it while the rest of the class remains seated. Each successive group should be set up in the same way, with the rest of the class remaining seated quietly. During this procedure, the teacher should remind the students about noise and tell them that they are to be as quiet as possible in moving their furniture. With younger students, when all the groups have been set up for the first time and before they are put to work, the teacher should have them return to their normal places in class, returning the furniture. When everyone knows where and how he is supposed to move, the teacher should have the class as a whole move. The procedures described to this point should be used whenever a new grouping arrangement of any kind is made. Like any new routine, grouping routines have to be taught.

The teacher should give all directions before the class moves into groups so that when they get into their groups, the students know precisely what they are expected to do and can start working immediately. Among the general directions that the teacher should give are the rules for decorum within the group. The first rule should be that only one person at a time may talk, the purpose, again, being to help reduce noise. In order for this rule to operate, each group should have a chairman to recognize speakers. Each group will also need a secretary, usually. The first few times that the teacher uses committees, he should choose the chairmen and secretaries for all groups. Subsequently, the groups can choose their own.

During the preliminary direction-giving, the teacher should specify the objectives of the group work. A paper of some kind required from the group as a whole—a list of words, answers to a number of questions, or the like—should specify the objectives. All members of the group should sign the paper, although the secretary alone may write what the group dictates.

The teacher should also indicate how much time will be allowed for the completion of the task. While the students are working, he should move from group to group, giving help as it is needed, answering questions, and evaluating the progress the students are making. A few minutes before the end of the allotted time, he should call for attention and ask if everyone will be finished within the specified time. He can then adjust the timing according to their responses.

In deciding how to put the groups together in the first place, the teacher's first problem is to decide whether he wants his groups to be formed homogeneously or heterogeneously in terms of the kinds of groups that he is using. There are three kinds of groups: ability groups, interest groups, and groups determined by some social criterion.

The teacher should use ability grouping when he is chiefly concerned about concept development or the use of previously developed skills needed to complete an assignment. Whenever the class is working on concept formation (as described in Chapter 13), the teacher should structure his groups heterogeneously in the following way. Suppose there are thirty students in the class. Because the optimum maximum size for a working committee is five, there will be six groups. The teacher should rank his students in order, strongest to weakest, and assign the six strongest as intellectual leaders of his six groups (these students are not necessarily the chairmen of the group). Next, he should place his six weakest students, so that the weakest and strongest members of the class are together in one group, the second weakest and second strongest are together in another group, and so on. Using the same kind of structuring, he should place the remaining eighteen students into the six groups.

Often, new learnings are contingent upon skills that have been previously developed. Whenever this situation arises, the teacher should group his class heterogeneously so that the more skilled students will support the less skilled. using the same structuring techniques described in the preceding paragraph. For example, suppose the class is going to work on a series of compositions in which some highly stylized material will be imitated. In the first composition in the series, everyone will imitate the same highly stylized material, such as a news dispatch. In order for the class to imitate the style, they will first have to analyze it; the quality of their analyses will depend upon reading skills that have already been developed. Obviously, there will be a range in levels of development of the necessary skills. Therefore, the groups should be structured heterogeneously so that the more skilled students will support the less skilled.

In the matter of *skills development* or remediation, the groups should be structured homogeneously. The value of this structuring is that the teacher can more easily get to the students who need his help most and spend more time with them.

Groups can be put together on the basis of interest. This is an especially useful technique when working with classes of weaker students. In motivating reluctant readers to read, for example, a baseball book group might be formed, an automobile book group might be another, a horsewomanship group could be another, and so forth. Whenever motivation is the central problem in instruction, the teacher should think about forming interest groups.

The final set of principles to consider in structuring groups is the various social principles. If a considerable amount of the work of the group will be done outside class, as in preparing a play for presentation, for example, the best course of action is to set up the groups along lines of friendship. The teacher should simply allow those who want to work together to group themselves together. In the lower secondary grades, such groups will usually arrange themselves along sexual lines, all boys or all girls. In the seventh and eighth grades the boy/girl basis for grouping usually results in the most enthusiastic kind of work.

Sometimes, however, friends do not help one another work but rather keep one another from working. In forming friendship groups, the teacher should discuss this problem with the students; and when he arranges such grouping himself, he should keep apart those students who distract one another.

Sometimes committees engage in long-range projects—such as making an 8 mm. film—that are rather complicated and depend for their success on the leadership of one or two committee members. How can a teacher find leaders to build groups around? Often, students that a teacher chooses as leaders are not regarded as leaders by the peer group. The device that is used for finding peer-group leaders is the sociogram, which is made in the following way: The teacher distributes index cards and asks each student to fill in the names of two persons he would like to work with and the names of two he would not wish to work with. The teacher then collects the index cards and tabulates both the names listed as desirable co-workers and the names listed as undesirable co-workers. Next, he makes a chart indicating all those people who choose to work together and those who are rejected from such groups. Those repeatedly mentioned as desirable co-workers are the social leaders. This technique reveals not only the leadership in a class but also what the friendship groups are.

As indicated above, while groups are working in a classroom, the teacher should move from group to group keeping his fingers on the pulse of things. One of the important evaluations he must make is which students dominate their respective groups; this is particularly important when the dominant individuals tend to lead the group astray. If the teacher's purpose in forming the group is to withdraw his support, he must use a technique that is not authoritarian in suppressing the influence of dominant students. If he uses authoritarian techniques such as telling the dominant student not to talk so much and to give the others a chance, his broader purpose of withdrawing his support is defeated.

The teacher's best approach is to lead the group to its own analysis of who the most influential members are through the use of a flow chart. In order to prepare the flow chart, one of the group members acts as an observer/recorder while participating in the group work. This student draws a seating diagram of the group, identifying the members on the diagram by their initials. As a student makes a contribution, the observer/recorder marks a symbol beside his name. The symbols for statements are plus signs; symbols for argumentative or contrary statements that arise in response to these are minus signs; questions are indicated by question marks; and answers to questions are indicated by check marks. When the group discussion is completed, the role of each member of the group can be analyzed in terms of his typical contribution. It quickly becomes obvious to the group which members say nothing, which members typically contribute questions, which usually make an answering response only, which make statements, and which persons' contributions come in the form of reaction to statements made by others. A review of the discussion will indicate which types of contributions were most influential in determining group decisions and group activities.

There is no way to predict which member will be the most influential. Sometimes it is the questioner who will illuminate a course of action; sometimes it is the verbal counterpuncher. Through the analysis of the flow chart, the group gets insight into who the dominant person is, and individual members of the group who make no contributions are also pinpointed.

Whatever class a teacher faces, the inventory results will inevitably show that this planning must include provision for differentiating instruction. The function of grouping is to aid in this differentiation. For example, let us assume that an eleventh-grade teacher has a heterogeneously grouped class with a wide range of ability in reading. He is teaching a thematic unit on physical appearance as it relates to character change and personality. During the early stages of the unit the class had read a number of myths and fairy tales having change in physical appearance as a central feature of the imagery. During the current period class members have been doing outside reading assignments in various works. Each student was assigned a specific selection on the basis of his reading ability. There are twenty-seven students in the class, and the grouping and reading assignments were made as follows:

four fluent readers—*Richard III*

six functional, high ability girls—*Cyrano de Bergerac* by Edmond Rostand

five functional, high ability boys—*The Portrait of Dorian Grey* by Oscar Wilde

five functional, reluctant readers—*Planet of the Apes* by Pierre Boulle

four functional, average readers—*Rhinoceros* by Eugéne Ionesco

three very weak to dysfunctional readers—*The Snow Goose* by Paul Gallico

When the assignments were made, reading guide questions and vocabulary were distributed to help the students through the material they were to read independently. Key questions for all the readings were the following:

1. Does the physical appearance help or hinder the protagonist in his relationship with members of the opposite sex? How does he respond to their physical appearance?
2. Does his appearance change? In what ways? What are the results of his changes in appearance? What are the results of the failure of his appearance to change?
3. To what extent are his physical defects symbolic? Do you find symbolic meaning in the appearance of other characters? Explain.

Additionally, each selection has questions relevant to it alone.

Fluent readers were assigned *Richard III* because it is the most difficult in terms of readability. The very weak readers were assigned *The Snow Goose* because it is quite short and relatively easy. The reluctant group were assigned *Planet of the Apes* because of considerations of interest; at one level of interpretation the book is science fiction, and the satire is not subtle. *Rhinoceros* is not too difficult; the characters are stereotypes, and the symbolic significance of the rhinoceroses is not profound (although the moral to the allegory is somewhat obscure). The remaining assignments were differentiated on the basis of interest and readability.

When the outside readings are finished, each group meets to discuss its assigned reading, the discussion being channeled by the guide questions. (There are six members in one group, a bit larger than the recommended optimum maximum size. But sometimes such operational compromises are unavoidable.) When the discussions are completed, a restructuring of the groups takes place.

Now heterogeneous groups are formed, the grouping principle being the titles that were read. Each member of each new group has read a different book. After each person briefly summarizes the plot of his book, he answers the key questions on the guidesheets that were common to all the books. Clearly, one function of the earlier homogeneous grouping was to prepare students to make contributions to the heterogeneous groups. During the period of homogeneous groupwork the teacher spends most of his time with the weaker groups.

Student-Teacher Conferences

Grouping helps to differentiate instruction and thus to individualize it. But true individualization is accomplished only on a one-to-one basis as in a tutorial. From time to time, various exigencies will point to the necessity for a pupil-teacher conference.

Good conference experiences will do very much to help strengthen rapport, increase understanding of specific learning problems, and generally improve individual performance. A poor conference experience, on the other hand, will have the opposite effect. Therefore, each conference must be planned as carefully as any other kind of lesson. Let us consider conferences of two general types: those initiated by students, and those initiated by teachers.

Very often a student initiates a conference just before or just after class. Usually some very specific problem is bothering him, and sometimes he is unaware of its complexities. For example, a student may request a time extension on a composition assignment. Before any decision is reached, the teacher must know what is prompting the request and must weigh the request against his general planning and objectives. His immediate response, therefore, is to ask the student why he needs more time, and the answer to this question will determine whether a more lengthy and formal conference is indicated. Consider the two following incidents that might occur just before class:

Student: Would it be O.K. if I turned in my composition on Monday instead of Friday?

Teacher: Why won't you be ready on Friday? What's the problem?

Student: Well, we're leaving to visit my uncle Thursday afternoon, and I won't be in school till Monday.

The problem is simple, and obviously, no follow-up conference needs to be scheduled. The teacher simply answers the question. The second incident:

Student: Would it be O.K. if I don't turn in my composition on Friday?

Teacher: Why won't you be ready on Friday? What's the problem?

Student: Well, I don't know just what you want, and I need more time.

In this case, the student needs help, although he may be unaware of it. Obviously, his problem cannot be reviewed in a few minutes before class begins. The situation signals the need for a conference. The teacher's response at this point should be to indicate that he'd like to talk the assignment over with the student at greater length and then arrange for some mutually convenient time for the talk. The student has invited the conference, although he is unaware of his need for it. (Of course, the teacher must be perceptive of the need.) On occasion, students initiate conferences directly and formally. However the case may be, whenever a student initiates a conference, he will have some specific purpose in mind, usually a learning problem of some kind. His immediate needs will give direction to the conference.

It is more often the case that the teacher initiates a conference. Consequently, the teacher must control and give direction to the situation. The first problem that the teacher faces is that of time: When can he get together with a student on a one-to-one basis? Some fortunate teachers have conference periods regularly scheduled as part of the school day, and the time problem is solved. More often, however, the teacher's day is full. Should the teacher have a "free" period in his schedule or study hall supervision, this time might be used for pupil conferences, provided that the student is free at the same time. Otherwise, before-school time or after-school time can be used, provided that the teacher has no assigned responsibility during these hours and the student is free. In many instances, because none of these time blocks is available, conferences must be held during class time.

When? Whenever the class is engaged in independent study, there is time for a conference. If the teacher makes a regular practice of using the last fifteen minutes of the class hour for beginning homework, conference time will be built into class routine. When the class is engaged in committee work, there is also time for a conference.

Some conferences might touch areas in a student's experience that are delicate to him. If the teacher is sensitive to this possibility, the conference will not be scheduled during class time, of course, but rather during some time when problems can be talked out in privacy.

Most conferences, however, deal with specific learning problems in an intellectual way and can be held in the classroom while other class members are engaged in other things. Nevertheless, many students are somewhat shy about the conference situation in the classroom, feeling as though all eyes are on them. This problem is mitigated to some extent if the conference is held at the back of the classroom, especially if the student's back is kept to the class.

Each conference should have a clear purpose and a highly specific conference objective. The student should be aware of both. That is, he should understand *why* the conference is necessary and *what* is supposed to be achieved by it.

Usually the teacher should plan a series of student conferences on some specific problem—style in composition, spelling improvement, progress reporting on long-term assignments—a problem that faces many in the class, but one that has individualistic overtones. When the teacher has decided to have the series of conferences, he should explain to his class that during the next several days he will schedule conferences with individuals during class and indicate their general nature—spelling problems, for example. At this time he should lay the ground rules and announce that not all students will be called into conference, only those who have specific problems. He should indicate that he expects people to work on their own during the conference period and that he won't be able to give much help because he will be in conference with someone. The teacher should also let the students know that any who want to have a conference on the problem should make an appointment.

The next step is to make a list of students who have spelling problems that will yield to specific suggestions.* The teacher should post the list of names and dates on the bulletin board and indicate that students with whom conferences are scheduled should think about what their problems in spelling are. Thus, when a student is called into conference, he knows that the purpose of the conference is to effect improvement in his spelling. Additionally, he prepares himself by thinking about his particular problems. It is crucial, then, that the teacher have some phase of the student's work analyzed and be ready with constructive comments. Otherwise, the situation is pointless and artificial and will result in wasted time, loss of confidence in the teacher, and destruction of rapport.

The teacher must prepare for the conference. He must have concrete examples of the student's work to focus on, which should show specific examples of the topic under discussion. In addition, he must have some clear course of action to suggest to the student—better yet, alternative courses.

During the conference, although he is following his own plan, the teacher must not be didactic or authoritarian in any other way and must avoid any overtone of threat. The very fact that he is giving special and complete attention to his student is overwhelming enough. He must be "soft" in his general approach and manner, using questions whenever he can. He should establish

---

* A discussion of spelling instruction may be found in Chapter 22.

the objective of the conference at the outset, and when he feels this is clear to the student, the conference should proceed.

From time to time during the course of the conference, the teacher may need to break away momentarily to give attention to the class. But he must be careful not to show pique at these interruptions, and he must be especially careful to avoid expressing negative feelings toward his conferee. Let us consider a typical student-teacher conference on a spelling problem; the class is working on committee projects—say, reading a play:

Teacher: Sit down, Pete. Have you been thinking about your spelling problems?

Student (tentatively):   Yeah.

Teacher: Have you been able to pinpoint any particular problem?

Pete: I don't know. There's a lot of words I don't know how to spell.

Teacher: But there's one mistake that turns up over and over on your papers. Look at these. (He has several papers ready. Pete looks at them.) You have some trouble handling the apostrophe, don't you?

Pete: I guess so.

Teacher: I know it doesn't seem like a serious problem, but it is one that can be licked. Can we review a little?

Pete: O.K.

Teacher: The main problem is with the possessive. Know what that is?

Pete: Yeah. When somebody owns something.

Teacher: Right. Now, how do you show the possessive?

Pete: Add apostrophe *s*.

Teacher: Good. Excuse me, Pete, it's getting a little noisy. (Raise voice.) Class . . . Class! I know you're working on a play, but you're getting a little loud. Keep your voices down, please. (Lowering voice.) Sorry, Pete. Where were we? O.K. You've got the rule. Can you give me a couple of examples?

Pete: O.K. . . . Uh . . . Mr. Brown's coat. The boy's hat.

Teacher: Good. You seem to know how to handle it. It looks as though your problem is keeping the error out of your compositions. How long does it take you to proofread a composition?

Pete: I don't know.

Teacher: Have you been proofreading?

Pete: I guess not.

Teacher: O.K. That's probably the real problem. Pete, will you try to do this: On your next three compositions, will you try to work in some possessives. And definitely proofread. I think you can catch all the errors then.

Pete: O.K. I'll do it.

Teacher: O.K. Now let's go over this. What problem have we talked about, and how are you going to work on it? . . .

The teacher had the conference planned. He had isolated a single specific problem, forming the singular possessive. He checked on a series of things to get at the root of the problem: Did Pete understand what the usage was, did he know the critical rule, could he give specific examples? The answers Pete gave indicated that he had the appropriate learnings. The teacher did not insist on a formal statement of rules at any time. The short conference indicated that Pete's trouble was something other than what might be solved by spelling instruction or drill. The proofreading habit was the next point checked—and proved to be the culprit. Finally, a concrete course of action was indicated. The student review was to clarify that the conference objective had been met.

Because so much of English instruction requires individualization, the teacher must have various differentiating techniques in his repertoire. In some cases administrative grouping may help by reducing the degree of diversity in skills in a particular class. However much this diversity is reduced, it will not be eliminated, or even nearly so. Consequently, there will always need to be some methods of differentiating in leading discussion, some need for grouping within the class, and some need for individual conferences.

The Tragic Hero

The unit that follows illustrates various methods of differentiating instruction in a particular unit. In the course of their study students work in various small group situations with a variety of purposes: library research, discussion of plays read by the whole class and those studied by only a few students, criticism of each other's writing, and discussion of play productions attended. In addition, the teacher confers individually with students about their reading and their writing.

The Tragic Hero, as it appears below, was planned for functional twelfth-grade, college-bound students. It has been presented successfully to very fluent ninth graders as well. However, for the vast majority of ninth, tenth, and even eleventh grade students it is difficult. Recordings of the plays, the filmed Stratford Theatre version of *Oedipus Rex,* and live productions are very useful in helping less accomplished readers dealing with the language of the plays. Christopher Marlowe's *Dr. Faustus* and Eugene O'Neill's *The Emperor Jones* were originally selected as whole class readings for two reasons: they were relatively short and they were both being performed by local theater groups. Alternate plays can be used. For instance, one popular play with high school seniors is Arthur Miller's *Death of a Salesman.* (A good film version is available.) In selecting plays for the whole class to read, the teacher should keep in mind what films are available, but especially what plays are scheduled for production locally by amateur, college, and professional theater groups.

This unit on the Tragic Hero is predicated on the idea that if a student is to understand a concept, he must encounter it in its variety of shapes and contexts. Reading a single tragedy such as *Macbeth* gives the student only a minimum background in tragedy. He will have only a vague idea of what the form of tragedy is. He will know about only a single tragic hero. He will be unaware of the possible range of heroes, situations, and plot structures available to tragedy. By examining a number of plays, however, the student can begin to comprehend not only the actions of a single hero involved in a particular situation, but the nature of the tragic view of man. If the student reads a number of plays, he can consider such questions as: What kind of man can become involved in the tragic situation? Why does the pursuit of what man believes to be his destiny sometimes result in tragedy? What is the view of man that tragedy conveys?

The emphasis on extensive reading; however, does not and should not prohibit intensive study of appropriate works. In the course of the unit, the class reads three plays as a group, each of which is read and studied in detail for plot, character, themes, patterns of imagery, major conflicts, philosophical and cultural ideas, and so forth.

The first activity of the unit involves background reading in the library about the Greek and Elizabethan theaters and about major Greek and Shakespearean playwrights. Following reports on the library reading, the class proceeds to an intensive study of Sophocles' *Oedipus Rex*. The discussion of the play centers in the plot, the characters, the themes, and the ideas. The broader questions concerning the nature of tragedy are reserved until the students have read additional plays. As the study of *Oedipus Rex* draws to a close, the students select a Greek play from a list to read individually. Usually from four to five students read a given play, and they can be grouped together for discussion after they have read the play. It is sometimes very helpful to ask various faculty members to read and discuss a play with one of these small groups. This technique assures a reasonably intensive study of even the outside plays.

The next step in the unit involves the intensive study of Marlowe's *Dr. Faustus,* followed by the selection of another Elizabethan play for outside reading. The approach in this section of the unit is similar to the approach to the Greek section.

By the time the students have read four plays, they can begin to approach the larger questions concerning the nature of tragedy. A class discussion at this point should attempt to isolate significant elements, such as the nature of the hero, the structure of the plot, and the use of irony. The class as a group then begins to examine each of these elements. After the examination of the various elements is under way, a composition is assigned in which the students attempt to define tragedy. Two approaches are possible: (1) Either the student analyzes all the various elements or (2) he chooses the quality that he feels is most central to tragedy and builds his essay around that central idea.

When the students have completed their own definitions of tragedy, they examine a few excerpts from published critical writings on tragedy to determine what aspects they had not considered.

The final section of the unit is a test of what has been accomplished, for here the student reads modern plays which may or may not be tragedies. The first modern play, *The Emperor Jones,* is examined by the entire class as a play. The students are on their own to decide whether or not it is tragic. Their conclusions are usually of three kinds. Some wish to call it tragic. Some say that Jones is far too ignoble to be a tragic figure. And some say that in some respects the play is tragic, while in others it is not. Following his analysis of *The Emperor Jones,* the student chooses a second modern play and analyzes it without the help of the teacher or other students. Once again he asks himself the question, can the play I have read be considered tragic? The conclusions reached are important only as they reflect the method used in reaching them. If the student examines the play carefully, brings what he has learned about tragedy to bear on this particular play, and presents evidence to support his argument, the unit and the student have been successful.

TIME REQUIRED

Approximately six weeks.

TERMINAL OBJECTIVES

To identify the stage conventions of the Greek, Elizabethan and Modern theaters.

To write a composition defining the nature of tragedy and the characteristics of the tragic hero.

To write (outside class) an analysis of a modern literary work read independently, determining the extent to which it can be considered tragic.

MATERIALS

Essays:

Aristotle, from *The Poetics,* trans. by L. J. Potts in *Eight Great Tragedies.* ed. Sylvan Barnet & others (New York: The New American Library, 1961).

Emerson, Ralph Waldo, "The Tragic," in *Eight Great Tragedies.*

Hume, David, "Of Tragedy," in *Eight Great Tragedies.*

Krutch, Joseph W., from *The Tragic Fallacy,* in *Eight Great Tragedies.*

Richards, I. A., from *Principles of Literary Criticism,* in *Eight Great Tragedies.*

Tillyard, E. M. W., from *Shakespeare's Problem Plays,* in *Eight Great Tragedies.*

Reference:
Hamilton, Edith, *Mythology* (New York: The New American Library, 1959).

Plays:
Marlowe, Christopher, *Doctor Faustus,* ed. Louis B. Wright & Virginia A. Lamar (New York: Washington Square Press, Inc., 1959).
O'Neill, Eugene, *The Emperor Jones,* in *Four Modern Plays* (New York: Holt, Rinehart and Winston, 1961).
Sophocles, *Oedipus the King,* translated by Bernard M. W. Knox (New York: Washington Square Press, Inc., 1959).

Recording:
Tragical History of Dr. Faustus, Richard Burton, Capitol Records.

Duplicated Materials:
Study Guides for *Oedipus Rex* (I and II), *Prometheus Bound, Medea, Hippolytus, Oedipus at Colonus, Antigone,* Greek Tragedies, *Dr. Faustus,* and *The Emperor Jones.* (Guides for *Julius Caesar, King Lear, Hamlet, Othello, Macbeth,* and for the essays listed above have not been included here.)
Selected Bibliography for Outside Reading.

STUDENT LOAD

1. Preparation of oral report and outline.
2. Reading and discussion of six plays.
3. Reading and discussion of seven essays.
4. Writing of major compositions:
   a. Characteristics of Greek tragedy.
   b. Definition of tragedy.
   c. Analysis of *The Emperor Jones.*
   d. Analysis of outside reading selection—final evaluation.

Lesson 1

OBJECTIVE

To identify dramatic conventions of Greek, Elizabethan and Modern stages.

PROCEDURES

A. To give the students a background in different periods of drama and to initiate the research work, ask the class if they know the differences between Greek, Elizabethan, and Modern staging. Ask them if they know what changes might have to be made in a play if it were produced on each of these three stages.

After a brief discussion, tell the class that in order to understand the Greek, Elizabethan, and Modern theater they must understand not only the kind of stage the dramatist had at his disposal, but they must also understand what kind of audience the dramatist wrote for, what kind of costuming and actors were available, and what the role of the dramatist was in his society.

List the topics on the board in the following manner:
Role of the dramatist in all three societies.
What is drama?

Greek stage	Elizabethan stage	Modern stage
Greek audience	Elizabethan audience	Modern audience
Greek actors & costuming	Elizabethan actors & costuming	Modern actors & costuming

Have the students choose topics and group the class according to their topics.

B. Tell the students that the information they gather will be presented to the class by their group. To insure that the other students are able to follow the talk and have notes to refer to after the talks, the groups will be expected to make outlines for distribution to the class.

C. Take the students to the library, or tell them to go to the library in the evening and get three or four books apiece on the subject they are working on. The next day, group the students to discuss their topics or to read. When the groups have gathered enough information on their topics, have them make a rough outline of how they are going to present their material.

Review the outline with each group and make suggestions for improvement. After the outlines are satisfactory, duplicate them.

D. As each group presents its discussion, allow the class time to ask questions and draw parallels. If the students giving the talk leave out important information, ask questions that will bring it out, or supply the information at the end of the discussion.

EVALUATIONS

Are the outlines satisfactory? Do the oral reports supply the necessary information?

Lesson 2

OBJECTIVES

To identify the characteristics of Greek tragedy.

MATERIALS

Oedipus Rex
Mythology (selection)
Reading list

PROCEDURES

1. To give the students a background for reading *Oedipus Rex,* distribute copies of Edith Hamilton's account of the Oedipus legend as it appears in her book, *Mythology.* Have the students read the selection, and answer any questions they may have.
2. Distribute *Oedipus Rex* and its study guide. Have the students read the study guides. Answer any questions they may raise. Start the reading of the play together, asking a few questions about the plot along the way. After they are well into the plot, have them finish the reading on their own.
3. Divide the class into small groups to discuss the simple plot questions. Have them appoint a recorder to write down their answers. Circulate to be sure that the students do not get too involved in any one question to the detriment of the others.
4. Discuss with the class the *essay and discussion questions.* It is helpful for students to refer constantly to specific sections of the play to support their answers. For variety it may be useful to have the class work on a few of the questions in groups. Question number 11 is useful as a writing assignment. Its directions are self-contained.
5. To allow students a chance to work on their own and to draw comparisons between plays, distribute the list of Greek plays and let the students select the play they are interested in. Give the students a brief synopsis of each play to help them in their choice. Form groups of not more than five students on the basis of their play selections. Distribute the general study guides and the study guide for the specific plays. Allow them sufficient time to read the study guides and ask questions, and then give them the rest of the class time to read.
6. After the students have read their plays, have them discuss the specific study guide questions first, followed by the general study guide questions. Circulate among the groups to insure that the students draw comparisons between the plays. The important thing is the nature of tragedy as it is exhibited in the plays. The students should begin to formulate a definition of tragedy from the comparisons they make.
7. After the class has finished its group discussions, begin whole class discussion of the general study guide. As the students point out characteristics that are similar, write them on the board. Then have the students summarize in a short paper the characteristics of Greek tragedy. Tell them to use specific examples from the plays they have read to support their position.

EVALUATIONS

Does the paper comment on the Greek dramatic conventions, the characteristics of the tragic hero, the nature of the tragic situation? Are specific examples used to support the generalizations?

Study Guide I *Oedipus Rex*

The following questions will give direction to your reading of the play.

1. In the beginning, what clues do we get to Oedipus' character?
2. What faults in his character are revealed as the play progresses?
3. How is Creon related to Oedipus?
4. According to Creon's report, what was the cause of Thebes' misfortunes?
5. Upon what gods does the chorus call in its prayer for help for Thebes? Why is each god significant?
6. Oedipus' proclamation sets what form of punishment for the murderer of Laius?
7. What is Oedipus' reaction to Tiresias' prophecy? Does he believe it?
8. Whom does Oedipus blame for the supposed plot against him?
9. What, says Creon, are his reasons for not wanting to be king?
10. What is Oedipus' physical defect? What caused it? How does he feel about it? What does his name mean?
11. How and why had Oedipus killed Laius?
12. What seems to be Oedipus' chief reaction to the news of Polybus' death?
13. How does he think he might have been the cause of Polybus' death?
14. How does Oedipus interpret Jocasta's reluctance for him to learn his true identity?
15. Why are Oedipus' children referred to as "monstrous"? For which of them is he most concerned?
16. According to Oedipus, what superhuman power urged him to blind himself?
17. Describe Creon's attitude toward the blinded Oedipus.
18. What final warning and advice does Creon give Oedipus?
19. How does each of the points of Tiresias' prophecy come true?
20. What moral does the chorus draw from Oedipus' story, at its close?

Study Guide II *Oedipus Rex*

ESSAY AND DISCUSSION QUESTIONS

1. A Greek audience would have known the Oedipus legend before seeing the play. How would that knowledge have affected their responses to the play in the opening scenes and later?

2. What kind of leader does the situation in the city call for? Is Oedipus this kind of leader? Is Oedipus a heroic character? Support your position.
3. What importance to the play is Oedipus' decision to have Creon give the oracle's reply in public? In questioning Creon, what trait does Oedipus reveal? What does Oedipus do as a result of the information that Creon brings?
4. How does the decision to send for Tiresias influence the plot? In his questioning of Tiresias, what additional character trait does Oedipus reveal? Note especially the speech on p. 27 of the text. What is his reaction to what Tiresias tells him? Why?
5. What does Jocasta's speech on p. 50 reveal about her attitude toward religion? Oedipus' speech on pp. 66–67? How are they similar? What other statements by them do you find in the play which support your inference?
6. When does Oedipus turn from interest in finding the murderer to interest in learning his own identity? In what sequence does Oedipus learn his fate? How does this affect audience response to the play?
7. What is the ultimate irony of the play? List the plot episodes and show how each results from the preceding one, except in the arrival of the messenger from Corinth. What does the interrelationship of the episodes contribute to the irony of the play?
8. How is the play unified in terms of time, space, and character? How does the phrase *in medias res* relate to this play?
9. What are two important roles played by the chorus?
10. Take notes on each of the prophecies indicating what is predicted about Oedipus' life. What in the play is not predicted about Oedipus? Since the play proves the truth of the prophecy, how can Oedipus be said to have acted as a free agent with a free will?
11. Apollo is the god of light, of the sun, of intellectual achievement, the god who controls disease and health. What is Oedipus' relationship to these aspects of Apollo?
12. Who appears to have controlled destiny—Oedipus and Jocasta, the prophecy, or the gods? What evidence supports your contention?
13. Comment on the symbolic significance of the blindness imagery throughout the play.

Study Guide *Prometheus Bound*

1. What is the nature of Prometheus' punishment?
2. Why is he to be punished? Could he have avoided punishment?
3. What is his immediate reaction?
4. Is Prometheus greater before or after he brings man fire? Why?
5. Which punishments does Prometheus enumerate?

6. Describe the Wanderer.
7. What is the main problem of the actress who plays the role?
8. What doom for Zeus does Prometheus prophesy?
9. For what reason does Hermes visit Prometheus?
10. Describe Prometheus' final punishment.
11. Does Prometheus at any point regret his earlier action? Explain.
12. Who triumphs in the end, Prometheus or Zeus? Defend your position.

Study Guide *Medea*

1. Who is Medea's husband?
2. Why does Medea despair?
3. What is the order Kreon gives to Medea? What is his reason for giving this order?
4. Who is Aigeus? What agreement does he make with Medea? (When Aigeus exits, we see the chorus in one of its classic roles; it comments on Aigeus, the comment having little to do with the action of the play. What do you suppose is Euripides' purpose in so flattering Aigeus?)
5. By what method does Medea plan to kill her rival?
6. Why does she plan to kill her children?
7. As a director, how would you develop the murder-of-the-children scene?
8. What is Jason's reaction?
9. What does Medea finally refuse him?
10. Many critics believe that tragedy is resolved with a final suggestion of nobility (or affirmation). How is this view substantiated or repudiated in *Medea?*

Study Guide *Hippolytus*

1. What is the purpose of Aphrodite's prologue?
2. Which goddess does Hippolytus worship and whom does he refuse to worship?
3. Which member of the household is ill? What is the reason for her illness?
4. What is the nature of the cure the nurse suggests?
5. What is Phaedra's reaction when the cure fails?
6. Who is Theseus and why does he turn against Hippolytus? What is the ironic element in his return?
7. What are the circumstances of Hippolytus' injury?
8. Who intercedes for Hippolytus and what are the results of the intercession?
9. Does the play end on an affirmative note? Explain.

10. What is the most difficult scene in the play to produce? If you were a director, how would you produce it?

Study Guide   *Oedipus at Colonus*

1. Why is Oedipus asked to leave the sacred grove and then the town?
2. How does Oedipus regard his fate?
3. What message does Ismene bring to him?
4. How does Oedipus feel about having been banished from Thebes? Why?
5. What bargain does Oedipus make with Theseus?
6. What reasons does Creon give for asking Oedipus to return to Thebes?
7. What is the situation which prompts Polyneices to go to his father?
8. Why is it important to Oedipus that he successfully deny the requests of both Creon and Polyneices?
9. How does Oedipus find peace and tranquillity at the end of his agony?
10. Is this play a tragedy in the same sense as *Oedipus the King* is? In what ways is it similar or different?

Study Guide   *Antigone*

1. Why does Creon decree that Polyneices must not be buried?
2. Why does Antigone insist on disobeying this decree?
3. How does Sophocles raise this specific conflict to a universal one?
4. What is the conflict between Haemon and Creon?
5. Why do we tend to sympathize with Creon?
6. What part does Tiresias play?
7. Creon relents of his decree and of his sentencing of Antigone. Why is it too late?
8. Who is the real tragic figure of the play, Antigone or Creon?
9. What are the multiple causes of Creon's tragedy?
10. Near the beginning of the play, the guard bringing news of the burial to Creon says, " 'Tis sad, truly, that he who judges should misjudge." In what respects does this apply to Creon?

Study Guide   Greek Tragedies

1. What specific problems do the major characters of the plays confront?
2. Is each problem due to external forces, forces which are internal to the characters, or both? What precisely is the nature of these forces?
3. Do the events of the play lead to a resolution of the conflict? Is the resolution external in the events, internal in the minds and emotions of the characters, or both? What is the precise nature of the resolution?

4. If there is no resolution, a continuing unanswerable question must be presented. What is the precise nature of this question?
5. What is the theme of the play? State the theme as carefully as possible.
6. What role does each character play in the enactment of this theme?
7. In what ways is the play similar and different from *Oedipus Rex*—in plot development, in character, and in theme?
8. From your reading of the two plays write out notes toward a definition of tragedy. Include the nature of the hero, his personality, his social position, and his relationship to other characters. Also include the nature of his experience and its relationship to the nature of the audience's experience during the course of the play.

Lesson 3

OBJECTIVES

To identify the characteristics of Elizabethan tragedy.
To compare Greek tragedies and *Faustus*.

MATERIALS

Doctor Faustus, book and record
Macbeth
Othello
Titus Andronicus
Hamlet
Julius Caesar
King Lear

PROCEDURES

1. To begin the analysis of Elizabethan drama, review with the class their notes on the Elizabethan theater, paying particular attention to Marlowe and the history of the Faust story. Distribute copies of *Dr. Faustus* along with the study guide.
2. To aid reading comprehension, have the students read the play in class along with the recording. Advise the class before they begin that the record omits some of the scenes, telling them which scenes to pass over as they follow along. Following the class reading, tell the students to reread the play at home, using the study questions as a guide.
3. To insure knowledge of important details and simple inferences, conduct a whole class discussion based on the first sixteen study guide questions. Cut off discussion when it is clear that students understand the literal level of the play.
4. To begin interpretation of the play, divide the class into groups and assign each group two or more of the essay questions. After the groups

have discussed the questions, ask them to prepare a report of their ideas for the class. As each group reports, involve the whole class in discussion of the particular questions answered by the group.

5. To compare the tragedy of Faustus to the Greek plays in the previous lesson, ask the class questions which will lead them to select similarities and differences.

    a. How does Faustus' situation at the beginning of the play compare to the situation of Oedipus? Other Greek heroes?

    b. What is the general movement of the action in *Dr. Faustus?* How does this compare to the general movement of Greek tragedies?

    c. In *Oedipus,* what is reestablished by the fulfillment of the hero's fate? Is there a similar reestablishment in *Faustus?*

    d. How do Oedipus and Faustus differ in their attitudes toward their destinies at the end of the play? Does this affect the audience's interpretation of the two characters?

    e. Compare the problem of man's free will and fate in *Faustus* and the Greek plays.

       (1) To what point is man in control of his destiny?

       (2) Can the gods defeat man?

    f. Compare the characteristics of Faustus and Oedipus. Are they in any way similar? In what ways are they different?

    g. Is the fluctuation of Dr. Faustus' will parallel to the action of Oedipus? Does Oedipus at any time doubt himself or his intentions?

    h. What portions of the Elizabethan play assume the function of the chorus in Greek tragedy?

    i. What elements common to all the plays read thus far would indicate the essential nature of tragedy?

6. To provide for individual analysis of an Elizabethan tragedy, list the titles of supplementary plays on the board. After the students have selected the plays they wish to read, distribute the corresponding study guides. When the students have read the plays, assign the composition of a short essay in which they discuss the tragic elements of the play they have chosen and make pertinent comparisons with previous readings. Allow time for individual or group conferences during this part of the unit to discuss problems which arise in the reading, giving students an opportunity to test the ideas they have formed.

EVALUATIONS

1. In Procedure 5, are discussion responses pertinent?

2. In Procedure 6, are the generalizations, contrasts, and comparisons in the compositions supported by parallel references to Greek and Elizabethan plays? Are these references specific? Do the generalizations follow logically from the specific references?

Study Guide   *Dr. Faustus*

1. Where was Faustus born? Is he low-born or of high birth? How do you know? What is the connection between Faustus and Icarus? Does this give a clue to Faustus' tragic flaw? What do you expect it to be?
2. In Scene I, where is Faustus? What is he doing? What are Faustus' ambitions? What do you think would be the purpose of such acts? Would they be at all practical?
3. The First Scholar refers to Faustus as a man "that was wont to make our schools ring with *sic probo*." What does this indicate about his character?
4. Does Faustus oppose or give in to temptation? What shape does Faustus order the devil to take? Why? What quality in Faustus does the incident reveal?
5. Why does Mephistopheles appear before Faustus the first time? What is the tone of Faustus' conversation with Mephistopheles? How does the spirit react initially to Faustus' desire to sell his soul to the devil? What is Mephistopheles' definition or description of hell? Faustus' reaction?
6. What do Wagner and the clown discuss?
7. What is the purpose of the good and evil angels in Scene V? As Faustus writes his pact with Lucifer, his blood ceases to flow from the wound. How does he interpret this? What remedy does Mephistopheles offer?
8. What means does Mephistopheles use to distract Faustus? Does he succeed?
9. In the agreement, what benefits will Faustus receive? What must he do in return?
10. Why will Mephistopheles not tell Faustus who made the world?
11. Whose spirit does Faustus conjure up for Emperor Carolus?
12. After he buys the horse from Faustus, what warning is the horse-dealer given? What happens to the horse when the man disobeys? How does the man "pay" for his disobedience at that moment? Later? What moral would you infer from this incident?
13. What does the Old Man tell Faustus? What is the meaning of Faustus' request to see Helen of Troy? What does this show about the depth of Faustus' sin?
14. Did the scholars approve Faustus' bargain? What is the unpardonable sin Faustus commits?
15. What is the moral drawn by the chorus at the end?

ESSAY AND DISCUSSION QUESTIONS

1. Who are the principal characters? What is the function of each character; that is, what does he contribute to the drama?
2. What is the principal conflict in the drama? What is the course of the development of the conflict? List the six episodes in which Marlowe tells the tragedy of Faustus.

3. What is the story of Lucifer? Why is it related? In what respects does Faustus resemble Lucifer?

4. How is Wagner's part in the drama a comic commentary on Faustus?

5. What is the irony of Mephistopheles' remarks about God, hell, heaven, etc., to Dr. Faustus in Scenes III and V?

6. What powers had Faustus been granted by Mephistopheles? How does he employ them? What does this suggest about the significance of those powers?

7. Is Faustus' corruption the outcome of his interaction with evil, or were the seeds of decay always in his character? Explain and find evidence to support your position.

8. Could Faustus have been saved by repentance? Find the lines which support your answer. Why was he unable to repent?

9. What analogy can be drawn between Faustus and contemporary scientific investigation? In this, consider knowledge apart from moral considerations, then as part of moral considerations.

10. To what extent is Faustus glorified, that is, made to be a superman? For what purpose? Explain.

11. What aspects of Faustus' character are revealed first by his bargain with Mephistopheles and later by the uses that he makes of the powers he is granted?

12. Choose one scene that might be difficult to produce, for instance, the scene of the contract signing. If you were a director, how would you stage the scene?

Lesson 4

OBJECTIVES

To write a paper defining tragedy, using examples from the plays as supporting evidence.

MATERIALS

Model essay.

PROCEDURES

1. Before assigning the composition, a number of procedures should be followed in order to prepare the students for the assignment. A general synthesizing discussion of tragedy, based on the works read in previous lessons is the first step in such a preparation.

2. Divide the class into small groups and distribute copies of the following general discussion questions to the groups. Assign each group the discussion of *one* of the questions, since an adequate discussion of each question would require too much time. When the groups have finished

their discussions, ask each group to report its ideas to the class. Along with each report there should be an open discussion of the material presented and of the question which served as a basis for the report. Require each group to make specific references to plays as supporting evidence, and to provide quotations for the class in their reports.

GENERAL DISCUSSION QUESTIONS—TRAGEDY

1. What are the qualities common to the tragic hero? How is he a type which can be identified in literature?
2. What is the role of fate in tragedy? How is it related to the free will of the hero? In what forms can it appear?
3. What common elements are found in tragic plot structure? What is the movement of the plot from the beginning to end?
4. How does tragedy make use of irony? How does irony contribute to the tragic experience?
5. What emotions are experienced by the audience in tragedy? How are the emotions aroused by the writer?
6. What is the tragic writer's view of the universe and man's place in it? Does it change from play to play, or is there a basic philosophy consistent with tragedy? Explain.

3. Once the entire class has had an opportunity to discuss the previous questions in some detail, explain that each student will be required to write a paper defining tragedy. There are several approaches to the topic, and time should be spent discussing various methods of organization and topic formulation.
4. Some students may wish to write an over-all view of tragedy, enumerating each of the major elements of the genre and then giving examples and other evidence to support their thesis. Others may wish to choose the one element they consider central to tragedy and focus on it, showing all other elements in relation to this one. To provide a model for analysis of structure and theme, distribute a sample outline, such as "The Nature of Tragedy," below. In addition to commenting on organization, the students should discuss the validity and clarity of the content.

Sample outline of "The Nature of Tragedy," as part of the analysis of the model essay.

1. Introduction—problem of definition.
2. Aristotle's theory—summary and examples.
3. Specific tragic flaws and downfall.
   a. Oedipus
   b. Creon
   c. Faustus

    d. Hamlet

    e. Macbeth

4. Tragic emotions—pity and fear.

5. Tragic Irony.

6. Ennobling of hero through suffering.

7. Conclusion—summary of major points. Final statement on essence of tragedy.

Assign the composition on tragedy, allowing time in class for formulating topics and for writing introductions. This enables the teacher to assist students who have difficulty getting started. Conferences should also be arranged with individual students to discuss their progress on the assignment. Before students turn in a final draft, divide the class into heterogeneous groups of three. Ask students to criticize the papers written by the other members of their groups. Then ask them to prepare a written analysis of a paper written by another student. Following this activity, students may revise their own papers if they wish.

EVALUATIONS

Is the composition well organized? Is the thesis adequately defended? Does the content reflect the work of the unit to this point? Does the definition of the tragedy include a discussion of the tragic hero as a central feature? Is the tragic hero carefully characterized?

Lesson 5

OBJECTIVES

To analyze and compare some theories of tragedy.

To examine various tragedies in the light of critical essays in order to revise the definitions of tragedy established by the students.

MATERIALS

Selection from *The Poetics*—Aristotle
        "Of Tragedy"—Hume
        "The Tragic"—Emerson

Selection from *Shakespeare's Problem Plays*—Tillyard

Selection from *Principles of Literary Criticism*—Richards

Selection from *The Tragic Fallacy*—Krutch

PROCEDURES

1. Distribute copies of the selection from *The Poetics* with the study guides. When the students have read the selection, conduct a class discussion using questions such as those on the study guide.

2. The essays by Emerson and Hume are difficult; so it is helpful for the teacher to read the essays aloud while the class reads along. Questions as to Emerson's and Hume's meaning are asked while the reading is in progress. Use the general questions in the study guide for whole class discussion when the reading is completed.
3. Have the students read both Richards' essay and Krutch's essay in small groups. Have them answer the study guide questions and prepare to present a summary comparing all the essays they have read. They should select those points in the essays they agree with and attack logically those that seem inadequate or incorrect. Each presentation should focus on one particular selection while taking the others into account. Whether they agree or disagree with the writer is less important than the discussion which should arise during and after each presentation.

EVALUATIONS

The group reports and the ensuing class discussion should re-examine and revise the definitions of tragedy constructed in the previous lesson. The teacher can direct this re-examination and revision by asking questions such as the following:

1. What do the critics say about tragedy that your definitions neglected?
2. Are these elements important to tragedy?
3. Should your concept of tragedy be revised in light of these comments?
4. Do your definitions disagree with what the critics say? How?
5. Are your ideas about tragedy reinforced by what the critics say? How?
6. In what ways do the plays you have read support or detract from the generalizations presented in the critical essays?

Lesson 6

OBJECTIVES

To write an analysis of a modern drama, determining whether or not and why it should be considered tragic.

MATERIALS

The Emperor Jones
Selected Bibliography

PROCEDURES

1. The purpose of this lesson is to present the students with a problem which will allow them to make use of what they have already learned about tragedy. The problem is first to decide to what extent particular modern plays adhere to and deviate from traditional tragic patterns, and then to decide what effect such adherence or deviation has on the

play. For instance, while the plot structure of O'Neill's *The Emperor Jones* is very like the structure of Greek and Elizabethan tragedies, the nature of the Emperor as a ruler and as a man differs markedly from that of the heroes of most Greek and Elizabethan tragedies. This combination of character and plot produces an effect which is far removed from the effect of Greek or Elizabethan tragedy. In the process of dealing with this problem, the student reinforces his previous learning as he uses it in making rather complex inferences.

2. Distribute copies of *The Emperor Jones* and the study guide questions. Following the reading of the play, either orally in class or as a homework assignment, conduct a class discussion involving characterization, plot, dramatic techniques and interpretation of specific passages. The study guide questions will be useful as a basis for this discussion. A review of the description of modern theater as presented in the first lesson may be useful at this point.

3. After students have completed their study of *The Emperor Jones* and their outside reading (see Evaluations 2), raise the following question: Some critics feel that tragedy cannot flourish in the modern theater. What do you think? What characteristics of our time might preclude the development of tragedy?

EVALUATIONS

1. Assign the writing of an analysis of *The Emperor Jones*. The students may take various positions: the play is a tragedy or it is not, or it is tragic in some respects but not in others. The composition will give evidence to support one of the positions, drawing on not only the drama in question, but also the other tragedies read in the unit and the definitions of tragedy developed by the class.

2. Ask the students to select a work from the bibliography. Ask each student to write an analysis of the work as tragedy—giving his definition of tragedy and explaining to what extent the work can be considered tragic.

Study Guide *The Emperor Jones*

1. How might you describe Jones' personality? His ambitions?
2. How does Jones view his subjects? How do they view him?
3. What is the relationship of Jones to his society on the island? To his society in the United States?
4. How does O'Neill reveal significant events in Jones' past?
5. Consider each of the events. What does each of the events reveal about Jones' personality? What does each reveal about his relationship to his society? How has each contributed to Jones' ambitions, his attitudes towards the islanders, and his attitudes towards others in general?

6. In what ways is Smithers like Jones? What advantages does he have that Jones does not have?
7. Does Jones change during the course of the play? If so, how?
8. Why does Jones fail in his attempted escape?
9. In what ways is his failure ironic?
10. To what extent or in what ways can this play be considered tragic?

Selected Bibliography for Outside Reading

Anouilh, *Antigone*
      Becket
      The Lark
Chekov, *The Cherry Orchard*
Conrad, *Lord Jim*
Eliot, *Murder in the Cathedral*
Hardy, *Tess of the D'Ubervilles*
Ibsen, *The Doll's House*
      An Enemy of the People
      Ghosts
      Hedda Gabler
      The Master Builder
Kazanzakias, *The Last Temptation of Christ*
Lorca, *Blood Wedding*
      The House of Bernarda Alba
      Yerma
Miller, *Death of a Salesman*
O'Conner, Edwin, *The Last Hurrah*
O'Neill, *The Hairy Ape*
      Mourning Becomes Electra
Shaw, *Saint Joan*
Steinbeck, *The Grapes of Wrath*
Wharton, *Ethan Frome*
Williams, *The Glass Menagerie*

Lesson 7 (Optional)

OBJECTIVE

To criticize the production of a tragedy by a local theater group.

PROCEDURES

1. This lesson is necessarily optional because in any given area live productions of plays may not be available. However, the effect of visiting a live

production, when it is reasonably well done, is so powerful that the teacher should make every effort to include attendance in his unit.

2. The unit should be scheduled around production dates so that students will be familiar with the play before they attend the theater. Otherwise, many lines and even whole sequences of events will be lost on them, especially with Elizabethan plays. If they have not read the play, they should be given a fairly detailed plot summary before they attend. Such precautions are not so necessary with modern plays.

3. Assuming they read the play before attending, divide students into small groups and ask each group to plan the production details of a scene that particularly appeals to them, including such things as where actors will stand, how they will move and behave, what the set will be, what lighting will be used, and how actors will deliver particular lines. Following the production, ask the groups to compare their production notes for that scene with what they observed in the theater.

4. Assign a composition evaluating the real production of the scene which they prepared. Their evaluation will be largely subjective but should consider the effectiveness of various elements in the scene, how well they related to each other, and how effectively the production of that scene supported the play as a whole.

NOTES

1. A recent extensive study purporting to show among other things that there are no advantages to students in racially homogeneous classes is the following: James S. Coleman, *Equality of Educational Opportunity* (U.S. Department of Health, Education and Welfare, 1966).

2. "The Thorny Garden of Ability Grouping," *Overview,* 1 (June 1960), pp. 36–38.

SUGGESTIONS FOR FURTHER READING

1. For discussion of administrative grouping and its implications for curriculum: CONANT, JAMES B., *Shaping Educational Policy* (New York: McGraw-Hill Book Co., 1964).

2. For a discussion of questioning and response classifications: GETZELS, JACOB W., and PHILIP W. JACKSON, *Creativity and Intelligence* (New York: John Wiley and Sons, Inc., 1962); and GUILFORD, JOY PAUL, *Personality* (New York: McGraw-Hill Book Co., 1959).

3. For discussion of grouping techniques and theory, and additional bibliographies: CARTWRIGHT, DORWIN PHILIP, and ALVIN ZANDER, *Group Dynamics: Research and Theory* (New York: Harper & Row, 1960).

4. ORTON, JOHN W. ed., *Readings in Group Work* (New York: Selected Academic Readings, 1965).

4

Purposes, Concepts, and Objectives

After the teacher has assessed the abilities of his students, he must begin planning for instruction. Creating an environment in which students can respond freely, read critically, discuss energetically, and write creatively takes careful planning. The teacher must consider the concepts and skills he wishes to teach in relation to the materials he will use and both of these in relation to his students. And he must consider all of these in relation to his general purposes.

The unit on "Animals in Literature" which appears at the end of this chapter was developed for seventh-grade classes and has been used extensively by many teachers in various forms with considerable success. But what general purposes would a teacher have in using such a unit? What concepts in literature, language, and composition would he attempt to develop? What should the students be able to do by the end of the unit that they could not do prior to having studied it? These questions are extremely important in the development of any instructional sequence.

General Purposes

A seventh grade teacher's decison to begin the year's literature study with a unit on animal stories is governed by several purposes. First, he wishes to begin the year with material that will have immediate interest for the students, and he knows from experience and from research findings that most seventh graders have a strong interest in animals. Second, he wishes to provide an easy transition from elementary school reading to junior high reading. He knows that seventh graders are faced with many adjustment problems. Stories about animals provide familiar territory and thus help to reduce anxiety. Third, he wishes to introduce some concepts basic to the literary study the students will meet in the seventh grade and important to the reading and interpretation of literature in general.

Any course of work in English exists as an alternative to other courses because time alone prevents the study of all things that might conceivably be studied. At every phase of curriculum planning, the planner must make choices. When all other exigencies governing his choices are held equal, his purposes will determine his choices.

For example, if there is a possible choice in course content between studying the work of Poe or of Hawthorne, and the teacher is aware that at a later stage in the curriculum the students will study the French symbolists, his broader purpose will invite the option of Poe because of his influence on the French school.

Again, considerations of purpose will indicate directions to avoid. In the study of Shakespeare's sonnets, for example, if the sonnets are to be used only as models for writing, then having the class read Shakespeare's biography would not be a useful procedure.

Concepts

We must ask two basic questions in selecting concepts for the curriculum or for an individual unit. First, are the concepts underlying the proposed unit of instruction important to the understanding of the subject and to the development of skill in that subject? Second, is the proposed unit of study appropriate to the background, ability, and knowledge of the pupils so that it is likely to be of interest to them? If the teacher can answer these questions positively, his next step is to determine specifically what he intends to teach—to formulate terminal objectives.

Are the concepts underlying the proposed unit of study important to the understanding of the subject and to the development of skill in the subject?

Jerome Bruner, in *The Process of Education,*[1] has suggested that every subject matter has a discoverable structure and that a subject is best taught by teaching its structure. All too frequently a course presents a student with isolated bits of information, which if he learns them in the first place, he will soon forget. He has no conception of an underlying structure that will enable him either to remember what he has learned or to cope with new situations. Obviously, a student who understands the concepts underlying the operation of the English language—that is, how it has meaning—will be better able to cope with new language situations than one who has only bits and pieces of information about the language.

Frequently, when teachers are most convinced of the usefulness of what they teach, their instruction is least useful. For example, many teachers believe that a knowledge of traditional school grammar is not simply important to composition but prerequisite to it. Yet an important report from the National Council of Teachers of English states unequivocally that there is no relationship between the study of grammar and the ability to write—except perhaps a negative one.[2]

The teaching of literature offers numerous similar examples. High school courses that seem to be related to the nature of literature are, in reality, concerned with little more than the chronological ordering of a few selected works. Students may learn the plots, characters, themes, and occasionally even the chronological ordering of these works, but such study does not increase the student's ability to read *other* works. If their ability to read other works of literature improves at all, it does so only by chance. In part, this has happened because high school teachers have been so concerned with explaining the meanings of specific works that they neglect to plan instruction so that the students *themselves* learn to derive meaning from literature.

In short, a teacher should think very carefully about the ideas and concepts he wishes to teach. They should be productive in the sense that the student can put them to work for him in interpreting, analyzing, and evaluating his language. They should help the student to produce or unlock various language structures on his own.

Units on animals appear very frequently in seventh grade anthologies. Ordinarily they are shallow because they do not attempt to convey concepts important to the understanding of literature. Instruction is primarily concerned with what happens at the literal level of a given story, and discussion centers on telling about experiences with pets. The students might be highly motivated, but the unit provides nothing that will be useful in their later reading of literature.

Yet a unit on animals need not be empty. The one outlined at the end of this chapter introduces four concepts important to the study of literature, important and useful beyond the immediate confines of the unit.

1. ANIMALS AS CHARACTERS, IMAGES, AND SYMBOLS An animal in a story or poem can be either a main character as in Kipling's "Rikki-Tikki-Tavi," or he can be a secondary character such as Lady in James Street's story "Weep No More, My Lady." When the animal is a main character, the action and thought of the story revolve around it. If the animal is a secondary character, it usually contributes to the understanding of other characters. Other animals play only an incidental role in the action of a story. For instance, the cat in Edgar Allan Poe's story "The Black Cat" is not really a character, but an image that helps to produce the horror of the story. In some works animals are used symbolically. Fables and some poems such as Blake's "The Tiger" and "The Lamb" make use of animals that have emblematic value in our culture: The lion usually equals courage, honor, kingliness; the lamb equals innocence; the fox and the snake equal cunning and/or treachery, and so on. Although the distinctions among animals used as main and secondary characters, images, and symbols may seem rather simple, they are not so simple to

seventh graders for whom they can serve as the beginnings of rather sophisticated literary concepts.

2. THE AUTHOR'S TREATMENT AND DEVELOPMENT OF CHARACTER The author's treatment of animals as characters can be anthropomorphic (attributing human characteristics to nonhumans) as in Kipling's "Rikki-Tikki-Tavi" in which a mongoose thinks, feels, and acts like a human being with emotional and rational faculties, or it can be naturalistic as in Jack London's *Call of the Wild,* in which the animals act primarily on the basis of instinct. Students can also examine the ways in which the author develops the "personality" of the animal. Do we see the inner workings of the animal's mind, its fears, motives, desires, and the like? Does the author say explicitly that the animal is good or bad, friendly or vicious, cowardly or courageous, straightforward or treacherous? Or does he let the reader know such characteristics only through the actions of the animal or through what humans say about the animal? If we must infer the "personality" of the animal, then what do various circumstances of the plot reveal about the animal? Questions such as these are of utmost importance, not only to seventh graders but to literary critics. Note the critical difficulty with *Hamlet.*

3. THE ANIMAL AND HIS ENVIRONMENT Perhaps this short title sounds as though it ought to be a part of someone's science curriculum, but think for a moment how much literature is concerned, at least in part, with a man's or animal's attempt to confront, adapt to, or conquer his physical environment: to name a few, Jack London's works, Defoe's *Robinson Crusoe,* Kipling's *Captains Courageous,* Ole Rölvaag's *Giants in the Earth,* and, at a much more complex level, William Golding's *Pincher Martin.* An examination of the relationship between the animal and its physical environment can serve as an introduction to the relationship between man and his physical, social, and cultural environments, and these relationships are extremely important in almost any extended literary work.

4. THE IDEA OF CONFLICT A plot of any sort does not arise without conflict. The interpretation of conflict is one of the most important aspects of reading literature. In junior high and high school, teachers frequently expound three kinds of conflict in literature; man against the elements, man against man, and man against himself (the internal conflict). This analysis is so superficial, however, that students are easily misled by the activity. The identification of a conflict as "man against man," for instance, tends to obliterate the specificity of conflict in a given work and homogenize all works. The conflict might involve individuals, an individual and a group, an individual and a whole society, or any number of other combinations. It might arise out of petty jealousy, greed, or various other conflicts in personal values. Or it might arise out of an individual's or group's rejection of social or cultural values. The

conflict might be presented in gross physical terms or in emotional or spiritual situations.

Any generalization that an author suggests in his work is likely to reside in the specific nature of the conflict, its causes, and its resolution. Therefore, the reader must ask such questions as the following: What is the initial cause of the conflict? What signs of conflict exist before the outward manifestation appears? What is the essential nature of the conflict? Is the conflict resolved? If so, how does the resolution come about? If not, what is the effect of its remaining unresolved? Finally, what is the significance of the conflict in terms of the work as a whole? All these questions and more need to be asked if the analysis of conflict is to be worthwhile. Although seventh graders may not be capable of answering all these questions, one of the primary purposes of an English teacher is to enable students to do so. A unit on "Animals in Literature" is admirably suited to this purpose because it can present a wide variety of conflicts for the student to examine.

Of course, any study unit may touch briefly on any of the ideas suggested above. An occasional question about conflict, a discussion about theme, a note on point of view—all are likely to be included somewhere or other. But such incidental examination of literary problems does very little to help the student become adept at handling them on his own. Units must *focus* on one or more of the concepts if the students are to apply them in later reading and writing situations.

Is the proposed unit of study appropriate to the ability and knowledge of the pupils so that it is likely to be of interest to them?

Obviously, decisions about what to teach cannot be made only on the basis of whether or not the concepts are important to the structure of the subject matter. A teacher who falls into that error is likely to meet disaster within weeks, days, or even minutes of the opening day of school. His classes will be noisy at the wrong times or will achieve a silence so profound that it can only be the result of utter boredom. He is likely to present either material that is far too difficult or material so easy that the students ridicule him for it.

There are two aspects to the problem of insuring that instruction is appropriate. First, the teacher must determine the abilities of the students (see Chapters 2, 11, and 21). Second, he must determine what abilities and knowledge are requisite to the unit he is planning. Units he decides to teach should move from what the students know and can do to the things they don't know and cannot yet do. Following these procedures has a great deal to do with maintaining student interest.

Everyone knows students who are indifferent to English, who make an effort to look bored and unimpressed regardless of what the teacher presents. These students are largely responsible for the hands-in-the-air postures of their despairing teachers. Yet consider for a moment why they are that way. They have been eminently unsuccessful in academic areas for at least six years—a long time for even an adult to experience frustration and failure.

If they display interest, try hard, and *then* fail, their stupidity, their worthlessness is confirmed in their own eyes. But if they do not care, if they do not try, then failure can be attributed to something other than incapacity. A good bit of the "I-don't-care" syndrome can be overcome by carefully assessing student ability, selecting appropriate materials, and structuring lessons from the simple to the complex.

Interest inventories ordinarily ask students to indicate what kinds of books they like, what kind they would write, or which books they have actually read. Some teachers, in their desire to have students love literature, use these responses as a basis for curriculum planning. Yet although the responses may be an aid to curriculum building, they do not form an adequate base for it. For instance, if students have never heard of myth, they cannot indicate it as an interest on a survey. The mere fact that it does not appear should not lead inevitably to the conclusion that students would not be interested in it.

In general, the teacher should ignore stereotyped thinking about student interests. He should select materials that the students will learn to handle in the unit. Then he should watch for signs from the class. Are more students than usual staring out the windows? Is the class discussion lively? Do students' faces indicate boredom? Or do they appear interested and alive? Finally, at the end of the unit the teacher might distribute a questionnaire on which students can anonymously indicate their interest in the unit as a whole and in specific parts of it. (See Chapter 14.)

EVALUATION Whatever the concepts taught in a unit or in a curriculum, the teacher must continuously evaluate their validity and appropriateness. They must be valid in light of the definition of the subject. They must be appropriate in terms of student ability and interest, and students must be able to put them to use. To select the concepts for a unit or a curriculum once and consider the task complete will not do. Population shifts cause changes in the character of students in particular schools. Scholarly progress may invalidate or add to the teacher's original definition of the subject. More than likely, a curriculum will tend to invalidate itself. If the curriculum works, what the students learn in one grade will make certain learnings unnecessary in the next. To a certain extent the culture of a school creeps downward from grade level to grade level. Tenth graders teach ninth graders what they have learned. No one objects to this sort of change, but it is another reason for continuous evaluation of the decisions about the concepts we teach.

Specific Objectives

When the teacher has determined the purposes of his instruction and selected concepts important to the study of literature, composition, or language and appropriate to the abilities and interests of his students, he enters the next phase of deciding what to teach. He must decide what his students should be able to do by the conclusion of the instruction. In other words, he must formulate objectives.

There are two classes of objectives. The first, *terminal objectives,* are attained when a unit of study is completed. Assume, for example, that the objective is "to write a Shakespearean sonnet." When a student can write one, his unit of study is completed because he has *attained the objective.*

In order for him to write a Shakespearean sonnet, he would have to be able to characterize one. This then is another objective: "Characterize a Shakespearean sonnet." Because getting to the point where he can write a Shakespearean sonnet depends upon his first being able to characterize one, the objective of characterizing the sonnet is called a *medial objective. Terminal objectives* depend on *medial objectives.*

When the teacher plans work for a year (or longer), the terminal objectives of one unit can become the medial objectives for another. For example, the objectives for composition for the year might be: "To write sonnets of all forms." In that case, writing a Shakespearean sonnet, although a terminal objective in its own unit, would be a medial objective for the year.

Needless to say, determining the terminal objectives for the whole English studies curriculum is a central task for the whole profession. Beyond this, determining terminal objectives for American education is an absolutely crucial task.

Advantages of Specific Objectives

Defining the specific objectives of a given lesson is extremely important to both teacher and students for a number of reasons. First, the teacher's planning becomes far easier and more meaningful once he knows what he can expect his students to be able *to do* by the end of the instruction. He can then plan procedures and select materials appropriate to his purposes with a minimum of labor. Attempting to build anything without a specific plan in mind means a waste of time and energy in false starts, unexpected detours, repair of damage resulting from unforeseen obstacles, and so on. A shipwright does not begin to build a boat without a blueprint—an abstract representation of his *objective.* Medical doctors do not treat a patient haphazardly; they must know what conditions they wish to alleviate or what diseases they wish to cure— their *objectives.*

Those who argue against setting terminal objectives claim that teaching is an art and is not so mechanical as shipbuilding or medicine. Therefore, they say, objectives are either irrelevant or confining, or both. It is true that good teaching must grow out of the interaction of teacher and student. But even a sculptor does not begin hammering away at a block of stone without first making some sketches that represent his *objectives.* Da Vinci's sketches, for example, are famous. Any teacher who is a greater artist than Da Vinci may claim exemption from objectives—perhaps.

There is no question that objectives must and do change through the interaction of artist and material or of teacher and students. The sculptor may make certain concessions to his block of stone. As he gets to know his material better, he will find that there are certain soft spots, cracks, and the like, and he will change his plan accordingly. A painter may have a sudden insight about the color or shape of some object, and instantaneously his objectives change. Similarly, a teacher confronting a group of students will necessarily learn more about them. He will detect ambiguities and omissions in his original objectives, or he may discover that his original plan is inadequate. He must change his objectives accordingly.

A second advantage of precisely formulated objectives is that they reduce frustration and insecurity by enabling the teacher to evaluate what has been accomplished in the classroom. Of all the subject-matter teachers, the English teacher is least likely to know whether or not he has accomplished anything. The math teacher can simply count the number of problems his students solve correctly. The foreign language teacher knows his students cannot speak a language at the beginning of a semester but will be able to use certain words and phrases at the end of a certain number of weeks. The English teacher, on the other hand, is frequently reduced to counting errors in compositions or rationalizing that though students don't like Shakespeare in school, they will later in life when they reflect upon it. Evaluation of this kind is not very satisfying to an honest teacher, and most English teachers are honest and conscientious. Part of their reward lies in watching their students grow.

Carefully formulated objectives help an English teacher to evaluate what the students have accomplished in the course of a unit. If the objectives are clearly stated, the teacher need only observe his students to determine the extent and quality of their learning.

It is the student who is best served by the careful formulation of objectives. Obviously, if the teacher knows what he wants the students to be able to do by the end of the instruction, he can convey the goals to them. They in turn will learn more easily and with less frustration.

Nearly everyone has experienced considerable uneasiness at the hands of teachers who know only intuitively what they expect of students and cannot explain assignments. Successful students handle this problem by "psyching out" the teacher, and it is their compositions that help the teacher to define what it was he wanted in the first place. The other, less fortunate students are doomed to partial or complete failure from the beginning. The teacher who formulates objectives carefully will not have to wait until he reads the compositions to decide specifically what he wanted; he will know at the beginning of the lesson and will be able to teach his students far more efficiently.

There is a second advantage to the student. If the teacher knows what he wants his students to do, he is less likely to teach the student one thing and test him on another, a very unfair but common practice in English classrooms. For instance, many teachers drill students on the meanings of vocabulary words and test them on their ability to write the words in sentences that illuminate their meanings. They justify the test on the basis that students do not understand the words unless they can use them in a sentence. Yet learning definitions and writing words in sentences are quite different tasks. A clear statement of objectives might have changed either the test or the instruction. If the teacher plans to test students' ability to write words in sentences, it is only fair to teach them how to do it.

Formulation of Objectives

The formulation of specific terminal objectives is not a simple task. They should be stated so clearly that two competent teachers could agree *in advance* about what students need to do to fulfill them. The following objectives are typical of those that frequently occur in English curriculum guides. As you read them, ask yourself if you would agree with another competent person in deciding which students had fulfilled them.

1. To understand the nature of the English language
2. To make the student aware of the literary heritage of the United States and England
3. To improve vocabulary

Everyone will agree that these statements express the general purposes of an English course. But in most English curricula such statements are intended to serve as the terminal objectives for a unit of instruction or for a year's course. If they do not help us evaluate instruction in terms of student progress, then they are useless as terminal objectives. A brief examination will reveal their uselessness.

1. TO UNDERSTAND THE NATURE OF THE ENGLISH LANGUAGE This objective poses a number of questions. The most specific parts of it are the words "English language." But what does the word "nature" mean? Does it refer to dialect differences, usage in composition, the sound system, syntax, morphology, connotative problems, biases implicit in the language, all of these, or something else? The word "understand" is also ambiguous. What level of understanding must the student display, and how must he display it? If the word "language" refers to grammar, does "understanding" entail writing definitions of parts of speech? Must he label the nouns, verbs, adjectives, and so on, in a given passage? If so, how complex will the passage be? Will it include nouns used as verbs, prepositions used as nouns?

2. TO MAKE THE STUDENT AWARE OF THE LITERARY HERITAGE OF THE UNITED STATES AND ENGLAND This objective tells what the teacher will do,

not what the student will do. If terminal objectives are to be useful in planning and evaluation, they must tell what the *student* must do. The word "aware" presents even more problems than "understand" did in the previous statement. Should the student simply know that literature exists? Should he recite or recall authors, dates, titles of works, plots, and characters? Or should he write a composition about his literary heritage? In brief, the word "aware" in an objective permits practically any standard, any nonsense in the classroom, no matter how shallow or pernicious.

3. TO IMPROVE VOCABULARY Although this objective is more specific than the preceding one, the word "improve" offers problems of its own. How will the student's vocabulary level be measured to begin with? What degree of change will be regarded as improvement? Will recognition of new words in reading be satisfactory? If so, how must the student demonstrate his recognition of new words? Must he write definitions of them, pick synonyms, antonyms, or definitions from lists that he is given? Will the words that he must recognize appear in context or in lists? How many words will he have to recognize? Will the student have to use the words in his writing or in his everyday spoken language?

A satisfactory set of terminal objectives for vocabulary development as one phase of a year's English program might read as follows:

GENERAL PURPOSE

To improve vocabulary

TERMINAL OBJECTIVES

1. Given a list (the list should be appended) of 300 words studied during the course of the school year, to choose the correct synonym from a list of four alternatives for at least 70 percent of the items. (The test or sample items should be appended.)
2. Given a set of passages utilizing 50 of the 300 words studied during the school year, to write adequate, short definitions (the phrase "adequate, short definitions" should be defined or examples should be supplied.) of 35 of the 50 words as they are used in context.
3. To use correctly the 50 key words (a list of key words—such as "plot," "conflict," "resolution," "prose"—should be appended) that are introduced by various units of study in compositions written throughout the course of the year.

Clearly, a teacher can use any or all of these or other specifically stated objectives. The point is that objectives stated in this way are useful for both planning and evaluation. First, they tell precisely what the student must do—for example, he must choose the correct synonym from a list of four alternatives for 70 percent of 300 words. Second, they tell the conditions of the evaluation—he will receive a list of 300 words with four alternative answers for each one. Third, they indicate the minimal performance required.

Thus, if a teacher adopted the second objective, he would know how to plan vocabulary lessons for the year. Students would work with words in context. Preliminary tests would require the student to write definitions of certain words underlined in various passages. Therefore, it would be necessary to teach students how to write definitions.

This problem brings us to another important aspect of terminal objectives, *criterion statements*. The criterion statements enable the teacher to judge consistently the extent to which his instruction has been successful. For instance, criterion statements should define the phrase "adequate, short definitions" in the second objective above in such a way that the teacher can immediately recognize a successful definition. If he teaches and requires formal definitions, then the criterion statements might read as follows:

1. The definition must take the sentence form.
2. The word to be defined must be the subject.
3. The definition must indicate the class to which the word being defined belongs. The class should be neither too broad nor too narrow. For example:
   A hammer is a thing . . .
   A hammer is a carpenter's tool . . .
4. The definition should differentiate the word being defined from other members of the class.
5. Neither the word indicating the class nor its modifiers may include the word being defined or a derivative of it.
6. Additional statements should be used if necessary to make contrasts with similar words.
7. The following definition by a tenth grader represents an adequate definition: "A hammer is a tool with a handle attached to a head made of metal, rubber, or plastic, used for striking other objects such as nails, wood, metal, etc. A hammer is different from a mallet in size and shape. The head of a mallet is much larger, and usually made of a softer material. A hammer is different from a hatchet in that a hatchet has a cutting edge."

Writing objectives for vocabulary study, punctuation, and spelling is relatively simple because the objectives tend to deal with specific bits of information that can be committed to memory. Writing objectives for composition and literature study is considerably more complex. The objectives should never dictate the precise ordering of specific words for a composition, nor should they indicate specific responses to a literary work. They should, however, specify the processes and/or forms that a student should use in producing his composition and in approaching a work of literature. Such objectives may include several alternatives. For instance, a twelfth-grade literature student might be required to approach a poem from any one or a combination of several points of view. A ninth grader who may have learned two modes of organization might be asked to use either one in writing a composition. An eighth grader learning to write formal definitions must observe the form and choose whatever details and language are relevant to his problem in definition. But any one of a number of definitions may meet the requirements. Tenth graders could be asked to examine *Antigone* in terms of the conflicts existing in the play and to specify what the conflicts are, defend and explain their choices, and determine which conflict has most significance for the play as a whole. Obviously, a variety of answers of equal validity are possible. In most cases the teacher should be less concerned with eliciting some particular response from a student than with seeing that the student use a sound argument for defending his conclusions.

The following terminal objectives and criterion statements for the unit "Animals in Literature" illustrate how objectives for literature and composition can stipulate processes and forms while allowing considerable latitude in fulfilling the tasks. Note that no specific responses are required in any of the objectives.

OBJECTIVES

1. To write an essay analyzing a book selected from the unit bibliography. Criterion statements
   a. The essay must be written and revised during class time.
   b. The analysis must answer the following questions:
      (1) What is the conflict in the book? What is its cause? How is it resolved?
      (2) How does the author treat the animal? To what extent is the animal anthropomorphized? To what degree is it treated as an animal? What evidence is there to support your position?
      (3) What generalization does the author imply?
   c. The essay must include a statement of the book's theme and answer the above questions in explaining the theme.
2. To write a paragraph essay analyzing the symbolism of a fable not studied in class.
   a. The reading and writing must be done in one class period.
   b. The student must identify the referents of the symbols in the fable, explain their relationship and how they contribute to the moral.
   c. He must evaluate the appropriateness of the author's choice of animals in terms of the conflict in the fable and in terms of the moral.
3. To write an original fable.
   a. The animals must be personifications of human characteristics.
   b. They must be generally appropriate to the qualities they represent.
   c. The fable must include a moral.

The terminal objectives stated at the beginning of the "Tragic Hero" unit contain no criterion statements, and that creates a problem. For instance, the final objective reads, "To write (outside class) an analysis of a modern literary work read independently, determining the extent to which it can be considered tragic." The problem arises because the terms "analysis," "modern literary work," and "tragic" are rather vague. The selected bibliography at the end of the unit helps define "modern literary work," and the teacher can easily clarify that anyway. The whole unit deals with the concept of the "tragic," but even so, if the teacher wishes to require that the student makes use of specific characteristics in his analysis, then the objective should convey them. "Analysis," however, is the chief problem which the following criterion statements help to clarify:

1. The essay must include a definition of tragedy which enumerates the major characteristics of tragedy. The definition may be formal or informal.
2. The essay must explain which characteristics of tragedy the modern work and its hero display and which they do not.
3. The essay must explain what characteristics the work displays which are not those of tragedy.
4. Assertions must be supported with specific examples from or allusions to the work.

Further, if the teacher will base his evaluations in part on organization and mechanics, he must include criterion statements to that effect unless such criteria are standard for all work of this type. Even then, he should be sure that students know how to organize and proofread. Such criteria not only clarify the assignment for the student but clarify what the teacher's instructional emphases will be.

The various objectives above are stated in *behavioral* terms. That is they stipulate what students must *do*. If the students cannot perform the tasks described in the objectives by the end of instruction, then the teacher knows that some aspect of his instruction has been inappropriate or inadequate. But if he has no objectives or if the objectives do not describe clearly what the students must do, then the teacher has no way of evaluating his instruction.

Objectives must emphasize what the student must do or perform because, as the first chapter pointed out, there is absolutely no way to examine the internal thinking processes themselves. But the emphasis on external behavior does not imply lack of interest in internal processes. On the contrary, English teachers must examine external behavior as the *only* means of determining what thinking has taken place.

Nor does the emphasis on behavior require mechanistic responses. Too many English teachers, primarily those who have not analyzed their objectives, write tests that require only recall of information: the names of authors, the content of poems, interpretations thoroughly discussed in class. Objectives can be written at many levels, and *recall* is the least sophisticated because it requires the least understanding. The objectives for English should require the student to put what he has learned into operation in new situations. For example, the first and second objectives for "Animals in Literature" require analysis of a book and a fable, which the students read on their own, applying the principles learned in the unit. The third objective requires synthesis, creating something new, which, at the same time, reflects what has been studied in the unit. Objectives such as these go far beyond rote learning and enable the teacher to make a real assessment of *understanding* and *creativity,* terms that are too often mouthed and then ignored because the teacher has no clear idea of what he means by them.[3]

Unfortunately, it is not always possible to write useful terminal objectives before planning a unit of instruction. Some teachers must plan a unit in some detail before they can formulate specific objectives. As long as they begin their planning with the specific concepts of the unit in mind, they can usually write objectives later. Examining the materials they will use, the questions they will ask, and the assignments they will make helps to clarify the goals of the instruction and to suggest the criterion statements. If the teacher writes objectives as the final stage of unit planning, he must check his plans to be sure they are in line with his objectives. If he does not check his plans, then the students may suffer. The teacher may teach one thing and expect the students to do another. After teaching a unit and examining student responses, the teacher can revise terminal objectives, criterion statements, and procedures. For instance, requiring formal definitions of words in context to indicate knowledge of meaning is probably unduly severe. Formal definitions of concrete words such as "hammer" are difficult enough to write. Presumably, a vocabulary test would include many abstract words, but chances are that many students would fail the test because they could not write adequate formal definitions. Therefore, a less formal definition would be more appropriate to the test. Thus, a teacher who had required formal definitions and realized their difficulty might wish to revise the criterion statements.

The following rules are useful in formulating terminal objectives:

1. The objective should take the infinitive form, for example, "To write haiku."
2. It should be written from the student's point of view, explaining what he must do.
3. Another competent person should be able to select students who have fulfilled the objectives. His selections should be in agreement with the teacher's.
4. The objective should avoid such ambiguous terms as understand, examine, appreciate, interpret—unless they are defined either in the objective or in the criterion statements.

5. The objective should specify what the learner must be able to *do* or *perform* when he is demonstrating his mastery of the objective.

6. The objective should specify the conditions imposed upon the learner while he is demonstrating his accomplishment of the objective. For example, "Given an unfamiliar poem such as 'Ozymandias,' to write . . . in a fifty-minute class period."

Although it is difficult, writing objectives for literature, composition, and language study is absolutely imperative. Literature and composition study suffer horribly because teachers have not decided what to do in specific terms. For example, one assignment required eleventh graders to write a letter to the employer who had fired Walt Whitman. The teacher was dissatisfied with the results, but he had no right to be because he had had no specific objectives in mind and no criteria to define what an acceptable letter would be when he had made the assignment. Therefore, no instruction had taken place. The students had learned no techniques, no methods of approach and had no idea of what the teacher really expected. In class one day, they produced the best letters they could under the circumstances, and they received low grades. The low grades punished the students for what the teacher had failed to do.

On the other hand, the teacher must be wary of attempts to standardize objectives for all students at particular grade levels. The teacher himself must prepare clear objectives appropriate for his own students in his particular classes.

ANIMALS IN LITERATURE*

Lesson 1   Identifying Unit Concepts

OBJECTIVE

To identify key unit questions

MATERIALS

Overhead projector

PROCEDURES

1. The teacher begins the unit by asking students what pets they have and how they treat their pets. He guides the discussion to the question of how human beings think of animals (as having human characteristics or only animal characteristics). He encourages students to talk about

---

* This is simply an outline, not a complete instructional unit. Study guides and the bibliography for outside reading have been omitted. The unit was first developed by the authors and teachers at Euclid Central Junior High School (Euclid, Ohio) and was subsequently distributed by the Project English Demonstration Center at Euclid Central and Western Reserve University.

the animal stories they have read and leads into the problems of what conflicts animals encounter, why human beings become attached to animals, and the relationship between animals and their environment.

2. The teacher explains that the students will be reading animal stories and asks them to suggest questions that they might use as they read the stories. From the discussion above and with some prompting from the teacher, the class develops a set of questions such as the following. The teacher will record the questions on the overhead as they are suggested and reproduce them for use throughout the unit.

a. Conflict

(1) What are the various kinds of conflict present in the story? (Animal vs. animal, animal vs. man, animal vs. nature.) What are the specific conflicts?

(2) What are the causes and results of the conflict?

(3) Through what abilities, characteristics, and opportunities does the animal resolve the conflict?

b. The animal in his environment

(1) What characteristics of the animal enable him to adapt to his environment in finding food and shelter and in protecting himself against environmental threats?

(2) How does the animal react to threatening situations—through fear or planning?

(3) In what respects can we say that animals plan?

(4) What characteristics of man enable him to adapt to nearly any environment whereas most animals can survive in only some environments?

c. The author's treatment of the animal

(1) Is the animal given the position of a main character, a secondary character, or a symbol?

(2) Does the author attribute human characteristics to the animal, or does the animal remain a creature of instinct?

(a) How does the animal learn from experience?

(b) How does he communicate with other animals?

(c) In what situations does the author attribute possession or lack of any of the following to the animal: loyalty, generosity, kindness, cruelty, helpfulness, obedience, rebelliousness, courage, or justice?

(d) What motivates the animal to be loyal, kind, courageous, and so on?

(e) If a giraffe runs from a lion, is the giraffe cowardly? If two lions fight until one kills the other, can we say that either or both are courageous? If a small animal fights back when cornered by a larger animal, is the small animal courageous?

(f) Why is it questionable that virtues such as courage and loyalty can be attributed to animals?

(g) What characteristics of man prompt him to attribute such qualities to animals?

Lesson 2 Conflict and Environment

OBJECTIVES

To identify and explain the causes, results, and resolutions of the conflicts in the stories and poems

To analyze the relationships between the animals in the materials and their environments

MATERIALS

John L. and Jean George, "The Hunt"
Jim Kjelgaard, "Snow Dog"
Liam O'Flaherty, "The Wild Goat's Kid"
Samuel Scoville, "The Cleanlys"

PROCEDURES

1. The teacher provides guide questions for "The Hunt" and assigns it to the whole class. When the reading is complete, the teacher leads a discussion that focuses on the problems of conflict and environment as suggested by the questions in parts 2 and 3 of "General Study and Discussion Questions" above.

2. The teacher then divides the class into three homogeneous groups and assigns the strongest readers "The Cleanlys," the next strongest "The Wild Goat's Kid," and the weakest "Snow Dog." Each group reads the story, discusses it in terms of the special reading guide questions and parts 2 and 3 of "General Study and Discussion Questions." If the groups have seven or more students, it will be necessary to divide them in two for discussion. Each group then presents its findings to the rest of the class *or* assigns the class its story and elects representatives to lead the whole class in a discussion of it.

Lesson 3 Author's Treatment of the Animal

OBJECTIVE

To identify and explain the way in which the author treats the animals as characters

MATERIALS

Robert P. Tristram Coffin, "The Spider"
Rudyard Kipling, "Rikki-Tikki-Tavi"
Howard Maier, "The Red Dog"

Beryl Markham, "Wise Child"
Sterling North, "The Great Dan Patch"
Walt Whitman, "A Noiseless, Patient Spider"

PROCEDURES

1. While the reading and discussion of this lesson focus on part 3 of the "General Study and Discussion Questions," the questions in parts 1 and 2 continue to be considered.

2. The teacher assigns "Rikki-Tikki-Tavi" in which Kipling anthropomorphizes the animals. The discussion focuses on how the animals are given human characteristics and what the result is. The teacher leads the students in comparing and contrasting "Rikki-Tikki-Tavi" with stories in previous lessons. For more specific contrasts he reads aloud the poems by Coffin and Whitman. After discussing each poem, the two views of spiders can be compared with each other and then contrasted to the treatment of animals in the Kipling story.

3. The teacher then assigns "The Red Dog," "Wise Child" and "The Great Dan Patch" to homogeneous groups from strongest to weakest respectively. The procedures for Lesson 2, part B, apply here.

4. When discussions are complete, the teacher leads the class in developing the opening paragraph for a composition discussing the various unit problems as they apply to "Rikki-Tikki-Tavi." The teacher uses the overhead projector to record student suggestions. When the first paragraph is developed, the teacher leads the class in developing an outline for the remainder.

5. Each student then selects a different story already discussed and, following the model developed by the class, writes an essay in which he answers the questions concerning conflict, environment, and the author's view of the animal.

6. When the essays are complete, the teacher divides the class into small groups to evaluate the essays. The groups criticize each essay in terms of how adequately it answers the various questions. Students have a chance to revise in light of the criticism.

Lesson 4 Animals As Symbols

OBJECTIVES

To identify the referents of animals used as symbols
To write an original fable

MATERIALS

Aesop, *Fables*
Edward McCourt, "Cranes Fly South"
James Thurber, *Fables for Our Time* (selections)

PROCEDURES

1. The detailed lesson plans in Chapter 5, on introducing symbolism through fables are satisfactory here. The seventh-grade teacher will have to use additional fables and more group work, however.
2. Following the examination of fables, assign "Cranes Fly South" and discuss the significance of the cranes to the reader as well as the characters in the story.
3. Before writing a fable, the students objectify the characteristics of the fable, and compile a list of them:
   a. Each animal represents a human characteristic or quality.
   b. The animals frequently represent opposite traits, for example, wise-foolish, brave-cowardly.
   c. The reader knows only a few characteristics of the animals.
   d. The fable has a moral, either implicit or explicit.
4. After suggesting ideas for fables, the students begin writing their own fables. If necessary, the teacher suggests combinations of animals and situations such as the following:
   a. The giraffe teases the donkey about his long ears.
   b. The alligator tempts a turtle to examine his teeth.
   c. The rooster announces to the animals that he should be the king of the barnyard.
5. When students have completed their fables, they criticize one another's fables in terms of the characteristics listed above. They should have an opportunity to revise in light of the criticism.
6. The teacher may select a committee of students to select fables and to produce a dittoed collection of fables written by students.

Lesson 5   Synthesis

OBJECTIVE

To apply the major unit questions to a series of short poems

MATERIALS

Dunning, Lueders, and Smith, *Reflections on a Gift of Watermelon Pickle*

PROCEDURES

1. The teacher makes a selection of six or seven poems dealing with animal subjects in *Reflections on a Gift of Watermelon Pickle*. He reads the poems aloud while the students follow in their copies.
2. Each student fills out a card indicating his first and second choice of poems he would like to study. The teacher organizes groups of three or four students according to their preferences, and each prepares a discussion of its poem for the class. The unit questions developed in Les-

sons 1 and 4 are applied to the poems. Each group decides how to present its poem: by organizing a debate on some aspect of the poem; by asking questions or presenting a series of views to stimulate class discussion; by using audio-visual equipment.
3. Some classes may take only a day or two for the presentations. Others may take a week. The teacher permits the class to move at its own pace.

Lesson 6   Synthesis

OBJECTIVE

To analyze novels in terms of the unit questions

MATERIALS

Jack London, *The Call of the Wild* (fluent readers)
Jack London, *White Fang*
Fred Gipson, *Old Yeller* (slow readers)

PROCEDURES

1. The teacher divides the class into three groups according to reading ability and distributes novels and study guides accordingly.
2. To use students' previous knowledge of the North as a basis for motivation and involvement, students reading the books by London are given a map with two trails marked from California to the Yukon.
   a. Students write a short description of the physical environment of the area covered by these trails on the back of the map.
   b. When they are finished, they are divided into small groups to share their ideas.
3. To secure student participation and motivation, students with lower reading ability will begin *Old Yeller* with a short period of oral reading by the teacher.
4. The class will vary daily within the groups according to the pace each group sets. The following activities may be used in any combination or sequence at the option of the teacher and students:
   a. Oral activities:
      (1) Discussion of themes treated in a chapter (for example, the conflict in "Dominant Primordial Beast" in *The Call of the Wild*)
      (2) Discussion of main ideas in a chapter (for example, the force of hunger in Chapter III of *White Fang*)
      (3) Discussion of character (for example, the man in the red shirt in *The Call of the Wild*)
      (4) Discussion of vocabulary (for example, "venison" from *Old Yeller*)
      (5) Discussion of study guide questions

(6) Discussion of the themes as treated compared to other chapters and other selections studied

b. Written activities for individuals or groups:
   (1) Answers to study guide questions
   (2) Analysis of a particular theme or themes in a chapter
   (3) Rewriting of a section from another point of view
   (4) Composition concerning the student's experience with animals
   (5) Listing the sequence of events
   (6) Comparing the treatment of a particular theme in the novel to the treatment of the theme in a short story

c. Activities for slow students
   (1) Drawing illustrations of scenes from the book
   (2) Building models of animals or scenes
   (3) Preparing a bulletin board display
   (4) Drawing maps of the area covered in the book
   (5) Viewing and writing reports on television animal programs

5. To maintain interest, the classroom activities also vary within each daily period. Each group participates in as many as three different activities in one class period. For example:

Group I White Fang	Group II Call of the Wild	Group III Old Yeller
1. Silent reading	Writing paragraph	Oral discussion of study guide questions
2. Oral discussion	Reading	Writing paragraph
3. Writing paragraph	Oral discussion	Reading

6. Each student writes a paper discussing the novel he reads in terms of the unit concepts.

Lesson 7 Final Evaluation

OBJECTIVE

To write a book report analyzing a novel in terms of the unit concepts

MATERIALS

Bibliography

PROCEDURES

1. The teacher prepares a bibliography of books dealing with animals that are available in the school or local public libraries. He distributes this and helps students make appropriate selections.

2. The teacher provides some class time for reading so that he may confer with students to help develop a topic about which the student can write his report. The student prepares to answer the questions listed under terminal objective 1 at the beginning of the unit.
3. The teacher reserves class time for writing and revising the essay.

NOTES

1. Jerome S. Bruner, *The Process of Education* (Cambridge: Harvard University Press, 1960).
2. Richard Braddock, *et al., Research in Written Composition* (Champaign: National Council of Teachers of English, 1963), pp. 37–38.
3. Benjamin S. Bloom, *et al., Taxonomy of Educational Objectives: Cognitive Domain* (New York: David McKay Co., Inc., 1956). A very useful analysis of levels of objectives in six major categories: knowledge, comprehension, application, analysis, synthesis, and evaluation.

SUGGESTIONS FOR FURTHER READING

1. RALPH MAGER, Writing Instructional Objectives (San Francisco: Fearon Publishers, 1961).
2. JEROME S. BRUNER, *The Process of Education* (Cambridge: Harvard University Press, 1960).
3. NORMAN E. GRONLUND, *Stating Behavioral Objectives for Classroom Instruction* (New York: Macmillan Co., 1970).

5 | Creating an Environment for Active Learning

*There is an odd paradox in the teaching process which sounds,
at first, as though teaching were an art of noble hypocrisy, like
the noble lie of Plato's state. There can be no sense of excitement
or discovery, no glimpsing of new worlds of the mind, without
dramatizing for the student a mental attitude that is inductive
and empirical, putting the learner into the same psychological
position as the most original of thinkers.*[1]

For generations teachers have assumed that the most
efficient method of teaching the young is to impart knowledge directly. Since the invention of printing, the two primary sources of knowledge have been the teacher and the
texts he assigns. The primary goal has been for the students to absorb as much as possible of what the teacher
and text have to say. Classic examples are common on
nearly every college campus in the country. The professor
speaks. The students write in their notebooks. They read
the assigned texts. At the end of the course, when the professor finally asks a question, the students copy the answer,
presumably from memory, into little blue books. Some
shortcomings of this model of teaching should be evident
to anyone with experience in our educational system. First,
this model assumes that education is simply a matter of
accumulating knowledge. The tests that most high school
and college students encounter are evidence of that. Second, it assumes that all students are capable of accumulating knowledge in the same way and at the same rate. This
assumption, along with economic exigencies, has given
rise to the mass lecture, common at many large universities and, unfortunately, in more and more high schools.
Third, the model ignores, almost completely, other means
of learning, especially that of discussion with other students.

The lecture as a method of instruction is not always or
necessarily bad. Some lectures are very stimulating indeed.
Some secondary English teachers are able to talk their
students through a literature and composition course. But

when lecture is the only method, the student is never more than a passive agent in the learning situation. He may be able to recall what the teacher says, but only infrequently and incidentally does he learn to cope with new problems independently. And when he does, it is usually through some chance circumstance, related tenuously, if at all, to his classroom experience.

Typically, the literature student who has been taught by this method may know the meaning and structure of a particular poem or novel that his instructor has treated in class, but the student is unable to cope efficiently with a new literary experience. He may know a few adjectives by which he can characterize Poe's style, but he is unable to show how those words have specific application in one of Poe's tales that his instructor has not discussed. He has had neither the challenge nor the opportunity to approach a literary work on his own. The instructor has always done it for him.

Since it is clearly impossible for English teachers to deal specifically with all the language situation in literature and composing that his students might encounter outside the classroom, it is imperative to teach so that students learn how to examine and use their language independently. That, of course, requires active participation by the student and a different model of teaching. The method must be largely inductive, putting the learner in what Northrop Frye called "The same psychological position as the most original thinkers."

Clearly, we can never use a completely inductive method in the classroom. If the student were to start from scratch and explore his subject inductively, it might take him years to formulate a single, useful generalization. Further, most students would find the process far too frustrating. But it would be a foolish teacher who did not allow his students to benefit from what man has already learned. The teacher can use his knowledge to arrange problems, materials, and situations so that his students *rediscover* for themselves and gain understanding on their own, a method capable of taking advantage of what man already knows without losing the pride and excitement that comes with discovery for oneself. If the teacher who uses this method is a hypocrite, his is a noble hypocrisy. He knows in general where the students are going, and he organizes the material so that they can have insights for themselves.

Picture such a classroom. Students are actively engaged in discussing subject-matter problems with the teacher or other students. Most students participate in the discussion. At times students work independently; at other times they work in groups. They examine additional materials and discuss them. Gradually, having learned to approach problems of a particular type, they no longer need the guidance of the teacher in that respect. Unfortunately, such classroom situations do not come into existence by magic. Most teachers, at any rate, do not know the magic words. Most must plan carefully and be prepared to change the plans once the lesson is begun. Further, most teachers should strive to be aware of how they themselves behave during a lesson and how that classroom behavior affects the learning and attitudes of their students.

The remainder of this chapter will deal with two major aspects of creating environments for active learning: planning—what the teacher does to prepare the lesson; and teaching—how the teacher behaves once the lesson has begun.

Planning for Active Learning

Two aspects of planning for active learning are extremely important for both experienced and inexperienced teachers: (1) beginning at a level of sophistication appropriate to the students, and (2) selecting and arranging appropriate materials and questions. In addition, the inexperienced teacher must plan all procedural details the first time he uses a particular lesson or else he runs the risk of losing his students' attention while he is searching for materials, thinking of appropriate questions, and so on.

BEGINNING AT THE APPROPRIATE LEVEL

Chapter 4 emphasized the importance of determining the prerequisite knowledge or skill for reaching terminal objectives. If the student has not met the prerequisites, the medial objectives, then instruction must begin with them.

If the composition inventories at the beginning of the year indicate that students are functional writers, the teacher may want to introduce the concept of "audience" to his students. His purpose is to help them learn to write for particular audiences. The terminal objective may be "to write three versions of a composition, each designed for a particular audience." One prerequisite or medial objective is "to analyze an audience." But even prior to this the students must have some conception of "audience" and the importance of making the analysis. So the most basic objective is "to identify factors responsible for breakdown in communication." If students are unfamiliar with the concept, the teacher probably cannot begin by introducing the term "audience" as an abstraction. He must present it in as concrete terms as possible, perhaps by asking students how communication breaks down when one person in a conversation is not familiar with a term that another is using or by asking how they would speak to parents as opposed to the school principal or a clergyman concerning some currently inflammatory topic.

SELECTING AND ARRANGING
APPROPRIATE MATERIALS AND QUESTIONS

Once the teacher has determined the appropriate level at which to begin instruction, he must decide how to increase gradually the difficulty of the problems his students encounter. This decision involves both materials and questions. An ordinarily sound rule is to move from the more simple and concrete to the more complex and abstract. The teacher should begin with materials that present as few problems (apart from the major instructional concern) as possible. Similarly, he should begin with the simpler questions, those that will prepare students for the more difficult questions that follow.

Let us suppose that the teacher wants his class to learn to identify and interpret literary symbols. In order to do this, they will have to have some concept of what a literary symbol is. Let us assume further that this area of learning is an entirely new one to the students and that the students are eighth graders.

Since this learning is relatively complex and at the same time central and crucial to serious literary study, the teacher knows that a single lesson cannot do the job. Consequently, he must develop a unit of related lessons. The unit must provide an opportunity for analysis of literature in terms of symbolic intent. To have the students simply develop a definition of literary symbol would defeat his underlying purpose; the reason for pursuing this study in the first place is to enable the students to deal with interpretation problems caused by symbolism in all their reading.

In order to avoid possible confusion, the teacher must limit consideration of symbolic imagery to images of the same type. And although problems of the evaluation of literature will be ultimately important to his students—not all symbolic work is per se worthwhile—to engage the class in evaluation problems at the stage of concept formation might cloud their thinking and perception. So he will delay considerations of critical evaluation to some later time.

Since he has decided to limit the symbolic imagery to imagery of a single type, his next task is to choose the type and then select works that contain that kind of imagery. He decides that there are many literary works containing animal imagery in which the animal images might legitimately be interpreted as symbolic. Among the many works that he is considering are *Aesop's Fables* and *The Rime of the Ancient Mariner*.

It is intuitively obvious that *The Rime of the Ancient Mariner* involves harder learning in every way than *Aesop's Fables*. The length of the poem alone makes it harder. The greater vocabulary load makes it harder. The greater number of interrelationships among the many more elements in the imagery makes it harder. (How to interpret some of the elements is still perplexing scholars.)

Since his students will have enough problems forming the concept of literary symbol alone, it would be a strategic error to begin their study by having them read a work that presents so many other difficulties, which might well represent a block to learning. Anticipating this, he schedules the experience so that they will deal with the easier material, *Aesop's Fables,* first, and later, when the concept of literary symbol has been formed, perhaps they will study *The Rime of the Ancient Mariner.*

Scheduling materials in terms of difficulty is an extremely important aspect of planning for inductive teaching. Because of considerations of concept formation, easier materials are used before harder materials. And all materials must relate in an obvious way to the concept under consideration. New concepts are harder to deal with than familiar ones. Since this is undeniably true, learners will need a great deal of support when they begin to learn a new concept.

At the beginning of his work on literary symbols, the teacher must be careful to use only materials that contain clear instances of symbols. He anticipates ambiguity and deals with it before students themselves become aware of it. His questions move from the simple to the complex. He teaches using similar instructional patterns so that new things in the instruction itself do not present learning problems; thus, the instructional pattern itself supports the learning. When students begin to anticipate the whole pattern, volunteering answers to questions even before they are asked, it is time to withdraw support and allow them to work more independently.

REDUCING STRATEGIES TO CONCRETE PLANS

The teacher begins the study of the literary symbol by using *Aesop's Fables*. He selects a number of fables for class consideration. Among them are "The Fox, the Crow and the Cheese" and "The Dog in the Manger."

Let us consider the general structure of the procedures:

1. A fable is distributed to the students.
2. Before they begin reading, the teacher presents guide questions for the reading.
3. The students read the fable silently. The teacher may read the fable aloud (optional).
4. The teacher conducts a discussion beginning with the reading of the guide questions.
5. The teacher continues the discussion with other questions that lead to forming the concept of "literary symbol."
6. The term "literary symbol" is introduced after the concept is formed.
7. By a review of the discussion, the term is tentatively defined. (As work progresses, the definition will be both refined and expanded.) The lesson is a short one; perhaps two or three such lessons are possible in a class period. Let us see how this outline is realized in terms of the two fables, "The Fox, the Crow and the Cheese" and "The Dog in the Manger."

Lesson 1 "The Fox, the Crow and the Cheese"

1. The fable is distributed to the students.
2. Before they begin the reading, the teacher presents guide questions (which are directed at explicating the literal level of the fable):
   a. What does the crow have that the fox wants?
   b. How many arguments does the fox use with the crow? What are they? Which one works?

3. Students read the fable.
4. The teacher begins the discussion with the reading of guide questions.
5. The teacher continues the discussion with other questions that lead to forming the concept of "literary symbol."

(The next set of questions requires inference from the learners. They are easy inferences, to be sure. But inferring is harder than responding to things specifically reported in the reading. Therefore, at this stage of instruction, inference questions are handled under teacher direction.)

   a. Why did the fox compliment the crow on his singing?
   b. Why did the crow start to sing?
   c. What human character traits does the crow have? The fox?
   d. What is a "foxy" person like? What is "vanity"? What is "gullibility"?
   e. What human character traits does the crow represent? What traits does the fox represent?
   f. When one thing represents something else—such as our flag (point to it) represents the United States—what is the term used for the thing doing the representing, the flag in this case? (If the students don't know the term "symbol," introduce it by writing it on the chalkboard and spelling it aloud. Have the students write it in their notebooks.)
   g. What are some other symbols? (Wedding ring, the cross, and so on.) What do they represent?
   h. The thing that does the representing is called a "symbol." What do you call the thing it represents? (Students will probably not know the term "referent." Follow the same procedures used in introducing "symbol" in *f* above.)
   i. We said that the fox and the crow represented human character traits. Which traits did each represent?
   j. In this case which are the symbols? (Fox and Crow.) Which are the referents? (Character traits.)
   k. In literature, things are often used to represent other things. When something represents something else, what is it? (A symbol.)
   l. Because the symbol occurs in literature—unlike the flag in this room —it is called a "literary symbol." (Follow the procedure in *f* above for introducing the term.)
6. The term is tentatively defined.
   a. Let us look at these literary symbols and see what they are like. Who wrote this fable? (Somebody, the author, Aesop.) Does the author tell us what the animals are supposed to represent? (No.) How do we know? (We figure it out. It's obvious.) Does the author tell us what the referent for a literary symbol is? (No.) But he may give us a clue. What clues does Aesop give us?

b. So we see that the referent for a literary symbol doesn't have to be expressed.

(Later work can involve literature in which the referent is expressed.)

c. We could classify things as "concrete" and "abstract." (If these terms seem unknown to students, introduce them as in 5*f* above.) Name some concrete things. Name some abstract things.

d. What are the literary symbols in the fable? (Fox and crow.) Are they concrete or abstract? (Concrete.) What are the referents for these symbols? (Character traits.) Are character traits abstract or concrete? (Abstract.)

e. Let us review what you have learned about literary symbols. What is the term used for the thing the symbol represents? (Referent.) Does the author have to present a referent for a literary symbol? (No.) Will the symbol be concrete or abstract? (Concrete.)

The next lesson follows a similar pattern; the fable used is "The Dog in the Manger." The procedures vary slightly because students are now familiar with both the concept and the general procedures themselves.

Lesson 2 "The Dog in the Manger"

1. Distribute fables.
2. Introduce reading guide questions and vocabulary as follows:
   a. *Vocabulary.* What is a manger? (If students do not know, explain it. They cannot understand the reading without knowing the term.)
   b. *Questions.* What animals are involved in this story? Where is the dog? Why does the cow want him to move? Does he move? What is the dog's purpose in acting the way he does? What human character traits does the dog have?

(The set of guide questions is made a bit harder in the second lesson. Support is being withdrawn.)

3. Silent reading.
4. & 5. Discussion begins with reading guide questions and continues: What does the dog symbolize? What does the manger symbolize? (If it is necessary, judging by responses, the same careful detailed pattern of the previous lesson can be followed.)
6. & 7. Symbols in this fable are checked against the definition that was developed in the previous lesson.

If necessary, other fables can be read in teacher-controlled situations until responses are quick and sure. Usually, three such lessons will suffice.

When responses in the teacher-led discussion are good, the next stage in withdrawing support begins. Duplicated sets of reading-guide questions and discussion questions are prepared and distributed with fables. The class is divided into small groups for discussion. A student chairman leads the small-group discussion.

The teacher is no longer giving direct support because the general procedural pattern is known. The only new elements are in the content of the fables. In small groups more students have a chance to respond. Disagreements in interpretation can be resolved by the peer group, which can, if it is necessary, seek help from the teacher. The teacher moves from group to group giving help as it is needed. After the small-group discussions, the class is re-formed, and the questions are taken up again so that responses can be compared. Since the territory is familiar and the questions are before everyone, a student can lead the whole-class discussion, thus allowing the teacher to comment in a general way. This procedure continues the withdrawal of support and allows students greater intellectual independence.

The next stage of the group work is changing from fables to other short forms. Such poems as Whitman's "A Noiseless Patient Spider" and Blake's "Chapel All of Gold" can be used. Guide questions at this stage can go directly to the analysis: "What are the symbols and their referents in this poem?"

When students are responding well in groups, independent work begins. Such a story as "The Masque of the Red Death" by Poe can be assigned as homework with guide questions leading to the identification and interpretation of various symbols in the story. The problems are now being handled independently. There is a follow-up discussion in class the next day.

The final stage is the independent reading of such longer works as *Lord of the Flies, The Pearl, Animal Farm,* and *The Rime of the Ancient Mariner.* The reading is assigned, and a book report type of composition is required. The report must discuss literary symbolism in the work chosen for the reading.

Thus, all phases of the work are now being handled in an independent way. There is virtually no teacher support. But the central concept of "literary symbol" is formed, and the objective is attained. Because the work was structured, because pupils gradually came to stand on their own feet, because the materials and questions used at first were easy and clearly showed the principle under attack, blocking was minimized; and the curriculum works.

PLANNING PROCEDURES

In day-to-day instruction, neither purposes nor objectives nor evaluations take up a very great share of planning or classroom time. Evaluations in the form of tests hang like a cloud of doom over the heads of all, true enough. But in the day-to-day routine, the *procedures* dominate the curriculum. Procedures are what the teacher does and what the students do, and what order these things are done in. They will also include the materials that are used.

Although procedures absorb the lion's share of time and require the longest preparations, when purposes have been determined, objectives carefully expressed, and evaluative techniques and devices decided on, the procedures will follow almost as a matter of course.

To a certain extent many teaching procedures are a matter of routine—such things as collecting papers, distributing books, leading discussions, and so on. These routines vary from teacher to teacher and even from class to class of the same teacher.

A beginning teacher must not assume that any class will operate any routine without instruction. An experienced teacher in writing lesson plans will subsume a number of operations under a simple statement like, "Divide the class into committees." Such a statement supposes a great deal of preplanning (setting up the committee on some basis) and earlier teaching (how to arrange furniture, how to function in small groups, and so on). The first time any procedure that will become routine is used, a carefully detailed, step-by-step lesson plan must be thought out. If class behavior indicates the need, instruction based on the plan must be carried out even after the initial lesson employing the routine is finished.

An important routine has to do with giving directions. When directions have been made explicit, the teacher should ask if there are any questions. When the questions are answered, or if there are none, the teacher should then ask the class to repeat the directions. Only after directions have been restated by students are activities begun. This procedure should be followed whenever directions are given.

Finally, the objectives of the instruction should always be made clear to the class. There is no reason to keep students in the dark about the goals of their learning; nor is there reason to assume that they are so sophisticated that they just naturally perceive the objectives. A failure to clarify objectives can result in students working pointlessly (or feeling that they are), working toward wrongly conceived objectives, or in some cases working against the teacher. When objectives are clear, students can help in overcoming deficiencies in materials and procedures and often will short-cut extraneous steps. Consequently, at the inception of an instructional sequence, objectives should be discussed (and if it is appropriate there should be a discussion of purposes also).

These items are the nuts and bolts of instruction, philosophically trivial. Dealing with them ultimately becomes automatic behavior with a teacher. Failure to exercise care in handling the nuts and bolts invites disaster.

THE DAILY PLAN

When the teacher has done all the planning outlined above, he must prepare a daily lesson plan, a procedure that beginning teachers find particularly trying.

Time is the controlling element in daily planning. Conceptually, a lesson may be so short that several may be taught in one class period, as with the fable lessons detailed above. Or it may stretch over a number of class periods.

Thus, the teacher must anticipate how much of a lesson is to be covered during the class period; to do this, he must first make a time estimate for each procedure. Because it is often difficult to anticipate response times, there must be provision in the plan for changes: additional activities for occasions when the class moves faster than expected, or strategic changes for occasions when the responses take longer than expected.

The plan should include a statement of objectives and a list of all necessary materials. It must also include a list of procedures in the sequence in which the class will experience them. The procedures should indicate at what point during the lesson the objectives should be revealed.

Teachers who are just starting out should express, in detail, how even trivial procedures are to be carried out, how the paper is distributed, for example. When this sort of thing has become so routine that it is second nature to both class and teacher, careful explanations can be reduced to such a note as "distribute paper."

A good plan for beginners, and experienced teachers who are trying a lesson for the first time, is to arrange the plan in three columns: the first, very narrow for a notation of anticipated time; the second, the statement of procedures; the third, a statement of the reasons for the procedures. The act of expressing the reason often indicates a weakness in the procedure or in the sequencing of procedures.

An important part of many lessons is making the homework assignment, which should be made as close to the beginning of the lesson as possible (pp. 35–38). A major shift in strategy that may be necessary, however, is to cancel the assignment if its completion is contingent on completing all the planned activities and time runs out unexpectedly.

Let us examine a daily lesson plan that has been used widely and with great success, a plan for teaching the writing of haiku. Parenthetical comments refer to the plan and are not a part of the lesson.

The Haiku Lesson

OBJECTIVES

To analyze haiku
To characterize haiku
To write haiku

MATERIALS

Chalkboard model of haiku for analysis:

Someone lights a moon;
Then angels with silver chalk
Draw on their blackboard.

Sheets of duplicated haiku for analysis and criticism
Scratch paper

Estimated Time	Procedures	Reasons
2 min.	1. Preliminary to lesson, write model for analysis on chalkboard. Have board clean with enough space for results of analysis. Class must be able to identify figures of speech and write them. (Lesson timing begins here.)	1. Don't slow down the lesson for this—class control may suffer or interest may lag.
3 min.	2. Call class to order. Talk a little about characteristic simplicity in Japanese culture, art. Relate haiku to tradition of economy and simplicity. Write word "haiku" on the chalkboard. Explain that this is both singular and plural form.	2. Introducing vocabulary and key ideas.
2 min.	3. State objectives of lesson and make homework assignment: "I would like you to write four haiku on a single theme of your choice for tomorrow. To be able to do this you will first have to know the characteristics of haiku. So we will analyze the one on the chalkboard together." Have class repeat the assignment and what will happen during the lesson.	3. Objectives should be clear to students. Homework assignment should be given with plenty of time in an unhurried way. Class repeats so that teacher is certain everything is clear.
1 min.	4. Indicate that many questions will seem easy but answers are not to be spoken out. Hands must be raised.	4. Otherwise answers will be shouted out. Avoid danger of wrong answers. This pattern is especially important for step 13.
2 min.	5. Instruct class to read the poem silently, and ask a pupil to read	5. Begins with perception of poem as a

Estimated Time	Procedures	Reasons
	it aloud. Ask, "How many lines does a haiku contain?" As answers to this and other analytical questions are forthcoming, write them on the chalkboard. Answer: "Three."	whole. Sets pattern of analysis. Responses written on board for later pupil reference as they find necessary.
2 min.	6. "How many syllables are in the first line?" "Five." "How many syllables in the second line?" "Seven." "How many syllables in the third line?" "Five." "What kind of letter does a line of poetry begin with?" "Capital." At this point indicate that this is the usual convention in all poetry, not just haiku.	6. Analysis begins with mechanical elements as these are easiest to detect.
2 min.	7. Indicate that in much familiar poetry, words at ends of lines rhyme. Ask if lines do or do not rhyme in haiku. Answer: "Do not rhyme." Point out the possible dichotomy in word classification: strong/weak. Explain that "strong" words carry a clear meaning—like "red," "boy," "city." "Weak" words do not carry a clear meaning—like "of," "and," "that." Ask if haiku lines end in strong or weak words. Answer: "Strong."	7. Calls attention to first composing problem that is distinct from specific tradition. Single words are easier to deal with than ideas; more difficult than mechanics or counting.
2 min.	8. Indicate that the haiku must contain at least one figure of speech. Ask if the model does. There are three in it; and the poem as a whole is a metaphor for nightfall. Answers: " 'Someone lights	8. Beginning of image analysis is with general poetic devices. Because figures are highly conventional, they are easier to

Estimated Time	Procedures	Reasons
	a moon' may be personification or hyperbole"; " 'silver chalk' is metaphoric for stars"; " 'blackboard' is metaphoric for night sky."	deal with than other elements in imagery. Also, this is review material. Phrases are harder to deal with than words as indicated in previous step.
2 min.	9. Indicate that the haiku must contain a clear reference to time. This is usually a seasonal reference but it may be any passage of time: minutes, years, days, forever, and so on. Ask if the model contains any such. Answer: "Night."	9. Getting away from structured elements and into "meaning." This aspect is conceptually not very difficult.
2 min.	10. Indicate that the haiku must give the reader a clear picture or "image" and that the image should contain one stable element and one changing element. Ask if this haiku meets the criteria. Answer: "Yes. Stable element: sky; changing element: stars and moon going on and off."	10. Most difficult conceptual aspect of analysis.
2 min.	11. Quickly review all elements needed in haiku. Students may refer to notes on chalkboard.	11. Pulls together all elements in the tradition.

(First medial objective has been attained. Lesson time should be about half gone.)

5 min.	12. Distribute duplicated sheets of haiku.* Ask class to read them and find out if there are any that break the rules. Answers: a. " 'Daydreams' may or may not be a clear reference to	12. Can be done only after rules are articulated. Work with several whole patterns helps to fix concept strongly.

* These are appended to the Lesson (p. 115).

time."

b. "Line 1 contains four syllables."

c. "Line 3 contains four syllables."

d. "Line 2 contains six syllables."

e. "Line 1 contains six syllables."

Responses need not come in sequence.

(Second medial objective has been attained.)

| 5 min. | 13. Distribute scratch paper. Indicate that class is to supply titles for these haiku. Since they are now familiar, you will allow only one and one half minutes for titling. When the time is up, compare titles. | 13. Introduction to idea of theme. Also an activity of high interest. |

(There will be a consistently strong convergence in response, surprising the class. For example, most will title the first "daydreams," the second "the moon," and so on.)

| 3 min. | 14. Point out that the reason for the strong similarity of titles is that class was responding to the *theme* of the poem in titling it. Ask for suggestions for other possible themes that haiku might be written on and as these are suggested write them on the chalkboard under heading "theme." | 14. To give class some ideas of themes they might use. Support in a basic conceptual area on which assignment hinges. |

Estimated Time	Procedures	Reasons
1 min.	15. Indicate that class will now write their first haiku and that the first line will be supplied. Write it on chalkboard— "Winter trees are hands" Suggest that class think of characteristics of hands to complete poems: fingers, gloves, beckoning, and the like.	15. First line supplied to eliminate as much frustration as possible.
2 min.	16. Before writing begins, analyze line by questioning: "How many syllables does this line contain?" "Five." "Does it end in a strong word?" "Yes." "Does it contain a figure?" "Yes: metaphor." "Does it refer to time?" "Yes: winter." "What must you add?" "Two lines of seven and five syllables." "What must you be careful about?" "Lines should not rhyme and must end with strong words."	16. Review helps clarify immediate task.
5–10 min.	17. As class is writing, circulate and give help as needed. As poems are finished, read them aloud and ask for comments. Commend good poems.	17. Recognition and support in a new kind of task.

(Some evidence that terminal objective has been attained.)

balance of time	18. Review homework assignment and permit students to begin in class.	18. Uses up remaining time. Teacher help available.

(Finished homework is evidence of terminal objective.)

Haiku Sheet for Analysis

1. Daydreams are fingers
   Reaching to grasp far-off thoughts
   Of silver and gold.

2. The moon's a lantern
   That sheds beams of golden light
   Showing Night his way.

3. Are cats' eyes daggers
   Flashing through the black of night
   Seeking their prey?

4. Sparkles of fresh dew
   Lingering in the dawn
   Make morning a gift.

5. Twilight, a calling card,
   That announces the nightfall,
   One last flickering.

6. Barren trees shiver.
   The icy winter has come:
   Time to sleep once more.

7. Autumn trees are men
   Stately, old, and awaiting
   Winter's long, long sleep.

Teaching the Lesson: Encouraging Student Participation

It should be obvious that the planning described above is aimed at encouraging student response by beginning instruction at an appropriate level, organizing materials and questions from simple to complex, and providing support until students are ready to work independently. But other factors are also important. The teacher who hopes for active learning in his classroom must consider the physical organization of the room and his own behavior as they affect the responses of the students.

In a traditional classroom, the desks are arranged in rows with all students facing the front of the room, with the result that the attention of the students is focused on the teacher. If the dominant method of instruction is the lecture, such an arrangement is necessary. But if the method is teacher- or student-led discussion, some other seating plan is preferable. When seats are arranged in rows, students see only the teacher's face, not the faces of other students, and their tendency will be to respond primarily to what the teacher says, not to what other students say. For an active, engaging discussion, the students should respond to one another. Arranging the desks in a hollow square, a circle, or a horseshoe shape will support such discussion. The students will be able to see one another and will not be forced to direct their questions to the teacher.

The teacher's verbal behavior, what he says to encourage response, is a significant factor in both the attitudes and achievement of students. A study by Ned Flanders[2] demonstrated that students whose teachers encouraged response had more positive attitudes toward their subject matter and learned more than did students whose teachers' verbal behavior tended to preclude student response. Flanders used a system of ten categories to describe the verbal behavior of both teacher and students in a classroom. The first seven of these have to do with teacher talk in the classroom. Categories 8 and 9 refer to student response, and 10 indicates silence. Every three seconds, the classroom observer indicated, by recording the number of one of the categories, what type of verbal behavior had taken place during the preceding three seconds. Observers worked and practiced together until they could apply the categories with a high reliability (usually over 0.9).

The categories of major interest here are the first seven, those that concern teacher talk.

1. ACCEPTANCE OF STUDENT FEELINGS When a student reports his reaction to the work in class, the teacher can ignore it, accept it, or reject it. For instance, a student may say, "This is really a dumb story." The teacher may ignore the remark. Or he may reject it with what he regards as witticism: "Perhaps what you say tells us more about you than it does about the story." If he does this or bluntly disagrees with the student, he will significantly diminish the possibility not only for real evaluation of literature in his classroom but for discovering how his students react to the works he teaches. On the other hand, if he accepts the student's remark and encourages students to talk about their reactions, he may be able to lead them to increased understanding and perhaps to more sophisticated evaluation. At the very least, his students will be willing to express their feelings in class.

2. PRAISE OR ENCOURAGEMENT If a teacher desires the continued response of his students, he must express encouragement and praise when it is warranted. Encouragement is a simple matter: "Yes," "Go ahead," "I see what you mean," or even "Uh-huh." There are degrees of praise and the teacher should use them with discretion. If he praises everything equally, his students will cease to value his commendations. On the other hand, he can indicate approval of most student efforts while reserving stronger praise for special insights and for outstanding efforts. Such expressions as "O.K.," "All right," "That's interesting," and "Good" will indicate approval. When the response warrants it, the teacher can use the student's name and emphasize the praise:

"John, that is a very important idea." If the teacher explains why the response is worthwhile, both the praise and the learning are reinforced.

3. ACCEPTANCE OF STUDENT IDEAS Sometimes the reponses will be inappropriate. Sometimes there will be several different responses to the same question or problem. In both cases the teacher will want to accept the responses and lead the class to examine them. If the responses must be rejected, it is much more effective for the peer group to reject them than for the teacher to do it. This sort of behavior by the teacher encourages students to examine their own responses—a crucial part of the learning process.

Sometimes the teacher will want to build on the response of a student: "That's an interesting idea and leads us to the heart of the problem. Now, if we consider that idea in relation to the other aspects of the problem . . ." The teacher can also build upon student responses by reviewing what has been said, showing the relationships and moving to a problem that grows out of the responses. This category represents an important teaching strategy that allows every student to feel that what he thinks is worthy of intellectual consideration by the group.

4. QUESTIONS When they are carefully planned, questions are an important means of eliciting response. Too frequently, however, a teacher who has not considered very carefully what his lesson involves will ask questions that get no response. They are ambiguous, or they are too difficult because the teacher has not prepared adequately for them. When no response comes, the unprepared teacher tends to answer the question himself. The most important part of preparation is not simply knowing the answers to the questions but considering what questions to ask in order to help students to have their own insights into the problems. Certain questions will require a good deal of thought, and the teacher should allow the students enough time to think out their responses. There is nothing inherently bad about silence in a discussion—if the participants are considering what is relevent to the discussion.

5. LECTURE Most teachers talk during a class period far more than they are aware. They lecture, they answer their own questions, they give examples. Teachers may think they use a discussion technique simply because they break up a lecture with an occasional question. But the discussion is terribly one-sided with one participant, the teacher, talking 60 to 99 percent of the total class time. Some lecturing is unavoidable, and some lecturers can be very powerful in influencing their listeners. But it is folly to think that a class is really discussing something simply because a teacher intersperses his remarks with a few questions.

6. GIVING DIRECTIONS The directions included in this category are those that require physical compliance: "Go to the board and write," "Answer the question," "Read the next passage aloud." When the teacher requires students to think about a particular problem, student compliance is not observable and

the teacher's remark is included in category 5. Clearly, some directions are necessary, but when a teacher's comments to the class have a high proportion of directive language, the students are likely to feel inhibited and coerced.

7. CRITICISM There are times when criticism of students is unavoidable. A few students who disrupt a classroom will respond to direct rebuke only. If a teacher finds a great deal of disruptive behavior in his class, he must examine the probable causes: Are the tasks too difficult for the students? Are the materials and activities such that they retain interest? Are the classroom procedures planned to move smoothly, so that the students do not have an opportunity to become unruly? Does the teacher's behavior increase the anxiety of the student?

At this point, however, the concern is with criticism of student responses to a lesson. A teacher must assume that when a student responds, he is making the best attempt he is capable of at that moment and in those circumstances. If the teacher responds with criticism of what the student says, the student's desire to respond again will certainly diminish. Such remarks as "What have you been dreaming about?" "I don't see how you can possibly say that," "That is incorrect," "It's easy to see John has been thinking of something else" can be very discouraging. When teachers react frequently with such comments, the students defend themselves by ignoring the instructor.

The first four categories described above represent the kinds of verbal behavior by the teacher that are conducive to student response. The last three tend to limit not only the opportunity but the desire to respond. Flanders' study demonstrated that teachers who accepted, encouraged, and elicited student response were more successful in terms of student achievement and attitude than were those whose tendency was to inhibit response.

Let us examine the behavior of a teacher who encourages active learning in his class. The tenth-grade students in this particular class are studying a unit similar to, but more sophisticated than the unit outlined earlier in this chapter, and after studying certain poems and short stories in which symbols are relatively clear, they begin reading *Animal Farm*. The guide questions for the first three chapters are as follows:

1. What is the basis for Major's complaint against human beings?
2. What do Farmer Jones and Manor Farm represent?
3. How does the rebellion come about?
4. Which of the Seven Commandments should be regarded as the most important? Why?
5. What do the various animals represent? Napoleon, Snowball, Squealer, Mollie, and so on?
6. What evidence is there that the animals will or will not obey the Seven Commandments?

Because the teacher wants the students to respond to one another, the class is seated in a hollow square so that they do not focus on the teacher alone but on the person speaking.

The class discussion begins with the first guide question. Commentary on the teacher and student responses appears in italics.

Teacher: What is the basis for Major's complaint against human beings?

Sam: I think he doesn't like the way people treat animals.

Teacher: Uh-huh. What do you mean? *Encourages elaboration.*

Sam: Well, you know, the way a lot of people hurt animals and don't treat them right.

Teacher: All right. *Accepts response.* Does anyone see some other basis for Major's complaints?

Carol: Well, Major says that man takes everything from the animals but doesn't produce anything himself.

Teacher: Yes, go on. *Encourages elaboration.*

Carol: Man takes the milk and the eggs and slaughters the animals and sells them. And that's not fair because . . .

Richard: What do you mean it's not fair? That's just the way things are.

Carol: Sure, in real life, but this story is not real life.

Teacher: What difference does it make that the story is not real life? *Accepts Carol's response and at the same time moves discussion toward symbolic interpretation.*

Carol: Well, in real life the animals would not be able to speak or anything. They wouldn't have a point of view. They wouldn't know that they are being used unfairly. And here they represent something.

Teacher: Good. What do the animals as a group represent?

Pamela: They represent any group of people that someone else takes advantage of or controls.

Teacher: O.K. Is that how you would describe Jones' treatment of the animals?

Sam: No, 'cause he does worse things than just control them.

Teacher: Right. What do you mean by "worse things"?

Sam: Well, he takes away everything. I mean, he even kills them.

Richard: But he has to do that. That's what farmers do.

Pamela: Oh, Richard, don't be silly. Don't you see the animals aren't just animals. They represent people—people who are under the absolute control of someone else.

Teacher: That's a good point, Pamela. *Gives extra reinforcement for a key element of the meaning.* Farmer Jones controls things in an absolute way to the extent that the animals have nothing for themselves. Can any of you think of any real life situations in which one person exercises complete control over everyone?

Richard: Yeah, school.

Teacher: All right, how is that similar, Richard? *Accepts what appears to be a challenge.*

Richard: Everyone has to do what the teachers say—or what the bells command. They tell you when to get up and sit down, when to work, and what to study.

Teacher: Good. Is there any difference?

Frank: Nope, it's just the same.

Carolyn: Not quite. The school only controls you part of the time—not all the time. And the school doesn't take our money the way Jones takes what the animals produce.

Sam: Yeah, and they don't kill us either. At least, not really.

Teacher: Can anyone think of any other real life parallels? *Responses to this question will help in understanding the idea of absolute control or tyranny and, at the same time, will prepare for later symbolic interpretations.* (During this phase of the discussion students mention feudal life, communism, sharecropping, and the French Revolution. The class examines how each is similar and different. Obviously, such digressions cannot be planned but are important. Following this, the teacher returns to the initial question.)

Teacher: Let's get back to the first question. What is Major's key objection to human beings?

Pamela: He objects to the way Jones controls everything without any consideration for the animals.

Teacher: George?

George: That's what I was going to say. Except Orwell uses the words "tyranny of human beings." He is really objecting to totalitarian forms of government.

Teacher: Very good. Let me note that on the board. (Teacher writes: Objection is to totalitarian forms of government.) *Reinforces the key point and gives strong support to the student.* Now then, what do Manor Farm and Jones represent? *Several hands go up, but since this is an easy question at this point, the teacher waits for students who respond less frequently than most.*

Joe: Well, the farm must represent a country.

Teacher: Very good. *Joe does not answer very often, and the teacher offers more praise than he might to a more able student.* Joe, what do you think the farmer represents?

Joe: He must represent . . . like the government.

Teacher: Very good. What is wrong with the government that Jones represents?

Sally: It's really bad.

Teacher: Why?

Sally: Well, he does not treat the animals well. He doesn't even feed them. And he kills them.

Sam: Yeah, that's what started the rebellion. He hadn't fed the animals 'cause he was drunk.

Teacher: Good. There are three questions that I think we might debate at this point. I'll suggest each one, and you decide which point of view on one of the questions you would like to take. The first problem is in the guide questions. Which of the Seven Commandments is most important and why? Would anyone like to take a position on that?

Richard: The animals themselves boil them down to "Four legs good, two legs bad." So it must be the first two that are important.

Carolyn: Ohhh! Richard, what's the matter with you? The seventh is most important, "All animals are equal." The first two don't guarantee anything for anyone.

Teacher: All right. We have two points of view. Alice, will you act as secretary and write down the names of people who want to prepare an argument for each point. No more than five people on a committee. Does anyone want to volunteer now? Or do you want to wait until you hear the other problems? (Some students volunteer.) The next problem I had in mind involves what the pigs represent. Will they be good leaders? What do they represent? Are they appropriate animals to represent what they do? Does anyone want to make a statement?

Frank: The pigs have to be the leaders. They are the smartest. Snowball is really good because he cares about what happens to the other animals.

John: But you don't think of a pig as being a marvelous example of leadership. I mean you usually think of pigs as greedy, dirty, and lazy.

Teacher: There are two points of view to consider. Anyone want to volunteer? (Some do and Alice records the names.) The third problem is also in the guide questions: What evidence is there that the animals will or will not obey the commandments?

Linda: I think some will and some will not.

Teacher: Which will?

Linda: Boxer will. He is already working harder than anyone else. But the cat won't probably, because it runs away when it's time to work.

Teacher: Does anyone have a different view?

Sam: I think they will all work. It says they are all really cooperating.

Teacher: Anyone else?

George: The pigs have broken the commandments already. They reserved milk and apples for themselves. They don't believe that all animals are really equal.

Teacher: Fine. We have three points of view on that question. Volunteers? (More volunteer.) Is there anyone who is not on a committee? I would like each committee to spend the remainder of the class period preparing to present its point of view. Examine the first three chapters carefully to get all the evidence for your case, but you had better examine the evidence that your opponents are likely to use. Tomorrow, we will take one problem at a time. Each committee should take no more than five minutes for its presentation. And after you hear your opponent, you will have one minute for rebuttal. Then the discussion will be open to the class. Ed and Alice, I would like you to serve as the discussion leaders for tomorrow. You do the timing and lead the class discussion. Any question? Committee?

The discussion above and the follow-up plans illustrate three different processes for inductive teaching: the teacher-led discussion, the small-group discussion, and finally the student-led discussion. Because the teacher recognizes the importance of response, he does not limit his procedures to the teacher-led discussion. There will be more student response and hence greater involvement through both the small-group and student-led discussions. At the same time, the problems posed and the debate format will force a very close examination of the text, perhaps even closer than if the teacher himself had led the discussion.

To summarize, the most important considerations for creating an environment conducive to active learning and participation by the students are the following:

1. Beginning at a level appropriate to the abilities and experience of the students
2. Selecting and organizing materials and questions that proceed from easy to complex
3. Planning the procedures (especially those new to the teacher) in concrete terms
4. Encouraging student response through the verbal behavior of the teacher and through appropriate seating arrangements and discussion techniques

In exploring new problems it is necessary to examine the data from as many vantage points as possible and to forgo established procedures—in short, to think creatively. Getzels and Jackson describe two cognitive modes in their study of creativity and intelligence:

> The one mode tends toward retaining the known, learning the predetermined, and conserving what is. The second mode tends toward revising the known, exploring the undetermined, and constructing what might be. A person for whom the first mode or process is primary tends toward the *usual and expected*. A person for whom the second mode is primary tends toward the novel and speculative. The one favors certainty, the other risk. Both processes are found in all persons, but in varying proportions. The issue is not one of better or worse, or of more or less useful. Both have their place.[3]

Creating a classroom environment for active learning involves the use of both cognitive modes. The student who questions and explores is not rebuked for his failure to choose a "correct" answer. The teacher's role is not so much to reward and punish correct and incorrect answers as it is to help the student reexamine his ideas and responses in the light of the data and decide for himself the adequacy of his answers, generalizations, and hypotheses. The teacher is not simply an authority figure who imparts information in the form of facts, theories, or interpretations. He is, to use Plato's figure, a midwife whose job it is to assist at the birth of ideas in the minds of his students.

NOTES

1. Northrop Frye, "Elementary Teaching and Elemental Scholarship," *PMLA,* LXXIX (May 1964), p. 15.
2. Ned A. Flanders, *Teacher Influence, Pupil Attitudes, and Achievement, Co-operative Research Monograph No. 12* (Washington: U.S. Office of Education, 1965).
3. Jacob W. Getzels and Philip W. Jackson, *Creativity and Intelligence* (New York: John Wiley and Sons, Inc., 1962), pp. 13–14.

SUGGESTIONS FOR FURTHER READING

1. PLATO, *Meno,* tr. Benjamin Jowett (New York: Bobbs-Merrill Co., Inc., 1949).
2. NORRIS M. SANDERS, *Classroom Questions: What Kind?* (New York: Harper & Row, 1966).

6 | Evaluation in the Curriculum

During the course of a year's work, a teacher must make different kinds of evaluations of his students' work and use different kinds of evaluation instruments: inventories, quizzes and examinations, compositions, and questionnaires. These help him to assess each student's learnings. Taken together, their results help to assess the instruction the teacher provides.

Let us consider these evaluation instruments—how the teacher should devise and use them, his purposes in using them, how he should interpret them, and what action he should take after making the evaluation.

Evaluation Instruments

TEACHER-MADE TESTS

The design of any teacher-made test should depend on its purpose. Teachers sometimes develop very short quizzes for spot-checking students' learning. Ordinarily, the purpose of such a quiz is to determine to what degree each member of the class understands a small but crucial bit of the course content. Sometimes, a quick quiz is used as a method of checking on how well students attend to outside assignments. Such tests are simple to construct, for the pertinent test items (questions) are suggested by the purpose. Trick items or catch questions are out of place in such short quizzes, since responses to them will not give the desired insights. In other words, the questions will not be valid.

The test intended to evaluate longer periods of study and more complex learnings requires much more care in its development. For this discussion, let us assume the teacher wants to evaluate the learnings in a literature unit. In developing the test, he must consider what kinds of information he wants the test to give him and how he will treat the information when he gets it.

What kinds of information should the test give? First of all, it should indicate to the teacher whether or not his objectives have been attained—or how closely they have been approached. Moreover, the test should be diagnostic to some extent—that is, if the responses show that the class does not have the desired learnings, the test should give the teacher some clue as to what needs to be done. For example, if some reteaching is necessary, the test should be constructed so as to indicate at what points the original teaching went wrong.

Let us suppose that a teacher wishes to construct a test to be given at the conclusion of a unit on symbolism. The terminal objectives of the unit were "to interpret literary symbols in a work" and "to support the interpretation." Therefore, there must be items that present materials containing symbols, that request an interpretation of them, and that request support for the interpretations. In order for a student to handle such items, he must know what symbols are and be able to identify them. Probably, these learnings were medial objectives in the unit; let us assume so. Therefore, there must be questions testing for these earlier learnings, as well. Does the student know what symbols are *in general?* Can he identify specific imagery as symbolic? The responses to these questions will determine if the instruction has broken down at this point in the learning sequence.

Assuming that the test reveals that these learnings have not taken place, the next problem is to determine why. Presumably, the concepts were developed inductively during the course of the unit as a result of the analysis of specific materials. If learning blocks occurred at this point in the instruction, some of the items should be designed to show whether students are familiar with the classroom materials and whether they were understood.

Thus, the test must contain items of the following kinds:

1. Items that test the students' familiarity with, and understanding of, the content material used in direct instruction
2. Items that test their knowledge of the general concept of literary symbol
3. Items that test their skill in identifying symbols
4. Items that test their skill in interpreting symbols
5. Items that require support for their interpretations

The forms these items should take should be determined, in part, by considering how the teacher will deal with the responses, once the tests are turned in. When the tests are turned in, the first problem he will face is scoring them. Insofar as possible, the entire scoring procedure should be consistent from test to test. Therefore the items should be designed to allow for maximum consistency in scoring. Although multiple-choice items allow a very high degree of scoring consistency, it is often difficult to make valid multiple-choice items that test skills.

The use of any multiple-choice items—whether they be true-false, matching, or selecting from a series of multiples of the *a, b, c,* or *d* genre—says something about how "deep" the learning is expected to be. If a tester uses multiple-choice items, he presents both correct and incorrect information, and the student is required only to recognize that the information is correct or incorrect. Generally, recall items are more demanding than recognition items because they require the student to produce information with the cues implicit in the instructions and questions as his only helps. For example, it should be more difficult to respond to the question, "Who wrote 'Crossing the Bar'?" than to choose the author's name from the list, "Wordsworth, Tennyson, Keats, Shelley." Therefore, the next consideration in designing test questions is the "depth" with which the teacher feels it is necessary for a student to know information. Assuming that a skill can be thought of as a cognitive learning, the only way that a teacher can be sure that a pupil "knows" a skill is to require him to "recall" it; that is, be able to use it on request.

Planning recall items introduces another important consideration; ambiguity in responses and in the questions themselves. In administering the test, a few minutes at the beginning of the testing period should be planned for clearing up ambiguities. However, questions that invite divergent responses cannot be handled as readily. For example, think of the possible legitimate answers to a question like this:

"A symbol is _____."

How could one maintain much consistency in scoring these possible answers (and there are many other possibilities):

"something that has a referent."
"used to represent something else."
"a figure of speech."
"often used by authors."
"sometimes capable of many interpretations."

Some types of questions must be somewhat open-ended, inviting various responses, such as the type asking the students to support the assertion that an image is a symbol. Many forms of support may be reasonable in a particular instance. In such cases, the teacher must anticipate all the pertinent responses in advance.

Next he must decide on the order of the items within a section. As noted in the discussion of reading inventories in Chapter 11, questions should be presented in an order ranging from easy to difficult. Although the structure of the question (multiple choice vs. recall) tends to predict relative ease, as does the task that the question implies (recall of key specific information vs. inferences), the only way that a teacher can be certain of the relative difficulty of an item is by noting the frequency of correct responses. Obviously, a question that everyone always answers correctly is easier than a question that hardly anyone can ever answer. Over a long period of use, tests and other instruments can be redesigned so as to yield more reliable information.

Next, the teacher must make a crucial decision about the scoring of the test. There were five types of questions that were to be included, each testing a different learning. The teacher must decide which of the learnings, if any, he feels is the most important and whether there are different degrees of importance that can be assigned to the various items. Such decisions are not easy. For example, he may decide that the students' ability to identify certain imagery as symbolic in some new reading is the essential feature of the unit or that the character of the support they provide for their interpretations is more important. If the unit included the reading of literary masterworks, the teacher may decide that familiarity with their structure or content is of overriding importance. His decisions about relative importance will determine how the individual items or sections on the final test will be weighted, that is, how much each will count. The more important a given response, the more heavily it should be weighted in the final scoring.

The administration of the test must be considered now. Some time in the testing period must be reserved to check inadvertent ambiguities, both in the expression of the items and in the directions that are part of the test. Students must be made aware of the weighting given to the various parts, since they have only a limited amount of time for writing the test, and should have information that will help them in planning their time. Otherwise, they may use too much time in places where the returns—both in terms of final scores for them and diagnostic information for their teacher—will not justify the time spent. (This consideration suggests that in any curriculum design there ought to be provision for lessons teaching students how to take tests—that is, how to prepare for them, how to attack them, and how to deal with the results.)

While the class is writing the test, the teacher should circulate and watch to see that directions are being followed. If the students respond badly because of ambiguous directions, the test results will not be useful (unless one purpose of the test is to evaluate the student's ability to follow directions). From time to time during the testing period, the teacher should indicate how much time there is remaining.

In designing a test for a unit, it is clear that the teacher must pull the unit into perspective. All the main concepts, the objectives, all experiential elements, and their relationships must be viewed both independently and as a complete pattern. One important function of a test for a student is that he is forced to do the same thing. All too often, however, students are not sophisticated enough to put all these elements into the proper perspective by themselves. A good technique, therefore, is to have *the class* design the final unit test or sections of it. This activity also helps them to gain sophistication in preparing for tests, generally.

The procedures are easy and logical. First, the teacher leads a discussion about the appropriateness, use, and design of test items. Then the content of the unit is briefly reviewed. Next, heterogeneously grouped committees are formed to design items, each group working on one section of the test. When each group has finished its work, the class is regrouped so that each new committee contains at least one member from each of the previous committees. Each member presents his section of the test to the new group. Then, when the whole class is familiar with all parts of the test, the teacher leads a whole-class discussion on weighting. Finally, using student-made items as a base, the teacher completes the final test design. The procedure requires about three class periods.

COMPOSITIONS

The test is not the only tool that the teacher has to help him evaluate learnings. Student responses in discussion can serve as a basis for general evaluations as can worksheets and homework papers of various sorts. Probably, compositions are the most important of these other evaluation instruments. We shall discuss here the type of composition that is intended to communicate information, including an expression of the writer's feelings and opinions.

One purpose of literature study is to develop critical faculties. Only by analyzing the informational content of his students' compositions can the teacher evaluate the success of his students in developing their critical faculties—that is, the extent to which they bring their total life experience, independent intelligence, and personal sensitivity to their reading. In the classroom, it is composition alone that permits an adequate and appropriate critical response from all the students.

If the teacher wants to make such an evaluation, he should, under ideal conditions, attend only to the informational content of the finished composition. In most secondary school classes, however, such ideal conditions only rarely obtain. English teachers teach composition as well as literature, and consequently a composition must be evaluated *as a composition,* even though the teacher's purpose in assigning it had been to assess the students' other learnings.

Therefore, the finished composition will usually be judged on the basis of its informational content; the techniques of organization, definition, and logic used in presenting that information; the writer's aptitude in handling the mechanics of the written language—the spelling, punctuation, and capitalizing conventions; and the language style.

The weighting that a teacher should give to these elements depends on the type of student doing the writing, the previous instruction of the class, the objectives in instruction, the purpose of the assignment, and the material that the writer is discussing. To the extent that the whole program has been individualized, composition grading should be individualistic. This is especially the case in classes where the inventories (Chapter 22) have shown a wide spread in writing ability among the class members. Then, in extreme contrast to the scoring of tests, the grading of compositions should not, and could not, be based on rigid paper-to-paper scoring consistency.

Suppose that the inventories have revealed that the class is weak in the techniques of organization (Chapter 22), and the teacher therefore decides to teach a composition unit that will have as its objective a mastery of the techniques for presenting data. When the writing is evaluated, the heaviest weighting should be given to those organizational techniques. Some papers will show control of all the techniques; others will show control of some of them and weakness of varying degrees (including omission) in others. The weaknesses will vary from paper to paper: some students will have poor definitions, some will not be able to support generalizations, and so on.

Next, the teacher must decide on what action to take as a result of the evaluation. Obviously, in this case, some individualizing of instruction will be necessary—probably in the form of notes on the compositions indicating which parts need to be revised and what directions the revisions should take. Thus, the evaluation will not be completed until the teacher has read the *revisions*.

Although in reading the compositions the teacher gives the heaviest weight to organization and the like, he will also have to take account of such other features as information, the spelling, punctuation, and capitalizing conventions, and style.

Some teachers are uncomfortable in assigning a single mark to a composition and may give a composition two letter grades (one for "content," one for "mechanics"); in fact, it is conceivable that a whole series of grades could be used. Even without so elaborate a marking apparatus (and what it implies for recording marks and averaging them for report cards), the act of reading and responding to compositions is terribly time- and energy-consuming. However, any teacher who feels comfortable only with multiple composition grades and who is willing to take the additional time and effort required to deal with them should do so. On the other hand, many teachers feel that one mark suffices. The question is essentially one of teacher comfort, and any alleged "rationale" to the contrary is really rationalization.

Whether one mark or multiple marks are used, the teacher must rank the compositions. Ordinarily, the most convenient technique for ranking is to place the compositions in piles, each pile containing papers of about the same general merit. Then, the only problem is deciding which mark or range of marks to assign to each pile.

On occasion, there will be a highly problematic paper. For example, consider an otherwise fluent composition that displays a disheartening number of spelling errors. Probably the best marking procedure in this case is to give two marks, one for spelling and one for the rest of the paper. This procedure helps to drive home to the student the feature of his writing that he must particularly attend to.

Difficult as it may be to evaluate information-oriented compositions, this job is simple when compared to grading more clearly belletristic work. The great danger in judging belletristic writing is that the teacher will make an entirely personal appraisal, judging the composition only and not considering the process that generated it. In order for a student's composition skills to improve, the teacher must consider the composing process—especially in connection with belletristic writing.

In marking such papers, the elements discussed in connection with more utilitarian writing should, of course, be considered when they are pertinent. Beyond this, the aesthetic merit must be judged. In order to make consistent evaluations, the teacher must try to visualize the writer's composing problem as the writer himself saw it. Only then can he make helpful comments on his general approach to the aesthetic problem. Perhaps the weakness in a paper is in some feature of the writer's approach, but perhaps the student perceived his problem inadequately to begin with. Whatever the case may be, the teacher should try to put himself in the writer's place so that he can evaluate the paper from a point of view that will be relevant to the writer.

Evaluating the Curriculum

Individually, an inventory, a test, or a composition are used to assess student learnings. Collectively, they can be used to make assessments about the curriculum. Assuming that English skills are cognitive in character, these instruments are the principal means of evaluating the success of the curriculum in producing appropriate cognitive learnings. As indicated in Chapter 4, evaluative judgments are made in terms of criterion statements, which describe the implications of attaining objectives. Therefore, one measure of the curriculum as a whole is whether objectives are being met.

Assuming that the objectives are worthy and need not be altered, two conditions are possible: the students generally attain the objectives, or they generally do not attain them. In the latter case, either methods or materials (or both) should be changed. Even if the objectives are being attained, there may yet be some question about materials and/or methods: that is, the procedures, although effectual, may not be efficient.

An example may help to discriminate between these concepts. Consider a problem of moving ten tons of sand from one place to another. One man with a wheelbarrow and shovel might do the job in two weeks. The same man with a steamshovel and a dump truck could do it in half a day. In both cases the sand would be moved. Therefore, both methods are effectual because they get the job done. The second method, however, is the more efficient in terms of time and the worker's effort.

Consider the problem of eliminating run-on sentences from the compositions of a group of thirty students. Six years of grammar book drill might result in eliminating the faulty usages from the work of twenty-five students. Another approach might be to teach a few lessons in proofreading and have a series of short conferences—of about five minutes—with each student. During the conference, the student would read his work aloud, and when his stress, pitch, and juncture patterns indicated the need for terminal punctuation, he would insert it. Assuming that this procedure would also be effectual with the twenty-five students in terms of curriculum time and effort, it is more efficient by far than the endless drill.

Another dimension of curriculum evaluation has to do with the affective (rather than cognitive) responses of the students. Assuming that the objectives are attained, how do the students feel about the program? Do they like, for example, drilling on run-on sentences year after year for six years, even though the drill eliminates run-on sentences from their writing, and they are aware of both the objectives of the drill and success of the procedures?

To an important extent cognitive learning is conditioned by the emotional climate that surrounds it. Negative feelings about experiences can result in learning blocks, whereas positive feelings can help to eliminate blocks. Whether or not cognitive learnings take place in a curriculum, affective responses must be assessed. It is important to maintain an instructional climate that is appealing.

Much of the assessment of student feelings can be done informally. The frequency and tone of responses in discussion can suggest inferences to the teacher. Students will usually let a teacher know how they feel. If they do not do this—with both positive and negative responses—this is itself evidence of negative reactions and may mean that they are afraid to express their feelings. Needless to say, discipline problems of the other kind—rudeness, unruly behavior—are likewise evidence of negative feelings. Students' thoroughness in preparing outside work is another good clue to affective response. Requests for more time are also clues; when the extensions result in work that is very well done, this is an indication that the worker has been highly motivated. A good device for gauging affective response is the questionnaire (as described in Chapter 14).

One further evaluation of the curriculum is necessary, an evaluation of the quality of the students' experience. Suppose that objectives are being met, and students obviously enjoy the work. Suppose further that the procedures seem both efficient and effectual. Now let us postulate a tenth-grade class working on a unit in this happy situation.

The unit will deal with literature about adolescent love, a topic that ought to be appealing to tenth graders. The reading ability of the class is such that, with proper instructional techniques, they might read *Romeo and Juliet*. The teacher is versed in these techniques. Obviously, they could also deal with contemporary books aimed at the adolescent market. All other things being equal, the teacher should choose *Romeo and Juliet* since the quality of the reading experience it provides is so much higher than that of the adolescent novel.

How does one judge this quality difference? To a large extent, the value judgment has ultimately been made by society as a whole. A teacher's own experience, including his own education, enables *him* to make the judgment. Probably, it is a question of taste as well as knowledge, and presumably an English major, a college graduate, has the appropriate background for making the necessary discriminations.

The choice of materials and teaching methods will be discussed in detail throughout the balance of this book. Challenging, even difficult, materials and tasks do not in themselves predict negative affective responses. Feelings of pride and accomplishment can accompany the knowledge that a hard task has been mastered. However, if the task is *not* completed because it is inherently frustrating, quite the opposite feelings can be generated. The tightrope between challenging and frustrating curriculum content is a difficult one for teachers to walk.

The evaluation of a curriculum cannot take place all at once. Usually, very poor elements are obvious. In another year, these may be modified or dropped, and alternatives are substituted, which in turn must be evaluated.

Even when a teacher feels comfortable about the validity and reliability of his homemade evaluation instruments, and they show that his objectives have been met, that student feelings about his program are positive, and that the content of the program is rich in quality, he cannot yet be sure that his instruction alone is responsible for this outcome. Suppose, for example, that one of the objectives in his program is to teach his class to write sonnets. After he proceeds through the unit and everyone is able to write an acceptable sonnet, how does he know that *he* has taught the material? He cannot know, unless he had first established that writing sonnets was not in his students' repertoire before he started the unit. Therefore, any sound system of evaluation must provide for pretesting for previous learnings. This pretesting need not be formal; using the example of the sonnet unit, the teacher might simply ask his class: "How many of you know how to write sonnets?" Certainly, not a very formal or elaborate device, but one that nevertheless produces the appropriate information.

Finally, evaluations are judgmental. Although this is not the same thing as saying that they are random, absurd, useless, or wasted, the judgments of evaluators are naturally subject to change. As a teacher's experiences accumulate, the character of evaluative instruments should change. Probably the value system of the teacher will change as well, and the relative importance of various elements in his experience will shift. In addition to these changes, as time passes, the culture changes, and with cultural changes come changes in the reactions of students.

The evaluation process must be dynamic, not static. Let us reconsider the elements in that process in a general way:

1. An evaluation rests on an appropriate observation of whatever is to be evaluated. A test must be valid, first of all.
2. The observation must be rated in some way. Generally, the rating should be as consistent as possible. The consistency need not derive from the scoring technique but may reside in some other phase of the treatment of the observations.
3. When the observations are made and rated, subsequent behavior should be conditioned by the information that has been derived. This is the purpose of engaging in the evaluation process in the first place.

A teacher's curriculum experience will, more and more, assume the character of a constant evaluation of all phases of that experience. Evaluations are often judgmental, and whatever guidelines a teacher may use, in the end the quality of his evaluation will be determined by the character of his judgment.

SUGGESTIONS FOR FURTHER READING

The following pamphlets are useful guides for many phases of test construction and treatment of test results:

1. From the Educational Testing Service, 20 Nassau Street, Princeton, New Jersey: *Making the Classroom Test* (1959), and *Short Cut Statistics for Teacher Made Tests* (1960).
2. From NCTE, Champaign, Illinois: *Building Better English Tests* (1963).

Teaching Literature

Instruction in literature has two major functions: (1) to enable students to gain the skills and literary experience necessary for the independent comprehension of the full range of literary meanings (cognitive, affective, and aesthetic); and (2) to help them to find the literary experience—whether it be reading, viewing drama, acting, or some other—that they will enjoy and will seek again. When instruction is successful, it eliminates the need for itself. As the student becomes more and more sophisticated in his response to literature, he should become decreasingly dependent on the teacher and various instructional aids.

The first chapter of this section examines the traditions of teaching literature and attempts to assess their effectiveness in reaching the goals listed above. These various approaches have had a singular concern for the "facts of literature" at one extreme and the social adjustment of the student at the other.

Before developing an alternative approach to teaching literature, it is necessary to determine what literature is, how it differs from other verbal statements, what its values are, and what all this implies for instruction. Accordingly, Chapter 8 attempts to answer some of these questions and to suggest a rudimentary philosophy of literature.

Next, Chapter 9, "The Reading Situation," examines what the elements in any reading situation are: the reader's literary background and experience, the ways in which a text conveys meaning, the immediate reading situation that can be influenced by the teacher, and the responses of the reader. The remaining chapters of Part II examine each of these elements in detail.

Chapter 10, "The Text and the Reader: Levels of Meaning and Response," examines the various aspects of meaning in a text to which a reader responds. The chapter moves from consideration of literal aspects of meaning through inferential meanings to affective and aesthetic responses. These aspects of meaning and response suggest a hierarchy of skills that can inform the structure of a unit of instruction for a given group of students at a particular time, a course of instruction for a year, or a whole curriculum. If a teacher fails to consider these elements, his instruction runs the serious risk of being inappropriate to his students.

Clearly, if instruction is to be appropriate, the teacher must have more than an intuitive grasp of his students' abilities in responding to literature. Chapter 11, "Assessing the Reader's Literary Experience: The Reading Comprehension Inventory," presents a method for determining the sophistication of a group of students in dealing with the sort of questions about a literary work that they are likely to encounter during the course of a year's work.

Chapter 12, "Designing the Literature Unit, Part I," examines those considerations that are preliminary to the design of a unit for a particular group of students. These include analysis of the unit content, the unit pretest (the function of which is similar to that of the reading comprehension inventory), and the selection of appropriate objectives and materials.

Chapter 13, "Designing the Literature Unit, Part II," focuses on the arrangement of materials and activities for instruction. The chapter recommends beginning with the simplest materials, frequently with materials that students encounter as part of the popular culture, and with activities and procedures that give them maximum support and confidence in their initial contacts with new materials, problems, and concepts. The next phase of the unit promotes independence from the teacher as the students approach a variety of problems in small-group, student-led discussions. The final phase involves totally independent work for which the student must rely on his experience in the preceding parts of the unit.

Chapter 14, "Teaching Literature: The Affective Response," focuses on those classroom processes and activities that are likely to result in positive responses to the reading of literature. The classroom need not be dominated by the teacher. The materials for instruction must not always be verbal. Students should participate in a wide variety of activities, from leading discussions themselves to role-playing and acting, from viewing and discussing movies to making a movie or slide-tape collage. A unit, "Courage," developed in detail demonstrates how the various methods and materials suggested in the chapter can be utilized in a single unit of instruction.

Chapter 15, "Curricula in Literature," examines various considerations and models for developing curricula in literature. It presents a sample scope and sequence outline for grades seven through twelve plus a more detailed outline of units at one grade level and an outline of related units from seventh to twelfth grades. In addition, the chapter examines a model for an elective high school English program. A unit on "The Literature of Black Protest" demonstrates how varied curricula can be developed to meet special needs.

Finally, Chapter 16 takes up the special difficulties and techniques of helping students who have rather serious reading problems. Obviously, this book cannot deal with all aspects of reading retardation. The chapter offers practical suggestions for dealing with students who cannot read successfully at the literal level.

7 | Traditions in the Teaching of Literature

Neither English nor American literature has existed as a subject in the schools for very long, yet there has been time for two rather distinct traditions to develop: a conservative approach that has its roots in the humanistic tradition of Western civilization and the teaching of Latin and Greek literature, and a progressive approach that has been traced to the philosophy of John Dewey and the distortions of some of his disciples.[1] Various elements of these traditions may be observed in the practice of teachers in almost any school, although many teachers are unaware of their origins. Some teachers combine aspects of the two traditions in their teaching, but most are either primarily conservative or primarily progressive. It seems only fair to students for a teacher to be cognizant of some of the traditions that affect his teaching.

The goals of the two approaches are superficially similar in that both view the study of literature as a means of understanding one's self and the relationship of the self to others and to the universe. But the differences between the two in procedures and in emphasis are tantamount to a difference in purpose. Whereas the conservative avoids didacticism, the progressive attempts to use the literature didactically to help individuals adjust to society. Literature, he believes, is a tool to inculcate moral and spiritual values, to bring about an understanding of one's self and others, and to promote mental hygiene and wholesome attitudes. This major difference in belief about the use of literature is responsible for six other points of cleavage between the two schools.

First, the conservative focuses attention on the work itself. The progressive, on the other hand, is concerned primarily with the emotional effect the work has on his students or with the extent to which the work can help solve extraliterary problems. The conservative's class will be expected to concentrate mainly on the meaning, structure, and artistic merit of the literary work. Ordinarily, however, the conservative tends to ignore the background of his students in his selection of works and problems for discussion. For instance, he may decide to discuss the epic characteristics of *Beowulf*. But because his students know nothing at all about epic poetry, the "discussion" becomes a lecture, which the students view as dull and irrelevant. Thus, while the conservative conducts a close reading of the work, the progressive avoids close reading for fear the students will lose interest and become frustrated with careful analysis, what the progressive is likely to call "tearing the work to pieces." He tends to believe that whatever meaning a student takes from the work is valid, no matter how distorted his interpretation may be. "After all," the progressive would argue, "what we really want to do is establish healthy attitudes."

Second, because the conservative recommends intensive reading of a few works by all students, the works read are usually of relatively high literary merit. He ignores the obvious problems that arise when all students in a particular class are not equally capable of reading the same works. The progressive curriculum, on the other hand, features extensive reading organized rather loosely into expansive units with the result that emphasis is placed on the quantity of material rather than the quality. "Literature" recommended in progressive curricula frequently includes nonliterary materials and material of low literary quality. Much would not pass the conservative test as literature at all.

A third difference is that the conservative advocates a common curriculum for all students, whereas the progressive emphasizes the individual differences among students and attempts to vary curricular offerings accordingly. The conservative hopes that a common background in literature can thwart the centrifugal influence of a culture in which *change* may be the dominating force. Paradoxically, he hopes that the students will maintain their individualism despite his attempt to ignore differences in offering the same curriculum for all and in demanding the same response from all. The progressives compound this paradox, for although they express concern about individual differences, they use the school and its curriculum to "socialize" the students, to make them sensitive to, and directed by, those around them, thereby reducing, if not eliminating, individualism. This result of progressive educational policy has been widely criticized by Riesman, Friedenberg, and others.[2]

Fourth, the conservative views literature as a distinct subject matter, but to the progressive, literature is a distinctly subordinate part of an experience in problem solving. In the progressive curriculum, subject-matter lines disappear, and literature is integrated with social studies or other subject matters. The conservative, however, arranges work by author, type, or chronology, arrangements that have little intrinsic relationship to the abilities of the students and have little power to increase their literary competence. As a matter of fact, his arrangements are based on only a very superficial analysis of what learning to read literature involves. Because his students read and explicate a number of short stories, the conservative is willing to assume that they have learned how to read short stories. Unfortunately, understanding the meaning of one or several short stories after class discussion is not in any way the same as being able to interpret a short story independently of the teacher. The progressive espouses units or projects such as those in the 1935 *An Experience Curriculum in English,*[3] which suggests several "Experience Strands," such as "Enjoying Action," "Exploring the Physical World," and "Exploring the Social World." In units such as these, the emphasis is on the informational content of the work rather than on the work as literature.

Fifth, the conservative selects and assigns nearly all the material that the students read, whereas the progressive commonly believes in student-teacher cooperative planning, which frequently means little or no planning at all. This, of course, has been one of the major misinterpretations of Dewey's philosophy, which held that the teacher should not abdicate his responsibility as a mature individual to plan carefully for the learning experiences of his students. Despite Dewey's emphasis on careful planning, the progressive classroom frequently displays a criminal waste of time. One teacher reports that after five weeks of discussion, his English class decided that its only real concern was in getting grades necessary to leave the school. The class then embarked on a study of the "Great American Grade System."[4]

On the other hand, although the planning of the conservative appears to be detailed, it is frequently shallow and perfunctory. The conservative teacher plans only in the sense that he decides in advance which pages in the text will be read on particular days, when to introduce background material, and how to proceed with discussion. But the selection and arrangement of materials is likely to be arbitrary. All students, regardless of differences in ability, are likely to read the same materials. He assumes that reading and discussing a series of works will have the desired effect on the students' ability to read literature. But he seldom, if ever, attempts to test his assumption.

The sixth difference between conservative and progressive lies in the area of evaluation. The conservative bases his evaluation on the student's knowledge of content. His literature tests frequently do not involve more than recall, from the level of simple stated fact to the levels of interpretation and evaluation. That is, the answers to the various questions he asks have been presented either in the text or in classroom discussions. The student need only be possessed of a good memory to answer them. There is some justification, of course, in requiring students to know what has been said in class. But if all testing is of the content variety, the teacher has no right to assume that the ability of the students to read literature has been enhanced by the instruction.

The progressive, however, would not evaluate on the basis of content since he regards the content of his instruction, insofar as there is any at all, as instrumental to reaching other goals. His objectives deal with establishing healthy attitudes. Ordinarily the objectives are phrased in such loose and ambiguous language that any evaluation at all is virtually impossible. The objectives of the unit from "Exploring the Social World," for instance, are stated in procedural terms, for example, "To discuss social forces." They describe what the teacher and students will do during the course of instruction. Therefore, the evaluation can be, and frequently is, made only in terms of the number and diversity of activities, the number of students taking part, and the amount of material they read.

Although the evaluation procedures of conservatives and progressives differ widely, they are alike in one negative respect. Neither makes any objective attempt to determine the effect of instruction on the students' ability to read literature. Both are content simply to assume that the activities and materials have some effect.

These two traditions continue to influence the teaching of literature in the secondary schools. Both are frequently evident in the practice of a given teacher, so that the approaches they engender cannot be rigidly separated. The three groups of approaches that we will consider have been selected, not because of the traditions behind them, but because of their frequency. The first, the guidance approaches, displays a sort of traditional influence (but not a reputable one), on the one hand, and a progressive philosophy, on the other. The second, the social studies approaches, represents a decidedly progressive point of view. The various appreciation approaches display the influence of both schools.

The Guidance Approaches

There are two guidance approaches, one that is very old and another that is of relatively recent vintage. The first is in the tradition of the *McGuffey Readers*,[5] whose purpose was not only to teach the child to read but to shape his mind and morals. This tradition dates much further back than that, however. In the Renaissance, Sir Philip Sidney, building on a classical critical tradition, declared that the function of literature was to "teach and delight." But the moral purpose of literature as it is suggested by Sidney's "The Defense of Poesie" is far different from the straightforward didactic morality of the *McGuffey Readers*. Sidney believed with Aristotle that literature was a *mimesis,* an imitation of life, or as he puts it, "a representing, counterfeiting, or figuring forth: to speak metaphorically, a speaking picture. . . ."[6] Although Sidney insists that the end of all knowledge, including literature, is "virtuous action," he points out that the most important aspect of knowledge stands in "the knowledge of a man's self, in the ethic and politic consideration."[7] To Sidney, literature more than philosophy or history produces "This purifying of wit, this enriching of memory, enabling of judgment and enlarging of conceit, which we commonly call knowledge."[8] It is knowledge in this sense that leads to "virtuous action." The McGuffey tradition is much more narrow. Here a poem is "used" to illustrate a precept or moral truth. For Sidney, the presentation of precepts lay in the realm of philosophy, not of literature. The moralistic teacher in the McGuffey tradition, on the other hand, sees literature as a useful tool for shaping the conduct of his students to conformity with preconceived standards. For Sidney and the humanist critics who followed him, the problem was not that simple. For them, the knowledge imparted by literature helps man attain an ethical position that helps to guide his actions.

The modern critic, of course, avoids the use of a phrase such as "virtuous action" altogether. For him literature is not and should not become a didactic instrument of morality. We read literature partly for the aesthetic experience that a work of art offers and partly for the insight we gain into the nature of man's existence in the universe. Obviously, though, some works do have a didactic intent. The medieval allegories *Everyman* and *Piers Plowman* are certainly didactic. Their intent is to teach men the attitudes and conduct that will enable them to attain heaven. But after the Middle Ages, literature became less and less didactic in the narrow sense. The bulk of English and American literature is didactic only in the sense that it helps man to understand himself, but certainly not in the sense that it presents specific instructions for behavior.

Literary works do present generalizations about moral problems, but the great power of such works usually lies in their examination of the complexities underlying those generalizations. But if we select and teach works to emphasize a moral, then we give answers without raising the appropriate questions. We put a stop to what ought to be healthy discussion and inquiry before it has had an opportunity to get started. We ignore one of the most powerful insights that literature offers: an examination of the complexity of human existence. And we deprive our students of that insight in two ways. First, we force him to generalize and, therefore, to oversimplify the theme of a work. Second, when we focus on the "moral" of a work we deprive the student of an opportunity to learn *how* to deal with the complexities of the work and to learn *how* to get at its full meaning. The study of literature has always been a "liberal art." If the teacher attempts to use literature as a tool for moral indoctrination, literature ceases to be liberal, and it ceases to be art.

The second "guidance theory" has come into the public schools within the last thirty or forty years. This theory views literature as an appendage to the school's guidance program. The proponents of the theory view a literary work as a jumping-off point for a group therapy session. The students read the work, identify the problem with which the work deals, and then suggest similar problems in their own lives. The discussion proceeds to the attitudes and behavior of the students in such problems and moves further and further from the work that fostered it.

Obviously, there is motivational value in a brisk discussion of the problems that students encounter in their own experience and that the work at hand examines. Students frequently turn from a discussion of such problems to an enthusiastic reexamination of the literary work. Furthermore—and this is obvious too—evaluation of a work cannot take place in a vacuum. The best readers and critics bring their full experience to bear on a work and evaluate both the aesthetic aspects and content of the work in terms of their experience. The guidance approach, however, ignores both of these values. Its proponents use the work to motivate discussion; they do not use the discussion to motivate an examination or reexamination of the work. And for their purposes, evaluation of the work per se is irrelevant. In short, this theory does not embody an approach to literature. It is an approach to group guidance. The English teacher *must* make the distinction.

The Social Studies Approaches

The 1935 *An Experience Curriculum in English,* which was mentioned earlier, provides a clear example of the social studies approach to teaching literature. The curriculum is made up of what it calls strands, one of which is called "Exploring the Social World." The fifth unit in this strand offers the following objectives.

PRIMARY OBJECTIVE

To observe man's industrial expansion.

ENABLING OBJECTIVE

To compare industry as it was before our time with our own industrial age; to participate vicariously with men and women who worked and are working under conditions both good and bad; to analyze our present economic system, and to compare it with systems of other days.[9]

The unit includes *Silas Marner* and *David Copperfield* as means of achieving these objectives. Obviously, although both books contain some economic information, neither of them was written for the purposes suggested by the objectives. There might be merit in studying economic systems to enable students to read certain pieces of literature more intelligently. But nowhere does *An Experience Curriculum in English* attempt anything of that sort. Literature is clearly regarded only as a means of fulfilling other purposes.

More than thirty years after the publication of *An Experience Curriculum in English,* this progressive philosophy is still the basis for many literature texts, especially for seventh through tenth grades. A recent eighth-grade text includes units about pioneer life, the founders of our country, America the melting pot, getting along with others, and so on. Two common "social studies" approaches to literature appear frequently in the schools: the "literature is history" approach and the "other lands and people" approach.

The teacher who adheres to the "literature is history" approach asks his students to read a novel like *Johnny Tremain* for an understanding of life during the period of the American Revolution, the works of Washington

Irving for an understanding of the Dutch settlements in New York, and *The Scarlet Letter* for background on Puritan New England. Similarly, the teacher who operates under the "other lands and people" theory brings literature to bear on the geography lesson: Kipling for life and customs in India and Homer for attitudes, religion, customs, and even architecture among the Greeks.

Let us assume that the goals set by the proponents of these theories are important and worthwhile. Our question now is whether the study of literature is the best method for attaining those goals. For example, if a teacher wants his students to learn about the conditions of slavery in the South before the Civil War, should he assign *Uncle Tom's Cabin?* Probably not. Harriet Beecher Stowe wrote *Uncle Tom's Cabin* as a piece of propaganda to influence Northerners against the institution of slavery and to gain sympathy for the slaves. Thus, what the student will have after reading the book is a rather biased view of the conditions. Pretend for a moment that Harriet Beecher Stowe had written an unbiased novel. Would the study of *Uncle Tom's Cabin* then be an efficient method of learning about the conditions of slavery? Would the hours spent in reading the novel yield a quantity of information sufficient to justify the expenditure of that time? The information-time ratio would be much more favorable if the student spent his time on original documents and appropriate secondary sources. In short, reading *Uncle Tom's Cabin* for the picture of slavery that it offers is about as impractical as reading spy stories in order to become a spy. What the adherents of these theories do not realize is that the informational content of a literary work is ordinarily secondary to the main purpose of the work and necessarily limited by that purpose.

As teachers of English, however, we are not really concerned about the inefficiency of the study of literature for historical, geographical, or sociological information. We are concerned about the damaging effect that such an approach has on the student's attitude toward literature. The student is very likely to view literature only as a means to some more or less irrelevant end, such as historical or geographical knowledge. And chances are if he accepts this view, he will tend to reject any work without informational content that can be "used" for some similar utilitarian end. This view excludes most fiction, most poetry, and most grammar. The danger that the "social studies" theories build false expectations is too great to be ignored. If the student expects to find immediate practical values in literature, he is almost bound to be disillusioned, and rejection of literature follows almost of necessity.

On the other hand, if we succeed in convincing students to read literature for utilitarian purposes, our literature will suffer too. For years scholars riveted their attention on *Beowulf* as a cultural artifact. They probed the poem for what it could reveal about the language, philosophy, social organization, dynastic lines, armor, mores, eating habits, and architecture of the Anglo-Saxons. Undergraduates are constantly amazed that a single poem of 3,182 lines could contain the material for so many articles and books. Yet even with all this attention, the poem suffered. The critics neglected to examine its integrity as a work of art. Its monsters were deplored as "unreal" or "juvenile." Its allusions were attacked as irrelevant. Its structure was condemned as merely episodic and disunified. Some of these attitudes spilled over into twelfth-grade treatments of the poem. Finally, J. R. R. Tolkien's article "The Monsters and the Critics"[10] rescued the poem. Tolkien argued that the poem was not merely a cultural artifact, a storehouse of historical and anthropological information. He argued for its artistic integrity and won. Since the appearance of that article, *Beowulf* criticism has taken a new shape and the poem has gathered new stature as a work of art. Perhaps a handful of high school teachers teaching mediocre students cannot detract from great literature. Perhaps only critics can do that. But who wants to test the destructive power of even a handful of English teachers?

Surely the skillful teacher of literature will instigate whatever discussions and learning situations bring his students to a greater understanding of the text at hand, but he will just as surely bring the fruit of the discussion to bear on the text. A discussion of Puritan morality in New England can inform a student's reading of *The Scarlet Letter,* just as a discussion of communist theory and practice can inform a reading of *Animal Farm.* For the English teacher, the error lies in using *Animal Farm* as a vehicle for teaching Russian history or communist doctrine. If he does that, he is no longer teaching literature. In short, he must make the distinction between using other subject areas to illuminate literature and using literature to illuminate other subject areas. The former can be both valid and valuable, but the latter is necessarily misleading and inefficient.

The Appreciation Approaches

Nearly every English teacher hopes that his students will enjoy the literature he assigns, and as a result nearly every English teacher teaches partly or exclusively on the basis of one of the "appreciation theories." There can be no doubt that their goal is an important one, and therefore the approaches are worth a careful examination. Though the goals are the same, the methods that supposedly lead to appreciation are rather diverse in nature. It is possible to divide the "appreciation theories" into two main groups: the "traditional" approaches and the "progressive" approaches. For the purpose of analysis, we will subdivide these two main groups of approaches into alternative approaches to appreciation. However, it is common to use some combination of the approaches. The combination is arbitrary rather than organic. That is, the use of one approach to a work does not influence the use of a second or a third approach.

LITERARY APPROACHES

There are three literary approaches to appreciation: the emotive approach, the famous authors approach, and the approach through analysis of technique. The first of these is widely used and has been subject to more ridicule than all of the others put together. But it is tenacious. It can be used at any point in a lesson and in combination with any one of the other approaches. The theory underlying it is that enthusiasm for or appreciation of a literary work can be communicated from teacher to student by word of mouth. Knowing that the student *should* like the work, the teacher assumes that the most efficient method of bringing him to a sense of appreciation is either to explain its emotional and aesthetic qualities or to dramatize his personal response. The questions for our consideration, of course, are whether or not the student is influenced by the emotive language of the teacher and whether the influence is positive or negative.

There are some few individuals who can convey their own emotional responses to a class. Such teachers are actors who can achieve a direct empathic response from their students, whom they hold enthralled lecture after lecture. Their students achieve an emotional response not only to the teacher but to the work; and that response may be genuine, even though their involvement with the work comes as a secondary effect of their involvement with the teacher. Such teachers capture their audience by reading aloud or by lecturing in a dramatic way that is irresistible to the students.

A less dramatically talented teacher resorts to pronouncing value judgments directly to his students. He tells them how great the work is and may even work himself into a state resembling certain forms of hysteria in his zeal. These teachers want to spellbind their students, just as their less numerous but more talented counterparts do. More frequently, their effect is just the opposite: to drive students away from any appreciation of the work at hand.

For the time being, let us assume that the approach is generally effective, that is, that students will accept their teachers' judgments about the beauty of a poem or the intricacy and artistry of a story. Is the students' acceptance of the teacher's evaluations desirable? The danger of accepting the teacher's evaluation if it is "wrong" is obvious. But if his evaluation is "right," there is still a danger. First, the students may develop standardized responses to literary works. If the teacher enjoys certain poems, certain styles, certain authors, or certain genres, the student too will respond favorably to those, and perhaps only to those. Second, if the students accept their teacher's emotional response and evaluation, they are clearly deprived of an opportunity to respond emotionally and aesthetically as individuals. If they are to become mature readers of literature, they must respond independently to both aspects of literature.

Fortunately, however, the student will more often feel free to reject his teacher's opinion before, after, or during his reading of the work in question.

If he rejects it before he reads the work, then there was little point in the teacher's giving it in the first place. If he rejects the teacher's evaluation during or after his reading of the work, it won't be long before complete disillusionment sets in. Thus, the teacher praises a work; the student reads it but finds nothing praiseworthy in it. His expectations have been raised only to be disappointed. After a few experiences of this sort, the student will be conditioned to expect incomprehensibility when the teacher promises beauty, dullness when the teacher mentions artistry, and general frustration and boredom when the teacher pleads enjoyment.

Every effective teacher of literature attempts to involve students in what they read, but he does it in subtle ways both by his personal responses and by his pedagogical approach. He reveals his enthusiasm for literature by the respect he pays it as something worthy of close attention, but his enthusiasm is neither boisterous nor intimidating. He encourages and propagates emotional and aesthetic responses in his students, not by emoting and declaiming, but by organizing his instruction in such a way that his students become more and more sophisticated as readers capable of emotional and aesthetic responses of their own.

A second approach to literary appreciation is through a study of famous authors and their works. Many teachers assume that, to a certain degree, appreciation is synonymous with knowledge of authors and their works. They feel that in order to appreciate literature students must be familiar with "great" literature—usually its content and the lives of its authors. They assume that such knowledge will make students more discerning and appreciative readers. The curriculum is devised by making a list of famous works and/or authors organized randomly in seventh through tenth grades and chronologically in eleventh and twelfth.

The supposed advantages of the chronological organization of works and authors are that students will learn more of their literary heritage and that the study of a literary period will illuminate the works read. Both arguments are vacuous. High school literature surveys are notoriously shallow affairs that do little more than alienate most students who have to sit through them. And even if students do learn a list of authors and works and can recite the content of some of the works, what good is it? The "investigation" of any literary period in a high school course is so perfunctory that it can give no special insight into any work read. Worst of all, the arrangement of works has nothing at all to do with either student interest or ability. The most complex material comes early in the year (*Beowulf, Paradise Lost,* poems by John Donne) whereas the easier materials are scheduled last (a play by Galsworthy, stories by Maugham and others). The problems of interpretation in any one work are likely to be entirely different from the problems that students encounter in the works assigned before or after it. In such courses teachers ordinarily do not even think of organizing the materials so that students accumulate higher level interpretive skills in a systematic way. Their attention is riveted to the explication of individual works. As a result, although the students may learn the content of individual works—and many do not even do that—very few become more competent in dealing with a text independently.

The method of evaluation is to test the student's knowledge of facts about an author's life and times and the content of his works. If a student can pass the test, then the approach is deemed successful. Apparently no one ever attempts to determine whether or not the students have become more discerning or more appreciative readers. As a matter of fact, there has probably been no attempt to determine what those phrases mean. If the student had become more appreciative or more discerning, how would the teacher know?

Of course, it is possible to prepare a productive instructional unit based on the writings of a single author. But such a unit would have to last for a few weeks, and the author would have to be chosen with care, since there are not many whose work will sustain the interest of high school students over a relatively long period of time. But good units could be developed on such authors as Poe, Mark Twain, Hemingway, and Stephen Crane, whose works include a fair variety of material in terms of difficulty and type. The purpose of such a unit would be to learn how to approach the body of works of a given author. A unit on Poe, for instance, could include examples of his tales of horror, mood, and ratiocination, his poetry, criticism, and biography. Students could examine special influences on Poe's writing, including the writer's personal life and critical theories. It would not be a simple unit, but neither would it be superficial.

A third approach to literary appreciation is through analysis of technique and/or genre as that word is used to refer to "the short story," "the novel," "poetry," and so on. The assumption is that if the student is aware of an author's artistry, he will appreciate the "author's craft" and thereby enjoy the literary work in question. If the assumption were warranted, one would expect the curriculum in literature to be built around a sequence of investigations into technique—a sequence in which each succeeding lesson builds upon the preceding lesson and contributes to the following one. This is almost never the case. On the contrary, the techniques examined at a given point in the curriculum depend on the work being read, and the works are not ordinarily selected to teach increasingly complex problems in technique. The result is that the approach to technique is haphazard. One week ninth-grade students may read Poe's "The Tell-Tale Heart" and examine the rhythm of the prose and the nature of Poe's vocabulary. Next they may read a Sherlock Holmes story in which they examine the development of suspense and plot structure in terms of introduction, development, complication, crisis, and denouement. They may even learn to make plot diagrams at this point. Next, they may turn to poetry and learn how to scan lines and identify rhyme schemes. Perhaps the next reading will be a novel by Dickens in which the students will examine the art of caricature. Thus, their work is fragmented. There is little or no attempt to apply what is learned from the reading of one story to the reading of another. The teacher may point out the rhythmic patterns in Poe's "The Tell-Tale Heart," but the students are not likely to hear about rhythmic prose for the rest of the semester. If they have learned anything at all about rhythmic prose from reading Poe's story, they have no opportunity to make use of it and are likely to forget it very quickly.

A second, perhaps even more serious, charge against this approach is that individual lessons such as those mentioned above are likely to be superficial and are likely to appear so to the students. For instance, once the students have taken note of Poe's imitation of heartbeat rhythm in the story, they are likely to ask "So what?" And this question (it is more likely to be a statement) is justifiable. The teacher has directed their attention to prose rhythm in one limited part of one story. The students have not examined prose rhythm in other parts of the story, nor are they likely to examine rhythmic prose in other stories by Poe, nor will they have an opportunity to view this particular phenomenon against Poe's aesthetics. Isolated as it is, it hardly has a chance to be more than superficial.

Let us examine one of the most common approaches to technique: metrical analysis of poetry. Ordinarily, the teacher proceeds to teach metrical analysis by teaching first the differences between iambic, trochaic, anapestic, dactylic, and perhaps some of the less common feet (metrical units) such as the spondee, the amphibrach, or the amphimacer. Once the differences have been taught, the student proceeds to the scanning of poetry, that is, the marking of metrical units in various lines of poetry. Many teachers will be satisfied when their students can scan accurately—or at least with some degree of accuracy. But we cannot really blame the students for saying, "So what?"

Some teachers of course, attempt to go beyond simple scansion. They have been influenced by a tradition expressed in Pope's line in his "Essay on Criticism": "The sound must seem an echo to the sense." Of course, the relationship of sound to sense is much more obvious in some poems than it is in others. Ordinarily, teachers choose the obvious examples for beginning such a study. This is as it should be. However, most teachers who teach their students to scan poetry, seem to assume that such a relationship always exists, even in poems where a particular metrical unit is clearly traditional or arbitrary. The result is that interpretations are frequently forced.

As Pope says earlier in his "Essay on Criticism," "A little learning is a dangerous thing." The teacher of scansion frequently becomes so absorbed with the idea that the sound should reinforce the sense that he fails to realize that it is often the other way around: as Samuel Johnson pointed out, frequently the *sense* leads us to attribute certain characteristics to the sound. Pope himself unwittingly illustrates this problem. At one point in the "Essay on Criticism," he condemns the Alexandrine, a line composed of six iambic feet:

A needless Alexandrine ends the song
That, like a wounded snake, drags its slow length along.
(11. 356–357)

What is it that makes the second line sound long and slow? Is it the fact that it has six feet? Or is its languishly slow appearance the result of the image of the wounded snake coupled with the words "drags," "slow," "length," and the somewhat redundant use of "along" to fill out the line? Sixteen lines later Pope, apparently unwittingly, uses an Alexandrine again—this time to illustrate a method of conveying a sense of swiftness:

Flies o'er the unbending corn, and skims along the main.
(1. 373)

This line has the same number of feet, and only the second foot is not iambic.

Failure to realize the influence that sense has over apparent sound can result in some fairly peculiar assignments. One ninth-grade text, for instance, includes Browning's poem "How They Brought the Good News from Ghent to Aix." The students are told, "The poem sounds like a galloping horse." After reading the poem they are asked to "compare the sound of the first stanza with that of the last. How does the sound fit the sense?"[11] In the first stanza the ride to Aix is just beginning. In the last, Roland—the only horse to arrive at Aix—is on the ground dying. The meter of the two stanzas is almost exactly the same. Here are the stanzas; decide for yourself about the wisdom of the question:

I sprang to the stirrup, and Joris, and he;
I galloped, Dirck galloped, we galloped all three;
"Good speed!" cried the watch as the gate bolts undrew;
"Speed!" echoed the wall to us galloping through;
Behind shut the postern, the lights sank to rest,
And into the midnight we galloped abreast.

.   .   .

And all I remember is—friends flocking round
As I sat with his head 'twixt my knees on the ground;
And no voice but was praising this Roland of mine,
As I poured down his throat our last measure of wine,
Which (the burgesses voted by common consent)
Was no more than his due who brought good news from Ghent.

Not only are such analytical approaches frequently inadequate in themselves, they also take the life out of literature. The student begins to feel that reading poetry is a matter of finding figures of speech or scanning metrical lines, and that short stories are intended as exercises in plot diagrams. Of course, figures of speech and elements of structure cannot be avoided because both help to provide meaning, which might escape the student if he cannot, for instance, interpret a metaphor. But it is much more meaningful for students to talk about the "turning points" (and there are several possibilities) of Jack London's story "To Build a Fire" than to diagram the story. It is more interesting and rewarding to spend a few days learning and discussing two or three figures of speech and using them in the Japanese poems called haiku than to spend two or three weeks learning and identifying all figures of speech, some metrical patterns, onomatopoeia, and the like, in poem after poem. Students can be interested in a poem for itself and in the devices, say contrast, imagery, or symbol, that contribute to its meaning. But to study many devices in a few days is to divorce them from meaning. If a student learns what metaphors are and how to interpret them, he needs time to see them working, to discuss their meanings, to use them in his own writing. The all-at-once approach might lead to identification, but it leads to little else except boredom.

THE "ENJOYMENT FIRST" APPROACHES

There are a group of theories that hold that the most promising method of teaching literature lies in ensuring that students enjoy what they read and that the principle of enjoyment should not be violated at any cost. Classroom activities and the literature read should be geared to what students normally enjoy. No one will deny that the enjoyment of literature is extremely important if reading is to be established as a habit. The problems arise over what we mean by enjoyment and over the methods of helping the student enjoy the reading of literature. The teacher who adheres to the approaches under consideration here tends to equate enjoyment with entertainment and to put his classroom in competition with television, the movies, parties, athletics, and so forth. "After all," he says, "these are the things students enjoy. If we want them to read, we've got to make them like it." Such approaches fall into two major divisions: the "fun and games" approach and the "interests" approach.

The teacher who uses the "fun and games" approach will organize classroom activities before, after, or during the reading of particular works in order to attract the interest of the students. Miss Soma's approach to *Treasure Island* and myth is common (see pp. 4–5.) For instance, a few years ago a teacher from a large city system reported a method of interesting a class of bright ninth-grade students in mythology. The students read stories of the Greek gods and heroes and stories of Arthur and his knights, whose number, according to her, included Beowulf. They collected advertisements using the gods and emblems of Greek mythology (Ajax, Pegasus, etc.) to see how Greek myth is "relevant to life today." They made posters and displays showing Greek and Arthurian heroes in action and held contests to learn the pronunciation of the Greek names. The whole business was topped off with an "Olympian party" to which the students came dressed as gods and heroes.

Perhaps both these examples are extreme. But they illustrate a phenomenon that takes place in many English classes with varying degrees of elaboration. Our problem is whether or not such activities are really worthwhile. Do they bring the students first to enjoyment, then to understanding, and finally to appreciation? In the "fun and games" approach to mythology, what did they learn of the significance of myth? How did myths come about? Why did people continue to tell the stories? How did succeeding ages use the materials of myth? Why do we find similar myths in disparate cultures? Why is there so much interest in myth in the twentieth century? Are not these questions, or at least some of them, interesting in themselves? The teacher who uses the "fun and games" approach seems to deny that the material itself is interesting, and students are quick to catch the implications. "The stuff is pretty dull," they say, "but the teacher tries to make it interesting."

Certainly, students enjoy games. They are pleasant breaks from the tedium of school and can be used discreetly to increase interest and learning; but the teacher must always test them against the question of their worth in conveying subject-matter concepts and skills. If they teach neither concepts nor skills, if they attract attention only to themselves, then they have no place in the English program. As long as our classroom activities deny that literature is interesting in itself, as long as we focus student attention on more or less irrelevant activities, we are short-changing our students and the literature we teach. If we were science teachers and wanted our students to learn about microscopes, we might ask them to build one, or use one, or take one apart. We would not ask them to come to school dressed as lab technicians or to draw pictures of famous scientists. If the science teacher and his students can deal directly with an area of inquiry, why can't we?

The second of the "enjoyment" approaches is the approach through the students' interests, and perhaps this is the most valuable or potentially useful of all those mentioned so far. In general the approach is predicated on three related assumptions: (1) students at a given age have normal and natural interests for that age group, (2) those interests change as the students grow older, and (3) the students will learn to like literature if the teacher simply follows their interest patterns.[12] If these assumptions are true, the procedures requisite to success should be obvious. First, discover the interests of students. Second, select materials as indicated by those interests. Third, let nature take its course.

There are several methods of discovering student interests. The first and, in some ways, most reliable method is simply to keep a record of books that students withdraw from a library. The titles are then classified—biography, adventure, love stories, and so on—to determine what kind of books they prefer to read. Another method is to ask students to list books they have enjoyed reading. Some interest inventories offer brief synopses of plots of various types, and students are asked to select among them. Others simply ask direct questions such as the following: "What do young persons like you want most to read? What kind of book or article would you choose to read above all others?"

Most of these studies yield similar results. In general very young children prefer stories about animals, other children, and fantasy or fairy tales. Beyond the primary grades, sex differences begin to appear, with boys showing interest in adventure and science and girls in material about home and school life. A study by Ruth Strang in 1946 reported that the favorite reading among seventh graders included animal stories and stories of adventure and mystery.[13] In later grades the animal stories lose prominence, and the "big three" take over for several years: adventure, mystery, and romance. Boys show preference for adventure, mystery, science, sports, and outdoor life. Girls continue to prefer stories of romance, problems of home, school and adolescent life. In the upper grades (the studies seem to hedge here) students show more interest in reflective works, historical novels, current events, travel, and best sellers.

Strang reports asking students the following questions as well: "Suppose you were going to write a book or article that persons your age would all want to read, what would be its title?" The answers, of course, indicate interest in romance, adventure, and mystery as well as in material concerning problems of the age group: parent problems, adolescent problems, school and teacher problems, and so forth.

The Strang study also asked students why they disliked books and why they liked books. The responses to the two questions were correlatives of each other. They liked simple books and disliked difficult ones. Strang reports statements such as the following as typical of the reasons students give for liking books: "Written in simple words that everyone can understand. A person can hardly enjoy something if he doesn't understand it." There should be "as little description as possible," and the author should not "beat around the bush" to get at the point. A good book "tells a story in a straightforward manner; presents the idea and lets you judge for yourself." When students did not like books, they objected to "books I can't understand," "too much description," "too much detail about surroundings," "idle conversation," "not enough action," "slow plodding plot," and so on. Strang summarizes, "In brief they wanted accurate facts, stated quite directly and clearly. They did not want to wade through irrelevancies."[14]

Armed witn the results of interest surveys, many teachers and textbook writers set about building an interest-centered curriculum with a view to making the students like literature. Unfortunately, such texts have failed. The great majority of students have not learned to like literature.

There seem to be several difficulties involved. First, any teacher or anthology that emphasizes vicarious excitement and adventure as the major reward of reading tends to equate literature with the popular media of mass culture and to ignore the aesthetic and intellectual values of literature. Those teachers apparently think that literature competes for student attention in the same way that movies and TV dramas do. Literature demands more and offers more. But even if it did compete in the same way, most students, including college students, would much rather watch TV than read a story for adventure, mystery, and romance.

Second, most of the interest studies appear to assume that the interests they discover are somehow inherent in the sex and age of the child. Should we assume that these are natural or inherent interests? Isn't it more likely that they are conditioned interests, conditioned by teachers, parents, and the culture? Ninth-grade boys may like sports stories because their experiences in our culture dictate that boys be interested in sports. The emphasis that the mass media gives sports implies a lack of masculinity in those who are not interested. Twelfth graders may begin to be interested in literature about social problems because high school courses have introduced them for the first time to such problems. A few researchers argue that reading interests are not instinctive or inherent, but the result of various kinds of conditioning.[15] This seems much more reasonable. Our experience tells us that it is possible to create or motivate new interests. If this is true, there is no real need to center all classroom work in the areas indicated by the reading interest surveys. If we do make the surveys our guide to building curriculum, we may actually hinder a student's acquisition of reading skills and inhibit his interests. If we ask students to read mystery, adventure, romance, and adolescent problem tales, and if we reward them for doing so, can we really expect them to become interested in something else?

Third, it is a physical impossibility for a single anthology to appeal to the interest of all or even most of the students in a given class—let alone in a given school or city. Some of the interest studies make this point very clear. One study of the voluntary reading of eighth-grade students concludes that "the voluntary reading of an individual [is] complex, dynamic, and unique."[16] If this is true and if a teacher wishes to appeal to the interest of his students, he must make the appeal through a program of voluntary, *individualized* reading—not through a text that strives to meet the interests of thousands of students in the confines of a few hundred pages.

Finally, anthologies developed from interest surveys are frequently based on the assumption that interest is the key to the teaching of reading. The books seem to suggest that if we just give a student materials he is interested in, he will automatically become a better reader as he grows older. Unfortunately, the assumption is simply not true. A boy might begin reading mystery stories when he is in junior high school and read them until he reaches old age, but he won't ever be able to read more sophisticated literature as a result of having read them alone.

Reading is a complex process of getting meaning from a printed page. If students don't get that meaning, if they don't understand the words, if they can't follow a complicated plot or see the relevancy of details, if they can't make inferences about imagery, symbols, or subtle relationships, we can't expect them to find such material interesting. A tenth-grade student once condemned Orwell's *Animal Farm* as "a silly kid's book about animals." The boy condemned the book, not because he wasn't interested in social problems, but because it had no significance for him. Lack of interest or active dislike is often a direct result of an inability to comprehend. Obviously, if interest is strong enough, it will help a student overcome an edge of frustration in the reading he undertakes. But even strong interest cannot do everything.

There is value in determining the interests of individual students, especially of reluctant readers, and the research suggests some methods for discovering those interests. The immediate interests of students can be a jumping-off point for expanding old interests, creating new ones, and for increasing comprehension skills. The research also suggests the value of assessing student response to the literature studied in the curriculum, and it provides techniques for making that assessment. We do want students to enjoy literature, and if they indicate they don't like what they read, we need to change either our teaching method or the materials or both. In short, any literature program must provide for an assessment of student responses to the material, but a program based on interest alone is not likely to do the job.

In one respect, the method of instruction suggested in what follows is conservative. It holds that literature is a distinct way of knowing and should be treated as a distinctive subject matter, just as philosophy and the sciences are treated as distinctive subject matters. Instruction should be directed toward learning to read literature. Literature should be neither an appendage to other subject matters nor an instrument for social control.

In another way, however, the units of instruction suggested here are progressive. They require tailoring instruction to the abilities and needs of the students in a particular classroom. The common curriculum advocated by the conservative is patently absurd, and its absurdity should be apparent to even the most casual observer. It is simply not possible for each student in a given grade level to read the same material in the same way. Some students, even in the tenth, eleventh, and twelfth grades cannot read at all, and others can barely read. If a teacher ignores those students, he is not fulfilling the terms of his contract. If, on the other hand—and this is more often the case—he selects materials suitable for his average and slower students, he cheats the students who are above average. In other words, sound instruction must help the slow student and challenge the bright student. There must be provision for varying materials, goals, and methods according to the abilities of the students in particular classes.

In the matter of purpose, however, the instruction presented here is in firm agreement with the statements of both conservative and progressive. A statement from a 1955 bulletin issued by Kenyon College displays a typical conservative point of view. The bulletin states explicitly that "power" to read literature should be the student's primary goal.[17] John Dewey uses the word "power" also, though not explicitly in relation to literary study: "The planning must be flexible enough to permit free play for individuality of experience and yet firm enough to give direction towards *continuous development of power* [italics added]."[18] Power is a key word, but to develop power in reading literature, it is necessary to depart from both the conservative and progressive approaches to teaching literature.

NOTES

1. Dorothy E. Moulton, *The Teaching of Literature in the Senior High School: An Historical and Critical Study of Recent Trends, 1911–1955* (unpublished doctoral dissertation, Ann Arbor: University of Michigan, 1959). Dr. Moulton's work has been invaluable in preparing the summary comparison of the conservative and progressive approaches.
2. See especially Edgar Z. Friedenberg, *Coming of Age in America* (New York: Random House, 1965).
3. The Curriculum Commission of the National Council of Teachers of English, W. Wilbur Hatfield, Chairman, *An Experience Curriculum in English* (New York: Appleton-Century, 1935).
4. Holland D. Roberts, Walter V. Kaulfers, and Grayson N. Kefauver, *English for Social Living* (New York: McGraw-Hill Book Co., 1943), pp. 237–238.
5. See for example *McGuffey's Fifth Eclectic Reader: 1896 Edition* (New York: New American Library, 1962).
6. Sir Philip Sidney, "The Defence of Poesie," *Tudor Prose and Poetry*, ed. J. William Hebel, *et al.* (New York: Appleton-Century-Crofts, 1952), p. 806.
7. *Ibid.,* p. 808.
8. *Ibid.,* p. 808.
9. The Curriculum Commission of the National Council of Teachers of English, *op. cit.,* p. 49.
10. J. R. R. Tolkien, "Beowulf: The Monsters and the Critics," *Proceedings of the British Academy,* XXII (1936), 245–295.
11. William Eller, Betty Yvonne Welch, Edward J. Gordon, *Introduction to Literature* (Boston: Ginn and Company, 1964), pp. 463–465.
12. For a recent, and sounder approach in this tradition, see G. Robert Carlsen, *Books and the Teen-Age Reader* (New York: Bantam Books, 1967).
13. Ruth Strang, "Reading Interests, 1946," *English Journal,* 35 (November 1946), pp. 477–482.
14. *Ibid.,* p. 481.
15. Evan R. Keislar, "Learning Sets in a Stimulus-Response View of Classroom Motivation," Paper read at AERA meeting, Atlantic City, 1960, reported by George D. Spache, *Toward Better Reading* (Champaign: Garrard, 1963), pp. 170–171.

16. Mary H. B. Wollner, *Children's Voluntary Reading as an Expression of Individuality* (New York: Teacher's College, Columbia University, 1949), p. 80.
17. Moulton, *op. cit.,* p. 31.
18. John Dewey, *Education and Experience* (New York: Macmillan, 1950), p. 65.

8 | Toward a Philosophy of Literature for Teachers

The readers of this book will probably meet a good many people on their faculties, in their classrooms, on boards of education who are skeptical of the values of literature. "Why bother to read literature?" they ask. It is an irritating question, which we are tempted to answer with the response Louis Armstrong gave to someone who asked him what jazz was. He said, "Man, if you have to ask, you'll never know." But the question of value in literature has been raised by responsible thinkers since, and probably before, Plato decided to banish poets from his perfect state. It cannot be dismissed by teachers who are theoretically and legally responsible to the public they serve. Louis Armstrong justifies his existence every time he gives a concert or sells a record. We neither receive applause nor sell records, but we must justify our existence. Our intuition tells us that literature is unique; it is one of the highest and most valuable activities of man. However, in the face of responsible skepticism, declarations of faith will not be sufficient. But if teachers never encounter anyone bold enough to ask the question, they still need an answer. They need an answer to give direction in building a curriculum and in developing a theory of instruction.

This chapter will raise two major questions: (1) What is literature? (2) Why read it or why teach it? We will attempt answers and explore their ramifications. It would be foolish to pretend that our answers are either complete or final, but they do provide a beginning toward the development of a philosophy of literature for English teachers.

What Is Literature?

For our purposes, the term "literature" does not refer to everything that is in print. If it did, we might find ourselves responsible for teaching students to read scientific writing and math problems, as many of our colleagues believe we should. Not that the kind of reading we teach does not overlap in some significant ways the kinds of reading taught by a history teacher, a math teacher, or a science teacher. It does, and many points of overlap might be exploited to the advantage of both teacher and student. But, essentially, the reading taught by the English teacher should be the reading of literature. The word "literature" therefore requires at least a working definition. Traditionally, in the schools, it has meant poetry, fiction, drama, biography, myth, folk tale, essay, and whatever else the anthologist wished to include. This is not a very sophisticated definition—if it is a definition at all—and the word "essay" opens the door to all kinds of writing. Still, it is useful in delineating our subject matter. If we require a definition that tells us something of the nature of that subject matter, the most useful approach is probably to examine the language of literature. How does that language differ from everyday language or from language whose purpose is primarily utilitarian? If we confine our concept of literature, for the time being, to poetry, fiction, drama, and some essays, we can make some useful distinctions.

An explanation of molecular weights, a philosophical work such as Spinoza's *Ethics,* a recipe for apple pie, and a history of World War I all have something in common that imaginative literature does not share: The referents are outside the work. The function of such works is to direct our attention to objects, processes, systems, events, and so on, that exist apart from the work in a world that we like to think has an empirical, objective reality. The ideal of pragmatic or scientific language is a complete absence of ambiguity: one term, one referent. Such language is purely denotative and receives praise for accuracy. The recipe for apple pie must direct the cook's attention to the flour, shortening, sugar, and apples in the proper order and in the proper quantities. We judge the recipe on the basis of whether or not it produces a good pie. The language of the recipe is the kind of language that René Wellek and Austin Warren call "transparent";[1] it calls little or no attention to itself. The language of imaginative literature (poetry, fiction, drama), on the other hand, calls attention to, and stresses the importance of, the language. The poet wants his reader to be acutely aware of his words as words. His language has an expressive and connotative side that pragmatic language minimizes as much as possible.

Furthermore, the reference or denotation of literary language is within the world created in a given work. There is no necessity for the characters of a short story to exist in the real world. They exist in the world of the story. Northrop Frye's discussion of this problem is useful:

> . . . verbal structures may be classified according to whether the *final* direction of meaning is outward or inward. In descriptive or assertive writing the final direction is outward. Here the verbal structure is intended to represent things external to it, and it is valued in terms of the accuracy with which it does represent them. Correspondence between phenomenon and verbal sign is truth; lack of it is falsehood; failure to connect is tautology, a purely verbal structure that cannot come out of itself.

In all literary verbal structures the final direction of meaning is inward. In literature the standards of outward meaning are secondary, for literary works do not pretend to describe or assert, and hence are not true, not false, and yet not tautological either, or at least not in the sense in which such a statement as "the good is better than the bad" is tautological. Literary meaning may best be described, perhaps, as hypothetical, and a hypothetical or assumed relation to the external world is part of what is usually meant by the word "imaginative." . . . In literature, questions of fact or truth are subordinated to the primary literary aim of producing a structure of words for its own sake, and the sign-values of symbols are subordinated to their importance as a structure of inter-connected motifs. Wherever we have an autonomous verbal structure of this kind, we have literature.[2]

The way in which we can test reading comprehension points up the difference between nonliterature and literature. The cook's ability to comprehend a recipe can be tested in terms of what she produces: the apple pie. An auto mechanic's comprehension of a book on carburetors can be tested by his ability to repair or modify a carburetor. A chemist's comprehension of an article on the corrosion of steel can be tested on the basis of how he makes use of the information. But we cannot expect to test comprehension of literature in that way. Reading literature will influence our attitudes, heighten our perception, and create an emotional state in us, but reading *The Adventures of Huckleberry Finn* will not teach us how to civilize Huck. We cannot test a student's comprehension of Kipling's "Rikki-Tikki-Tavi" by his ability to raise a mongoose. Nor can we test his comprehension of Poe's "The Pit and the Pendulum" by the student's ability to survive the horrors that Poe depicts. We do not even think of testing the comprehension of literature in that way. The particular denotations, the referents, of a literary work are important as they exist in the literary work; whether or not the characters and events of a work may have existed in the real world is a matter of relatively little consequence.

The definition requires three qualifications. First, certain types of works usually considered at least peripheral to literature do have specific referents in the real world: biography, true adventure, and personal essays, for instance. To the extent that these works project an internal world of their own, they are literary. To put it another way, although the language of such works is about real people, events, conditions, and so on, they are also literary insofar as the language creates a self-contained reality, apart from the external reality that it represents. Thus, a biographical sketch in *Who's Who* is nonliterary because it directs attention *only* to external facts about its subject, whereas Carl Sandburg's biography of Lincoln is literary because it creates its own internal world while concomitantly representing the real world. Similarly, a newspaper account of Thor Heyerdahl's voyage across the Pacific is nonliterary, directing the reader's attention *only* to the external truth, but Heyerdahl's *Kon-Tiki* is literary insofar as it attempts to create an internal world of its own. Again, although the events and emotions of Orwell's "Shooting an

Elephant" may have occurred in the real world, their use is literary because, for the purpose of the essay, their force is centripetal, directing attention inward to the central theme of the essay rather than outward to specific external events. This suggests two bases for evaluating such material: (1) the degree of accuracy in reporting real events, and (2) the extent to which the language of the work presents a self-sufficient, consistent internal reality.

Second, although the referents of a literary work (characters, events, setting, and so on) exist primarily within the boundaries of the work, the words that make up the work have agreed-upon meanings apart from it. The word "fox," for instance, has a meaning that most English speaking people accept. The use of that word conjures up the image of an animal with reddish brown fur, extended canine teeth, and a bushy tail. These animals do indeed exist in reality. But the particular fox in Aesop's fable (who spies grapes on an arbor, attempts to reach them, and fails) exists only within the bounds of that fable.

Third, the idea that the referents of the work exist within the work *does not* suggest that the interpretation of literature need be or should be entirely subjective. Because no two readers are alike, elements of subjectivity in the interpretation and evaluation of literature are unavoidable. The New Criticism, which placed so much emphasis on careful reading of the *text,* may inadvertently have given rise to irresponsible reading in the classroom. The reader is encouraged to interpret what is there, but, unfortunately, he can interpret only what he *thinks* is there. The result is that time and again students base interpretations on private, irrelevant associations, false analogies, misreadings of words, and the like. In professional criticism we see twentieth-century meanings forced on fifteenth-century words, images, and symbols. It is no easy matter to read Chaucer without a twentieth-century bias. But if we accept the definition above, we must consider both *text* and *context.* Our interpretations of a given work must be based on careful examination of the text and whatever outside sources illuminate its meaning. In short, the definition does not validate the "anything goes" philosophy of interpretation.

This definition of the nature of literature, which seems to be nearly axiomatic in contemporary criticism, carries with it at least two corollaries of which literature teachers ought to be aware. They concern reading difficulty and the problem of reality or truth in literature.

Ordinarily, teachers of junior high and high school literature fail to make any distinctions among the works in a given anthology on the basis of difficulty —at least, they make no distinction in practice. At most, they are vaguely aware that students have more difficulty with a poem by Wordsworth than with a short story by Edgar Allan Poe and more difficulty with an essay by Emerson than with the poem by Wordsworth. In general, among most teachers, reading difficulty is a very vague concept. The foregoing distinction between literary and nonliterary works gives us some clues to the problem. The purpose of what Northrop Frye has called descriptive or assertive writing (comparable to what is called information-oriented writing in the section of this book on composition) is to convey information. The author of such a piece of writing ordinarily attempts to be as clear as possible. For the most part, he defines his terms when necessary, avoids ambiguity, and makes the implications of his argument explicit when he is aware of them. Except for occasional stylistic effects, he leaves as little as possible to the inference-making capacity of his audience. The literary artist, on the other hand, uses words and images because of their ambiguity, that is, their multiple meanings. He requires that his reader make inferences at many different levels about the actions of characters, about relationships between them, about images, about the structure of the work as a whole. The major "meanings" of a literary work are usually implied and emerge through the texture of the whole work. In short, the artist relies heavily upon the inference-making capacity of his reader.

This is not to say that inference making is unnecessary in reading information-oriented material. Information-oriented writing requires application, extrapolation, and evaluation just as literary works do. But in understanding *what* it has to say, inference making is ordinarily minimal—by the very nature of the material. In comprehending literary material, on the other hand, inference making is maximal. The difficulty of understanding what information-oriented material has to say ordinarily resides in the vocabulary, the syntax, the relative familiarity of the concepts that a writer uses, and in the level of abstraction of those concepts. Nearly any beginning student of statistics will agree that his text material is difficult. The vocabulary is technical and unusual, and the concepts are highly abstract. Technical research in astrophysics would be difficult reading for anyone who is not a physicist, and it may be difficult for physicists who are not specialists in astrophysics.

Of course, literary works can present similar difficulties in vocabulary and syntax. Teachers complain that students are not interested in *Ivanhoe.* Is it any wonder? Sir Walter Scott was fond of using the Norman-French terms for pieces of armor, fighting gear, and general attire. He wrote one hundred and fifty years ago, time enough for some of his words to go out of general circulation. In addition he tended to use a high proportion of relatively unusual words and very long sentences. Yet this is the most obvious kind of difficulty, and frequently the only kind that teachers help their students overcome. Although such difficulties cannot be ignored, the real problems in reading literature lie beyond the level of vocabulary and syntax in the nature of literary art as we have defined it. They lie in what the writer does not say, in what he implies. Before we can decide how to teach literature, we will have to determine as precisely as possible what problems readers encounter or, to state it positively, what levels of meaning readers must comprehend to come to a full understanding of a work. Chapters 9 and 10 will discuss this problem in detail.

A second corollary of the definition of literature has to do with the nature of truth or reality in literature. We have already commented on this problem in the previous chapter during the discussion of the social studies approaches to literature. To recapitulate in part, the study of literature as history and geography is inefficient because the literary artist chooses details and incidents, not because they are true in fact, but because they help to accomplish his central purpose. If we studied Shakespeare's history plays in order to learn about English history, we would have a highly inaccurate view of what actually happened before and during the Wars of the Roses. Shakespeare felt no necessity to make a play conform to the facts of English history. He was primarily concerned with the production of a work of art, as are all literary artists.

If literature is not restricted to actual fact, it is also not limited to the probable or even the possible, although writers frequently pretend to restrict themselves in such a way. Witness Orwell's *Animal Farm,* Shakespeare's *Tempest,* and Swift's *Gulliver's Travels.*

Although the mature reader knows that pigs cannot walk and talk and read and write, he accepts these unreal elements of *Animal Farm* to let Orwell tell his story in the way he wishes. The mature reader does not expect factual reality. The truth that he expects in literature is not the truth of empirical knowledge. Although he may not be able to state the definition of literature that Northrop Frye gives us, the ideal mature reader ordinarily recognizes that the reference of a work does not move outward to the real world, but inward to the microcosmic world produced by the artist. In more ordinary terms, he accepts the conventions of the literary work for its duration. He indulges himself in what Coleridge called "the willing suspension of disbelief." Thus, the characters of a fictional work need not have existed in reality. The events need never have occurred.

Still, literature involves a kind of truth that mature readers demand. First, a good literary work is true to itself on its own terms. When an author creates a work of fiction, he makes a series of postulations. He says given this character and these conditions, certain results will be forthcoming. The work has internal consistency. Aristotle makes this point in regard to character in the *Poetics.* If a character is going to be inconsistent, he must be "consistently inconsistent."[3]

The second kind of truth is what critics from Aristotle to Sidney to the moderns have called truth to life. This is the truth that Archibald MacLeish seems to refer to in "Ars Poetica" when he says a poem is "equal to: not true."[4] The problem is that this notion of truth to life gives rise to many misconceptions about literature—for instance, to the social studies approaches to literature discussed in the previous chapter. If literature is "true to life," people say, then it must be a valid approach to history, geography, economics, psychotherapy, and so on. However, the people who consciously or unconsciously believe that forget that an author wrote the particular work—an author who may or may not have been an historian or psychiatrist, but who, at any rate, is attempting to create a work of art and not an historical document or a treatise on psychiatry. The work is dominated by an aesthetic purpose. Still, critics insist that the poet must be "true to life." There must be essential truth and internal consistency in the illusions he creates. The reader must leave the work saying, "Yes, I see how this is true. I understand this view of life. The vision of this artist whether it corresponds with mine or not is comprehensible and meaningful. It reflects essential truth through its internal consistency."

Such truth resides in the function of the work as metaphor or symbol. In her essay, "The Art Symbol and the Symbol in Art," Susanne K. Langer discusses the work of art as a symbol.[5] A literary work is not simply a construct of verbal symbols. It is itself, taken as a whole, a symbol. The truth it has may be expressed as the soundness of the comparison it establishes to life. Remember MacLeish's words: a poem is "equal to: not true." We can evaluate literary truth as we evaluate a metaphor. Look for a moment at the first four lines of Shakespeare's Sonnet 73:

> That time of year thou mayst in me behold
> When yellow leaves, or none, or few, do hang
> Upon those boughs which shake against the cold,
> Bare ruined choirs where late the sweet birds sang.

Old age is compared to a season of the year, and the metaphor is appropriate in all its details. Shakespeare has established a relationship that goes beyond the simple terms of the metaphor's comparison in indefinable ways. It is true and useful. Similarly, a whole work has truth if its reflection of life is valid. The concrete referents of a scientific work lie outside the work, and the truth of the work is judged according to how accurately its symbols correspond to the outside objective reality. The concrete symbols of a literary work have their referents only in the work, not in outside reality. But the abstractions of the literary work—the quality of the experience represented in concrete terms, the judgment and interpretation of that experience, the ultimately indefinable aspects of life—all these have referents outside the particular work. And here lies the symbolic truth of literature.

As every English teacher knows, the nature of truth in literature presents problems in the English class. On the one hand, some students accept everything they read as gospel. On the other, some students reject anything that is not what they consider "true to life." Ordinarily, the latter are the most irritating to the teacher. They are the young skeptics who grow into adults who reject *Hamlet* because they do not believe in ghosts. Strangely enough, the same students who never are willing to accept literary conventions will sit enthralled for hours over comic books or TV cartoons without ever raising a suspicious eyebrow about the "reality" of the material. For this very reason, however, the problem is not altogether impossible. A unit on fantasy and reality in literature, through the use of cartoons and fantasies such as *Alice in Wonderland* and various works of science fiction as well as "realistic" works, can demonstrate the uses of literary conventions and the difference between fantasy and realism in art.

Our definition of literature and its two corollaries can give some direction in planning the content of the literature phase of the English curriculum. In the first place, the selection of reading material should be primarily the material of literature as we have defined it—poetry, fiction, drama, biography, and some essays. Essays on heredity, computer systems, hot-rod building, and homemaking should not receive the primary emphasis in our English classes. Their referents are outside the work and belong more properly in the science, mathematics, industrial arts, and homemaking curricula. For decades reading experts have been saying, "Every teacher should be a teacher of reading." They have been saying it for so long that it has become a cliché. Still, there is a good deal of truth in it. Reading is an extremely important method of increasing knowledge in every area of endeavor. Students who can't read are likely to flunk math, science, and history as well as English. But this fact does not make the English teacher responsible for teaching the reading skills appropriate to other subjects. Confining reading instruction to the English class gives students the mistaken impression that English is the only place in the curriculum where reading matters. Including essays on scientific discoveries and hair styling in the English curriculum allows the teachers of other areas to continue in their misconception of English as a *general* reading course. Actually, we cheat our students by allowing those teachers to abdicate their responsibilities as teachers of reading. A second objection is the disservice we do ourselves and our profession. The random inclusion of such materials tends to destroy the integrity of what we profess to teach.

However, there is no need to exclude rigorously all nonliterature from the English curriculum. In general, we will want to include a good deal of nonliterature in the content of classes devoted to corrective reading. Students in such classes (reading two years or more below grade level) still need to learn the reading skills common to both literature and nonliterature. They still have difficulty with unusual words, with complicated syntax, in locating key ideas and important details, and in drawing simple inferences. Seventh graders who are reading at grade level will need continued instruction in these areas, but they can begin to be concerned primarily with learning the skills and accumulating the background necessary to read literature intelligently. In a curriculum for functional and fluent students, nonliterary materials should be included when there is an explicit purpose for using them. There are two general reasons for their inclusion: to convey information relevant to some aspect of the English curriculum, such as an essay on language, or to serve as the subject for analysis of style, problems in meaning, form and the like. Naturally, the interests of the students should be considered when the teacher selects an essay, but to include it *simply* because of its potential interest to students or because the science teacher or principal wants such material in the curriculum is an insidious kind of prostitution.

Why Read Literature?

When anyone asks the question, "Why read literature?" he is really asking about the function of literature, and the answers attempted here will be in terms of that function. When we are building a curriculum, we must first ask what the function of education is and then determine which subjects of study are most likely to fulfill that function. In this country we believe that the major function of public education is to prepare the individual for successful participation in society. But there are other important functions, too—to advance the frontiers of knowledge, to improve social conditions, and so on. Some of the most persistent problems in American education have arisen out of attempts to formulate and then interpret statements such as those above.

Despite the hazards, it is necessary to attempt an interpretation of the phrase "to prepare the individual for successful participation in society." The most obvious sorts of preparation are those that are strictly utilitarian in nature. For successful integration within our society, some skill in reading and arithmetic are absolutely essential. Illiterates ordinarily, and almost literally, "have a hard row to hoe." But the ability to read road signs, receipts, directions, application forms and bank statements and the ability to add and subtract are subsistence level skills. The concept of "successful participation" goes beyond them.

Apparently we believe that "successful participation" involves knowledge of man and his estate. Students study history, aspects of anthropology, geography, biology, and the natural and physical sciences. Although these studies have fairly obvious utilitarian values, they imply our belief that the "proper study of mankind is man"—though Pope might object to our taking his line out of context. What does the study of man involve? Can we justify the study of literature as part of that study?

Man's Need To Symbolize

Susanne K. Langer in *Philosophy in a New Key* argues that while man is an animal, he is different from other animals in both degree and kind. The difference is due not simply to his ability to exert pressure against the palm of his hand with his thumb. Nor is it simply due to his use of language. This difference is due, she argues, to

> . . . a primary need in man which other creatures probably do not have, and which actuates all his apparently unzoological aims, his wistful fancies,

his consciousness of value, his utterly impractical enthusiasms, and his awareness of a "Beyond" filled with holiness. Despite the fact that this need gives rise to almost everything that we commonly assign to the "higher" life, it is not itself a "higher" form of some "lower" need; it is quite essential, imperious, and general, and may be called "high" only in the sense that it belongs exclusively (I think) to a very complex and perhaps recent genus. It may be satisfied in crude, primitive ways or in conscious and refined ways, so it has its own hierarchy of "higher" and "lower," elementary and derivative forms.

This basic need, which certainly is obvious only in man, is the *need of symbolization.* The symbol-making function is one of man's primary activities, like eating, looking, or moving about. It is the fundamental process of his mind, and goes on all the time. Sometimes we are aware of it, sometimes we merely find its results, and realize that certain experiences have passed through our brains and have been digested there.

*   *   *

The fact that the human brain is constantly carrying on a process of symbolic transformation of the experimental data that come to it causes it to be a veritable fountain of more or less spontaneous ideas. As all registered experience tends to terminate in action, it is only natural that a typically human function should require a typically human form of overt activity; and that is just what we find *in the sheer expression of ideas.* This is the activity of which beasts appear to have no need. And it accounts for just those traits in man which he does not hold in common with the other animals—ritual, art, laughter, weeping, speech, superstition, and scientific genius.[6]

If Dr. Langer is right, then literature is one of our most sophisticated methods of fulfilling a basic need, just as architecture, medicine, and agricultural science have become highly sophisticated methods of fulfilling basic needs. But there is more to it than that. As a part of man's need for symbolization, literature embodies a distinct method of knowing that neither philosophy nor the empirical sciences can provide. Perhaps this is its most important function. Literature makes the quality of experience concrete for us and allows us to examine and evaluate it within an aesthetic frame. It heightens our perceptions, takes us momentarily out of our own necessarily restricted sphere, and permits us to see with the eyes of another. It breaks down the physiological and spiritual barriers among individuals and gives us some understanding of how it feels to be another person. But it is not anthropology, or history, or geography, or psychology, each of which embodies an approach to knowledge different from that of literature.

Literature As a Distinct Way of Knowing

Literature is a *distinct* way of knowing on the basis of our definition alone: A literary work is a verbal construct whose referents exist within the confines of the work, which may be regarded as a symbolic transformation of experience. But it is distinct also because of the nature of the interaction between an audience and a given work. There are at least three dimensions to the interaction: the cognitive, the affective, and the aesthetic. The cognitive dimension includes the decipherment of the explicit and implicit meanings arising out of the author's rhetorical stance and his deployment of words, images, characters, events, and so on in a given work. The affective dimension involves the arousing and/or soothing of "passion" or emotion by a given work—its cathartic effects. The aesthetic dimension of our interaction with a work is the pleasure we feel in the art and artifice of the work; it involves the appropriateness of words, images, characters, and the like, the internal consistency of the work as a whole, and intellectual honesty and freshness. Although each dimension of the reader's interaction with a work is discernible, no one of the three can be totally isolated from the others. It is the inseparability of these three dimensions that makes literature a distinct way of knowing.*

COGNITIVE RESPONSE

Teachers of literature must be concerned with all three dimensions. The cognitive is important for several reasons. First, if the cognitive response to a work is inadequate, the affective response may be inappropriate. At a rather simple level, for instance, students reading the word "Brother" in the name "Brother Timothy" as a statement of kinship rather than as a clerical title can easily misinterpret James Hanley's story "The Butterfly."[7] One student who read the word in this way made a series of inadequate intellectual responses based on her misinterpretation of that single word. Her emotional response to the characters was, as a result, completely inappropriate.

More complex cognitive failures bring about inappropriate emotional responses as well. For example, in Stephen Crane's story "An Ominous Baby," which we will examine in detail later, the narrator quite obviously sets out to build and sustain sympathy for the tattered child who is the main character of the story. Towards the end of the story when the tattered child steals a toy fire engine from a rich child, the sympathy is maintained in what are, at least for the mature reader, rather obvious ways. But some readers—even at the college level—side with the rich child, condemn the tattered child as a "dirty thief," and believe that Crane also condemns the child. In part, this inadequate emotional response is the result of a cognitive failure to understand the author's attitude. Sometimes, negative affective responses (those that move counter to the sympathies of the work) are the result of a marked difference between the reader's values and those of the work.

The second reason for emphasizing the cognitive response is to help guard against the students' accepting everything they read or hear on the basis of emotional appeal. Many teachers place primary emphasis on the emotional

---

* Empiricist and logical positivist traditions in Western philosophy and science attempt to exclude emotion rigorously. Religion involves both cognitive and emotional dimensions, whereas the aesthetic dimension is important only indirectly; however, religion permits an additional avenue to knowledge—special revelation.

response to literature and above all else want their students to have rewarding emotional experiences with the work. To such teachers, the phrase "rewarding emotional experiences" means experiences that are in accord with the teacher's experiences. A study by Walter Loban, however, indicates that some students enjoy reading sadistic stories.[8] That is, they seek out and have "rewarding [for them] emotional experiences" with books emphasizing cruelty. Ordinarily, teachers neither encourage nor approve this sort of "rewarding emotional experience." In encouraging emotional response, even if only to stories and poems that they approve of, teachers frequently neglect intellectual examination of the emotional response. Consequently, students might very well learn to accept everything they read on an emotional basis. But students must learn to examine, evaluate, accept what is good, and reject what is not.

Since teachers trust and approve their own emotional reactions, they see no danger in encouraging the emotional reactions of their students, often to the total neglect of intellectual analysis. They tend to forget that a student may encounter works that cannot be accepted without careful examination and evaluation: propaganda of types ranging from ads to short stories, for instance. The writer of propaganda neither expects nor wants a careful evaluation of his material but hopes to program a set of values into his readers. People living in an electronically oriented culture are bombarded with materials that require evaluation.

Some writers deny the efficacy of rational evaluation. As evidence that "conceptual" awareness is not "useful," one writer quotes a young student, after her class had devised criteria to evaluate newspapers, as saying, ". . . that paper we get at home is rubbish, and we've proved it—but I feel sure I'll go on reading it."[9] The change in behavior that this writer wishes requires an affective response at a very high level (see Chapter 14)—developing a value system. He does not realize, apparently, that affective responses have already taken place in the student. At the lowest level, the student is aware of the problem. Beyond that, the student has already made a value judgment about the paper—which she apparently believes. Although she may, and probably should, go on reading the paper, she will never read it in the same way again. If the instructional goal, as this writer implies, were really for the girl to stop reading the newspaper, and if rational evaluation is ineffective in producing that effect, then the alternative procedure involves tinkering with the child's emotions and values—a procedure closely akin to propagandizing, whether it appears as the "hard sell" or the "soft sell."

AFFECTIVE RESPONSE

Although the cognitive response has importance as a base for affective response and as a means of evaluating the affective, the affective itself should not be ignored by the English teacher. On the contrary, talk in the classroom must encourage students to tell how they "feel" about characters, events, images, and so on. But talk cannot remain for long at that level, for as soon as it becomes an explanation of *why* students feel as they do, it becomes cognitive. The two types of responses are so closely related, leading one to the other and back again, that they cannot be treated exclusively. Any teacher who tries to do so distorts literature, making it something other than it is.

Further, ignoring one or the other types of response to particular literary works frequently results in a negative reaction to reading literature. If, at the one extreme, a teacher focuses on analysis of literary devices and forms, students are likely to find literary study dull and meaningless, to regard it as they do grammar. If, at the other extreme, the teacher encourages only statements of affective responses, the students are likely to regard literature as superficial. They are quick to see that if the teacher's concern is only with what they feel, there is no real need for discussion ("Isn't everyone entitled to his own opinion?") or reading ("What difference does it make?"). If literature study is to be meaningful, a good part of the discussion in class must turn on the meaning of a work as it relates to the experience of the students.

For instance, a discussion of Browning's "My Last Duchess" might begin with a question about the ways in which some people dominate others, ignoring their personal aspirations, interests, and feelings. Then, what happens to people who are dominated in that way? What are the possible reactions? The class might then proceed to read the poem and discuss such questions as the following:

1. What kind of person was the Duchess?
2. How did the Duke treat her?
3. Did she deserve that treatment? Why?
4. What kind of person is the Duke?
5. What are the things he really cares about?

Each of these questions involves considerable talk by the students.* There are many lines to reread and speculate over, actions and attitudes of both Duke and Duchess to evaluate. This sort of talk provides a base for a discussion of the technique of the monologue, the irony, the frame imposed by the first line and the final three, or various other formal aspects of the poem, if the students are ready to move in one of these directions. But there is no necessity for exhaustive analysis of the poem. With some students the teacher should not use the poem at all; with others the first set of questions will suffice; still others can move from the formal problems to aesthetic evaluations (for example, are the last three lines of the poem necessary or useful? Why?).

---

* Although the questions appear to be relatively simple, their answers will be obscure to many students because of the irony of the poem. Many will take the Duke's critical statements at face value, for example, "She had/A heart—how shall I say?—too soon made glad,/Too easily impressed . . ." Thus, the teacher should probably not introduce the poem unless he is reasonably sure that his students are capable of responding to, though not necessarily identifying, the irony.

But whatever the group of students, the teacher must encourage examination (or validation) of the insights offered by the work in terms of the students' experience.*

AESTHETIC RESPONSE

The aesthetic response derives from what appears to be a combination of both the cognitive and emotional aspects of literary experience. That is, we seem to appreciate what a writer has done with language as we respond to his work with understanding and feeling. An aesthetic response demands a certain distance. The reader must stand back to view the work as a whole. If his energies are wholly absorbed in attempting to understand what a work states and implies, or if he is totally involved with a work emotionally, he is too close to it to understand, let alone evaluate, how an author achieves his effects.

Thus, prerequisite to a reader's aesthetic response is a degree of sophistication on his part in relation to the work. Although many young readers can respond aesthetically to Steinbeck's *The Pearl* or Richter's *Light in the Forest* or Anne Frank's *Diary of a Young Girl,* only a few would be likely to respond similarly to Thackeray's *Vanity Fair.* When a reader understands the content of a work and reacts emotionally to the imagery, events, or characters, he can examine the effects the author is attempting to achieve, how he selects and organizes the parts of his work to achieve them, and how effective this arrangement has been in controlling his own response. This process is evaluative, but the evaluation is personal rather than absolute.

There was a time when aesthetics was dominated by the search for universal laws of beauty and harmony. Presumably, if the laws could be established, the judicial response to art would be a relatively simple matter, and art could be judged in absolute terms. Either the work displayed the laws or it didn't. Neoclassic criticism reveals the fallacy in such thinking. The universal laws turn out to be no more than a description of the taste of an age. Hence the neoclassic critics considered Shakespeare's plays to be flawed because they did not observe the unities.

The modern study of aesthetics is concerned with the effects of a work on a viewer, reader, or listener and how those effects are achieved. This concern is evaluative even though there is no attempt to rank works in order of artistic merit. The judicial function is perhaps best reserved for the book reviewers, who are paid to make such distinctions; for as most reviewers would admit, their judgments of art are personal, not absolute, even though their tastes may be catholic and their experiences broad.

Although a wise teacher refrains from forcing his personal tastes and

---

* The discussion of affective response in this chapter has been in terms of response to individual works rather than to reading literature as an activity. Both are important. The latter is treated in Chapters 12 and 14.

evaluations on his students, a still wiser one recognizes that his reaction to a work and his treatment of it in class will inevitably influence his students' responses. The wiser teacher does what he can to insure positive evaluations of truly great literature. He presents it only when the students are sophisticated enough to understand it and respond to it, and he helps them reach that level of sophistication. He does not require them to interpret material that he has not prepared them for. He teaches a work in such a way that the students understand and appreciate the work through their own insights. What goes on in a classroom can have a profound influence on a student's aesthetic response not only to individual works but to literature in general.

The chapters that follow suggest procedures for helping students attain not only full access to literature as a distinct way of knowing in its cognitive, emotional, and aesthetic aspects but a positive attitude toward it as well. The answers to the questions raised in this chapter are intended primarily as a basis for the approach to teaching literature that follows. But they are intended also as a defense of literature against the skeptics.

NOTES

1. René Wellek and Austin Warren, *Theory of Literature* (New York: Harcourt, Brace & Company, 1956), p. 11.
2. Northrop Frye, *The Anatomy of Criticism* (Princeton: Princeton University Press, 1957), p. 74.
3. Aristotle, *De Poetica* in *The Works of Aristotle Translated into English,* ed. W. D. Ross (Oxford: Clarendon Press, 1924), XI, 1454a.
4. Archibald MacLeish, "Ars Poetica," *A Pocket Book of Modern Verse,* ed. Oscar Williams (New York: Washington Square Press, 1963), pp. 373–374.
5. Susanne K. Langer, *Problems of Art* (New York: Charles Scribner's Sons, 1957), pp. 124–139.
6. ———, *Philosophy in a New Key* (New York: New American Library, 1959), pp. 45 and 47.
7. James Hanley, "The Butterfly," *Seventy Five Short Masterpieces,* ed. Roger Goodman (New York: Bantam Books, 1961), pp. 116–120.
8. Walter Loban, "A Study of Social Sensitivity Among Adolescents," *Journal of Educational Psychology, 44* (February 1953), pp. 102–112.
9. John Dixon, *Growth Through English* (Reading, England: National Association for the Teaching of English, 1967), pp. 73–74.

SUGGESTIONS FOR FURTHER READING

1. CHARLES KAPLAN, ed. *Criticism: Twenty Major Statements,* San Francisco: Chandler Publishing Company (n.d.). Includes Plato, Aristotle, Horace, Sidney, Dryden, Poe, T. S. Eliot, etc.
2. SUSANNE K. LANGER, *Mind: An Essay on Human Feeling.* Baltimore: Johns Hopkins University Press, 1967. A discussion of art as a symbolic projection of feeling.

The Reading Situation | 9

An important question for a teacher of literature to ask is this: What is involved in understanding a literary work? Unfortunately, there is no way to answer this question empirically. The best we can do is to observe two kinds of phenomena that are related to the process of reading but essentially outside it.

First, we can observe the elements in a reading situation and their relationships. Second, we can examine stated responses to literary works. The results of these observations together with our impressions of our own reading experiences give us some understanding of the process.

In exploring the reading process, we must examine these elements: the general environment, the specific reading situation, the reader, and the text. Finally as teachers of literature we should determine the extent to which we can or should make use of or influence each of these elements. They are shown in Figure 9.1.

The General Environment

Any reading situation will be influenced by various aspects of the general environment which prompt reading and condition responses. For instance, the cultural and social values of a reader may prevent his establishing empathy with a literary character whose values are different from his. Readers with certain sets of values will reject some literature completely. Note the negative responses of some individuals in some communities when their young people are assigned *1984* or *The Catcher in the Rye*. Topical interests and publicity for movies and books will prompt reading. Some environments, on the other hand, will completely discourage it. In short, the individual's cumulative experience with selected aspects of his environment will condition his attitude toward reading as an activity as well as his attitude toward specific reading experiences.

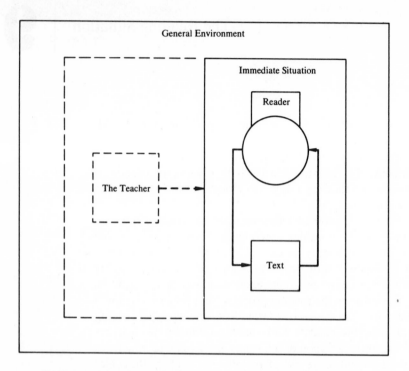

FIGURE 9.1   General Elements of the Reading Situation, 1

The Specific Reading Situation

Any act of reading takes place under some set of specific circumstances. Sequences of such situations comprise the reader's background, his literary experience. The reading may be prompted by internal stimuli. For example, a person may read because he simply wants to escape reality for a while with a detective story, he may have a problem that he wishes to solve, or he may wish to enjoy the full intellectual, emotional, and aesthetic experience that some readers seek in great literature. If he reads for escape, he may either choose something that is easy for him to read or choose something difficult but ignore the dimensions of the work that make it difficult for him. Proficient readers, of course, find a kind of escape in the full reading of a work; as they read, they solve the literary problems that the work presents, and the work becomes more than a means of escape.

Unfortunately, in educational settings the stimulus to read is likely to be consistently external to the student. A teacher *assigns* the work for reasons that frequently appear arbitrary to the student and then uses a grade to force him to complete his work and report or be tested on it. It is not a situation conducive to positive attitudes.

The Reader

The reader's first approach to any text is primarily physiological and intellectual. He must perceive the symbols on the page, translate them into the sounds for which they stand, and then supply the semantic content of the symbols. Problems for the reader can appear at any point in this process. He may not be able to see the printed symbols adequately. As a matter of fact, undetected vision problems are responsible for the failure of many students to learn to read. Even if he can see the letters, he may not be able to discriminate among them, to tell *m* from *n* or *p* from *q,* for example. If the student is able to perceive the symbols, he may not be able to translate them into sounds, and if he can translate them into sounds, he may not know their meanings. How many readers of this book know the denotations of such words as "anacrusis," "amphibrach," or "picaroon"?

Although a reader's first approach to a text may be simply physiological, it is more likely to be complicated by his past literary and nonliterary experience. For instance, if reading has been a distasteful experience in the past, the reader is likely to approach any new work with some misgivings. On the other hand, if he has read several seventeenth-century poems, he is likely to approach a poem by John Donne with certain expectations about the imagery and may expect to find it intriguing.

Aside from any negative or positive attitude toward reading as an activity, the reader's initial responses contribute to more complex cognitive responses and to affective and aesthetic responses. But the cognitive responses at all levels remain basic to the emotional and aesthetic responses. Beyond the initial intellectual translation of printed symbols to meaning, it is impossible to determine any absolute order of response. The various responses contribute to one another in so subtle and complex a fashion for the proficient reader, that they must ultimately be viewed as concomitant. Still, it is possible to discuss the meanings of a text as they have been interpreted by a reader, and it is possible to describe the emotional and aesthetic experiences that derive from reading. It is also possible to determine to some degree what cognitive responses must precede others if a student is to have a full understanding of a text. Thus, he must discriminate letters before he can translate them to sounds; he must supply literal meanings of words before he can deal with implications of incidents; he must understand the implications of words, details and imagery before he can understand literary symbols. By understanding a student's responses in these areas, it becomes possible to determine some of the reasons why students fail to interpret a text appropriately.

In the late 1920s I. A. Richards confronted the problem of inappropriate cognitive, affective, and aesthetic responses to poetry. Even though his subjects were of "advanced educational standing," he found that they misread poetry rather consistently and that their emotional and aesthetic responses to the poems were governed by those misreadings. Richards notes four types of meaning in a poem (for that matter, they exist in any literary work, perhaps in any piece of writing, to some extent): (1) *sense,* by which he means the "plain sense" of what is said; (2) *feeling,* the "personal colouring of feeling" of the writer toward his subject; (3) *tone,* the attitude of the writer toward his audience; (4) *intention,* the aim, conscious or unconscious, that the writer is attempting to promote.[1] All these aspects of meaning are interdependent, and a misunderstanding of any one can result in serious distortion of the others.

In addition to faulty apprehension of any one of these aspects of meaning, a reader's comprehension can be blocked by what Richards calls irrelevant associations and stock responses. A reader may encounter a poetic image that has a very personal, subjective connotation for him. If he allows his personal response to the image to interfere with the *sense, feeling, tone,* or *intention,* the poem is lost upon him. He converts it to something that it is not. Obviously, since every reader approaches a text from the context of his own experience, a personal response to a poetic image is natural, but the more sophisticated reader winnows out the chaff of his response and retains the kernel that is relevant to the context of the work. Nor is the work any less a personal experience as a result of the winnowing process. The reader's response is still conditioned by his own experience, or should be, and not by the responses of others. And yet, the more literary experience a reader has, the more likely it is that his interpretation will have large areas of agreement with the responses of other experienced readers.

The stock response is another block to comprehension. If a reader fastens on certain elements of a work as relating to particular stock situations or stereotypes, his understanding of the work is likely to be cut off before it reaches culmination. He is likely to ignore other elements of the work that deny the validity of his stock response. For instance, in a recent study of adolescents' responses while reading short stories, James R. Squire found that students tended to blame a mother for the criminal tendencies of her son. They were responding to the cliché in pop culture which says that juvenile delinquency is caused by parental delinquency. This premature judgment about the story led the students to ignore completely the author's sympathy for the mother and condemnation of the son.[2] Both the irrelevant association and the stock response represent failures to respond adequately to the text, as well as an unwarranted response to a kind of static from the outside. The sophisticated reader ignores the static so that the sound and sense of the work come through to him.

No one can deny that even the most sophisticated critics may disagree as to the *sense, feeling, tone,* and *intention* of a work. But there are large areas of agreement. Some literary works are so complex that critics continually discover new aspects of meaning and structure in them, but, ordinarily, they agree as to the primary or basic meanings. When divergent interpretations arise, they are usually the result either of variant manipulations and emphases of textual evidence on the basis of internally or externally established assumptions or of special philosophical or aesthetic evaluations of one or more aspects of the text. For instance, John Dover Wilson's particular interpretation of *Hamlet* in *What Happens in Hamlet?*[3] comes as a result of a careful exegesis of the text, supported by external historical data. Ernest Jones' Freudian treatment of *Hamlet* brings assumptions from an external discipline to bear on the evidence of the text. Jones' diagnosis of Hamlet is based on his isolation of the symptoms that his work in Freudian psychology preconditions him to seek.[4] T. S. Eliot's reading of the play results from two primarily evaluative ideas: first, the assumption that the *objective correlative* is necessary to effective drama; second, the judgment that there is no objective correlative to warrant Hamlet's behavior. His aesthetic decision that the play is defective is based on external criteria that may or may not be relevant.[5]

Variant responses are inescapable. The responsibility of the English teacher is not to insure similar responses but rather to teach so that his students respond to the structured data of a text in all its aspects of meaning: intellectual, emotional, and aesthetic. If a student is to read successfully, he must see and feel the result of the author's strategies and accept and follow the rules of the language game that the author is playing—at least until he has comprehended the *full meaning* of the work. Then he may reject it all. But as he enters the work and progresses through it, he should be able to say, "Yes, I recognize this. I see what is going on here."

In other words, although nonliterary experience is important to reading, literary experience is at least as important. A long, eventful life does not necessarily produce a sensitive reader. It is impossible, after all, for us to experience all that life has to offer. And in a sense literature makes it unnecessary to do so, for we can have a fairly complete understanding of various experiences through literature. We need not have had the specific experiences to understand them when they appear in literature. Not many of us have killed our fathers and married our mothers, but we can understand Oedipus and emphathize with him in his plight. Our empathy is based partly on our culturally ingrained horror of patricide and incest and partly on the fact that we have all, at one time or another, felt completely trapped by our own irreversible actions and their inescapable results. Even relatively young students have had such experiences.

But if our literary experience is limited and we do not know the story of Oedipus, or understand the function of the chorus, if we misconstrue the personality of Oedipus or fail to grasp the implications of his lines that reveal his fear and courage in discovering his identity, in short, if we fail to grasp the tremendous irony expressed in the language and structure of the play, the full force of a great tragedy is lost upon us. The fault is not in our lack of life experience, but in the barrenness of our literary experience.

The Text

In order for the teacher to determine the sorts of literary experience that will engage his students, he must know how a text reveals meaning to a reader. He must also ask in what order the understanding of some meanings precedes the understanding of others. Readers' responses to literary works, together with what we know of our own experience, provide insight into the problem. The student responses to the following short story by Stephen Crane illustrate, at least in part, the levels of comprehension involved in understanding literature.

AN OMINOUS BABY by Stephen Crane

A baby was wandering in a strange country. He was a tattered child with a frowsled wealth of yellow hair. His dress, of a checked stuff, was soiled and showed the marks of many conflicts like the chain shirt of a warrior. His sun-tanned knees shone above wrinkled stockings which he pulled up occasionally with an impatient movement when they entangled his feet. From a gaping shoe there appeared an array of tiny toes.

He was toddling along an avenue between rows of stolid, brown houses. He went slowly, with a look of absorbed interest on his small, flushed face. His blue eyes stared curiously. Carriages went with a musical rumble over the smooth asphalt. A man with a chrysanthemum was going up steps. Two nursery-maids chatted as they walked slowly, while their charges hob-nobbed amiably between perambulators. A truck wagon roared thunder-ously in the distance.

The child from the poor district made way along the brown street filled with dull gray shadows. High up, near the roofs, glancing sun-rays changed cornices to blazing gold and silvered the fronts of windows. The wandering baby stopped and stared at the two children laughing and play-ing in their carriages among the heaps of rugs and cushions. He braced his legs apart in an attitude of earnest attention. His lower jaw fell and disclosed his small, even teeth. As they moved on, he followed the car-riages with awe in his face as if contemplating a pageant. Once one of the babies, with twittering laughter, shook a gorgeous rattle at him. He smiled jovially in return.

Finally a nursery-maid ceased conversation and, turning, made a ges-ture of annoyance. "Go 'way, little boy," she said to him. "Go 'way. You're all dirty."

He gazed at her with infant tranquillity for a moment and then went

Reprinted from *The Arena,* B. O. Flower, ed., 9 (1893), 819–21.

slowly off, dragging behind him a bit of rope he had acquired in another street. He continued to investigate the new scenes. The people and houses struck him with interest as would flowers and trees. Passengers had to avoid the small, absorbed figure in the middle of the sidewalk. They glanced at the intent baby face covered with scratches and dust as with scars and with powder smoke.

After a time, the wanderer discovered upon the pavement, a pretty child in fine clothes playing with a toy. It was a tiny fire engine painted brilliantly in crimson and gold. The wheels rattled as its small owner dragged it uproariously about by means of a string. The babe with his bit of rope trailing behind him paused and regarded the child and the toy. For a long while he remained motionless, save for his eyes, which followed all movements of the glittering thing. The owner paid no attention to the spectator but continued his joyous imitations of phases of the career of a fire engine. His gleeful baby laugh rang against the calm fronts of the houses. After a little, the wandering baby began quietly to sidle nearer. His bit of rope, now forgotten, dropped at his feet. He removed his eyes from the toy and glanced expectantly at the other child.

"Say," he breathed, softly.

The owner of the toy was running down the walk at top speed. His tongue was clanging like a bell and his legs were galloping. An iron post on the corner was all ablaze. He did not look around at the coaxing call from the small, tattered figure on the curb.

The wandering baby approached still nearer and, presently, spoke again. "Say," he murmured, "le' me play wif it?"

The other child interrupted some shrill tootings. He bended his head and spoke disdainfully over his shoulder.

"No," he said.

The wanderer retreated to the curb. He failed to notice the bit of rope, once treasured. His eyes followed as before the winding course of the engine, and his tender mouth twitched.

"Say," he ventured at last, "is dat yours?"

"Yes," said the other, tilting his round chin. He drew his property suddenly behind him as if it were menaced. "Yes," he repeated, "it's mine."

"Well, le' me play wif it?" said the wandering baby, with a trembling note of desire in his voice.

"No," cried the pretty child with determined lips. "It's mine! My ma-ma buyed it."

"Well, tan't I play wif it?" His voice was a sob. He stretched forth little, covetous hands.

"No," the pretty child continued to repeat. "No, it's mine."

"Well, I want to play wif it," wailed the other. A sudden, fierce frown mantled his baby face. He clenched his thin hands and advanced with a formidable gesture. He looked some wee battler in a war.

"It's mine! It's mine," cried the pretty child, his voice in the treble of outraged rights.

"I want it," roared the wanderer.

"It's mine! It's mine!"

"I want it."

"It's mine!"

The pretty child retreated to the fence, and there paused at bay. He protected his property with outstretched arms. The small vandal made a charge. There was a short scuffle at the fence. Each grasped the string to the toy and tugged. Their faces were wrinkled with baby rage, the verge tears. Finally, the child in tatters gave a supreme tug and wrenched the string from the other's hands. He set off rapidly down the street, bearing the toy in his arms. He was weeping with the air of a wronged one who has at last succeeded in achieving his rights. The other baby was squalling lustily. He seemed quite helpless. He wrung his chubby hands and railed.

After the small barbarian had got some distance away, he paused and regarded his booty. His little form curved with pride. A soft, gleeful smile loomed through the storm of tears. With great care, he prepared the toy for travelling. He stopped a moment on a corner and gazed at the pretty child whose small figure was quivering with sobs. As the latter began to show signs of beginning pursuit, the little vandal turned and vanished down a dark side street as into a swallowing cavern.

The following responses to "An Ominous Baby" are selected from a large number of responses collected from eighth graders and high school seniors in suburban schools and from college sophomores. Significantly, the range of eighth-grade responses was very similar to the range of responses from high school and college students. All students who responded had fifty minutes to read the story and write an essay "explaining the meaning of the story." The students had never seen the story before or at least did not remember it. The student essays are printed without corrections.

Response 1.1   (Twelfth-Grader)

The story begin when a young child is walk down the street the child is dirty and pull a peice of string he find.

As he walk he saw baby carriage with little children in them.

One of the children started to laughter and want to play with him but his nursery maid chase him away. Later he found a another child play with his fire engine and pull it down the street. The baby went after he until he caught up with him.

When baby met him he ask if he can play but the another child said no with out even looking then the child look up and see him and the rope. Then baby ask again if he can with it the other boy said yes and started to hand him the toy and started for the rope the baby have.

The baby saw what he wanted and hold on the rope tighter until there was a fight for it.

Then the baby got the toy and run down the street but later find he miss a booty and wrong he did he went back for the booty and started to play with the toy.

The little boy then came running after him with a little fighting power to get it back.

When the baby saw this he run leaving the toy behind.

Response 1.2   (Eighth-Grader)

In the story "An Ominous Baby" the two main characters are children. One is dirty with scratches and ragged clothes. The other is pretty, dressed in fine clothes and playing peacefully with a toy.

The ragged child is turned down by everyone. He has only a piece of old rope as a toy or something to play with. The other child has a tiny fire engine painted brilliantly in crimson and gold.

When the ragged child sees this he forgets his little piece of rope and runs as quickly as he can to ask the pretty child if he might *just* pull the fire engine for a while. When he gets there the pretty child says no, and both children get in a scuffle. They tugged and tattered trying to gain control of the string from which the fire engine was pulled by. Finally the ragged child got the string and ran away with the toy.

At the end both children were crying, The ragged child was weeping because he had seen that he had done wrong in getting what he wanted. The pretty child was squalling because he seemed helpless now that the ragged child has his toy.

As a whole, this story tells about people in different classes and how they react to certain situations.

Both writers are primarily concerned with the literal level of the story, that is, with the events that took place. The twelfth grader clearly has a writing problem, the omission of word endings, which is *not* due to her natural dialect. However, while this student can comprehend the literal meaning reasonably well, the essay displays a few serious misreadings. The student apparently confuses "booty," which means loot in the context of the story, with baby booty. She has also apparently confused the string on the toy with the bit of rope which the tattered child carried. The eighth grader's writing is more sophisticated than that of the high school senior, but his comprehension of the story is at about the same level. His response displays some misreadings, but they are not so serious as those of the high school senior. The eighth grader does not attempt an interpretation of the story as a whole until the final line, and as an interpretation that line is rather vague. With all their shortcomings, these two responses represent an important level of comprehension, for without an understanding of the literal level of a work, the inferences drawn are likely to be irrelevant and erroneous.

Response 2.1 (Eighth-Grader)

"An Ominous Baby" is an illustrious account of why a child might turn delinquent. If a small child from the lower class is walking in the upper class district it is pretty obvious that he will be shunned. To be allowed to be there is a sign that his parents don't really care too much about him.

When a child is deprived of the things he wants such as the fire engine, he might steal to get that thing.

The child begins to feel hurt and unwanted when the nursery maid tells him, "Go 'way. You're all dirty." He carried the rope with him to try to gain security. When he saw the upper class child playing with the fire engine the child from the "other side of the tracks" began to feel inferior and to want that fire engine. He wanted the fire engine enough so that he dropped his "security" rope and begged· the other child to let him play with the toy. When he is told firmly many times, "It's mine!" by the other child the wanderer decides to advance and take the toy away. The boys had a short fight and each was so mad he was ready to cry. When the lower class boy finally got the fire engine and started to run away he was "weeping with the air of a wronged one who has at last succeeded in achieving his rights." The wanderer was proud of himself for stealing the toy and when the other boy began to chase him the wanderer ran down a dark street and disappeared.

The dirty child wanted the fire engine enough to steal it and with this accomplished he was proud of himself. This will probably begin his life as a delinquent because now he thinks it is all right to steal.

The eighth grader who wrote response 2.1 is concerned with theme: "why a child might turn delinquent." However, the statement of this theme is derived as much from stock response as it is from analysis of motives: "When a child is deprived of the things he wants . . . he might steal to get that thing. . . . This will probably begin his life as a delinquent because he now thinks it is all right to steal." Many respondents at both the eighth-grade and college levels interpreted the story as a portrayal of incipient delinquency. Apparently, they were reacting to certain details of the story that identify what they regard as the archetypal causes of delinquency: no parents mentioned, economic deprivation, rejection by others, and so on. The writer of 2.1 has gone beyond the literal level of the story to a concern with why the child took the fire engine, and he attempts to support his interpretation by reference to the text. However, the stock response—the quick identification of the delinquency pattern—has cut off his thinking at that level with the result that he interprets details in terms of his first reaction. For instance, he infers that the child "begins to feel hurt and unwanted" at the rebuff of the nursemaid. Although 2.1 quotes one of the most significant lines of the story (". . . weeping with the air of a wronged one who had at last succeeded in achieving his rights."), he does nothing with it. Even though he refers to the tattered child as "the lower class boy," he does not see the broader social implications of the story.

Response 2.2 (College Sophomore)

The baby represents a person or possibly even a country that is rugged and yet gives the outward appearance of being wronged. He will search around innocently looking for someone he can overpower. Those that he can not overpower, after observing them to be sure, he will quietly and innocently leave be.

This is shown in this story by the baby's wandering. And while he wandered he observed things carefully, the carriages, man going up a step, a truck wagon roaring in the distance. He observed things until he came upon something that interested him, two children in their carriages. He could not take advantage of these two weaklings because they were protected by their nursery maid much like weak people are that can afford to or can gain the favor of the strong. After being closed off he quietly continued his innocent search until he came upon a weakling that was unprotected. Following his usual path he tried peacefully to overcome the toy owner but when this failed he resorted to force tactics. After having succeeded he showed no emotion. He ran to be sure he would get away, looked back and then continued on into a dark place to remain unseen for awhile.

This baby or person has to better himself at the expense of others. He carried his greatest prize, a rope, with him until he found something better and then he forgot about the rope. He did nothing to earn the rope and he did nothing legal to earn the toy.

Response 2.2, by a college sophomore, attempts to deal with theme and the motivation of the crime. The reader sees the motivation as somehow inherent in the personality of the tattered child, who "represents a person or even a country that is rugged and yet gives the outward appearance of being wronged. He will search around innocently looking for someone he can overpower." The remainder of the interpretation, which is concerned with the implications of various incidents in the story, is predicated on this basic assumption. How did such an erroneous assumption come about? Simply by ignoring what Richards called *feeling,* the attitude of the writer toward his subject. Writer 2.2 completely ignores all the words and images that convey the author's sympathy for the tattered child: "frowsled wealth of yellow hair," "suntanned knees," "tiny toes," "toddling," "smiled jovially in return," and so on. These are not words that describe an object of contempt. The reader has not realized the effect of the individual words. Such a reader needs training in observing the connotations of individual words and images and their effect on the work as a whole. He needs to observe how apparently slight changes in the choice of words can change entirely the emotional impact of the passage. Change "frowsled wealth of yellow hair" to "twisted mass" of yellow hair, "suntanned knees" to "grimy knees," "tiny toes" to "dirty toes," and sympathy toward the child diminishes considerably.

This reader's response is a vivid example of how cognitive understandings influence the affective response. Of course, it is his prerogative to reject the social implications of the story; but as a reader, his first obligation is to interpret the story adequately.

Response 3   (Twelfth-Grader)

The poor child in this story has been mistreated, so he thinks a child of fate and misfortune. This child seems to be lost in a world he can't even begin to understand or cope with. He wanders around the streets and looks for excitement. He seems to have no one to care for or look after him. He seems to think that the whole world is against him and nobody cares. He is looked down upon by older people. He is shabby and dirty and no one wants him around. Not even children of his own will have anything to do with him. Perhaps under his dirty clothes and scratched soiled face there is a clean neat little boy who can look just the same as any other little boy. Act like any other little boy. But no one has given him a chance to compete with the others. He has no friends and not even adults will try to help him. At his tender age he cannot even begin to understand why he has been treated as an outcast. He can see no difference between himself and the little boy who is clean and has nice clothes and most of all a shinney fire engine. He can't understand why he shouldn't be able to play with the fire engine. At first the other little boy just ignored him. The little boy made it a point to make himself known, but this did no good. The pretty child flatly refused him and made it clear to the poor dirty little boy that it belonged to him and he was the only one who would use it. The poor boy made it a point to start an arguement once the pretty child protected his property against anything who might bring harm to it. At this point in the story both children were very upset and just about on the verge of tears. All at once the poor little boy grabed the truck from the other child's steady grip and began to run. At last he had achieved what he believed to be his rights. He had at last got what he thought should be his. The hurt which he had held inward for so long was finally released. All the feeling of this small confused child seemed to rush out all at one time. A feeling of achieventt (*sic*) swept over him. He had rebelled against being discriminated against. He was in a sense like a "Negro" who had fought and gave of himself to attain a goal. The boy had at the moment he grabbed the truck taken all he could from the cold cruel world. He was going to show the owner of the truck as well as the world that he had taken enough, and that he was now a different person. No more feeling sorry for himself and no more of being an underdog. He was just as good as any boy. He wase equal to the little boy with the clean face and pretty clothes. This was the turning point in this boys life. He could now grow into a man, a man equal to any other man regurdless of his wealth. He knew what it was to be poor and to never have anyone to care for him. Perhaps he would do his best to make sure that he always cared for any children that he might have and to make sure that all his children were taught not to judge a person by the clothes he wears nor by the amount of money he has. I think that this little boy learned the hard way. A lesson he will never forget.

The writer of response 3, in contrast to the writer of 2.2, is very sympathetic toward the tattered child. In fact, while she clearly understands the literal elements of the story, her interpretation is directed at explaining the tattered baby's feelings about his environment and his motives in stealing the toy. Some of her inferences are unjustified or irrelevant, for instance, the comments explaining how the tattered child will care for his own children. She makes some tentative movements toward explaining the story's theme, but does not, as she fails to deal with the symbolic significance of the two children. Still, this is the most sophisticated response so far and its inferences about feelings and motives represent an important level of comprehension.

Response 4.1   (Eighth-Grader)

The baby represents anyone with no meaning, someone always on the loser's end. Society won't give him a chance to get what he wants and so he becomes a menace to that society.

The baby is wonderous at the new things it sees. The comfort and luxuries present, that were never introduced to him. When a nurse tells him to "Go 'way, little boy. Go 'way. You're all dirty," it was being told they wouldn't let him have the "good" things in life.

Finally he meets with someone who has just what he wants. But he can't get it by persuasion. So he uses force, symbolically against Society, and takes what he wants.

Overall, I think, this means that the baby was rejected by Society personally when the nurse adminished him to "Go 'way . . ." Then he rebelled against the boundaries of Society and threatened it with his violence. Forcefully takes his 'reinbursement' from Society, in the form of a little fire truck, and tactfully, disappears.

Symbolically this is the rejection of and rebellion against Society of any socially ostrasized peoples, lower classes, Negroes, sometimes Jews, etc.

The writer of response 4.1 has approached the story with considerable sophistication. Not only does he understand the literal level and infer the implications of key incidents and imagery but he comprehends the basic symbolism of the story. Clearly, there are other elements of the story that are worthy of comment and undoubtedly influenced the response. But in its handling of the major symbolism of the story, this response is more sophisticated than many of those from high school and college students.

The main concern here, however, is the aspects of a text to which a reader at any level must respond to come to a full understanding of literary work. First, he must comprehend the work at its literal level. If he does not, any inferences he draws from the work may be inappropriate. Second, he must recognize the implications of the language, imagery, details, and incidents of the work. Third, he must make appropriate inferences about the rhetoric and structure of the work. Fourth, when necessary, he must view the work against various contexts. His affective responses come as the result of his understanding of any or all of these levels. Finally, when he has arrived at an adequate understanding, the reader evaluates the work as a whole. The accomplished reader approaches all these levels of significance more or less concomitantly. But even he must come to terms with the literal level of a work before making inferences, and he must attempt to suspend his judgments of the work until he has sifted the evidence. His reading raises questions at each level of significance about the total meaning of the work. He moves with comparative ease from one level to another and back again to answer those questions.

Response 4.2   (Twelfth-Grader)

"An Ominous Baby" by Stephen Crane is an ingenious attempt by the author to express in the guise of infants what is perhaps a basic part of human nature. It concerns itself with the human impulse to gain at all costs what one has been denied, with that thing being at the same time what one most desperately needs.

In the wandering baby is perhaps represented the "vagabond" (if one wishes to call him that) who has been deprived of what may be termed "essentials." In the case of the child, it is pretty clothes, cleanliness, a toy. But in deeper perspective, the child is those of this earth who are deprived not so much of food, or clothing, but of their very humanity— the security of a toy or happiness—the security of being a person in the sense of not being hooplessly turned away—by people, by others of his own kind. (This happens a no. of times—ie. the nursemaid, the other child).

And, when the child strikes out at the other child, the story may have an overtone of war. (ie: "He clenched his fat hands and advanced with a formidable gesture. He looked like some wee battler in a war).

In this, however, is represented the human tendency to strike out, reach for, grasp for, that which one needs, which one must have in order to be —whether it be a toy as in the case of the story, or security, or love or whatever it may be. The story says: One does not resign oneself to hopelessness; one fights it.

And there is an indication that the author does not feel this is completely understood, that we treat it obliviously, without regard or attempt to understand it (ie. we know that it happens but don't really care why): "the little vandal turned and vanished down a *dark side street as into a cavern*" [italics added].

This dark cavern is the realm of human misunderstanding of the fact that men must be men (ie. in the philosophical conception of the word) and if not allowed to be so, they will not resign themselves to that fate. And this is a basic insight into war or conflict: that we must have what we must have, whether it be a toy or a land to call our own, or our dignity as men and that we will do anything to attain it.

Response 4.2 is somewhat more sophisticated than 4.1, dealing with the symbolism and the theme but reaching beyond social conflict to suggest why Crane chose babies as characters to represent what is essential to man's nature. Perhaps the chief difference between this response and 4.1 is in the more explicit, better organized treatment which the high school senior gives her interpretation of the story's theme.

It is significant that, while very few students in several hundred wrote responses of this caliber, the difference, in terms of literary understanding, between one of the strongest eighth-grade responses and one of the strongest twelfth-grade responses is not very great. At the very least it reveals that the traditional methods of determining course content by grade level is foolish. The teacher may have eighth graders who read and write more effectively than most seniors, or he may have twelfth graders who read and write at the level of eighth graders or below. The teacher must examine the abilities of the students in his own classes.

For the immature reader, however, the various levels are more nearly hierarchical. A few students cannot understand the literal level of the simplest story. Some cannot draw even simple inferences about character and incidents. Clearly, they must learn to solve these problems before proceeding to the more complex aspects of literary interpretation. At the same time, each level has its own range of difficulty. For instance, evaluation of simple works, such as fables, may be a less demanding task than understanding the literal level of a work like *Paradise Lost*.

The Teacher

Although the teacher is present only in specific reading situations in educational settings, his presence should be of vital importance. At least, he has a great deal of power in influencing the students. The danger of direct attempts to influence student attitudes toward particular works was examined closely in Chapter 7. Declaiming to students about the virtues of a particular work or reading as an activity is likely to do far more damage than good. Nor can the teacher transfer his own ability to read directly to his students.

What can the teacher do then? First, he can make use of various aspects of the general environment. Second, he can create a series of specific reading situations through which his students can become more and more sophisticated as readers.

THE TEACHER AND THE GENERAL ENVIRONMENT

Although the teacher cannot (and would not want to) control the total environment, he can take its influences on his students into consideration when he teaches. If he finds, for example, that his students have strong negative values toward reading as an activity, he should find unit ideas and materials that relate directly to strong positive interests and values. If he finds that his students reject characters whose value systems are different from theirs, he may wish to develop a unit through which the students learn why different groups have different values.

Beyond that, the teacher can make use of specific elements of the total environment in his teaching. He might select news stories, cartoons, movies, or television programs to prepare students for reading a particular text. The strength of this technique is obvious; it not only prepares the student for reading but also helps make the relevancy of the text apparent. The student can see the connection between literature and other aspects of his environment. Methods and materials for capitalizing on the general environment of the students are enumerated in Chapter 14.

THE TEACHER AND THE SPECIFIC READING SITUATION

The teacher's role in developing instructional units and in selecting texts is complex. He must know what reading literature involves; he must learn to what extent his students can cope with a text; and he must design immediate reading situations that are based upon his and his students' knowledge of literature.

His instruction must move students from what they can already do to the easiest tasks they cannot already do. For instance, if they can barely comprehend what is directly stated in relatively simple material, the unit of instruction should present questions that focus on what happened when and to whom. The inference questions relating to the text should be fairly simple. Class discussion, however, relating what is read to student experience has immense value for weak readers and might involve rather complex inferences. Once the students can deal adequately with the literal level, the teacher's units of instruction can begin to focus on making more complex inferences from the text. First, then, the teacher must determine what his students observe and what inferences they can make. Systematic inventories (discussed in Chapter 11) will give him a fairly clear idea of what reading experiences his students need. His next problem is to design a unit of instruction that will help his students become more sophisticated readers.

Obviously, sophistication as a reader does not pertain simply to cognitive understanding of a text. It has a great deal to do with affective responses, which to a large extent are dependent upon intellectual understandings. But while the teacher strives to improve the students' ability to understand a text cognitively, he must be acutely aware of affective responses. There is no point, for instance, in using material that students reject or are neutral toward affectively—even if that material helps to improve cognitive understandings. The teacher must select materials and activities that will excite the students' interest and response. At the same time, the materials and activities must help to improve the cognitive aspects of reading. The task, which is discussed explicitly in Chapter 14, is not particularly easy.

Figure 9.2 summarizes the various aspects of a reading situation. First, the reader's general environment, the cumulative effects of all his experiences both in and out of school, not only gives rise to specific reading interests but may significantly influence his understanding of what he reads. For instance, a great many responses to Crane's "An Ominous Baby" associated the conflict in the story with racial conflicts. Some, apparently ignoring the tattered child's "frowsled wealth of yellow hair," stated that he "represented" the blacks. While it is clear that no element of the story specifically represents racial conflicts, there are some clear analogies between racial conflict and various aspects of the story's meaning. And seeing how literature reflects real life is an important part of literary experience. Thus, a teacher can make effective use of various elements of the environment to increase reading interest and skill with all students, but especially with slow or reluctant readers.

Second, any act of reading takes place in some particular, immediate situation, which may have given rise to the reading. The reader's response to the text in that situation will be influenced by various aspects of the situation itself, such as the reader's purpose, whether it be to learn how to fix an automobile or to understand and enjoy a poem. Other apparently superficial elements, such as lighting, noise level, and physical comfort are also important.

The reader's response to the text will be affected by his physiological functions (his vision and control over eye movements, for instance) and by his literary and nonliterary experience. His cognitive, affective, and aesthetic responses are all closely interdependent and, at the same time, depend upon his past experience, his physiological functions, various influences in the immediate situation, and selected aspects of the general environment.

Dotted lines are used to represent the teacher as an optional element. He may influence the immediate situation in a number of ways, by his general demeanor in the classroom, by the kinds of pre- and post-reading activities he generates, by the types and appropriateness of the instructional units he develops, and so forth. He often has a decisive influence over all texts that

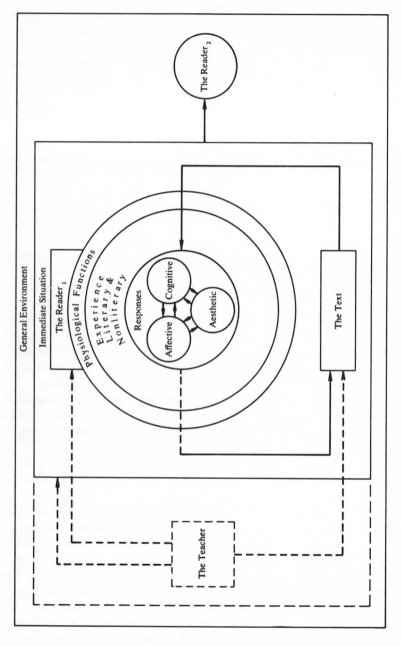

FIGURE 9.2 General Elements of the Reading Situation, 2

a student reads in class; too often that influence is negative because the texts are inappropriate for the students. Finally, he may attempt to influence the reader's attitudes, purposes, and even cognitive understandings directly in authoritarian ways. While such influence may be appropriate for some students, for many more it is only destructive, resulting in negative attitudes toward both particular texts and reading as an activity. The teacher has his most positive influence over the situation in which the reading takes place and over the selection of appropriate materials.

Each reader emerges from every reading experience as an essentially new reader (indicated as Reader$_2$ in Figure 9.2). Often the change is so slight that it is barely noticeable. But when a reader encounters a series of reading situations in which he treats similar reading problems with increasing independence, he gradually gains proficiency in that particular respect. Thus, when a first or second grader encounters a word such as "locomotive" for the first time, he may have to sound it out syllable by syllable. After he has worked through the word several times, however, he will know it at a glance. In a similar way, tenth graders, given appropriate reading experiences and discussions in literary symbolism (see Chapters 4 and 5), become more and more adept at interpreting symbolism. In such a sequence of reading experiences the teacher maintains indirect influence over the situations, rather than direct control over the students themselves.

Figure 9.2 suggests four areas that demand careful exploration before instruction proceeds: (1) the elements of the text to which a reader must respond, (2) the reader's literary experience as reflected in his ability to deal with a text, (3) the construction of individual units that will improve reading, and (4) a sequence of instructional units that will produce readers capable of responding as intelligently and sympathetically to a text as their abilities permit. These areas will be examined in the chapters that follow.

A teacher planning a specific unit of instruction such as "The Outcast," which follows, should be concerned with all the elements of the reading situation. He decides upon the unit topic because of his analysis of his students' literary experience and their concerns with their own environment, and also because he knows it is appropriate to the study of literature. His reading inventories and classroom observations have revealed that although most of his students read reasonably well at the literal level and handle simple inferences fairly well, they have difficulty with implied relationships and the interpretation of character. He has also noticed that tenth graders are concerned about belonging to a group; they are afraid of being ostracized. He realizes that the unit on "The Outcast" will give them considerable experience in dealing with implied relationships and character. At the same time the unit should have strong interest for them because it deals with a topic that concerns adolescents in their total environment. In planning the unit, he finds materials that will be suitable to the various ability levels of his students and that have high interest potential and permit strong affective responses. He plans to help students relate the unit and the literature to their own lives (their environment) by making use of their personal experience, TV shows, films, newspaper and magazine articles, and so on, wherever possible. He organizes the unit so that the students begin with a discussion of a high-interest story in terms of what they already know of ostracism and increases the difficulty of materials and problems gradually, giving sufficient practice to enable the students to handle the unit problems independently. This procedure encourages affective response while developing increasingly complex intellectual (cognitive) understandings. Finally, to determine whether or not the students can actually make the inferences about character and implied relationships that are stressed in the unit, the test will be over material that the students read and interpret independently—full length works selected from a bibliography.

THE OUTCAST*

Teaching the Unit

Great writers have often studied the outcast and the group from which he is ostracized in their works; Shakespeare's Hamlet, Ibsen's Dr. Stockman, O'Neill's Yank are all examples of the outcast. Although every student could not handle the intricate and delicate situations in such works, all students can benefit from an awareness of the outcast, the scapegoat, and the group and its prejudices as used in literature. Treatment of the outcast theme in easier works will lead to the student's eventual understanding of the alienations of a Hamlet and awareness of the social implications in O'Neill's treatment of Yank.

The unit is introduced with an obvious physically grotesque outcast in "Born of Man and Woman" and an obvious ethnic outcast in "The Charivari," so that the student can recognize and begin to develop the concepts of how being different and not being in accord with group standards affects the individual. The unit then moves into the study of short stories that involve various reasons for ostracism—religious, ethnic, racial, social, and physical—some obviously and some subtly.

In this unit, it is particularly essential that some work be done with vocabulary that is related to the unit, as much of it will be unfamiliar to the student; scapegoat, ostracize, prejudice, social, ethnic, religious and racial are all terms that should be analyzed and discussed in terms of student experience with references to actual or fictional incidents.

---

* This unit was first developed by the authors and Mrs. Betty Lou Miller for use in the Euclid (Ohio) Public Schools. It was later printed and distributed for the Project English Demonstration Center at the Euclid Public School and Western Reserve University through the support of the United States Office of Education. It has been revised for inclusion here.

The student can apply "outcasting" to the present-day and real life situations through newspaper reading and writing. The students can bring into class examples from newspapers of present day "outcasting," which are discussed in class. The student is then asked to write an editorial, a feature story, or a news story from some experience that he has had or witnessed involving some form of ostracism. Some techniques of newspaper writing are taught along with this lesson.

For individual analysis, longer short stories whose themes are more fully developed allow the student to explore the detailed ramifications of the unit problems and concepts. "The Snow Goose" is read individually by all students and then discussed in class. For those students able now to work independently, "The Blue Hotel" is assigned. Students who have not fully grasped the concepts might read another long, but simple, short story to clarify concepts. When a majority of the class has become aware of the concepts, they are ready to examine poems, which give fewer clues to meaning than the other forms of literature. The teacher may use a variety of poetry and divide the class into homogeneous groups with the "most clue" poems going to the slowest and the "least clue" poems to the fastest students. The entire class then hears the reports of each group so that the class may share in the interpretation of all poems.

For this particular unit, *To Kill a Mockingbird* is appropriate reading for most functional readers. Students enjoy the book and are able to apply unit concepts to the novel. Every student will not obtain the same level of understanding, but each will come to valid conclusions at his own level. When the students complete the novel, the class is divided into homogeneous groups, and each group chooses a discussion topic upon which the group will write a paper to be presented to the class.

The final step and culminating point of the unit is the student's selection of a novel from a bibliography and his application of all the concepts to his selection. An individual conference with each student helps him to choose a topic relating the concepts learned in the unit to his book. The topic is then developed and used as the basis of the student's essay.

These various steps lead the student to an awareness of the conflict between individual and group standards and the effects of the group upon the individual in life and literature and the effect of the individual on the group. More than this, however, the unit offers both background and practice that will engender understanding in the student's later reading of literature.

TIME REQUIRED

Approximately seven weeks.

TERMINAL OBJECTIVES

To write an analysis of a novel, identifying and explaining the relationships between individual characters and the groups that ostracize them. The analysis must include a discussion of the causes and effects of the ostracism as they relate to the individual and the group. (See objective for Lesson 9.)

To write a newspaper story (feature story, editorial, or news story) whose subject is a real or imaginary experience concerning the ostracism of an individual or a group.

MATERIALS

Teacher Source

Frazer, J. G., *The New Golden Bough,* abridged and edited by T. H. Gaster, New York: Criterion Books (1959).

Poetry:

Field, Edward, "Tulips and Addresses," *The New Yorker,* April 27, 1963.

Hughes, Langston, "Brass Spittoons," in Louis Untermeyer (ed.), *Modern American Poetry,* New York: Harcourt, Brace & World (1950).

Robinson, E. A., "Mr. Flood's Party," *Modern American Poetry.*

Rosenberg, Isaac, "The Jew," in Louis Untermeyer (ed.), *Modern British Poetry,* New York: Harcourt, Brace & World (1950).

Sassoon, Siegfried, "Does It Matter?" *Modern British Poetry.*

Thomas, Dylan, "The Hunchback in the Park," *Modern British Poetry.*

Short Stories:

Crane, Stephen, "The Blue Hotel," in *Twenty Short Stories,* New York: Knopf (1940).

Gail, Zona, "The Charivari," in *Yellow, Gentian, and Blue,* New York: Appleton-Century-Crofts (n.d.).

Gallico, Paul, *The Snow Goose,* New York: Alfred A. Knopf (1941).

Gorky, Maxim, "Her Lover," in Roger B. Goodman (ed.), *75 Short Masterpieces,* New York: Bantam Books (1961).

Harte, Bret, "The Outcasts of Poker Flat," in Matilda Bailey and Ullin W. Leavell (eds.), *Worlds to Explore,* New York: American Book (1956).

Matheson, Richard, "Born of Man and Woman," *75 Short Masterpieces.*

Parker, Dorothy, "Clothe the Naked," in Ernestine Taggard (ed.), *Twenty Grand Short Stories,* New York: Bantam Books (1961).

Peretz, I. L., "The Outcast," in *The Book of Fire,* Joseph Leftwich (tr.), New York: Thomas Yoseloff (n.d.).

Peretz, I. L., "The Seventh Candle," *The Book of Fire.*

Novel:

Lee, Harper, *To Kill a Mockingbird,* New York: Popular Library (1960).

Duplicated Materials:

Study guides for "The Charivari," "The Seventh Candle," "Clothe the Naked," "Her Lover," "The Outcasts of Poker Flat," "The Outcast," "The Snow Goose," "The Blue Hotel," and *To Kill a Mockingbird.* (Only sample guides are included here.)

Bibliography for individual reading.

Selected cartoons from "Peanuts" with Charlie Brown as the "scapegoat." (Not included here.)

1. Reading and discussion of eight short stories, six poems, and two novels.
2. Writing of compositions:
   a. Newspaper story.
   b. Analysis of one short story.
   c. Analysis of one aspect of *To Kill a Mockingbird*.
   d. Analysis of outside reading selection.
3. Preparation of one part of class discussion of a poem.

Lesson 1

OBJECTIVES

To identify some causes of ostracism.

MATERIALS

"Born of Man and Woman"
"Charivari"

PROCEDURES

1. Distribute the story "Born of Man and Woman" and have the students read it in class before any discussion takes place.
2. Check on reading accuracy by finding out through questions such as the following the major details of the story on the literal level:
   a. Who is the speaker?
   b. Where and how does he live?
   c. Is there anything unusual about the speaker?
   d. Who are the "little mothers" and "little fathers"?
3. Develop inferences about the story and the concept of outcast by asking such questions as:
   a. Why did the character call children "little mothers" and "little fathers"?
   b. Why do you think the speaker was forced to live in the cellar?
4. The students will recognize this story as an exaggeration of the way a deformed person might be treated. Lead them to relate the concept to personal knowledge by telling them a story from personal experience in which you have known or heard of an outcast. Ask them to mention situations they've heard about.
   a. Do you know of other situations like this? (Children locked in attics by their parents, children kept under sedation by parents, and so on.)

b. Why do people treat other people in this way? (Fear, shame, ignorance.)

5. Assign "The Charivari" and the study guide questions. To explore the causes of prejudice, discuss the study questions in class.

6. After reading and discussion of the stories, introduce the word "ostracism" and its related forms.

Study Guide "The Chariviari" by Zona Gail

VOCABULARY

hypocritical   mementos   wit   charivari

1. How did the people treat Obald, and how did they think about him before Edward Muir entered his house? How much did they really know about him?
2. Why did Muir go inside Obald's house?
3. Describe the interior.
   a. What things in particular interested Edward?
   b. What was Obald's reaction to Edward's interest?
4. Whom did Edward tell about his visit?
5. After they found out about the chest, what did various people say about Obald? How did they act toward him?
6. Why did they react as they did?
7. What was Obald's reaction to the townspeople? Did this help or hurt his acceptance by the group?
8. What is a charivari? Considering the end of the story, why was it ironic that the boys gave Obald a charivari?
9. What effect does the ending have on the reader?
10. What are the causes of prejudice in this story?
11. How do the same forces cause prejudice in real life situations?

Lesson 2

OBJECTIVES

To identify the reactions of the outcast to his situation.
To identify the causes of ostracism.

MATERIALS

"The Seventh Candle"
"Clothe the Naked"
"Her Lover"
"The Outcasts of Poker Flat"
"The Outcast"

Selected cartoons from "Peanuts"
(Study guides are not included below.)

1. Introduce the concept of the scapegoat by having the class examine selected cartoons from "Peanuts" in which Charlie Brown is the scapegoat for his ball team. The discussion deals with why the others blame Charlie Brown, how he feels, and so forth.
2. Direct the students in the recognition of concepts by assigning each story the day before class discussion and giving the students the study questions to use as a check on understanding. This work is to be done individually.
3. Using the study questions as a basis for discussion, analyze each story with the class, objectifying the concepts that each one exemplifies. At the discretion of the teacher, some stories can be discussed in small groups.
   a. "The Seventh Candle"—ostracizing a member of a group for religious differences
   b. "Clothe the Naked":
      (1) Scapegoating in the aggression of the boys against Raymond.
      (2) Prejudice in the treatment of Lannie by her employers and in the attitude of whites toward Negroes.
      (3) Reactions of the outcasts:
         Big Lannie—acceptance of fate.
         Raymond—bewilderment and fear.
      (4) Ostracism for reasons of physical deformity, for difference in dress, and for reasons of race.
   c. "Her Lover":
      (1) Reaction of outcasts by creation of a fantasy world.
      (2) Change in attitude of group (represented by student after familiarity and understanding is achieved.
      (3) Outcast for reasons of physical appearance and social status.
   d. "The Outcasts of Poker Flat":
      (1) Several individuals as scapegoats for a town.
      (2) Variety of social outcasts: prostitute, gambler, drunkard, and the like.
      (3) Reaction of the outcasts to their situation: fear, aggression, courage, and so on.
   e. "The Outcast":
      (1) A character outcast from more than one group.
      (2) Ostracism of an individual by nature of the individual's inability to function in a role assigned him by the group.

Lesson 3

OBJECTIVES

To define the vocabulary of the unit.
To identify unit concepts in literature and personal experience.

PROCEDURES

1. Give examples of scapegoating from *The New Golden Bough,* "Scape-goats." Then discuss with the class their personal and literary experiences with scapegoating.
   a. How does scapegoating go on today?
   b. What examples of scapegoating were there in the stories we have read?
   c. What is a definition for modern scapegoating? Refer to the theoretical sources to guide the students in formulating their definition.
2. Examine related vocabulary by putting the term "prejudice" on the board. Ask the class to identify its base forms (judge).
   a. What does "pre" mean?
   b. What does "judge" mean?
   c. When you are prejudiced toward something, what have you done?
   d. What might be a good definition for "prejudice"?
3. Brainstorm with the class for reasons *why* people prejudge. Refer them them to the stories they have read. Suggest reasons that the students fail to develop.
4. Introduce the concept of group standards by asking the students to think of incidents in their lives in or outside of school in which someone has been cast out of a group. If student responses are weak, ask about causes.
   a. What can cause a person to be ostracized?
      (1) Standards of dress.
      (2) Standards of physical appearance.
      (3) Standards of home background.
      (4) Standards of speech.
      (5) Standards of ability (academic, sports, mechanical).
   b. Why was the person outcast in the examples suggested? (Violated idea of group standards.)
5. Help the students to think of these causes by listing five qualities that might cause isolation from a group and discuss their distinctions:
   a. physical
   b. social
   c. ethnic
   d. religious
   e. racial

6. Relate these ideas to literature even further by asking the class the following questions about "Born of Man and Woman":
   a. What standards of our society did the speaker fall below?
   b. What evidence is there of "scapegoating" in the story?
   c. What type of outcast was the speaker?
   Continue the discussion with other stories until the class has objectified and synthesized the concepts.

Lesson 4

OBJECTIVES

To write an editorial, news story, or feature story whose subject matter is real or imaginary experience concerning the ostracism of an individual or group.

MATERIALS

Newspaper and/or magazine articles

PROCEDURES

1. Ask the students to obtain newspaper and/or magazine articles in which a person or group is outcast. This assignment should be made *a week in advance* of the lesson. In class, let some students read their articles and lead discussions of them. They should emphasize various reasons for outcasting, such as social differences, ethnic differences, religious differences, racial differences, and physical handicaps. (It is helpful to collect articles ahead of time so as to have one example of each cause.)
2. Divide the class into heterogeneous groups, and have the groups discuss their newspaper articles in the terms of the unit. To show the students that outcast situations apply not only to others but to themselves as well, lead the groups, while circulating among them, from these life situations to individual situations where they have been an outcast or have a friend who was an outcast.
   a. Have you ever known any one who was outcast by his parents?
   b. Outcast from friends or peer group?
   c. Outcast from groups by reason of race, religion, or physical difference?
3. Prepare for the written assignment by distributing an editorial, a feature, and a news story dittoed from the articles the students have brought in.
   a. Read these articles carefully to see how they differ.
   b. What are the differences among the three articles?
   The students may apply many of the concepts learned in other units in this type of analysis. List the students' comments on the board in three columns and conclude the discussion by heading the columns with the appropriate word.

   (1) Feature writing:
      (a) Human interest stories, not necessarily "newsworthy" or "front-page material."
      (b) Appeals to a certain audience, for example, teenager, businessman, housewife.
      (c) First paragraph attention-getting devices: questions, exclamations, quotations.
      (d) Use of clever, highly connotative language.
   (2) News story:
      (a) Who, what, when, where, why usually in first paragraph.
      (b) Use of denotative language.
      (c) Newsworthy material.
   (3) Editorial:
      (a) Article commenting on a subject; opinions.
      (b) Should be backed up with facts and logic as well as opinion.
      (c) Used either to inform the public, influence opinion of others, or entertain.
      (d) Use of slanted language, connotative words.
      (e) May be accompanied by letters to the editor or cartoons.
4. Make the assignment: Write about a personal experience with ostracism similar to those discussed in class. Use the form of a newspaper editorial, feature story, or news story.
5. To further prepare for the writing assignment, have each student write an outline of what he wants to say, and then help him decide which form would be best to present his topic. For slower students the straight news story might be best.

Lesson 5

OBJECTIVES

To analyze both the reasons for outcasting and the reaction of the outcast. To write an analysis about one aspect of the story.

MATERIALS

"The Snow Goose" by Paul Gallico

PROCEDURES

1. Prepare for reading by distributing the study guide and previewing the vocabulary of the story:

hamlet	oblivion	apparition	girl
bulwark	barnacle	plummeted	derelict
inarticulate	unerringly	askance	extant

tendrils	buffeted	pinioned	meandering
ogre	breached	ply	estuaries

2. After the students have read the story individually, divide them into heterogeneous groups and have them discuss the study guide questions in their groups. (Answers to the questions may be written if the teacher feels this is necessary to keep the groups moving. If the discussions seem to be progressing adequately, written answers are unnecessary.)
3. To prepare students for group writing, bring the class together for a discussion to review the concepts of the unit briefly.
4. Group the students homogeneously and suggest topics according to ability, for example:
   a. Low ability—Rhayader, as an outcast from society, builds his life around Fritha and the world of nature.
   b. Middle ability—The parallel characterizations of Rhayader and the snow goose.
   c. High ability—The symbolic meaning of the snow goose.

Study Guide "The Snow Goose" by Paul Gallico

1. Describe the setting of the story. How does it fit the main character and create the mood?
2. Describe Philip Rhayader. Where does he choose to live? Why?
3. Who is the narrator? How does he know the story?
4. How did the people react to Philip? Why was he outcast?
5. What kind of personality did Philip have? How did he react to people who rejected him?
6. To what did Philip turn to replace human companionship? Explain his life in the lighthouse.
7. Describe Fritha. What brings her to Rhayader?
8. What is Fritha's attitude toward Rhayader when she first meets him? What changes her attitude?
9. What is the background of the snow goose? How does the bird become attached to Rhayader?
10. Describe the relationship built up between Rhayader and Fritha. What is the function of the bird in this relationship?
11. During what period in history does the story take place?
12. What does Rhayader plan to do with his boat? Why is this particularly important to Rhayader? How does he carry out his plan?
13. What techniques does Gallico use to describe the heroic efforts of Rhayader?
14. What does the snow bird symbolize? Use as guidelines the snow bird's connection with Fritha, its role in the relationship between Fritha and Rhayader (and the nature of that relationship), its actions during the rescue, and Fritha's thoughts at the end of the story.

Lesson 6

(An optional lesson to be used in place of Lesson 5 with fluent readers.)

OBJECTIVES

To write an analysis of "The Blue Hotel" in terms of the unit concepts.

MATERIALS

"The Blue Hotel" by Stephen Crane (Study guide not included below.)

PROCEDURES

1. Distribute the study questions and assign the reading of "The Blue Hotel."
2. Have the students discuss the study guide questions in their groups. Have each group develop several questions that could be discussed in a report on the story.
3. Help the group make a final selection of a suitable topic for a report.
   a. How does Crane use the setting to develop the story's theme?
   b. What are the causes of the Swede's isolation from the group and of his death?
   c. What are the attitudes of the other characters toward the Swede?
   d. Who is the scapegoat in "The Blue Hotel"? What evidence supports your opinion?
4. After group discussions, ask each student to choose a particular topic and begin work on his composition. Help students as necessary. Some analyses might be presented orally to the class.
5. Close the lesson by discussing the story with the entire group.
   a. Explain the significance and meaning of the second paragraph in Section VIII. How does the vain man separate himself from the rest of the world? What does the blizzard symbolize? How does Crane feel about taking refuge from life?
   b. What is the significance of "blue" in the story?
   c. What is the effect of Section IX on the story? Would the story be stronger or weaker without it? Why?
   d. Compare the Swede to Robinson's Richard Cory.
   e. Crane frequently writes about an "outcast." He never tries to protect the outcast from the natural forces that surround him; he usually tries to explain the outcast and what forces made him an outcast. How has he done it in this story?

Lesson 7

OBJECTIVES

To apply the concepts to poetry.
To organize and present oral reports.

MATERIALS

"Tulips and Addresses"	"The Hunchback in the Park"
"The Jew"	"Brass Spittoons"
"Does It Matter?"	"Mr. Flood's Party"

PROCEDURES

1. Familiarize each student with all the poems in this lesson, dividing the class into homogeneous groups and having them read the poems. Then have each group select one poem that they as a group will study and report on to the rest of the class.
2. Increase independence and develop some understanding of an author's attitude by having each group study its poem looking primarily for the concepts learned in the unit:
    a. The type of outcast.
    b. The reason for outcasting.
    c. The reaction of the outcast.
    d. The attitude of the author toward the outcast and toward the group that casts him out.
    e. The relationship between the speaker and the outcast.
3. Develop skill in oral activities by having each group present its poem and its interpretation to the class. The group presentation might go this way:
    a. One person reads poem.
    b. One person discusses type of outcast.
    c. One person discusses reason for outcasting.
    d. One person discusses the author's attitude.
    e. One person discusses the reactions of the outcast.

Lesson 8

OBJECTIVES

To identify and interpret the causes and results of prejudice and ostracism as they affect the characters of *To Kill a Mockingbird*.

MATERIALS

To Kill a Mockingbird (Study guide not included below.)

PROCEDURES

1. Distribute the novel and, before reading begins, discuss the book in general terms to arouse interest. Ask the students to develop major problem questions (based on unit concepts) that they may be able to answer in their reading. (Type of outcasts; reactions of characters; characteristics of groups from which individuals are outcasts; reasons for aggression by certain individuals against others.)

Allow time in class the first day for reading. For further reading, assign a reading schedule according to the ability of the class.

2. Approach the study of the book through whole-class discussions, small-group discussions, and individual reading time in class. Use the study guide questions as the basis for discussions.

3. Check the reading progress of the students by having them write out some of the study guide questions in a quiz situation. (In the study guide there are many inference and comprehension questions that may be used in teacher-directed discussion.)

4. After the novel has been read begin structuring the group writing assignment by reviewing the outcasts in the novel: Scout, Tom Robinson, Boo Radley, Mayella Ewell, and Delphas Raymond.
   Discuss the elements of prejudice in the novel.
   Discuss the social structure of the town and its effect on scapegoating and prejudice.

5. Develop analytic skill by using the above discussion as the basis for helping the students develop such theme topics as:
   a. Scout Finch was an outcast because of her age.
   b. Boo Radley was a victim of scapegoating and prejudice.
   c. If Tom Robinson had been a white man he would have gone free.
   d. The Negro population of Maycomb was the victim of prejudice.
   e. The old saying about killing a mockingbird adds meaning to the theme of the novel.
   Have each student develop at least one discussion topic.

6. Divide the class into homogeneous groups, and ask each group to choose a topic and prepare to lead a class discussion of it, citing passages in the story that will help develop the topic in a paper. A composition may then be written by each student or by the group with each student developing and writing one phase. If the composition is a group project, make sure each group has developed a specific, equitable plan for dividing the work. Perhaps all students may help in writing the introduction and conclusion, whereas various parts of the body of the composition may be developed by individual students but revised and fitted to the whole by the group.

Lesson 9

OBJECTIVES

To write an analysis of the relationships between individual characters and groups from which they are ostracized.

Criterion statements:
1. The student must select the book and read it independently.
2. He must identify the outcast(s) and the ostracizing group(s).

3. He must identify and explain the causes and effects of the ostracism in terms of the unit concepts.

MATERIALS

Bibliography

PROCEDURES

1. Distribute the bibliography to the students. Review the titles, providing information about the difficulty and content of the books wherever possible. Remind the students to read the cover blurb to help them choose a book. Take the class to the library to select books and provide reading time in class for two to three days. Allow students to choose books not on the bibliography if they are appropriate to the unit content.
2. Assign a deadline day on which the book should be *near* completion, and allow two days after deadline for finishing of books in class.
3. Arrange an individual conference with each student during the reading time to discuss his novel and the topics for his paper. Also provide one or two days in class after completion of the reading to work on outlines and the beginning of compositions with teacher assistance.
4. Note: The bibliography following includes books at a wide variety of reading levels. The teacher should help students to find books appropriate to their reading levels.

The Outcast A Bibliography for Individual Reading

Aleichem, Sholem	*Mottel, the Cantor's Son*
Allen, Merritt	*The White Feather*
Arnold, Elliott	*Blood Brother*
Arnow, Harriet	*The Dollmaker*
Baldwin, James	*Go Tell It On the Mountain*
Baruch, Dorothy	*Glass House of Prejudice*
Bell, Margaret	*The Totem Casts a Shadow*
———	*Daughter of Wolf House*
Bonham, Frank	*Durango Street*
Bontemps, Arna	*Chariot in the Sky*
Brecht, Bertolt	*Galileo*
Conrad, Joseph	*Lord Jim*
Crane, Stephen	*Red Badge of Courage*
DeHartog, Jan	*The Inspector*
Dickens, Charles	*David Copperfield*
———	*Great Expectations*
Doss, Hellen	*The Family Nobody Wanted*
Douglass, Frederick	*Narrative of the Life of an American Slave*

Dumas, Alexander	*The Count of Monte Cristo*
Edmonds, Walter	*Two Logs Crossing*
Eliot, George	*Silas Marner*
Ellison, Ralph	*The Invisible Man*
Faulkner, William	*Intruder in the Dust*
———	*The Unvanquished*
———	*The Old Man*
Field, Rachel	*Hepatica Hawks*
Fuller, Iola	*The Shining Trail*
Gibson, Althea	*I Always Wanted To Be Somebody*
Gould, Jean	*That Dunbar Boy*
Gregory, Dick	*nigger*
Hansberry, Lorraine	*A Raisin in the Sun*
Hawthorne, Nathaniel	*The Scarlet Letter*
Hersey, John	*The Wall*
Holt, Rackham	*George Washington Carver*
Hugo, Victor	*The Hunchback of Notre Dame*
Jackson, Jesse	*Anchor Man*
Kroeber, Theodora	*Ishi, Last of His Tribe*
LaFarge, Oliver	*Laughing Boy*
Lewiton, Mina	*A Cup of Courage*
Little, Jean	*Mine for Keeps*
Lowery, Bruce	*Scarred*
Malcolm X	*The Autobiography of Malcolm X*
Martin, Betty	*Miracle at Carville*
Means, Florence	*Great Day in the Morning*
———	*The Moved Outers*
O'Flaherty, Liam	*The Informer*
Paton, Alan	*Cry, the Beloved Country*
Petry, Ann	*The Street*
———	*Harriet Tubman: Conductor on the Underground Railway*
Piersall, Jim and Al Hirschberg	*Fear Strikes Out*
Plato	*The Apology* and *The Phaedo*
Rostand, Edmond	*Cyrano de Bergerac*
Rosten, Leo	*Capt. Newman, M.D.*
Sackler, H.	*The Great White Hope*
Sams, J. B.	*White Mother*
Schoor, Gene	*Willie Mays, Modest Champion*
———	*Roy Campanella, Man of Courage*
Sinclair, Upton	*The Cup of Fury*
———	*Dragon's Teeth*
Smith, Betty	*A Tree Grows in Brooklyn*
Steinbeck, John	*Grapes of Wrath*

————	*Of Mice and Men*
Stevenson, R. L.	*Dr. Jekyll and Mr. Hyde*
Stolz, Mary	*The Day and the Way We Met*
————	*Pray, Love, Remember*
————	*The Sea Gulls Woke Me*
Stuart, Jesse	*The Thread That Runs So True*
Tarry, Ellen	*The Third Door*
————	*Young Jim: The Early Years of James Weldon Johnson*
Tunis, John	*The Keystone Kids*
Twain, Mark	*Pudd'n'Head Wilson*
Vance, Marguerite	*The Jacksons of Tennessee*
Viscardi, Henry, Jr.	*A Man's Stature*
Walden, Amelia	*A Girl Called Hank*
Walker, Mildred	*The Quarry*
Wier, Ester	*The Loner*
Wouk, Herman	*The Caine Mutiny*
Wren, Percival	*Beau Geste*
Wright, Richard	*Black Boy*
Yates, Elizabeth	*Patterns on the Wall*
Young, Jefferson	*A Good Man*

NOTES

1. I. A. Richards, *Practical Criticism* (New York: Harcourt, Brace and World, Inc., n.d.), pp. 175–176. For types of misunderstanding see pp. 12–15. For analysis of these see pp. 173–287.
2. James R. Squire, *The Responses of Adolescents While Reading Four Short Stories* (Champaign: National Council of Teachers of English, 1964).
3. John Dover Wilson, *What Happens in Hamlet* (New York: Cambridge University Press, 1951).
4. Ernest Jones, *Hamlet and Oedipus* (New York: Anchor Books, 1955).
5. T. S. Eliot, "Hamlet and His Problems," *The Sacred Wood* (New York: Barnes and Noble, 1950).

10 The Text and the Reader: Levels of Meaning and Response*

A careful analysis of what the intelligent reading of literature involves can provide a basis for sequencing instruction in literature. Once the teacher has determined what abilities his students already have, he can design units that begin at that point and help them to become more sophisticated readers. The model in Figure 10.1 summarizes the various responses. It indicates the three major types of response, the cognitive, affective, and aesthetic, that were examined in Chapter 8. The model indicates the dependency of emotional and aesthetic responses on the cognitive. Within the general category of cognitive response, it indicates various levels of response, from literal meanings to structure and thematic meanings. In addition, more sophisticated readers will approach particular texts through a variety of contexts such as that of genre, a particular historical period, and so on. This chapter will examine the types of response and approaches to literature indicated in the model.

Cognitive Responses

Literal Meanings

At the literal level the reader is concerned with what is directly stated by an author. The teacher needs to ask, "Can my students understand most of the words? Can they follow unusual syntactic patterns in which the verb is separated from its subject or object by a series of modifiers?" The difficulty of a work's literal level is a function of the complexity of both sentence structure and vocabu-

* Parts of this chapter appeared in an article by George Hillocks, Jr., in the *English Journal,* September 1964, entitled "Approaches to Literature: A Basis for a Literature Curriculum." They are reprinted here by permission of the National Council of Teachers of English.

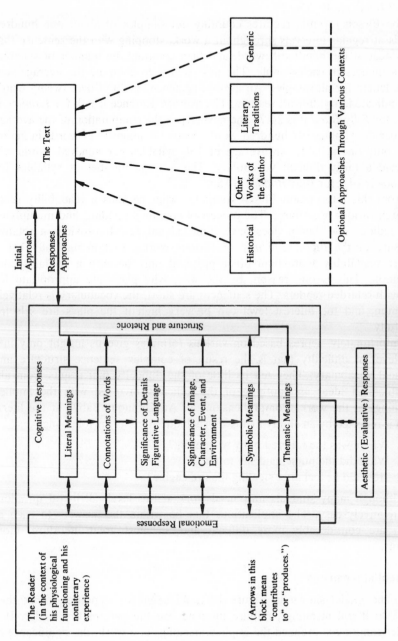

FIGURE 10.1 The Reader's Responses to a Text

lary. A number of formulas have been developed to measure relative literal difficulty.[1] One for adult materials was developed by Rudolf Flesch in *The Art of Readable Writing*.[2]

The Flesch formula requires counting out samples of about one hundred words at regular intervals throughout a work, stopping with the sentence that ends nearest the hundredth word, and then counting the number of syllables and sentences in each sample. The next step is to compute the average sentence length for all samples. An average sentence length of over twenty words will indicate fairly difficult reading. The average sentence length for *Ivanhoe* is 27.8; for *Billy Budd* it is 24.7. The next step is the computation of the average number of syllables per hundred words. Since the majority of words in fiction have only one syllable, an average of 130 syllables per hundred words will indicate a fairly difficult vocabulary. The average number of syllables for *Ivanhoe* is 141; for *Billy Budd* it is 155.

From this information Flesch computes what he calls a readability score through various procedures. The process of counting, dividing, and multiplying is a tedious one, but it does have some advantages. It provides a relative measure of the *literal difficulty* of various works. Fiction naturally has a higher readability score than other prose, if only because it contains conversation. This is one reason, by the way, why plays are appropriate for use with retarded readers. The sentences are short, the vocabulary is relatively common, and the interest level can be very high if the plays are selected carefully.

Unfortunately, scores based on various formulas give us insight only into the level of difficulty that is the result of complex sentence structure and unusual vocabulary. They tell us little of the difficulty that results from abstractness of ideas and nothing of the difficulty involved with the implied meanings of the work. Comprehension of "An Ominous Baby" at the literal level is reflected by an ability to answer such questions as the following:

1. Where was the tattered baby wandering?
2. What did the nursemaid say to him?
3. How did he feel after stealing the fire engine?

Although many students may need work at this level, all literal questions are relatively easy. The implications that lie within the answers to each of them are considerably more difficult and, in most great literature, more important.

Inferential Meanings

In the model shown in Figure 10.1, all cognitive responses, other than those to literal meanings, require inference on the part of the reader. If a reader cannot comprehend the implied meanings of a work, the significance of that work will be lost to him. A misunderstanding of even part of the implied meaning may distort the rest. At this level, the reader must respond to what an author implies by his choice and arrangement of words and imagery in his development of scenes, incidents, characters, and symbols. Stephen Crane's "An Ominous Baby" affords a clear example of how all these work together. Each child in the story is symbolic, just as their quarrel is. The imagery that Crane uses to develop the children and their battle for the toy contributes directly to their meaning as symbols. The words that he uses contribute to the significance of the images. All these help produce the meaning of the whole.

Most students must learn to interpret such implications. In a total curriculum it is useful to introduce each level of implication in a simple, objective fashion so that students can examine how each contributes to the total meaning of a linguistic structure.

A. CONNOTATIONS OF WORDS

Even very young students can understand that different words tend to have different meanings for different people and that various words that have similar denotative meanings may have entirely different connotative meanings. The teacher can make this point clear simply by putting a list of words such as the following on the board: policeman, teacher, unintelligent, home, and so on. Students can then make new lists of words that "mean the same thing but sound better or worse." After an exercise of this sort, the teacher can introduce the words "connotation" and "denotation" if he wishes because the students will have concrete examples to which they can tie those words. Additional exercises might include the examination of advertising copy, which notoriously uses words primarily for their connotative meanings. Again, students can write two or three descriptions of places, people, or events in which they vary the point of view by choosing sets of words with differing connotative values. For instance, they might write about what they study in English from the point of view of an interested student, an uninterested student, and an English teacher. After a systematic introduction to the nature of connotation and how it reflects the point of view of a writer or speaker to his subject and audience, the teacher (and the curriculum) should continue to make use of the students' knowledge in ensuing instruction. Knowledge of connotation is extremely important to the student as both writer and reader and should receive careful and continued emphasis.

B. SIGNIFICANCE OF DETAILS AND FIGURATIVE LANGUAGE

Although it is ordinarily much easier for a reader to comprehend a simple detail than a figure of speech, the two have been classed together because both contribute to the meanings of images, characters, scenes, and events, and because the significance of both is influenced by the connotations of the individual words that convey them.

Students should discuss the significance of details from the time they begin reading, or perhaps from the time they begin to hear stories read aloud. In almost any intelligently organized unit of study, there is a necessity to focus on the meaningful details of a literary work, especially those that are keys to the meaning of imagery and to the interpretation of character and events.

In approaching an individual work, say *Treasure Island,* one of the primary questions for consideration might be, "What details of Long John Silver's appearance, conversation, and actions signal the kind of man he is? Which details, if any, contradict others?" At another level, the student can examine the problem of apparently contradictory or paradoxical features in a single character. In a thematic unit on "Survival," a recurring question might be, "What details of a character's appearance, conversation, or actions predict his ability or inability to survive a given type of crisis?" Similarly, questions can be raised about how details effect a reader's response to a setting, image, or incident.

Certain effects of details may need separate treatment, however, especially when they indicate the writer's attitude toward his subject and his attitude toward his audience. This is especially true for poetry, satire, and propaganda and, in reality, hardly less true for fiction, drama, and biography. Young readers must learn to observe the details a poet has selected to promote a certain tone or feeling or to note the effects of a satirist's use of detail as a devastating weapon. They need to observe how a propagandist can bias an issue simply by focusing on some detail and ignoring others.

Metaphor or figurative language is ordinarily an integral part of the whole work. Its function is more than simply to make an image more vivid to the reader. It adds a layer of meaning to whatever was there before and, in many instances, becomes part of a configuration of details and metaphors that reinforces, complements, or even produces the full meaning of a work. Take Crane's first simile in "An Ominous Baby" for instance: "like the chain shirt of a warrior." The simplest function of this simile is to make clearer Crane's description of the child's clothing. He also wishes to show that this child, awed as he is by the splendid surroundings, has something of the calm courage of a warrior about him. But more than that, Crane suggests by the simile that the child is a tough, experienced fighter. In addition, the use of the specific words "chain shirt" and "warrior" lend an aura of nobility to the tattered child. This simile is the first of a whole series of allusions to battle: "covered with scraches and dust as with scar and powder smoke"; "he looked some wee battler in a war"; "he clenched his fat hands and advanced"; "the pretty child retreated"; "the small vandal made a charge"; and so forth. There is something absurd and pathetic in applying these allusions to babies: absurd because they are children, but pathetic because they are so like grown men at so young an age. The pattern is a clear sign of why and in what respect the baby is ominous.

The most common way to introduce figurative language to students is through a textbook unit on poetry. For "enrichment" the teacher provides a list of figures (metaphor, simile, hyperbole, personification are the most common) with a definition and examples of each. The students then "pick them out" of various poems. The approach is not only deadly, but it may be the reason students think that figurative language is superficially decorative. By using this approach, the teacher tells his students that figurative language actually is something to be "picked out of poetry."

A more reasonable approach is first to examine what effect figurative language has in poems and short stories. Most anthologies supply appropriate materials for such an examination. The teacher can then ask questions such as these:

1. What effect does the comparison have on the reader?
2. What effect does it have in addition to making the meaning clearer or the description more vivid?
3. Why did the author choose this particular comparison?
4. In what way is the comparison appropriate or inappropriate?
5. Is the comparison part of a pattern of details? That is, does it have anything in common with any other comparisons or details in the work? (It may be necessary to help students locate related details.)
6. If there is a pattern, what meaning does it suggest for the work?

When possible, it is useful to examine figurative language in the students' own writing or in the writing of other students. If the school has a literary magazine, it is usually possible to find two or three poems in back issues that are worthy of examination. Using student materials has the double advantage of making figurative language appear less esoteric and encouraging students to use it in their own writing.

Once the students have examined the effects of figurative language, it will seem sensible to name the different kinds of figures and discriminate among them. The discriminations can be taught inductively by comparing, for example, a group of metaphors to a group of similes. This instruction can be followed by the haiku lesson described in Chapter 5.

C. SIGNIFICANCE OF IMAGERY, CHARACTER, EVENT, AND ENVIRONMENT

Up to this point the concern has been with literal meanings and the implications of individual words, details, and figurative language because these aspects of a work contribute heavily to the significance of the larger elements: imagery,* character, events, environment, and setting.

---

* The term "imagery" raises a number of problems. Characters are images. Figurative language evokes images. Details are sometimes images. What an image is and how it operates psychologically is a problem this book cannot even pretend to investigate, let alone resolve. We should like, however, to impose an arbitrary definition by example. For the purpose of this chapter, an image is an elaborated and/or recurrent sensory entity, animate or inanimate: for example, the albatross, the sun, the moon,

Nearly any unit of instruction should deal with the way the implications of individual words, details, and metaphors contribute to the significance of imagery, character, and setting. Certain thematic units are especially appropriate for work with character. In a unit on "Courage," for instance, students should attempt to determine whether or in what ways certain characters are courageous on the basis of their actions and speech and on the basis of details. It is useful for a student to begin a serious examination of character with an analysis of the stereotypes he encounters in his daily TV fare: the heroic guy, the bad guy, the well-meaning bumbler, the sidekick, and so forth. Students enjoy establishing the stereotype patterns and identifying characters who belong to them. The procedure involves an examination of the details, action, and speech used to create and support the stereotype. A comparison of the stereotypes with the characters of more serious fiction can promote insight into both the stereotype and the more original characters. The students will see that a writer relies on his audience to respond to a few rather common details that create the conventional image of the detective, Western-gunslinger-turned-good, and so on. The writer who creates the more original character does not rely on the conventions to so great an extent and asks his audience to respond to the character he presents rather than to some standard, prefabricated character.

Thematic units built around such themes as courage, justice, and survival are useful in helping students observe the relationships between character and event, between image and character, and so on. One of the central problems for such units is: What do the actions of the character reveal about his personality (courage, justice, moral values, and the like)?

The relationship of a character to his environment presents a particular kind of difficulty to the reader. This general problem of man and his environment can be separated into three focal areas: the physical, the social, and the cultural environments. In reality, of course, these three form a matrix of influences that operate dynamically in influencing the personality, desires, and aspirations of man. Since the author's task involves a commentary on man, his work necessarily involves the relationship of man to his environment —a relationship that may be seen lying somewhere in the continuum extending from the character as controller of his environment, as in the case of the mythic protagonist such as Prometheus, to man as subject of his environment, as in the case of many modern protagonists such as Willy Loman in *Death of a Salesman*. No character in any work can be abstracted from his setting, for even the values of the mythical hero who is basically in command of his environment are influenced by it.

An arbitrary separation of the areas that constitute the environment

---

the skeleton ship in "The Rime of the Ancient Mariner"; the snake, the gates of Hell, the Tree in *Paradise Lost;* the blood imagery in *Macbeth;* the animal imagery in *Volpone;* the fire engine in "An Ominous Baby."

simplifies analysis, promotes understanding, and facilitates teaching. At the same time, however, it is essential to realize the inseparability of the physical aspects of environment from the cultural and social aspects.

1. THE PHYSICAL ENVIRONMENT A teaching unit that focuses on the physical environment might examine a series of such problems as the following: (*a*) How does man react and adjust to his physical surroundings? (*b*) What abilities, physical and psychological, enable man to adapt to conditions of privation and to conditions imposed by location—jungle, desert, mountain, sea, farm, and city? (*c*) What psychological effects do isolation and physical torment have on man? (*d*) Why do the effects of similar experiences vary from one individual to another? (*e*) How does exposure to various physical conditions influence the growth of character or personality? More complex problems arise when the focus changes to that part of the physical world that is man's own creation. It is this part of the physical environment that is so frequently the subject of the literature of protest: slum conditions, intolerable working conditions, economic oppression.

In addition, man's concept of nature also requires examination because it is frequently a matter of primary concern in literature. Primitive men see nature as a force upon whose good will they are dependent. Modern man sees nature as a challenge and as a refuge where the rights of the individual are unmolested and where the soul can reconstitute itself for renewed contact with the world of men and affairs.

2. SOCIETY AND ENVIRONMENT No attempt to understand the human element in literature can ignore the fact that man is a social animal. Knowledge of the bases of social organization is fundamental to the full comprehension of some works and helpful in the comprehension of others. For instance, some knowledge of class stratification, mobility from class to class, and the effects of status and power in social situations will greatly faciliate the understanding of such novels as Galsworthy's *The Man of Property* and the novels of Louis Auchincloss. Not that the terminology or concepts need be objectified for the mature reader, but the word "mature" implies the ability to comprehend and be sensitive to the distinctions of status, power, and wealth that shape the lives of people as well as literary characters. The "mature" reader has had enough experience to enable him to understand. The problem is that, for many people, even experience fails to be useful in reading or observing. Why? We do not know, but we do know that professors of English find it necessary to explain the meanings of novels like *The Great Gatsby* and *The Adventures of Huckleberry Finn* to their students.

A unit on "Man and Modern Society" might open with a story such as Aldous Huxley's "Fard," which portrays two characters, Sophie, an overworked maid, and Madam, her pampered mistress who has no conception that Sophie might have feelings and desires of her own. Students could proceed to a discussion of class structure and the factors that support it: wealth, power, status. They should examine how the possession or lack of wealth, power, status permits or denies certain kinds of life patterns, gives rise to varying sets of values, and so forth. In the course of the unit students should discuss how and why people attempt to change from one social class to another, what happens when they do, how their values are affected, and why some have no mobility. Students can apply such insights to plays ranging from James M. Barrie's *The Admirable Crichton* to Tennessee Williams' *A Streetcar Named Desire;* to novels from Dickens' *Great Expectations* and Thackeray's *Vanity Fair* to Claude Brown's *Manchild in the Promised Land* and Richard Wright's *Native Son;* and to nonfiction from Oscar Lewis' *The Children of Sanchez* to Dick Gregory's *From the Back of the Bus.* Clearly, the range of material available would permit teaching such a unit to students from the tenth to twelfth grades, depending on the unit requirements and the abilities of the students.

3. CULTURE AND ENVIRONMENT Man's cultural milieu may be distinguished from the social as the composite of all the forces that cut across social boundaries to delimit the behavior of an individual and to organize patterns of behavior for the whole society. For a given society the class system is operative within the boundaries of the various cultural forces that influence it. Much of the behavior of an individual is determined by the culture into which he is born. Superficial cultural patterns, such as habits of eating and dress, are obvious; but cultural patterns that are the basis for modes of thought are, to the outsider, neither obvious nor acceptable. The idea of progress, for instance, which pervades Western civilization, is not accepted in many Far Eastern cultures.

Cultural conditioning is reflected in all literary works, but especially in those dealing with cultural change or cultural conflict, for example, Pearl Buck's *The Good Earth,* Conrad Richter's *The Light in the Forest,* E. M. Forster's *Passage to India,* Alan Paton's *Too Late the Phalarope* and *Cry, the Beloved Country.* Whatever the institutions existing in a given culture, an individual born into that culture is influenced by them and in turn influences them. His adherence to the ideals of the culture is rewarded; his digressions from its standards are punished. When an individual moves from one culture to another, he will be caught in a conflict of customs and values, as is Trueson in *The Light in the Forest.* Here a white child, indoctrinated into an American Indian culture, is transplanted into the white culture. Since his customs and values are not the same as those of the other whites, he is unable to adjust. When a culture changes, even minutely, new customs and mores must be learned, and this is often difficult for older people, as it is for Wang Lung in *The Good Earth.* Most individuals adhere to the standards of the various institutions in which they are involved; but when they depart from them or when they are in conflict with them, they will be punished by official or unofficial social disapproval.

A knowledge of culture as a factor that influences and differentiates the behavior and thought of individuals supplies a background from which the reader is able to infer the cultural forces active in a literary work and tends to create a sympathy for cultural values different from his own.

At a more sophisticated level, the reader should learn to be aware of the cultural and social values that operate on the author. Frequently these can be inferred from a careful examination of the work. When a piece of writing is not contemporary, however, such an inference sometimes requires considerable research into the period—the examination of a work in its historical context.

D. SYMBOLIC MEANINGS

Although the difference between an image and a symbol is not theoretically clear among critics, most would agree that symbols are images, but not all images are symbolic. This is the distinction used here. A symbol is an image that takes on meanings other than its content. It represents something external to it. Aesop's animals, for example, are not simply animals. Spenser's knights and monsters represent abstract, complex concepts. Symbolic meanings, when they exist in a work, arise directly from the literal content of the text and its implications. To understand symbolic meanings, the reader must first understand the text in all of its simpler dimensions. If he misconstrues the literal level, the connotations of words, the implications of events, and so on, his reading of the symbolism is likely to be inadequate. This is true whether he is dealing with concrete allegorical symbols or highly abstract archetypal symbols.

To introduce students to the problem of symbolism it is easiest to begin with what the student already knows. Even the average seventh grader can tell how to respond to signs in the streets, various religious signs and symbols, national and military insignia, and various other conventional signs. A discussion of how these work leads to a working definition of "symbol." From their work with connotation and with metaphoric language, students will know how the qualities of one thing, a rose for instance, became associated with another, a girl. As a part of general cultural knowledge, they know what animals are associated with certain characteristics and vice versa. From here it is an easy step to the examination of fables.

The fable, of course, uses the simplest kind of symbol—the allegorical symbol, the meaning of which is usually rigid and easily grasped by the reader. For instance, in a medieval morality play, gluttony might be represented by a fat man riding a hog across the stage holding a bottle of wine in one hand and a side of bacon in the other. Generally in this kind of allegory, in addition to the rigidity of the symbol, there is what can be called a one-to-one relationship between symbol and referent. The man on the hog represents a single concept. This does not exclude the possibility of two or more levels of allegory existing side by side, as in Spenser's *Faerie Queene,* where Gloriana represents both the Virgin Mother at the religious level and Queen Elizabeth at the historical level. At each level the one-to-one relationship still exists. Furthermore, in medieval allegory there is a tendency for each event, object, and agent to be symbolic and for each symbol to be related to each other symbol in a direct and clear manner.

In contrast to the allegorical symbol, the symbols in such works as *Moby Dick, The Scarlet Letter,* and *The Rime of the Ancient Mariner* tend to be less rigid and to represent a syndrome of meaning. They may or may not be related to other symbols in the same work, and every event, object, and agent in the work is not necessarily symbolic. Such symbols ordinarily do not depend upon public acceptance of conventional symbolic values; rather the symbol is developed throughout the context of the work as the author suggests symbolic meaning through the interplay of various elements in his work.

The value of the archetype or universal symbol depends neither upon local convention nor upon the author's manipulation of his material; rather, its meaning is dependent upon its universal recurrence in the life patterns of mankind. Such symbols seem to arise out of the basic needs, desires, and experiences common to all men of all cultures. The most famous archetype, that of death and rebirth, which Maud Bodkin[3] tells us is present in *The Rime of the Ancient Mariner* and which other critics have seen in other works, is central to all of the great and many of the minor religions. Many archetypes figure prominently in myth: the birth of the hero; the pattern of his journey, task, and return; the crone who refurbishes the powers of the hero; and the mother goddess.

Although it is obvious that symbols convey a heavy burden of meaning in literary works, the particular meaning suggested by them in any one work is not always obvious. To the unpracticed reader even an obvious allegory may be obscure in the details of its implications; the same reader, while reading for plot, will be completely unaware of more subtle symbolic content, and he will reject a work as incomprehensible when its meaning is the function of complex symbols. If a student is to approach a symbolic work successfully, then he must have a program that will make him aware of the existence of symbols, help him to explore the ways in which they function, and give him practice in interpretation. See the lessons on symbolism described in Chapters 4 and 5.

E. RHETORIC AND STRUCTURE

As the model "A Reader's Responses to a Text" on page 209 suggests, the rhetorical and structural aspects of a work control, emphasize, or reinforce the meaning at each of the levels described so far. The rhetoric of a work refers to the voice of the author and the stance that he adopts. Structure refers to the arrangement of the parts of the work.

The rhetoric that an author adopts for a given work has a direct bearing on the meaning of the work as the audience responds to it.[4] For an adequate response to the work, the reader must understand who is speaking, why the author has adopted that particular persona, and what the attitudes of the persona are toward both subject and audience. The persona who speaks of himself helps carry the major impact of the work; in Browning's "My Last Duchess," Burns' "Holy Willie's Prayer," Salinger's *Catcher in the Rye,* in *Huckleberry Finn,* and in many of Poe's short stories, what the narrator reveals about himself carries the intellectual and emotional weight of the work.

Fielding, Dickens, Dostoevsky, and many other writers assume stances that allow them to intrude into the narrative to direct the reader's attention and control his responses. Conrad, Swift, and others invent persona who tell the story of others but are themselves important to the works. Authors who seem to withdraw from the narrative retain control over the reader's reactions by the use of carefully selected details and vocabulary.

The analysis of point of view most common in the secondary schools is too oversimplified to be useful. The teacher merely asks whether the narration is in the first person or the omniscient or limited third person. The problem is much more complex than that and might be introduced to the student through a series of comparisons. For example, *Huckleberry Finn* and *Great Expectations* are both first-person narratives. But a simple recognition of this fact tells us nothing of their differences and nothing of the uniqueness of each. Why does Mark Twain make Huck his narrator? Huck is an outsider, an "uncivilized" boy whom society would dearly love to "civilize." But since Huck is inherently good, he cannot and will not adopt the hypocritical stance of the society he sees everywhere. His "lack of sophistication" in the mores of his society enables him to think for himself. Even while he believes himself to be wrong and society to be right, he must defy society and accept punishment in hell rather than turn Jim in. Huck's point of view may be simple and naïve, but it knifes past the double standards of society. The great irony lies in the fact that Huck never knows that he is right and society is wrong. He only knows that he can't understand civilization and must "light out for the territory." Only the reader knows. Dickens, on the other hand, uses a first-person narrator who is wise and mature and who can understand his experiences from a more or less detached point of view. The older, wiser narrator can recount experience, interpret it, and interpose himself between the experience and us to prevent it and us from becoming maudlin. A horrifying, heartbreaking experience comes to the reader through the filter of Pip's mature sense of humor, which creates an aesthetic distance.

Although the sophisticated reader can understand the effects of an author's rhetorical stance partly as a result of his wide experience in reading, readers who lack experience are less likely to comprehend these effects.

The teacher must help them to develop a frame of reference. Comparing and contrasting the effects of point of view in some of Poe's stories, in the opening chapters of *Huckleberry Finn* and *Great Expectations,* and in various short stories and poems can develop the concepts rather quickly and in depth. What is the effect of Watson's narration of the Sherlock Holmes stories? Why does Shirley Jackson narrate from the point of view of a child's mother in some of her stories? Why does Richard Matheson narrate "Born of Man and Woman" from the point of view of a monstrous child? Any number of works in most common anthologies make use of narrational techniques that illustrate the concept.

The structure of a work contributes to or controls its meaning in special ways. First, and probably most important for high school readers, is the problem of form as it applies to individual works—the way in which the arrangement of the parts of a work contribute to and reinforce its meaning. Second, knowledge of form from the point of view of mode of presentation (fiction, lyric, drama, and oral epic) helps the reader to understand and accept the conventions derived from the limitations and advantages of a particular mode of presentation.

1. ARRANGEMENT OF PARTS The arrangement of the parts of a work influences the meaning and impact of the work at all levels, from the choice of words and their syntactic arrangement to the arrangement of incidents, images, and symbols.

The effects of word choice and syntax in one passage are likely to be most clear to students when they see them in contrast to another. For example, the passage that describes Kino's awakening at the beginning of Steinbeck's *The Pearl* provides an interesting contrast to the passage in *Great Expectations* that tells of Pip's awakening as he gathers food to take to Magwitch in the swamps. From *The Pearl* by John Steinbeck:

> Kino awakened in the near dark. The stars still shone and the day had drawn only a pale wash of light in the lower sky to the east. The roosters had been crowing for some time, and the early pigs were already beginning their ceaseless turning of twigs and bits of wood to see whether anything to eat had been overlooked. Outside the brush house in the tuna clump, a covey of little birds chittered and flurried with their wings.
>
> Kino's eyes opened, and he looked first at the lightening squares which was the door and then he looked at the hanging box where Coyotito slept. And last he turned his head to Juana, his wife, who lay beside him on the mat, her blue head shawl over her nose and over her breasts and around the small of her back. Juana's eyes were open too. Kino could never remember seeing them closed when he awakened. Her dark eyes made little reflected stars. She was looking at him as she was always looking at him when he awakened.[5]

From *Great Expectations* by Charles Dickens:

As soon as the great black velvet pall outside my little window was shot with gray, I got up and went downstairs; every board upon the way, and every crack in every board, calling after me, "Stop thief!" and "Get up, Mrs. Joe!" In the pantry, which was far more abundantly supplied than usual, owing to the season, I was very much alarmed by a hare hanging up by the heels, whom I rather thought I caught, when my back was half-turned, winking. I had no time for verification, no time for selection, no time for anything, for I had no time to spare. I stole some bread, some rind of cheese, about half a jar of mincemeat (which I tied up in my pocket handkerchief with my last night's slice), some brandy from a stone bottle (which I decanted into a glass bottle I had secretly used for making that intoxicating fluid, Spanish liquorice-water, up in my room; diluting the stone bottle from a jug in the kitchen cupboard), a meat bone with very little on it, and a beautiful round compact porkpie. I was nearly going away without the pie, but I was tempted to mount upon a shelf, to look what it was that was put away so carefully in a covered earthern-ware dish in a corner, and I found it was the pie and I took it, in the hope that it was not intended for early use, and would not be missed for some time.

There was a door in the kitchen communicating with the forge; I unlocked and unbolted that door, and got a file from among Joe's tools. Then I put the fastenings as I had found them, opened the door at which I had entered when I ran home last night, shut it, and ran for the misty marshes.[6]

The semantic differences between the two passages are obvious. But even young readers can detect differences in the functioning and tone of the syntax and in the choice of vocabulary. The teacher might begin by asking how the passages differ in tone and what makes the difference. He might ask next what syntactic differences the students can detect. They may be able to enumerate a number of differences. If not, the teacher might ask about differences in the length of the sentences. Clearly, Dickens' sentences are much longer. Questions such as these might follow:

a. How many words are there in the first sentence from Dickens? (Over forty.)
b. How many main clauses (basic sentence patterns) are there in that sentence? (One.)
c. How many main clauses are there in the first forty words from Steinbeck? (Four, and a fifth one has begun.)
d. How many main clauses are there in the first forty words of the second paragraph from Steinbeck? (Four.)
e. How often does Steinbeck use the word "and" to connect his clauses in these two forty-word passages? (Five times.)
f. How does Dickens' syntax differ from Steinbeck's? (It is more complicated. It uses more modifiers.)

When the quantitative differences in the syntax are clear, the teacher should begin to ask about the qualitative effects of the differences. The students should come to see how the simple syntax of Steinbeck promotes the peaceful, fable-like quality that his semantic content provides, whereas Dickens' complex syntax allows the humor of the older Pip who is recalling the episode to interpose itself between the fear of the child and the audience. The subordinated remarks, both in and out of parentheses, in Dickens' lines hold the veil of humor. At the same time this complex syntax can convey a note of urgency through its relatively short parallel structures: "no time for verification, no time for selection . . ." and "I stole some bread, some rind of cheese . . ." Steinbeck's syntax on the other hand moves slowly, peacefully, and with utter simplicity.

In *The Pearl,* of course, Steinbeck's syntax never becomes very complex, but when the trackers are searching for Kino and his family later in the story the tempo increases considerably, partially through syntactic devices that any student can detect:

> Kino was not breathing, but his back arched a little and the muscles of his arms and legs stood out with tension and a line of sweat formed on his upper lip. For a long moment the trackers bent over the road, and then they moved on slowly, studying the ground ahead of them, and the horseman moved after them. The trackers scuttled along, stopping, looking, and hurrying on. They would be back, Kino knew. They would be circling and searching, peeping, stooping, and they would come back sooner or later to his covered track.[7]

In addition to examining the syntax in such passages, the students can also examine the selection and arrangement of detail. Why does Steinbeck mention the roosters, the pigs, and the birds? What do these details reveal about the immediate scene? about Kino's total environment before the events beginning with the discovery of the pearl? Why does Dickens select the particular details he uses? What effects do they have? An exercise that will illuminate the use and arrangement of detail is the comparison of the first few paragraphs of the third chapter of *Great Expectations,* in which Pip goes to the marsh with food for Magwitch, with the opening paragraphs of Poe's "Fall of the House of Usher." Although the details of the physical description of the terrain have certain qualities in common, the two authors use them in entirely different ways. Or students may compare the way in which Stevenson treats the one or two awakenings of Jim Hawkins in *Treasure Island* with Kino's and Pip's. There are few details in *Treasure Island.* Jim simply awakes and moves into action. But one does not miss the detail. The sequence of events is succinct, direct, and clean.

The arrangement of images, scenes, and characters is also of vital importance. Shelley's "Ozymandias" is an obvious case in point. It is the juxtaposition of images in the final six lines of the poem, not either image by itself, that conveys the essential meaning.

And on the pedestal these words appear:
  "My name is Ozymandias, King of Kings:
  Look on my works, ye Mighty, and despair!"
  Nothing beside remains. Round the decay
  Of that colossal wreck, boundless and bare
  The lone and level sands stretch far away.

The contrast between the words on the pedestal and the reality not only reveals the emptiness of Ozymandias' boast but gives *despair* a double meaning: After the lapse of centuries, the words of Ozymandias are no longer a boast but a cry of warning and lamentation. It is a double-edged irony.

The reader must think about, and respond to the arrangement and function of scenes, characters, and events. What is the function of the Grangerford sequence in *Huckleberry Finn?* The function of the last eleven chapters of the book, in which Tom helps Huck "steal a nigger" he knows to be free, is still debated by critics. But that is no reason why the question can't be put to students.

The reader will miss much of the richness of a book if he does not recognize modulation of character and the use of such techniques as the double or doppelganger. In Conrad's "The Secret Sharer," for example, the narrator comes to view Leggatt as an embodiment of the primal urges that lay hidden deep within himself. In Dickens' *Great Expectations* a similar technique helps define the moral universe with a set of characters who reflect the urges in Pip's own personality. There is a polarity of inherent goodness in Joe and inherent evil in Orlick, and Pip fluctuates between the two. This modulation of character is repeated in various sets of characters: Miss Havisham's treatment of Estella has much in common with, but is different from, Magwitch's treatment of Pip; Estella's social consciousness is contrasted to Biddy's sincerity and humility; the theme of commitment is amplified through the comparison of Pip's guardians—Jaggers and Joe—and in Wemmick, who has one set of values for the office and another set for the "castle"; and Pip himself has his counterpoint in Herbert.

The reader must also ask about the shape of the work as a whole. What holds it together? How do the parts relate to each other? The compact structure of *Oedipus Rex,* for example, has the effect of driving the attention to the immediate, central problems of the play: man's role in creating his own destiny, his struggle against it, and his submission to it. The whole impact of these problems is conveyed through the figure of Oedipus, the other characters being only the machinery, as it were, for staging the events of the play and the emotions of the man. Oedipus is the focal point of the play's meaning, the purveyor of emotion and theme. More specifically, the steps of the plot by which Oedipus seeks and learns the truth about himself thrust home the ineluctable nature of his fate.

Dostoevsky's *Crime and Punishment* is closely structured, but in a different way, and this difference in structure helps to achieve different effects. The central plot line moves directly from consideration of the crime through commission, suffering, and punishment. The major themes and interest center in Raskolnikov and the workings of his morbidly introspective and philosophical mind. The themes of crime and its casuistry, or moral responsibility, and of human depravity and dignity find their primary expression in Raskolnikov. But in contrast to the dramatis personae of *Oedipus Rex,* the characters of *Crime and Punishment* are important in themselves as well as in the development and variation of the major themes of the book. A number of characters commit "crimes," but some are depraved and some are not. Through the secondary characters Dostoevsky explores a number of related themes, including the causes and effects of "crimes" committed out of helplessness, necessity, egotism, and depravity. Thus the moral questions raised in the book exceed those raised in *Oedipus Rex* not only in number but in precision. *Oedipus Rex* raises large questions. *Crime and Punishment* raises large questions and proceeds to refine them by raising smaller, related questions.

2. MODE OF PRESENTATION[8] *How* a work is to be presented to an audience has a considerable influence over both the form and content of the work. The writer of fiction has his audience at his disposal for a period of several hours, whereas the dramatist has his audience for only two or three hours at most. This rather obvious fact has several important consequences. First, the novelist can explore not only those questions that are a major concern to him but a multitude of less important, related questions as Dostoevsky does in *Crime and Punishment.* The dramatist has time to explore only the major questions. The time factor allows the novelist to present a much more complex character analysis than the dramatist. Moreover, the characters of a novel can appear in an unlimited number of situations, each of which can increase their complexity.

The fictional mode allows an author to explore the mind of a character as he encounters various situations, other characters, and himself. The dramatist is far more limited in this respect. The same advantage allows the writer of fiction to intrude into the narrative in various ways: to explain the significance of what has happened, to persuade the reader in a direct way to accept the values on which the work may be based, and to invest the setting with significance. The dramatist can never talk to an audience as a novelist does to his reader, except by means of a chorus, and even that is a far less direct method than that available to the novelist. On the other hand, the dramatist has the advantage that his characters become incarnate on the stage. He is not nearly so dependent on the reader's imagination to put the dry bones together so that they may walk around. Establishing empathy is not entirely his responsibility; in part, at least, it falls to the director and the actors and to the audience, who respond directly and immediately.

Both lyric and oral epic also have their restrictions and advantages. In fiction the author is partly concealed from his audience but can speak directly through the characters and the narrative voice he adopts. In drama the author disappears behind the voices of the actors. With the oral epic, however, the artist confronts his audience directly. The convention of telling and listening is always present. The singer of epic was not simply a vehicle for carrying a previously composed tale to his audience. On the contrary, he composed as he sang and as he watched the reactions of his audience. Thus, depending on his mood or the mood of the audience, he could shorten or lengthen the poem by hundreds of lines. His composition moved very rapidly. Rather than memorizing a piece several thousands of lines long, the singer had at his command scores of what have been called "oral formulaic patterns," stock phrases that could be added or deleted and rearranged internally as the singer proceeded. Thus, certain phrases were commonly used to describe battles, horses, armor, and the like. A talented singer could use the formulas to elaborate or digress at length. The exigencies of the oral method of composition are obvious, and when students read *The Iliad, The Odyssey,* or *Beowulf,* an understanding of the oral technique involved can be very useful.[9]

If oral epic speaks directly to an audience, the lyric pretends to allow the reader to eavesdrop on the private thoughts of its author, and the effect is to produce a somewhat precise emotion in the reader through a process of association. The compact, rapidly developed imagery ordinarily demands far more inference of the reader than any other mode of presentation. The writer of a lyric presents the concrete material of experience, and the reader must respond maximally to a minimum of clues. In contrast, even a story as short as "An Ominous Baby" provides enough clues so that a reader can remain impervious to many and still respond adequately. A novel presents even more. The reader of a lyric must do without explanations from authors and characters. He cannot skip words, phrases, or chapters. He must read carefully, listen to the sound and sense of what he hears, and allow himself to come under the spell of the poem, at least momentarily.

An intelligent understanding of these modes of presentation can be achieved by even young students. They can see that a narrator's voice emerges frequently in fiction, never in drama, indirectly in the lyric (so that it might appear that the author does not care that no one understands him), but that it is always present in the oral epic. Even this idea, as a bare minimum, can lead to more intelligent reading. But the teacher must allow students to explore the differences themselves when they are ready. *Lectures will not do.*

F. THEMATIC MEANINGS

Understanding the "theme" of the work involves responding to the work as a whole, to the total of literal and inferential meanings that the work conveys. The theme of a work becomes apparent to the reader when he answers two questions: (1) What is the meaning of the work? and (2) How is that meaning produced? Answers to both are important. If a reader answers only the first, he is likely to oversimplify; but if he attempts answers to both, he must bear most of the evidence in mind in his attempt to derive the central significance of the work. The theme, or central significance, is the product of the organization of the whole work.[10] In order to get at this significance, the reader must respond to the elements discussed above. Further, he must evaluate his perceptions of theme against the evidence of the text. Most sophisticated readers do this as they read. They make inferences about central meanings and alter those inferences as they continue to read. A young, less experienced reader is less likely to alter his concept of the work as he encounters new evidence. If someone offers an alternative interpretation, he is likely to reject it in favor of his own. For this reason and others, it is wiser to guide the students' examination of aspects of a text in a discussion than to simply present the student with an interpretation in a lecture.

The carefully constructed instructional unit will help to do just that. It will provide the student with a basis for the examination of a series of texts. At first, the examination will be under the direction of the teacher, but finally it will be the student himself who conducts the examination. One argument against unit teaching has been that it tends to distort the meaning of individual works by emphasizing certain aspects while neglecting others. When that happens, the unit is at fault. The works have not been carefully selected, the student has not had careful preparation for reading them, or the teacher does not understand them himself. A unit should be so designed that it enables the students to get at the central significance and the organizational principles of the works it contains.

For example, Harper Lee's novel *To Kill a Mockingbird* might be used as a major reading in a unit dealing with point of view. If the students are concerned only with that problem, the central significance of the book is almost bound to be overlooked. They will have to understand a good many other aspects of the text as well as the point of view. On the other hand, the same novel appears in a unit called "The Outcast" in Chapter 9. One of the major concerns of this unit is the relationships among various sets of characters and their attitudes toward one another. Obviously, point of view is one aspect of the problem. But the concept that is central to the unit is also central to the book, so that the unit helps the student to arrive at an understanding of the book.

In another sense, however, the objection to unit teaching is somewhat ridiculous. It implies that a reader should always get everything possible from what he reads. To do that he would have to understand everything about reading before he read anything. The idea also results in practical failure. When a teacher attempts to squeeze every bit out of a work, the work and the students die a slow and agonizing death. The teaching unit, however, is designed to prepare students for handling particular problems in meaning, so that when they do arise, they can be dealt with by the students themselves. Each unit of instruction in literature should help the student acquire additional skills and concepts to use in his reading. Eventually, he will be able to approach a text and understand its theme and its principle of organization without the support of an instructional unit or teacher.

Contexts of the Text

Sometimes it is useful, if not necessary, to examine a work from the point of view of one of the several contexts in which it exists.

1. HISTORICAL For most texts written before the twentieth century, certain kinds of historical information are necessary to more complete understanding. Unfortunately, the kinds of historical information provided in surveys of English and American literature are only indirectly relevant to the works studied. What a student usually needs is historical information that is directly applicable to the texts he will read—and not simply publication dates. He needs to know the iconography and philosophy of the age, or at least those aspects of it that are reflected in the works he will read. If he reads *Richard III,* he needs to know that the Elizabethans regarded Richard as a villian immediately upon his first appearance on the stage. His deformities were the signs of villainy much as the moustache, high hat, and black cloak were the signs of villainy in nineteenth-century melodrama. If they read Augustan satire, then they need to know the political situations that gave rise to the satire. If they read "The Nuns' Priest's Tale," then they need background on medieval medical theory and the conflicts between certain religious orders. Students can read the texts without the background, of course, but their reading will be more complete with it.

Either the teacher or the text may provide such information, but in either case the student should not be swamped with irrelevancies. It is easy to read or recite long lectures from college notes, and it is even easier to bore the students by doing that. Probably the best method is to present historical information briefly and concretely in the form of a problem that the students attempt to solve in their reading and discussion of the work. If Shakespeare introduces Richard as a sort of melodramatic villain, to what degree does he remain so throughout the play? What internal evidence attests to Richard's villainy? What aspects of the play might cause an audience to empathize with Richard despite his villainy?

In addition to presenting historical information relevant to individual works, the teacher of advanced school students might wish to teach his students how to examine the literature of an age—or one type of literature during a given age. High school survey courses pretend to do this, but most do not. If an historical approach of some sort is imperative, it would be more productive to give up the impossible task of the survey and prepare two or three units on such topics as Elizabethan tragedy or comedy, the Elizabethan lyric, the Metaphysical poets, Augustan satire, and man and nature in the Romantic movement. Such units could focus on the impetus, ideology, techniques, content, and results of a particular literary movement. By the end of one or two such units, students would know something rather specific about a particular historical phase of literature and good deal about the nature of literature in general.

2. GENERIC A more important context for most students is that of genre, in the sense that Aristotle used the term to refer to tragedy, comedy, and epic. A study of genre in this sense introduces the student to the problem of form and provides a matrix of experience against which he can examine a particular work. Gilbert Highet has pointed this out: "One of the best ways to study the problem of form in literature is the method used by Aristotle. This is induction. First, collect as many examples of a given phenomenon as possible. Then, by observing resemblances and differences and contrasts and alliances, extract from these particulars a few general descriptive principles."[11] Nearly any secondary school student can make worthwhile generalizations about the nature of blues, fables, detective stories, and science fiction. From these relatively simple genres, the student, having learned the techniques of comparison and contrast, can advance to more complex Aristotelian genres of tragedy, comedy, epic, and satire. Sooner or later, he will begin making comparisons and contrasts by himself.

The principles that he detects in specific genres are frequently widely applicable to literature in general. For instance, any work of science fiction is based on extrapolations from known scientific principles to the unknown. These extrapolations are the hypotheses on which the story is based. The author of science fiction says, "If . . . , then . . . If . . . , then . . ." Science fiction can serve as a clear-cut, concrete introduction to an examination of the idea that each literary work poses its own world, which is extrapolated from the real world. Thus, the principles that a student learns from the study of science fiction should become operative in his reading of all fiction.

Affective Responses

As the reader encounters the literal level of a text, as he draws inferences from the parts individually and as they relate to one another, he is likely to respond emotionally to the work or some part of it. Empathy or emotionl response arises, not from the main action of a drama or novel, but from the details of character and event. If Crane had written that a dirty child wandered in a strange neighborhood, encountered another child with a toy, and stole the toy, our sympathy would not necessarily be with either child. If there were any sympathy at all, it would most likely be a superficial sympathy with the child who lost the toy. The implications of language, details, and events, however, give rise to immediate and continued involvement with the tattered child. It is possible, however, for the implications to go unrecognized and for the reader to remain impervious to the emotional effects of the story. Similarly, a summary of the main action of *Macbeth* would be likely to result in utter condemnation of Macbeth. Shakespeare's language, details, and imagery, create empathy with the character. Unfortunately a reader cannot respond with emotional sympathy to words he does not comprehend, connotations he does not recognize, or implications he does not grasp.

Any empathic response, whether it is reflected in tears, laughter, verbalization, or in some other manner, must result from at least a momentary acceptance of the value structure of the work, resulting in turn from at least a partial understanding of the text. If we detest murders without qualification or for some reason fail to respond to the value structure of *Crime and Punishment,* we can have no empathy with Raskolnikov. Similarly, if we do not share Mark Twain's fondness for the tricks and irreverent escapades of a little boy and do not respond to his text, we can have little use for *Tom Sawyer.* In short, a good deal of any text is directed to the creation or reinforcement of certain attitudes in the reader toward the values expressed or implied in the text. But the reader cannot respond with the desired attitude if he does not comprehend the text.

Paradoxically, although a reader can easily reject any text he does not understand, there are some that he may not reject *unless* he fully comprehends them. Successful propaganda is a case in point. Trite newspaper doggerel is another. If a reader succumbs to the words and images, trite or otherwise, that are intended to provoke particular emotions, he will become little more than a mechanical instrument. Strike the keys (mother, home, old age, sickness, death) and the response comes forth.

Obviously, a teacher cannot talk his students into giving what he (the teacher) considers appropriate responses to *Macbeth,* although many teachers try. If students do not respond as he hoped they would, the teacher must determine why, back away from the particular work at hand, and teach a sequence of materials, perhaps over a period of several months or years, that will prepare the students to comprehend a text intellectually, emotionally, and aesthetically.

Many teachers are fond of arguing that some works are beyond the experience and emotional capacity of the students. They resolve to present only those works that the students can automatically "appreciate" and to save the others until later. But the students get older, and many still detest the works that they could not "appreciate" earlier. A majority of adults, if they could be convinced to read in the first place, would be bored silly with Shakespeare, Dante, Dostoevsky, Hawthorne, Melville, and even Mark Twain. Surely their boredom is not the result of inexperience in the world. It is very likely the result of inexperience in literature. They do not know how to read, how to interpret the complex implications of language, imagery, character, and event. And because they cannot comprehend those implications, no empathy is possible and the work is boring to them.

It is too simple, too easy, to say that a student cannot comprehend a text or have empathy with it because he has had too little experience in his short life. The argument implies a lack of responsibility for teaching anything, as though birthdays were an index to the collection of appropriate experience. In hundreds of American schools, students are not regarded as ready for anything very "mature" at age fifteen. But at age sixteen they suddenly and miraculously come of age. They read *The Scarlet Letter,* or more accurately, their teachers assign it. If teaching literature were that simple, there would be no need for English teachers. The students could simply pick up a reading list at the beginning of the seventh grade and read the appropriate texts on their appropriate birthdays.

In reality, of course, most students who read *The Scarlet Letter* at age sixteen find it dull and irrelevant, and not because they have never been adulteresses. Although the school cannot promote experience in such matters, it can provide carefully planned experiences with literature that lead to the skills and concepts necessary to the full comprehension of great literary works, among them *The Scarlet Letter*.

Aesthetic Responses: Evaluation

Perhaps the most effective way to encourage aesthetic response is through the processes of evaluation. If literary evaluation is to be more than a statement of prejudice or preference, then evaluation is the most complex task that a teacher can require of his students. Evaluating a work subsumes all the skills that this chapter has attempted to describe. No wonder, then, that teachers are continually frustrated by book reports that state only that the reader has liked or disliked the book. Such statements, while valid as statements of preference, are not really evaluations. An evaluation must use criteria, or at least pretend to use them, as a basis for evaluation.

Sometimes, aesthetic judgments are made on the basis of preconceptions. The folly of such judgments is apparent from the results of neoclassical dramatic theory. Shakespeare's plays suffered major revisions at the hands of critics and directors who preferred that a play conform to the classical unities. Similarly, if critics were to accept Poe's theory of the short story as a basis for the judgment of non-Poe stories, a great many stories would be condemned. If a critic claims that a writer's irony is heavy-handed, the critic has some preconceived notion of what irony should be and condemns a writer whose notion of appropriate irony is not the same as his. It is like saying Turner's colors are too bright or Rembrandt's shadows are too heavy. Such decisions are matters of personal taste and difficult to defend or attack but frequently easy enough to rationalize.

Teachers are on safer grounds if they direct the attention of their students to evaluations on the basis of other criteria. Two approaches warrant concern: (1) the validity of literary statement, and (2) the artistic design of the work.

1. The validity of literary statement is the degree to which the concrete evidence of the text, whether realistic or fantastic, reveals or generates truth about the real world. For example, the language, characters, events, and design of George Orwell's *Animal Farm* work together very efficiently in depicting the deterioration, even perversion, of certain political and social ideals. And although the world of *Animal Farm* is a fantasy world in which animals think and talk like humans, it reflects considerable truth about the real world. The text corresponds hypothetically to the real world. If animals were endowed with rational abilities and if they should attempt to develop a socialistic farm, then the events that follow in Orwell's book would ensue in reality. Many popular songs, on the other hand, frequently rely on single lines for their emotional effects while the remaining words simply fill up the space. Consequently, most people can remember only a line or two of most popular lyrics. Neither the concrete text nor the derived generalizations have much correspondence to the real world. Their correspondence is usually to some imagined emotional state. The same is true of inferior poetry. It does not take a heap of living in a house to make it home, as Edgar Guest would have us believe. There are many houses in which marriage, childbearing, and death take place without their ever becoming very satisfactory homes. Edgar Guest's poem says, Wouldn't it be nice if . . .? His emotional content does not derive from concrete imagery but from standard connotative words that he can rely upon to arouse certain emotions. The patter of children's feet, the laughter of childish voices, the death of a beloved one—all these, in the popular imagination and Edgar Guest's, make a home. But to anyone who stops to think, to anyone who does not simply submerge himself in a Norman Rockwell vision of "home" at the instance of a word or two, the language does not create a concrete world within the poem that, in turn, generates truth about the real world. On the contrary, the language presents ready-made generalizations that bear little or no relationship to the real world.

The process of determining the degree of relationship between the hypothetical world of a literary work and the real world, then, is primarily an evaluative task. This kind of evaluation must be preceded by another task that the textbooks and reading experts sometimes call "application," a task that most sophisticated readers perform almost automatically and that teachers can impose to check comprehension: application of the work's theme to other situations. When teachers ask their students such questions as the following, they require application: "Can you think of any situations in real life like the one in this story? Have you ever seen people behave like this in real life?" Questions such as these are frequently an important aid to understanding. Their danger lies in the fact that they lead away from the text rather than to it, and classes may spend a disproportionate amount of time in recounting experiences that are only broadly similar. But as long as the experiences recounted are examined in light of the text, and as long as application leads back to evaluation of the text, the exercise is essentially literary.

2. The artistic design of the work involves the consistency, appropriateness, and efficiency of its various parts in accomplishing what the work set out to do. Therefore, an evaluation of artistic merit is inseparable from a rather careful analysis of the whole work. This is an important point for the teacher to bear in mind. As students evaluate a work, they must return again and again to the text for verification.

The task of evaluating the consistency, appropriateness, and efficiency of the parts or aspects of a work as they combine to accomplish its apparent purposes is not so abstruse as it sounds at first. Elementary school students can discuss intelligently the appropriateness or inappropriateness of Aesop's use of animals in particular fables. At a more advanced level, students can attempt to answer such questions as the following in relation to a story such as "An Ominous Baby": (1) To what degree is Crane's choice of words in the first paragraph effective in producing a favorable disposition on the part of the reader toward the tattered child? (2) To what extent is the eruption of a fight between the two children convincing—that is, has Crane prepared the reader adequately? Defend your answer. (3) In what way is the final line of the story (in particular the phrase "into a cavern") appropriate or inappropriate to the rest of the story? Questions 1 and 2 are much simpler to answer than the final question, simply because the last requires a rather thorough understanding of the story as a whole. The teacher must attempt to discriminate the easy questions from the difficult ones and design evaluation questions appropriate to the abilities of his students. If there is a wide range of abilities in a class, then the brightest students can deal with the most difficult problems. As the students become more and more able readers, they should become increasingly competent as evaluators of what they read.

Even if evaluation questions are carefully incorporated into every lesson, however, students may respond only in a superficial way. Many students, even those who are not very bright, can detect a teacher's attitude toward an assigned work. Many will assume that the teacher would not assign it if it were not good. Therefore, they voice an evaluation that they expect to be in agreement with the teacher's, or they make no comment at all. Any teacher who really wants his students to evaluate and not simply parrot back the teacher's ideas must remember two cardinal rules: (1) Never grimace at any negative evaluation from a student. (2) Never smile approvingly at positive evaluations when they are unaccompanied by a defense or explanation. Either reaction gives away the teacher's position. The teacher has already evaluated the work; it is only fair to give the students a chance. There is a third rule as well. When a student does make an attempt at an intelligent evaluation, accept it. Once when a group of seventh graders were deciding whether

Aesop used appropriate animals in his fables, a young man raised his hand, a somewhat wicked grin on his face. "Well," he said, "he used a fox in that fable, and, man, everybody knows that foxes don't eat grapes."

"That's a good point," his teacher said. "What should he have done instead?" The young man considered a moment.

"Well, he could'a used a different animal, maybe a bear, or he could'a used somethin' instead of grapes."

There are a number of ways to prevent evaluation from becoming a mechanical, superficial procedure. Among them are the following:

1. As a means of establishing criteria for evaluation, present two poems or stories involving similar content or theme but of fairly disparate literary value. No author's name should be revealed. Ask students to decide which is better and to explain why. An immature reader will tend to rate the more difficult work lower. Therefore, the works should be of approximately equal difficulty and within the comprehension of the students. Ninth, tenth, or eleventh graders will benefit from a comparative study and evaluation of works by the same author: Poe's "The Cask of Amontillado" and "The Premature Burial," for instance. Both stories deal with someone's being entombed alive. The first allows only a line or two for introduction before entering on the main action of the story, which presents all the horror one could wish for. The second begins with an extremely long passage in which Poe explains over and over the horror of premature burial, as though attempting to convince his reader. By the time the main action begins, the reader is bored. The difference between the two stories is glaring, but students beginning their careers as literary critics learn more from glaring differences that they can objectify than from subtle ones they cannot detect.

2. Every now and then bring a work of inferior quality into a unit. Most school anthologies can supply at least two or three. Let the students tear them up. They need to be convinced that at least sometimes a teacher will listen to their evaluations.

3. Ask the students to find stories to include in a unit of instruction. After the unit is under way, let them search through anthologies for stories and poems to use in a lesson of their planning. Require them to find several possibilities, to select two or three, and to defend their selections in terms of quality as well as appropriateness to the unit. For below-average groups it is best to suggest the possibilities and allow the students to make the selections. If the students actually teach the selections, their motivation will be that much higher.

4. Prepare with the students a unit dealing with fiction they enjoyed in the past. They will suggest such materials as the Hardy boys, *Hot Rod, Seventeen,* and *Sue Barton,* and many of the students will be able to bring such books to class. Let them study the books with a view to comparing

them, not to Shakespeare or Conrad, but to each other: the Hardy boys adventures series against *Hot Rod* and *Street Rod; Seventeen* against the Nancy Drew mysteries; or any of the lot against *The Light in the Forest, The Catcher in the Rye,* or some other relatively easy book of high quality. Although the comparison might begin with the expression of preferences, the teacher should use the preferences to establish criteria. Why do you prefer this book over that? Is it personal taste? (You don't like westerns, period.) Or is it the quality of the book? After studying the plot patterns, characterization, and style of their old favorites, students will enjoy writing parodies of them, and stories like the Hardy boys adventure series are relatively easy and certainly amusing to parody.

If a teacher allows, encourages, and approves evaluation, his students have a chance of learning how to evaluate. But a single year will not bring much sophistication. Evaluation must begin when readers are young. If they can understand what they read, they can evaluate it. The question about the appropriateness of the fox in Aesop's fable may not seem very sophisticated, but critics still argue the appropriateness of the final eleven chapters of *Huckleberry Finn.* The difference is only one of degree.

Throughout this chapter the problem of inference making has been prominent. And so it should be. But the English teacher must do more than teach his students how to make inferences. He must teach so that the student, through interaction with the curriculum, begins to understand the nature of literature. He must teach in a cumulative way so that the student becomes increasingly aware of what to expect of literature and what to look for. It is, after all, the knowledge of what to look for that provides the most pleasure to the reader and produces the best reader. Edgar Allen Poe once said of the good whist player what is also true of the good reader: "He makes, in silence, a host of observations and inferences. . . . the extent of the information obtained, lies not so much in the validity of the inference as in the quality of the observation. The necessary knowledge is that of *what* to observe."[12]

NOTES

1. Jeanne S. Chall, "Readability: An Appraisal of Research and Application," *Bureau of Educational Research Monographs,* No. 54. (Columbus: Ohio State University, 1958).
2. Rudolf Flesch, *The Art of Readable Writing* (New York: Harper, 1949).
3. For a discussion of some archetpyes, see Maud Bodkin, *Archetypal Patterns in Poetry* (New York: Vintage Books, 1958) and C. G. Jung, *Psyche and Symbol,* ed. Violet S. de Laszlo (New York: Anchor Books, 1958).
4. The problems of the author's voice and control of his material has been brilliantly discussed by Wayne C. Booth, *The Rhetoric of Fiction* (Chicago: University of Chicago Press, 1961).
5. John Steinbeck, *The Pearl* (New York: Bantam Books, 1956), pp. 1–2.

6. Charles Dickens, *Great Expectations* (Boston: Houghton-Mifflin, 1962), pp. 12–13.
7. Steinbeck, *op. cit.,* pp. 97–98.
8. For a more detailed analysis of this problem, see Northrop Frye, "Rhetorical Criticism: Theory of Genres" in *The Anatomy of Criticism* (Princeton: Princeton University Press, 1957).
9. For a complete discussion of the oral technique and oral formulaic patterns, see Albert B. Lord, *The Singer of Tales* (Cambridge: Harvard University Press, 1960).
10. For a further commentary on this idea of *theme,* see Northrop Frye, "Literary Criticism," in *The Aims and Methods of Scholarship in Modern Languages and Literature,* ed. James Thorpe (New York: Modern Language Association of America, 1963).
11. Gilbert Highet, *The Anatomy of Satire* (Princeton: Princeton University Press, 1961), p. 13.
12. Edgar Allan Poe, *Great Tales and Poems of* (New York: Washington Square Press, 1960), p. 104.

SUGGESTIONS FOR FURTHER READING

1. EDMUND REISS, *Elements of Literary Analysis.* New York: World Publishing Company, 1967.
2. I. A. RICHARDS, *Practical Criticism.* New York: Harcourt, Brace, and Company, 1929.
3. NORTHROP FRYE, *The Well-Tempered Critic.* Bloomington: Indiana University Press, 1963.
4. RENÉ WELLEK AND AUSTIN WARREN, *Theory of Literature.* New York: Harcourt, Brace and Company, 1942.
5. ALAN C. PURVES, *The Elements of Writing about Reading: Research Report #9.* Champaign: National Council of Teachers of English, 1968.

11 | The Reading Comprehension Inventory

Once the teacher understands what the reading of literature involves, he is ready to plan an instructional unit for a specific group of students. His first step in planning is to determine, through the use of a reading comprehension inventory, the literary experience of his students as reflected in their responses to a text that is new to them. He needs to know the sorts of meanings they can and cannot deal with. The reading comprehension inventory is simply a short story, essay, poem, or drama with a series of questions, each of which illustrates one aspect of reading comprehension.

The unsophisticated person tends to regard reading in holistic terms: A person simply picks up some reading matter and reads it. This is far from the best instructional thinking, however. Various kinds of reading require various kinds of skills. Our attention in the reading inventories centers on study-type reading rather than leisure reading. The reading *matter* under consideration is the shorter prose piece, such as short stories and essays. The short-story will be discussed in this chapter.

The main considerations in developing reading inventories are the components of reading difficulty. There are four components to consider: (1) the readability of the selection, (2) its length, (3) the instructional context in which the reading is done, and (4) the purpose(s) of the reader in reading.

It is intuitively obvious that some reading matter is "easier" than other material. A popular mystery novel, for example, is less challenging than *Paradise Lost*. The preceding chapter dealt in detail with the elements of reading that make one text more difficult than another, elements that range from vocabulary and syntax to the interpretation of a text in the light of its various contexts.

All other things being equal, simple length is a measure of reading difficulty, for it is easier to read ten pages than it is to read one hundred. The principle reasons for the difference are the inherent fatigue associated with the longer task and the difficulty in grasping the greater number of interrelationships it presents.

The third consideration is the general instructional context. For example, only one element in this context is the background of the student. Consider two undergraduate students doing outside reading in an advanced course in philosophy, one an English major, the other a philosophy major. The philosophy student handles the reading in a routine way, whereas the poor English student plods through with copious note-taking and rereading. Obviously, the general background, previous course work, interests, previous reading, buzz sessions with his peers, and the like, are of great advantage to the philosophy student, although both students may possess equivalent "native" ability at reading. The general instructional context in which one student finds himself cannot be equated with that of the other. Many elements are present in any instructional context—in addition to individuals' backgrounds.

The final consideration is that of purpose. For example, suppose a teacher in the primary grades is trying to decide which of two trade books is the more appropriate for second grade supplementary reading and which is the more appropriate for third grade. Obviously, measured readability presents no difficulty to her own reading of the two books; and if they are of about the same length, this consideration will not impede her. But think of the highly complex nature of the inferences she will be drawing about things like measured readability, vocabulary load, life experiences of the intended readers, sequential appropriateness, the relation of these books to others the children will read, and the like. Because of her purpose in reading, this college graduate literally spends hours reading and rereading little, second-grade books.

Let us now consider the role of each of these aspects of difficulty in developing the inventory, which is based on four short stories chosen from one of the anthologies used in class. The selections are as nearly similar in length as possible, and they contain some common thematic element or elements.

1. MEASURED READABILITY If there is a choice of anthologies available for use in class, select the easiest one from which to develop the inventory. If only one anthology is available, select the easiest stories in it. The emphasis is on materials of easy readability for rather negative reasons. If the inventory uses difficult stories and pupils show weak performance, the teacher gains no real insight because difficult materials predict weak performance. Additionally, the general structure of curriculum content logically moves from easy to difficult in any experiential sequence. The new teacher can ask reading specialists, librarians, or teachers experienced in using the materials about their difficulty. If these sources are unavailable or seem unreliable, the teacher has recourse to the reading formulas. Probably, a concert of these authorities will prove most reliable in selecting stories.

Many contemporary anthologies group their contents thematically into units. But beware of one pitfall in selecting stories: It is often the case that the anthology editor will not have considered the relative difficulty of the stories in terms of readability in sequencing the materials. Because a story appears early in a book is no guarantee that it is easier than (or as easy as) one appearing later. In fact, because a story appears in a seventh-grade anthology, it cannot be assumed that the story is easier reading than one in a "later" anthology. (Case in point: *Split Cherry Tree* by Jesse Stuart appears in different anthologies intended for seventh, ninth, and eleventh graders.)

2. LENGTH OF SELECTIONS In choosing shorter selections, the most pertinent referent for the "length" consideration is the amount of time the students will need to read it. Ordinarily, one finds a variety of reading rates in a given class. But a safe, general, rule-of-thumb estimate for secondary school readers is 300 words per minute (not a high rate, to be sure).

Most teachers (and many schools), as a matter of policy, assume a certain time period as "reasonable" for outside, homework assignments—about thirty minutes per course, per student. Again, most teachers assign reading on the basis of some "complete" unit of work, such as one story for overnight reading. Unfortunately, few teachers check to see if the students can actually read a fifteen-page short story within the "reasonable" amount of time. Having the students read a "typical" story drawn from the anthology *in class* under the teacher's supervision is a check on how well the reading rates of the students working on his materials match his notion of the amount of time needed.

3. INSTRUCTIONAL CONTEXT Often, the learnings derived from a reading assignment are not gained from the reading experience *alone*. Preparations and discussions of various kinds occur in addition to the reading; and it is from the total of these experiences that the learnings develop. Let us postulate four different general patterns of reading lessons: the unsupported reading assignment; the reading assignment with specific preparation; reading with preparation, followed by a teacher-led discussion; and reading with preparation followed by small-group discussion and a summary, teacher-led discussion. This sequence is designed to move from a context in which maximum responsibility rests on the student to a context in which maximum support is provided. In addition to the supports that are manifest in the contexts described, there is the latent support of the thematic relatedness of the stories: Sequential experiences with thematically similar material should tend to support one another.

4. READING PURPOSES Reading purposes can be rather closely specified in terms of the kinds of questions about the reading that students are expected to answer when they have completed an assignment (assignment here meaning the reading in its complete instructional context).

The questions on the inventory should be in an order ranging from easy to difficult (as they should on any evaluation instrument). The reasons for this scheduling relate to the student's attitudes toward the test. If he encounters a difficult question early in the sequence, the difficulties he has with it are likely to color his responses on easier items that he encounters later, thus biasing the results and tending to invalidate the instrument. For example, he may use too much time on an early item and not have ample time for later ones. He may "get stuck" on an early item and not answer later (and easier) ones at all. He may, because he experiences difficulty, lose confidence in himself and become otherwise "rattled," lowering his general performance. Scheduling items from easy to hard helps to diminish the probability of this kind of blocking and to provide some support. In addition, such structuring simplifies the interpretation of results.

What is the general rationale for developing questions in terms of difficulty? Generally, those that require responses based on specific statements contained in the reading material are easier than questions involving inferences. The further an inference is from the literal content, the more difficult is the question involving the inference. Thus, a question about the author's presumed purpose (not directly expressed in the reading) is more difficult than one about the probable reasons for a character's behavior (implied in the behavior); and this kind of question is more difficult than one requesting information on some physical characteristic of the character (as specifically described in the reading).

The questions in the inventory that follows are based on Jack London's story "To Build a Fire." They are scheduled from easy to difficult.

1. What is the setting of this story?
2. What kind of matches did the man use?
3. What made the springs dangerous to the man?
4. How did he know it was colder than fifty below zero?
5. When he stopped for lunch, what part of his journey lay before him, if his start were at the beginning of the story?
6. Why was he glad to feel pain in his fingers when he struck them?
7. What is the turning point of the story? Support your answer.
8. Jack London suggests that both men and animals have certain characteristics and capabilities that help them deal with unfriendly elements in the universe. Give evidence that he believes one of these (name which one) is superior in this respect.
9. Name another piece of literature in which a person or group is brought into conflict with his physical environment. What is the *significance* of the outcome of the conflict in the other story as compared with "To Build a Fire"?
10. In the first parts of the story, the man makes some assumptions about self-sufficiency that are in opposition to the evidence of the experience of others. Show how what befell the man in this respect is consistent

(or inconsistent) with the true-life experience of someone known to you (including yourself).

Analysis of the Questions

1. "What is the setting of this story?" *Basic Stated Information:* A question getting at basic information in a story is one whose answer the teacher feels is so absolutely apparent and obvious that no one could possibly miss it. Ordinarily, in constructing evaluation instruments, many teachers would not even consider including questions of this kind ("They're *too* easy!"). Consider, then, the implications involved if a pupil misses this kind of question (see *Interpretation,* below). Another question of the same type might be: "What was the weather like that day?"

2. "What kind of matches did the man use?" *Key Detail:* Many teachers in constructing evaluation instruments use a preponderance of questions that require recall of details. Unfortunately, in many instances, their questions request information about relatively unimportant details. The importance of the information requested in this question resides in the fact that because of the fumes given off by the *sulphur matches,* the man cannot light a match with his teeth, thus apparently sealing his doom. Compare this *key* detail with another related one: "How many matches were in the bundle he dropped?" The answer (seventy-five) is irrelevant to the action, and thus is not worth eliciting. One supposes that the reason for the inclusion of questions requiring knowledge of inconsequential details on many teacher-made tests is explained by the desire to find questions with high discriminatory power. Since unimportant details *are* unimportant, they are readily overlooked or forgotten by readers; hence, questions involving them do tend to discriminate. Surely, there are better ways to develop questions of discriminating power.

   Another question of the same type might be, "What kind of weapon did the man carry?"

3. "What made the springs dangerous to the man?" *Expressed Relationships:* This type of question is intended to get at the relationships (particularly as found among the details) expressed in the reading. The previous question (2, above) gets at details *independently perceived.* There are many kinds of relationships open to questioning: time, spatial, size, family, cause/effect, sequential, and so on. Often, relationship questions are cued by words such as "when," "where," "how many," "how often." Care must be taken, at this point, that the answer to the question is explicitly stated in the reading. (See 5, below.) This question deals with the relationship between the man and

a specific aspect of his environment. The springs represent a danger because they are covered by "ice skin" and snow and because they can cause the man to get wet (as they do). Getting wet in such extreme cold results in freezing. Since all this can be regarded as part of the answer, the teacher must decide in advance how much constitutes a "complete" answer. Part of the discussion following the inventory should attempt to establish answer patterns so that students learn how much to include. Note, however, that no inference is necessary to produce any part of the answer. It is all stated explicitly in the text.

4. "How did he know it was colder than fifty below zero?" *Expressed Inference:* An expressed inference is one made by a character (or by the voice of the author) that is explicitly explained to the reader. The process involves noting details (as in question 2), understanding the relationships involved in these (as in 3), and drawing conclusions based on these understandings. (Sherlock Holmes often illuminates this process for Dr. Watson in the stories of Conan Doyle.) Again, care must be exercised so that the question elicits a response that is explicit in the reading. It is possible that a character may make an erroneous inference. The correctness of the inference has no bearing on the fact that the process *is* inference. For example, toward the end of the story the man infers that he can run along the trail and make it to camp or restore his circulation, or both. This proves to be incorrect; but it *is* an inference. "Why" is often a cue to inference questions. Almost always, the response to such a question includes two parts: the premise(s) and the conclusion(s). Thus, the answer to this question will be something like (premises), "The spittle froze in the air. At fifty below spittle freezes on the ground." (conclusion) "So it must be colder than fifty below for the spittle to freeze in the air." Another question of the same type might be, "Why couldn't the man kill the dog, once he had caught him?"

5. "When he stopped for lunch, what part of his journey lay before him, if his start were at the beginning of the story?" *Implied Relationships:* The background for this question is essentially the same as in question 3 above, except that the relationships have *not* been made explicit by the author. The relationships are implicit in the information in the reading. Doubtless, inferential thinking is required of the responder, but premises are spelled out for him, and his job is to relate them adequately. Some such answer as "two-thirds" is appropriate. The answer is short, but the mechanism required in arriving at it makes for the difficulty. Another question of the same type might be, "How did the man's attitude toward the dog change during the course of the story?" or "The man's attitude toward the old timer's advice changes at least three times in the story. Explain the reasons for one of the changes."

6. "Why was he glad to feel pain in his fingers when he struck them?" *Reader Inference:* The general background for this question is essentially the same as in question 4 above, except that the inference pattern has not been explicated by the author. Sometimes the reader will have to refer to experiences outside the story (such as his direct life experiences) in order to complete the inference procedures. The answer to this question should be something like this: "When his fingers were without feeling, he knew they were freezing. When he felt pain, he felt *something,* so the freezing was stopping, so he was glad." Another question of the same kind is, "Why didn't the man cast a shadow at noon under a cloudless sky?"

7. "What is the turning point of the story? Support your answer." *Structural Generalization:* This question requires a response to the reading as a whole rather than to discrete elements within it. Although question 1, above, does the same, the kind of response required in that instance is not nearly so sophisticated. "Basic stated information" is hammered at the reader over and over throughout the story. A question requiring a structural generalization requires a pattern analysis of the work that depends on perception of story patterns in general. Such a response usually requires experience with other works of the same type.

It may also imply experience with a certain kind of instruction. Since this inventory is not intended as a survey of previous instructional experience (such as is the case with the content inventory), care must be taken in wording the question so that its terms do not block responses. For example, had this question been phrased, "What is the *climax* of the story?" the student would have to understand the technical term "climax" in order to respond. On the basis of intuitive power combined with critical analysis, he might be able to specify the climax in this plot without having the conventional term for it in his vocabulary. Such power is what this type of question is designed to assess. Even the term "turning point" may need some explanation by the teacher, especially in lower grades; but this term has the advantage (in this instance it *is* an advantage) that it is not technical.

Many times conventional critical concepts do not apply to a particular work of art in a way that is so ideally specific as to obviate alternative discussions. Such is true in this case. Does the turning point of this story occur when the protagonist decides to travel alone (that action taking place even before the story begins); when he decides to follow the creek bed; when he falls through the ice; when he builds the fire beneath the tree; when the fire is blotted out; or at some other point? Hence, the response requires not only the naming of "the point" but also some support for selecting that point.

Another question of the same kind is: "The author prepares the reader in a number of ways for what happens at the end of the story.

Name one comment or event at the beginning of the story and explain how it prepares for the ending."

8. "Jack London suggests that both men and animals have certain characteristics and capabilities that help them to deal with unfriendly elements in the universe. Give evidence that he believes one of these (name which one) is superior in this respect." *Author's Generalizations:* This question looks at a philosophical generalization of some kind made by the author. A worthwhile work of literature will be, in one aspect, an exemplification of one or more philosophical generalizations made by the author. The reader may or may not agree with the generalization, but he will have to be aware of it and aware that it represents the view of the author (rather than of a character) before he can objectify his agreement or disagreement. Accordingly, this question is intended to get at the author through his work.

One weakness in the question presented here is that the particular philosophical generalization is presented to the student. However, a question asking the student to *form* such a generalization himself is likely to result in a statement so ambiguous that it cannot be evaluated readily ("Life can be hard at times," for example). This wider type of question might prove valuable, however, in the case of advanced students in advanced grades if the teacher knows for certain that they have had the appropriate instructional experience previously.

The question as it is phrased presents enough difficulties, however. The student must decide which of the two indicated views is the one entertained by London. Then he must ascertain which elements in the story have led him to his decision.

Another question of the same type, which is somewhat more difficult because of its symbolic nature, is "What, if anything, does London's referral to the central figure as 'the man' and to the dog as 'the dog' (not naming either) indicate about London's use of these figures to represent all mankind and all animals? Support your answer."

9. "Name another piece of literature in which a person or group is brought into conflict with the natural environment. What is the *significance* of the outcome of the conflict in the other story as compared with 'To Build a Fire'?" *Relating Reading to Other Reading Experiences:* This is the first question that requires the reader to go completely outside his experience with the story in question. He is asked to make the same kinds of formulations as in question 8 with respect to another, thematically similar work in his previous literary experience and then compare this analysis to that of "To Build a Fire." His response can break down anywhere along the line.

The key word for the teacher in evaluating the response here is *significance*. The student is likely simply to compare outcomes. Of principal concern, however, is what generalizations the authors are implying rather than how the action mechanically works itself out. The teacher must be sure that the students focus on the appropriate aspect of the question. It will probably be necessary to comment to the class on the question. Such comment does not invalidate the question since explaining the focus gives very little assistance in performing the mental operations required in the response.

Another question of the same kind: Name another piece of literature in which the central figure succeeds in overcoming environmental obstacles. What are the basic elements that are different in the situation of that story and "To Build a Fire"?

10. "In the first parts of the story, the man makes some assumptions about self-sufficiency that are in opposition to the evidence of the experience of others: For example, the old timer from Sulphur Creek tells him that it is dangerous to travel alone in extreme cold. Yet the man assumes that he can. Show how what befell the man in this respect is consistent (or inconsistent) with the true-life experience of someone known to you (including yourself)." *Application to Life Experiences:* The kind of thinking required to answer this type of question is somewhat similar to that required to answer question 9, in that direct life experience is substituted for the vicarious experience of reading. A major difference is that the reader must make a judgment concerning the consistency of the story material with real life. The most profound block to responding will relate to the relative inexperience of the student or his lack of sophistication in analyzing his experiences, or both. One intent of the question is to illuminate a potential value of reading—that of gaining insight into one's own life. In addition, as explained in the previous chapter under "Aesthetic Responses: Evaluation," this type of question is the first step in evaluating the validity of literary statement.

Frequently, teachers, in attempting to construct questions of this kind, neglect the evaluative aspects of the question and develop questions of a superficial nature. "Have you ever been in serious difficulty like this man? What did you do?" The failure of the question results *not* from any lack of importance of the life experience of the responder, but rather from the failure to suggest a suitable analogous case in literature together with the pertinent generalization. The example above might just as well read: "What did you do in some situation that was very serious?" Thus, the response requires no reference to reading experience of any kind.

As in question 8, an inherent weakness in the formulation of question 10 is that of cuing the generalization. The same qualifying remarks apply here.

Another question of the same type: "Later in the story the man makes assumptions about what his danger would be if he had human companionship. Cite some comparable life situation known to you in which what happened to *groups* of people supports (or refutes) the man's assumptions."

Many teachers intuitively regard questions of the type exemplified by questions 8, 9, and 10 as "thought" questions. In planning and scoring their routine tests, they are prepared to give full credit to *any* reasonable answer and are chagrined when students write no response whatever, thus depriving themselves of "free" credit. Hopefully, the analysis suggested for these inventory items sheds some light on this apparently cavalier behavior of students.

The Items in Summary

The items on this reading comprehension inventory are very easy at the beginning and much more difficult at the end, the question's relative difficulty being determined by its reference to explicit statements in the reading, whether the reader responds to a part of the reading or the piece as a whole, the structure of the response, the kind of thinking that leads to making the response, and the character of the reader's previous experiences. The question types can be generalized following Figure 11.1.

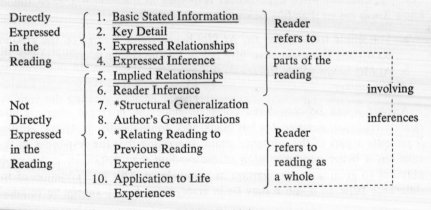

FIGURE 11.1

Underlined items mean the answer has one part (other items usually require answers of more than one part).

Starred items mean the answering requires certain kinds of experience previous to reading (other items can be handled with reference to this experience alone).

This inventory structure is intended for use in a relatively heterogeneous class, and it supposes that the teacher is interested in a general survey of reading comprehension. There are no questions testing the reader's ability to deal with connotative language, metaphor, imagery, symbolism, and the like. Such items might require a different reading passage; "An Ominous Baby" discussed in Chapter 9 is highly susceptible to questions of this type. Moreover, no question requires the student to evaluate the internal consistency of the story or to rate it against other literary works.* (Questions dealing with some aspects of evaluation were, however, suggested in the preceding chapter.) Nor are there questions testing the ability to handle vocabulary. Changes must be made if the principal interest in a given class is not prose fiction but some other form, say, critical essays or poetry. Individual teachers may note deficiencies of other kinds in thinking of their particular informational needs. However, the general principle enunciated in developing items of relative difficulty (directly expressed information vs. implied information, and so on) and, in general, structuring from easy to more difficult items is useful.

Scoring the Responses

As opposed to the procedures of most standardized tests, it behooves the teacher to treat responses in terms of degree of correctness rather than in an absolute way—that is, either all right or all wrong. For example, consider three hypothetical responses to question 4 ("How did he know it was colder than fifty below?")

a. The spittle froze in the air. At fifty below spittle freezes on the ground. So it must be colder than fifty below for the spittle to freeze in the air.
b. At fifty below spittle freezes on the ground.
c. No answer.

Answer *a* can be considered complete since the inference chain is adequately reported. Answer *c* is left blank and, consequently, is wrong. Answer *b* presents a part of the inference chain, suggesting that the responder in this case has a better comprehension of the reading than responder *c* but probably not so good a comprehension as responder *a*. This interpretation of the difference between *a* and *b* may be in error, since *b* may simply be respond-

---

* Questions asking students to rate literature are generally more difficult than any on this model. Rating requires the reader not only to go outside a particular piece of writing for purposes of comparison but also to develop a systematic rating system of some kind based upon his experiences and to place the work in question on that rating scale. As Northrop Frye and others have pointed out, such criticism, even among responsible critics, is usually dependent upon the prevailing tastes of the age. Frequently, questions that require attempts to rate literature are irrelevant and inconsequential. Is Pope's "Rape of the Lock" a better poem than Milton's *Paradise Lost?* The question is irrelevant because the poems do entirely different things. When an item involving comparative merit is relevant, the task is extremely complex: For example, consider *Macbeth* and *Othello* in terms of poetic language and explain which is the stronger.

ing inadequately and may have understood the reading completely. (Hence, the inventory involves experiences with more than one story, allowing the teacher, in the interim between reading experiences, to discuss response patterns. See "Inventory Procedures," below.) In scoring responses, however, the teacher must score the response given and not infer the responder's probable knowledge that led to only a partially adequate answer.

Let us now consider a fourth hypothetical response:

d. The dog was trying to tell him that it was too cold to be out, and if he paid better attention to the dog's behavior, he would know that it was colder than fifty below, a "safe" temperature.

In terms of the question "How did the man know?" this response is inadequate. The responder is answering a question not asked, although the general pattern of his response is acceptable. He may, however, be coming closer to the mark than is *c* who could not answer at all. Since one of the controlling aspects of reading difficulty is purpose, and since in this inventory purpose is controlled by question type, let us consider the "wrong" responses, *c* and *d,* in terms of the probable psychology governing the responses.

Either something in the phrasing of Item 4, or the reading purpose itself, or the readability of the story (or perhaps the readability of the item, though this seems unlikely) has completely blocked *c.* The block is so profound that he cannot offer any answer. On the other hand *d,* although blocked, is not so completely blocked as *c,* since he is able to respond in some way.

Therefore, the four types of response may be ranked:

a = correct
b = partially correct
d = incorrect
c = no answer

In scoring the responses, therefore, a marking system that accounts for this kind of variation in responding (and the teacher's interpretation of the responses) is employed:

$$correct = +$$
$$partially\ correct = \sqrt{}$$
$$incorrect = -$$
$$no\ answer = 0$$

To an extent, the scoring will rest on the subjective judgments of the teacher. But the judgments used in scoring the inventory should reflect the judgments that the teacher will use in his marking throughout the year and thus have a high degree of validity to him, although perhaps other teachers might score the results somewhat differently. The teacher who develops and scores the inventory will be thinking of the kinds of things he will be doing and not doing in his class as suggested by the inventory results and his interpretation of the results.

Needless to say, the scoring procedure is complex. Therefore, a practice that many teachers follow in dealing with tests is categorically *ruled out:* that of having students correct one another's papers. In other situations this practice can be considered useful, in every way quite legitimate, even indicated as being generally beneficial to learning. But in this case, the scoring is so delicate and of such great import that the teacher must do it all.

Inventory Procedures

The inventory is administered in four stages. A story is read in class as the central activity in each stage. As noted above, all four stories should approximate each other in terms of measured readability and length. The length should be such that students can finish the reading within a single class period, reading at a rate of about 300 words a minute.

STAGE 1 Explain the purpose of the inventory, and then assign the reading of the first story. While the class is reading, circulate among the students and notice gross indications of frustration such as lip movements (mouthing of words), finger pointing, extreme lag (some readers getting pages behind), distractions from the reading (gazing about the room, out the window, and so on). Note these symptoms on the seating plan (or some convenient place —remember you will not know students' names early in the year) by making check marks (or some convenient symbols). After the predetermined number of minutes has elapsed (calculated by dividing the approximate number of words by 300), ask how many have finished. If a number have not finished, extend the reading period. After that, have class close books. Administer first set of questions. The questions may be administered orally or in duplicated form, but for general efficiency the latter practice is recommended, although this intensifies the general difficulty of the entire reading experience. The first question, however, *is* asked orally: "Did you finish?" The students write "yes" or "no." If they question the items and the difficulty appears to lie in an unintended ambiguity in the expression of the question, clear the matter up. When the students have finished, collect the papers. It is a good idea to have supplementary reading available for fast workers. Leisure reading in the anthology will suffice for this purpose, provided the class is warned off other stories that will be used in the inventory.

If time permits, lead a discussion based on the inventory questions. If not, have the discussion at the beginning of the next meeting. In addition to the obvious pedagogical reasons for going over the questions in this way, it will help to discharge the anxiety and hostility that are involved in any testing situation. During the discussion, get into the problem of appropriate patterns in responses (as discussed in connection with Item 4 and others above in this text).

STAGE 2 Before in-class reading begins, supply students with inventory questions for the day's story, which more clearly specify their purpose in reading. Go over the questions to clear up unintended ambiguities. Review the discussion on response patterns. Then proceed as in Stage 1.

STAGE 3 Initial procedures are followed as in Stage 2. When the class has finished reading, have them leave the books open for reference. Conduct a teacher-led discussion using the inventory questions. When the discussion is completed, the books are closed, and the class writes the responses, as in Stage 1. The same procedures are used in completing the activity.

STAGE 4 Initial procedures are followed as in Stage 2. When the class has finished the reading, divide it into small groups for discussion (see Chapter 3 on "Grouping for Instruction"). The groups will base their discussions on the questions in the inventory. When group discussions are completed, return to a teacher-led discussion with the whole class, summarizing the small-group discussions. When the teacher-led discussion is finished, proceed as in Stage 1, completing all activities.

Score the papers from each stage as they are returned.

Interpreting the Inventory Results

As indicated earlier, some teacher interpretation is involved in the scoring procedure itself. Beyond this, a more systematic and thoroughgoing interpretation is mandatory. The teacher will want to know how each pupil responds to each type of question and how the response is conditioned by the instructional context. In addition, he will want an overview of class performance in these respects. A two-dimensional charting device on which class results are recorded is useful in developing these interpretations and others. A page in the gradebook can be devoted to such a chart (as well as other inventory data), which should look like the one shown in Figure 11.2. Reference to the chart provides a quick, graphic way of assessing individual and class performance.

RATE A low rate was used in the original timing for the reading, and easy reading material was chosen. Therefore, pupils who consistently do not finish the reading have a reading rate that is below normal for their age group. There are many reasons for slow reading rates. The immediate things to check are symptomatic evidence of frustration and the character of responses on the

FIGURE 11.2

Names	Symptoms	Item 1 phases				Item 2 phases				Item 3 phases				Item etc.	Item 10 phases				Totals				Notes
		1	2	3	4	1	2	3	4	1	2	3	4		1	2	3	4	1	2	3	4	
Adams, J.		+	+	+	+	✓	+	+	+	✓	✓	+	+						7	8	9	9	
Brown, C.		+	+	+	+	+	+	+	+	+	+	+	+						9	10	10	10	leader?
Deleone, P.		+	+	+	+	+	+	+	+	✓	✓	✓	+						7	7	8	8	
Kauffman, B.	✓	-	-	+	+	0	0	+	+	0	-	-	✓						1	2	5	5	check records now
Etc.																							

Beginning at the left, and reading from left to right, the chart is constructed and utilized as follows:

first column: Students' names.
second column: Observations of gross symptoms of reading frustration.
next ten columns: Record of responses to items; each of these ten columns is subdivided into four columns, one for each phase of the inventory; scores (+, ✓, —, 0) indicate type of response in appropriate phase.
next to last column: Subdivided into four columns for approximate "total score."
last column: For any notes.

early items in the inventory. If weak performance is noted here, the slow rate is part of a complex of behaviors indicating that this reading is too difficult for the reader. If no gross evidence of frustration is noted and the responses are good, the readability of the material is probably not beyond the power of the student. Probably he should be involved in a program designed to increase his rate in a mechanical way. If this is the case, the teacher should seek consultation with a reading specialist for help in developing the program.

Interpreting Responses to Specific Items

ITEMS 1 AND 2   These questions should be answered correctly and completely—at the very least from Stage 2 throughout. If this is not the case, the reading is unquestionably too difficult for the reader. Consequently, the year's work for such pupils will have to be done with materials of easier readability, at least until such time as the pupils demonstrate enough improvement in power to handle the regular class work. Very likely, the teacher will have checked these names as evincing gross symptoms of reading frustration. If possible, he should consult with a reading specialist for techniques to use in working with these pupils. In the abence of a reading specialist, advice may be sought from elementary school principals or skilled teachers in the elementary schools.

ITEMS 3 AND 4 Pupils whose scores show check marks and worse on these questions (while showing plus marks on questions 1 and 2) as a consistent pattern should be regarded as weak normal readers at best and perhaps in need of remediation. Look for evidence of gross symptoms of frustration, and seek consultation with the reading specialist or other appropriate personnel. It is conceivable that these students are simply intellectually incapable of going beyond reading for main ideas and details but have no actual mechanical difficulty with reading. It is also possible that they can learn the more sophisticated reading tasks. Only the teacher's carefully evaluated subsequent experience with these pupils can indicate which of these possibilities is realizable.

ITEMS 5 AND 6 For most students, questions 5 and 6, will be the ones on on which plus marks disappear, at least in Stages 1 and 2. Normal readers should achieve at least partial answers to these questions in Stages 3 and 4 (after discussion).

ITEMS 7 THROUGH 10 To a great extent, success on these items in Stages 1 and 2 will be determined by previous instructional experiences. If pupils are accustomed to handling reading in the manner suggested by the questions, blocking should be minimized. Students who fail these items in the early stages of the inventory and show some success in later stages are displaying readiness for the kind of instruction implied in the items. If no improvement is evident in later stages, written responses to literature should be limited to the kind of classroom experiences indicated by earlier items on the inventory.

Generally, plus marks should characterize early questions. These should fade to check marks in the middle items. Minus signs and zeros will probably appear in later items. If the general response pattern supports this prediction, the teacher should feel quite comfortable with his inventory in terms of validity. Should some particular question elicit a surprising general response in either direction (responses that seem relatively too strong or too weak), it should probably be revised before it is used in another year.

From stage to stage, class responses should improve. In the final stage they should be markedly better than in Stage 1. Should responses for the class be very strong (nearly all plus or check) in an early stage, there is no need to go through all of the inventory. Furthermore, such response patterns will indicate that group discussion and teacher-led discussion during the year should deal with something other than review of reading for the purpose of strengthening comprehension.

Should a particular student (or group) show strong responses in an early phase, his papers in the later phase need receive only perfunctory attention in scoring, thus effecting some saving of time and energy.

Implications for Planning Instruction

Characteristic responses will change from one type of item to another. The area in which checks begin to predominate indicates the kinds of questions that should be used as study guide questions for reading assignments. Wherever minus signs and zeros begin to predominate, the indication is that teacher instruction and class discussions should focus here. Areas characterized by nothing but minus signs and zeros suggest that involvement in this kind of reading problem is best delayed until the less difficult skills are more nearly mastered.

In addition, the results of the general reading comprehension inventory suggest the kind and focus of instructional units that will be most beneficial to the class as a whole. For instance, a class whose responses are weak on Items 2, 3, and 4 should probably work on a unit that focuses on the literal level of the materials but involves some simpler inferences as well. A unit suggested by the central conflict of "To Build a Fire" might be appropriate: "Man Against Nature." Such a unit would involve materials whose meanings were primarily literal. At the same time, however, the teacher-led discussions and the small-group discussions might well deal with questions aimed at implied relationships, reader inferences, simple structural generalizations, and generalizations made by the author (question types 5, 6, 7, and 8). The kind of unit proposed in the chapters that follow will involve a comparison of literary materials (question type 9) as well as the application of reading experiences to life (type 10). Such questions, however, should remain simple for weaker students, and the teacher should be careful not to lose sight of the text at hand in discussing previous reading or life experiences.

If the students do well on the first four types of questions and reasonably well on types 5 and 6, they can probably do considerable work involving inference and should deal with units of work, materials, and questions that require inferences involving connotation, figurative language, structure, the relationship of structure and theme, and other aspects of literary meaning discussed in the previous chapter.

The reading comprehension inventory, then, is an extremely important device for beginning the year's work. It will give the students immediate practice in some of the activities important to that work; and it will offer relatively successful experience in the later stages. Most important, however, it will provide a sound estimate of the general literary experience and skill of the class as a whole and will identify students who need special correctional help as well as those who read fluently. In short, it provides a basis for planning the year's work in literature.

SUGGESTIONS FOR FURTHER READING

1. BENJAMIN S. BLOOM, ed. *Taxonomy of Educational Objectives: Cognitive Domain* (New York: David McKay Co., 1956).
2. NORRIS M. SANDERS, *Classroom Questions: What Kinds?* (New York: Harper & Row, 1966).

12 | Designing the Literature Unit: I. Preliminary Planning

One of the most important things that any literature unit can do is to provide a conceptual matrix against which the student can examine each new work he reads. Insights into any given work are partly the result of experience in reading others because concepts grow by comparison and contrast. In defining even simple objects, knowing what the object is *not* is as important as knowing what it *is*. A rubber mallet is like a claw hammer in some ways but unlike it in others. When a child begins to learn what an apple is, he sees it as a red, more or less spherical piece of fruit. If he should see an orange or a tomato, he is very likely to call it an apple. On the other hand, if he should see a yellow or green apple, he may not call it an apple. But as he comes into contact with more and more apples, oranges, and tomatoes, he will become increasingly adept at discriminating among them, regardless of variations in color, size, or shape.

A similar process takes place in reading literature. If a student is confronted with a series of related literary situations that require similar (but not the same) inferences, he will learn what to observe and how to make the necessary inferences. If he reads only one satiric work, however, he has no basis for comparison and contrast, with the result that his concept of satire will be severely limited. Like the child who has seen only one apple, he will probably not be able to interpret another satire adequately, if at all. If he reads several, he learns what to expect, what to look for, and how to make the inferences. Similarly, if the student has practice in observing the actions and in inferring the traits of a spectrum of characters from the courageous to the foolhardy, he will make such inferences more completely afterward.

The province of the unit, then, is to arrange materials and the examination of them in such a way that the student accumulates the background necessary for knowing what and how to observe and for making appropriate inferences. If the unit is to develop the student's power to read literature, planning must be very careful. First, a unit's content depends upon the teacher's analysis of both the literature and the abilities of the students. In regard to the unit on satire, which will be used as an example throughout this chapter, the teacher must know what satire is and how it works. At the same time, he must determine what the abilities of his students are and plan the unit content in terms of those abilities. The arbitrary, conservative arrangement of materials by type, chronology, or author will not suffice because it ignores both the student and the skills and knowledge required to read literature. Nor is the broad topical unit of the progressive school designed to teach literature. As we have seen, it uses literature to teach something else.

Second, the teacher must set down the objectives and criteria for student performance so that he knows as precisely as possible what he expects his students to do and know at a minimum by the end of the unit. If he does not work out his goals in advance, he runs a risk, in the first place, of teaching nothing and, in the second place, of being unable to evaluate it if he does teach something.

Third, the materials should be so arranged that the reading of each one contributes in specific ways to the reading of the next. Since the objectives will describe some specific problem in the reading of literature, the materials should illustrate the problem and be so arranged that the student learns to cope with the problem at an appropriate level of sophistication by the end of instruction.

Fourth, evaluation should be an attempt to determine whether or not the student has learned to do the tasks described by the objectives, to read something new, for instance, something that he has not seen before. Further, evaluation should determine how well students respond to the unit affectively.

Analysis of Unit Content

Obviously, the teacher must first analyze the unit topic before deciding that it is appropriate to the abilities of the students. Intuitive decisions about appropriateness are often completely inadequate. For instance, teachers who refuse to teach satire because they did not study it until college may have no qualms about offering a complex play like *Macbeth* (only a few Shakespearean plays are more complex) to all twelfth graders.

A second important reason for researching and analyzing the unit topic is to prevent superficiality in the unit. A teacher should explore a topic as far as he can before designing his unit. For instance, the teachers who planned "The Outcast" unit at the end of Chapter 9 read about ostracism and scapegoating in books on psychology, sociology, and myth and ritual in addition to reading many literary works. The unit on "Courage" at the end of Chapter 14 was planned only after reading commentaries on courage by philosophers such as Aristotle and Marcus Aurelius. *The Syntopicon,* which comprises the first two volumes of the *Great Books* series published by Encyclopaedia Britannica is a very useful source in approaching some fifty themes such as war, love, and courage. The more the teacher knows about the unit topic, the better. He may not be able to use the product of all his researches directly in his planning, but it will prepare him to help develop discussion of ideas that students raise in class and to explore the dimensions of the unit problem as far as his students' interests permit. Unfortunately, most college curricula offer only period or major figure oriented courses, which provide information and models of instruction inappropriate to the vast majority of secondary school students. Thus, *the teacher must do the necessary learning on his own.*

Once the teacher has examined the unit concepts thoroughly he will know intuitively which aspects of his initial idea, if any, might be useful with his own students. A cursory understanding of satire that suggests only works by Pope and Swift should automatically preclude satire as a topic for study for most students. But a more complete understanding of satire reveals that satire might be taught at many levels of sophistication. Similarly, a perfunctory knowledge of the structure and style of adolescent literature of the Hardy boys or hot rod variety precludes such materials as too unsophisticated. But a teacher who has considered such material carefully might note that it is prime stuff for the analysis of structure and style to be followed by the writing of parodies. It is surprising how much students can learn from the analysis of such simplistic material!

The teacher must analyze the unit topic for another reason: to determine whether it is appropriate to the study of literature. Although it is relatively easy to justify the teaching of satire because it illustrates how literature examines values and behavior, other unit topics are not so easily justified. The teacher must be sure that the unit's content is literature and not social studies, geography, or history. As we have seen, however, even an unlikely topic such as "animal stories" can illustrate key literary concepts. (See Chapter 4.)

Carefully planned units can contribute a great deal to the students' understanding of literature. To begin with, the teacher should choose a theme that appears in literature rather frequently, the problem of conflicting social and cultural values, for instance. Then he must decide whether there is material available that is not too difficult for his students. He may have to begin with material that presents conflict in cultural values in a rather straightforward manner, perhaps a story like Ernest Haycox's "A Question of Blood,"[1] which tells of a white settler in the West who marries a Crow girl before civilization creeps to the frontier. He is later caught amid the disapproval of the new white community, his moral responsibility toward the girl, and his inability to understand her customs or her language. The reading of a story like this might be preceded by a discussion of how the groups to which an individual belongs influence his system of values in rather subtle ways—ways that are frequently not apparent to adults, let alone adolescents. The students can examine their own experiences in the groups to which they belong, the sanctions that those groups exercise over them, and the conflicts that arise because they have different roles to play in different groups and because those groups have different sets of values. Most students have experienced tension or anxiety because their roles as students conflict with their roles as members of adolescent groups. Students know that the school expects a certain set of behaviors and the adolescent group expects, perhaps demands, a different set. This sort of discussion extended to cultures other than the students' will prepare the way for understanding the problems of a character caught between conflicting sets of values or the problems of characters who cannot understand or accept the values of others. Although the students may not be able to understand the complex cultural conflicts in E. M. Forster's *A Passage to India,* they will better understand the problem of Trueson in Conrad Richter's *The Light in the Forest,* and eventually they will be able to approach more difficult material.

Assume, then, that the teacher decides that a unit on satire might be appropriate for his classes. His first step will be to find out as much as he can about it for himself. The most common definition of satire is in terms of its purpose: to ridicule and so correct the follies and vices of mankind. The aim of a social satirist such as Fielding was to laugh men out of their follies and vices. But not all satire provokes outright laughter or even amusement. On the contrary, some of the best satire involves the bitterest humor. Alvin B. Kernan has called the satirist's muse "cankered."[2] Swift's description of the Yahoos is funny only briefly—before it turns to gall. Though it may be gentle, the humor of satire is never sweet. It burns as it cuts, and its wounds can be inflicted with the refinement and delicacy of the rapier or with the spine-splitting blows of the two-handed broadsword.

In Roman literature satire was, at first, a genre in the same sense that epic or tragedy were genres. It could be defined by its structural characteristics and its purpose, and, as a result, has been called formal verse satire or diatribe. Such satire was usually an abusive monologue in verse that made no attempt at subtlety. The speaker was always direct and emphatic in denouncing the objects of his criticism, using whatever weapons came to hand to make others scoff with him. He ranted and barked his scorn; he used imagery intended to disgust his audience. He barbed his criticism with vituperative humor. The foremost exponents of formal verse satire in Roman times were Juvenal, whose satires exemplify the most brutal methods, and Horace, whose satires are considerably more gentle.

Another sort of satire developed in which the criticism emanates indirectly from a story rather than directly from a harangue delivered by the satirist. The audience has to infer the satire from the nature of the characters, plot, and setting. Although the implications are not necessarily difficult to detect, only occasionally does the author make explicit satiric comments in his own voice; instead, the satire, for the most part, is implicit. This sort of satire, which became known as Menippean satire, after a Roman satirist who supposedly invented the form, is the type most widely used in English literature. Pope's "The Rape of the Lock," Dickens' *Nicholas Nickleby,* Mark Twain's *The Mysterious Stranger,* H. G. Wells' *Tono-Bungay,* and Orwell's *Animal Farm* are all examples of Menippean satire, insofar as they are satire.

Since the criticism emerging from Menippean satire is largely implied, it is more difficult for unsophisticated readers to understand than formal verse satire. Frequently, though, many Menippean works are short and fairly easy to read: fables, short poems, and some novels. The satiric techniques used in some Menippean satire are rather obvious. For instance, Dickens' satire of Squeers in *Nicholas Nickleby* is blunt in its exaggeration of the schoolmaster's ignorance and vice, and it presents a number of explicit condemnations from the voice of the omniscient author.[3]

The Unit Pretest

If the teacher believes that his unit idea might be workable, his next step is to plan a pretest for his unit. The reading inventory given at the beginning of the year will obviate certain choices, of course. For instance, if inventory responses on early items are minimal even in the later stages (see Chapter 11) there will be no point in planning a unit on satire in which students will have to deal largely with inferences—unless the teacher intends to use materials that involve very little or no reading, such as films, TV programs, cartoons, and so forth. (If this is indeed the teacher's intention, his pretest should use the same sort of materials.) On the other hand, if students do very well in response to the reading comprehension inventory, the pretest is still necessary, for it will give a clearer indication of the level at which a unit can begin. Teachers sometimes give themselves credit for having taught a great deal when in reality their students had already learned and were capable of doing with ease most of what the teachers thought they were teaching. A unit pretest helps to eliminate such errors. In addition, because it reflects the type of learning involved in the unit, it will serve as a base for the evaluation of instruction. In conjunction with final unit evaluations it will provide some notion of how effective the teacher's instruction has been. Without a pretest, he will have no way of knowing whether the students' achievements can be attributed to his efforts or to their prior learning.

A unit pretest should attempt to examine both extremes of a teacher's expectations for his class. That is, it should present materials and questions that the teacher feels will be very simple as well as those which he thinks will be difficult for his students. As in the reading comprehension inventory the items should be arranged from easy to difficult. The following items for a unit pretest on satire include a far greater range than necessary for most classes. An eighth grade teacher need use only the first two or three selections, while a twelfth grade teacher might use only the last three, or, depending on the results of the reading inventory and other observations he has made of his students, he too might use the first three selections. Obviously, the difficulty of the pretest can be modulated by varying both the selections used and the questions following them.

The following items were designed to answer some fairly specific questions: (1) What level of familiarity do the students have with the term "satire"? (2) Can they identify the target of ridicule in fairly obvious satire? (3) How adequately can they explain why the author believes the target deserves ridicule? (4) To what degree do they recognize the extension of the satire beyond the context of the specific work? (5) To what extent can they understand how the effects of the satire are achieved?

Unit Pretest: Satire

A. Read the following fable and answer the questions:

THE FOX AND THE CROW

A crow was sitting on a branch of a tree with a piece of cheese in her beak when a fox observed her and set his wits to work to discover some way of getting the cheese. Coming and standing under the tree he looked up and said, "What a noble bird I see above me! Her beauty is without equal, the hue of her plumage exquisite. If only her voice is as sweet as her looks are fair, she ought without doubt to be Queen of the Birds." The crow was hugely flattered by this, and just to show the fox that she could sing she gave a loud caw. Down came the cheese, of course, and the fox, snatching it up, said, "You have a voice, madam, I see: what you want is wits."[4]

1. What did the foolish animal do that revealed its foolishness?
2. Explain *why* the foolish animal did what it did.

B. The following passage is from a novel by Charles Dickens. The scene is a nineteenth-century private boarding school for boys. Mr. Squeers, the headmaster (principal) and owner of the school, is showing Nicholas Nickleby how he runs the school. Read the passage and answer the questions that follow.

"This is the first class in English spelling and philosophy, Nickleby," said Squeers, beckoning Nicholas to stand beside him. "We'll get up a Latin one, and hand that over to you. Now, then, where's the first boy?"

"Please, sir, he's cleaning the back parlour window," said the temporary head of the philosophical class.

"So he is, to be sure," rejoined Squeers. "We go upon the practical mode of teaching, Nickleby; the regular education system. C-l-e-a-n, clean, verb active, to make bright, to make bright, to scour. W-i-n, win, d-e-r, der, winder a casement. When the boy knows this out of the book, he goes and does it. It's just the same principle as the use of the globes. Where's the second boy?"

"Please, sir, he's weeding the garden," replied a small voice.

"To be sure," said Squeers, by no means disconcerted. "So he is. B-o-t, bot, t-i-n, tin, n-e-y, ney, bottinney, noun substantive, a knowledge of plants. When he has learned that bottinney means a knowledge of plants, he goes and knows 'em. That's our system, Nickleby; what do you think of it?"

"It's a very useful one, at any rate," answered Nicholas.

"I believe you," rejoined Squeers, not remarking the emphasis of his usher. "Third boy, what's a horse?"

"A beast, sir," replied the boy.

"So it is," said Squeers, "Ain't it, Nickleby?"

"I believe there is no doubt of that, sir," answered Nicholas.

"Of course there isn't," said Squeers. "A horse is a quadruped, and quadruped's Latin for beast, as everybody that's gone through the grammar knows, or else where's the use of having grammars at all?"

"Where, indeed!" said Nicholas abstractedly.

"As you're perfect in that," resumed Squeers, turning to the boy, "go and look after *my* horse, and rub him down well, or I'll rub you down. The rest of the class go and draw water up, till somebody tells you to leave off, for it's washing-day tomorrow, and they want the coppers filled."[5]

1. At one point in the passage, the following conversation takes place:

Squeers: "Third boy, what's a horse?"
"A beast, sir," replied the boy.
"So it is," said Squeers, "Ain't it, Nickleby?"
"I believe there is no doubt of that, sir," answered Nicholas.

What does this conversation indicate about Squeers' ability as a schoolteacher? Explain your reaction.
What other parts of the passage support your judgment of his ability as a schoolteacher? Find two examples and explain how each supports your judgment.

2. How does Squeers probably treat the boys in and out of class?
3. Explain Dickens' attitude toward schools such as the one run by Squeers. What parts of the passage help you to explain what his attitude was?
4. What technique or method does Dickens use to convey his attitude toward schools such as the one run by Squeers?

C. The following passage is from Jonathan Swift's *Gulliver's Travels.* During his third voyage Gulliver visits the Grand Academy at Lagado where he watches scientists at work.

The first man I saw was of a meagre aspect, with sooty hands and face, his hair and beard long, ragged, and singed in several places. His clothes, shirt, and skin were all of the same colour. He had been eight years upon a project for extracting sunbeams out of cucumbers, which were to be put into vials hermetically sealed, and let out to warm the air in raw, inclement summers. He told me he did not doubt in eight years more he should be able to supply the Governor's gardens with sunshine at a reasonable rate; but he complained that his stock was low, and entreated me to give him something as an encouragement to ingenuity, especially since this had been a very dear season for cucumbers. I made him a small present, for my lord had furnished me with money on purpose, because he knew their practice of begging from all who go to see them.

I went into another chamber, but was ready to hasten back, being almost overcome with a horrible stink. My conductor pressed me forward, conjuring me, in a whisper, to give no offence, which would be highly resented, and therefore I dare not so much as stop my nose. The projector of this cell was the most ancient student of the Academy. His face and beard were of a pale yellow; his hands and clothes daubed over with filth. When I was presented to him, he gave me a very close embrace (a compliment I could well have excused). His employment, from his first coming into the Academy, was an operation to reduce human excrement to its orginial food by separating the several parts, removing the tincture which it receives from the gall, making the odour exhale, and scumming off the saliva. He had a weekly allowance from the society of a vessel filled with human ordure about the bigness of a Bristol barrel.

I saw another at work to calcine ice into gunpowder, who likewise showed me a treatise he had written concerning the malleability of fire, which he intended to publish.

There was a man born blind, who had several apprentices in his own condition. Their employment was to mix colours for painters, which their master taught them to distinguish by feeling and smelling. It was, indeed, my misfortune to find them at that time not very perfect in their lessons, and the professor himself happened to be generally mistaken. This artist is much encouraged and esteemed by the whole fraternity.

In other apartment I was highly pleased with a projector who had found a device for ploughing the ground with hogs, to save the charges of ploughs, cattle, and labour. The method is this: In an acre of ground you bury at six inches distant and eight deep a quantity of acorns, dates, chestnuts, and other mast or vegetables whereof these animals are fondest; then you drive six hundred or more of them into the field, where in a few days they will root up the whole ground in search of their food and make it fit for sowing, at the same time manuring it with their dung. It is true upon experiment they found the charge and trouble very great, and they had little or no crop. However, it is not doubted that this invention may be capable of great improvement.[6]

1. *Gulliver's Travels* was first published in 1726. What was the basis for Swift's attitude toward the scientific research of his day? Explain your answer by specific references to the passage.

2. To what extent are his ideas applicable to scientific research in the twentieth century? Defend your conclusions.
3. What devices does Swift use to convey his feelings about that research?

D. Arthur Hugh Clough

THE LATEST DECALOGUE

Thou shalt have one God only; who
Would be at the expense of two?
No graven images may be
Worshipped, except the currency:
Swear not at all, for, for thy curse
Thine enemy is none the worse:
At church on Sunday to attend
Will serve to keep the world thy friend:
Honour thy parents; that is, all
From whom advancement may befall;
Thou shalt not kill; but need'st not strive
Officiously to keep alive:
Do not adultery commit;
Advantage rarely comes of it:
Thou shalt not steal; an empty feat,
When it's so lucrative to cheat:
Bear not false witness; let the lie
Have time on its own wings to fly:
Thou shalt not covet, but tradition
Approves all forms of competition.[7]

1. What is the target of Clough's ridicule in "The Latest Decalogue"? Explain both the target of the ridicule and the reasons for it.
2. How does Clough organize the poem to convey the ridicule?
3. To what extent does your own experience or the experience of another support the poet's ideas? Name a particular experience and explain how it supports or denies the poet's contentions.

E. John Donne

SONG

Goe, and catche a falling starre,
   Get with child a mandrake roote,
Tell me, where all past yeares are,
   Or who cleft the Divels foot,
Teach me to heare Mermaides singing,
   Or to keep off envies stinging,
         And finde
         What winde
Serves to advance an honest minde.

If thou beest borne to strange sights,
   Things invisible to see,
Ride ten thousand daies and nights,
   Till age snow white haires on thee,
Thou, when thou retorn'st, wilt tell mee
All strange wonders that befell thee,
      And sweare
      No where
Lives a woman true, and faire.

If thou findst one, let mee know,
   Such a Pilgrimage were sweet;
Yet doe not, I would not goe,
   Though at next doore wee might meet,
Though shee were true, when you met her,
And last, till you write your letter,
      Yet shee
      Will bee
False, ere I come, to two, or three.[8]

1. What do the images of the first stanza have in common?
2. Explain how the first stanza established the tone of the speaker's comments for the poem as a whole.
3. How does the paradox in the line "Things invisible to see" continue the tone of the opening stanza and intensify the central ridicule of the poem?
4. To what extent is the imagery of the final stanza appropriate as a climax to the first two stanzas? Explain your evaluation.

F. The selections you have read on this test are satires. From your previous knowledge of satire and from your reading of these selections write as clear a definition of satire as you can.

The fable and the passage from Nicholas Nickleby are both relatively simple and straightforward examples of satire. Still, some students at all grade levels will have difficulty with the later questions, especially with A4 and B4.

Although the selection from *Gulliver's Travels* is funny, the object of the satire will be obscure to many. Many have a very high regard for modern scientific research and will not see the passage as applicable in any way to modern research. In answer to the first question following this selection many readers are likely to write that Swift thought scientists dealt with silly problems. While such an answer displays some insight, a much stronger response would explain why he thought so. In discussing the devices that Swift uses, a good answer will deal with exaggeration in relation to the sort of problem the researchers work on as well as their personal condition.

Unsophisticated high school readers may take Clough's poems literally; that is, they may understand it as a set of real recommendations. Some may even see it as an attack on the Ten Commandments. The difficulty lies in recognizing that Clough is suggesting, through irony, that the old commandments are followed only perfunctorily out of self-interest and hypocrisy. The poem by John Donne is by far the most difficult of all the items, because of its language, syntax, and its somewhat complex imagery. Most high school seniors will have difficulty with the questions listed. Many will not understand the poem at all.

A number of contemporary poems which are widely anthologized can be used in place of some of the selections above: Cummings' "pity this busy monster, manunkind," "(of Ever-Ever Land i speak," or "the Cambridge ladies who live in furnished souls"; W. H. Auden's "The Unknown Citizen"; T. S. Elliot's "The Hippopotamus"; and so forth.

In preparing the pretest, the teacher must strive to include a range of selections and questions. His selections and questions should provide insight into how well his students already comprehend aspects of the unit topic. The use of only difficult materials and questions predicts weak responses. The use of only very easy materials and questions predicts strong student responses. Neither approach reveals the entire range of student abilities.

Levels of Interpretation

English teachers tend to assume that if a student has reached the tenth grade, he is ready for *Julius Caesar,* and if he has reached the twelfth grade, he has sufficient preparation for whatever snippets of English literature the anthology has to offer. This highly generalized view of prerequisite training may be at the heart of our failure in English. If we intend our students to be able to read and appreciate certain works by the end of their training in English, we must determine what skills and concepts are prerequisite, when they can be introduced, and how they can be best developed— a task that is much easier in other academic areas than it is in English. Even the worst algebra teacher does not try to teach the solution of quadratic equations before students can solve for x. A first-grade teacher, similarly, does not give written spelling tests before her students have learned to form the letters. But English teachers frequently assign *Macbeth* to students who cannot read much beyond the fifth- or sixth-grade level. They try to teach the irony of *Huckleberry Finn* and the symbolism of *The Scarlet Letter* before their students are capable of interpreting either irony or symbolism, for themselves, in even the most obvious forms.

For the most part, however, English teachers do not decide consciously to ignore prerequisite knowledge and skill in teaching specific works. The problem simply does not occur to them—for three major reasons. First, they think of prerequisite knowledge and skill only in a very general way. For example, tenth-grade learnings (whatever they are) must take place before eleventh-grade learnings (whatever they are). Individual teachers cannot be blamed for that, perhaps. The problem of sequencing skills and knowledge for teaching students to read literature has only recently been confronted by a few of the U.S.O.E.-sponsored English projects. Chapter 10 of this book is an attempt to define some of the skills and knowledge necessary to the successful reading of literature. The definition of these skills and their appropriate scheduling into a spiral-like curriculum that is susceptible to change by virtue of changes in the students is a task that should confront the profession for some years to come.

Second, English teachers tend to think that the stories and poems appearing in anthologies have been placed there because of some inherent appropriateness. They believe that a poem in a ninth-grade anthology is there not because the anthologist could think of nothing else, but because that poem is *right* for ninth graders. Teaching literature becomes a matter of "covering" the material in the anthology. This attitude is reinforced by a teacher's very broad statements of objectives: to inculcate an appreciation of literature, to increase competency in reading short stories, and so on. The objectives are so broadly stated that the teacher has no real means of evaluating them. Since he believes, for the most part, that the anthology represents "literature" for a given grade level, he assesses his performance on the basis of the amount of material he covers.

Third, the traditional orientation of English teachers is primarily to the content—aesthetic, intellectual, and emotional—of individual works and secondarily to the historical context in which the individual work occurs. And so it should be—in part. Unfortunately, this orientation *alone* is not very useful pedagogically. The concern for the meaning of individual works often results in the teacher's explaining those works to his students. But a teacher's explanations, no matter how thorough and precise, will not enable most students to become successful, independent readers.

Without relinquishing the values he sees in individual works, the English teacher, for instructional purposes, must begin to think of a series of works, similar in the kinds of critical or interpretative problems they present but graduated in complexity. But he must also begin to think in terms of where the student *is* as reader and what he can learn next. A literary skill, concept, or theme can be introduced in a simple, though not superficial way to very young students and reinforced and developed at succeeding grade levels. Thus, it is possible and necessary for students to deal with a problem like satire from several increasingly sophisticated points of view. The following set of statements about Aesop's "The Fox and the Grapes" suggests a paradigm of increasingly sophisticated interpretation.

1. The fox is funny (possibly grade 2 or 3).
2. The fox is funny because he changes his mind about the grapes.

3. The fox is funny because he is really only making an excuse for himself when he says the grapes are sour.
4. Aesop is making fun of the fox because the fox makes an excuse for his own incompetence.
5. Aesop ridicules people who, like the fox, etc.
6. Aesop uses symbolism and irony to satirize people who, like the fox, etc.
7. Aesop's use of symbolism and irony to satirize people who make excuses in order to ignore their failures is gemlike in its compactness and precision (possibly college).

Obviously, it is a long way from the first to the seventh statement, but each is true and none is essentially superficial. Presumably, one goal of our literature curriculum is to help each student attain the highest level of interpretation he can. Each unit of instruction, then, must begin with what the student can do and help him move as far as possible. If the teacher finds that his students cannot report what the fox does and says, he would be foolish to demand that they make statements like 5, 6, or 7. But if they can report the plot of the fable adequately, perhaps he can help them learn to interpret other fables at levels 2, 3, or even 4.

Similarly, a literary concept may be introduced in a relatively simple way and developed in an increasingly sophisticated fashion. Table 12.1 illustrates the principle.

Level I on the table, satire as humorous criticism, can be easily taught to students at the fifth- or sixth-grade level. But they need only to understand satire as *humorous criticism*. Later on, if the curriculum is articulated, they can learn to objectify the moral purpose of satire, to distinguish the two basic types of satire, and to interpret satire which uses more and more complex devices. Note, however, that the levels on the table are cumulative, that the student must know level I before he moves to level II, and so on. Thus, if the students have not had previous training in satire, and if the teacher wants his class to study Augustan satire, he would be wise to ensure that they have the requisite knowledge and skills. The levels suggested on the table can be taught in several units at various grade levels or in one unit at one grade level. (Teaching all of the concepts at one grade level obviously requires rather sophisticated students.) Most students in secondary schools can comprehend those concepts most basic to satire that are illustrated by levels I and II on the table. But even this level of comprehension is dependent on what the students can do when they enter the class.

Setting Objectives

If the students can read only the literal content of the material in the pretest, the teacher probably should not bother with satire. But if many can make some of the inferences adequately, he can probably take

TABLE 12.1. Satire Units for Various Levels of Ability

	Concept	Objective	Materials	Contingent Abilities
I.	Satire as humorous criticism: exaggeration, allegory.	To identify the target of criticism.	Caricatures and fables.	To cope with simple inferences.
II.	Simple ironic satire with both elements of contrast expressed; diatribe.	1. To write a definition of satire. 2. To identify the device used to make the satiric criticism. 3. To identify a satiric work according to the criteria of the definition. 4. To write a satire using one or more of the devices studied.	Selections from Juvenal or Philip Wylie; ironic poems no more difficult than "Ozymandias"; *Animal Farm.*	To cope with inferences about author's purpose, author's generalizations.
III.	Complex ironic satire with only one element of contrast expressed; short parody; two basic types of satire: diatribe and Menippean.	1. To identify diatribe and Menippean satire according to the criteria. 2. To identify and explain the devices through which satire is accomplished. 3. To identify and explain the operation of simple parody.	Satires of Juvenal, Philip Wylie, Horace; ironic monologues; selections from Dickens, Mark Twain; *The Physician in Spite of Himself*; short parodies.	To use previous learnings about satire; to analyze style; to analyze literary structures of irony, paradox, etc.
IV.	The satire of the Augustan Age: burlesque, complex parody, the mock heroic.	1. To identify the interrelationships of satire as genre with other aspects of the Augustan age. 2. To identify and analyze the satiric techniques of various writers of that age. 3. To analyze mock heroic works in terms of the …	Satires by Pope, Dryden, Swift, Fielding, Johnson, *et al.*	To use previous learnings about satire; to make and use generalizations about a literary era; knowledgeable in classic epic and some seventeenth century epic theory.

them a reasonable distance. For instance, he can set the following terminal objectives for students who answer the simpler inference questions on the pretest adequately.

1. To identify the specific target of ridicule within the work in each of the following:
   a. a simple example of formal verse satire
   b. a simple story or poem using exaggeration
   c. a simple poem or short story using satiric irony
   d. a simple fable
2. To explain how the satirist uses character and event to ridicule the target.
3. To explain how the ridicule of the target within the work applies to the real world through generalization or application.

Although these objectives are reasonably specific, the teacher should clarify them by deciding more specifically what he means by "simple" in objective 1. To be simple enough for the students concerned here, the works should not require any specialized knowledge of social institutions or customs. They should not involve complex patterns of imagery or abstract ideas. They should deal with common, recognizable follies and vices, for example, greed, stupidity, pride, gullibility. Although many of Aesop's and some of Thurber's fables qualify, *Animal Farm* is not simple in these terms. In addition, the teacher needs to specify the manner in which the student is to display his understanding: choosing the correct answer from multiple-choice questions, writing out brief answers to a series of questions, or writing a paragraph to satisfy all the objectives. The latter is the most difficult. For average eighth-grade students, short-answer questions are probably the most satisfactory.

If the students do rather well on the pretest, the teacher can require written paragraphs and increase the difficulty of the selections upon which the students will be tested. He might also include the following objectives:

4. To name the satiric devices used in the selections and to explain them by allusion to the text.
5. To write a short definition of satire, explaining its function and chief characteristics, illustrated by examples.

If the students are capable ninth graders, the teacher might make the first four objectives more complex by requiring not only that the students interpret and explain satire but that they attempt to discriminate satiric works from those that might appear to be satiric because of similar devices or similar intent. For instance, the objectives and criterion statements for a lesson on satiric irony might read as follows:

1. Given an unfamiliar ironic poem not more difficult than "Ozymandias," to write a composition explaining how the irony works in terms of the ironic contrast.

2. To explain in the composition why that poem should or should not be regarded as satire in terms of the definition of satire previously established in class.

The criterion statements for the first objectives are as follows: The student must

1. Name the parts of the ironic contrast and quote pertinent lines from the poem.
2. Explain the effects of the irony.

For the second objective, the student must

1. Answer each of the following questions:
   a. Does it make a criticism?
   b. Does it use one of the satiric devices?
   c. Does it involve some degree of humor?
2. If the answers to any of the questions are "yes," identify the criticism, the satiric device, the humorous element, or some or all of these.
3. If the answers to any of the questions are "no," explain what the work does that precludes a criticism, a satiric device, humor, or some or all of these.

Parts of these statements need further qualification. The teacher may wish to add criterion statements concerning the form of the composition, but that is the province of another section of this book.

The major emphasis for a lesson with these objectives is the interpretation of irony. Note, however, that a *correct* decision as to whether or not a poem is satiric is not required. A decision supported by appropriate arguments is the major goal.

For these students, the objectives dealing with the interpretation of types of satire are medial rather than terminal. That is, the students must learn to deal with exaggeration, irony, satiric allegory, and diatribe individually, before approaching a longer work that might use all of the devices. Fulfillment of the following terminal objectives is contingent upon them. If the students cannot perform at the level of the medial objectives satisfactorily, there is not much sense in attempting to reach the terminal objectives.

1. To write an essay interpreting the satire of a play, novel, or series of essays or short stories by a single author. (May not use material studied in class.)
   Criterion statements: the student must
   a. Decide on the basis of criteria in a definition whether or not the work is satiric.
   b. Identify the targets of satire and explain why they are satirized.
   c. Explain how plot, character, imagery, and satiric techniques provide the satire.

    d. Identify the values that the author regards as good or appropriate in contrast to those he condemns.
2. To write an extended definition of satire.
   Criterion statements: the student must
   a. Explain the purpose of satire.
   b. Discriminate adequately between formal verse satire (diatribe) and Menippean satire.
   c. Explain the devices (those studied in class) used in each kind of satire.
   d. Illustrate each point with examples from material studied in the unit.
3. To write an original satire.
   Criterion statements: the student must
   a. Choose a target to satirize.
   b. Use one or more of the devices studied to implement the satire, which may be either diatribe or Menippean satire.
4. To write an original parody.
   Criterion statements: the student must
   a. Choose a style characteristic of a writer or publication, for example, *Time,* Poe, primers.
   b. Imitate the point of view, syntax, vocabulary, and so on, in retelling a well-known tale.
   c. Satirize the style imitated.

These objectives can be met by fluent ninth graders who can deal with such aspects of literature as implied relationships between characters and their environments, connotation, figurative language, elementary symbolism, and the simpler aspects of structure. The various student compositions in Chapter 13 are from above-average ninth graders with the kind of background suggested. Obviously, the same unit might be taught to very bright eighth graders or to average tenth, eleventh, or twelfth graders. The point is that the adoption of specific terminal objectives for any unit is dependent on the abilities of the students in a given class and on the nature of the literary problem involved.

Throughout the discussion of objectives, there has been an emphasis on *specificity,* an emphasis that some teachers will object to as being narrow and limiting. But when teachers fail to develop specific objectives, their instruction wanders, students become frustrated, then bored because they are confronted with too many unfamiliar tasks at once, and evaluation of teaching is impossible.

A unit of instruction should present only a few clearly defined aspects of literature that are new to the students. If the goal is independent reading, then the unit should be organized so that students learn to respond to those aspects, without the aid of a teacher, by the conclusion of the unit. At the same time, only a foolish teacher allows his objectives to restrict his students. If, once the unit is launched, the teacher discovers that his objectives are inappropriate to the students or the subject, he should revise them. Once formulated, the objectives should not confine the students in terms of interests or responses. If students develop special interests in some aspect of a unit, obviously a teacher should encourage them. And although a unit focuses on particular understanding, as reflected by certain kinds of responses, it will necessarily involve many other kinds of responses as well. For instance, although the unit on humor described in the first chapter of this book focused on various aspects of structure, it is clearly concerned with literal meanings, connotative language, evaluation, and so on. In short, the purpose of specifically stated objectives is to facilitate instruction: to make planning and evaluation easier for the teacher and to make learning less frustrating, more rewarding, and more efficient for the students.

NOTES

1. Ernest Haycox, "A Question of Blood," *Seventy Five Short Masterpieces* (New York: Bantam Books, 1961).
2. Alvin B. Kernan, *The Cankered Muse* (New Haven: Yale University Press, 1959).
3. For an analysis of satire, see the following: Robert C. Elliott, *The Power of Satire* (Princeton: Princeton University Press, 1960). Gilbert Highet, *The Anatomy of Satire* (Princeton: Princeton University Press, 1962). Alvin B. Kernan, *op. cit.*

The materials cited in footnotes 4–8 can be found in many sources; these sources are suggestions:

4. Aesop, *Fables,* trans. V. S. Vernon Jones (New York: Doubleday, Page and Company, 1926), p. 6.
5. Charles Dickens, *Nicholas Nickleby* (London: Oxford University Press, 1950), pp. 90–91.
6. Jonathan Swift, *Gulliver's Travels* (Oxford: Oxford University Press, 1904, rpt. 1948), pp. 216–218.
7. Arthur Hugh Clough, "The Latest Decalogue" in *The Penguin Book of Satiric Verse,* ed. Edward Lucie-Smith (Baltimore: Penguin Books, 1967), pp. 242–243.
8. John Donne, "Song" in *The Complete Poetry and Selected Prose of John Donne,* ed. Charles M. Coffin (New York: Random House, 1952), pp. 8–9.

13

Designing the Literature Unit: II. Procedures

After determining the terminal objectives, the next step in unit design is to plan procedures and select materials. In most cases, the task of writing terminal objectives will suggest, if not demand, ideas about both. The materials selected should be appropriate to both the students and the unit concepts. In general, an instructional unit should consist of four types of activity, each with a different purpose: (1) introductory activities to arouse interest and establish confidence; (2) teacher-led instruction to develop unit concepts initially; (3) student-led small-group activities to extend the development of the concepts and, at the same time, to allow the students to work somewhat independently of the teacher; (4) independent activities for the purpose of evaluating instruction. For the most part, the activities should develop in that order. The movement from teacher-led discussion to student-led small-group activities and then to independent work gradually weans the student from the teacher, putting increasingly more responsibility on the student. At the same time, it gives the students adequate practice in performing the tasks described by the terminal objectives. Thus, at the beginning of a unit, when the students are exploring a new province, they receive maximum support from the teacher. By the end of the unit, when approaches to the new territory have become more familiar to the students, they begin to approach similar, but new and more complex, problems without the aid of the teacher.

In some units, such as the one on satire in which several related concepts are developed, the progression from teacher-led activity to individual activity may take place several times as each new aspect of the concept is introduced. The following lesson on satiric irony exemplifies the process. When this lesson takes place, the students have already been introduced to satire, have formulated a simple, working definition of the term, and have examined some rather obvious examples of satire. The lesson is a microcosmic unit from introduction to evaluation. Its objectives were stated in the preceding chapter.

Teacher-Led Activities

Ideally, any unit should begin with an introduction that the students can readily understand. Although irony may seem rather complex, its basic structure is really little different from the blunt sarcastic remark that most ninth graders can deliver deftly and viciously, if not too subtly. The teacher can introduce the lesson by composing several lines that are complimentary when delivered with normal intonation but murderous when delivered with ninth-grade cunning—murderous to another ninth grader at least. Simple lines will do:

Isn't that the most beautiful dress you've ever seen?

In this school he's what's called a good teacher.

After practicing saying the lines for various effects, the class can make up some of their own. Although this activity could go on forever, only a few examples are necessary. As soon as feasible after the students have the idea, the teacher should ask what turns essentially complimentary remarks into insults. Class discussion and analysis should reveal that the important thing is the difference between the words and "how" you say them. The element of contrast is crucial. The teacher then writes "contrast" on the board and distributes copies of the following poem by Sara N. Cleghorn and asks students to read it.

The golf links lie so near the mill
    That almost every day
The laboring children can look out
    And see the men at play.[1]

Teacher: Does anyone know what golf links are?

Student 1:   A golf course.

Teacher: Good. What is a mill?

Student 2:   That's a place where you get wheat and corn ground up.

Student 3:   It can be a factory.

Teacher: What kind of factory?

Student 4:   It could be a steel mill.

Student 5:   It's probably a textile mill. That's why kids are working in it.

Student 2:   Why can't kids work in a steel mill?

Student 6:   The poem says children. And they used to use child labor in textile mills because children were cheap.

Teacher: Good. Do you notice any contrast in this poem?

Student 2:   Naw.

Others: Yes.

Teacher: What is it?

Student 7:   Between the children working and the men playing.

Teacher: Why is that a contrast?

Student 7:   It should be the other way around. At least that's what most people think nowadays.

Teacher: Does the poem criticize anything?

Student 5:   Yes.

Teacher: What?

Student 5:   The whole idea that men are playing while children are working in a mill.

Teacher: How does the poem get that across without stating it directly?

Student 8:   (Tentatively) By contrasting the men and the children.

Teacher: Right, at least in part. But the poet also expects something of his reader. What does he expect?

Student 6:   To feel that men should be working while children are playing.

Teacher: Good point. Is there anything else?

Student 3:   The second line makes it sound as though some days the children are too busy to look out.

Teacher: Good. Is there anything humorous about the poem.

Student 2:   Work is never funny. (He finally gets a laugh from the class.)

Teacher: All right. For the most part the poem is serious. Is there any element of humor at all? (Silence . . . finally . . .)

Student 5:   In a way. Partly because it's over so fast. The last line really hits you.

Teacher: That's a good point. You don't laugh, do you? You smile, perhaps. Why do you smile? Because the men are playing? (No response.) How would you describe the smile? What is it like?

Student 4:   It's the kind you don't really mean.

Student 9:   Yeah, like when something happens you don't expect. And you say, I might have known.

Teacher: Good point. I think that describes it nicely. Can anyone add to that?

The teacher-student dialogue will not always go this smoothly. On the other hand, it will not always take so long. The most difficult part of the discussion involves the problem of humor. If the students understand that humor can have a strong admixture of bitterness, the problem disappears. Primarily it is a problem of definition. Students frequently understand and apply the word "humor" in a very narrow sense. Once they see that the word can apply to something other than farce and television situation comedy, the major hurdle is past.

The students should examine at least one additional ironic satire before the teacher introduces the word "irony." Edward Arlington Robinson's "Miniver Cheevy" is useful, in part because its contrasts are clear and its humor more obvious. Note the sixth stanza, for instance:

Miniver cursed the commonplace
    And eyed a khaki suit with loathing;

He missed the medieval grace
  Of iron clothing.[2]

The absurdity of any kind of grace in iron clothing is apparent to even the most obtuse students, and through the examination of such contrasts, they see the folly of Miniver's longing for the past.

When the students have had sufficient opportunity to see how contrasts work, the teacher can introduce the term "irony," explaining that the contrasts in the poems are called *ironic* contrasts. He writes both words on the board and clarifies the use of each. He then can mention other contrasts between a white card and black card, between a tall student and a short student, between a high game score and a low game score, and so on, and ask how such contrasts are different from those in the poems. The ensuing discussion should develop the idea that when a contrast is arranged to surprise or disrupt our expectations, it is an ironic contrast. When the same contrast makes use of humor and reveals folly or vice, it is called satiric irony.

The teacher can now direct the attention of the students to another poem, perhaps the following one by Siegfried Sassoon:

BASE DETAILS

If I were fierce, and bald, and short of breath,
  I'd live with scarlet Majors at the Base,
And speed glum heroes up the line to death.
  You'd see me with my puffy petulant face,
Guzzling and gulping in the best hotel,
  Reading the Roll of Honour. "Poor young chap,"
I'd say—"I used to know his father well;
  Yes, we've lost heavily in this last scrap."
And when the war is done and youth stone dead,
I'd toddle safely home and die—in bed.[3]

The students can begin the discussion by identifying the contrasts existing in the poem, some of which are obvious. Because others are subtle, the teacher may have to direct the attention of the students to particular lines. From the identification of contrasts the discussion will automatically move to the target of criticism: the tendency of war to kill youth while the older men who give the orders lead lives of comparative luxury. The next problem is whether the poem involves humor and is satiric. The teacher should ask key questions and respond to student statements with additional questions:

1 Who is the speaker in the poem?
2. What are the contrasts?
3. Are the contrasts ironic? In what way?
4. What is the target of criticism?
5. What degree of humor is in the poem?

6. What contributes the humor of the poem?
7. Should the poem be considered satiric? Why?
8. To what extent is the criticism of officers justified?

The teacher should take the class through additional poems until they begin to make the analyses very quickly. Sassoon's "They," "Does It Matter?" and Southey's "Battle of Blenheim" serve this purpose nicely. When the students display relative proficiency, the teacher can divide the class into small groups for additional, somewhat more complex work. (See Chapter 3 for procedures on grouping.) Heterogeneous groups are best here since all students will read similar material.

Group Activities

If the teacher wishes to expand the students' understanding of the satiric use of irony to the soliloquy, two poems are particularly useful. "The Admiral's Song" from Gilbert and Sullivan's *H. M. S. Pinafore* is a rather simple ironic soliloquy in which the Admiral reveals his own ineptitude. A more difficult poem that students should understand with relative ease by this point is Browning's "Soliloquy in a Spanish Cloister." These are more difficult because the ironic soliloquy requires the reader to expect certain traits or characteristics of the speakers. We expect an admiral to be intelligent and to have had experience at sea. We expect a friar to be humble and loving. If we do not expect these things, the irony of the poems may be completely lost. At any rate, the students should approach the poems with a set of key questions like those listed for "Base Details." As the students read and discuss the poems, the teacher should move from group to group. He cannot sit at his desk to grade papers. He must be available if students bog down on a problem, and he must evaluate the discussions to determine how well the students can proceed on their own.

Once a unit concept has been clearly established, it may be useful to contrast the idea with related but different ones; courage with foolhardiness, for instance. In this case the students should examine poems that are ironic but not necessarily satiric. This activitiy is important to prevent what is sometimes erroneously called overteaching, which, in this case, might result in the students' thinking that everything ironic is satiric. Actually, it is the result of underteaching. Students must learn when irony is satiric *and* when it is not. Two useful poems are Whitman's "When I Heard the Learn'd Astronomer" and Edward Arlington Robinson's "Richard Cory." (Other useful materials are stories by Shirley Jackson and O. Henry.) The discussion groups should approach these with a list of key questions:

1. Does the poem contain irony? If so, what?
2. What does the irony accomplish? Does it criticize anything? If so, what? If not, what does it do?

3. Is the poem satiric? If so, explain how it meets the criteria for being considered satiric? If not, explain what it does accomplish.

The key questions are phrased to permit, even encourage, disagreement, and if time permits, the teacher should take full advantage of any disagreement, that arises. If one group's analysis diverges from another's, the teacher might pit one group against the other in debate while the rest of the class serves as judge. When both sides are forced to argue their positions, they have to review everything they have learned about satire and apply it carefully to the poems and in their presentations. The disagreement can serve to reinforce the learning. As indicated before, a "correct answer" is not necessary, perhaps not even desirable. The main requirement is a decision supported by careful analysis of the texts.

Individual Activities—Evaluation

The final activity of the lesson requires the individual students to examine a poem that they have not seen before in the light of what they have learned. Actually, the teacher can require as many individual analyses as he deems useful. If he requires a written statement, he may wish the students to write about several works so that he can teach certain aspects of composition before the final evaluation activity. At any rate, this activity is important as an evaluation of how effective the teacher has been in instructing students to deal with satiric irony. The objectives of the lesson call for the student to interpret irony and to decide, according to certain criteria, whether or not the work is satiric. If the work is not satiric, the student is to decide what the work does do, what effect the irony has. All this is to be done in a brief essay illustrated by quotations from the text. A group of ninth graders were presented with Shelley's "Ozymandias" and the question that follows it below. They had forty minutes to read it and write a brief essay answering the question. Three of their responses with a brief analysis of each follow:

OZYMANDIAS

I met a traveler from an antique land
Who said: Two vast and trunkless legs of stone
Stand in the desert. Near them, on the sand,
Half sunk, a shattered visage lies, whose frown,
And wrinkled lip, and snear of cold command,
Tell that its sculptor well those passions read
Which yet survive, stamped in these lifeless things,
The hand that mocked them, and the heart that fed:
And on the pedestal these words appear:
    "My name is Ozymandias, King of Kings:
    Look on my works, ye Mighty, and despair!"
    Nothing beside remains. Round the decay

Of that colossal wreck, boundless and bare
The lone and level sands stretch far away.

PROBLEM

Write a brief essay explaining why this poem should or should not be considered a satire. If the poem is not a satire, explain what the poem means and how that meaning is achieved.

Response I

The poem "Ozymandias" is not a satire, but an ironic poem. Through this irony a theme is built. The theme suggests that man cannot attain perfection, and omnipotent power, and when man does attain something close to perfect power he cannot keep it.

The author set up a contrast in the last five lines of the poem. The king's sculpture reads "Look on my works, ye Mighty, and despair," but nothing of his empire remains, except in ruins and barren lands. This contrast is also the irony of the poem in the fact that he was Mightiest of kings and that his kingdom lay in a "colossal wreck," also "boundless and bare." This shows further that nobody even the "King of Kings" can hold on to perfect power.

Through the poem the author expresses that no one can have perfect power, control all empires of the world, and hold these things. The author conveys his idea through an irony which contrasts the power of Ozymandias "King of Kings" to the remains of his empire and power.

Ninth-grade boy

The young man who wrote this response handled the irony of the poem well. He quotes or alludes to all the pertinent lines, interprets them in terms of the ironic contrast, and makes a statement about the theme of the poem as a whole. The only requirement he did not fulfill was to explain why the poem should not be considered a satire.

Response II

In the poem "Ozymandias" ironic contrasts are used to bring out the poem's dual targets, those people who think their own culture is the greatest, and the idea that of all the former "eternal" greatness only the sneering face is left. The two targets are interwoven, and occur simultaneously. Irony is used to develop these targets together with some details of Menippean satire.

The ironic contrast is between the former glory of the empire that would cause Ozymandias to say, "My name is Ozymandias, King of Kings: Look on my works, ye Mighty and despair!" and what is now left of that empire, "a shattered visage . . . frown-wrinkled lip and the sneer of cold command." Even these few remnants are covered by sand and surrounded by "lone and level sands" that "stretch far away." And yet of all the greatness only a "sneer of cold command" remains for the ages to comment on.

"Ozymandias," while not strictly Menippean, does contain some elements of Menippean satire. The poem is abusive, and subjective, with a few traces of a bitter humor. The abuse seems to be directed towards Ozymandias and what he stands for, and stood for. While there is no real plot, the satirist is not speaking directly, but through the traveler. The satire also follows an indirect course, not coming out with a "factual" statement as in Juvenal, but pointing instead in the right direction. Thus the type of satire is unknown currently, but is nearer to Menippean than diatribe.

Ninth-grade girl

The young lady in writing this response dealt quite adequately with the irony of the poem and its central meaning. Her analysis of the poem as satire is less effective. Although she makes clear what the poem criticizes, she leaves her remark about "a few traces of bitter humor" unexplained. She does attempt to make a discrimination between diatribe and Menippean satire, a discrimination that her class was not yet prepared to make. The terms had been introduced only incidentally. Still, she had remembered them and makes reasonably good use of them. Her comment that "the type of satire is unknown currently" was meant to apply to her, of course, not to the world at large.

Response III

"Ozymandias," by Shelley, is satirical because it contains an ironic contrast, a target, and the essence of humor. The ironic contrast is achieved by the words of Ozymandias, "Look on my works, ye mighty and despair." These words applying to the rubble shown in the rest of the poem certainly are contrasted, and also inject a note of humor into the poem. The target of the satire is the artificial greatness of men, that is in time overcome by nature, to slump into oblivion. This is reinforced by the desert that the statue is found in. It is as far from greatness as possible, and is referred to as an "antique" land.

Ninth-grade boy

The third response is certainly the most concise of the three. One wishes that the young man had been a bit less concise, that he had explained the humor that he sees in the poem more carefully, and that he had developed the theme more completely. Still, response III meets the criteria of the terminal objectives more completely than either of the others, and, in that sense, is the best of them.

Responses such as these help the teacher to gauge the success of the unit instruction. If the remainder of the class responses treat humor in the same way, the teacher may need to spend more time with the students in determining whether, why, and how a line conveys humor. Simply by checking the results of such a test against the terminal objectives of the unit, the teacher can determine aspects of his teaching that require revision.

The Unit As a Whole

The unit as a whole should display this progression from introduction to evaluation. One effective method of introducing the concept of satire is through the use of cartoons. The teacher can collect satiric cartoons dealing with various topics: the President, pollution, political radicals, the schools, and so on. If he can obtain copies of the etchings of Hogarth, Rowlandson, and Daumier, the cartoons of Goya, and some of the paintings of Hieronymus Bosch and Pieter Brueghel, students may be interested in seeing them. In many, the satire will be as clear as the satire of some of the modern cartoons. There are two main advantages in introducing satire through cartoons. First, they attract immediate interest. Second, they can help the student understand not only the major goals and characteristics of satire but some of the specific techniques. (Similarly, the concepts of other units may be introduced through the use of cartoons or other popular media.)

Once students have examined and discussed several cartoons, the teacher can introduce the term "satire." As the results of the pretest indicate, some students may already be familiar with the term. If the teacher explains that the cartoons the class has examined are examples of satire, the students can begin to formulate a working definition of satire that includes a statement about the function of humor. Note that new vocabulary should be introduced after students have experience to which they can attach the terms.

The lessons following the introduction should each deal with a separate unit concept, beginning with those that are easiest to understand. The first lesson following the introduction to satire might be a brief examination of diatribe from Juvenal's *Satires* and from Philip Wylie's *Generation of Vipers*. The students can read selections of each, perhaps sections concerned with the same follies: women's make-up, education, and so on. The discussion that follows should deal with questions such as these:

1. Who is speaking?
2. What is satirized?
3. What techniques does the author use to accomplish the satire?

Ensuing lessons can take up exaggeration and allegory as the lesson described previously takes up irony. In contrast to exaggeration, it might be useful to introduce examples of understatement. Dickens uses both deftly. Aesop, La Fontaine, Thurber, John Gay, and Ivan Krilof are good sources of satiric fables.[4]

By the time the students have read and studied examples of diatribe, exaggeration, irony, and fables, their original definition of satire will have been expanded considerably. They may then learn to discriminate between the two major types of satire: diatribe, the satire of direct attack; and Menippean satire, the satire of indirect attack. The teacher can begin the lesson by asking the students to compare the passages from Juvenal and Philip Wylie to the satires they read later and explain how they differ in the method of attack. The students should be able to list several significant differences. The teacher should accept each suggestion and ask questions that require the class to examine the suggestion against the various works studied. Following the discussions, the students can examine brief examples of each type of satire as a check on their list of differences. There are, for example, a number of short, epigrammatic pieces by Swift, Pope, and others that are essentially the satire of direct attack.

Students Evaluate Works

Although a special lesson can focus on problems of evaluation, to a certain degree each of the lessons beyond the introductory ones should include questions that force the students to evaluate both the validity and the effectiveness of the works being studied. For instance, the following questions would be appropriate in the satire unit: (1) Does the target of the satire deserve the criticism it receives? (2) How effective is the satire? As mentioned before, the lesson dealing with diatribe and exaggeration early in the unit might make use of various selections attacking similar targets such as women's use of makeup. Students are always amazed to see that satirists as widely separated in time, space, and culture as Juvenal, Oliver Goldsmith, and Philip Wylie are concerned with similar problems. Passages in Juvenal's Sixth Satire,[5] Goldsmith's Letter 3 in *Letters from a Citizen of the World*,[6] and in Wylie's *Generation of Vipers*[7] all attack female vanity.

After reading the selections, identifying the targets of the satire, and discussing the techniques involved, the students can turn to evaluative questions: Which satire is the most convincing? What makes them convincing or unconvincing? To what extent do the satirists use techniques effectively? To what extent is the criticism valid? Obviously, if the students are to consider the problems of effectiveness and validity seriously, they must have criteria on which to base their judgments. But the consideration of the questions will lead to the formulation of criteria. The teacher, however, must continually pose the question Why? Why is the satire effective? Why is it ineffective? Why is it valid or invalid?

The examination of validity must follow a discussion of the work's theme and an application of its ideas to real life. For instance, with Sassoon's "Base Details" students should discuss the following questions: What is the central idea of the poem? What events in real life parallel those in the poem? To what extent, then, is the criticism offered by the poem valid? Questions such as these should give rise to the type of discussion that makes literature meaningful.

Artistic merit does not and should not depend totally upon the validity of the value system. Certainly no one should argue that Buddhist painting has little artistic merit because he does not hold the values that Buddhist painting reflects. The same is true of literature. Most Americans do not desire a monarchical form of government, nor do they believe in the divine right of kings, but none condemns Shakespeare's history plays for that reason. Thus, students must consider validity in two contexts: that of the real world as they see it, and that of the literary work as its own world. Examined in this way, questions of validity become congruent with those of effectiveness and artistic merit. Students can evaluate the artistic merit of a satire, or any literary work, by assessing the appropriateness, consistency, and efficiency of its parts as they work together to produce the total effect.

The teacher must remember how little influence is necessary for the student to make the judgments he thinks the teacher desires. For both types of evaluation the student should have an opportunity to make his own evaluations and defend them. For a further discussion of evaluation in the classroom, see Chapter 10.

The importance of evaluation in any unit, especially in satire, cannot be overemphasized. It is not enough to interpret, to comprehend the meaning. The students will want to debate questions of effectiveness and validity. If the teacher fails to allow time for such discussion, if he fails to promote it, the students are likely to view literature merely as a puzzle that is useless once the meaning is determined. Certainly, a student's evaluations will be subjective, but whose are not? His evaluations, as well as those of the most sophisticated critic, can be supported by textual analysis, personal reaction, and by comparison to the student's value system and to reality as he sees it.

Study of a Major Work

The lessons to this point serve as a preparation for the reading of a major work, perhaps *Huckleberry Finn, Pudd'nhead Wilson,* Leonard Wibberly's *The Mouse That Roared,* Orwell's *Animal Farm,* or Swift's *Gulliver's Travels.* The selection of the major works depends to a certain degree on the ability of the class. The ninth graders whose writing appears in this chapter studied both *Animal Farm* and *Huckleberry Finn.*

The presentation of a longer work offers special problems simply because of length. First, there is a temptation to dwell on every page of a novel as though each page were a separate lyric poem. Second, there is a temptation to assign a set number of pages per night and to discuss that number of pages for a class period whether or not the importance of the pages warrants more or less discussion. The result is that reading and discussion may take many days longer than necessary so that the instruction becomes tedious and boring. Fortunately, such techniques are not necessary.

In the first place, the teacher should probably assign the whole novel at once, suggesting a date by which the students should have completed their reading and intermediate dates as well, by which time they should have completed a certain minimum number of chapters. Since everything in the unit so far has led to the reading of this major text, the students are likely to be interested in the problem that the work presents and knowledgeable in the techniques the writer uses. If they are neither interested nor knowledgeable, then either the instruction up to this point has failed rather miserably or it has been inappropriate as preparation for reading the particular book.

Second, the teacher should decide on the key scenes and episodes in order to focus class discussion on them, rather than proceeding page by page. For instance, if the novel for study is *Huckleberry Finn,* the teacher might divide the novel into the following sections for reading and discussion: Chapters 1 and 2, one day for introduction; Chapters 3 through 15, two days of discussion on the major characters and the river; Chapters 16 through 31, two days on the satire of society; Chapters 2, 6, 15, 16, 23, and 31, one day on Huck's growth as an individual; Chapters 32 through 43, two days on the denouncement and satire of society. An additional two days might be reserved for discussing the novel as a whole or for additional time to treat one or more of the divisions suggested above. This plan holds class time spent on the novel to two weeks.

As mentioned above, the first two chapters introduce the book on the first day. They are short enough for the students to read quickly in class, and they illustrate themes, techniques, and targets of satire that run throughout the novel. By asking appropriate questions about the chapters, the teacher can introduce concepts that are basic to the book's satire: Huck as an outsider viewing the mores of a society he cannot completely comprehend; the hypocrisy of the society illustrated by the widow's taking snuff while refusing to let Huck smoke; the blind obedience to custom and tradition; Miss Watson's religion of fear; and Tom's role in the novel as a foil for Huck. If Huck is to be "civilized," he too must learn hypocrisy, custom, and the religion of fear; he must learn not to question what society has established; he must learn to follow the dictates of tradition as blindly as Tom follows the fictional robbers' code in Chapter 2. Tom, the widow, and Miss Watson have been so thoroughly indoctrinated into the value patterns of their society that they cannot see clearly. Huck, on the other hand, has not been "civilized." He can examine the values of the society objectively, but when his conclusions are negative, he attributes it to his being "so ignorant, and so kind of low-down and ornery." In short, most of the ideas and targets of satire that are central to the novel are introduced embryonically in the opening two chapters. The following key questions might be used for the introductory discussion of the novel.

1. What are the widow and Miss Watson planning to do to Huck?
2. In what ways do they plan to change Huck?
3. How does Huck feel about the widow's saying grace and taking snuff? Is Huck justified in feeling this way?
4. What is the basis for the beliefs and customs of Miss Watson and the widow?
5. What is the basis for Tom's decisions about the organization and activities of the robber band?
6. What is Tom's greatest concern in directing the activities of the robber band? (Is he more concerned with procedures or with attaining certain goals?)
7. Does Tom regard himself as civilized? Why? Does he regard Huck as civilized? Why?
8. In what way is Tom's behavior with the robber band similar to the behavior of the widow and Miss Watson? (Refer to the answer to question 4 if necessary.)
9. In what way is Huck different from all three in this respect?
10. Is Huck really ignorant? In what sense is he ignorant? In what sense is his ignorance an advantage unavailable to Tom, the widow, or Miss Watson?
11. What are the targets of Twain's satire in these two chapters?

Since most unit activities should have served as a preparation for understanding the special problems of meaning in the novel, a study guide can pose only the central questions and problems. The teacher should, however, have some simpler questions in reserve to use when the students have difficulty dealing with the central problems. These questions should be used to lead to a fuller comprehension of the study guide questions. The position of a work in the unit makes a difference. If it appears early in the unit, while the unit concepts are being developed initially, study guides should proceed from the simplest questions to the most difficult. Note that discussion questions for Chapters 1 and 2 of *Huckleberry Finn* move from literal questions to complex inference questions. The simple ones, whether literal or inferential, should bring the students' attention to those aspects of the work that must be considered in order to answer the more difficult questions. Their function, in short, is to help the student comprehend the details of the central unit problems. The study guides for a work coming late in the unit, after the concepts have been established and developed, can use questions that focus only on the major problems. For slower students, however, some of the simpler questions may be necessary even then. The following study guide for *Huckleberry Finn* focuses on major problems. Most of the questions lead to an examination of satire in the novel, but some deal with important, related problems such as Huck's growth as an individual.

CHAPTERS 4–15

Huck, Pap, Jim, and the River.

1. What advantage does Mark Twain have in telling the story from Huck's point of view? What advantages does Huck's dialect have over more formal speech patterns?
2. In what ways is Huck like his father? In what ways is he different?
3. In view of Pap's behavior both as a father and a citizen, what does his tirade against the free "nigger" suggest about him? What does the tirade satirize? The "nigger," Pap, or both? What form of satire is it?
4. What is the function of the scene aboard the *Walter Scott?* How does it contribute to Huck's education? What does it satirize?
5. What passages in these chapters best characterize Huck's attitude toward Jim?
6. What are Jim's essential characteristics? Which passages best reveal them?
7. What importance does the river have to Huck? What importance does it have for the novel as a whole? A good deal of the action takes place on the river. With what does Mark Twain contrast the river? For what purpose?

CHAPTERS 16–31

Society.

1. What values, vices, and follies of the society are satirized in the following incidents and episodes?
   a. Huck's stay with the Grangerfords—the interior decoration of the Grangerford home with its mementos of the deceased daughter, the church attendance, Huck's comment on the pigs in church, the feud.
   b. the Sherburn-Boggs incident.
   c. the King and the Duke—the camp meeting and the theatrical performances.
2. At the close of Chapter 24, Huck says, "It was enough to make a body ashamed of the human race." To what does his comment refer? In what sense do Huck's reasons for being ashamed multiply in Chapters 25 and 26?
3. What is the chief characteristic of the crimes perpetrated by the King and the Duke? What do their crimes reveal about their victims?

4. What do the crimes of the King and the Duke have in common with the follies and foolishness revealed in Miss Watson, the widow, the Grangerfords, and Tom? What does Twain satirize in relation to all of them?

CHAPTERS 2, 6, 15, 16, 23 AND 31

The Character of Huckleberry Finn.

1. In Chapter 2 Tom tricks Jim. In Chapter 15 Huck tricks him. Compare Huck's attitude toward the two tricks. What does the difference in attitude reflect about the change in Huck?
2. In Chapter 16 Jim thinks about his approaching freedom and considers stealing his two children from the man who owns them. Huck begins to feel guilty about helping Jim escape and remarks, "Thinks I, this is what comes of my not thinking. Here was this nigger, which I had as good as helped to run away, coming right out flat-footed and saying he would steal his children. . . ." What is the irony of Huck's remark? What does it satirize?
3. In the same chapter Huck considers turning Jim over to the authorities, but he cannot bring himself to do it. Between what two sets of values is Huck caught? How are these sets of values similar to the "two providences" mentioned at the beginning of Chapter 2? What does the simultaneous existence of the two sets of values indicate about the society?
4. In Chapter 23 Huck and Jim discuss the nature of kings. Their discussion is followed immediately by Jim's story of his deaf daughter. What does this story reveal about Jim? What does the juxtaposition of the two suggest about kings? About slaves? In view of this, why is it ironic that Jim is a slave?
5. Toward the end of Chapter 23 Huck remarks that he believes Jim "cared just as much for his people as white folks does for ther'n. It don't seem natural, but I reckon it's so." What changes does this remark reveal in Huck? Why is the remark ironic? What does it suggest about the society?
6. In Chapter 31 Huck fights with his conscience again. What is a conscience? How does it develop? What does Huck's conscience represent? What does his final decision represent? What does Huck's decision reveal about the changes he has undergone as a person since the beginning of the book? What is the target of Twain's satire in this scene?
7. Trace the development of Huck's personality to the end of Chapter 31 in light of his relationship to Jim and his view of the society.

CHAPTERS 32–43

1. What is Huck's plan to steal Jim? What is Tom's plan? What differences in the two boys do the plans reflect? Which plan is better? Why?
2. In what ways is Tom a representative of society as reflected by his reason for helping Jim escape and by his plan for doing it?

3. What does the fact that Tom knew Jim had been freed before he put his plan into action reveal about Tom's feelings for other people? What was the purpose of his gift of forty dollars to Jim? What does the money reveal about Tom's view of human dignity? What does the incident satirize?
4. What differences between Huck and Tom do the final eleven chapters reveal? In terms of their review of reality, society, and human dignity? How do these differences serve Mark Twain's purposes as a satirist?
5. Could Mark Twain have made Tom the hero of the book? Explain your answer.
6. Some criticis have argued that the final eleven chapters mar the artistic unity of the book because they are farcical and unrelated to the first thirty-one chapters. How would you defend or attack this judgment?

The teacher need not lead the discussion on each of the focal points. He can and should lead the discussion of Chapters 1 and 2, and thereafter he should lead discussions of focal points that illustrate problems arising for the first time. For instance, the first division after the introduction focuses in part on personality: Huck, Tom, Pap, Jim. Thereafter, discussions of character might profitably take place in small-group sessions. The students can discuss the problems of character that arise in Chapter 23 when Huck and Jim discuss royalty and when Jim tells his story of his deaf daughter. However, when the discussion shifts to the structure of the chapter, the problem of why the two conversations are juxtaposed, the teacher might take over or at least lead a class discussion after the student groups have dealt with the problem. Again, the teacher should lead the discussion that focuses on Huck's first feelings of guilt as he reflects on the evils of helping Jim escape in Chapter 16. But students working in small groups can examine the similar scene in Chapter 31 in which Huck makes his decision to help Jim and go to hell. Although the irony of the scene is very complex, the study of irony early in the unit and the earlier discussion of Huck's qualms as they reflect on society should enable the students to handle the scene efficiently. Similarly, if the students discuss the purpose of the final eleven chapters and attempt to evaluate them in terms of the artistic design of the whole book, they should have examined the effects of the juxtaposition of scenes and chapters earlier in the book, probably with the help of the teacher.

In the whole-class discussion following the small-group discussions, two or more groups may find themselves diametrically opposed. Such a situation is invaluable because the teacher or students can then organize a debate, with each of two or more groups presenting its point of view, while the remainder of the class acts as arbiter. Each group should present its conclusions, explain the textual evidence upon which the conclusions are based, and prepare to examine the conclusions and evidence of the other groups. The class should be permitted to ask questions of the groups after their presentations. What is important is the close examination of the text that will precede and follow the presentation of conclusions.

Finally, the teacher can reserve a group of important scenes for students to examine independently. For example, the Boggs-Sherburn incident, the dramatic productions of the King and the Duke, the events aboard the *Walter Scott,* and Huck's reaction to the tarring and feathering of the King and Duke are all appropriate for comment in a classroom test or outside essay situation. The students should explain the significance of the scene in itself and as it relates to the novel as a whole.

The procedures suggested here are useful in approaching any longer work: careful teacher-led study of the opening scenes; selection and arrangement of focal points throughout the work for discussion; small-group discussion of appropriate problems; individual analyses of scenes, events, images, and so on, after the discussion of similar problems by the class or by small groups. A careful study of the first thirty-two lines of the *Odyssey,* for instance, reveals the essential plight of Odysseus, the main plot of the story, and a good deal about his character. Similarly, the first short chapter of *The Pearl* presents the story's main characters, the event that instigates the action (the scorpion stings Coyotito), and the contrast beween the idyllic countryside and the evil of the city. Richard's opening speech in Shakespeare's *Richard III* and the opening scenes of *Macbeth* present, in microcosm, the major characters and the themes that will be developed later. Each work is divisible into sections that extend and develop the opening section or that introduce additional complications. The teacher can select various focal points for discussion and reserve some for individual analysis. Thus, the study of even a single long work can usefully take the unit shape: (1) introducing and establishing major concepts in a discussion led by the teacher; (2) small-group discussion of certain portions of the work focusing on concepts already developed; and finally (3) individual analysis and interpretation.

Individualized Reading

The final phase of the unit, individualized reading, has two separate functions: first, to allow the students to pursue reading that is of special interest to them and at or near their own level of comprehension; and second, to provide a means of evaluation for the unit as a whole. Near the conclusion of the unit, the teacher should distribute a list of books related to the unit topic. If possible, he should comment briefly on the various titles to note their relative difficulty and to suggest those which might be of particular interest. It is useful to take the class to the school library for this assignment, especially if the librarian will put the books on a special shelf so that the students can look them over and withdraw the ones they prefer on the same day. When the list of books is long, the teacher might wish to comment on the titles on one day and take the class to the library on the next.

The bibliography should provide a fairly wide range of satirical books. The weaker students should be directed to such titles as *The Mouse That Roared, The Mouse on the Moon, Planet of the Apes, The Prince and The Pauper, H.M.S. Pinafore, Fail-Safe,* or *The Decline and Fall of Practically Everybody.* The more advanced students might deal with Austen, Dickens, Swift, or Thackeray. The students should have as much leeway as possible in selecting what they want to read. A student will read a book that is too difficult for him if he is interested enough in it, and in any case, it is not necessary that every student comprehend every aspect of the book he selects. As long as the student can determine the targets of the satire and how the satire works, the teacher need not demand complete explication of every passage. Robert Southey once said, "What blockheads are those wise persons, who think it necessary that a child should understand everything it reads." Obviously, a student reading a book on his own may overlook the significance of certain details, but then even sophisticated adult readers do that. On the other hand, the students should understand the major aspects of the unit topic as they are reflected in the books they have chosen for individual reading and have enough understanding of details to support their interpretations.

Although the more he knows about the books the better, a teacher should not restrict an outside reading list simply because he has not read all the titles personally. He knows the unit and can judge a student's comprehension of a book by his application of the unit concepts to the book. A reading list can be compiled by a group of teachers working together and with the aid of the school librarian, who is frequently a very helpful source of information about books. As a matter of fact, if the teacher explains the concepts and purposes of a unit to the librarian, she can sometimes produce a long list of appropriate titles that are available in the school library. She can also recommend sources of reviews and/or summaries of all sorts of books that can be invaluable in composing the lists. Most teachers have no compunctions about not being familiar with all the books students read for conventional book reports. There is even less reason for concern in this situation because the student cannot use some other student's report on a book, simply because the unit plus the student-teacher conferences provide a special focus through which to view the book.

Student-teacher conferences on outside reading are valuable for three reasons. First, while the teacher confers with individual students, the rest of the class can read their books. Devoting in-class time to outside reading is a solid demonstration that the teacher regards that work as important. Second, by the point in the unit at which the outside reading is beginning, some of the major unit compositions may be in progress. The conference session can provide time for working on compositions in class. Third, the conference itself is important. The teacher ought to know by this time how well each student has progressed in the unit. During the conference, therefore, he can help the student focus on the particular unit problems that are appropriate to his level of sophistication. The teacher can also determine whether or not the student has chosen a book suitable to his reading skill and interest. Assuming that the teacher knows his students' abilities, each conference need last only five or six minutes and should proceed as follows: The teacher situates himself at a vantage point that ensures both a degree of privacy and a view of the class. As each student comes to speak with the teacher, he brings his book. The teacher checks the title and asks a series of questions:

1. What is the book about?
2. Do you think it is a satire?
3. What does it satirize?
4. What evidence leads you to think the book is satiric?
5. (If the student is hazy in answering 2, 3, and 4) Are there any scenes or incidents that puzzle you?
6. (If there are) Tell me about the scene. (Then examine the scene or incident briefly with the student. Ask a few appropriate questions.)
7. Do you prefer to continue reading this book, or would you rather find another?
8. Do you have any questions about the book?

In view of the answers to these questions, the teacher can evaluate the student's responses to the book and, by asking a few questions, suggest directions for the student to take in his reading.

Even with a class of forty students, the teacher should be able to complete individual conferences in five or six days. If several students are reading the same book, the teacher can confer with two or more of them at a time, thus speeding up the conferences. At any rate, by the time the conferences have been completed, most students will be far along in their reading, and many will have finished.

The report that the student writes on his individual reading not only takes the place of the traditional book report but is usually far more interesting to read. As a result of the unit, the student has a point of view and can observe evidence and draw inferences more intelligently. He also has a stronger base for evaluation because in the course of the unit he has read other works, similar in some ways, against which he can evaluate his individual reading. Most important, the student's essay will provide a basis for evaluating the effectiveness of the unit as a whole.

Sometimes, the teacher may wish to use other methods of evaluation. For instance, a less sophisticated unit on satire than the one described here might be evaluated through a test on a group of short selections that are similar to, but more difficult than, those on the pretest. Or the teacher may ask the students to read three or four poems and short stories in preparation for an essay test in class. Occasionally a unit will require a special project such as the investigation and comparison of several works by one author. In each case, however, the students work with material they have not previously studied. In short, what the students have learned *to do* in the course of a unit becomes an important measure of the unit's success.

Differentiating Assignments

This unit structure allows, and in a sense demands, the differentiation of assignments. We have already described one assignment that allows each student to choose a book from a list distributed by the teacher. Obviously, this technique differentiates assignments. But ordinarily, it may be necessary or useful to differentiate at other points in the unit as well. When the teacher is leading the class activity in order to develop a concept, all students need to read the same material. But after the initial development of concepts when students are working in small groups or individually, it is both useful and desirable to differentiate assignments. For instance, while the teacher begins the lesson on satiric fables with a series of three or four very simple ones, he might select fables of varying degrees of complexity for analysis by small groups and individuals. Aesop's fables are almost uniformly simple, some of Thurber's are more sophisticated, and the eighteenth-century fables by John Gay and Christopher Smart are the most complex, at least in terms of vocabulary and syntax. Very bright students might be assigned to work with a translation of Chaucer's "Nuns' Priest's Tale," the story of Chanticleer and Pertelote. Similarly for purposes of evaluation, the slower students might be asked to interpret the irony of "The Battle of Blenheim" instead of "Ozymandias," provided that it has not been used earlier for instruction.

Additionally, it is frequently necessary to differentiate the assignment of major works. Many students will find *Huckleberry Finn* boring. Students who do not read ordinary language fluently cannot be expected to read unfamiliar dialects fluently. Listen to Jim: "I crope out all a-tremblin', en crope aroun' en open de do' easy en slow, en poke my head in behine de chile, sof' en still, en all uv a sudden I says *pow!*" A great many unusual words there. Besides such problems at the literal level, the irony and structural aspects of the book are complex. Thus, while one group studies *Huckleberry Finn,* it might be useful for others to read an easier novel such as Leonard Wibberly's *The Mouse That Roared.* It is possible for a teacher to guide as many as three or four groups reading different major works, but careful planning is necessary. While one group meets with the teacher for the introductory discussion of the opening portion of its novel (see previous discussion), the other groups of ten or more can read their opening sections or work on composition assignments. Later, discussions with five or six students can take place around the teacher's desk. For the most part, however, the discussions can take place in small groups with only the occasional assistance of the teacher. Naturally, this procedure requires study guides for each group involved. But once the guides for each group are written, the teacher need only revise them as revision proves useful. When a variety of materials is not available, it is possible to differentiate assignments by assigning various questions to various groups of students as described in Chapter 3.

Selection of Materials

Selections used to introduce concepts should be relatively free of problems that the students have not learned to handle previously. If the teacher can think of no other vehicle for the introduction of imagery than *King Lear,* he should probably abandon the idea of teaching imagery. Fortunnately, in most of the conceptual areas of literature there is a wealth of simple material available. Imagery and symbolism can be introduced through the use of fables and simple poetry. Concepts of character, plot, and environment can be introduced through animal stories. The idea of structure can be examined through the study of relatively simple but powerful poetic forms such as haiku and blues. Genre can be studied through the analysis of detective stories and science fiction. Most important literary themes, motifs, and archetypes abound in myth, fairy tales, and in quality literature written expressly for adolescents. For instance, the theme of alienation in Joyce's *Portrait of the Artist as a Young Man* also appears in a more obvious form in Paul Gallico's *Snow Goose.* On the other hand, some genres present special difficulty. To study either tragedy or epic, one must read tragedies or epics. But it is possible to prepare students for tragedy and epic. Many of the myths of Greek heroes (for example, Jason, Perseus, Theseus) display the themes, motifs, and to some degree the plot structure that will appear in the great epics from *Gilgamesh* to *The Odyssey* to *Paradise Lost.* Others display the outlines of the tragic plot: the pride of Bellerophon and his fall from Pegasus, and the like.

That the materials exist is important; that they are worth reading in themselves by particular students at a particular time is equally important. If we ask poor readers to fight through *The Return of the Native,* they are likely to have little reward for their efforts despite whatever critical and pedagogical stature it may have. Although *Johnny Tremain* and *The Bronze Bow* are not such great historical fiction as *A Tale of Two Cities* or *Henry Esmond,* they undoubtedly will offer a great deal more to certain students at certain points in their development than will novels by Dickens or Thackeray.

Writing

Any literature unit should contain a wide variety of writing experiences for the student, and each of them can be an integral part of the unit. For example, composition is an important phase of the unit on satire, and each composition lesson or activity arises directly out of the study of satire. As the objectives indicate, the unit involves four major writing assignments: a definition of satire, an analysis of a satiric work, an original satire, and a parody.

1. DEFINITION The work on definition begins with the first lesson of the unit. After the students have examined and discussed the cartoons, the teacher asks them to compose a working definition. Then, using a chalkboard or an overhead projector, the teacher writes out a working definition based on the contributions of the class. It is extremely useful for the students to have previously studied and written genus-specie definitions. The first attempt at the definition may be clumsy, and it certainly will be incomplete. One ninth-grade class composed the following: "Satire is a form of literature which ridicules something by the use of humor. The humor may be subtle or obvious, gentle or violent." The students who composed this were not aware of how appropriate their use of the word *form* was. They used it as a synonym of *kind,* but as the unit progressed they came to understand *form* in a more technical sense.

After each lesson on an aspect of satire, the students add to and revise the definition in terms of what they have learned in that lesson. Note-taking is important to this process, and the teacher should exercise care to give the students the time to take notes. In inductive teaching, there is a tendency for the teacher to move on to the next lesson as soon as students reach the appropriate conclusions. But he must take the time to review the lesson, consolidate what the students have learned, and provide note-taking time.

One important aspect of the extended definition is the inclusion and discussion of examples for illustrative purposes. Students frequently do not know how to incorporate or refer to examples smoothly. The result is either no example or a clumsy statement: "Irony is used as a satiric device. This is shown in 'Base Details.'" The teacher can use models written by other students to illustrate better techniques.

The major problem for writing the definition of satire, of course, is organization. If the students have already studied patterns of organization, there will be no problem. If they have not, the teacher must introduce appropriate models. A brief class discussion of possibilities for organization is helpful. One group of ninth graders suggested the following pattern:

a. Brief statement about the nature of satire.
b. Distinction of two kinds of satire: diatribe and Menippean satire.
c. Discussion of each type with examples.

The student who wrote the composition below departed from this suggested approach somewhat but met all the criteria stated with the second objective for the unit—to write an extended definition of satire.

Criterion statements: the student must
a. Explain the purpose of satire.

b. Discriminate adequately between formal verse satire (diatribe) and Menippean satire.

c. Explain the devices (those studied in class) used in each kind of satire.

d. Illustrate each point with examples from materials studied in the unit.

THE NATURE OF SATIRE*

The division of literature which, in its essence, ridicules and criticizes man and his works or some other target is known as satire. Satire can be classified into two main groups, Diatribe and Menippean. Both types involve the use of such elements as humor, sarcasm, exaggeration and connotation, but these elements are used in different degrees in the two types.

The attacking of a target by ridicule, irony, or some other form of criticism appears to be the main purpose of satire. However, the opinion of the author as to what is good or right is usually conveyed, and often the author may suggest a solution to the problem. The opinions and suggested solutions may not be very obvious in Menippean satire, but in some diatribe, such as Juvenal's Satire VI, one can easily see the author's opinion, and from this a solution to the problem may be conveyed.

Diatribe is related in the first person, is usually subjective, has no plot, and makes use of specific detail, connotation, humor, sarcasm, exaggeration, harshness and abusiveness. These elements can be observed in Juvenal's Satire VI, which is told in the first person. Although there is no real plot, Juvenal's opinion criticizing women's use of cosmetics is conveyed. He sharply exaggerates with connotative phrases the various uses of make-up and ornamentation.

. . . she rings her neck with emeralds
and hangs to her ears gold links
. . . her face is foul, each contour
Grotesquely puffed by beauty packs,
and she reeks and drips
With thick Poppaean creams . . .

Humor is achieved through the greatly exaggerated passages in the satire. The constant harsh and abusive treatment of women and their use of make-up leads to the final sarcastic statement, "Questionable? What shall we call it—a face or an ulcer?"

Menippean satire makes use of some elements which are found in Diatribe, such as connotation, exaggeration, humor, and detail, but there are some differences. Unlike Diatribe, Menippean satire has a plot and is not told in the first person, but makes use of an omniscient author. Since the satire has a plot and is often in the form of a story, like *Nicholas Nickleby,* the opinion of the author may not be obvious on the literal level. In *Nicholas Nickleby,* Dickens uses exaggeration and connotation to de-

---

* This and the compositions that follow in this chapter were revised and polished by their authors for inclusion in class or school publications.

scribe the treatment of a group of boys in a boarding school, but the credibility of the situation is not as distorted as in Juvenal's works. Menippean satire may make use of a bitter, or, as in *Nickleby,* a pathetic sort of humor which is directed at Squeers, the man who is in charge of the school.

Another element of Menippean satire is irony. In satires like this, there is an ironic twist at the end of the selection. This is true of *Animal Farm.* In the beginning, the pigs on the farm denounce men, and vow never to act like humans. As the story progresses, the pigs gradually take on more and more human characteristics—wearing clothes, walking on two legs, living in houses, and drinking alcoholic beverages. In the end, it is almost impossible to distinguish the pigs from the men. Irony is achieved in "Ozymandias" in the fact that something great and outstanding is eventually forgotten. It criticizes man's vain attitude that he will never be forgotten, that people will forever remember him and his so-called outstanding accomplishments:

'My name is Ozymandias, King of Kings.
Look upon my words, ye Mighty, and despair!'
Nothing beside remains. Round the decay
Of that colossal wreck, boundless and bare,
The lone and level sands stretch far away.

Another type of Menippean satire is that which is found in fables. These fables use symbolism or allegory with the basic Menippean elements. The fables sometimes make use of irony and often contain a moral. Animals are often used in fables. This is true of *Animal Farm,* where the animals are given human characteristics in order to satirize some human institution.

Doth Diatribe and Menippean satire use the techniques of exaggeration along with specific examples to make their satires effective. Both types use highly connotative and precise words. The main difference in the structure of the two types of satire is the person who is speaking. In Juvenal the satirist speaks for himself, while in *Nicholas Nickleby,* Dickens makes use of an omniscient author whose criticism evolves from the plot and the characters. Satire, while it seems to be only ridiculing a target, can be subjective and suggest solutions to given situations. This is achieved through two main divisions of satire, Diatribe and Menippean. Both have many similar elements, but use them in different ways, creating the two different satirical structures.

Ninth-grade girl

2. ANALYSIS Throughout a given unit students write interpretations of literary works. And although the written analysis of literature is customary in nearly every curriculum, unknowing teachers throw up their hands at the word "analysis." They are afraid of what the word connotes to them. They recall uncomfortable experiences in college when they were asked to write analyses, and not knowing how to do it or what the professor wanted, they

found themselves frustrated, demoralized, and losing interest in the course. Even the most traditional and the most modern teachers require analyses of their students constantly: book reports, responses to poems, short-answer tests, précis writing, and the like. All these require analysis at some level of sophistication.

Analysis need not be a frightening term. One function of any unit is to enable the students to interpret (analyze) literature at a more sophisticated level. If the unit begins with what students can already do, introduces concepts in their simplest form, and gradually increases in complexity, the students will be neither bored nor frustrated by the work. Further, they will know what the teacher expects because the whole unit is directed toward helping the student learn to interpret.

Just as the unit develops from simple to complex concepts, the first writing task is relatively simple whereas the final ones are more complex. Thus, the analyses required early in the unit will be concerned with a short example of diatribe, perhaps a selection from Juvenal or the poem by Swift mentioned earlier. As the lessons deal with more complex concepts, the composition problem becomes more complex. By the end of the unit, the student should be able to write an analysis of a longer work in terms of the criterion statements for the first objective of the unit—to write an essay interpreting the satire of a play, novel, or series of essays or short stories by a single author. (May not use material studied in class.)

Criterion statements: the student must
a. Decide on the basis of criteria in a definition whether or not the work is satiric.
b. Identify the targets of satire and explain why they are satirized.
c. Explain how plot, character, imagery, and satiric techniques provide the satire.
d. Identify the values that the author regards as good or appropriate in contrast to those he condemns.

The composition that follows fulfills all the criterion statements. The young lady decides that the work is a satire, designates the targets of criticism, explains briefly how the satire works, and identifies the values that the author regards as better—all in a smoothly written composition. The only thing that one might ask is that she explain the workings of the satire more fully. But even the way it stands, the composition is more than adequate.

PRIDE AND PREJUDICE: A Review

Jane Austen's novel, *Pride and Prejudice,* written in the eighteenth century, looked at various phases of English upper class society with a satirical eye. The author subtly criticized the life in a small town, with its gossips and marriage minded mothers, the higher society with its pride and snobbish traditions, and the "marriage market" of that era on which young ladies were placed to make sure they had a home and someone to care for them in their later life. In her indirect and simple way, she brought her characters to life and wove them into her story, giving them the same "pride" and the same "prejudices" they would have had, had they been real.

Miss Austen had no qualms about showing ". . . a small town, with its gossips and marriage minded mothers," and plunged right in by wrapping them both up in Mrs. Bennet. She and her sister, Mrs. Phillips, were the town gossips. Nearly every event that happened in town was known to them within the hour. They were the first to know who had rented Netherfield Park and what Mr. Darcy's and Mr. Bingley's yearly incomes were. To Mrs. Bennet, this was extremely necessary because she had ". . . five worthy daughters to get rid of." It was her greatest aim in life to have all five of them settled down with rich husbands, and consequently, she was always on the look-out for this type of man.

"The higher society, with their pride and snobbish traditions" was epitomized in Mr. Darcy, Elizabeth's suitor. His pride, conceit and so-called superiority were woven by Miss Austen into every action and word which he spoke. At the first ball he went to in Meryton, he absolutely refused to dance with any of the women there, because they were too inferior for him and were unable even to carry on a decent conversation. He felt ". . . there is not a woman in the room whom it would not be a punishment to me to stand up with." When he finally proposed to Elizabeth, he told her how he had fought with himself to keep from loving her because ". . . of the inferiority of her connections . . . whose condition in life is so decidedly beneath my own." These traditions which made men marry into their own class were something which Jane Austen found insupportable.

The "marriage market" of that era was a thing that was rather depressing. Property could go only from father to son. If a man wasn't fortunate enough to have a son, his property went to his next of kin. Because the Bennets did not have a son, their five daughters were forced to get married, for in the event of their father's death, they would be put out of their home. For many years, authors like Jane Austen wrote about and satirized this law which made it nearly impossible for a woman to own property. When this law was finally revoked, the marriage market slowly disappeared because women found they no longer had to get married to get along in life.

Pride and Prejudice summed up three of the major defects of English society. Wrapped up in its satire, it was like a sugar coated pill for people to swallow. Even though it may not have done anything to improve conditions, it has proven a good example of satire and will continue to entertain people with its humorous criticism in disguise.

Ninth-grade girl

While this particular terminal objective calls for students to write about material not studied in class, other objectives might call for a student to use material that was used in class without simply regurgitating class and group discussions. There are at least two possibilities. First, the student can select a particular image or scene not discussed in class and examine its meaning in terms of the whole work. Second, he can compare or relate a work studied in class with one studied outside class. In the following composition, a ninth-grade boy compares the philosophy of Machiavelli's *The Prince,* selections of which he had read in the eighth grade, to the view of man underlying Golding's *Lord of the Flies.* For this project he read more extensively in *The Prince* on his own. The *Lord of the Flies* was studied in class.

THE NATURE OF MAN IN
LORD OF THE FLIES AND *THE PRINCE*

Though they lived four and one-half centuries apart, William Golding and Niccola Machiavelli exhibit many similarities in both theory and in their works *Lord of the Flies* and *The Prince* (respectively). Exemplifying those similarities is the fact that both authors believe that man is innately evil: Machiavelli revealing this directly and Golding indirectly through the plot of his work. In theory Machiavelli and Golding show other similarities, too, as much of Golding's work corresponds directly with the theory related in *The Prince.* Contrasts in the works are also evident, though they are minor in consequence. *Lord of the Flies* is written to be interpreted through its fictional value on the symbolic level, whereas *The Prince* is written and interpreted literally, as Machiavelli supports his theories with fact. Another contrast in the works is that Golding's work is written on a microcosmic scale and Machiavelli's portrays a true-to-life scale. Though these contrasts are clearly defined, they are unimportant to the theory behind the work.

Golding, in *Lord of the Flies,* tells of a group of boys' reversion to savagery after losing physical ties with civilization. By this fact alone Golding infers man's evil nature. He tries to reveal that if man is apart from civilized society for any lengthy duration, he will eventually revert to his inborn savagery and lose all cultural ties. This change is slow, though, as Golding explains it.

After a short period of separation from society "Roger's arm was conditioned (still) by a civilization that knew nothing of him . . ." This explanation of a boy throwing stones at another displays the time involved, as Golding must feel that man's degeneration is a slow process. He believes that the only force holding man in existence is society and that this, too, in time, will degenerate greatly. To Golding, therefore, man's "Golden Age" must have been in the past, as it seems obvious that Golding's theory (and Machiavelli's, too) is in opposition to the Doctrine of

Progress, or that man as an individual is basically good and that he is constantly progressing.

To interpret Golding's theory on man further (if this can be done), the extreme or complete degeneration of man would lead to the extinction of the human race. If mankind were to follow the example set by the boys in *Lord of the Flies,* it would soon lose much of its knowledge (through lack of records) acquired by it and sent down from the "Golden Age." If such a complete reversion occurred, men could be found destroying each other, and soon going into extinction. As denoted in *Lord of the Flies,* in a short period, presumably a year or so, the boys had lost most all ties with civilization and were madly killing one another. "He tried to convey the compulsion to track down and kill that was swallowing him up." In summary, then, Golding obviously feels that society modifies and purifies Man who is basically evil, rather than perverting and corrupting Man who is basically good.

Machiavelli, too, believes that man is innately evil, and in *The Prince* he tries to tell man how to overcome the wickedness of others. Man will always look out for himself before others and will not care about the well-being of others if his personal goal gets in the way. "For it may be said of men in general that they are ungrateful, voluble, dissemblers, anxious to avoid danger and covetous of gain; as long as you benefit them they are entirely yours." As a result Machiavelli might modify the Golden Rule to read: "Do Unto Others Before They Can Do Unto You." Man must not live just by his morals or goodness for "A man who wishes to make a profession of goodness must necessarily come to grief among so many who are not so good." To interpret his statement then, Machiavelli believes that man corrupts society and not vice-versa. Therefore it is reasonable to say that if man were innately good, the boys in *Lord of the Flies* would not have become savage.

Many other Machiavellian theories can be directly compared to Golding's book. Within the book a power struggle occurs between two good leaders, Ralph and Jack. Ralph, the elected leader, was kind, courteous, and democratic in his ways. He sought "to make a profession of goodness." Jack, on the contrary, lived in a completely different world. He was clever, absolute, and military in his doings. His life revolved about his love for fighting and hunting, whereas Ralph stuck to governing. According to Machiavelli, those two types of leaders must conflict. "For one being disdainful (Jack towards Ralph) and the other suspicious (Ralph of Jack's army), it is not possible for them to act well together." As a result the masses (the boys) had to take sides, and Jack becomes a much more successful leader than Ralph. Why? This, too, can be related to Machiavelli. To begin with, Jack made himself both feared and respected by his subordinates. He developed a reputation for his skill in hunting; a reputation is "very profitable" in the eyes of Machiavelli. To develop a fear in the boys, Jack made them believe that if they didn't do as he told them a beast might attack and kill them. Because of this fear they obeyed him. Ralph neither gained respect nor fear from the boys he "governed." He preferred love to fear as shown in his democratic rule. With this government nothing was accomplished, as the boys easily broke their promises to work, for "men have less scruples in offending one who makes himself loved than one who makes himself feared; for love is held by a chain of obligation which, men being selfish, is broken whenever it serves their purpose; but fear is maintained by a dread of punishment which never fails." Jack was successful for another reason. He always kept his boys on guard and ready for Ralph, even though he knew Ralph would never and could never attack. This action united the boys against a common enemy and kept them under his control. "A prince should therefore have no other aim or thought . . . but war and its organization and discipline." Thus, through these three main Machiavellian concepts: 1) a leader should be feared rather than loved, 2) a leader should develop a reputation, and 3) a leader should constantly be thinking of war, its organization and discipline, Golding shows Jack to be a far more successful ruler than Ralph.

Four and one-half centuries. What has happened to man in that long span of time? Has he basically changed at all? According to these authors, no. Alike in this respect, they both feel that men shall ever be "ungrateful, voluble, dissemblers, anxious to avoid danger, and covetous of gain."

Ninth-grade boy

---

3. ORIGINAL SATIRE Any unit can be organized to incorporate what is commonly called creative writing. The unit on satire includes the writing of an original satire.

Criterion statements: the student must

a. Choose a target to satirize.

b. Use one or more of the devices studied to implement the satire, which may be either diatribe or Menippean satire.

The assignment writing a satire should come late in the unit, after the students have had an opportunity to read and study a variety of works that use a variety of techniques. The first step is picking something to satirize. It is useful to have a brainstorming session with every person suggesting possible, specific topics as fast as possible. The teacher selects three students to write on the board and then calls on students in rapid succession until everyone has had two or three opportunities to suggest an idea. Every student should suggest something. To get the brainstorming off to a good start, the teacher should give everyone a moment to think and demand that the first student make a suggestion. In ten minutes, the board will be covered with examples. Next, the teacher should let the students work in pairs to discuss and develop the ideas. Is the problem really worthy of satire? What weaknesses should be attacked? How might the satire proceed? The teacher should speak with as many students as possible in the time available, helping them to limit the possible targets of their satire to real weaknesses. Slower students tend to pick rather broad topics without thinking about them long enough to determine where the weaknesses lie. For instance, the idea that school is like a prison has possibilities and appears to be a favorite with slower students. The teacher rather than rejecting the idea should ask the students to list all the ways in which the school is prison-like: appearance, the bells, rules concerning what not to do, lack of real responsibility, and so on.

Next the students must decide how their satires will proceed—what devices or tactics they will use. One student, for example, decided to have a man from Mars visit the school and comment in a letter to his friend back home. (Interestingly, this student had not read the Goldsmith selection mentioned earlier.) Once these decisions are made, the teacher should allow time for the students to begin their satires in class, so that he will have an opportunity to work with students who may have trouble.

One interesting result of this assignment is that various teachers and administrative practices receive a good many well-wrought and well-aimed satiric barbs: the principal, school dances, guidance counselors, gym teachers. Nothing should be sacrosanct. The following satires take on a variety of targets:

Original Satires

I. Diatribe

THE OMNIPOTENT MALE

There are many different shapes, sizes, and varieties. They vary from the slim to the flabby, from the muscle-bound to the 98-pound weakling, but they still have one basic thing in common—their infallible ego. The male ego is that which is supposedly the most invulnerable thing on the face of this Earth, yet if it is in anyway harmed, a most radical unbalancing takes place in the mind of the male, and he becomes "emotionally disturbed."

When he is undisturbed, he is preoccupied with building up muscle—to show the other guys who's boss—and collecting girls. He follows a rigorous training program and sometimes comes looking like one of those greased mountains of men you have seen on "Guides to Body Building" magazines. In this case, however, he is often all brawn and no brains. His patterns in girl-watching are fairly obvious. He is either a suave, sophisticated Don Juan, a fast talking smoothie who leads you to believe he knows the ropes, or a bumbling dunderhead who falls head-over-heels if a girl says "hello." Most men would like to be considered Don Juans, but usually turn out to be bumbling dunderheads who don't really know the score.

You may have decided that no males you know fall into any of the previously mentioned categories. If not, there is yet another. Here we have the guy who think's he's sharp if he wears pants that fit him like a second skin, boots with ridiculously high heels and hairdos that make him look like the girl next door. At this stage whether he had simply given up, or whether he is just rebelling against the world is the question. These observations lead me to believe that men are becoming more and more feminine. I ask you, where are the days when men shaved themselves with straight razors once a week and didn't bother with all sorts of potions and pomades for their razor burn. Nowadays, men are properly talcum powdered, deodorized, splashed with various after-shaves, pre-shaves, face conditioners, etc. And out of this they emerge smelling like lilies of the valley and fresh as the morning dew. It always was hard to tell the men from the boys but now who's going to be able to tell the boys from the girls?

Ninth-grade girl

II. Menippean Satire

A. FABLE

A MOUSE EYE VIEW

Now, as all this may seem rather strange to you, I will tell you what I did not find out until much later. The farmer had been told that animals, like people, need social activity. This "togetherness atmosphere" would increase work and productivity. So the farmer had decided to let the animals have a party if they would take care of the decorations and clean up afterwards. The farm animals agreed. To make sure that nothing went wrong, the farmer had sent his farm hands to keep an eye on things.

A great deal of noise and general air of festivity pervaded the barn. As the evening wore on, though, I felt that everything was not as it should be. Though there were groups of animals milling around, it certainly seemed as if they were segregated—groups of chickens, groups of ducks, groups of horses—no mixture. Of course, I'm only a mouse, so I might be wrong.

Anyway, these groups struck me as slightly amusing. There were the chickens, standing in a corner, clucking and cackling about some of the other animals. Every once in a while, a couple of them would get together and start scratching in time to the music, but none of the other animals paid any attention to them.

Then there were the geese. They started out in a little group the way the chickens did. Pretty soon, though, they began waddling to one of the stalls. When they got there they would start preening themselves and washing their bills and, later on, they even began powdering their bills with straw dust to keep them from shining. It didn't do them any good. The only people they talked to were themselves.

I think the group that took the cake was the horses. They were lined up against one side of the barn looking as if they were holding up the wall. Each one had on a harness that had been waxed and polished until it shone but looked as if it choked its owner. They had been re-shoed but they fidgeted as the shoes pinched their hooves. On the whole, they looked so uncomfortable that I wished they had been in their stalls asleep.

The farm hands saw all this too, and decided to try to stop it. There was a long trough of food outside for refreshments and they decided to bring it in, in hopes of getting the ball rolling. Those poor, deluded men. If I had been just a little slower I would have been trampled to death. I hadn't seen the hogs, standing in a dark corner, but they saw the food and dashed out so fast that it made my head swim. They pushed and shoved and elbowed everyone else out of their way until they got to the trough where they settled down to enjoy themselves.

Meanwhile, outside, the farmer's hounds had met some desperate-looking wolves and, instead of running them off the property, had joined them to raid the chicken coop. Luckily, one of the roosters had stayed behind and, when he saw the danger coming, had set up an alarm that brought the whole farm. The farmer came running out of the farmhouse with his gun held high and his lantern swinging. He took a pot shot at the fleeting pack but missed them.

His farmhands filled him in on the details of the wolves *and* the party. He finally realized that this "social atmosphere" would not improve work or productivity and this thought made him so mad that he called off all parties then and there.

Ninth-grade girl

B. EXAGGERATION

NEMO'S NEMESIS

Gazing up at the fifty foot neon sign "Super Colossal Super Market," Nemo C. Cow marvelled at this ultra-modern establishment. He entered quickly, but timidly, and stared incredulously at the size of the store. As he looked down at the mat he was standing on, he observed that it resembled a conveyor belt. Gliding along, he suddenly felt cold steel fingers grasp his shoulders and put him in an atomic powered shopping cart, which then careened down a seemingly endless aisle.

Recovering from the shock of this experience, he gazed in wonder at the innumerable varieties of food and other articles. The store contained everything from the simplest food to atomic fired spark plugs. Astonished and over-awed with the beauty of the most attractive packaging and arrangements, he felt compelled to buy many items he saw.

Leaping from his cart, he began heaping items into the conveyance, as though he were hypnotized. There was nothing unusual about his actions in the Super Colossal Super Market, for everyone was stuffing his cart with luxuries, because all the merchandise was so enticing.

Propelling the vehicles down the aisle, he found it crowded with people. To his delight he discovered he was in the "Free Sample" aisle. The featured article of the day was a miniature can of America's newest sensation for the home-owner, Instant Striped Paint. After picking up his free sample of the item no home should be without, he noticed that the line was slowing up. As he moved farther along, he learned the cause of the disturbance. An irate customer had jumped upon a soap-box, and was shouting above the murmur of the crowd that Instant Striped Paint should be taken out of the Super Market and returned to the hardware store where it belonged.

Leaving the free-sample aisle, he wandered aimlessly until he found a rack which featured a road map of the Super Market (for a mere $1.50) without which he could not find his way out of the market.

Forging ahead, Nemo found his way to the aisle which led to the check out counters. While waiting for a traffic light to change, his attention was drawn to a large sign with bright red letters. It announced the beginning of a nation-wide contest, in which the grand prize was fifteen minutes to collect all the merchandise one could gather in the super market. The directions were simple: Just complete in thirty-three words or less "I like Ravishing Rose green, phosphorescent finger-nail polish because ———— ————." Although Nemo was not acquainted with the product, he took an entry blank.

Upon reaching the check-out counter, he realized how much merchandise he had accumulated. The cashier totaled the bill which came to an over-whelming $76.69. Nemo jokingly told the cashier to charge it to the management, but after a menacing look from the cashier, he quickly pulled out his wallet. After paying his bill, Nemo was thrilled to learn that because he had purchased over $69.00 worth of items he was given a coupon worth $5.00 off the final purchase price of a new automobile. Along with this ticket, he was given some Summit Value Stamps. When a book of these stamps was completed, it could be redeemed for valuable premiums.

As Nemo walked home, toting five bags filled with groceries and other items, he recalled his recent experience. The Super Colossal Super Market and all its superfacilities made him proud to be a citizen of his country, great because it developed such fine modern conveniences.

Ninth-grade boys

C. IRONY

JOHNNY (in the style of e. e. cummings)

> 'and that's the way it happened'
> and that's the way it happened
> old johnny now marched home
>   from war
> hup
> two

three
for   what reason i am not quite sure
.it wasn't the american Way of Life
or Aunt Jemima's pancakes
why Johnny
               ?he was asked   po
                                    lite
                                    ly.
why said Johnny,
topreservedemocraticidealswithlibertyandjustice-
forallofcourse
                (he didn't even stutter like he
usually did
               —before he left)
johnny don't leave us again
stay
warm and safe in your rocK-
ing chair by the fire
stare blankly into it all day
your eyes reflecting the backward images.
we lov   (ed)
you johnny
don't go again,

Ninth-grade girl

D. EXAGGERATION AND IRONY

FUN AND GAMES

There was a hurried consultation lasting as usual only a few seconds, after which Alice, our nine-year old and the oldest of the four, turned and announced, "O.K. We've decided to watch my show this time and Billy's tomorrow. So turn on 'Fun and Games' now, Mom."

I sighed. Alice always won over her younger brothers and sisters, and Billy's turn probably would never come. However the program was one of the best on the air, and I was pleased that they wanted to watch it. I heard that it brought history down to the level of the child, and I wanted them to get a firm base in history. History always was my worst subject.

The T.V. flicked on and a clown dressed in a soldier costume appeared and said, "Hello, Kiddies. I'm sure glad that you decided to listen to us today. We have a treat for you today, real live movies of the big one, W.W. II. Won't that be fun? Gather 'round now, cause after this word from our sponsors we'll start showing those fun movies!"

The announcer, a tired man in an equally tired clown suit appeared.

"Kids, be the envy of your friends and enemies alike! Get Mom and Dad to give you just ten dollars and send it along with your name and address to Box 111, N.Y. 1, N.Y., and soon you'll receive a dandy, authentic machine gun from our 'War of the Week,' W.W. II! Of course, no ammunition comes with the gun so that it is perfectly safe! There are only a few left so be sure to send your ten dollars now to Box 111, N.Y. 1, N.Y. and hurry!"

That was nice to hear about. I had wondered what in the world to get for Tommy's third birthday. Perfect!

"And now back to Fun and Games!"

"Before we start those great films, kids, just so you can enjoy them more, W.W. II or the Big One was started by a nasty man named Hitler. Whenever the movie mentions Hitler, let's all boo real loud, O.K. kids? Anyway, this Hitler declared war on all our peace-loving imperialistic allies, and pretty soon we were in the war! You probably all know that we won, and we took it out on the skins of those dirty war-mongers! Japan was on the side of Hitler and Germany, but we took care of those war-mongering Japs when we finally dropped the atomic bomb, and all of Hiroshima went up in that big mushroom cloud that we have grown to know and love. And now on with the film! I'll narrate, pointing out all of the nice bloody parts so you don't miss anything. Incidentally those dirty war-mongering Japs have disappeared completely, and the new peace-loving Japs are in power."

As I watched the film I noticed how quiet the kids were. Maybe this would be my salvation since I was trying desperately to finish my housework while the kids were home. I hoped so.

"Notice, kids, how all the soldiers are going into the fight? And notice how none are coming back? That's called the risk involved in battle. Now see how the peace-loving Russians, our allies, are marching all the German prisoners across the land? Look out, one of those dirty Nazis is trying to escape! That's good, hit him again! Oh, too bad, he died."

It was so quiet that I must have gone to sleep for awhile. When I woke up awhile later I heard the clown talking about the atom bomb.

"Well, kids, after this message we'll see previews of the next show with the dropping of the atom bomb! Won't that be nice?"

The same tired announcer appeared, and began his pitch. "Well, kids, we have a special offer. For a limited time now we have ammunition cheaply priced. The ammo will fit any W.W. II weapon, and is on sale for a short time now for only $1 a box! Send your money to Box 222, N.Y. 2, N.Y. Be sure to send now!"

Back to the clown.

"Kids, it's time for us to leave now. Well, kids, it's been a fun show, and be sure to have fun! And Games, of course."

Well, Easter was coming up and the kids would sure get a kick out of real ammunition. And only a dollar! Another shopping problem solved. I decided that this was indeed a worthwhile show.

Ninth-grade girl

E. PARODY

THE FALL OF HUMPTY-DUMPTY (In the Style of Edgar Allan Poe)

I cannot, for my soul, remember when it was that I first met the narrator of this tale. He approached me in one of those many taverns which dot the streets of London, as I was meditating on many dark and ancient subjects. When I inquired as to his business, he related to me the following tale of ancient woe:

"The tyrant had long oppressed the people of the land I was entering. His greed and evil ways had devastated the simple farmers who inhabited the region. The soldiers of this king roamed the countryside, bringing ghastly tortures to all who dared even speak a word of malcontent.

"I was passing through this singularly barren and dismal country on my way to the castle of the king, which was set in a misty mountain region some great distance away. At length, I approached the castle, which rose dark and forbidding from a deep and dank tarn. The castle was remarkably small, being in appearance more of a walled tower than a manor. Its stones were separated by cracks, where the ravages of long ages had washed away the mortar, and filaments of minute fungi criss-crossed the barren, decayed face of the wall. Atop the wall I beheld the awesome figure of the tyrant himself, his great egg-shaped body perched above my head on the very highest wall, gazing out upon the valley. Even as I approached, I was seized unexpectedly by his guards.

"The king feared the approach of an army from a neighboring kingdom, and all my attempts at persuasion could not divert his mind from the fear that I was one of Them.

"I was imprisoned in a minor tower, some distance from the castle, my cold, clammy chamber affording me (within the limitation of my chains) a view of the king's fortress. I was at this window one dark evening, mourning for my vanished freedom, as the red, garish light of the moon illuminated the tarn surrounding the castle.

"All at once, there came a clamor of trumpets and of horses. The King's men swept out of their castle to do battle, and the clash of steel on steel and the anguished shrieks of downed men and horses filled my ears. I stared in transfixed horror as the armies surged back and forth across the causeway to the castle. Sickness swept through me as I saw the blood flow in streams from the bridge over the tarn.

"Suddenly the moon, which had set behind the castle, again lit the landscape with its red light. I stared as the castle walls shook—as the very stones flew to ruin—the king tottered from his height—the castle wall itself was rent asunder—there was a long tumultuous shouting like the voice of a thousand waters, and the deep and dark tarn at my feet closed swiftly and silently over the fragments of the tyrant king, "Humpty-Dumpty."

Ninth-grade boy

The compositions written by the students might well be saved throughout a unit or the year and published inexpensively in dittoed or mimeographed form for the class as those quoted above were. Classroom publications can be quite attractive on minimal budgets. Various color dittos can be used for the cover; P.T.A. mothers or high school business departments sometimes will do the typing; some illustrations can be included by using dittos or by having drawings burned into stencils.

A publication not only gives its writers considerable pride but can be used effectively with other classes. Obviously, the student writings quoted above can serve as models and incentive for students in other classes; they also present materials for analysis and provide a painless introduction to criticism. Scholars read and respond to criticism written by their peers. Why shouldn't high school students do the same? Within a very short time, an English department can build a fairly extensive file of materials to which students can respond and from which they can take off in new directions. The idea of debating one another's views has a great deal of motivational force for students. When a teacher or a professional critic presents his views, students are too readily awed, and their own thinking stops. But, they regard the views of another student as only the views of another human being, which can be challenged with impunity.

NOTES

1. Sarah N. Cleghorn, "The golf links lie so near the mill," *Portraits and Protests* (New York: Holt and Company, 1917).
2. Edward Arlington Robinson, "Miniver Cheevy," *The Town Down the River* (New York: Charles Scribner's Sons, 1910).
3. Siegfried Sassoon, "Base Details," *Collected Poems* (London: E. P. Dutton, 1918).
4. Diane di Prima, ed. *Various Fables from Various Places* (New York: G. P. Putnam's Sons, 1960).
5. Juvenal, *The Satires of Juvenal,* tr. Hubert Creekmore (New York: New American Library, 1963), p. 109.
6. Oliver Goldsmith, "Letter 3," *Letters from a Citizen of the World* in *Oliver Goldsmith: The Vicar of Wakefield and Other Writings,* ed. Frederick W. Hilles (New York: Modern Library, 1955), pp. 87–90.
7. Philip Wylie, *Generation of Vipers* (New York: Pocket Books, 1964), pp. 191–192.

SUGGESTIONS FOR FURTHER READING

1. GEORGE HENRY, "The Unit Method: The 'New' Logic Meets the 'Old.'" *English Journal,* 56:3 (March 1967), pp. 401–406.
2. WALTER LOBAN, MARGARET RYAN, JAMES R. SQUIRE, *Teaching Language and Literature, Grades 7–12.* New York: Harcourt, Brace & World (1961).
3. JEROME BRUNER, *et al., A Study of Thinking.* New York: John Wiley & Sons, 1956.

Teaching Literature: The Affective Response

14

Most English teachers want their students to enjoy reading literature. Most will agree that positive affective response to individual works and to reading as an activity is extremely important. As we have seen in Chapter 7, many teachers and publishers base their literature programs almost exclusively on student interest.

If we wish students to enjoy reading and to respond to what they read affectively, there are two problems that we must consider. First, what do we mean by interest, enjoyment, or affective response? Second, what can we do to promote enjoyment?

Levels of Affective Response[1]

It is self-evident that there are various levels of enjoyment, satisfaction, or appreciation. Some people enjoy a short story but would not read it again. Others read it many times, discuss it with their friends, write about it, and so on. Whatever these levels are, they must have a cognitive base. At the very least, the reader must be aware of the existence of the story. For his response to be a valid, personal response, he must have read it and be aware of some aspects of its meaning. Some children read *Huckleberry Finn* very early and enjoy it well enough to read it again and again. They enjoy it at the level of a humorous adventure story and may be totally unaware of its irony, its criticism of society, and its symbolic meanings. Even this affective response, however, has a cognitive base because the reader knows what happens in the plot. The cognitive base is thus a prerequisite of any positive affective response, but a reader need not understand all aspects of what he reads to enjoy some aspects of it.

Huck's decision to go to hell in Chapter 31 provides a specific example. If a reader cannot read the words of Huck's decision, "All right, then, I'll *go* to hell," he can have no positive affective response at all. Unless he infers from these words the fervent loyalty Huck has for Jim, he cannot empathize with Huck on that particular account. Unless he realizes the essential irony of Huck's remark, he will not infer the criticism of the society. He will feel no impatience or disgust with the society and no commiseration with the plight of an outsider who feels unnecessary guilt. Indeed, he will miss the basic comedy of the entire situation.

Of course, there is no guarantee that an adequate cognitive response will bring the appropriate affective response, be it disgust, satisfaction, grief, laughter, or so on. However, every teacher's experience indicates that hostility, rather than appreciation, results when the student cannot handle the cognitive aspects of a work. Even the most skeptical must admit that affective response at basic levels has a strong cognitive component.[2] Still, the teacher must remember that *understanding does not necessarily result in positive affective response.*

The most basic level of affective response is the simple willingness to receive a particular stimulus. The behavior is almost completely passive. The organism does not seek the stimulus, nor does he necessarily receive any satisfaction from it. His reaction may be one of complete indifference. The initial problem in teaching English to many students is getting through the screen they have erected between themselves and the subject.

At a somewhat higher level, the student does not simply receive the stimulus, but he attends to it as a particular stimulus, as differentiated from other stimuli in his immediate situation. With some students the teacher must make a special effort to select materials or activities that have enough intrinsic interest to receive the controlled or selected attention of the students. Those who have been bored by English for a year or two require special persuasion to focus their attention—materials that will strike their attention, focus it, and induce them to the next affective level, that of responding.

Many students will respond if the teacher requires it, but a forced response does not help to involve the student. On the contrary, it frequently has the opposite effect. The student must respond because he wants to. Many students fail to respond because they have not read the material. Some fail to respond because they see no point in it, others because they fear reprimand. Responding requires more than materials; it requires an atmosphere in which the student feels that his own response is not only welcome but worthwhile. A student is responding willingly when he actively contributes relevant information, ideas, and questions to group discussion, when he *voluntarily* seeks material relevant to classroom activities, when he reads and writes independently of teacher assignments, and when he does assigned work willingly and with vigor. With such response, students ordinarily feel some degree of satisfaction.

At a level beyond voluntary response and satisfaction, the student begins to value certain activities. It is possible to designate three levels of value: acceptance, preference, and commitment. The student may believe that reading literature is a valuable activity (acceptance) without preferring it to other activities, or he may prefer reading to another activity without being committed to it. The student who *accepts* the value of reading literature will respond positively in a consistent manner to what he reads. If he *prefers* it to other activities, he will elect to read when confronted by other activities that he may also value. At the level of *commitment,* however, he will actively seek reading, discuss what he reads, and attempt to convince others that the activity has value.

At still higher affective levels, the individual conceptualizes or objectifies his values and organizes them into a system. The reader of literature identifies the characteristics of what he admires and adopts or develops a theory of criticism. The development of such a value system for literature has been beyond the reach of most schools, although it probably need not be. Teachers are usually satisfied if their students express satisfaction with the individual works they read. Teachers can be pleased with some students if they advance at least one level. To change active hostility to a willingness to read, even though that willingness is characterized by indifference, is a meritorious achievement.

Teaching and Affective Response

Teaching so that students will demonstrate positive affective responses to literature is a complex task that involves the curriculum, the teacher's behavior, the activities and the materials. The teacher, of course, is responsible for all of these.

1. The Role of the Curriculum

The importance of a carefully planned curriculum in attaining positive affective response cannot be overemphasized. The teacher must examine the abilities of his students and plan their work in accordance with what he finds. He must gradually raise their level of sophistication in interpreting literature, for if students are not cognizant of the elements of a text, they cannot respond affectively to them. For example, a student who reads *Lord of the Flies* might enjoy it as an adventure story, but he cannot receive satisfaction from its symbolic meanings unless he recognizes, at least intuitively, the existence of symbols in it. Yet, obviously, he needs to go beyond simple recognition of the symbols.

Teaching this involves analysis or interpretation—but analysis appropriate to the students' level of development as indicated by inventories and pretests. Analysis need not be anathema. When a third grader says that the boy should not have cried wolf, he makes a simple analytical statement, and a generalization to the effect that lying leads to distrust—a more sophisticated analytical statement—is not very far away. The trick is to help the student move from one level to the next with a minimum of frustration. Analysis is frustrating when too many interpretative tasks are beyond the ken of the students or when the teacher does not prepare them for it. He must help the students to acquire the cognitive base, but he cannot expect them to handle all cognitive tasks at once. Moreover, his curriculum must be flexible enough to permit changes in the direction of simplicity or complexity as the abilities of the students indicate the need.

2. The Role of the Teacher in the Classroom

Various studies have shown that the more direct a teacher is in his influence over students the less his students learn. Thus, the more time he spends in lecturing, in giving directions and commands with which the students must comply, in criticizing them, and in justifying his own authority, the more he restricts their freedom and the less they learn. His time is put to better use in teacher-led discussion than in lecturing. If he asks questions to clarify or develop the ideas of the students and praises and encourages them, he will create an atmosphere that tends to enlarge their freedom to think in the classroom. The more students contribute, the more involved they become, and the more they learn.[3] The inductive or discovery approach to teaching described in Chapter 5 is designed to encourage student contribution and involvement. At each step the teacher must build on what a student has to say. It involves the students in problem-solving situations, which some psychologists believe result in the desired affective response.[4] Besides teacher-led discussion, other activities are important in maintaining and encouraging student involvement. Most of the activities discussed below tend to diminish the authority of the teacher and place the responsibility for learning in the hands of the students.

3. The Role of Activities

a. SMALL-GROUP DISCUSSION The importance of small-group discussion in attaining cognitive goals was emphasized in the last chapter, but this type of discussion is equally important in attaining positive affective response. If you observe a classroom discussion, you will notice that relatively few of the students take part and that a very small group tends to dominate the discussion. In an authoritarian classroom, there is likely to be no student talk at all, at least none that is relevant to the subject at hand. Even in a classroom characterized by the discovery method and indirect patterns of influence, a teacher is lucky if more than 50 percent of the students respond. But in small-group discussion (limited to four or five students), when the problem is appropriate, nearly every student participates, and few, if any, remain uninvolved. Procedures for small-group discussion appear in Chapter 3.

b. STUDENT-LED CLASS DISCUSSION Invariably, when small groups of students discuss similar problems or materials, different groups will reach different conclusions. In these situations, the teacher should arrange to have one or more of the groups present their ideas to the class and request that the class direct questions to them. Students who have arrived at conclusions different from those presented will very likely ask discerning questions. Heated discussions should be allowed to develop.

Similarly, when the groups examine different reading materials, each group can teach its material to the class. For example, if the students are studying the lesson on satiric irony outlined in the last chapter, one group might study and present "The Learn'd Astronomer," another "Richard Cory," still another O. Henry's "The Cop and the Anthem." Each group could explore with the class whether or not the work is ironic, whether or not it is satiric, and what the evidence is to support the conclusions.

Other student-led discussions are useful as well. For example, groups of students could prepare reports on special background information relevant to the unit. Students who have read the same outside materials, or materials by the same authors, could make presentations or give panel discussions. There is no need, however, to require every student to give an oral presentation of some sort in every unit. Requiring every student to give a five-minute talk is a marvelous way to kill interest—and five to seven days. Probably, the plan should be used only in extreme emergencies—when the teacher is planning a wedding, and so forth. However, the teacher should meet with those students who do make oral presentations (reports, panels, discussions) to ensure that their presentations will be of maximum benefit to the others in the class.

c. ROLE-PLAYING For some students a straightforward discussion of a text or of some abstract concept during each successive class meeting is not a very satisfactory procedure. Role-playing can help to bring literature alive for such students, and at the same time it provides a more concrete and immediate base for discussion. It can be used in connection with literature or in developing abstract concepts. For example, various students can assume the roles of the Widow Douglas, Tom Sawyer, Pap, and Jim, as they are revealed in the opening chapters of *Huckleberry Finn,* and discuss what ought to be done about Huck. To dramatize the conflicting emotions that Scout feels toward Atticus in *To Kill a Mockingbird,* the students can adopt the points of view of the various characters and improvise other characters to represent their own reactions as readers. The resulting discussion not only illuminates Scout as a character but other problems as well. A similar approach can be readily adapted to *Richard III,* a play that has considerable intrinsic appeal to high school students. Because Richard takes special care to give a variety of impressions of himself to various characters and is himself a superb player of roles, what the other characters think of him and what he thinks of himself at various points during the play offer a compelling role-playing situation.

The technique can be used to examine thematic problems as well. For example, the short story "Born of Man and Woman" by Richard Matheson, used as an opener for the unit on "The Outcast" (see Chapter 9), is written from the point of view of a monstrous child whose parents confine him to the cellar. The physical appearance of the "child" is totally inhuman, but its mind is human in its desire to understand and be understood. The pro and con roles are obvious. Should the child be confined? Should the parents be censored? What is the author's attitude? Similarly, role-playing can help to establish the central ironies of *Animal Farm*. After reading the opening chapter, the students might adopt the roles of various animals, farmers, and outside observers and explore the following questions: Should the animals be allowed to rule themselves? In what ways will their lives be better because of self-rule? The ensuing discussion should establish the idealism with which the animal revolution begins.

Role-playing is extremely useful in developing the concepts of point of view, connotation, and propaganda. It can be extended to the evaluation of specific works, of genres, and of literature as a whole. Students are usually reluctant to verbalize their negative feelings toward what is studied in class, though they often reveal it through their looks and attitudes. Unfortunately, they have learned through experience that it is best to keep silent on such matters. However, if they are assigned the role of attacking a story or poem as weak, satire as ineffectual in promoting change, or literature as useless, they will do it with more gusto than one might hope. Ultimately, verbalizing these negative feelings has positive effects. Perhaps the best way to dissipate hostility is to express it.

d. PRODUCING PLAYS Although every high school has one teacher who is responsible for the production of plays and some schools offer a course or two in drama, these dramatic productions and courses involve only a very small percentage of the students. Dramatizations in class, on the other hand, provide an opportunity for almost every student to walk through a scene or two at least and can be a tremendous means of motivating the students.

The classroom production need not be a chore. Scenery is not necessary—only basic props. (If Shakespeare could do without scenery, so can the high school teacher.) Students can bring in old clothes to improvise costumes. They should have a chance to practice their lines ahead of time, but there is no need to memorize.

Once a year, at least, the teacher should attempt to obtain an audience—a school or grade level assembly, another class, a class in another school, or a group of parents. Here, too, the keynote is simplicity. Abstract settings and basic props will suffice. If students want make-up, keep it simple unless a student in the class is skilled in its application. If the audience has read or is reading the play, the class can present selected scenes. The teacher's time should be devoted to helping the actors, but he should have the students help with the blocking and directing. The actors should be encouraged to develop their own "business" to achieve the effects they want. Class or group discussions can center on how a character or scene should be presented. Furthermore, the class should identify the problems in characterization or blocking, develop solutions, and plan ways of implementing them. The report of a student teacher who had her ninth graders produce the bumpkins' production of "Pyramus and Thisbe" from Shakespeare's *Midsummer Night's Dream* appears at the end of this chapter.

Reading plays aloud in class is useful in covering difficult material, for example, Shakespearean plays. Allow one day for each act, and assign parts the night before so that the students can practice. Although the strongest readers should have the longest parts, every student should have an opportunity to read aloud, if possible. In dealing with these difficult plays, the students should have a set of key plot and character questions to answer for each act, not necessarily to be written out, but to be discussed briefly in class. The reading should proceed as far as possible during class, with pauses for dealing with unfamiliar words, syntax, or special information. Whatever reading of the act is not completed in class can be finished at home. Reading through a play in this way helps students to see it as a whole, and the later discussion, in depth, of particular lines, scenes, and characters is far more meaningful.

As a special complement to producing plays, the teacher might wish to involve the class in writing and producing radio plays of their own. Most schools have tape recorders. Turning a short story into a radio play presents special problems in form from which students learn a great deal. Let them decide how and when to use a narrator, sound effects, and background music. Students can also produce parodies of television shows and their commercials and, in the process, learn a great deal about the uses and effects of language and dramatic clichés. If the school system has portable television equipment (hand cameras, and the like), it is worthwhile to explore the possibility of making videotapes of various dramatic productions. Some companies sell lightweight, relatively inexpensive cameras and complementary equipment that yield fairly high quality tapes. The incentive that such equipment provides for writing and producing dramatic materials is well worth the extra effort by the teacher.

e. STUDENT PLANNING AND EVALUATION It is obviously foolish to believe that students can or should plan or evaluate all aspects of instruction. If they could do it, there would be no need for specialists in English, and a monitor trained in group dynamics would suffice. However, although the students lack the background to do all the planning, they can take part in it at various points during the instruction and can be active in evaluation.

If the teacher does not provide the basic structure within which students plan, they are likely to grope for weeks, blindly attempting to reach a consensus about what to study. Even then, there is no guarantee that they will be any more interested or involved than if the teacher made *all* of the decisions. Nor is there any guarantee that what they decide on will have much relevance to the subject matter of English. On the other hand, if the teacher provides a structure within which the students help to plan, the affective results will be just as positive.

For instance, the teacher may decide on the basis of pretests and his estimate of class interests that satire would be a useful area for study in a particular class. He has a unit outline in mind, has selected the materials, and decided on what compositions the students will write. But not all the planning has been done. For example, after the first lesson involving cartoons, the students can bring various cartoons to class that they believe are satiric. They can examine their cartoons in small groups, select some to show the class, and devise questions for discussing them. In addition, they might examine the cartoons to discover whether they all "work in the same way." With a little guidance from the teacher, the students can discover that some cartoons use exaggeration, some incongruity or irony, some symbols, and so on. The class can then decide the order of study for the ensuing lessons. The teacher simply asks, "If we are going to study satire, what satiric device should we study first?" The teacher can make suggestions and explain what the difficulties will be. Once the students have a working definition of satire, they can begin to look for materials for the class to study. They can begin to outline the goals in composition in a general way, decide what kinds of writing they should do, when it will be due, and so on.

The activities outlined above (small-group discussions and presentations, student-led discussions, role-playing, and producing plays) involve considerable student planning. In each the students must plan what they are going to do and how they are going to do it.

An activity closely allied to student planning is evaluation. Asking the students to make an exam covering the content of a unit is extremely effective in motivating them to review and in reinforcing what they have learned. The student-made exam should not be regarded, however, as a device for alleviating the teacher's work load. On the contrary, it may increase it. Procedures for developing and using student-made exams appear in Chapter 6.

Some teachers fear that student-made tests contribute to cheating, but if they worry about this, they are probably asking the wrong sort of questions. If the student must provide specific bits of information or check true-false or multiple-choice questions, cheating is not only possible but probable. If, on the other hand, he must demonstrate comprehensive knowledge by analyzing, applying, synthesizing, or evaluating what he has learned, then cheating becomes almost irrelevant. As a matter of fact, the student should have a good knowledge of the kind of question to expect because knowing the specific nature of the questions is valuable in learning. British universities, for example, make a practice of printing and binding end-of-year examinations, which are kept in the library for anyone to see. The student is expected to examine the questions carefully, to practice writing answers to them, and to extrapolate the nature of the exam he will take from those that have been given in the past. He who does not avail himself of old exams stands a better than average chance of flunking.

The value of having students make up their own examination far outweighs any danger of cheating. The students will have less fear of the exam and less hostility toward it because they helped to write it, and they will have a much clearer notion of what to study for. In addition, they will have a more comprehensive, better organized knowledge of the subject, simply because writing an examination forces them to consider all that has been covered, weigh the relative importance of the parts, and determine the relationships existing between them. Besides, it is a cliché that those who set their own goals work harder and more willingly to attain them than those whose goals are set by others.

4. The Role of Materials

The materials of a unit must not only strike a balance between the background of the student and what he must learn if he is to become more sophisticated but must also appeal to him affectively if he is to develop positive values toward the subject matter. At the very least, the student must receive the stimulus—the materials, which means that the materials must compete with other stimuli in the immediate instructional situation. For many teachers the major problem lies in arresting the student's attention even momentarily. Carefully selected introductory materials help a great deal. Beyond that, reading materials should be chosen in view of their relevance to the lives and problems of the students. Many students who are unable to communicate with their more verbal teachers are helped considerably by carefully selected nonwritten materials that help to make ideas clear and to stimulate verbal response.

The Selection of Reading Materials

a. The materials used to introduce a unit should have a very *high interest potential*. The unit entitled "The Outcast" in Chapter 9 begins with a story called "Born of Man and Woman." Many teachers prefer no special introduction. They simply distribute the story and ask the students to read it. Some read a paragraph or two aloud to help the students begin reading. The monster who tells the story drips green on the floor, is chained to the wall in the cellar, and walks on the ceiling. In other ways he is human. The immediate response is one of bewilderment. What is it? What is the green? How can "it" walk on the ceiling? The questioning is lively. They demand an immediate explanation of physical facts, but the teacher can lead to the more relevant questions of why the author used a monster, how the monster feels, whether or not the parents should treat him as they do. This discussion leads to a general discussion of ostracism, its effects on the individual, its causes, and its effects upon the group. These problems, which are central to the unit, are introduced rapidly and in some depth through a single, short story that appeals powerfully to the students.

b. The materials should be appropriate to the abilities of the students—unless the interest value is *so high* that a student will read on despite factors that would normally frustrate him. If the students are slow readers, the average sentence should be relatively short, and the vocabulary should be relatively familiar. The *implied meanings of the work should be of a kind the students can already handle or of the kind in which the unit has offered instruction.* The exceptions here are those works that can be read meaningfully on several different levels—*Huckleberry Finn* and *Robinson Crusoe,* for example. In such cases, the teacher can decide to ignore certain aspects of the implied meanings in the work if his students have not yet learned to handle them. For instance, he has the option of ignoring the patterns of imagery in *Macbeth* if his students know nothing about imagery, or if he wishes to have his students examine the imagery, he must then teach them how to do it. On the other hand, the teacher cannot ignore the irony of the key situations in *Huckleberry Finn* without distorting the meaning of the book.

c. If the students display negative attitudes toward poetry or literature in general, the teacher must do his best to find material that does not use conventions, especially of language and imagery, that the students do not understand and might regard as foreign or artificial. The best possibility is to use poetry written since 1900—or perhaps since 1950—until the students have learned to understand the conventions.

d. If the students are "reluctant learners" or are from deprived backgrounds, the material should be highly relevant to their life situations. It should deal with the kinds of problems that concern them, although the problem need not be depicted in an environment identical to theirs. For instance, in a ghetto school a unit intended to examine the power and effects of language might profitably begin with a discussion of the language of prejudice and move into reading and analysis of the literature of protest from the points of view of both the right and the left. Students can approach the problems of connotation and imagery in a poem such as Langston Hughes' "Brass Spittoons."[5] Richard Wright's *Native Son* would be a good focal point for the study of connotation, imagery, and character development. Besides, the material has *immediate* relevance because it deals with problems the students care about. Although the same problems might be examined in *Silas Marner, Ivanhoe,* or *Treasure Island,* those books have no intrinsic relevance to the lives of many students.

e. With reluctant readers it is frequently necessary to select materials that are not only relevant to their lives in general but *relevant to specific interests* that those students already have developed. These students frequently display a surprising breadth of interests, from automobile engines to coin collecting, from baseball to billiards. The teacher can obtain this information from the inventories described in Chapter 2.

A teacher in a depressed economic area who discovers that his students apparently have no interests at all, at least none they are prepared to admit, must experiment and observe. What problems do the students face in their lives? Are there literary or semiliterary materials that deal with those problems? Will such materials evoke an interested response from the students? What sort of movies do they enjoy? Is it possible to obtain movies or photographs to use as a jumping-off point into a unit? Have the students ever visited the public museums in the area? Can the museum evoke interest in a problem for the students to examine? These are avenues that the teacher can take to arouse the interests of students, for he must be willing to think beyond the four walls of the conventional classroom. All these keys to selecting materials apply to some degree to all students, but particular care must be exercised in choosing materials for those students who would just as soon not be in school.

Finally, the mere idea of a "selection of reading materials" may appear ludicrous to an English teacher who is hamstrung with a single text. The situation *is* ludicrous. The school system hires a professionally trained person to teach literature and gives him a single tool to work with. It is like giving a surgeon only a scalpel and urging him to operate. Despite his professional training, the surgeon stands a good chance of losing his patient. Just so, the literature teacher with only one text stands a good chance of failing to teach literature. Any English department confined to a single text ought to begin a concerted effort to bring pressure on the board of education to supply funds for additional materials. The initial cost of supplying each student with a literature text is only about three to four dollars per student, and frequently less, and the school system keeps a set of textbooks for at least three years, usually longer. Thus, the average cost per student per year is only about one dollar. Compare that sometime with the annual cost per student in a good science curriculum. Compare it with the cost of outfitting a boy to play football!

Until the board of education provides money for instructional materials in literature, there are ways to supplement the single text.

1. Check the school library for supplementary novels, short stories, poems, and so on, in multiple and single copies. Librarians sometimes are able to borrow extra copies of books from nearby libraries. Ask the librarian to make you a list of the books in the school library that might be of help.

2. Many poems, stories, and essays are in the public domain and may be legally copied for distribution to your class. A cooperative principal may

arrange to have a secretary help with the typing. P.T.A. mothers who can type are usually happy to cut stencils at home or at the school. The P.T.A. is organized for the purpose of helping the schools. Here is a way not only to get materials when money is unavailable but to call the attention of the parents to the need for additional materials.

3. It is possible to build classroom or departmental libraries by asking students and families to donate used books. Those that are not suitable for classroom use might be traded to secondhand book dealers for books that can be used in the classroom.

4. Some teachers report buying sets of paperbacks, which they give to the students during a unit. At the end of the unit they collect the books, allowing the students to purchase them. Because many students buy the books, the teacher is out very little money.

5. Some English departments sponsor book fairs and dances to raise money to purchase supplementary materials.

6. When and if the school system buys a new anthology, save fifty to one hundred copies of the old one.

Obviously, all these are interim measures. No English teacher should have to continue for very long begging, borrowing, or stealing materials. The unit-building suggestions for language, literature, and composition in this book require a variety of materials; some will be available in conventional texts, some can be typed and reproduced for distribution to students, and some are in paperback. The teacher who attempts to acquire new materials for an entire year's program is likely to meet frustration. Although collecting materials takes time, it is certainly possible to collect enough for one or two new units per year and to arrange those already available into a more effective teaching sequence. A curriculum cannot be written or revised overnight, or in a month, or even a year. Curriculum writing is a continuous process. If the curriculum is a good one, parts of it will make other parts outmoded. If the ninth-grade curriculum improves, then the tenth-grade program will have to change—and so on up through college. Under such conditions it is only logical to do a bit at a time.

The Use of Nonwritten Materials and the Mass Media

Teachers frequently overlook the valuable contribution that nonwritten materials and the mass media can make to a literature program. The use of photographs, films, recordings, magazines, and paintings not only make the study of literature more appealing to students but can be very effective in introducing new ideas and clarifying difficult concepts. For instance, the idea of kinds of imagery is not an easy one for students to grasp, but paintings and photographs can help to make the concept clear. Albrecht Dürer's "The Hare," for instance, has an almost photographic realism, but the animals painted by Franz Marc are totally different. Marc's horses are deep blue or red and are identifiable as horses only by their forms. His interest lies in an arrangement of forms and colors that has little to do with verisimilitude. The animal forms in the paintings of Hieronymus Bosch are used allegorically; they represent greed, lechery, the transitoriness of life, and so on. A surrealistic painter such as Salvador Dali produces dream or nightmare images; his painting, "Civil War," represents a woman on a barren landscape tearing herself apart. The imagery of primitive groups is usually highly stylized and representational; an image appears again and again in the work of the different artists, always with the same general delineation and the same meaning. Examining and discussing a series of paintings or representations by Dürer, Marc, Bosch, Dali, and primitive artists clarifies the differences between types and uses of imagery rather quickly. Afterwards, the students can turn with more insight to an examination of imagery and its uses in a work such as "The Rime of the Ancient Mariner." The discussion of the paintings for their own sake should be informative and stimulating, of course. The students can discuss why the artist uses the kind of imagery he does and evaluate the effects. Since some students tend to be hostile toward modern painters such as Dali, lively discussion is ensured.

MATERIALS FROM POPULAR CULTURE TO BUILD CONCEPTS

Comic book heroes, such as Batman and Superman, make a useful point of departure for a study of the hero. Students will be able to enumerate their moral and physical attributes, the kinds of villains they encounter, and the methods they use to overcome them. They can then discuss additional questions: How do adolescents respond to these heroes? Adults? What special powers do the heroes have that real men do not have? How do people respond to these powers? Why? How can the super hero be compared to heroes in the real world—the astronauts and sports heroes, for example?

Following such a discussion, the students can begin to read Greek myths and the myths and tales from other cultures. Their major concern might be how the mythic hero compares with the modern super hero. Then they should consider why the qualities and attributes of the heroes appeal to ordinary people. From this point a unit dealing with heroes could move in any one of several directions. For instance, a unit that involved popular conceptions of the hero might focus on mythic heroes, folk heroes, and western and detective heroes.

Materials from media other than print are relevant, useful, and interesting in English studies, and many are inexpensive. It is simply up to the English teacher to be aware of the possibilities and integrate them into his units of study.

a. PICTURES AND ADVERTISEMENTS Photographs and reproductions of paintings are useful in many ways. They can supply examples for discussion not only of imagery but of structure and style. Sometimes their content is relevant to a thematic unit. Photographs or paintings of war, of slums, of lonely people, of people interacting with one another can all be useful in developing ideas related to various units and in supplying the content or stimulus for certain composition assignments. They are particularly useful in teaching point of view. The students adopt different persona, for instance, to describe the same pictorial content. Or they can adopt the persona of someone in a picture to describe something else in the picture.

Advertisements from magazines are extremely helpful in studying the concepts of connotation, point of view, propaganda techniques, and audience appeal. In the study of connotation, for instance, the teacher first displays ads that have minimal text. The students discuss the use of the words that appear—"exquisite" in a diamond ad, "unique" in auto and airline ads, "romance" in perfume and lipstick ads. As they become adept at identifying and explaining words used because of their positive affective connotations, the teacher can move to audience appeal, for example, ads for the same car in a woman's magazine and a business magazine. The differences in the texts can be amazing. The students identify the audience to which the appeal is made and examine differences in the selection of words for the various audiences. Eventually, they should examine the basis of the appeal—a task that is not terribly difficult.

There are many sources of inexpensive pictures. Magazines use pictures that are relevant to various thematic organizations of materials. Large art museums such as the Cleveland Museum of Art, The Metropolitan Museum of Art in New York, and the National Gallery in Washington, D.C., will supply catalogs of inexpensive color and black and white reproductions. University Prints[6] carries an inventory of about 5,000 black and white 5½″ by 8″ prints, which are available for pennies each. It is possible to select individual prints from the catalog and have them bound with an inexpensive plastic binding, so that for a nominal cost individual students or small groups can work with a volume of specially selected prints. Each item in the University Prints Catalog is also available as a 2″ by 2″ or 3¼″ by 4″ slide.

Many large school systems have audio-visual departments that have the equipment for making transparencies for use with overhead projectors. Some can make 35-mm. color or black and white slides. In lieu of these, the teacher can use an opaque projector to throw a picture directly on a screen, but the quality is inferior to that of either an overhead or a slide projector. Lacking any of these, the teacher can have students mount the pictures for distribution to small groups for examination.

b. CARTOONS Cartoons can be used profitably in a number of ways. As previously mentioned, they can be used to formulate a working definition of satire, and to introduce important questions concerning the nature of the hero. But cartoons are relevant to many other aspects of English as well, both thematic and structural. For instance, a good many cartoons depend for their effects on visual exaggeration. Many depend on a visual contrast that results in incongruity. They can be used to objectify and illustrate both. They are especially useful in examining incongruity simply because visual incongruity is easier to sense and, eventually, formulate. Contrast permeates literature and is a rich source of implied meanings. Contrasting words, images, characters, and plots abound within a single work. At the same time, readers frequently overlook such contrasting elements and their significance. A study of appropriate cartoons helps make readers aware of the technique and prepares them to respond to the effects of the contrasts. Some examples: natives sitting in the door of a grass shack, with a medicine man dancing behind them, are reading *National Geographic;* two white explorers come upon a clearing in the jungle in which an otherwise primitive people are building a rocket ship. Examples of this type are easy to find.

Charles M. Schulz's *Peanuts* is an extremely fertile field for materials relevant to English: *Point of view*—Lucy gives Linus a long list of all his "faults." Linus calls them, not faults, but character traits. In another strip, Lucy tells Snoopy that he cannot have any of her ice-cream cone because it would be unsanitary. Snoopy muses to himself that she is right. He would be foolish to take a chance like that. *Connotation*—Lucy tells Charlie Brown that nobody likes his father. He denies it, saying that all sorts of people like his father. What kind, Lucy wants to know. Real people. Down-to-earth people. People people! (A recent *GM* ad states that General Motors is people making products for people.) In another strip, Lucy tells Charlie that she never wants to see him again. Never! Never! she shouts. Charlie Brown asks her to define "never." *Glittering generality*—Linus claims he loves everybody, every living creature. Lucy asks if he loves gila monsters. Linus says he doesn't know what they are, but if he knew, he'd love them.

Cartoons, *Peanuts* especially, can supply a good deal of relevant thematic material as well. In the middle of a ball game, which Charlie Brown's team is losing as usual, the players say that it is good to lose, that suffering is good for the soul; a discussion of suffering begins. It is a useful strip for getting at an important aspect of tragedy. Charlie Brown's bumbling, his refusal to quit, his near despair, his rejection by the group, Lucy's shrewishness and pessimism, Snoopy's refusal to allow his dancing to be deterred by others, Linus' faith in the Great Pumpkin and his need for security—all illustrate aspects of human nature in a simple, comic manner.

c. RECORDINGS Many teachers realize the value of recordings in teaching drama and poetry. For some students, they provide almost indispensable support in reading plays or poetry written in another era. Although a recording is not the same as a live production, the fluent voices of the readers will bring considerable meaning to materials that might otherwise be incomprehensible and lifeless to many students. A great range of drama, poetry, and prose is available on recordings, everything from the Greek cycles to *Every-*

man and the *Second Shepherd's Play* to very contemporary material. The *Schwann Long-Playing Record Catalog,* available at most record dealers, lists much of what is currently available. One section of the catalog is devoted to "Spoken and Miscellaneous." Additional recordings are listed in "Resources for the Teaching of English,"[7] published by the National Council of Teachers of English, and in the catalogs of such commercial educational suppliers as Educational Audio Visual, Inc.[8]

Recordings are especially useful for weak readers. The student can follow his text as he listens to the recording, and this helps him to respond to punctuation and vocabulary items that might block him completely if he were reading independently. The technique has the effect of making reading more enjoyable because it reduces frustration.

There are several recordings that are useful in language study as well. The National Council of Teachers of English publishes *Americans Speaking,* a recording of six American regional dialects. Each speaker reads the same passage in order to illustrate the contrastive features among the dialect areas, and he also discusses a subject of his own choice for a few minutes. A pamphlet that accompanies the recording provides a transcription of the common reading and the free speech of each speaker.

In teaching language history, nothing illustrates changes in pronunciation more readily than a reading from various historical dialects. A number of recordings of poetry in Old and Middle English are available. Those that use the same passage in various historical dialects are particularly useful. For instance, a two-record set prepared by Helge Kokeritz, *A Thousand Years of English Pronunciation,*[9] contains a passage from St. Luke (Chapter 7:2–9) as it appears in the *Anglo-Saxon Gospel,* the Wycliffe-Purvey translation, and the authorized version of 1611. A complete text accompanies the readings.

Such records are conventional for classroom use, but the teacher needs to consider less conventional recordings as well. *Pygmalion,* or its Broadway counterpart, *My Fair Lady,* is useful in gaining insight into the problems arising from snobbery about socially unacceptable dialects. Bill Cosby's recordings of such routines as "Buck Buck"[10] illustrate a number of comic techniques: exaggeration, understatement, situation comedy, and so on. Godfrey Cambridge, with "Blockbusting"[11] and other routines, provides good examples of topical social satire. These, used in conjunction with cartoons, can help to develop a very clear notion of the nature of satire.

George Carlin's recording *Take Offs and Put Ons*[12] includes one routine that makes a hard-hitting introduction to parody. "Wonderful WINO" is a parody of the typical adolescent-oriented station with its fast talking disc jockey, top tune lists, quickie newscasts, dedications, and rock-and-roll music. The parody and its purposes are entirely evident to students, who, no matter where they live in the United States, are familiar with that type of station. A discussion of the recording quickly identifies the characteristics or style of the stations that cater to adolescents, as opposed to those that cater to other audiences. Carlin's main parodic tools, exaggeration and irony, are abundantly clear. The record, then, can be useful as an introduction to the concepts of style and parody and can be used in conjunction with the parody lessons described in Chapter 1 or to stimulate ideas for writing parodies of radio and television shows.

Rock, folk-rock, and folk songs sung by adolescents' favorites can help to develop a feeling for, and even an analysis of, rhythm. The guitar and drum accompaniments objectify rhythmic patterns and in turn help make the student sensitive to the more subtle rhythms of poetry.

The use of popular songs has other advantages. Adolescents are concerned with the lyrics, which have an immediacy for them that poetry tends to lack until they learn to respond to it. In fact, the lyrics of many current favorites make very worthwhile listening. For instance, "An Ode to Billy Joe,"[13] written and sung by Bobbie Gentry, implies a great deal of its meaning. It protests the casualness and callousness with which all but one member of a family receive the news of Billy Joe's suicide. The concern of the mother and father is more with the food on the table. Apple pie, suicide, and bits of farm talk are juxtaposed in patterns that imply the central meanings of the song. Students know the words of such songs and can intuitively grasp their commentary. A discussion of the lyrics and the musical techniques not only flatters the students' taste but objectifies and makes meaningful a recurring pattern in literature: the juxtaposition of contrasting words, images, scenes, and characters. A discussion of "An Ode to Billy Joe" could be followed profitably by the reading and discussion of various modern poems that use a similar contrastive technique: for instance, Robert Francis' "Pitcher," John Updike's "Ex-Basketball Player," Wilfred Owen's "Arms and the Boy," and Theodore Spencer's "The Day."[14] By the way, a useful collection of rock lyrics is Jon Eisen's and Babette Low's *Rock Poetry Anthology* (New York: Random House, 1971).

The lyrics of folk, blues, and pop songs are appropriate to various thematic units. Many, for instance, lend themselves directly to a study of the literature of protest. Some of the old English and Scottish ballads are appropriate in units built around such themes as war, love, courage, alienation, power. "Sir Patrick Spens," for instance, tells of a man who is ordered to his death by a king who is unaware of the danger that his knight will confront. What are the implications for the use of power? The Robin Hood ballads[15] and others are relevant to units dealing with the mythic hero, popular conceptions of the hero, courage, and justice.

A comparison of blues verses to the lyrics of popular songs can give rise to interesting evaluative discussions. In the movie *The Semantics of the Popular Song* S. I. Hayakawa discusses the realism of the blues as opposed to popular lyrics.[16] Another good exercise is a comparison of "Chim-chiminee" from *Mary Poppins*[17] to William Blake's poem "The Chimney Sweep." The popular song sentimentalizes and idealizes the life of a sweep, whereas Blake deals with the harsh reality that is likely to bring death to a child sweep. In short, recordings have a great many uses in English other than the conventional, but still important, one of listening to the drama, poetry, and prose that the students will read.

d. TV AND MOTION PICTURES Many writers advocate special courses in TV and the "Art of the Film,"[18] but although the courses they recommend may be laudable, they are not the explicit concern of this book. *The concern here is with the study of TV and movies as it supports and parallels goals in the study of literature, composition, and language.* Therefore, certain specialized topics, such as the history of "cinematographic art," are irrelevant here. But the thematic or conceptual content, the techniques, and the language of TV and movies are both relevant and compelling to the English teacher's concerns and to those of his students. They are relevant for obvious reasons. They are compelling because the viewer can allow himself to be captured by the media and carried along with it.

Some motion pictures involve little or no inference. The villain in a black hat and moustache sneers and strikes an old lady. And in case the audience misses the implication, a character in a white hat (no moustache) comments, "What a wicked thing to do!" The same is true of many books. When movies do require complex inferences, unsophisticated students are hostile, just as they are to "difficult" poems and paintings. The viewer or reader must participate, must work out meanings for himself. The problem for teachers is to help students make the necessary inferences. Students are not "turned off" when instruction enables them to work out these meanings for themselves. They are bored or hostile only when the difficulties are overwhelming or when someone hands them predigested interpretations.

Beyond the signal level or basic format, the problems of meaning in written literature are remarkably similar to those of TV and the cinema: plot structure, juxtaposition of scenes, imagery, symbols, and so on. It is precisely for this reason that the study of literature and the study of movies parallel and support each other in that the study of cinematic structure, motif, imagery, and symbols illuminates their literary counterparts for students.

There are other reasons for including movies and TV in the English curriculum. Their immediacy for the students makes the study of similar problems in literature easier, and they produce a positive affective response, at least at the levels of awareness and attention, almost at once.

Movies have been used in the classroom to some extent for a long time. Ordinarily their use has been limited to didactic films, for example, The Encyclopaedia Britannica Films on the Greek theater, or to titles of works students are reading in class.[19] Many films are worth viewing, however, whether or not the students read the original—if there is one. Many are appropriate to various thematic units, such as those described throughout this book. Fine feature films are available for relatively low rental fees: *The*

Bridge on the River Kwai, All the King's Men, The Caine Mutiny, Death of a Salesman, The Last Hurrah, The Mouse That Roared, On the Waterfront, A Raisin in the Sun, Requiem for a Heavyweight, The Wild One,[20] and many others. *The Mouse That Roared* makes a fine addition to the unit on satire described in the last chapter. *A Raisin in the Sun* illustrates a number of social problems and would contribute a great deal to a unit dealing with social class and mobility. *On the Waterfront* might be viewed and discussed not only for its thematic content but for its use of camera angles (subjectivity), imagery, and symbolism.

Many fine short films are available at lower cost than the feature films and have the additional advantage that they can be shown in a single class period. Several are described below.[21]

The Eye of the Beholder (black and white, 25 min.) demonstrates how one's point of view distorts truth. The film presents an artist from the points of view of a headwaiter, who sees him watching women, of his mother, who believes he pays no attention to her, of a cab driver, who calls him a "crook," of a landlord, who suspects his sanity, and of a cleaning lady, who screams that he is a murderer. All these points of view are explained when the omniscient camera reconstructs the events at the end. The value of the film is obvious.

Flatland (color, 12 min.) is an animated film whose characters are geometrical figures. The people of the community belonging to different classes and castes are represented by various two dimensional figures. One day a sphere encounters a square and introduces him to the three dimensional world. When the square tries to explain what he has discovered, he is jailed as a heretic. The film should provoke a discussion of symbolism and is also useful in the unit on "The Outcast," which appears in Chapter 9.

The Hand (color, 19 min.) is a fascinating allegory whose two main characters are a puppet and a disembodied hand. The puppet's main pleasure in life centers in a flower for which he makes pots. One day the hand breaks into his peaceful existence, changing the pot on his potter's wheel to a hand. At first the hand, in a white glove, is persuasive in its demands, giving him gifts, luring him. But when the puppet refuses to carry out its commands, it returns, this time in a black glove, and forces the puppet to carve a giant statue of a hand. When the task is complete, the puppet flees to his home and dies tragically. The film is open to many interpretations. At first students might be somewhat hostile to a film with a puppet and hand as main characters, but as it progresses, they will become involved with the puppet. It will be reasonably clear to them that the hand represents controlling force. But the nature and causes of the relationship between the hand and the puppet should provide considerable material for debate. The students will return to the film to support their arguments, and they may wish to see it several times. Each time they return to it, their perceptions will be sharper because they will look for specific details. The discussion can profitably turn to the type of imagery used in the film, its purpose, and meaning. Viewing and discussing this film will demonstrate to students the need to watch closely. The carry-over to printed literature is obvious.

The String Bean (color and black and white, 17 min.) tells a wordless story of an old woman's cultivation of and devotion to a string bean plant, which is the only green, living thing in her otherwise drab flat. As the bean plant grows, she carries it to a park each day where it can get the sun. Eventually, she plants it in a corner of the park and visits it daily. A gardener, thinking that it is a weed among his flowering plants, pulls it and throws it away, but the old lady walks to the trash can, plucks some beans, and carries them home to plant. The film can stimulate writing from various points of view about the old lady, the gardener, and the bean plant itself. It can also lead to a discussion of at least one recurring pattern in literature, the death-rebirth archetype.

Hangman (color, 12 min.) is an animated film based on a poem of the same title. It concerns a hangman who comes to town and sets up his gallows, which takes the townspeople one by one. The tension of the film reaches a climax when the only person left, the coward who has allowed the others to die, becomes the Hangman's final victim. The film's fast-paced succession of stark images can compel lively discussion among students. Its emphasis on the responsibility of the individual to help maintain a just society makes it highly appropriate for a unit such as one on justice.

The following film distributors will send catalogs on request:

Contemporary Films
267 West 25th Street
New York, New York   10001

International Film Bureau, Inc.
332 South Michigan Avenue
Chicago, Illinois   60604

Encyclopaedia Britannica Films
425 North Michigan Avenue
Chicago, Illinois   60611

Films, Incorporated
1150 Wilmette Avenue
Wilmette, Illinois   60091

The Janus Film Library
871 Seventh Avenue
New York, New York   10019

National Film Board of Canada
680 Fifth Avenue
New York, New York   10019

Standard Film Service
4418 Pearl Road
Cleveland, Ohio   44109

Twyman Films, Inc.
329 Salem Avenue
Dayton, Ohio   45401

TV productions cannot be so readily used in the classroom as can motion pictures. Still, since nearly every student is likely to have access to a TV set, commercial TV programming can be used as an adjunct to various units of instruction. The humor unit outlined in Chapter 1, for instance, calls for watching various TV comedies with an eye to particular kinds of analysis. The alert teacher can also make use of various TV specials and movies. Dickens' "A Christmas Carol" and Menotti's *Amahl and the Night Visitors* make regular appearances near Christmas. Paddy Chayevsky's *Marty,* Faulkner's *The Old Man,* and special TV adaptations of musicals and plays reappear as the phoenix does. Many fine movies have appeared at a time when students can watch: for example, *The Bridge on the River Kwai, Death of a Salesman, Summer and Smoke, The Hustler,* and *Dr. Strangelove.* By asking students to watch TV presentations at home and then discussing them in class, the teacher can establish a bond between the classroom and the world outside. It is one more way of helping the student to see that the two are not entirely separate entities.

Assessing Interest in the Unit As a Whole

The usual technique for determining the likelihood of students' interest in advance is through some sort of interest inventory (see Chapter 7). Obviously, however, if we are planning a unit on satire, the results of ordinary inventories will be of very little help. Students who have never heard of satire can hardly be expected to express an interest in it. But in considering such a unit, there are some things we know even without the aid of inventories. First, we know that students enjoy humorous writing and cartoons, at least those they can understand. Second, whatever materials are selected for a unit on satire are not likely to condescend to students who are pleased to read material that is clearly for adults if they can understand it. Third, the materials would not be limited to the middle class, as so many stories written for adolescents are. Fourth, we know that most junior and senior high school students would find a series of lectures on the nature of satire extremely dull. The same material and concepts are far more interesting if they are arranged in sequence from simple to difficult and presented inductively so that the students can confront and solve increasingly complex problems in reading satire, an approach that promises to reduce frustration to a minimum.

One of the English teacher's greatest responsibilities is to create interest in literature for his students. Therefore, even when the prognosis for student interest in a unit is excellent, he must make both formal and informal evaluations of student interest during the course of the unit. Informally, he can look for signs of boredom. Do the students groan more than usual? Do only a very few students respond during class discussion? Do small-group discussions meander permanently away from the topic? Do students appear listless in class? Do they begin new assignments reluctantly?

It is wise to use a more formal technique as well. An anonymous questionnaire that calls for student evaluations of a unit and its parts can be very revealing. However, the teacher must exercise extreme care to avoid influencing student responses by his remarks as he distributes the questionnaire or gives directions. The following questionnaire was designed to follow a unit on satire.

A QUESTIONNAIRE ON THE UNIT

Your answers to the following questions will help in revising the satire unit for next year. Please do your best to give complete and honest answers. If you have additional comments that you think might be helpful, please add them on the back of this sheet. *Do not put your name on this questionnaire.*

1. Do you think you are a better reader of satire now than you were at the beginning of the unit?
2. Do you know more about how satire works now than you did at the beginning of the unit?
3. The following scales are for your evaluation of the unit *as a whole.* Put an X at the point on each scale that best indicates your reaction to the unit *as a whole.* Below each scale add a comment to explain your reaction.

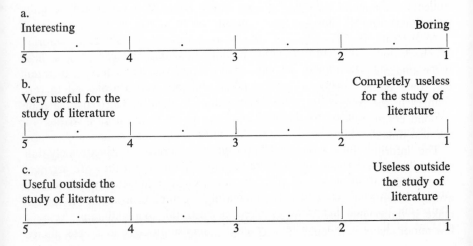

4. Which works did you enjoy reading? Why?
5. Which works did you *not* enjoy reading? Why?
6. Which of the works do you think students might enjoy reading in this unit next year?
7. If you were planning this unit for students next year, which works would you leave out?
8. Which activities of the unit outside the reading did you enjoy? Explain your preference.
9. Which activities of the unit outside the reading did you *not* enjoy? Explain why, if you can.
10. If you were planning this unit for another group of students, what changes would you make in the lessons, materials, and related activities?
11. Explain in what way the unit has most affected you—positively or negatively or both.

Since it is best not to rely on the responses to a single question to evaluate the unit, some of the questions here were designed to check on others. For instance, if a majority of the students mark the midpoint—3—on scale *a,* we can use the responses to other questions to obtain a clearer impression of student interest in the unit. If the students list many more works they did *not* enjoy than those they did enjoy in answer to questions 4 and 5, then the rating of 3 on scale *a* can be considered an indication of a lack of interest. The answers to questions 6 and 7 can be used as a check on 4 and 5. For if students say they did not enjoy certain works (question 5) but do not suggest taking those works out of the unit for other students (question 7), they must see certain values in using them. Even when student reactions appear to be positive, it is useful to cross-check the various questions. For instance, students may rate the unit very interesting because they like the teacher. If the same students recommend dropping several works from the unit, their rating of "very interesting" is automatically qualified.

At any rate, the questionnaire, despite its shortcomings, can be a very useful check on a teacher's general impressions of a class's response to a unit. If the students give the unit a middle rating on interest, list only a few works that they enjoy, suggest dropping several works, and recommend major changes in the procedures, it is clearly best to plan revisions. Even if they respond enthusiastically, their comments can be very useful in planning for the next time around.

The informal unit description that follows suggests how the kinds of materials and activities suggested above can be incorporated into the unit structure discussed in the previous chapter. The unit has been designed with average seventh or eighth graders in mind, but changes in the materials would make it thoroughly useful for average eleventh or twelfth graders. With a few minor changes, it could be used with slow high school classes. The quickest way to create a negative affective response among students is to choose a unit or materials for a class on some arbitrary or irrelevant basis. The following unit cannot be presented to a group of students simply because they are in the seventh grade. If they are poor readers, they might well lose interest in the reading materials, even though they remain interested in the general concepts and the other materials. The same holds true for each instructional unit described in this book: It must be adapted to the abilities and interests of the students in the particular classroom.

A UNIT ON COURAGE

TERMINAL OBJECTIVES

1. Given an unfamiliar novel or play appropriate to the unit theme, to write an essay explaining in what way or to what degree the characters are courageous.

   Criterion statements:
   a. The analysis must provide evidence in support of the judgment by allusion to or quotation from parts of the text.
   b. The analysis must distinguish between physical and moral courage, and among characters whose actions are truly courageous (the Aristotelian mean), those whose actions are foolhardy (excess), those whose actions are cowardly (defect), and those whose seemingly courageous actions are dictated by something that they fear more (defect).
   c. The analysis must consider the characters' knowledge of the dangers, their motives in performing the action, and their understanding of the possible consequences.
   d. The analysis must evaluate the author's treatment of courage in his presentation of characters, that is, it must determine whether the author has explored the character's reactions to the situations facing him in a realistic way.
2. To take part in a group's production of a one-act play.

   Criterion statements:
   a. The student must read a part, block, prepare sound effects, direct, lead a discussion of the production, and so on.
   b. The production will be a reading or a studio production for the class or some other class or a tape-recorded radio play.
3. To write a short story.

   Criterion statements:
   a. The story must describe a disaster (see model in Lesson 12, pp. 342–343) or some other situation in which a character is under extreme pressure.

b. The actions and thoughts of the character must display an inner struggle involving courage, cowardice, or rashness—or some combination of these.

Note: The criterion statements are very loosely framed. The student should be free to develop his story beyond or in a different direction from their requirements. The criteria are intended to help judge whether the student has met a minimal standard.

4. To write an extended definition of courage.

Criterion statements:

a. The definition must explain the characteristics of the courageous person or act.
b. It must contrast courage to cowardice and rashness.
c. It must distinguish between acts that appear courageous but are either cowardly or rash.
d. It must illustrate each point by allusion to materials read in or out of class and by allusion to television programs or motion pictures.

5. To write an analysis of the presentation of courage in a television show. (Criteria are the same as for objective 1.)

The Unit Problem

The problem of what courage is and what it is not is relatively complex. Most people believe that an athlete who hides a broken bone from his coach in order to stay in the game is courageous, even though his neglect might ultimately result in permanent deformity. Similarly, a seventh grader is likely to regard as courageous a peer who defies his teacher, even though the defiance might be a method of avoiding the ridicule of his fellows. Here is Aristotle on the relationship of courage to cowardice and rashness:

What is terrible is not the same for all men; but we say there are things terrible even beyond human strength. These, then, are terrible to every one—at least to every sensible man; but the terrible things that are not beyond human strength differ in magnitude and degree, and so too do the things that inspire confidence. Now the brave man is as dauntless as man may be. Therefore, *while he will fear even the things that are not beyond human strength, he will face them as he ought and as the rule directs, for honour's sake;* for this is the end of virtue. But it is possible to fear these more, or less, and again to fear things that are not terrible as if they were. Of the faults that are committed one consists in fearing what one should not, another in fearing as we should not, another in fearing when we should not, and so on; and so too with respect to the things that inspire confidence. *The man, then, who faces and who fears the right things and from the right motive, in the right way and at the right time, and who feels confidence under the corresponding conditions, is brave;* for the brave man feels and acts according to the merits of the case and in whatever way the rule directs.

. . .

Of those who go to excess he who exceeds in fearlessness has no name (we have said previously that many states of character have not names), *but he would be a sort of madman or insensible person if he feared nothing, neither earthquakes nor the waves,* as they say the Celts do not; while the man who exceeds in confidence about what really is terrible is rash. *The rash man, however, is also thought to be boastful and only a pretender to courage;* at all events, as the brave man is with regard to what is terrible, so the rash man wishes to appear; and so he imitates him in situations where he can. Hence also most of them are a mixture of rashness and cowardice; for, while in these situations they display confidence, they do not hold their ground against what is really terrible. *The man who exceeds in fear is a coward;* for he fears both what he ought not and as he ought not, and all the similar characterizations attach to him. He is lacking also in confidence; but he is more conspicuous for his excess of fear in painful situations. The coward, then, is a despairing sort of person; for he fears everything. The brave man, on the other hand, has the opposite disposition; for confidence is the mark of a hopeful disposition. *The coward, the rash man, and the brave man, then, are concerned with the same objects but are differently disposed towards them;* for the first two exceed and fall short, while the third holds the middle, which is the right, position; and rash men are precipitate, and wish for dangers beforehand but draw back when they are in them, while brave men are keen in the moment of action, but quiet beforehand.

As we have said, then, courage is a mean with respect to things that inspire confidence or fear, in the circumstances that have been stated; and it choses or endures things because it is noble to do so, or because it is base not to do so. *But to die to escape from poverty or love or anything painful is not the mark of a brave man, but rather of a coward;* for it is softness to fly from what is troublesome, and *such a man endures death not because it is noble but to fly from evil.* (Italics added.)[22]

If the students can comprehend these ideas, they can establish criteria for judging courageous action. Reading and discussion would be more meaningful and would lead ultimately to evaluation of a writer's thinking. They could deal with questions such as these:

1. To what extent is the character aware of all aspects of the situation and its possible consequences for him and others?
2. To what extent is the character's goal worthy of the action he undertakes?
3. In undertaking a particular action is the character more concerned with attaining some apparent goal or with avoiding something which he fears? What is his motivation for undertaking the action?
4. What evidence is there that the character is cowardly, rash, or courageous, or has these qualities in some combination?

5. To what extent does the writer present an honest evaluation of the problem? To what extent does he rely on popular beliefs or clichés for his solution? (Is the character treated as courageous when he is really foolish or cowardly? Were there other more sensible actions that the author might have attributed to the character? Does the character display reasonable fear?)

These are fairly abstract and complex questions for students at nearly any level. The problem for the teacher is to introduce them and develop them at a level that will appeal to the students.

Lesson 1 Introduction

The teacher opens the unit by asking students what they think courage is. Their explanations and examples are likely to focus on physical acts of derring-do. He leads the class in constructing a "temporary" definition of courage with examples. This definition* should be duplicated and distributed so that each student has a copy. As the unit progresses, the students will add to it and revise it. After building the first tentative definition, the teacher should capitalize on any disagreements among the students to keep the problem open. If there are no disagreements, they can be asked to validate their ideas by checking other sources: How might you check this definition? Where would you look? They should suggest dictionaries, encyclopedias, teachers, parents, their friends. Their first assignment is to collect ideas that will be used to revise the tentative definition.

Lesson 2 Basic Unit Concepts

After this easy introduction the teacher introduces the Aristotelian ideas. He shows pictures of a bull fighter in action. (Pictures of any other dangerous sport will do. The central figure must jeopardize his life. Close calls are useful. The rewards ought to be questionable.) The pictures can be found in magazines, on airline posters, and so on. The teacher proceeds with questions: Is the matador courageous? Hopefully, there will be disagreements.

Student 1: Yes, it takes a lot of courage to stand that close to the bull's horns.

Student 2: Naw. He's a nut.

Teacher: Why do you think he is foolish?

Student 2: What's it gonna get him besides a horn in the belly?

Student 3: Money.

Teacher: If a man does something for money, is he courageous?

* Obviously, the class should have had training in writing definitions.

Student 5: Yeah, but them guys do it every Sunday. I mean, they're trained for it. It's just like deliverin' milk to them.

Student 6: Yeah, he's no braver than somebody who takes risks everyday—like cops or steeplejacks.

Teacher: Is it possible that he isn't courageous at all? Maybe he only fights the bulls to escape doing other kinds of work?

Student 7: I don't think so. He must know the danger he is in.

Student 8: I don't know. He might have become a matador only because he was afraid not to. Like maybe somebody teased him into it, or his parents expected it.

Obviously, a good class. Most will not develop the basic ideas so rapidly. The teacher will have to provide more questions—perhaps a point of view for the students to argue with. But any class, with the help of the teacher's questions, will eventually develop the ideas with which Aristotle is concerned: courage and its relationship as a mean to the extremes of cowardice and foolhardiness.[23] Once the idea has been developed in class, the students can read the selection from Aristotle if the teacher thinks they will be able to comprehend it.

Whether they read Aristotle or not, their use of the ideas will help them avoid superficial inferences, for they will have to examine the character's motives, his goals, and his awareness of the danger. For instance, if a character undertakes a dangerous action because he fears the alternative more, he is not truly courageous. If he undertakes a dangerous action toward an unnecessary goal, he is, in Aristotle's view, not courageous, but foolhardy. Careful consideration of these questions helps to eliminate stock responses and provide touchstones for discussion.

Lesson 3 Developing Unit Concepts

MATERIALS

Carl Stephenson, "Leiningen Versus the Ants"[24]
Lucille Fletcher, "Sorry, Wrong Number"[25]
Jack London, "To Build a Fire"[26]

The materials for this lesson illustrate the three qualities with which Aristotle is concerned. The teacher assigns the stories and directs discussion. "Leiningen Versus the Ants" displays a classic example of courage in the Aristotelian sense. Leiningen knows the danger, fears it, but acts with confidence to defeat a huge swarm of ants that attack his plantation and nearly take his life. "Sorry, Wrong Number" is a one-act play about a rather disagreeable invalid woman who overhears a conversation about a murder that will be committed. She attempts to contact authorities but is so rattled that no one believes her. When she begins to suspect that she herself is the victim, she is reduced to complete panic. In addition to discussing the kinds of questions listed under "The Unit Problem," the students might consider the extent to which Mrs. Stevenson's panic contributed to her death. The hero of "To Build a Fire" ignores the warnings of an old-timer and travels alone in the severe cold of the Yukon. He is confident his journey will be successful, but as he travels, his confidence leaves him, and he becomes panicky and freezes to death. All three stories are compelling. "To Build a Fire" is the most difficult but has a high interest level for students. The teacher leads a discussion of each story in terms of the unit problems, and when all the stories have been read, he asks questions to help students compare the three.

Lesson 4   Developing Unit Concepts

MATERIALS

B. J. Chute, "Ski High"[27]
Stewart Alsop and Ralph E. Lapp, "The Strange Death of Louis Slotin"[28]
Homer, *The Odyssey,* Book 9[29]

In this lesson the students attempt to discriminate between courage, rashness, and cowardice in a given character. The class is divided into three groups according to reading ability. The high group reads and discusses Odysseus' adventure with the Cyclops, whose cave he enters out of curiosity but with dire results for his men. The middle group reads "The Strange Death of Louis Slotin," and the low group reads "Ski High." Each story presents a character who may or may not be considered courageous, depending on the circumstances and motives for his acts.

For instance, the "Strange Death of Louis Slotin" tells of a young man who, in the early days of the atomic bomb, was fascinated by an experiment that involved pushing two lumps of fissionable materials together to determine their "critical mass." If they were "critical," a chain reaction would begin. The trick lay in knowing when to stop it. It was an extremely dangerous experiment, but Slotin enjoyed it and rejected the safety devices that were developed for it. He would allow the lumps to stay together for as long as possible before pushing them apart. His final test resulted in his death. In demonstrating the experiment to a visitor, he allowed the materials to stay in juxtaposition for too long and threw himself on them to stop the chain reaction. In doing so, he saved the lives of the visitor and his co-workers but sustained radiation burns that resulted in his death a few weeks later. The authors of the essay call Slotin a brave man but imply that his actions were not altogether rational. The problem for the students is to determine if, when, and why his actions were courageous or foolish.

Following small-group discussion of these selections, each group plans a presentation to the rest of the class, explaining the events and supporting their judgments concerning the courage of the characters.

Lesson 5 Evaluation

MATERIALS

Leo Tolstoy, "The Raid"[30]

The class reads "The Raid," which is based on the Aristotelian concept of courage. The teacher provides a study guide for the reading. Then the students write a brief analysis explaining why each of the three characters is courageous, cowardly, or rash. They should contrast the three characters in their analysis. If the students have not done this kind of written analysis previously, the teacher must include a composition lesson prior to this or allow the students to write out brief answers to particular questions instead of writing a composition.

Lesson 6 Moral Courage

MATERIALS

Transparencies of cartoons
Recording: *You're a Good Man, Charlie Brown*[31]

The materials up to this point in the unit have emphasized acts of physical courage. This lesson will introduce the idea of courage in situations other than the physical. The lesson uses sequences of cartoons for the purpose. Charlie Brown is a loser, but he continues to try. His kite-flying ends in disaster. His ball team never wins. But a few pages later he is trying again.[32] Is Charlie Brown courageous? Some students will think he is not. Others will argue that he is. The students should be encouraged to debate the matter after collecting evidence to defend their positions. In this connection, they can discuss the title song of *You're a Good Man, Charlie Brown*. For example, why do the writers of the song believe that Charlie Brown has a sense of humor? The lesson should result in the realization that many people display courage though they are never subjected to physical danger. The class should define this aspect of courage and add it to their notes for a definition of courage.

Lesson 7 Moral Courage

MATERIALS

Zona Gale, "Bill"[33]
Ernest Hemingway, "A Day's Wait"[34]
Mary E. Wilkins Freeman, "The Revolt of Mother"[35]
Pearl Buck, "Guerrilla Mother"[36]

This lesson has two parts. In the first, the students read "A Day's Wait" and "Bill" and discuss the stories in terms of all the aspects of courage developed in the unit. In the second part, the students working in small, heterogeneous groups read and discuss "Guerrilla Mother" and "The Revolt of Mother." The teacher supplies appropriate study guides for the group discussions.

Following the discussions, which should focus on moral courage and the issues involved, the teacher assigns a composition defining courage. To make the assignment, he calls the attention of the class to their notes toward a definition and asks them what ought to be included in a complete definition. He continues the discussion, asking leading questions when necessary, until the students have listed all the criteria for writing a definition of courage. (They are listed at the beginning of the unit.) If necessary, the teacher provides the appropriate composition models and instruction.

Lesson 8   Synthesis of Unit Concepts

MATERIALS

Movie, *Captains Courageous*[37] (black and white, 116 min.)

After viewing *Captains Courageous,* the students make use of all aspects of the unit concepts in their discussion of the movie, examining the courage or lack of courage displayed by the various characters at various times. To support this discussion, they also discuss why and in what ways specific scenes and actions of characters were convincing or not convincing. The problem is good preparation for producing one-act plays, which follow.

Lesson 9   Producing a Play

MATERIALS

Lucille Fletcher, "Sorry, Wrong Number"[38]
Holworthy Hall and Robert Middlemass, "The Valiant"[39]
Pearl Buck, "The Rock"[40]

A number of one-act plays are appropriate for this unit. Two that might be used as alternatives to those above are Lady Gregory's "The Rising of the Moon"[41] and Eugene O'Neill's "In the Zone."[42] "Sorry, Wrong Number" is repeated here on the assumption that it be assigned to slower students in the class. Of the three plays, "The Valiant" is the most difficult and should therefore be assigned to the better readers.

The groups assigned to each play first read and discuss the play with the help of a study guide supplied by the teacher. Then they plan and execute a production of the play. They may choose to make a radio play—especially good for the group working with "Sorry, Wrong Number." Or they may decide to do either a reading or a studio production. They elect a director and an assistant and begin to discuss how each character should be presented, what the special production problems are, and so on. For instance, if "Sorry, Wrong Number" becomes a radio play, how will the various phone calls be handled? What special sounds are necessary? Once the various problems have been identified, the director can assign the parts on the basis of tryouts and assign specific jobs such as sound effects or blocking to some of the students. While the actors are practicing their parts, other students can work out their special problems. At first, all this activity can take place in the classroom, but eventually the teacher will have to find spots for rehearsal—a vacant classroom, the auditorium lobby, the hall outside the English class itself. If some students want to rehearse after school, the teacher should welcome the enthusiasm. If all students cannot be involved in the production of a play, a few members of each group can be responsible for leading a discussion of their group's play after its production. The teacher must visit groups regularly and check with his directors on progress.

If the teacher does not plan procedures carefully, chaos may result. If, on the other hand, they are carefully planned, the teacher will find himself free to confer with students over the rough drafts of the compositions assigned in Lesson 7.

Lesson 10   Evaluating a Work and Television Productions

MATERIALS

Rudyard Kipling, "Gunga Din"[43]
Recording: "Gunga Din"[44]

Students listen to the recording of "Gunga Din" while they follow a mimeographed text. They discuss first whether the speaker's judgment of Gunga Din's courage is justified. Does the poem present enough evidence to make a judgment? To what extent is Kipling concerned with the motives for Gunga Din's courage? What is there to indicate that Gunga Din fears what ought to be feared and acts courageously in spite of that? Questions such as these lead to the second major point of the discussion, an evaluation of Kipling's treatment of Gunga Din's courage. The opening question is: With what aspects of courage is Kipling concerned? Although the students may not use such words as "romantic," "idealistic," "popular," or "superficial," they are likely to arrive at similar judgments. The discussion should then turn to television treatments of courage and proceed in a similar manner. The teacher requests that the students watch a particular television production that night. The next day, the students can discuss the show in small groups, asking the same questions about the show that they asked about "Gunga Din."

The teacher then asks the students to decide which and how many television programs they might watch in order to write a critical paper, analyzing the treatment of courage on television. The student may draw examples from one show, a series, several shows from different series, and so on. Fluent writers are encouraged to work on papers comparing one show or series to another or a book or story to a television show, and so on.

Lesson 11   Outside Reading

MATERIALS

Bibliography of books suggested for outside reading.

The teacher distributes a list of books for outside reading. The students may either choose a book from the list or select some other book with the teacher's approval. The teacher makes an appointment to take his class to the library, asking the librarian to place the books on the unit bibliography together on a table so that the students may browse through them. Although the teacher may suggest appropriate titles for slow, functional, and fluent readers, the final choice is the student's own. When the choice is made, he registers the title with the teacher, and if he decides to change books, he keeps the teacher informed. The teacher encourages the students to change when and if they wish because there are always some who make inappropriate choices.

Following the trip to the library, it is wise to devote a session or two to reading in class. During these reading periods the teacher may confer with students on their written definitions of courage, which will be due shortly, or the critical papers described in the preceding lesson. The trip to the library and the days following signal the formal end of the unit activities in class. While the teacher begins the next unit, the students can complete their outside reading and write their "book reports." The reports will not be book reports in the usual sense, however. They will make use of the main unit concepts as described in objective 1 and its criterion statements.

Lesson 12   Writing a Short Story

MATERIALS

"Death of a City," student model.

This lesson can appear at various points in the sequence after Lesson 4 and may very likely be taught in two parts, separated by another lesson. The students develop their short stories in two installments. They first read the model and analyze its parts. They identify the two major sections of the essay, its descriptions of the same characters in each section, its use of highly specific details, and so on. Following the analysis, the students suggest similar situations that may effect entire communities—for example, flood or fire—or individuals—snake bite, drowning. Each student then writes a composition in which he describes a scene before and after the coming of some sudden, frightening event. He must include specific details about two or three people in particular. In the second stage, he selects one character for special development. The first part of his story, the peaceful scene, should give some clues as to how the character will react when disaster strikes. Some of the materials read in class provide good examples, "To Build a Fire," for instance. The story should let the reader see not only the actions of the character but what goes on in his mind—an inner struggle involving courage, cowardice, or rashness, or some combination of them.

The model for the first stage follows:

DEATH OF A CITY

May 8, 1902, dawned magnificently in the small West Indian port, St. Pierre. The sun shot shafts of gold and pink across the azure Caribbean and touched the top of Pelie, the long-restless volcano towering above the village, and edged its floating banner of vapor with gold.

The plump padre of the white-washed church on the plaza gazed up at it in wonder. "A most fortunate omen for the day to come," he muttered, and turned back into his sanctuary for morning prayers. Lolling back in a wickerwork chair on a magnolia-shaded veranda, a French planter absorbed the beauty of the sunrise along with a glass or two of port. On the bridge of a small sloop riding at anchor in the bay a ship captain leaned against a mast and let the soft sea breeze caress his face. A half-drunken carter staggered from his shack in the slums and strode unsteadily toward his cart.

Morning grew old and flowed into early afternoon, and the town began to awake from its mid-day rest. Stretching wearily, the carter rose from his nap in the shade of his cart. The French planter stepped out of a shop on the plaza and strode easily down the square. A small boy sprawled idly in the dust nearby, making formations of rudely carved wooden soldiers. A feeling like that of a man newly awakened from sleep ran through the town, and people prepared to take up again what they had left undone that morning.

It began so slightly as to be almost unnoticeable, a slight trembling of the earth that set the palm-fronds dancing and the boy's soldiers sprawling in the dust. It grew, and rocked walls and sent people stumbling. And with it grew a sound, at first a mere sigh, a small mutter, that swelled to a roar that drowned everything else in its vastness. The earth itself seemed to cry aloud in agony as groan after groan was wrenched from its very heart.

An explosion shook the sky, and a flaming cloud boiled upward from Pelie's mouth, then settled and flowed down the mountain like a great flood bursting from a broken dike. Billowing and eddying like an angry river, it swept all before its raging flood.

The priest fled from his church, and stumbled toward the shelter of a crumbling wall. The carter hauled frantically at his burro, but the fear-stricken beast refused to move. He turned and fled toward the church. Tripping against a curb, the French planter fell, and lay where he struck, holding his head as if to shut out the roar of the volcano. Crying for mother, the small boy cringed in the shadow of a shrub. Searing all before it into oblivion, flames flowed through the doomed city and rolled into the sea. Where it passed, the waters of the bay spouted and boiled, and the ships it touched exploded into flames. Those that had time fled for their lives. The cloud pushed a scorching wind before it, and the fleeting ships were assisted in their flight by the very death they were attempting to escape. City, ships, men, all were lost for one infinite moment in one glowing cloud of fire blotting out all things within it.

And then it was over. Where once a city had lived only dead ashes remained. Yet down in the deepest dungeon of the city jail a prisoner pounded his cell door and shouted for a jailer who could not come. Of all the thronging multitudes that had been living but a moment before, only the most wretched, despised of them all remained.

Ninth-grade girl

In building and teaching this or any other unit, the teacher must be concerned with both the affective and cognitive responses of his students. Although the cognitive may be primary, no one doubts that students learn more in the cognitive realm if they enjoy what they are doing. The teacher must do a great deal to ensure positive affective results. He must adapt particular units of instruction to the abilities of the students; he must teach inductively, so that the students can become involved in learning processes; he must find a variety of instructional materials and devise a variety of activities for his students. Above all, he must order the learnings so that the students progress from the simple to the more complex and from the teacher-supported activity to the independent one. All this demands considerably more of the teacher than lecturing on or discussing one story after another in a single text. But the extra effort accomplishes far more.

The following report by a student teacher describes her experience in using and her classes' responses to certain of the activities and techniques suggested in this chapter.

Notes on the Production of "Pyramus and Thisbe"

Charlene McMahon

I look around room 33 the day before the play and find five sets of costumes, swords, mulberry bushes, jars of ketchup, lanterns and one large painted refrigerator box (which happens to be a wall) all over the room. How will one hundred fifty kids find what belongs to them in all this? Somehow five different classes did, with just a few mix-ups. Fifth period borrowed fourth period's lantern which was found in seventh period's pile of props; second period's costumes ended up with first period's (they were returned to second period) and seventh period's mulberry bush completely disappeared until Brooks ran across the stage with it on play day shouting, "I found it; I found it!" *after* the mulberry scene was over. But together 150 ninth grade students and I produced a play, the Pyramus and Thisbe story, taken from the last act of *Midsummer Night's Dream* on stage with lights, costumes, make up and audience. The five plays were presented the same day and if anyone in my classes had a studyhall during one of the plays he could come and watch.

I used a recording of the last act which gave the students a general idea of how the acting sounded. Then we began our three-week practice. Auditions were held the first two or three days, giving a lot of the students a chance to read. To catch the students' interest, I chose one of the funnier parts of the play to read first rather than start at the beginning of the act. I chose the actors and appointed student directors. The play used thirteen of the students as actors in each of my five classes; the rest were placed in a costume, makeup, or prop group. Each group had a student appointed leader. Anyone not in a group was appointed curtain man and prompter. I helped the directors and suggested ideas for costuming and props, but they had to obtain whatever they wanted. The groups met in various corners of the room during rehearsal. I checked on different days to see that each person in the group was bringing in or working on something for the play. A group had class time to prepare props or costumes. From the first day of practice till stage appearance, the actors moved the chairs to the edge of the room and imagined themselves on stage. Everyone offered suggestions to the actors.

The play itself is funny! A group of men act out a love scene in which the tragic heroine is played by a male actor. (The record helps the ninth grade Thisbes to use a high girlish voice.) The bumpkins offer a ludicrous interpretation of the tragic mythological story, and interest in the play was no problem. Students were excited about appearing on stage, and the competition of five plays helped; each period wanted to be the best.

Practices were fun. Once students were familiar with their lines, they started putting more physical motions into their parts. The student directors gave stage directions, and I kept reminding the actors not to stand still and recite their lines, but to move around a lot. The more they hammed it up the funnier the play would be. Ninth graders have tons of enthusiasm and use lots of imagination in their roles. The teacher needn't tell them every move to make. Ninth grade Thisbes danced around lifting their skirts, lions swung tails and a "tragic" Pyramus swooned around an entire stage dying. Walls reached out and pinched Thisbes, and not to be outdone, one Pyramus kicked Wall and almost lost his balance. When introduced they strutted, danced around and bowed vigorously. Sometimes it was difficult to get an enthusiastic actor off stage once his lines were read. Variety in actor choosing helps. In a predominately female class a shy boy made a great Thisbe in an all girl cast; a chubby girl with a booming deep voice made a marvelous Pyramus paired with a skinny, shorter male Thisbe. An enthusiastic slow reader was an impressive swaying human mulberry bush.

With lots of time the costume groups collected elaborate costumes complete with wigs and skirts for Thisbe and fearful lion outfits. Costumes weren't chosen necessarily to fit the period. The mother of the human mulberry bush made a costume out of a sheet that came to the floor. When both lovers died, the mulberry bush turned around and the back sheet, dyed red, displayed the lover's blood. Balloons under a sweater produced a voluptuous Thisbe in one class and a girl lion wriggled onto stage in a sexy black leotard outfit. Eyes peered out of a fearful shopping bag lion's face. One Pyramus wore a plastic nose mask fastened by an elastic band with mustache and glasses attached. While leaning over her slain Pyramus, Thisbe lifted the mask, moaning, "These lily lips, This cherry nose, . . ." and let go of the mask, snapping the elastic band.

The audiences were comprised of my ninth grade students. (A few days before the play, I made a list of those from each class who wanted to come from a study hall to watch another production. Some students came to three different plays. The lists were then ready for anxious studyhall teachers on play day.) In addition, another teacher sent her English classes during some of the periods my plays were enacted. Two humanities classes also attended, as well as teachers who had free periods during some of the plays.

Backstage was a little hectic on the day of the play. Stage fright appeared for the first time, and students seemed to be running in circles. But the curtain went up, and the students were tremendous. The audiences loved them. The other English classes that watched congratulated them in the hallway afterwards, and one audience ran up on stage after the play shaking hands with the actors. Even mistakes were funny. One Pyramus pulled out his sword and his costume fell off. A lion got excited and threw his lines off stage and then had to crawl backwards and get them because he couldn't remember what he was supposed to say. The voluptuous Thisbe found a pin on stage and popped his balloons as "she" died. Lines recited incorrectly brought laughter and with laughter each group relaxed and swung into action.

I walked into a classroom the day after the play and somehow I had different classes. We had worked hard together on something that was successful for them. They were actually smiling? They were the success of the play. I can't tell you how excited I was for them. They had done a tremendous job and realized it. The fears of inability to act were gone and class enthusiasm was visibly evident. We could have studied grammar together after this, smiling! We had produced a play!

It is unrealistic to say that everyone was totally caught up. Some wanted a bigger part; some with bigger parts could have worked harder. Since the class had a more relaxed atmosphere during practices, discipline was sometimes a problem. One class in particular, predominantly boys, didn't get involved in the play till close to the performance. I had actors from the other classes come in to demonstrate and this provided motivation for them to do as well as the other classes. I also told students early about having an audience which makes a difference in their efforts. I found that some of the students with only minor participation in the play became bored or were discipline problems. Doing the play again, I would try to find something interesting for them to do. They could work on another group project from the humor unit of which this play was a part, and present this to the class. I would also try to give the student directors more freedom, discussing acting hints with them perhaps rather than the whole class.

As a group I feel the students benefited. Their personal reactions to the play can express better than anything I can say the actual value of producing a class play. The day after the performance I asked the students to write a review of the play they had watched and to tell me their personal reactions to producing their own play. They also filled out a questionnaire which made use of a seven point rating scale (one is the lowest and seven is the highest) for questions about their play, whether they wished to be in future plays, general questions about activities covered in English class and their opinions of Shakespeare.

The questionnaire was filled out by one hundred and thirty-three students, sixty-two boys and sixty-one girls. Ten had not signed names. Seventy students gave the play as a class activity a high rating of seven. One hundred and three of one hundred and thirty-three students rated the play with six or seven; only two gave the play the lowest rating of one or two. Of the seven activities listed for English classes "reading short stories" and "working in the literature book" rated as next favorites with thirty people giving a rating of seven to short stories and twenty-nine giving a seven rating to the literature book, far fewer than rated the play production 7. Students liked the stage experience. Reading a play in class was given a much lower rating than producing the play on stage. Only twenty-three gave the class reading of a play a seven rating. Speech and grammar were lowest with only nine people giving the highest rating to speech and six rating grammar high.

Not unexpectedly, the classes that were most co-operative in play practice rated the play higher than the less co-operative groups. In the all-boy class sixteen of the twenty-seven gave the play the higher rating (six and seven). The other groups were more positive as a whole.

Sex made a little difference in ratings. The lowest play rating for a girl was three; three boys rated the play one, two, or three. The girls were slightly more positive about the play. Thirty-nine girls gave the play a seven rating, and twenty-five boys gave the play the highest rating. (Interestingly enough, the boys were more positive about grammar than the girls. Five boys gave this extremely high ratings compared to one girl. Twenty-five girls gave grammar the lowest one and two ratings compared to eighteen boys.)

Desire to produce other plays was evident. One hundred and fifteen students of one hundred and thirty-three responded that they would like to participate in another play. They also seemed eager to take active parts in another production. Seventy-four students wanted to be actors and twenty-nine chose director. Only seventeen listed no participation.

Producing the play even had an effect on their response to Shakespeare. Only forty-four students stated that they liked Shakespeare before producing the play. Their reaction to Shakespeare after the production was remarkably different. One hundred and one students marked yes to the question, Do you like Shakespeare at this point after doing this play? Sex made almost no difference in this question. The responses were similar. In their choices for an introduction to Shakespeare in English class the play was overwhelmingly rated the highest. A teacher lecture was given a high (6 or 7) rating by only nine students. Reading a play received forty-two high (6 or 7) ratings compared to ninety-two students who rated producing the play with a high six or seven rating.

Their comments taken from the reviews were also impressive. Their writing has not been corrected.

1. "It showed me that there are different things that can be done with an English class. It was alot of work, but it was fun and worthwhile."
2. "I love to be part of a play. I was so excited about it that when it was my turn, I forgot all my lines and the rest of the kids went on. I felt so ridiculous!"
3. "I learned alot more about Shaskspear than if I would have just read it and answered questions."
4. "I got experant for being up in front of people."
5. "I learned that you can't goof around and then to do something right. Now I believe in the saying PRACTICE MAKES PERFECT."
6. "For the first time our class co-operated and really tried to make the play a success."
7. "Now I know what it means to see an actor on the stage that looks like his old dead grandmother came to wish him good-luck."
8. "It was more fun than just dreary old English class. I enjoyed being in the play because everyone likes to stand out and be noticed and being in a play like this certainly makes you stand out and be noticed."
9. "I learned to never give up at the last moment in doing something. What did I get out of it? I got enjoyment, satisfaction and a few ulcers."
10. "I didn't think it would be that good."
11. "You really have to know what's going on."
12. "I liked the whole play because everyone put alot of effort to make the play a success."
13. "You had to have responibility and it was fun to."
14. "When everybody puts their mind to do something everything can work out very well."
15. "I've never did this before. I got the expermentce from this play. When I get to be in the 11th and 12th grade it will be eaiser to try out for a part."
16. "The lines weren't hard and I was an important figure."

There were only a few negative comments about the play from the entire group.

17. "I didn't get anything out of it."
18. "I like being make up but I would have wanted to be an actor."
19. "I think this play was very effective except the parts that were supposed to be funny that we practiced in class because I had heard them for two weeks."
20. "I didn't like the weeks that were spent on it but it turned out really good."
21. "I really didn't get anything out of the play but it was fun."

Most rewarding of all were the changes of attitude in some students who found that they could succeed.

22. "I enjoyed working with the actors very much as a director. Last year if I would have said do this or that, I would have been the laughing stock of the whole school and my friends (supposedly) wouldn't have talked to me or let me forget about it just out of jealousy. But all the kids were wonderful and for the first time I wasn't afraid to voice an opinion. Everyone cooperated very well and I just loved it."
23. "I found that I was quite silly acting in the beginning about being afraid of acting the Pyramus part. I found that I greatly enjoyed acting in front of a group. I hope to play in a future play."
24. "I like being in the play because it give me a chanch to act and feel good like some of the pro-acters in the big time."
25. "I had fun with the class and I was happy that sonthing I helped do was so sececfule." (a hostile student at the beginning of the year)

Students discovered that English classes don't really have to be dreary; they can be fun and worthwhile at the same time.

26. "I thought it was *keen* because it wasn't English but yet it was English."
27. "I didn't get to much out of the play because I wasn't here. but what I did see in class was good I thought. And what I didn't see must of have been good of what other people said. I wish I could have seen the play. I would have laugh a lot."

NOTES

1. For a more detailed, but somewhat different, analysis see David R. Krathwohl, Benjamin S. Bloom, Bertram B. Masia, *Taxonomy of Educational Objectives, Handbook II: Affective Domain* (New York: David McKay Co., Inc., 1964).
2. *The Taxonomy . . . Affective Domain* argues that "awareness" is the base for cognitive response and calls it "almost a cognitive behavior." The commentary continues, ". . . we are not so concerned that with a memory of,

or ability to recall, an item or fact as we are that, given appropriate opportunity, the learner will merely be conscious of something. . . ." (p. 176) The distinction appears to be in the choice of words used to describe it rather than in reality. For example, let us assume we want to test the reader's "awareness" of Huck's decision. Our question has to be something like this, "What did Huck think the consequences of helping Jim would be?" Any adequate answer not only involves recall, "awareness," of certain specific details, but simple inference as well. Clearly this is a cognitive response. Their eagerness to claim the independence of the *Affective Domain* from the *Cognitive* results in this ambiguity.

3. For a study of direct vs. indirect patterns of influence in the classroom, see Ned A. Flanders, *Teacher Influence, Pupil Attitudes, and Achievement* (Washington: U.S. Government Printing Office, 1965).

4. Jerome Bruner, *The Process of Education* (Cambridge: Harvard University Press, 1960).

5. Langston Hughes, "Brass Spittoons," *The Book of American Negro Poetry,* ed. James Weldon Johnson (New York: Harcourt, Brace & Co., 1931).

6. For a catalog write to: University Prints, 15 Brattle Street, Harvard Square, Cambridge, Massachusetts.

7. "Resources for the Teaching of English" Champaign: The National Council of Teachers of English, 508 South Sixth Street, Champaign, Illinois 61820.

8. Ask for "Audio Visual Teaching Materials," Educational Audio Visual, Inc., Pleasantville, New York, 10570.

9. *Ibid.*

10. Bill Cosby, *Revenge,* Warner Brothers, W 1691.

11. Godfrey Cambridge, *Ready or Not,* Epic FLM13101.

12. George Carlin, *Take Offs and Put Ons,* RCA, LPM 3772.

13. Bobbie Gentry, *Ode to Billie Joe,* Capitol, ST 2830.

14. All in *A Journey of Poems,* ed. Richard F. Niebling (New York: Dell, 1964), pp. 95, 32, 78, and 157, respectively.

15. Ed McCurdy, Michael Kane, *The Legend of Robin Hood,* Riverside, RLP12-810.

16. See the Language in Action Series, *Education Film Catalogue,* Indiana University, Audio Visual Center, Bloomington, Indiana, 47401.

17. Julie Andrews, Dick Van Dyke, *et al., Mary Poppins,* Buena Vista Records, BV 4026.

18. John M. Culkin, S.J., "Film Study in the High School," *Bulletin of the National Catholic Education Association,* XXIII:3 (October 1965), pp. 1–35. J. Paul Carrico, C.S.C., "Matter and Meaning of Motion Pictures," *English Journal,* 56:1 (January 1967), pp. 23–37.

19. For films dealing with literature, language, and linguistics see *Educational Film Catalogue,* Indiana University, Audio Visual Center, Bloomington, Indiana, 47401.

20. All the films listed are available from Contemporary Films, 267 West 25th Street, New York, New York, 10001. Request catalogs.

21. All the films described below, except the first, are available from Contemporary Films.

22. Aristotle, *Nichomachean Ethics,* in *Introduction to Aristotle,* ed. Richard McKeon (New York: Random House, 1947), pp. 362–364.

23. For an explicit discussion of the Aristotelian mean, see Aristotle, *op. cit.,* pp. 338–347.

24. Carl Stephenson, "Leiningen Versus the Ants," *Worlds to Explore,* ed. Matilda Bailey and Ulhin W. Leavell (New York: American Book Company, 1956).

25. Lucille Fletcher, "Sorry, Wrong Number," *24 Favorite One-Act Plays,* ed. Bennett Cerf and Van H. Cartmell (New York: Doubleday and Company, Inc., 1963).

26. Jack London, "To Build a Fire," *Fifty Great American Short Stories,* ed. Milton Crane (New York: Bantam Books, 1965).

27. B. J. Chute, "Ski High," *Prose and Poetry Adventures,* ed. William J. Iverson and Agnes L. McCarthy (Syracuse: L. W. Singer Company, Inc., 1955).

28. Stewart Alsop and Ralph E. Lapp, "The Strange Death of Louis Slotin," *Man Against Nature,* ed. Charles Neider (New York: Bantam Books, 1963).

29. A poetic translation: Homer, *The Odyssey,* tr. Robert Fitzgerald (New York: Anchor Books, 1963). A prose translation: *The Odyssey,* tr. W. H. D. Rouse (New York: New American Library, 1949).

30. Leo Tolstoy, *The Cossacks and The Raid,* tr. Andrew R. MacAndrew (New York: New American Library, 1961).

31. *You're A Good Man, Charlie Brown,* MGM, IE90C.

32. See especially Charles M. Schulz, *You Are Too Much, Charlie Brown* (New York: Fawcett Publications, 1967) and *Let's Face It, Charlie Brown* (New York: Fawcett Publications, 1967).

33. Zona Gale, "Bill," *Adventures for Readers,* ed. Elizabeth O'Daly and Egbert W. Nieman (New York: Harcourt, Brace, & Company, 1958).

34. Ernest Hemingway, "A Day's Wait," *Adventures for Readers,* ed. Elizabeth O'Daly and Egbert W. Nieman (New York: Harcourt, Brace, & Company, 1958).

35. Mary E. Wilkins Freeman, "The Revolt of Mother," *Prose and Poetry Adventures,* ed. Elizabeth F. Ansorge *et al.* (Syracuse: L. W. Singer Company, Inc., 1942).

36. Pearl Buck, "Guerrilla Mother," *Prose and Poetry for Appreciation,* ed. Elizabeth F. Ansorge *et al.* (Syracuse: L. W. Singer Company, Inc., 1942).

37. *Captains Courageous,* listed in catalogue for Films, Incorporated.

38. Lucille Fletcher, *Ibid.*

39. Holworthy Hall and Robert Middlemass, "The Valiant," *Adventures in Reading,* ed. Jacob M. Ross and Blanche J. Thompson (New York: Harcourt, Brace, & Company, 1948).

40. Pearl Buck, "The Rock," *Adventures in Reading,* ed. Jacob M. Ross and Blanche J. Thompson (New York: Harcourt, Brace, & Company, 1948).

41. Lady Gregory, "The Rising of the Moon," *Thirty Famous One-Act Plays,* ed. Bennett Cerf and Van H. Cartmell (New York: Random House, 1943).

42. Eugene O'Neill, "In the Zone," *Thirty Famous One-Act Plays,* ed. Bennett Cerf and Van H. Cartmell (New York: Random House, 1943).

43. *Kipling: A Selection of His Stories and Poems,* ed. John Beecroft (New York: Doubleday and Co., Inc., 1956), II, 420–422.

44. *Gunga-Din,* Caedmon Records, 1193.

SUGGESTIONS FOR FURTHER READING

1. DAVID R. KRATHWOHL, BENJAMIN S. BLOOM, BERTRAM B. MASIA, *Taxonomy of Educational Objectives: Affective Domain* (New York: David McKay Co., Inc., 1964).

2. NED A. FLANDERS, *Teacher Influence, Pupil Attitudes, and Achievement* (Washington: U.S. Department of Health, Education, and Welfare, OE-25040, Cooperative Research Monograph No. 12, 1965).

3. MARSHALL MCLUHAN, *Understanding Media: The Extensions of Man* (New York: McGraw-Hill Book Co., 1964). For in incisive review of McLuhan's theories, see Anthony Quinton, "Cut-Rate Salvation," *New York Review of Books,* IX:9 (November 23, 1967), pp. 6–14.

4. NATIONAL COUNCIL OF TEACHERS OF ENGLISH, *Motion Pictures and the Teaching of English* (New York: Appleton-Century-Crofts, 1965).

5. DOUGLAS BARNES, *Drama in the English Classroom* (Champaign: National Council of Teachers of English, 1968).

6. JAMES HOETKER, *Dramatics and the Teaching of English* (Champaign: National Council of Teachers of English, 1969).

15 | Curricula in Literature

In this book considerable stress has been placed on the two major considerations in teaching English: (1) the ability and interests of the students and (2) the structure of the subject. Up to this point, however, the emphasis has been on individual lessons (lasting a few days) and units of instruction (lasting a few weeks). The same considerations are equally valid for curricula planned for several years' work in English. The idea that curricula, at least at the present time, must be based upon sound, carefully considered theory rather than experiment or intuition was stressed in the introduction to this book. The experimental trial of alternatives is so complex that it is a practical impossibility for the development of curricula. The other alternative, teacher's intuition, has demonstrated its weakness in innumerable schools throughout the country. There are simply too many teachers whose intuitions correspond neither to the subject nor to the students in their particular classes.

The two considerations of students and the structure of the subject imply a third, that of change. Obviously, students change. Shifts in population change the students in a given school, and the general environment changes them. Note how the vocabulary of young people entering school has changed. Twenty years ago, how many people were familiar with such words as "astronaut," "Apollo," and "Gemini," to take three obvious examples? Finally, the curriculum, if it works, changes the students. Once they learn to apply such concepts as "connotation of words" and "audience," they will tend to read and hear everything in a more sophisticated way. The successful curriculum outmodes itself. By the same token, different students require different curricula because they may not share the same cultural backgrounds. For example, a six-year-old youngster from one household may be able to identify paintings by such artists as Picasso, Van Gogh, Brueghel, and El Greco. Another will know the music of Thelonious Monk, Cannonball Adderley, and Josh White.

352

A third may not know any of that but may know the nearest source of marijuana and heroin. The backgrounds are different, but it might be difficult for people from such varied backgrounds to decide which of them is *deprived*. In short, because change or differentiation is such an important consideration, any curriculum must contain a built-in mechanism for change. The results of pretests and inventories, discussed earlier, provide the impetus, but the teacher in his attitudes and planning must provide the actual change.

The best a total curriculum can do, or perhaps should do, is to provide a general sequence within which the teacher can plan with considerable latitude, depending on the students he finds in his particular classes. At the same time, there is a genuine necessity for a sequence of study that begins with the student as he stands in relation to the subject and then moves toward increasing his sophistication. A sequence of this sort, however, requires careful inventory procedures prior to instruction and careful evaluation of the results of instruction. Any curriculum that goes its merry way regardless of the effectiveness of instruction is useless, except in the shallowest sense—it gives the teacher something to do.

In the 1960s the United States Office of Education sponsored a number of English curriculum projects that were intended to develop workable sequences of instructional materials. Recognizing that a curriculum must be far more than a list of works and interpretations to be consumed by unwary students, the participants in most of these projects took a hard look at both subject matter and students and attempted to go beyond the prevalent arbitrary and senseless offerings made by the workbooks and the generically or chronologically ordered anthologies that structured the literature curricula offered in most school systems.

These curriculum projects developed a variety of programs, ranging from a K-12 curriculum to a program for only a few grade levels. Some focused on a distinct segment of the population or on a single aspect of English. The University of Nebraska's English Curriculum Center, for example, offers a K-12 curriculum that uses thematic, generic, and historically centered units. The units on mythology and satire from the elementary through the secondary program are good examples of sequencing. The Northwestern English Curriculum Center has developed lessons on composition. The Hunter College center has focused on developing English units in a program for "educationally deprived urban children" with reading materials appropriate for the fifth-through the eighth-grade reading levels.[1]

The materials produced by the various centers can be very helpful to teachers, English departments, and school systems interested in developing units of instruction for their own students. The approach has been scholarly, and the concepts underlying the lessons and units of instruction have been rather carefully worked out. The units suggest materials and procedures that have been tried by a good many teachers. Furthermore, they suggest possibilities for sequencing materials and units within grade levels and from one grade level to another.

Their weakness lies in what is at least an implied rigidity. Many present no specific mechanism for varying curricular offerings, no pretests, and few methods of evaluating instruction beyond the level of recall. A notable exception is the Nebraska curriculum in which nearly all units at the secondary level require independent work in which students must make use of what they learned during the course of their study. But most present no means for differentiating work within a single classroom or even for differentiating between, say, one tenth-grade class and another.

Despite the danger that rigor mortis frequently sets in on curriculum documents, there is a need for the individual teacher, the English department, and the school system to develop curriculum structures. Rigidity can be prevented if there is provision for change at all three levels. The individual English teacher, after examining the results of inventories and instruction, must be willing and able to vary materials, procedures, and objectives as necessary. Both departmental and system-wide structures for review and change should be available and should be used regularly.

Sequence

In planning the curriculum for several grade levels, the areas for study in literature will be dictated by the theory that the department or school system has adopted. The theory of literary meaning that guides the units of instruction presented in this book has been presented in Chapters 8, 9, and 10. Given certain student skills and backgrounds, this theory suggests that units should be scheduled into the curriculum on the basis of the type of problem and the kind of materials emphasized by the unit. Thus, a unit emphasizing the study of connotative language in advertising would precede a unit dealing with the analysis of imagery in poetry. Similarly, a general unit on concepts of the hero would precede a unit on the heroic figure of myth, epic, comedy, and tragedy. Again, a unit dealing with the relatively concrete relationships between a character and his immediate circle ("The Outcast" or "The Leader and the Group") should precede units dealing with the more abstract relationships ("Man and Social Class" and "Man and Culture"). The unit on "Courage" in Chapter 14 puts considerable emphasis on what the writer says at the literal level and requires relatively simple judgments and inferences about the motives, intentions, and feelings of characters. "The Outcast" unit for ninth or tenth graders in Chapter 9, while demanding ability to deal with literal and simple inference problems, focuses on the more subtle relationships among characters and the effects of those relationships.

Types of Units

Since one of the important characteristics of literature is its search for and examination of values, some units will be thematic, focusing on major social and cultural values. At lower levels in the seventh through twelfth grade curriculum, these will probably be relatively simple, restricted to the examination of a single value construct: courage, justice, love, money, and so on. At higher levels, the units can deal with sets of related values as they are examined, developed, or criticized in literature. "The American Dream," for example, might focus on the sets of values that affected the pioneers (Ole Rölvaag's *Giants in the Earth,* John Steinbeck's "The Leader of the People") and contemporary, urban, industrialized man (Arthur Miller's *Death of a Salesman,* F. Scott Fitzgerald's *The Great Gatsby,* and Nevil Shute's *Trustee from the Toolroom*). Another unit in this series might focus on how science is changing the values of modern man, giving rise to conflicts between generations. A great deal of material for such a unit is available in magazines from *Life* to *Esquire.* Aldous Huxley's *Brave New World,* George Orwell's *1984,* and B. F. Skinner's *Walden Two* could be used in such a unit. The examination of values is so pervasive in literature that students will be concerned with that problem in any units they study.

The examination of man in relation to his several environments (physical, social, and cultural) also receives widespread attention in literature. A series of units dealing with man in relation to various aspects of environment was discussed in Chapter 10. Other units of that type might focus on the city and country as contrasting environments. Small-town environments have been the setting for a number of literary works in the twentieth century. The unit might examine the sort of treatment afforded the various environments: realistic, naturalistic, romantic, and satiric. And since writers are usually concerned with the effects of these environments on their characters' value systems, the units in this series can be easily related to those in the one directly concerned with values. Some of the units might focus on particular types of relationships among individuals, as does "The Outcast" in Chapter 9. A unit of this type for eighth graders might deal with "The Leader and the Group" and seek to identify the qualities, responsibilities, and results of leadership and to interpret the relationships existing between the leader and his followers, given certain characteristics of leadership and certain conditions. The unit could make use of biographical material at various levels of reading difficulty, traditional material such as *Tom Sawyer* and *Treasure Island* (note the battles for leadership in the latter), and contemporary adolescent novels such as Henry Gregor Felsen's *Hot Rod* and Frank Bonham's *Durango Street.* This unit would relate well to units in the value series such as "Courage" and "Justice." At more sophisticated levels of the curriculum there might be a unit on "The Uses of Power" in which students examine materials ranging from Machiavelli's *The*

Prince to Golding's *Lord of the Flies.* (See a fluent ninth grader's comparison of these works in Chapter 13.) The central problems in such a unit would be to determine, first, how and why men have used power over their fellow men and, second, when and if such uses of power are appropriate.

Another area to explore is imagery, defined broadly as in Chapter 10 to include character, and the like. Such a sequence might begin with "Animals in Literature," the seventh-grade unit described in Chapter 4, and proceed to the interpretation and writing of figurative language, also in the seventh grade or perhaps the eighth. A unit on "The Nature of Personality" might follow in the eighth grade with students examining various methods of interpreting personality, from the use of horoscopes to the more recently developed psychological approaches. A unit of this sort is outlined very briefly in Chapter 3. The unit on "Symbolism" outlined in Chapters 4 and 5 might follow at the ninth- or tenth-grade levels and be followed in the tenth or eleventh grade with an examination of "Types of Imagery." In the latter, students could examine painting, sculpture, photography, poetry, and prose as each makes use of various types of representation: Realism, Symbolism, Impressionism, Surrealism, and so on. A project for evaluation of instruction might require students to determine the types of imagery involved in "The Rime of the Ancient Mariner" and to explain how the imagery relates to the central purpose and impression of the poem. A final unit in this sequence might examine archetypal image patterns in literature.

A fourth concern of readers of literature is that of genre. Most major genres (tragedy, epic, comedy) are too complex for study at junior high level. Although it is fairly simple to find relatively easy satiric material for study at junior high level, the same is not true for tragedy and epic. However, other more popular genre are available for study in the junior high. Science fiction is extremely popular with some students. Detective fiction and the western also make effective units of study. In any of these, the purpose would involve not simply identifying the characteristics of the form but determining how writers use and vary them in conveying the central meanings of a particular work.

At the eleventh- or twelfth-grade levels or with advanced students, units concerned with the work of a particular author or with an historical literary period can be productive. An "author" unit on Poe was suggested in Chapter 7, and a "period" unit on Augustan satire was suggested in Chapter 12. It is important to remember, however, that the vast majority of junior and senior high school students do not share the interests of college English majors. Although high school students will be interested in what a work says and how it says it, they ordinarily care little about the history of blank verse, the historical, cultural, and literary forces that influenced the work of Alexander Pope, or the ways in which one novel by Thomas Hardy is related to others he wrote. As a matter of fact, it is probably safe to suggest that not even all college English majors are enthralled by such study. Still, a carefully developed unit on the English Romantic poets that examines the various ideals and methods of the movement and supplies the background for intelligent, independent reading of other Romantic poetry not studied in class can be a rewarding experience for students who have the appropriate reading skills.

Scope and Sequence Charts

The scope and sequence chart on p. 358 is an example of how a literature curriculum for grades seven through twelve might appear. It includes a strand of units on language, most of which have direct relevance to the literature program. Although the chart has the advantage of presenting an overall view of the program at a glance, it does lack detail. To be really useful, any scope and sequence chart should be supplemented by brief synopses of the units that it incorporates. Synopses of units for two vertical series of related units across grade levels follow the chart. The synopses have been included only for units not developed in detail elsewhere in this book. The relationships among the units are far more complex than the grade level (horizontal) rows and vertical columns on the chart suggest. For instance, the unit on "Semantics" at the seventh-grade level contributes skills and concepts necessary to all units in the chart. Concepts learned in the "Courage" unit will contribute to all units in "The Hero" strand, "The Outcast" unit, and so on. Similarly, the twelfth-grade unit on the "Iconography of an Age" will draw heavily on all units in the "Imagery" strand, the "History of the English Language" and the "Value Systems" sequence.

The numbers in parentheses on the chart indicate a possible sequence for units during a given grade level. The initial activity in each grade is the administration of appropriate inventories. The first unit is one to which students ordinarily have a strong affective response. In addition, nearly all of the first and second units are conceptually important to the other units for the year. The criteria for arranging the other units involve the ways in which they contribute to one another and the unit's level of difficulty. Thus, the tenth-grade sequence opens with "Stage Comedy," which is likely to have strong appeal for the students. The unit "Communications: Ambiguity and Redundancy" prepares the students for "Levels of Interpretation." Both contribute to "Point of View in Literature," and all three contribute to "Social Protest."

Synopses of the units in two vertical sequences, The Hero and The Problem of Change, follow below. However, synopses for units that have been developed elsewhere in this book have not been included. "The Tragic Hero" unit, for instance, appears in detail at the end of Chapter 3, while "The Outcast" appears in Chapter 9. Suggestions for developing a unit on "The Nature of Personality" appear in Chapter 3. With some changes in the materials suggested, that unit can readily be adapted for use in the eighth grade.

TABLE 15.1. Sample Scope and Sequence Chart

Grades	Language	Imagery	Humor	The Hero	Value Systems	Problem of Change
7	Semantics I, Reading: Connotation and Propaganda Analysis (1)	Animal Imagery in Literature (2)	Introduction to Humor (3)	Types of Folk Literature (4)	Courage (5)	Science Fiction (6)
8	Dialects (2)	Types of Characters (4)	American Humorists (3)	The Nature of Personality (5)	Justice (6)	Coming of Age (1)
9	Semantics II, Writing: Purpose, Audience, and Point of View (1)	Introduction to Levels of Meaning (5)	Satire (6)	Mythic Hero (4)	Survival: Values Under Stress (2)	The Outcast (3)
10	Communications: Ambiguity and Redundancy (2)	Levels of Interpretation (3)	Stage Comedy (1)	Archetypal Patterns (6)	Social Protest (5)	Point of View in Literature (4)
11	Language, Culture, and Perception (2)	Perceptions: Realism, Surrealism, Impressionism (3)	Picaresque Hero (5)	Epic Hero (4)	The Black Experience (1)	Approaching an Author: Mark Twain (6)
12	History of the English Language (2)	Evaluation of Experience: Pessimism, Optimism, Neutrality (6)	Theory of Comedy (5)	Tragic Hero (4)	Individual and Society: Alienation and Integration (1)	Iconography of an Age (3)

Initial Activity: Inventories at Each Grade Level

Numerals in parentheses indicate unit sequence during year.

Vertical Sequence: The Hero

Types of Folk Literature   (Seventh Grade)

UNIFYING CONCEPTS

Myth, defined as stories of gods who create the world and of men who do not create but who, by virtue of supernatural powers, can control the environment; myth as etiological tale; legends, stories of historical men to whom extraordinary powers and virtues have been attributed; tall tales of invented heroes (occupational and regional) to whom supernatural powers are attributed; the methods of creating and conveying all such stories; the function of the stories.

CENTRAL READINGS

Tales of Greek, Norse, and American Indian gods and heroes; etiological tales from Greece, India, Africa, and American Indian tribes; legends of historical American heroes; tall tales of American occupational and regional heroes.

COMPOSITIONS

Analyses of stories of each type read independently; original heroic myth, etiological myth, and tall tale.

DESCRIPTION

The unit begins with a discussion of comic book heroes such as Plasticman and Superman. The class identifies their special characteristics and discusses why they appeal to the popular imagination. Next, the class speculates on the types of heroes that might be present in other cultures, before beginning to read Greek, Norse, and American Indian stories of gods and heroes. Following the reading, the students identify the human and superhuman characteristics of the heroes and discuss the appeal of such stories. Next, they read one or two such tales of their own choosing and write a brief essay, identifying the characteristics of the hero, comparing him to others studied by the class, and explaining the appeal of the story. After discussing what sort of hero has appeal today, students write an original "heroic myth." The following sections of the unit on etiological myths, legendary characters, and tall tales proceed in the same way from class reading and analysis to independent reading and analysis to creative writing. A class committee prepares a booklet of the best stories and analyses written by the students.

The Mythic Hero   (Ninth Grade)

UNIFYING CONCEPTS

The nature and significance of the pattern of heroic myth as it appears in diverse cultures: birth, initiation, journey, triumph over the monster, marriage, return, kingship, and death. The relationship of the mythic pattern to corresponding ritual events.

CENTRAL READINGS

The Greek myths of Jason, Bellerophon, Perseus, Theseus, Oedipus, Orpheus; selected hero myths from other cultures; Norma Lorre Goodrich's *Beowulf* in *Medieval Myths*.

COMPOSITIONS

Essay examining and interpreting aspects of the heroic myth pattern in a work studied independently; other short preparatory essays.

DESCRIPTION

The unit begins with a discussion of what heroes are, why they are regarded as heroes, and what they have in common. The teacher encourages student talk about both contemporary and mythic heroes. The students then proceed to read the stories of the Greek heroes comparatively. The result is a formulation of the basic pattern underlying the stories. Then the students discuss the possible significance of the parallels. Following the discussion they read the stories of heroes in other cultures. The discovery that many of these adhere to the same pattern should prompt a discussion of why they do, thus focusing on the aspects of human experience that give rise to the patterns. At this point the teacher presents a lecture on the seasonal ritual. The ensuing discussion should first relate the mythic pattern to the ritual and then examine the significance of the correspondences. The final activity before the independent reading is the study and discussion of *Beowulf*. To what extent does it appear to make use of mythic and ritual patterns? How does it transform these patterns to its own uses?

Archetypal Patterns　(Tenth Grade)

UNIFYING CONCEPTS

There are certain universal aspects of human experience that all men, regardless of particular cultural patterns, undergo. These experiences are reflected in the archetypal imagery of myth, folk tale, and literature. This unit focuses on archetypes of the trickster, initiation, death and rebirth, and the Golden Age, all of which are related.

CENTRAL READINGS

Various Greek myths, selections from Grimm's Fairy Tales, *The Rime of the Ancient Mariner*, Faulkner's *The Old Man*.

COMPOSITIONS

Essay examining the significance of one of the archetypes in a work studied independently; an original piece of writing involving archetypal imagery.

DESCRIPTION

The unit begins by recalling the study of the mythic hero in the ninth grade. The archetypes examined in this unit are all present in the complex of the mythic hero pattern. The discussion proceeds by examining what the most significant occurrences were in the hero pattern. Each archetype is examined in turn as it is represented in the Greek myths, fairy tales, and other short works. How these archetypes appear in modern life should be a continuing focus of attention. The students should collect and discuss representations of the archetypes in painting, advertising, and so on. The unit should focus on two major problems: (1) What is the mythic and/or psychological significance of each archetype? (2) What is the function of each particular representation of the archetype in its context? The study of *The Rime of the Ancient Mariner* and Faulkner's *The Old Man* synthesizes the concepts developed throughout the unit before the students undertake their independent study of selected works.

The Epic Hero (Eleventh Grade)

UNIFYING CONCEPTS

The nature and function of the epic hero and the values he represents and seeks.

CENTRAL READING

The Odyssey.

COMPOSITION

An essay examining the nature and function of an epic hero and the values he represents in a work selected for independent reading; or an essay comparing the epic hero to the mythic or picaresque hero.

DESCRIPTION

The unit opens with a discussion of the mythic hero, his characteristics and values. The students then read and discuss carefully the first thirty lines of *The Odyssey,* which adumbrate the full story of Odysseus and present his character. Thereafter, these opening lines become a guide for the study of the poem. Following the study of *The Odyssey,* the teacher divides the class for small-group comparison of *Beowulf* and *The Odyssey.* The class then discusses the nature of the epic hero, his significance, his values, and so on. They then select a work that may or may not be an epic for independent reading. The reading list should include romances, frontier novels, epic poems, and the like.

Vertical Sequence: Problems of Change

Science Fiction (Seventh Grade)

UNIFYING CONCEPTS

The world of a science fiction story as an extrapolation from existing scientific knowledge; the uses of science fiction to suggest social problems.

CENTRAL READINGS

The Martian Chronicles, various short stories.

COMPOSITIONS

Essay examining the world postulated in a science fiction work selected for independent study; original short story using science fiction material; various other short pieces of writing.

DESCRIPTION

The unit progresses from whole-class study of science fiction to group and then independent study. Since this might be one of the first units that deals with a genre, special care should be taken to examine the structural characteristics of science fiction and how they influence the meaning of the works. Thus, extrapolation and prediction become important both scientifically and morally. The vast amount of material available is conducive to considerable independent study. No matter what the reading level of the student, he can select a work in which he can examine the nature of the world postulated, how the characters behave in that world, and what the author predicts for mankind.

Coming of Age (Eighth Grade)

UNIFYING CONCEPTS

Differences between younger and older persons' views of the world and reality; the causes of those differences; how views change as the person reaches maturity; relationships between adolescents and adults.

CENTRAL READINGS

Various short stories and poems. Esther Forbes, *Johnny Tremain.*

COMPOSITIONS

Photographic essay or collage with pictures selected to emphasize the conflicts or differences between the young and old (must be accompanied by one of a variety of analytical or affective texts); personal essay explaining how the author became more mature or gained some insight through a personal experience; analysis of "coming-of-age" problems illustrated in a novel or biography read independently.

DESCRIPTION

The teacher initiates a discussion of differences in points of view between younger and older people by recounting an experience of his own as an adolescent. Then he inquires about how the point of view of the students is different from that of adults. After the differences have been sorted and listed, the students read and discuss a series of stories, poems, and popular songs which display conflict between youth and age. Next they read a series which displays changes in the attitudes of adolescents as they encounter various sorts of problems. The following discussions should work toward explanation and resolution of the various conflicts between young and old and within the adolescent. Next students begin work on the photographic essays and personal essays. When these projects are underway the teacher introduces *Johnny Tremain*. This is followed by independent reading of a long selection which involves the kinds of problems typical of the unit. This unit affords a number of opportunities for role playing of situations invented by students and dramatizing the problems developed in the class readings.

Points of View in Literature   (Tenth Grade)

UNIFYING CONCEPT

The stance of the author as revealed by his language and the persona he adopts.

CENTRAL READINGS

The Eye of the Beholder (movie), various short stories and poems, *Great Expectations.*

COMPOSITIONS

Short analyses of point of view in a poem and a short story; adopting three personae to argue a controversial issue; analysis of aspects of point of view in *Great Expectations, Planet of the Apes,* or *The Prince and the Pauper,* depending on reading level.

DESCRIPTION

The unit opens with the discussion of *Peanuts* cartoons that illustrate point of view. One small group of students role-play an argument that leads to a fight. The roles are planned in advance without the knowledge of the rest of the class. Then the other students write a composition explaining what happened and who was at fault. The class compares the results, discussing the various points of view. The class views the film *The Eye of the Beholder* before reading and discussing various short stories and poems in which the point of view of the narrator is important. In each of these, the students discuss what the narrator knows of the situation, what his words reveal about his attitude toward it, and how his point of view influences or controls the meaning of the work as a whole. These problems are central to the discussions of the major reading listed above.

Approaching an Author: Mark Twain   (Eleventh Grade)

UNIFYING CONCEPTS

How to approach the body of an author's work: examining the development of his style, his literary interests, and the motifs running through his works; examining his works against the context of his life and times for changes in attitude, technique, and so on.

CENTRAL READINGS

Life on the Mississippi, Pudd'nhead Wilson, The Mysterious Stranger, selected short stories.

COMPOSITIONS

Various short compositions concerning aspects of individual works, the relationships among works, and so on; major paper examining some aspect of a series of works by an author of the student's choice.

DESCRIPTION

By the commencement of this unit, the students will have studied *Huckleberry Finn* in the "Picaresque Hero" or "Satire" and one other novel by Mark Twain as well as various short stories. In addition to the books listed, each student should choose one other major work or collection of short works to read independently. The unit begins with discussions of Mark Twain's writings that the students have read, with the teacher posing questions about his choice of subject matter, style, and the like. After reading parts of *Life on the Mississippi,* additional questions can be raised. Then students choose one of the questions for independent investigation. Class time will be devoted to library work or completing *Life on the Mississippi.* At the end of two weeks, the students can begin reporting their findings to the class. Reports should continue at intervals during the remainder of the unit, being scheduled to emphasize the changes in style, attitude, and so on, reflected in the central readings. Since the major purpose of the unit is for students to learn how to approach several works by a single author, the final unit activity is an independent project in which they examine several works by a single author. Authors who write for children and adolescents are a good choice because they afford opportunity for original research and commentary. The projects should be completed several weeks after the close of the unit on Mark Twain.

Iconography of an Age: Medieval Allegory and Modern Imagery
(Twelfth Grade)

UNIFYING CONCEPTS

An author can expect an audience of his contemporaries to react to various imagery, symbolism, and modes of expression in particular ways. To understand the works of another age, a reader must understand, insofar as it is possible, the symbology and modes of expression of that age.

CENTRAL READINGS

From *The Canterbury Tales,* "The Prologue," "The Nuns' Priest's Tale," and "The Pardoner's Prologue and Tale,"; *Everyman; Sir Gawain and the Green Knight;* paintings by Bosch and Brueghel; pictures of medieval cathedrals.

COMPOSITIONS

Essay explaining the extent to which late medieval or Renaissance work involves medieval forms of allegory and explaining the allegorical significance; essay on some aspect of contemporary iconography.

DESCRIPTION

The unit opens with an examination of pictures of medieval architecture and painting. The teacher raises the problem of why cathedrals were designed and decorated as they were. What was the significance of the seating arrangement? of gargoyles? What is the significance of the various elements in Bosch's "Hay Wain"? After speculating on such problems as these, either in class discussion or in small groups, the students proceed to library work to find some of the answers. They select problems, with the teacher's approval, and work either in teams of two or three or individually in preparing oral reports or panel discussions. Following key reports that focus on the allegorical significance of paintings and aspects of architecture, the students read *Everyman.* From this obvious allegory they proceed to selections from *The Canterbury Tales* and finally to *Sir Gawain and the Green Knight* (all in translation). Next, the students select a work for outside reading, which becomes the subject of a major unit essay. Students then turn their attention to modern iconography through an examination of modern art, advertising, photographs, and poetry. The problem is what images have conventional significance for modern man? Why do they? How are they used? Each student then selects a project for independent study, for example, the machine as monster. The differences in the value systems of the two ages as represented in the iconography and symbology should be a major unit focus.

A Model for an Elective Curriculum in English

Recently, as part of a movement away from the arbitrarily and rigidly structured English curricula formed in most high schools, some schools have developed elective programs in which students select out of thirty to forty courses those they wish to take. The first question from skeptics is the obvious one: If students choose what they want to take, how can you be sure they will take what they need? Certainly the question requires an answer, but against a background of courses founded on little more than accidentally developed traditions, courses that offer little of what students need and even less of what they want, the question becomes almost irrelevant.

One of the best models for an elective curriculum in English was developed at Trenton High School in Trenton, Michigan.[2] The program includes approximately thirty-five courses; each is one semester in length and is offered in at least one semester during the school year. The courses offer a wide variety of subject matter, from a "Seminar on Shakespeare" to a course called "Language and Human Behavior." In addition, the courses represent various levels of difficulty (the Trenton program describes five "phases" of difficulty) from "Fundamental English" to "Research Seminar." All courses are nongraded so that a student can elect any course, regardless of his grade level.

There are several advantages to such a program. First, because the students are given a choice of what they can take, they tend to see success in the course as primarily their responsibility. Second, when the students are thoroughly informed of the nature of the courses available, they tend to select those that are appropriate to their own needs, skills, and abilities as they see them or those courses in which they have a strong interest, or both. Thus, the students in an elective program tend to see the courses as more relevant to their own lives than do students in traditional programs. Third, the teachers in such a program have a greater opportunity to teach from the strengths in their own backgrounds. Fourth, the teachers are under greater pressure to identify the skills and interest of the students who are likely to select particular courses and they tend to select materials and plan activities accordingly. As a result of all these advantages, the students tend to have a far more positive attitude toward English. Of course, the fact that a program is elective does not guarantee positive attitudes and increased learning. The individual courses must be well planned and well taught.

As skeptics have pointed out, the major disadvantages of an elective program lie in the lack of sequence among the courses elected and the lack of balance that may occur when a student avoids certain courses and when a teacher favors some aspects of English and ignores others. Careful planning, however, can diminish these potential dangers. The courses should begin with appropriate inventories and pretesting so that the teacher can make his instruction appropriate to his students. Each course should include a variety of activities such as those described elsewhere in this book. In short, whether the curriculum is sequential or elective, the procedures and techniques for teaching and planning described above are essential.

Adapting Literature Curricula to the Students

The scope and sequence outline presented in this chapter can only be hypothetical because it cannot take into account the actual needs and abilities of the particular set of *students* a teacher may have in his English class. Many of the units on the chart, perhaps even the whole chart, could be adopted for use in many schools. Since it is sequential, it would have to be introduced one grade level at a time. Obviously, most eleventh and twelfth graders could not do the work suggested without the preparation suggested by other units on the chart.

In some schools, the outline will be only partly appropriate, and while parts of it might be used, a teacher (or department) will have to assess the backgrounds of the students very carefully before planning the curriculum. Even then, he would have to build slowly from one grade level to the next and change the curriculum as the students gain the necessary skills for more sophisticated work.

In some schools, such as those in central city ghettos, he will have to pay far more attention to affective response than to cognitive, at least in the early stages of curriculum development. Most students in such schools view the school and its program as totally irrelevant to their real lives. Many, fearing failure in their own eyes more than a teacher's disapproval, refuse to try anything a teacher requires. Most have little outside encouragement to succeed in school. Their futures, as they predict them, will have little if any connection with what goes on in a school. A discouraging number have met failure and rejection so often in the past that they have given up trying by the seventh grade, if not earlier.

Let us consider the problem of developing a curriculum for very reluctant, even hostile students, say eleventh or twelfth graders, in a large urban school. It is obvious that traditional programs in American and English literature are totally inadequate for the job, and the units on the scope and sequence table in this chapter are inappropriate, at least until the students have more background. When then can the teacher do?

A number of teachers have developed units on the literature of protest because of its current popularity, its high interest potential, and its social relevance. Such an area of study offers a number of optional approaches, a wide variety of literary materials, and a host of materials in the popular culture including songs, films, editorials, magazine articles, and cartoons. In developing such a unit, the teacher in concert with his students can select any one of a variety of approaches. The unit might deal with the broad range of protest literature in the last twenty to thirty years, incorporating novels as disparate as Claude Brown's *Manchild in the Promised Land* and Kurt Vonnegut's *Slaughterhouse Five or the Children's Crusade*. Or it might examine the history of protest in the United States including early documents such as the Declaration of Independence and the speeches of early American revolutionaries. It might include the early protests against slavery by both blacks and whites: Frederick Douglas, Henry H. Garnet, and John Brown. One teacher planned a unit on protest to include the protests of the *Old Testament* prophets against various conditions. The unit might involve the many protests against unethical capitalism and working conditions in the nineteenth and early twentieth centuries, including such material as Upton Sinclair's *The Jungle,* Frank Norris' *The Octopus,* and the many union songs of which recordings are available. It might include full-length plays such as Henrik Ibsen's *An Enemy of the People,* Bernard Shaw's *Androcles and the Lion,* and Lorraine Hansberry's *A Raisin in the Sun.* Clearly, a great many folksongs as well as folk-type modern songs would be interesting to study. The unit might open with discussions of current songs of protest and cartoons. It might begin with the screening and discussion of one or two short films such as "Night and Fog" or any of various documentary films such as the "CBS Reports" series. From such high interest material the unit might move to an examination of various areas of protest: war, poverty, pollution, big business deceit, working conditions, women's lib movement and so forth. The teacher's problem is to become familiar with the options, suggest at least some of them to his students, and then to assemble the materials most appropriate to the interests and abilities of his students.

Prior to the study of protest literature, it is necessary for students to have some background in the study of persuasive language, especially in connotation, audience analysis, and the like. However, it is a simple matter to teach that material separately.

The unit that follows focuses on "The Literature of Black Protest" for various reasons, but primarily because of the immediate social relevance such a unit has for both black and white students and because of the high interest of the reading materials. Some other such topical units would be on the women's liberation movement, pollution, drugs, and the rights of minorities in the United States.

The Literature of Black Protest

As Richard Wright pointed out in "The Literature of the Negro in the United States,"[3] black literature, with very few notable exceptions, has always been associated with the voice of protest, and it has been and is an angry voice. This unit focuses on that literature because it has relevance for the black students in ghetto schools. Not only does the black writer speak to their needs but, because he is black, he can give the students a sense of pride in their racial identity, a sense of pride that is frequently not otherwise available in the dreary schools they ordinarily attend. The literature in this unit also has obvious and great immediacy for whites. As someone has pointed out, the struggle against prejudice has focused on the black man, but should not some of the focus shift to the white community? The literature included in this unit certainly should create a new sense of awareness among white students.

Before undertaking this unit the teacher should become aware of the students' environment as it relates to the unit he is about to teach. Patient observation and experience are necessary but cannot provide the whole story. For this particular unit, the following books, in addition to those suggested for use in the unit, will be helpful, but they are not the whole answer.

1. "The Negro American," *Daedalus,* Vol. 94, No. 4 (Fall 1965). A collection of studies about the conditions of Negro life in America.
2. Elliot Liebow, *Tally's Corner.* Boston: Little, Brown, 1967. A study of the lives, frustrations, and aspirations of Negro "street corner" men—lower-class men with irregular jobs and sometime families.
3. Otto Kerner, *et al., The Report of the National Advisory Commission on Civil Disorders.* New York: Bantam, 1968. An analysis of the riots in 1967—what happened, why, and recommendations for the future. See especially Chapters 6, 7, and 8, which deal with the formation of ghettos, unemployment, and conditions of life in the ghetto.
4. Louis E. Lomax, *The Negro Revolt.* New York: Harper & Row, 1962. An analysis of conditions giving rise to the earlier Negro protests.
5. Eldridge Cleaver, *Soul on Ice.* New York: Dell, 1968. The book speaks in anger and contempt against the white society that has debased and exploited the black man in America and around the world.
6. Lerone Bennett, Jr. *Pioneers in Protest.* Baltimore: Penguin Books, 1969. A collection of short biographies of men and women who protested against slavery and discrimination in the United States. It includes biographies of Benjamin Banneker, Henry Highland Garnet, Harriet Tubman, W. E. B. DuBois, and others. Could easily be used by students.
7. Bradford Chambers, ed., *Chronicles of Black Protest.* New York: New American Library, 1968. A collection of original documents with commentaries and biographical notes chronicling the development of black protest. A very informative and useful volume which can readily be used by students.

The following may also be useful preparation for teaching the unit:

1. Addison Gayle, Jr. (ed.), *Black Expression: Essays by and about Black Americans in the Creative Arts.* New York: Weybright and Talley, 1969. An excellent collection of essays, this book will provide

useful information to the teacher approaching black literature for the first time and to those already familiar with it.

2. Barbara Dodds, *Negro Literature for High School Students*. Champaign, Ill.: National Council of Teachers of English, 1968. A thoroughly annotated bibliography of books for classroom use extending from adult fiction to literature for youngsters. The author indicates the level of reading difficulty for each book, gives her estimate of its literary quality, and presents a synopsis and brief analysis. A very useful source of materials.

3. Lawana Trout, "Teaching the Protest Movement," *Dialog* (a periodical), New York: Holt, Rinehart and Winston, Fall 1967, pp. 5–13. A teacher's description of her experiences in teaching a unit somewhat similar to the one that follows. The article also includes quotations indicating the reactions of students to whom she taught the unit and the reactions of teachers who observed it.

The unit is divided into two major sections that overlap to some extent but contribute to one another: (1) the targets and methods of black protest, and (2) the responses of individuals and groups. The second section will require the most class time and the most reading. Free and open classroom discussion, both small-group and whole-class and both teacher- and student-led, are extremely important to this unit because one major purpose is to create an atmosphere in which the students can express their own opinions about the relevancy of the unit materials to their own lives.

Since some students will be more competent readers than others, diversified reading is also important. Core readings (those read by all students) should probably be short and relatively simple unless all students in the class are competent readers. The unit offers students a number of options: whether or not to study black protest in the first place; which books to study; and which projects to work on. Since a major goal of the unit is positive affective response to the materials and to English, giving the students such options is very important.

For several reasons, the unit opens with a study of the power of language (connotation, "purr" and "slur" words, and advertising). First, it offers early involvement and success. (Students especially enjoy developing advertisements.) Second, such study offers a neutral base to work from. Third, an understanding of the persuasive uses of language is important to the unit.

The difficulty of the unit can be varied in several ways. To make it more or less sophisticated, the materials or the objectives (or both) can be changed. For instance, if the students are functional writers, the reports in terminal objectives 3 and 4 could be written. If they are good readers, more poetry could be studied by all of them. Of course, changing the core readings can also make the unit easier or more difficult. Bonham's *Durango Street* will be easier than *A Raisin in the Sun,* which in turn is easier than *Native Son.* To make the unit easier, certain lessons or parts of lessons could be deleted. For example, the research lesson on organized protest groups will require students to read or listen to speeches, to read sometimes dry articles that will not sustain interest as readily as the fiction in the unit, and to deal with rather abstract language and ideas. The unit would be considerably "easier" if that lesson were deleted. In short, the teacher should consider his students very carefully and plan the unit in view of his findings. Even after the unit has begun, he should feel free to change his plans to make the unit more appropriate to his students.

TERMINAL OBJECTIVES

1. To develop, administer, and score an examination on the content of the works and the protest techniques studied. (This is to be a student-made exam.)
   Criterion statements:
   a. The exam should be comprehensive enough to include questions on vocabulary, the content of the books read, the various solutions offered by different groups, and so on.
   b. A student committee or the class as a whole should decide what makes up an appropriate answer and how many a student must answer to pass the test.

2. To write a short protest concerning some aspect of environment, social conditions, and the like.
   Criterion statements:
   a. Both the target of, and the reasons for, the protest should be clear, although both may be either implied or stated directly.
   b. The student should use specific details either to make his point or to support it.

3. To present orally, alone or as a member of a panel, an interpretation of the protest in a major work.
   Criterion statements:
   a. The work should be selected from a short bibliography prepared by the teacher.
   b. The students who select a particular book should read and discuss it together and also plan the presentation together.
   c. The presentation should identify all the targets of protest, explain the methods used, and evaluate both the targets and the methods.
   d. The students may dramatize or role-play some aspect of the book or use other methods to convey its general content.

4. To present orally as a member of a panel an exposition and analysis of the solutions or line of action advocated by reform leaders or groups. (See criterion statements for objective 3.)

STUDENT MATERIALS

Anthologies (class sets):

1. Abraham Chapman (ed.), *Black Voices*. New York: New American Library, 1968. (This is by far the most widely used anthology in the unit. Abbreviated in the text as *B.V.*)
2. Clarence Major, *The New Black Poetry*. New York: International Publishers, 1969. (Abbreviated in the text as *NBP.*)
3. Haig and Hamida Bosmajian (eds.), *The Rhetoric of the Civil Rights Movement*. New York: Random House, 1969.

Fiction and Autobiography (three to five copies each):

1. James Baldwin, *Go Tell It on the Mountain*. New York: New American Library, 1963.
2. Claude Brown, *Manchild in the Promised Land*. New York: New American Library, 1965.
3. William Demby, *Beetlecreek*. New York: Avon, 1967.
4. Lorenz Graham, *South Town*. New York: New American Library, 1958.
5. Dick Gregory, *Nigger*. New York: Pocket Books, 1968.
6. Richard Wright, *Black Boy*. New York: New American Library, 1963.
7. Richard Wright, *Native Son*. New York: New American Library, 1961.
8. Malcolm X, *The Autobiography of Malcolm X*. New York: Grove Press, 1966.

Drama (class set):

Lorraine Hansberry, *A Raisin in the Sun*. New York: New American Library, 1964.

Miscellaneous Books (three or four copies each):

1. Louis E. Lomax, *The Negro Revolt*. New York: New American Library, 1963.
2. Dick Gregory, *From the Back of the Bus*. New York: Dutton Books, 1962.

Recording:

Godfrey Cambridge, *Here's Godfrey Cambridge* (Epic FLM 13101).

Other (see lessons for specifics):

1. Mimeographed passages from *Native Son* and the *Negro Revolt*.
2. Mimeographed study guides as indicated in lessons for short stories, fiction, autobiography, and so on.

MAJOR UNIT QUESTIONS

The following questions should be applied rather consistently to the various readings throughout the unit—the short stories, poems, play, novels, autobiography, and study by Lomax.

1. What physical, psychological, and moral conditions does the author protest?
2. What causes those conditions?
3. What are the psychological and spiritual effects of those conditions?
4. What techniques does the author use to make his protest?
5. How valid is his protest?
6. How effective is it?
7. What are your personal feelings about the targets of the author's protest?

Part I: Protest: Targets and Techniques

Lesson 1   Introduction

OBJECTIVE

To discuss the possibility of studying the "Literature of Black Protest."

PROCEDURES

A. Introduce the possibility of studying protest with a statement such as the following: The materials you have studied so far demonstrate how people use language to influence the attitudes and actions of their audiences. People also use language to limit others, and sometimes they limit themselves by the words they use to describe themselves. Black people all over the country have been protesting various conditions, sometimes through the use of violence but often through the use of language in poetry, short stories, essays, biography, and in many other ways. Would you be interested in studying the writing of black authors who have written such protests?

B. Allow students to express their opinions about the idea. Most of them will think it a good one. If they want to know what kind of materials they will read, read aloud a selection from Dick Gregory's book *Nigger* or from Richard Wright's *Black Boy*.

C. Obviously, if the class refuses to study this topic, the lessons that follow will have to be canceled.

Lesson 2   Some Forms of Protest

OBJECTIVE

To compare fictional, expository, and humorous forms of protest.

MATERIALS

1. Selections from *The Negro Revolt* by Louis E. Lomax and *Native Son* by Richard Wright. These two passages are quoted below.
2. Copy of Dick Gregory's *From the Back of the Bus.*
3. *Black Voices,* for Langston Hughes' "Cracker Prayer."
4. Recording: *Here's Godfrey Cambridge.*

Passage from *The Negro Revolt,* pp. 68–69:

Housing and job discrimination are the major barriers faced by Negroes outside the South. The disturbing results of these barriers are evidenced by the fact that the income of the average Negro family is only 55 percent of that of the average white family; when it comes to housing, although Negroes comprise 11 percent of the population, we are restricted to 4 percent of the residential area. And the residential areas for Negroes are, by and large, Negro ghettos; this leads directly to *de facto* school segregation. As of the mid-1950's, 74 percent of the Negro population of Chicago was restricted, by practice more than by law, to six community areas. The situation in Los Angeles is about the same. There was considerable premature rejoicing in Los Angeles when the 1956 Federal Housing Administration report showed that the nonwhite occupancy of dwelling units had increased more than the nonwhite population in the past five years. On the surface it appeared that progress had been made, that white areas were being opened to Negroes. Then came the brutal facts behind the report: the increase in nonwhite occupancy had been brought about by Negroes acquiring formerly all-white property strips. The white families had moved out; thus there had been no break in the segregation pattern. The same trend is evident in New York City, where there is every promise that by 1970 the larger part of Manhattan Island will be a non-white ghetto.

The effect of this residential segregation is alarming. The Chicago Urban League has argued and documented the following disturbing facts:

First, although housing available to the Negro is poorer than that available to the white applicant, the rents charged Negroes are nearly as great as those paid by the whites. This, coupled with job discrimination, means that Negroes can only acquire housing by "doubling up," many families sharing an apartment unit. And here is the root of Negro family breakdown and crime.

Second there is a direct correlation between housing discrimination and general community health. Chicago Negroes are 20 percent of the population, yet they account for 33 percent of the city's tuberculosis. City health officers have certified that this high TB rate is due to improper diet and poor sanitation. Referring to the 1956 polio epidemic that hit Chicago, the Chicago Public Health Service said: ". . . As the (polio) outbreak progressed, high rates developed only in those areas of the city characterized by a particularly dense population, a low socio-economic status and a high proportion of nonwhites." When the final sad total was in, Negroes, 20 percent of the population, accounted for 61 percent of the polio. And the hardest hit were the children under ten years of age.

Passage from *Native Son,* pp. 19–20:

"Kinda warm today."

"Yeah," Gus said.

"You get more heat from this sun than from them old radiators at home."

"Yeah; them old white landlords sure don't give much heat."

"And they always knocking at your door for money."

"I'll be glad when summer comes."

"Me too," Bigger said.

He stretched his arms above his head and yawned; his eyes moistened. The sharp precision of the world of steel and stone dissolved into blurred waves. He blinked and the world grew hard again, mechanical, distinct. A weaving motion in the sky made him turn his eyes upward; he saw a slender streak of billowing white blooming against the deep blue. A plane was writing high up in the air.

"Look!" Bigger said.

"What?"

"That plane writing up there," Bigger said, pointing.

"Oh!"

They squinted at a tiny ribbon of unfolding vapor that spelled out the word: USE . . . The plane was so far away that at times the strong glare of the sun blanked it from sight.

"You can hardly see it," Gus said.

"Looks like a little bird," Bigger breathed with childlike wonder.

"Them white boys sure can fly," Gus said.

"Yeah," Bigger said, wistfully. "They get a chance to do everything."

Noiselessly, the tiny plane looped and veered, vanishing and appearing, leaving behind it a long trail of white plumage, like coils of fluffy paste being squeezed from a tube; a plume-coil that grew and swelled and slowly began to fade into the air at the edges. The plane wrote another word: SPEED . . .

"How high you reckon he is?" Bigger asked.

"I don't know. Maybe a hundred miles; maybe a thousand."

"I could fly one of them things if I had a chance," Bigger mumbled reflectively, as though talking to himself.

Gus pulled down the corners of his lips, stepped out from the wall, squared his shoulders, doffed his cap, bowed low and spoke with mock deference:

"Yessuh."

"You go to hell," Bigger said, smiling.

"Yessuh," Gus said again.

"I *could* fly a plane if I had a chance," Bigger said.

"If you wasn't black and if you had some money and if they'd let you go to that aviation school, you *could* fly a plane," Gus said.

"Maybe they right in not wanting us to fly," Bigger said. " 'Cause if I took a plane up I'd take a couple of bombs along and drop 'em sure as hell. . . ."

They laughed again, still looking upward. The plane sailed and dipped and spread another word against the sky: GASOLINE. . . .

"Use Speed Gasoline," Bigger mused, rolling the words slowly from his lips. "God, I'd like to fly up there in that sky."

"God'll let you fly when He gives you your wings up in heaven," Gus said.

PROCEDURES

A. Distribute the passages from Lomax and Wright to the students. Point out that they are by Negro writers and that they use different techniques of protest. Have the class read the passages and compare them, asking themselves the following questions:
   1. What do the passages protest?
   2. How does each one convey the protest?
   3. How do they differ?
   4. Are these writers using propaganda techniques?
B. The ensuing discussion should note how Wright's characters and images protest conditions and how Lomax makes use of statistics for a similar purpose. Students should note that the reader has to infer ("figure out") the protest in Wright's passage, whereas it is directly stated by Lomax.
C. Ask students what other conditions, situations, or attitudes they would expect black writers to protest. Make a list on the board that can be kept for additions.
D. Divide students into groups of four, and ask each group to prepare a skit that will protest one or more of the conditions the class has listed. They may dramatize the condition as they choose by attempting to pantomime it, by having characters talk as in the Wright passage, and so on. After each group presents its skit, have the class discusss its effectiveness as protest.
E. Have the class discuss briefly the relative merits of showing characters in various conditions and a statistical approach. Are the methods equally effective? To what extent are they both useful?
F. Introduce humorous protest by playing a band or two from Godfrey Cambridge's album *Here's Godfrey Cambridge*. Ask the students if the band called "Block Busting" can be considered protest. In what way is it protest? How does the protest work?
G. Distribute pages from Dick Gregory's *From the Back of the Bus*. Ask each student to tell the class a joke from the pages he received that he regards as successful protest.
H. Have students read Langston Hughes' short piece "Cracker Prayer" (*BV,* pp. 108–109. A cracker praying for a segregated heaven with Negro servants). Is the selection protest? How does it work? (The cracker condemns himself through the illogical prayer.)
I. Encourage the class to discuss humor as protest. Is it as effective as a statistical approach? Is it as effective as a dramatic approach? Which approach is likely to have more impact on an audience?

Lesson 3   Targets of Protest: Language and Attitude

OBJECTIVE

To identify the ways in which language limits the conceptions of others.

MATERIALS

1. Excerpt from a speech by Stokely Carmichael, "Speech at Morgan State College," in *The Rhetoric of the Civil Rights Movement,* pp. 114–115.
2. *Black Voices* for Richard Wright's "The Ethics of Living Jim Crow," Section 1, pp. 288–292.
3. *The Autobiography of Malcolm X,* pp. 52–55.
4. *Black Voices* for poems listed in part F.
5. *The New Black Poetry* for poems listed in part F.

PROCEDURES

A. Read aloud or have the students read the excerpt from Carmichael's speech that examines the term "definition," that is, how a word tends to define or delimit aspects of human experience that it refers to. One part reads as follows:

I define this as yellow. *This* is not yellow. So that when I speak of yellow you know what I am talking about. I have contained this. And so for white people to be allowed to *define* us by calling us Negroes, which means apathetic, lazy, stupid and all those other things, it is for us to *accept* those definitions. *We* must define *what we are* and move from our definitions and tell them to recognize *what we say we are.* (Italics added.)

B. Have the students discuss the effects that various words have on how people see themselves and others.
   1. Is what Carmichael says here true?
   2. What experiences do you know of that support his ideas?
   3. Is it possible to break the habit of accepting the words attached to people without really examining them?
   4. How do such words influence the prejudices of people?
C. Introduce the term "stereotype" and examine how the words of prejudice operate as stereotypes of the type Carmichael described.
D. Read aloud or have the students read Section 1 of Wright's "The Ethics of Living Jim Crow." In this section he describes his experience working in an optical firm in Jackson. The white boss tells him he will have a chance to learn a trade. However, the men will teach him nothing because they think of their work as "white," and they succeed in driving him from the shop altogether. Ask questions such as the following:
   1. What stereotype do the whites hold of Richard?
   2. How does it affect him? How does he respond?

3. What do you think he should have done? What would you have done? How would you have felt?

The discussion should lead beyond the loss of the job to the effects the loss has on Richard's psyche—"his feelings."

E. Raise the question of how the students respond to such stereotypes. Do they accept it or reject it? After free discussion read aloud from *The Autobiography of Malcolm X,* pp. 52–55, in which Malcolm X describes his first "conk" and comments on it. Raise the question of what else Negroes do to be more like whites. Why do they do it? Should they? Let the students develop the discussion freely.

F. Ask all students to look over the following poems and decide which they would like to study and present to the class: Frank M. Davis' "Robert Whitmore," *BV,* p. 435; Mari Evans' "Status Symbol," *BV,* pp. 370–371; Abu Tshak's "Theme Brown Girl" *NBP,* pp. 71–72; Gloria Davis' "To Egypt," *NBP,* pp. 46–47. The speakers or characters in each of these poems represent blacks who have rejected or accepted the white man's stereotype. The next two poems show white men reacting from the stereotype: Countee Cullen's "Incident," *BV,* p. 385; Sterling A. Brown's "Southern Cop," *BV,* p. 413. When students have examined all the poems, ask them to indicate their first, second, and third choices on a slip of paper. Then divide students according to their preferences insofar as possible and have each group prepare the poem it has selected.

G. Each group should discuss the poem using the following questions as a guide:
  1. What stereotype is the poem concerned with?
  2. What is the speaker's or character's attitude toward the stereotype?
  3. How does the stereotype control the reactions of the speaker or characters in the poem?
  4. What other effects is the stereotype likely to have?
  5. How do you feel about the speaker's or character's attitudes toward the stereotype?

Other more specific questions will be useful for the individual poems. Each group should prepare a presentation to the class, which may include a panel discussion, role-playing, and so on, and it should also lead a whole-class discussion about the poem's meaning and how the students feel about it.

H. The lesson should close with a discussion of the extent to which stereotypes influence attitudes toward, and treatment of, others.

Lesson 4   The Targets of Protest

OBJECTIVE

To identify some of the major targets of protest.

MATERIALS

1. Dick Gregory, *Nigger.*
2. *The New Black Poetry* for the poems indicated.
3. *Black Voices* for short stories and poems indicated throughout.

PROCEDURES

A. Ask students to read or read aloud Section II of "Not Poor, Just Broke" in Dick Gregory's *Nigger,* pp. 25–35. In this short section Gregory protests against many things but mainly against the indignities to which the social system and the attitudes of others forced him to submit. Throughout this lesson the students should examine both the physical and psychological targets of protest. The major questions for discussion in each selection will be as follows:
   1. What are the targets of the protest?
   2. How is the protest made?
   3. How do you feel about the conditions and attitudes described?
   4. To what extent is the protest justified?
   In addition, each of the following selections will require specific questions in regard to the characters, situations, and so on. This first one, however, gets at a number of the targets that the others will attack.
B. The students next read Norman Jordan's "Feeding the Lions," *NBP,* pp. 78–79, which also protests the attitudes of social workers. Langston Hughes' "Ballad of the Landlord," *BV,* p. 432, protests the conditions of tenement living. The Gregory selection protests both.
C. For an examination of the rural conditions that give rise to protest, have the students read Arna Bontemps' "A Summer Tragedy," *BV,* pp. 88–96, the story of an old couple who, having worked the land as sharecroppers for forty-five years, find themselves unable to continue. It is a very powerful story that is bound to promote a discussion of rural problems and perhaps solutions to them. Along with this selection, students might also read and discuss Arna Bontemps' poem, "A Black Man Talks of Reaping," *BV,* p. 424.
D. Divide the class into three or four groups according to reading ability. Assign the best readers Ann Petry's "In Darkness and Confusion," *BV,* pp. 161–191, the story of a hard-working Harlem couple who find out that their only son has been court-martialed and sentenced to twenty years' hard labor. Assign the next best readers Jean Toomer's "Blood Burning Moon," *BV,* pp. 66–73, an excerpt, complete in itself, from *Cane* that tells of a knife fight between a white and a Negro and of the Negro's fate. Assign the autobiographical essay by Richard Wright, "The Ethics of Living Jim Crow," *BV,* pp. 288–298, to the third group. Most of the incidents here also appear in *Black Boy.* A group in between the second and third might be assigned Chapter 1 of Malcolm X's *Autobiography, BV,* pp. 333–347. Provide brief study and discussion guides

for each selection and have each group prepare a brief explanation of the targets of protest in their materials for presentation to the class.

Lesson 5 *A Raisin in the Sun*

OBJECTIVE

To examine the effects of racial bias on a family.

MATERIAL

A Raisin in the Sun by Lorraine Hansberry.

PROCEDURES

A. For reading and discussion of the play, follow the procedures outlined for *Midsummer Night's Dream* in Chapter 1 or those for reading drama in Chapter 14.
B. Following discussion of the play as a whole, allow the students to decide whether they would like to produce a scene or more from the play. If they would, divide the class into four groups, allowing each group to elect a director, choose a scene for production, and so on. (See procedures in Chapter 14.) Allow some classroom time for planning and rehearsal.

Lesson 6 Outside Reading

OBJECTIVE

To present an oral interpretation of the protest in a major work. (See terminal objectives on page 371 for criterion statements.)

MATERIALS

Multiple copies of the following works (the Roman numerals indicate the relative difficulty of the works):

1. Dick Gregory, *Nigger* (I).
2. Lorenz Graham, *South Town* (I).
3. William Demby, *Beetlecreek* (II).
4. Richard Wright, *Black Boy* (II).
5. James Baldwin, *Go Tell It on the Mountain* (III).
6. Richard Wright, *Native Son* (III).
7. Louis Lomax, *The Negro Revolt* (III).
8. Malcolm X, *The Autobiography of Malcolm X* (IV).
9. Claude Brown, *Manchild in the Promised Land* (IV).

Note: All these are in paperback. For easier materials see Barbara Dodds' *Negro Literature for High School Students*

PROCEDURES

A. So far in the unit, the students have become at least briefly acquainted with five of the nine books listed. Remind them of this and give them some information about the other books on the list. Reading brief passages aloud from each is a useful approach.

B. The teacher should permit the students to select the books they want to read but should make private suggestions to guide them to a book at an appropriate level. Allow the students to browse through the books, to decide on one, and to change to another if they wish.

C. Although the unit to this point will have provided background for this independent reading, study guides containing the major unit questions and questions that relate specifically to important aspects of the books will be useful.

D. The students should be allowed class time for reading and group discussion. However, for the longer books especially, considerable reading will have to be done outside class.

E. Group presentation of the books to the rest of the class should be ready in two or three weeks.

Part II: Personal and Organized Response to the Conditions Protested

Lesson 7   Personal Response to the Conditions

OBJECTIVE

To analyze and classify various responses to the conditions presented in the literature of protest.

MATERIALS

1. *Black Voices*
2. *The New Black Poetry*

PROCEDURES

A. After the students have had a day or two in class to launch into the outside reading, ask them how the various characters and people they have read about have responded to the conditions in which they found themselves. Have them classify and list their ideas on the board.

B. Read aloud to the class Langston Hughes' "Harlem," *BV*, pp. 430–431, which begins "What happens to a dream deferred." After a short discussion of the poem in preparation for panel presentations of other poems that focus on reactions of various kinds, list the following poems for students to look over. Then follow procedures F and G in Lesson 3 for grouping students according to their preferences.

Fenton Johnson, "The Daily Grind" and "Tired," *BV,* pp. 367–368, 370.
Claude McKay, "If We Must Die," *BV,* pp. 372–373.
Sterling A. Brown, "The Ballad of Joe Meek" and "Sister Lou" *BV,* pp. 414–418 and 404–405.
Langston Hughes, "As I Grew Older," *BV,* p. 426.
Lance Jeffers, "On Listening to the Spirituals," *BV,* p. 474.
Naomi Long Madgett, "The Race Question," *BV,* p. 477.
Harry Edwards, "How to Change the U.S.A.," *NBP,* pp. 48–49.
Gerald L. Simmons, Jr. "Make Tools Our Strength," *NBP,* p. 119.

The poems represent a range of response from the despair of Johnson's poems to the violence of "The Ballad of Joe Meek" and "How to Change the U.S.A." and from the religious solace suggested in "Listening to the Spirituals" to the self-sufficient dignity of "The Race Question."

C. In presenting the poems the student groups should consider the following questions.
   1. What are the special conditions to which the speaker or character responds, if any?
   2. What is the nature of his response?
   3. To what extent do you approve of the response? What is your response?
   4. To what extent is the response appropriate? inevitable?
D. The lesson should conclude with a discussion of the various personal responses before moving on to the question, What are the *organized* responses to the conditions?

Lesson 8   Organized Responses to the Conditions

OBJECTIVE

To learn the positions and methods used by organized groups in fighting the conditions faced by American Negroes.

MATERIAL

The Rhetoric of the Civil Rights Movement.

PROCEDURES

A. This lesson is a research lesson. The volume mentioned above serves as an introduction to the ideas of Martin Luther King, Jr., in "Letter from Birmingham City Jail," of James Farmer and Malcolm X in "A Debate at Cornell University," of Stokely Carmichael in "Speech at Cornell University," and of Floyd B. McKissick in "Speech at the National Conference on Black Power." The teacher should read brief selections from the various speeches and articles before asking the students to choose one movement or leader they would like to study. Then ask them to read the article representative of that leader or movement in *The Rhetoric of the Civil Rights Movement* to confirm their interests.

B. Group students according to interests and have each group do research on the following questions:

1. What is the position of the leader or movement in regard to Negro life in the United States?
2. What tactics have they used to improve the situation?
3. Where have they used them?
4. What persuasive techniques have they used?
5. How successful have they been?
6. What advantages does one movement have over others?

C. The teacher should take the students to the library, demonstrate how to use the card catalog and the *Reader's Guide to Periodical Literature* if necessary, and put the students to work.

D. In answering question 6 above, students can use *The Rhetoric of the Civil Rights Moment* as a guide to positions other than the one they are studying.

E. In a few days, after the research is completed, the students can present their ideas in a symposium. They should be encouraged to debate the relative merits of the various movements.

Lesson 9   Writing a Protest*

OBJECTIVE

To write a brief protest.

PROCEDURES

A. After the students have studied several examples of protest, lead a discussion of how the writers make their points forcefully. The discussion should develop a list of the characteristics of protest such as the following:

1. The use of appropriate connotative language.
2. The careful selection of details to make the point.
3. The development of characters for whom the reader has sympathy.
4. Picturing people, places, and events that the reader finds appalling or disgusting.
5. Presenting enough detail to involve the reader.
6. Use of some propaganda techniques.

B. Next, have the students suggest conditions that they might protest.

---

* This lesson can appear almost any time after Lesson 3.

C. Have them begin writing in class. Give help to those who need it. Ask the students to prepare a draft for criticism by other students.
D. Divide the class into groups for criticism of their own papers.
  1. Is the target of protest clear?
  2. Are connotative language and details appropriate to the writer's purpose?
  3. Do you have sympathy with the appropriate persons or things?
  4. What should be done to make the protest stronger?
E. Following the group criticisms, allow the students to revise if they wish before turning in the final draft.
F. A special committee might be appointed to prepare a booklet of student writings from this lesson.

Lesson 10 Evaluation

OBJECTIVE

To develop, administer, and score an examination on the content of the works and the protest techniques studied.

PROCEDURES

A. Follow procedures for student preparation of examination in "Introduction to Humor" in Chapter 1 and in Chapters 6 and 14.
B. In addition, develop a questionnaire to determine affective response to the unit. See Chapter 14 for an example and suggestions.

NOTES

1. For a more detailed introduction to the Curriculum Centers, see Shugrue and Crawley, *The Conclusion of the Initial Phase: The English Program of the USOE,* available from the National Council of Teachers of English, 508 South Sixth Street, Champaign, Illinois 61820, Order No. 01152. The NCTE/ERIC Clearing House on the Teaching of English has published a thoroughly annotated bibliography of materials from the Curriculum Centers: *A Guide to Available Project English Materials* by Donna Butler and Bernard O'Donnell (Champaign: NCTE, 1969). The *Guide* describes the materials and lists the addresses at which the materials are available.
2. For a detailed description of Project Apex at Trenton High School, see *Project Apex: A Nongraded Phase–Elective English Curriculum,* available from Trenton High School, Trenton, Michigan 48183.
3. Richard Wright, "The Literature of the Negro in the United States," in *Black Expression,* ed. Addison Gayle, Jr. (New York: Weybright and Talley, 1969), pp. 198–229.

SUGGESTIONS FOR FURTHER READING

1. PAUL A. OLSON, *A Curriculum Study Center in English. Final Report*. 1967. (Available from ERIC Document Reproduction Service, The National Cash Register Co., 4936 Fairmont Ave., Bethesda, Md. 20014.) This final report of the University of Nebraska Curriculum Center in English presents the rationale for the Nebraska curriculum itself.

2. FLORIDA STATE UNIVERSITY CURRICULUM STUDY CENTER, *Curriculum III*, (Available as above.) *Curriculum III* presents the units for a ninth and tenth grade English program based on certain cognitive processes.

16 | Teaching Reading Skills in the English Class

In most secondary schools there are a substantial number of "problem readers." In addition to the immediate instructional difficulties that such students present in the English class, another burden is related to teaching them: the English teacher's colleagues in other departments, school administrators, and the general public often equate English instruction with reading instruction and expect the English teacher to teach general reading skills. This is true despite the fact that many, if not most, English teachers are untrained in and ill-informed about the techniques of teaching reading. The purpose of this chapter is to offer guidelines for (1) teaching reading skills that are needed generally in teaching English and (2) helping problem readers overcome their deficiencies.

If some English teachers are ill-informed about reading problems and the type of instruction needed to correct them, many teachers of other subjects are even less informed. Consequently, they fail to select textbooks at an appropriate reading level, fail to create the appropriate instructional context, and fail to individualize instruction. When the students go to another class (social studies, for example) ill-prepared, that teacher may blame the English teacher for not teaching them how to read. Since the cover-to-cover reading of textbooks forms such a minor part of the English curriculum, the English teacher might easily answer that he is teaching his students the necessary skills to read successfully in his discipline and that if the other teacher does not know how to make effective assignments, it is his fault and not that of the English teacher. Although such an answer would be logical, it would be a disservice to the students. The fact is that they will be given poor assignments at which they may fail unless they have learned the skills of textbook reading. Since the English teacher is the one looked to for reading instruction, he must do the job, or it will more than likely not get done. Rationally, he may reject the task because he has his own discipline to teach. But since English and reading instruction are synonymous in most people's minds, he must accept the task as a necessary service to the students.

A natural question for the beginning teacher to ask is "Why are there so many problem readers at the secondary level?"

When students begin school in the first grade, they are much the same in their ability to read. But as they move through the grades the differences among them will constantly increase. In the second grade, for example, some will still be reading at the first-grade level, while others will have advanced to the third-grade level. In other words, in the second year of school the teacher should expect an achievement range of three years. Because the weakest advance slowly and the stronger students advance rapidly, the bottom of the range tends to move up very slowly whereas the top advances quickly; therefore, the range constantly grows broader. In the eighth grade, the teacher can expect a range of at least six years, with 13 percent reading at the fifth-grade level or below and 16 percent reading at the tenth-grade level or above.[1] Nancy Vick suggests as a rule of thumb that the range of reading will be approximately two-thirds of the age of the students.[2] If the eighth graders are thirteen, this rule of thumb gives us a range of eight and two-thirds years. High school seniors will have a range of over eleven years, with some reading at the sixth-grade level. Thus, the higher the level, the more complex the instructional task becomes, since instruction must deal with a constantly widening range.

The instruction of problem readers should begin as soon as they have been identified during the inventory period at the beginning of the school year. "Problem reader" is a general term; the inventories (see Chapter 2 and Chapter 11) will help subclassify problem readers by indicating the specific kind of deficiency each has. The teacher may find that the inventory battery has indicated four kinds of problems that he must deal with:

1. The reluctant reader. The problems of some reluctant readers do not result from failure to have developed the appropriate skills; they are simply not interested in reading. Others are made reluctant as a result of inadequately developed skills.
2. The student with poor study patterns. There are two general patterns besides inadequate skills development that result in consistent failure to do outside assignments. The first pattern is that of the student who may have neither the time (because of a part-time job) nor the place (because of overcrowded living conditions at home) to prepare outside study assignments. The second pattern is that of the student who has never developed a systematically organized approach to independent study.
3. The student with a low rate of reading. Many students who have no other deficiencies in reading skills read too slowly and as a consequence are unduly hampered by routine reading tasks. Some slow readers

have low rates as a result of frustrations caused by weaknesses in other skills.

4. The dysfunctional reader. All of the problems enumerated above may be the result of a general reading dysfunction, the failure (for whatever reasons) to have developed comprehension and skills of a more mechanical kind, such as the techniques for word analysis. These readers will be identified by a consistent failure to answer the first four questions on the reading comprehension inventory (see Chapter 11), and they cannot do grade-level reading tasks. In order to help such students it is first necessary to develop a more thorough diagnosis of their problems than the routine, whole-class inventories can provide. Frequently, the symptoms that a dysfunctional reader shows will indicate the direction that instruction should take.

Let us consider each of these problems and the relevant instruction in greater detail.

The Reluctant Reader

In planning instruction for reluctant readers who are functional at reading, the central problem is that of motivating them. Lack of motivation can be the result of the reader's uncertainty about the purpose of the assignment or being unable to "get into" a story because the first part seems dull. Let us assume that a teacher of a tenth-grade class has completed his inventories and has concluded that most of his students can read the kind of material he has preplanned for the year. His first task in presenting a reading assignment is to make the purpose of the assignment clear. If there are many reluctant readers in the class, it is wise to precede the first *reading* assignment with some other activity—one that will engage the students in the work of the unit generally and help motivate their early reading as well.

Suppose the teacher has chosen "Survival" as the theme for his first unit. The major goal of the unit will be to develop his students' ability to infer from a text the main points: the opposing systems of values that create conflict within the protagonist and the generalizations implied by the results of the protagonists actions to resolve his conflict. Within this framework, the first reading assignment has the more specific purposes of arousing the students' interest, focusing their attention on the problem, and helping them to begin to formulate the kinds of questions they will need to answer to complete the unit successfully. As the first reading assignment the teacher has chosen Carl Stephenson's "Leiningen versus the Ants"[3] because it is the best work that he knows of to accomplish these purposes. That is, the purposes have become criteria to guide him in his choice of materials. To determine what preparation his students will need to read the story successfully, and to help them establish purpose in their reading, he rephrases his purposes as student objectives: to state the choices Leiningen has, to decide why he made the choices he did, to recognize the values implied by the results of his choices.

There are many aspects of the story that these objectives do not deal with, but we cannot, after all, do everything at once. There is no more reason to carry on an exhaustive study of this particular story than there is to write a closely reasoned critical analysis of every mystery story that is read. Because what we do with a work is determined by our purpose or purposes in reading it, the problem is how best to help the students understand their purpose in reading a particular work. The clearest way is to tell them: "When you are finished reading this story, I want you to be able to answer the following questions . . ." The questions used are based on the pupil objectives, for example: "What choices does Leiningen make?"

Aware of his need to provide some preliminary activity that is engaging and relevant to the story and the unit, the teacher has planned a discussion based on a fictitious situation that he presents to the class:

A group of six soldiers are on patrol when an enemy movement traps them behind the lines. When the presence of the patrol is discovered, three of the six men are severely wounded by mortar fire. As the enemy closes in, the lieutenant in command is forced to make a decision. Should the three unharmed men make an effort to fight off the far superior numbers and fire power of the enemy, or should they make an attempt to escape the trap? The lieutenant is faced with three alternatives: (1) to remain and fight with the probability that all six men will be killed or at best taken prisoner and tortured; (2) to attempt to escape with the wounded men, bringing almost certain death to all; or (3) to attempt escape, leaving the wounded men to their fate but gaining safety for the three uninjured soldiers.

1. What decision *should* the lieutenant make?
2. What decision would *you* make?
3. What decision would most people make?
4. Is there a difference between what people should do and what they actually do in an instance such as this?
5. What values or beliefs would be reflected in either a decision to remain with the wounded men or a decision to leave them to their fate?
6. Do people actually make decisions on the basis of such beliefs? If not, on what basis do they act?

Because "Leiningen versus the Ants" is a long story and because there is a heavy load of unfamiliar vocabulary at the beginning, many reluctant readers may become discouraged. Anticipating this, the teacher could read the opening section to the class, stopping when it becomes obvious that they are caught up in the excitement of the story. Additionally, he may provide some class time for students' silent reading, thus shortening the amount of outside reading time they will require to complete the story. The discussion at the next class meeting should focus on the similarities between problems of value judgments involved in the fictitious incident and those in "Leiningen versus the Ants."

Another problem connected with teaching reluctant readers is that of encouraging them to read as a leisure activity. In his search for suitable materials the beginning teacher must proceed by trial and error to a considerable extent; no amount of available knowledge about the difficulty of material, the general interests of the age group, or the special interests of a particular student will guarantee the discovery of the particular materials that will spark a particular student. Nevertheless, there are works of high interest and easy readability that should appeal to these students. Two helpful guides to such titles are Spache's *Good Reading for Poor Readers*[4] and Ray Emery's *High Interest—Easy Reading for Junior and Senior High School Reluctant Readers.*[5] Most librarians know of many others and have lists of works in their own libraries that are both interesting and readable.

Moreover, in selecting books that are most likely to catch the interest of a particular student, the teacher can refer to the interest inventory, the student's folder, previous teachers, and casual conversation with the student.

Books, magazines, and newspapers should be available in the classroom, and the student should have time to browse among them. If he finds material in which he shows interest, he should be given at least enough time to begin reading it. In this way the teacher will create the best possible atmosphere to support and encourage the student's interest in reading.

The Student with Poor Study Patterns

The inventories will reveal which students have poor study patterns, and an early conference should be held with each student as he is identified. The symptoms of poor study patterns are usually failing to prepare outside assignments or preparing them inadequately. The aim of the conference is to determine the reasons for these poor patterns.

If the conference reveals that students do not have time for much home study because of conflicting responsibilities such as a part-time job or supervising younger brothers and sisters, very often the only solution is a reduction of the student's academic load so that he has more study time in school. In many such cases this solution is not available. Another touchy area is the case of a student whose home is overcrowded and noisy: there is simply no place for him to work at home. If for valid reasons he cannot use the facilities of a public library, the school library, or study halls during his out-of-class time, he will be unable to complete home study assignments If a teacher has many such students—and in some classes there will be many—he should plan alternatives to frequent or heavy outside assignments. The most obvious alternative would be to plan guided study sessions in class.

In the early secondary grades, however, it is more often the case that a student has a poor general study pattern because he has never learned to approach his outside assignments in a systematic way. It is a simple matter for a teacher to suggest ways of organizing a study corner, taking notes when assignments are given in class, and budgeting time. It is somewhat more complicated to help a student organize his approach to assignments once these more mechanical problems are out of the way.

Most reading study assignments in English will involve some sort of literary reading—short stories, plays, novels, poetry, essays—rather than the textbook-type reading assignments that are more typical of other courses. But there are certain special skills that are required for reading textbooks that are important to the student and must be considered part of the instructional responsibility of the English teacher.

Those special skills derive from the unique qualities of the genre. Although in reading a textbook the student must take into account its purpose, background information, and vocabulary just as he would with any reading assignment, the textbook has been organized to simplify the reading task. Normally, each chapter will include an explanation of its purposes and a set of guide questions to help the student focus on the important aspects of the textbook. Boldface type, indentations, numbers, spacing, and italics will be used to emphasize important points and will usually create an outline of the chapter as it develops. Key words often will be explained in the text or in footnotes, and the vocabulary load will be controlled. Finally, the chapter will be followed by study guides and suggestions for activities ranging from simple to complex. Because a textbook is specifically created to facilitate learning, it embodies the techniques of good reading instruction. It is created to be as self-instructional as possible, leaving to the teacher only a minimum of the procedures necessary to giving good reading assignments. Unfortunately, many teachers do not supply the minimal procedures necessary to make textbook reading successful. Thus, instruction in textbook reading consists primarily in helping students learn to take advantage of the reading clues that are built into the book. The instruction may be scheduled in a variety of ways. First, the teacher might set it as a medial objective of regular English instruction. Second, it might be introduced as part of the general inventory of study skills at the beginning of the year, although this will delay the start of regular English instruction. Third, it might be treated as an isolated unit of instruction later in the year. This scheduling has the advantage of following grade reports, which can serve as a diagnosis of which students need work in which subject areas. Fourth, it might be scheduled as practice reading exercises for weak readers. Since the relationships of ideas are cued by visual devices and the vocabulary is controlled, textbooks are a particularly good source of literal comprehension exercises for slow readers. In addition, the textbook from another subject area may have far more pragmatic value than the more or less diffuse exercises normally used in reading instruction.

Probably a combination of these scheduling methods is most effective.

During the inventory period, the teacher should use an inventory of textbook reading skills for diagnosis and beginning instruction. After he has identified weak readers, he should use textbooks from other subjects as the basis for skill-building sessions. Moreover, he should reinforce good textbook reading habits when they are needed in English class. Finally, he should develop a brief unit of instruction to be used after the students know what particular courses are giving them difficulty.

During the inventory of study skills, the teacher should select a particular textbook to use as the basis for diagnosis. He should then explain that an important study skill is the ability to learn from textbooks. The students should be asked to bring the textbook he has selected to class on the next day, so that the teacher can help them learn to read textbooks easily and well. On the following day, he should discuss briefly the general skills of textbook organization and then ask the students to fill out a diagnostic worksheet adapted to the particular book he plans to use. The following is an example:

DIAGNOSTIC WORKSHEET: Textbook Reading Skills

Directions: The purpose of this worksheet is to find out how well you can use a textbook for learning. All the questions are based on Chapter 6 of your social studies textbook.

1. What is the number of the first and last page of the chapter? (*Note which students use the table of contents.*)
2. On what page is there a reference to John C. Calhoun? (*Note which students use the index.*)

(Questions one and two are text organization skills, unnecessary if they have been previously inventoried.)

3. On what pages do you find a summary of the general contents of the chapter? (*Introductory statement, summary at end of chapter, questions after chapter; this question forces students to get an overview of the chapter.*)
4. On what page do you find the best short statement of the topic of the chapter? Write it down. (*Title; again forces overview.*)
5. Write down the major headings that give the major topics of the chapter. (*Major headings in boldface capital letters or other distinctive type; again forces overview.*)
6. Write a brief paragraph that explains the purpose of this chapter. (*Evaluates students' ability to use the information they have found; emphasizes purposeful reading.*)
7. Change each of the subheadings in boldface type on p. 136 into questions. (*Emphasizes purposeful reading skills.*)
8. Define the two key words in this subsection. (*Emphasis on important vocabulary items.*)

When each of the students has completed the diagnosis, the teacher should collect their answers and lead a discussion on them to explore why they are important to good textbook reading. Following this instruction, the students should undertake a second diagnostic worksheet. The teacher should use both sheets for determining which students need additional instruction. Two other approaches can be used following these inventories to furnish additional information. The students may be asked either to make up a test on a chapter or to outline the chapter. Both will give the teacher insight into the students' ability to work more independently. The request for outlining should not, of course, be used until the teacher has established that the students have the necessary skill at outlining. Otherwise he will be diagnosing outlining ability rather than the students' ability to see relationships within the chapter.

Fortunately, there is considerable empirical evidence concerning the effectiveness of various procedures in the study of textbook materials. Much of this evidence is summarized by Robinson in *Effective Reading*[6] and *Effective Study*.[7] These books also explain a system of study that has been tested empirically. Commonly called the SQ3R method, it consists of these steps:

Survey: Skim the chapter and read introductory and summary statements to get an overview of the chapter.

Question: Turn major headings into questions.

Read: Find the answers to the questions you have formulated.

Recite: Recite what you have learned in order to fix it in your mind. Repeat these procedures for each section of your reading.

Review: Review the reading at frequent intervals, spreading learning over many short sessions rather than a single intensive session.

The books contain many other valuable suggestions about study skills that can also be incorporated into a brief unit of instruction.

In any school the importance of textbook reading skills must be gauged by the actual practices in the school. Teachers who have been influenced by "discovery" teaching procedures will place less emphasis on textbooks than on experimentation, document reading, and so on. Those who are aware of appropriate practices in reading instruction will select textbooks carefully and make good assignments. If there is a reading specialist in the school, he may have instituted special instruction in textbook reading skills for weak students and may be working with teachers to help them improve their instructional practices and develop special materials for weak readers. To the extent that these conditions prevail, the English teacher may not need to give special instruction in reading textbook materials. But in most situations, he will find it necessary to give some special attention to these skills.

Students with a Low Reading Rate

Some students will have good reading comprehension but read very slowly. It is wise for the teacher to be alert to clues to which of his students have this problem. If he has had all the students stop reading the stories that make up the inventory after a specified amount of time, low scores in comprehension may disguise what is really only a matter of low reading rate. The pattern of not writing answers to the last few questions suggests that rate may be the student's problem. The diagnostic procedure to use with students suspected of having a low rate but no problem with reading comprehension is to allow students all the time they need for completing a reading assignment and to compare test results to those on a timed assignment. If there is considerable divergence between the two scores, the teacher may assume that the real problem is rate, not comprehension.

The treatment of such a problem is not an easy task. Usually students who read slowly but well are firmly convinced that if they speed up they will miss something. Unfortunately, there is a misleading element of truth in that assumption. If the teacher were to push such a student to a faster rate on a particular assignment, the result would probably be a drop in comprehension because the student's old habits would interfere, and he could not in fact comprehend as well at the faster rate. But if the student practices enough to develop different habits, he will find that a faster rate will become as comfortable as the slower rate used to be, and his comprehension will be as high as it was before. Hence, the teacher should allow this student enough practice at a faster rate so that he can convince himself that greater speed does not necessarily mean lower comprehension. There are a variety of activities that will help build the reading rate, but *none* of them should be used with school-assigned materials; the task of getting a student to read *any* material at a faster rate is difficult enough. Contemporary "teen" magazines, high school newspapers, or sports articles may prove useful. Getting him to increase his rate with school-assigned material for which he feels a responsibility would be even more difficult.

Students often read slowly because they backtrack or regress by rereading part of a sentence or an entire paragraph. Control of regression will help break this reading habit; for example, the student can read using a blank piece of paper to cover each line as he completes it. In this way he will get into the habit of not looking back.

Some students read slowly because they read one word at a time, whereas faster readers take in several words at a single glance. To build the habit of reading groups of words, the student can practice with flash cards containing phrases like "in the house," "had been running," "down the stairs," and so on. He can also practice marking such phrases in a running text. Practice with narrow-columned reading material like the newspaper and the *Readers Digest* can also help develop this skill. The student can practice by covering lines as his eye sweeps down the column while he tries to see an entire line in one eye fixation. Practice with such materials is particularly effective because the student knows that he has no responsibility for the contents. The purpose of the practice is to improve his reading *rate*. Consequently, comprehension tests should *not* be used at the end of each rate exercise. Instead, the student should continue practice *without* testing until he has become comfortable at a higher rate. Only then should comprehension checks be used.

Short practice drills against time will also build the student's reading rate. With a book of short stories, he can set a time limit per page and chart his results on a graph, gradually decreasing the time limit as he proceeds. Such private practice can be supplemented by timed reading tests that will help convince the student (by his test results) that his increased speed is not decreasing his comprehension.

Two important cautions: (1) *Do not use* school assignments as materials for increasing student reading rate. (2) Rate-building activities are *only* for students who have given evidence of high comprehension and a slow reading rate. Training in increased rate will only compound the problems of students whose reading comprehension is superficial to begin with.

The Dysfunctional Reader

By far, the teacher's most difficult instructional problem is teaching the dysfunctional reader—the student who cannot do grade-level reading tasks because, for whatever reasons, his reading comprehension skills are poor. Such students will usually be identified by their inability to answer the first four questions on the reading comprehension inventory (see Chapter 11). These questions are easy ones because the answers are explicitly stated in the text. When it is clear that the teacher has such students he must plan his subsequent procedure with care.

His first recourse must be to seek help from a trained specialist. If there is such a person on the staff the student should be referred to him; there is no doubt that the specially trained reading teacher will have more success in corrective instruction than a teacher without such training. Unfortunately, many secondary schools do not have remedial reading teachers on the staff, so the classroom teacher must be prepared to do the best job he can in dealing with dysfunctional readers.

But even if there is no specialist in the building, most school systems employ some staff members who are regarded as local reading "experts." Every administrator will know of such persons, usually elementary school personnel, who can be very helpful in many phases of planning and instruction. This expert undoubtedly has materials available that he can give or lend, and he can be of great assistance in deciding what supplementary materials to order. The teacher can rely on him for practical suggestions about building instructional materials and about pedagogical procedures for organizing the classroom. In addition, the expert can help with diagnosis and any specific problems that the teacher encounters.

If such help is not immediately available, the teacher must proceed on his own. He must first begin collecting supplementary materials to use with weaker readers, he must make a more thorough diagnosis of each dysfunctional reader to specify the weaknesses peculiar to each, and he must plan his routine classroom instruction so that their special needs are accommodated. Let us consider each of these procedures in some detail.

Finding Supplementary Materials

Fortunately, reading is an area of great interest to the teaching profession; consequently there are a multitude of sound commercial materials available. Harris,[8] Spache,[9] and Emery[10] list a tremendous variety of them. With this variety of materials readily available and with a bit of initiative, any teacher can develop a fine collection of materials. The following sources are commonly known, but perhaps the suggestions will serve as a reminder:

1. *Materials already available.* It is very likely that someone in the district already has a collection of materials. The curriculum director, the department chairman, another secondary teacher, or an elementary teacher may be able to loan or give many sound materials.
2. *Community sources.* Often the local newspaper will furnish educational services. Public libraries often have easy reading materials. A nearby college may have a curriculum library or a professor who has developed a collection.
3. *Correspondence.* Two dollars worth of postage will bring a flood of brochures, announcements, and examination copies from publishers.
4. *Outside financial aid.* Someone in the school district may be willing to spend thirty dollars for reading materials. Those thirty dollars might buy three copies of five or more different workbooks, enough material for a reasonable beginning program. The P.T.A. or local service groups are possible benefactors.
5. *Students and parents.* Students and parents can contribute old magazines and paperback books to a classroom library. Publications about automobiles, sports, and adolescent interests such as fashion, hair styling, and romance are especially desirable since these have strong motivating power for students.

In a very short time the use of these resources will result in an extensive collection of supplementary materials for the classroom library.

Diagnostic Procedures

The general inventory does not go far beyond identifying weak readers, so a more thorough diagnosis is now in order. Hopefully this second diagnosis will uncover the *cause* of the student's disability, and enable the cause to be removed, permitting a relatively quick correction. If the cause cannot be determined readily—and this is usually the case—the teacher must specify the symptoms and treat them.

The first step is examining the student's records that are kept on file in the office. The teacher should compare the scores on standardized tests with the scores on IQ tests. The student's test records may indicate that although his performance seems "poor" he is working to capacity.

The intelligence quotient is equal to mental age divided by chronological age. For example, a sixteen-year-old eleventh grader with an IQ of 80 has a mental age of 12.8. Consequently, if he is reading at the eighth-grade level, he is doing about as well as can be expected. In other words, within the group that the teacher has identified as slow readers, he will find both students who are working up to expectations and those who are performing below their expected level. Although both should have the benefit of a planned skill-building program, the teacher should not expect great improvement in the former group.

Of course, the IQ tests that are the basis for such judgments are usually paper and pencil tests in which the student must be able to read in order to do well. Consequently, the test may be measuring his reading ability rather than his native intelligence. Although the IQ score may generally identify students of limited ability, the teacher may investigate further by comparing the student's results when he does the reading and writes his answers, to the results when the assignment is *read to him* and he answers the questions orally. If the latter score is higher, the student has a reading problem. If the two scores are the same, the problem is not reading. However, whether the problem lies with reading ability or native intelligence, students who are generally handicapped will continue to need considerable support throughout the year. Perhaps the best support is the oral reading of assignments to the student. The logic behind this approach is that the weak reader's listening vocabulary exceeds his reading vocabulary—he knows words when he hears them that he does not know in print. Hence, his comprehension will be better if his reading of the assignment is supported by hearing the words as he sees them. Since such an approach would take an inordinate amount of the teacher's time, he can turn to two sources of assistance. Most schools have student organizations (particularly Future Teachers groups) that are willing to do tutoring. They will usually be quite willing to assist the teacher in this manner during study periods. If a private place can be provided for this activity, it will not be embarrassing to the slow reader. The second source of assistance is the P.T.A. Usually, many mothers are willing to tape-record reading selections. In this way the tapes will be available at any time, and if the school has earphones available, they may be used even in noisy surroundings. If the student has the opportunity to hear the words at the same time that he sees them, he will come to associate the meaning of the oral symbol with that of the written one. This procedure will help build his reading vocabulary and help him become a better reader.

Standardized reading tests will give a great deal of information about students, but the teacher must be sure that he understands that information and is not misled by his failure to interpret the test results properly. For example, the test results will be inaccurate for the low rate–high comprehension student, just as the teacher's diagnosis will be. With such students the test will give little useful information unless it is readministered without time limits.

Moreover, the teacher must remember that the reading level indicated by a standardized test is not necessarily the level of graded material that he should provide the student for either an instructional or an independent reading assignment; students read at different levels in different situations. The test situation is one of high pressure, high concentration, and limited time period. In such a situation most students will do significantly better than they will in less structured situations. The reading level in these highly structured intense situations is called the "frustration" level and is typically two years above the student's "independent" reading level, the level at which he can read without the support of a structured situation or teacher's direction. For example:

Frustration level	(standardized test)—eleventh grade
Instructional level	(teacher direction)—tenth grade
Independent level	(without support)—ninth grade

Standardized test scores will often offer reading profiles that subdivide the total score into subscores that are more useful diagnostically. But again, such scores must be carefully evaluated so that the teacher is sure his understanding of the score matches what the test actually measures. Suppose, for example, that the teacher finds that a particular student scores at the fifth-grade level in vocabulary and the ninth-grade level in comprehension. These results seem to imply the need for a particular kind of corrective program, but a closer look at the test may reveal that the vocabulary section included four major parts—mathematics vocabulary, science vocabulary, social studies vocabulary, and general vocabulary. A breakdown of the student's score may reveal that he was extremely low in the mathematics and science vocabularies, whereas his social studies and general vocabulary scores were very similar to other members of the class. In this case, the solution seems to be tutoring in mathematics and science, not special reading instruction in the English classroom. It is also possible that further analysis of the student's comprehension score may reveal weaknesses that are masked by the total grade-level score of ninth grade. For example, the high comprehension score may have resulted from excellent work in reading maps, charts, and diagrams, and from correct answers to questions that require the skill of finding specific facts in a paragraph; however, he may have failed to answer correctly questions that call for selecting the best statement of the topic of a paragraph. In this case the teacher should prepare special materials to treat this weakness, which is a particularly important English class reading skill. Thus, although standardized reading tests offer the teacher a great deal of information about student strengths and weaknesses, he must take the time to study the individual student's test performance carefully so that he will not be misled by the relatively superficial analysis of the generalized scores. In many cases he may find that the emphases of the test are relatively unimportant to him and that he would rather develop his own diagnostic devices for the specific problems in which he is most interested.

Although the office records of a student may contain reports from his previous teachers, these reports may be suspect. In some cases, they will be subject to a "halo" effect. If the teacher found the student generally pleasant and easy to work with, this general attitude may serve to mask the teacher's recognition of a reading problem. Contrariwise, if the teacher has found the student generally difficult, the appraisal may carry over into his evaluation of the student's reading ability. A second weakness of teacher reports is that they tend to be general. Quite often they are made out at the end of the year when the teacher is pressed by the many duties of closing school. Furthermore, a teacher trained as a secondary rather than as an elementary teacher may be unaware of the specific skills involved in reading. For all these reasons, the reports of previous teachers will be inadequate help in developing a good skills program. However, if the reports give evidence of a knowledge of reading skills and careful diagnosis, the teacher can place far more confidence in them than he can in a standardized test. A good teacher's report is the result of a year's work with the student and consequently is far more useful than a sixty-minute test. Also, a good teacher may include comments on procedures that have been helpful—information that the reading test cannot provide. If the teachers who have written good reports are still on the staff, it would be wise to schedule conferences with them to discuss approaches and materials to use with the students.

Classroom Observation

Observing students' behavior during routine class procedures can give a teacher clues to possible physiological problems. If a student misses directions such as to open books or to stop reading, if he turns to the wrong page, if he watches the teacher's face intently, if he frequently misinterprets statements or questions during class discussions, he may have a hearing disorder. A student who squints, who holds books very close, who loses the place, who covers an eye or reads with his head tilted at a peculiar angle may have problems that can be cured by glasses. The teacher should immediately check the records of such students to see if they have had a recent examination and, if not, should contact both the school counselor and the parents to encourage such an examination. If such previously undetected physiological disorders are the cause of reading disability, correcting the physical problem should result in correcting the reading problem.

Many specific reading weaknesses can be pinpointed by using a brief oral-reading diagnostic procedure. The teacher works with a student individually using an easy passage. The teacher follows the reading on his own copy of the passage. (See the example on page 401.)

Although this diagnostic step may seem complex in its application, it is relatively simple in classroom practice. Its administration will take about ten minutes for each weak reader. The follow-up of a second similar diagnosis will take about the same time. In other words, even if the teacher must use three progressively more difficult passages with each of eight students, he will have spent only four hours. If he manages one student a week, he will have an excellent diagnosis by the end of October and will have seven months to spend in carefully planned, specialized instruction that will have far more advantages for the students and for classroom management than the same amount of time spent in disciplining the students for being inattentive with materials they cannot manage.

Planning Instruction

The early inventory may have revealed one of two situations: either the whole class is weak in reading or a small number of students have reading deficiencies. In some ways the latter situation is the more difficult: in addition to providing different instruction for those in the weak group, the teacher must also take pains to prevent their embarrassment at having an "easier" program and thus suffering a real or imagined status loss. In many instances, to oversimplify, the teacher is faced with two major alternatives in organizing instruction. If he has all the students in the class read the same material, he must individualize instruction by focusing on different skills for the weak students. If, on the other hand, he focuses on the same skills for all students, he must individualize by giving different students different reading materials. Of course, the alternatives are not quite that simple: there are a great variety of solutions in between the two listed here.

Even if the whole class is weak there will still be present some range in differences of ability; consequently there will be a need to differentiate instruction. However, when the entire class has weakness in the fundamental skills, the teacher can openly devote class time to correctional drills and similar activities.

Whichever situation proves to be the case, there are two major avenues of instruction: (1) the development of vocabulary skills and (2) the development of reading comprehension skills. These skills are related and in a sense are hierarchical. That is, success in one skill makes possible success in an-

Many people were busy all week on an empty lot near the park. Several boys were cleaning it off. Seven of them picked up old boards, sticks, and dry branches. Others cut the tall grass and carried it away. Then all the girls raked the ground and made it smooth. At last two men came and built a strong fence. Then the children had a safe playground.[11]

1. As the student reads the paragraph:
   a. Underline any words, letters, or groups of letters that the student finds difficult to pronounce. **DIAGNOSIS:** Special instruction in basic vocabulary and phonics skills necessary. Use simpler materials for comprehension skill building. Do not bother with step 2; skip to step 3.
   b. Listen for lack of intonation, poor phrasing, and the like. **DIAGNOSIS:** Conceivably a vocabulary weakness; probably comprehension is poor. Use all questions to specify weakness.
   c. Note *good* reading fluency. **DIAGNOSIS:** Material too easy for comprehension work. Use questions a through d to support this analysis. Use more difficult material to recheck vocabulary-attack skills and find appropriate level for comprehension work. Skip steps 3 and 4.
2. Ask the following comprehension questions:
   a. What is the story about? (main idea)
   b. What are they doing? Why are they doing it? (main idea)
   c. What are the three steps in clearing the lot? Which comes first? second? third? (organization)
   d. Who cleaned the lot? (details)
   e. What did the boys do? The girls? The men? (details)

DIAGNOSIS: The student who answers "Preparing a lot to be a children's playground" to question *a* should move to more difficult materials. Skip steps 3 and 4.

The student who has difficulty with the first question but can be led to a good answer through the others is working at the appropriate level. Skip steps 3 and 4, but follow with a diagnosis of vocabulary-attack skills in more difficult material.

The reading level of the material is too high for students who have difficulty. Use steps 3 and 4.

3. Point to words in the passage and ask the student what they mean: empty, several, seven, branches, smooth.

   DIAGNOSIS: Success indicates that the problem is comprehension, not vocabulary, at this level of difficulty. Use step 4 and find assistance so that the student can continue these activities. Failure indicates a weak vocabulary. Training in phonics and basic sight vocabulary is appropriate; use easier materials for comprehension work.
4. Read the passage aloud to the student as he listens. Repeat steps 3 and 2 orally.

   DIAGNOSIS: Success indicates that the problem is reading. Continue with planned program. Failure indicates some other deficiency. Seek professional help.

other; success in a high-level skill is impossible without success in a low-level one. If a student does not know what the words in a story mean, he cannot understand his reading at the literal level. If he cannot comprehend the literal level, he cannot recognize the implications. And if he cannot recognize the implications, he cannot make rational valuations. Thus, all these higher-level skills depend upon the basic skill of knowing what the words mean. Yet this skill depends upon still other more basic skills. Given a word that he does not know, the student has a variety of possible word-attack skills available to him. He may attempt to pronounce the word, since he may know it orally but not visually; this attack requires skill with phonics. He may attempt to interpret its meaning from the context, which requires skill in recognizing context clues. Or he may refer to a dictionary, which requires knowledge of the order of the letters in the alphabet (which, unfortunately, some high school students do not have).

The oral reading diagnosis will indicate the kinds of vocabulary work most immediately needed by each student. If a student stumbles over common everyday words in his reading, he needs drill on the basic sight vocabulary. Flash cards with words and phrases of the basic vocabulary are readily available commercially. Pairs of students can drill with these, and students can drill with the help of their parents at home. If only the longer, less familiar words present the problems, the teacher can give instruction in simple techniques for word analysis as follows: with a word like "tripartite," the teacher might ask: "What does tri mean? What does it mean in tricycle? What does it mean in trio? What little word do you see in tripartite? What does part mean? What must tripartite mean?" If the student understands "tripartite" with this support, it is fair to assume that he will profit from additional study of prefixes and roots.

In addition there are the routine techniques for teaching the vocabulary of the course (see pp. 485–487). When preparing the class for a reading assignment, key vocabulary terms should be introduced before the student encounters them in reading. The teacher clarifies the meanings of these words, not with rigid, formal definitions, but in a way that communicates strongly to the students. Using the word in a variety of simple, clear ways provides the students with the best chance to understand the word.

The careful introduction of reading assignments is a central technique for strengthening the comprehension skills. The purpose of reading is specified by the preliminary guide questions, and the teacher develops questions of the type most needed by the students for practice at comprehension skills (see Chapter 11). In addition, during his search for supplementary materials the teacher will encounter many titles of commercial materials designed to provide practice in comprehension.

Practice is the key idea in the development of any skill. A person cannot learn to swim by watching instructional films and never getting wet. There is no way to improve reading skill without reading. However, practice and drill periods should be kept relatively short; the practice materials should be as interesting as possible; and they should be relatively easy.

Generally speaking, nothing is easier or more interesting to read than plays (those that are not period pieces). Since the lines reflect conversational speech, the vocabulary load is easy. Lines and speeches are short so that a reader's frustration does not have time to build. Since different readers read different roles, the relationships among characters are quite clear. Since drama is more compressed than fiction, the action moves along at a faster pace. The experience of many teachers in using plays that are read aloud in class with some opportunity for acting, is that interest in this dramatic activity does not flag. As many plays as possible should be read during the year, since in addition to the strengths enumerated, work with drama is a grade-level task.

The school grammar book can be used to advantage in working with weak readers. The exercises are usually composed of short, discrete sentences, permitting a student to read only a single sentence at a time, and thus preventing the frustration build-up. Additionally, because the sentences are written to demonstrate some principle of analysis, they exhibit parallel construction that proves to be supportive of the reading task. Again, the drill is oral, and again, the student is working at grade-level tasks. Lessons on capitalization, pluralizing, and punctuation can give real aid in developing reading skills. Of course, when the teacher's purpose in using the school grammar is to provide reading practice, he need not be overly concerned about weaknesses in the responses to the analytical portions of the lessons. Unfortunately, in contrast to work with drama, work with the grammar book is not very interesting to students and must be scheduled with some restraint.

There should be frequent opportunities for free reading and browsing in the classroom library of old magazines and paperbacks. If students find something they want to read in these periods, they should be given time and freedom to do so. Encouragement and support cannot be lavished too heavily on these students. They need this comfort more than most, and they respond to it more warmly than do other students.

As he gains experience, the English teacher must go as far as he can in diagnosing and treating individual problems in all the areas of English instruction. Since reading is the *sine qua non* of success in our educational system, he has a particular responsibility in this area.

NOTES

1. Harris, Albert J., *How to Increase Reading Ability* (New York: David McKay Co., 1961), p. 100.
2. Vick, Nancy, "The Role of a Reading Consultant in a Content Area Classroom," Perspectives in Reading No. 6, *Corrective Reading in the High School Classroom,* eds. H. Alan Robins and Sidney J. Raush, International Reading Association.

3. Stephenson, Carl, "Leiningen Versus the Ants," *Great Tales of Action and Adventure* (New York: Dell Publishing Co., 1959).

4. Spache, George D., *Good Reading for Poor Readers* (Champaign, Ill.: Garrard Publishing Co., 1966).

5. Emery, Raymond C. and Margaret B. Houshower, *High Interest—Easy Reading for Junior and Senior High School Reluctant Readers* (Champaign, Ill.: National Council of Teachers of English, 1965).

6. Robinson, Francis P., *Effective Reading* (New York: Harper & Row, 1962).

7. Robinson, Francis P., *Effective Study,* revised edition (New York: Harper & Row, 1961).

8. Harris, *op. cit.*

9. Spache, *op. cit.*

10. Emery *et al., op. cit.*

11. Gray, William S., *Gray Oral Reading Test, form C., Reading Passages,* (New York: Bobbs-Merrill Company, 1963).

SUGGESTIONS FOR FURTHER READING

1. ALBERT J. HARRIS, *How to Increase Reading Ability.* New York: David McKay Co., 1961. An excellent basic text on the principles and practices of reading instruction.

2. RAYMOND C. EMERY and MARGARET B. HOUSHOWER, *High Interest-Easy Reading for Junior and Senior High School Reluctant Readers.* Champaign, Ill.: National Council of Teachers of English, 1965. A slim pamphlet that contains a brief statement of principles, extensive lists of appropriate works, and an excellent bibliography of additional sources.

3. FRANCIS P. ROBINSON, *Effective Study,* revised edition. New York: Harper & Row, 1961. A basic source for improving study skills with principles based on extensive research.

Language

The major purpose of teaching language in the English class is to help students understand the way their language works and to develop in them an ongoing enthusiasm for studying it. Although this book is divided into four major parts, Instruction, Literature, Language, and Composition, these divisions are primarily organizational conveniences, for each part is about teaching language. The focus of the entire text and of the English teacher's work is to excite students' enthusiasm for language and to develop their skill in using it.

This part of the text is devoted to the direct study of language as an end in itself rather than as a tool for understanding a written work or as a means of improving writing. To be sure, the distinctions are often not clear-cut. The study of hyperbole as a technique of satire could easily be moved from the literature section to this section. Similarly, the study of semantics which is discussed here could be moved to either the literature or the composition sections. In short, the study of language is a constant process in the English classroom. It cannot be set apart from either literature or composition and thus, every English curriculum is language centered by definition.

This insight is not so useful in curriculum planning as it may seem to be. The English teacher's knowledge that language is the *sine qua non* of the English program is no more useful to him than the mathematics teacher's knowledge that numbers are central to the arithmetic program. However, the importance of language carries a significant implication: the English teacher should be trained in at least the rudiments of contemporary language study. Unfortunately, this is only rarely the case.

Traditionally, the content of the language portion of the English curriculum has been determined to a great extent by the content of the grammar books that the students have used: syntactic analysis, usage, spelling, punctuation, capitalization, some dictionary work, and letter writing, all presented in a prescriptive way. Teachers have often come to believe that these are all matters of grammar, and students have too often come to identify "English" as consisting only of such instruction. The purpose that has frequently been set forth for emphasizing these elements in instruction is that of "helping students to improve their communications skills especially in composition" with the "help" deriving from the view that departures from the prescriptions must result in unacceptable usages or corruptions of the language. Chapter 17 examines both this point of view that has controlled language instruction and the research on the results of the instruction which has been found to be ineffective with most students.

A teacher may be required to teach grammar to his classes, but the grammar that is required may not be that found in the traditional classroom texts. It may be that one of the newer schools of thought, structural linguistics or transformational generative grammar, has been chosen by local fiat to be the approach to grammar teaching. Chapter 18 explores the contrasts that exist among the three approaches and delineates the problems involved in instruction when each is used. The chapter strongly urges that grammar instruction be minimized.

Since the study of semantics has direct application to both literature and composition, and since this study increases the student's sensitivity to language generally, it should be central in the language curriculum. Chapter 19 reviews the most fundamental concepts in semantics instruction and presents typical materials and lessons that can be used in the teaching.

Perhaps the single most noteworthy feature of living languages is that they are in a constant process of change that is sometimes rapid, but more often is evolutionary. The English language has changed dramatically and to the extent that the vernacular of Chaucer's Age is incomprehensible to everyone but students of Middle English; in turn, the language of Beowulf, Anglo-Saxon (or Old English), would have been incomprehensible to most of Chaucer's contemporaries, as well as to all but students of Early Mediaeval English today. The fact that there are many dialects of English used throughout the world and even in the United States at present is evidence that changes in the English language are taking place today. Chapter 20 presents some approaches to teaching about language change generally, the history of English and dialects.

Grammar, Usage, and Composition | 17

There has been considerable research on the effect the study of grammar has on writing, on what teachers have called problems of usage, and on syntax in student writing. The results of this research should inform both what the teacher does in class and what he avoids.

Grammar Study and Composition

Traditional instruction in grammar included not only instruction in the parts of speech and syntactic analysis—legitimate grammatical studies—but also such usage matters as the difference between "like" and "as" and "there" and "their." Most traditional grammar texts also included rules and practice exercises on spelling, capitalization, and punctuation. The reason for including these in the grammar handbook was the assumption that studying the rules and practicing their application in exercises would improve the students' skill in composition. But studies dating from the early 1900s show that grammar and usage instruction are *not* effective. In 1913 Thomas H. Briggs presented such a study, in which he discussed the purposes that were propounded for the study of grammar and tested the effectiveness it had in accomplishing those purposes. He made the following comment about the textbooks being used at the time:

> The textbooks in current use may be roughly divided into two classes: the first professes to apply traditional grammar practically to language; the second, following the laboratory practice of other subjects, has made grammar an inductive science. . . . In the books of the first class many details persist by the sole authority of tradition. In those of the second they are justified, openly, or implicitly, as affording a general discipline of the mind.[1]

Since at that time grammar was often taught to "discipline the mind," Briggs developed tests on a variety of "mental disciplines." One area of the tests evaluated "the ability of the children to correct errors and point off sentences." The items emphasized subject-verb agreement, pronoun case, double negatives, capitalization, and punctuation. He administered the examination twice—first to classes in the Horace Mann School and then to students in two groups of public schools. In each instance one group of students had received considerable training in traditional grammar. With the other group such training had not been emphasized. He concluded:

> In ten out of eleven comparisons the schools that emphasize formal grammar make a poorer showing than the schools that do not. . . . In the Horace Mann School, it will be recalled the advantage lay with the room having formal grammar in six out of nine comparisons; but the overwhelming advantage in the western schools following instruction in language and composition makes it probable that their evidence is more conclusive. This is more readily accepted when one compares the advantage of the one Horace Mann grade over the other in each of these tests with the much larger averages in the other schools. The advantage seems conclusively with the schools not emphasizing formal grammar.[2]

Further, grammar instruction did not even teach grammar:

> In two cases out of three the school emphasizing formal grammar is a poor second in the grammar examination, and in the third it shows only a trifling superiority over a group of children six months younger. . . .
> As a result of this experiment it may safely be asserted that these particular children after the amount of formal grammar that they had, do not, as measured by the means employed, show in any of the abilities tested improvement that may be attributed to their training in grammar. . . . Indeed, the burden of proof now rests with those who believe in a strengthening mental discipline from formal grammar.[3]

In 1929 R. L. Lyman reviewed the research on kinds of errors in usage:

> Language items which cause pupils the greatest difficulty are usually the items which persist. The persistence of errors seems to indicate the ineffectiveness of present methods of teaching English.[4]

Such studies continued. Symonds in 1931 compared different approaches to teaching grammar. After citing previous research and pointing out that "grammar still has a somewhat thriving existence in our schools" in spite of that research, he "carried out some test-teach-test experiments in Grade VI of four New York City elementary schools." He divided the students into six different groups: (1) students who read correct sentences orally; (2) students who read correct and incorrect sentences orally, adding "is wrong" and "is right" in their recitation; (3) students who learned formal grammatical categories without application; (4) students who learned formal grammatical categories and practiced applying them; (5) students who practiced choosing correct constructions; and (6) students who used all the above techniques in combination. He concluded that:

> The development of ability to analyze sentences for grammatical constructions apparently had about the same influence on usage that memorization of rules had. Practice in choice of correct expressions had measurably greater influence than the learning of rules or analysis. More repetition of the right and wrong forms in succession so that the distinction between the two is clearly brought out, and so that it is definitely stated which is the right form, had greater influence on usage than any of the work with grammar. The whole program . . . results in improved usage better than any one single method alone. . . . Grammar does have an influence on usage, but at what cost? Without doubt, for most children the difficulty and trouble of learning grammar as a means for improving usage is so great that more direct attacks on usage are certainly more profitable. Our own results show that mere repetition of correct forms, where it is clearly indicated what is correct and what the critical point at issue is, has more influence on usage than any procedure with grammar.[5]

In 1939, Ellen Frogner reported on her doctoral dissertation, whose aim was

> . . . to compare the improvement made by pupils who were directed to approach problems of sentence structure entirely from the standpoint of adequate expression of thought with the improvement made by pupils who, besides having their attention directed to the clear expression of thought, were also given the drill needed to ensure an understanding of the grammatical construction of the sentence.[6]

The class taught by the "thought approach" used the traditional ideas of subordination and coordination in their discussion of sentence structure and then considered common types of errors in this light. The grammar classes analyzed sentences in addition to carrying on the same activities as the "thought approach" classes. These general approaches were pursued through a series of seven units. The experimental design used matched pairs of students. Miss Frogner reached the following conclusions:

> The pupils in the grammar class definitely learned more grammar than did those in the group using the thought approach. . . . In spite of this fact, the thought method brought about superior results in sentence structure, as measured by general tests covering the work of the semester. . . . Results of the study, therefore, lend no support to the claims made for grammar as being essential to improvement in sentence structure.[7]

In 1952 Anthony Tovatt asked eighty-six adults to diagram a complex sentence and to answer a brief questionnaire about English teaching and diagraming. His first point was that intelligent adults (fifty graduate students and thirty-six students in engineering English at the University of Colorado) do not use diagraming when they write and that, consequently, the teaching of diagraming is unimportant. His conclusion points out the phenomenal power of educational tradition and mystique:

> Aside from the fact that 96 percent of the group was unable to diagram the sentence, perhaps the two most significant findings revealed by the experiment are the following: (1) that only two of 6 persons who were able to diagram the sentence stated that they actually applied diagraming skills to their own writing and (2) that 57 of the persons who were unable to diagram the sentence still maintained that, when they wrote, they visualized sentence elements as they would diagram them! . . . Notable, too, is the fact that 86 of those who could not diagram the sentence still believe that more emphasis should be placed on the teaching of grammar.[8]

In 1960 G. Robert Carlsen reviewed the literature for the *Encyclopedia of Educational Research:*

> Summaries of research in the teaching of language have consistently concluded that there is no shred of evidence to substantiate the continued emphasis on grammar prevalent in most classrooms.[9]

In 1962 Roland J. Harris completed a doctoral dissertation comparing the effects of explanatory grammar instruction and functional grammar instruction in ten classes in five London schools. Using a carefully planned experimental design and matched groups (the explanatory grammar groups had a slightly superior IQ in three of the five schools), the study covered a two-year period in which one period per week was devoted to grammar instruction for the explanatory group and direct composition instruction for the functional group. He concluded that "It seems safe to infer that the study of English grammatical terminology had a negligible or even a relatively harmful effect upon the correctness of children's writing in the early part of the five Secondary Schools."[10]

In 1963, the Braddock study, *Research in Written Composition,* reviewed the research on the relationship between grammar and composition. Its conclusions were:

> In view of the widespread agreement of research studies based upon many types of students and teachers, the conclusion can be stated in strong and unqualified terms: the teaching of formal grammar has a negligible or, because it usually displaces some instruction and practice in actual composition, even a harmful effect on the improvement of writing.[11]

But any teacher who has taught grammar has had far more personal experiences with the failure of grammar instruction to improve composition. It doesn't take long to find a student who underlines the correct choice between "don't" and "doesn't" in the workbook exercises, who writes the correct word to fill the blank in the grammar book exercises, and who writes original sentences properly illustrating their use, but who writes "he don't" in the theme that he turns in the next day.

In the face of all this evidence, some teachers would still argue that we should continue to teach grammar as an aid to composition because it is a necessary tool for communication between the teacher and the student. That is, it's much simpler to explain an error by marking it C.S. (comma splice) than it is to attempt to explain the nature of the error for which the abbreviation stands. The weakness of such a position is obvious. If the student understands the error he has made, the problem is not grammar but proofreading and should consequently be treated differently. If he does not understand the error, the teacher's reference to it will be futile. In either case, this rationale for teaching grammar will not hold.

It is possible that the newer grammars, when accompanied by good instruction, may have an effect on composition, but it is still too early to tell. They have replaced traditional grammar study in only a minority of high schools, and studies resulting from materials that are new and different to both teacher and students may show positive results simply because the materials are new and different. But it would seem reasonable to assume that transformational generative (T-G) grammar may have an effect upon the students' syntax because the system is strongly syntax-oriented. The research of Bateman and Zidonis supports this assumption. They developed a two-year program of instruction in T-G grammar and tested the results:

> Comparison of Before and After scores, experimental and control classes, and interaction scores are all significant at the .01 level. The increase in production of well-formed sentences by the experimental class can unambiguously be attributed to the study of grammar . . . The clear relationship between increase in proportion of well-formed sentences and decrease in error production substantially supports the claim that the greater change of the experimental class is attributable to its study of the grammar. . . .
>
> It seems clear that claims must be presented tentatively, regardless of the statistical level of significance, when the total population was limited to forty-one pupils. Even so, the persistently higher scores for the experimental class in every comparison made strengthens the contention that the study of a systematic grammar which is a theoretical model of the process of sentence production is the logical way to modify the process itself.[12]

However, it would be premature to accept the conclusions of limited research studies in new grammars without reservation. So, although it is quite possible that we may discover in the long run that a newer grammar does have effect on student composition, any teacher must consider his attempts in this direction as at best experimental.

Usage and Dialectology

If grammar study is no help in improving composition, the teacher is still faced with the question of student composition problems of usage, syntax, and the like, a question of very real concern for every teacher of English. The first thing he should know is that the concept of usage correctness has been severely challenged. Structural linguistics, with its strong emphasis on the empirical study of the facts of language usage, has led linguists to collect a large corpus of real language material and to analyze it painstakingly to determine what are, in fact, the standards of American usage. The results have led to a severe decrease in the number of items that can be considered "incorrect."

For the linguist, usage as defined by the English teacher is part of the much larger problem of dialectology. The dialectologist is interested in describing the peculiarities of language performance and in doing so sheds considerable light on usage. Each individual has language performance peculiarities or idiosyncrasies that are his alone. These define his "idiolect." Those idiosyncrasies that he shares with other members of his family but that are again not shared by larger groups make up the family's "familiolect." In building the larger groups that share certain peculiarities of language performance, we typically find that an individual shares features that are accounted for by his geographical area, educational level, social level, vocational pursuit, age, and special interests. Most of the language peculiarities occur in pronunciation or vocabulary. The results of such analysis suggest that usage is a relative thing that is determined more by considerations of circumstance than by grammar. If our judgments about usage are to be useful, then, we must take the student's circumstances into account.

As an extreme example, consider the problem of a Harvard-educated Bostonian from an upper middle-class family who takes a secondary teaching job in the deep South. Should he judge his students on the basis of his predispositions? Or must he become aware of the standards of the community and use them in making his judgments? Even if he were to stay in Boston, he would have the same problem with students who move to his area and with those from different social and educational backgrounds.

Even if there were some arbitrary absolute standard of correct usage, it would still not be clear that the English teacher should press all his students to attain it. Insofar as the student's language performance identifies him with a certain group—geographic, ethnic, racial, educational, social, chronological —there is a question of whether either he or the teacher should desire a change in language performance. Obviously, his usage serves not only to exclude him from other groups but also to include him in his own. The usual conflict between teacher and student comes when the teacher works to change his pattern so he will be included in the "well-educated" group while the student resists the change so that he won't be excluded from his peer group. The teacher's efforts are even more futile when we realize that the student's interest in written communication (the usual area of the English teacher's concern about usage) is at best remote in comparison to his vital concern for talk with his friends. If he found that his usage in such vital situations were alienating him from them, he would quickly change it. (When students move, they pick up the new slang and language style very quickly.)

With all these pressures against the possibility of success in changing students' usage, we can at least say that the teacher should be very careful in selecting those items that he wishes to change. It suggests, in other words, that he should focus only on those that are the most blatant instances of "poor usage" in the student's language performance. This suggests again the extreme importance of techniques for diagnosing individual student problems and treating them individually. Even if the teacher undertook such a program, he must still expect to fail because the evidence against school-effected changes in usage is overwhelming. But in the continuing search for answers we should at least try to avoid the approaches that have been so often tried and so often proved wanting. There are, after all, other possibilities.

One has already been mentioned—individualized instruction—but the point is well worth emphasizing. If the teacher were to spend an hour a week talking with a student, the dialogue would diminish the distance that is usually present in the teacher-pupil relationship. The more personal note and the greater understanding on both sides would establish a different kind of rapport. In such a situation, there is a far greater chance that the student will be responsive and consequently a greater chance of effecting change.

Most usage problems will be a carry-over from oral usage habits to written language habits. If the teacher discovers that a particular error is part of the student's oral language patterns, then he has a different problem than he would have if the student made the error only in the written language. That is, if the student does not make the distinction in any form, it must be taught. If he is able to make the distinction in speech but fails to do so in writing, then the problem is a matter of attention or habit rather than understanding and suggests a proofreading problem. A failure to make the distinction orally, on the other hand, suggests a need for language drill following the oral-aural approach of foreign language instruction.

Suppose, for example, that the student makes a multitude of spelling errors. Listening to him read his theme or a selection from a test may lead to the discovery that he does not pronounce word endings such as "s" and "ed." Further investigation may indicate that he does not hear those endings when the teacher pronounces them. The same is true of some punctuation problems. If the student does not follow normal intonation patterns in reading his own writing or in reading an assignment, it is probable that he will be unable to punctuate items like introductory adverb clauses or nonrestrictive adjective clauses. Again, the treatment should attack the oral patterns before the written patterns. Thus, a second suggestion for approaching usage problems is to distinguish between those that are only written and those that are based on oral language difficulties.

A third possibility is to reduce the complexity of the task. In writing (or speaking) a student may be so involved in the task of getting his ideas out, that he has no power left to consider usage, even though he may "know" the correct and incorrect forms. In fact, an experience common to all of us is the garbled result of our efforts to express ideas that are, to us at least, complex. A speaker (or writer) also tends to regress from correctness when he is strongly involved emotionally. In both kinds of situations, if the pressures of emotional or intellectual difficulty were decreased, the verbal pattern might become more fluent. This explanation may explain what we normally refer to as a "lack of carry-over" from a test or drill situation to a real writing situation. The test or drill situation effectively reduces the problems so that the student may concentrate on each choice singly and succeed. He breaks down when he has many other problems on which to concentrate. It may also explain the complaints of some students who find that they get better grades on themes that they write hurriedly before class than on those which they spend a great deal of time. It is possible that the theme "off the top of the head" typically deals with a topic with which the student has considerable familiarity and consequently reflects both greater subject mastery and more attention to stylistic and usage matters, whereas the theme in which he grappled with ideas reflects an inattention to the more mundane matters of usage. Reduction of complexity may improve usage.

But this approach is not so easy as it sounds. Typically, the teacher who attempts this approach reduces the task to what are for him fundamentals while they are for the students still complex. For example, take the student whose spelling is consistently atrocious. When the student turns in his paper, the teacher hands it back to him and tells him to look up the words which might be misspelled so that he can turn in a paper with no misspellings. Certainly this task is simplified. Not so! In a theme of two hundred words the student may very well have to look up forty words. The task may take him as much as two hours, more than any teacher would reasonably demand for a homework assignment. Very well, then, the teacher reaches an absolutely fundamental level. He asks the student to simply ask someone else how to spell the words that may be misspelled. This avoids the problem of dictionary skill. Absolutely fundamental? Not so. Where will the student find someone to whom he can admit how badly he spells? No, an even more fundamental approach is possible. The teacher may ask the student to circle those words which he thinks *may* be misspelled. When he is able to do this, then the next step is to worry about correction. If we were to mark only those errors that really interfere with communication, we would have a more meaningful effect on the students (and much less work to do). The encouragement and stimulation necessary to get students started writing is far more important than the relatively trivial problems of usage.

A fourth approach to usage problems is to increase the student's general sensitivity to language. If he becomes more aware of the subtle distinctions of language usage by which people (including himself) unconsciously make judgments, we may hope that such a sensitivity will pay off in the long run. In other words, let's help him be able to say, "People use language differently; people judge other people by the way they use language." If he also becomes aware that people change their language patterns according to the situation, he may be better able to see the need for adopting a certain set of language patterns for the particular composition situation. There is some hope—though no research data—that such an awareness will have an effect on the way he uses language. Such a sensitivity to language might be developed through the study of dialects and language history. But any of these approaches to usage should be judged by their effectiveness. The teacher should devise some method by which he is going to measure that effectiveness. It is only in this way that he can make intelligent choices among different approaches. Although there is no tested formula for improving a student's syntax, there is considerable research going on in this area, and teachers should become familiar with it as the results become available.

First, sentence variety has come under the same empirical scrutiny as usage has and with the same results. The research of Christensen can be duplicated by English teachers or, for that matter, English students. He first found an article that suggested different ways for students to vary their sentence openings. (Many grammar handbooks include such a section.) He next turned to a body of writing that is generally considered high quality and counted the number of sentences that used the various beginning devices suggested by the handbook. He found that good writers do not do the things suggested in the handbooks:

> They place something before the subject in only one fourth of their sentences (24.47%), and . . . they use almost nothing but adverbial modifiers. They use adverbial modifiers before 23 sentences in 100 (22.98%), but they use verbal groups before only one sentence in 85 (1.17%) and the inverted elements before only one in 300 (0.32%).[13]

As has been the case with much of the teaching of usage, it appears that the prescriptions about sentence variety do not stand up to empirical testing.

A second approach to the problems of syntax in composition is the study of developmental patterns. Obviously, the written syntax of very young children is different from that of the professional writer. Kellogg Hunt studied the syntactic patterns of fourth graders, eighth graders, twelfth graders, and professional writers in an attempt to describe the patterns of development.[14] He found that specific structures and sentence patterns increase or decrease in use as students grow. Also, the patterns of professional writers seem to be an extension of the pattern that is evident in the development of secondary school students. His findings suggest that a teacher's attempts to help a student improve his syntax need not be based on arbitrary criteria about what constitutes better syntax, but can rather be based on specific knowledge of how students change. If we know what comes after what in the normal course of development, we have a sound basis on which to decide what goals we should have for the student in this area. The research to date is not adequate to allow us to make definite statements about many particulars of the pattern, but anyone who refers to the study by Mr. Hunt will find that such investigation is well on the way to helping us state specific syntactic "use" goals on the basis of students' regular developmental patterns.

However, in the early 1900s a great deal of research of the same kind was done on "usage errors." Voluminous studies report what errors were made with what frequency at what grade levels. But this knowledge was of little value since English teachers have been unable to teach correct usage no matter when the problems occur. The same may very well be true for syntax. Even though we may be able to determine precisely what the student should learn, we may be unable to teach it effectively. We are still faced with the problem of effective approaches to the student's usage and syntax problems.

NOTES

1. Briggs, Thomas H. "Formal English Grammar as a Discipline," *Teachers College Record*, 14: 251–343; p. 256.
2. *Ibid.*, p. 339–341.
3. *Loc. cit.*
4. Lyman, R. L., Summary of Investigations Relating to Grammar, Language, and Composition. *Supplementary Educational Monograph 36*, University of Chicago, 1929.
5. Symonds, Percival M. "Practice versus Grammar in the Learning of Correct Usage," *Journal of Educational Psychology*, 22: 81–95; 1931, p. 93.
6. Frogner, Ellen, "Grammar Approach Versus Thought Approach in Teaching Sentence Structure," *English Journal*, 28: 518–526; 1939, p. 518.
7. *Ibid.*, p. 526.
8. Tovatt, Anthony, "Diagraming: a Sterile Skill" *English Journal*, 41: 91–93; 1952, p. 93.
9. Carlsen, G. Robert, "English," *Encyclopedia of Educational Research*, third ed. New York: The Macmillan Co., 1960.
10. Harris, Roland J. "An Experimental Inquiry into the Functions and Value of Formal Grammar in the Teaching of English, with Special Reference to the Teaching of Correct Written English to Children Aged Twelve to

Fourteen." Unpublished Ph.D. dissertation, University of London, 1962, described in *Research in Written Composition*.

11. Braddock, Richard, Richard Lloyd-Jones, and Lowell Schoer, eds., *Research in Written Composition*, Champaign: National Council of Teachers of English, 1963.

12. Bateman, Donald R. and Frank J. Zidonis, *The Effect of a Knowledge of Generative Grammar upon the Growth of Language Complexity*, U.S. Office of Education Cooperative Research Project #1746, 1964, pp. 134–136.

13. Christensen, Francis, "Sentence Openers," *College English*, 25, 1, October 1963, p. 8.

14. Hunt, Kellogg W., *Differences in Grammatical Structures Written at Three Grade Levels, The Structures to be Analyzed by Transformational Methods*, U.S. Office of Education, Cooperative Research Project 1968.

SUGGESTIONS FOR FURTHER READING

1. RICHARD BRADDOCK, RICHARD LLOYD-JONES, and LOWELL SCHOER, eds., *Research in Written Composition* (Champaign: National Council of Teachers of English, 1963). Describes the requirements of sound research and the results of research concerning the relationship of grammar and composition.

2. KELLOGG W. HUNT, *Grammatical Structures Written at Three Grade Levels* (Champaign: National Council of Teachers of English, 1965). An analysis of the developmental patterns of students' syntax illustrating the values of transformational grammar for the teacher's improved understanding of student composition.

3. DONALD R. BATEMAN and FRANK J. ZIDONIS, *The Effect of a Knowledge of Generative Grammar upon the Growth of Language Complexity* (United States Office of Education: Cooperative Research Project 1746, 1964). A research project which shows a significant relationship between study of generative grammar and sentence structure.

18 | Grammar: The Structures of Language

Many teachers find that their problems related to teaching grammar have been simplified by the department chairman, the principal, or the curriculum committee. A course of study has been designed, a textbook has been chosen, the topics that must be covered have been made mandatory, and very little has been left to the individual teacher's discretion. Two decades ago this was the situation in most schools. Increasingly, however, this practice is being abandoned, and the grammar curriculum is a no man's land where fewer and fewer combatants dare enter. In 1968 the National Council of Teachers of English published *High School English Instruction Today* by Squire and Applebee who, after studying 158 high schools chosen "largely for their reputation in English," could write: "Virtually no sequential or well-planned programs in language were discovered."[1]

Should a teacher find that no grammar program exists in his school, he must consider carefully the wisdom of teaching one on his own. First he must narrow the field, recognizing that spelling, punctuation, and capitalization are, strictly speaking, matters of usage and not grammar (see Chapter 17). Limiting the concept of grammar, then, to language structures and their relationships only, he must consider his purposes: why should he teach this content at all; and in view of all the available content alternatives in language study, as well as in literature and composition, why select grammar for attention, thus limiting the time that is available for the alternatives?

Assuming he can answer the questions of purpose in a satisfactory way—no easy task!—he must deal with one far more telling: Is he equipped to do the job? Two studies published by the National Council of Teachers of English[2] indicate that most English teachers are not adequately trained to teach grammar. Even today many teacher training institutions do not offer courses in grammar. It is incumbent upon any teacher not to teach error. In the absence of appropriate training in grammar on the teacher's part, the teaching of error is all but inevitable.

During the past three decades grammar scholarship has been the fastest growing, most dynamic and exciting area in all of English studies. The conventions and dominant points of view have been in continuous flux, and the rate of change has been accelerating. These changes involve the whole of the discipline from techniques of analysis, to the results of the analyses, to the fundamental philosophical views of the nature of languages and language structures.

The implications for public school teachers can best be understood through an analogy. Let us suppose a teacher assigned to teach chemistry in some remote place had only a textbook in alchemy to guide him and no other background in the science. Such is the English teacher with only his own high school experience in traditional school texts. Or more realistically, assume that in some far place the schools had only pre-World War II vintage chemistry texts asserting that matter and energy were only and always separate entities and that there were ninety-two elements in existence once and for all. A chemistry teacher who was himself untrained in contemporary chemistry and physics would allow his students to learn what is now error but what was once regarded as basic truth.

If today's English teacher cannot deal directly, with or without the aid of a class text, in such matters as allomorphs of morphemes, paradigms, deep structures and embedded sentences, marked and unmarked forms, suprasegmental phonemes, deletion transformations, and linguistic universals, he must perforce delegate instruction in grammar to his colleagues who have sufficient training. Even if he is conversant with the matters named and like arcana, if he does not stay abreast of developments in the field, he runs the risk of teaching error. A person who is informed only by his coursework in structural linguistics taken in the early '60s, for example, will teach a grammar that no longer enjoys the approval of grammar specialists. In short, given any choice, *most English teachers must not teach grammar* because they are simply unequipped to do the job honestly.

Even the teacher who has sufficient training will be left to his own devices in much of his teaching since even the most recent secondary school grammar texts suffer from an apparently unavoidable cultural lag in grammar scholarship.[3] Then, too, as noted above, even an informed teacher must deal with the question of purpose in teaching grammar, and this question will be considered in some detail below.

To return to the situation described in the first paragraph of this chapter, a teacher, whether trained or not, may be required to do some grammar teaching in his classes. If this is the case, he will certainly find that he will be limited to one of three types of grammar and that his text in each case has organized the instructional sequences for him. One alternative might be the traditional school grammar familiar to us all. The second alternative might be the grammar that has come to be known as structural linguistics. The third might be transformational generative grammar. Let us examine each alternative in terms of the character of its academic tradition, the dominant point of view of the school, the pedagogical purposes ascribed to the teaching, and typical lesson materials and procedures.

Traditional School Grammar

The academic influence of traditional school grammar in the English language has been traced to the eighteenth century.[4] Having its roots in the classical grammars of Latin and Greek, the school grammar is modeled on these, and English is seen as an imperfect imitation of these purer archetypes. The intention of the grammarian is to present the rules of the grammar as prescriptions for the student to follow so that his speaking, and especially his writing, will not display incorrect forms and thus contribute to an unfortunate tendency towards the debasement of English that can frequently be found in careless users of the vernacular. The written language is viewed as the true language.

The sentence is the key form in analysis, and that analysis yields clausal and phrasal structures, subjects, predicates, complements and, in the most contemporary treatments, eight parts of speech. Each of these structures may be identified by reference to a set of definitions, and the instructional approach is to apply the definitions in a deductive analysis of syntax.

The tradition has been maintained with only minor variations since its conception, and the school student first encounters it in the third grade or even earlier. In schools where teachers are required to continue this tradition, appropriate textbooks will be provided for student use. Should the teacher be hazy about some of the niceties in the analyses, he need simply stay a few pages ahead of his students, and with the most moderate application, all will come back to him.

As Chapter 17 indicates, this form of grammar and the implied instruction has been thoroughly discredited by the empirical evidence of hundreds of studies relating to all phases of instruction and its lack of carry-over to the speaking and writing of the majority of students. In addition to these studies, the logical inconsistencies in the system have been demonstrated by many modern grammarians, most notably Charles C. Fries.[5]

If a teacher is required to teach this kind of grammar, he should minimize the time and energy that he and his classes expend on it. Additionally, it is his professional responsibility to bring to the attention of his superiors the research data and the theoretic attacks on the grammar in an effort to obtain a major curriculum change. In this case he must make absolutely clear the distinction between syntactic analysis and the study of usage including spelling, punctuation, and capitalization—in all likelihood his superiors will be unaware of the distinction and, in possibly invincible ignorance, will resist any change.

Structural Linguistics

It may be the case that as a result of a capital investment in textbooks, a teacher may find that his curriculum has a commitment to structural linguistics as the grammar that must be studied. Sometimes called descriptive linguistics, this school had its origins in the nineteenth-century work of cultural anthropologists and philologists.[6] In dealing with exotic and primitive languages, these workers developed techniques for describing them. Whenever a language previously unknown to European or American scholarship—such as the languages of interior South America and Indonesia, for example—was encountered, it was often not possible to describe the language through the medium of translation, which is an unreliable procedure at best. Therefore, the techniques used in describing and analyzing languages had to be, as far as possible, free of reliance on translation or other semantic considerations. Over the years such techniques were developed, and later the same principles were applied to previously-known languages, including European languages, one of which, of course, is English.

The basic technique involved finding a native speaker of a language and recording what he said. Originally, the recording was done by hand and by using a phonetic alphabet with various diacritical markings. Today, field workers use tape recorders for the recording, but the speaker must be native to the language under study. This procedure implies the dominant philosophical view that language is what comes out of the mouth of a speaker. There are two important corollaries to this axiom: a written language is merely an attempt to reproduce a spoken language; the current language must be analyzed without reference to historical influences on it since any speaker may be unaware of the history of his language. (For example, it matters little in understanding or analyzing current English that historically the words "host," "guest," and "ghost" were once the same word.)

When a sufficient sample of the spoken language has been collected in its phonetic form, the sample—called a corpus—is analyzed into three levels, the phonological (significant sounds or alphabet), the morphological (words and parts of words that carry distinctive meaning), and the syntactic (sentence structures and substructures such as clauses and phrases). Thus the grammar of a language is a description of all the elements in each of these levels.

In summary, structural linguistics rejects the use of meaning as a criterion for the analysis of language. Instead, it uses structural criteria to establish classifications of observed data. This discussion purposely skirts the controversy over the use of "meaning" in linguistic analysis. Some linguists would claim that phonological, morphological, and syntactic classification can be accomplished strictly on the basis of structural criteria as this discussion implies. Others would just as strongly contend that the structural techniques mask an appeal to meaning. That is, although the linguist may not know the meaning of a foreign language, his use of a native informant to make contrastive discriminations necessarily depends upon the native informant's knowledge of meaning.[7]

With its strong emphasis on oral language and the facts of language as it is actually used by native speakers, structural linguistics becomes almost necessarily involved in the analysis of differences among native speakers. Although the study of dialect patterns is a discipline with its own techniques and specialists, its close alliance to structural linguistics has led to its usual inclusion under this heading.

These, then, are the basic areas of structural linguistics—phonology, morphology, syntax, and dialectology. The discipline has had a profound effect upon the study of language because it gives a more scientific base to that study, freeing it from the incorrect, imprecise prejudices of early approaches and allowing a more accurate description of language.

The purpose for studying grammar, then, is simply to describe the structures in the language as it is observed in the speech of native speakers.

Ordinarily, secondary school teaching will ignore the level of significant sounds. Here are three sample exercises with parts of speech, in the domain of morphology. Since most students will know the traditional parts of speech, it is often necessary to expose the weaknesses of those preconceptions.

WORKSHEET

What part of speech do we usually call the following words?

barn	barns
door	doors
toy	toys
motor	motors
top	tops
table	tables
window	windows
taxi	taxis

As what part of speech are the underlined words used in the following sentences?

1. The barn door is open.
2. The door handle was broken.
3. The toy soldier stood on the shelf.
4. He bought a motor driven toy.
5. He bought a boat motor.
6. The table top was too high for the little boy to reach.
7. The top table was too high for the little boy to reach.
8. The window washer unhooked his safety strap.
9. The taxi driver looked tired.

These concepts can be extended by asking students to use them in other situations.

WORKSHEET

Name the part of speech of the underlined words:

This joke will <u>floor</u> you.
We must <u>table</u> the motion until the next meeting.
A painting <u>mirrors</u> the real world.
We should <u>bottle</u> this sunshine.
I <u>picture</u> her as a blond.
The police will <u>book</u> him for hitchhiking.
You must <u>face</u> the problem.
You shouldn't <u>horn</u> in on the conversation.
We can <u>nail</u> it shut.
They will <u>page</u> you on the loudspeaker.

If you saw the underlined words *without* a context, what part of speech would you call them? Why?

Put an X through the noun or pronoun that comes before the underlined word in each sentence.

Circle the other words that come before the underlined words. What kind of word do we usually call them? What two kinds of words often come before the main verb position?

If the students are determinedly attached to the traditional definitions, another approach is the use of nonsense language. In a sentence such as "The farplest brugerts grubbled forpingly" students can easily identify parts of speech. Such nonsense makes the point that they must be responding to clues other than the "meaning" of words. With such an example, we observe the use of positional and formal characteristics as bases for discriminating classes of words.

Enough of this kind of instruction effectively convinces both students and teacher that the traditional definitions are extremely difficult to work with. After such discussion, however, it is not necessary to *discard* the traditional definitions of parts of speech. The point is, rather, that such definitions have weaknesses, specifically that they are too vague to be operational, that they do not distinguish between form and function, and that they rely on other criteria such as position and form that are not made explicit. With these reservations, the students may continue to use the intuitions on which traditional definitions are based. Also, this procedure of identifying the weaknesses of a particular approach to the structure of language will be equally applicable to the other approaches. No presently available grammatical system solves all the problems of language structure, so students should get into the habit of discovering both

---

WORKSHEET

Column A	Column B	
1. boy	boys	
2. girl	girls	
3. dog	dogs	
4. book	books	
5. church	churches	
6. branch	branches	
7. trench	trenches	
8. ditch	ditches	
9. man		
10. child		
11. tooth		
12. mouse		

The change from Column A to Column B is not the same for items 1 through 4 as it is for 5 through 8. But we can show that the different changes "mean" the same thing by building two positions, or frames, one for Column A and the other for Column B.

Column A frame: One _____ is here.
Column B frame: Two _____ are here.

By using these two frames, fill in Column B for items 9 through 12. Underline the part of the word that shows the change.

Build three frames that will show that all the changes in these words have the same "meaning."

Column A	Column C	Column E
swim	swam	swimming
fold	folded	folding
sleep	slept	sleeping
fight	fought	fighting

Column A frame:
Column C frame:
Column E frame:

---

weaknesses and strengths. Such procedures also suggest the kind of testing that is appropriate to possible language principles. From this kind of beginning, both students and teacher are free to suggest and test assumptions about categories and relationships in language. The teacher should be warned, however, that students who have thus been put on their guard will be difficult to deal with. Their rigor and questioning will be extremely disconcerting if the teacher wants them to take something for granted. But with preconceptions reasonably well destroyed, the class can continue their study of language in an unbiased way.

Structural linguists use many approaches to the analysis of relationships within the sentence, but the most common one is immediate constituent analysis, usually abbreviated IC analysis. This method assumes that the sentence may be analyzed by dichotomous cuts to the level of individual words, and sometimes morphemes. This is an illustration:

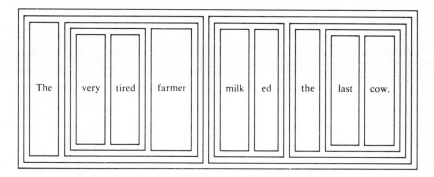

The diagram is often referred to as "Chinese boxes" and is far more easily and clearly illustrated by a branching tree diagram as follows:

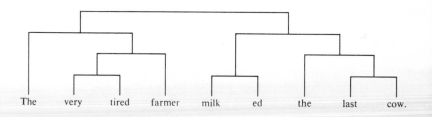

Although many sentences yield nicely to this kind of diagramming, many do not, and the teacher left to his own devices in the matter of producing practice exercise material is cautioned to test sentences before presenting them to the class. Presumably, the strength of IC analysis is that the technique does not require that the word order of the sentence be changed to fit the analysis as is the case with the familiar sentence diagrams of traditional school grammar. However, this advantage is not always possible with IC analysis. For example, the reader might try to develop a nice, neat tree diagram for the following:

I first saw them working on the road.

The problem, of course, is deciding with which constituent "working on the road" belongs, "I" or "them."

Transformational–Generative Grammar

American interest in transformational-generative grammars burst into full bloom with the publication of Chomsky's *Syntactic Structures* in 1957.[8] In addition to the problems involved in the IC analysis of such ambiguous sentences as "I first saw them working on the road," Chomsky pointed out a number of other difficulties.

The central difficulty of structural linguistics is the basic view of the fundamental nature of language. Transformational grammarians hold that language is not simply the spoken language. Any corpus can never represent the whole language no matter how large that corpus might be. Whatever anyone says will represent only a selection of all that it is possible for him to say. Thus, any recorded corpus of actual speech is essentially accidental. Furthermore, however accurate a description of what has been heard might be, that description does not explain how the sentences were formed nor does it predict what other sentences might be formed. Beyond not explaining what could occur, descriptive techniques, because they are limited to actual observations, can never explain utterances that *can not* occur in a language. For example, no English speaker would ever produce a word like *rlisw (the asterisk preceding a hypothetical form is a convention used in language notation). The form *rlisw cannot occur, not because the consonant clusters are themselves unpronounceable in English (since "swirl" contains the same clusters), but for some deeper reason. Likewise no English speaker would produce such a sentence as: *running stops of into tables from nothing over can house, although each word is an English word.

There are limitations to the use of frames (as in the third worksheet above) in generalizing rules about relationships of clusters within a sentence. For example, one adjective frame in English is as follows:

The _____ noun

Many adjectives will fit into the slot in such a phrase as "the _____ man": "old," "young," "decrepit," or "happy," as examples. However, if the noun in the phrase is changed to "typewriter" yielding "the _____ typewriter," we find that while "old," and possibly "decrepit" will fit into the slot, "happy" will fit only as a metaphor and "young" will not fit at all, since the semantically appropriate contrast for "old" with inanimate nouns is "new." The structuralists' avoidance of meaning and reliance on structure in analysis results in a failure of frames to account for such idiosyncracies of language.

Rejecting the view that the whole of language is contained in actually observed utterances, transformational grammars present the view that a language is an abstract entity and that the utterances actually spoken represent epiphenomenal evidence of the existence of the abstract language. Many regard the ideas of Ferdinand de Saussure who developed a similar dichotomy of *langue* and *parole* as the source of this view of the nature of language.[9]

Any grammar of a language should be understood as a theory of that language. Through his experience with his language the native speaker intuits the grammar of his language. The task of the grammarian is to state explicitly what the rules of this grammar are.

An English sentence is seen in essence as a "deep structure" containing elements of semantic content such as *boy play. The rules of the grammar act upon this deep structure and result in the "surface structure" that actually occurs: "The boy is playing." This sentence is only one of many possible surface structures that the grammar might generate: "A boy plays; a boy does play; a boy was playing; was a boy playing; where is the boy playing; etc."

The purpose of studying grammar, then, is to develop the rules that will explain how surface structures are generated from deep structures and to state these rules so that they have the widest possible generality in their application. It should be clearly understood that this grammar in no way should be related to the psychological processes behind human speech or writing, at least at the present stage of development of the science. For example, Emmon Bach wrote in 1964:

"A grammatical theory is not a direct model of the user of a language (either speaker or hearer)."[10]

Chomsky wrote in 1965:

"To avoid what has been a continuing misunderstanding, it is perhaps worthwhile to reiterate that a generative grammar is not a model for a speaker or a hearer. It attempts to characterize in the most neutral possible terms the knowledge of the language that provides the basis for actual use of language by a speaker-hearer."[11]

Ronald Wardhaugh wrote in 1969:

"It is important to reemphasize one crucial point about grammar and rules. The grammar and its rules are not a characterization of performance. They are not intended to be a model of how sentences are actually produced or understood by speakers—that is, a model of what speakers actually do in constructing sentences. The rules are not rules of behavior, nor do they have any necessary psychological correlates. Grammars generate sentences and descriptions; speakers produce sentences; generate and produce are not synonymous. It may eventually prove to be the case that the rules do correlate closely with psychological processes, but at the present time no such correlation is claimed for them. It may be the case, too, that a competence model of language underlies a performance model of language in some very simple way, but so far it is not clear how linguistic competence relates to the various kinds of linguistic performance."[12]

Instruction in transformational grammar begins with the assumption that a student has mastered certain fundamental concepts: he knows what the parts of speech are and can define these in an unambiguous way as well as being able to identify them in sentences; he knows what a well-formed Eng-

lish sentence is and what clauses and phrases are. The common procedure is
to present unproblematical sentences for IC analysis by students who use tree
diagrams. Next, students are taught a notation system that makes a branching tree diagram a more general statement of relationship. Take, for example,
a simpler version of the sentence used earlier: The farmer milks the cow.

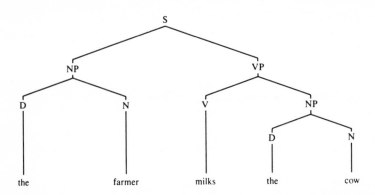

The abbreviations at the nodes of the branches have the following meanings:

S = sentence; NP = noun phrase; VP = verb phrase; D = determiner;
N = noun; V = verb.

When skill in such diagramming of simple declarative sentences is evident, the class is taught to reduce these to algebra-like formulations:

$$
\begin{aligned}
S &\longrightarrow NP_1 + VP \\
NP_1 &\rightarrow D + N_1 \\
VP &\rightarrow V + NP_2 \\
NP_2 &\rightarrow D + N_2 \\
D &\longrightarrow \text{the} \\
V &\longrightarrow \text{milks} \\
N_1 &\longrightarrow \text{farmer} \\
N_2 &\longrightarrow \text{cow}
\end{aligned}
$$

The abbreviations have the same meaning as in the tree diagram, and the
arrow should be read as: "may be rewritten as." Thus the student has learned
to use "rewrite rules" in formulating an abstract analysis of a sentence.

The next step is to recognize that any simple declarative sentence having
the verb in the active voice will always have as constituents the elements
NP + VP, and that the irreducible kernels of these constituents will be a
noun and a verb respectively. Thus the fundamental components of the deep
structure as presented in current secondary texts, are the noun and the verb.

The next step is learning how surface structures are generated from deep
structures. Given the same elements of the deep structure, farmer and milk,
how is the following surface structure generated?

Does the farmer milk the cow?

From the deep structure, "farmer milk," the surface structure, "the farmer milks the cow," was generated. If different rules had been applied, the surface structure, "the farmer does milk the cow," would have been generated. It is clear that one rule is necessary to transform the "milk" of the deep structure to "does milk" in the surface structure, a rule that governs introducing the auxiliary "does." In order to introduce the appropriate auxiliary, it is necessary to supply information about tense with the semantic input of the verb in the deep structure. Since "is milking" is an acceptable option to "does milk" a selectional rule is also applied to the deep structure.

In order to generate the question, in addition to transforming the verb to verb + auxiliary, it is necessary to use a rule that shifts the auxiliary to a position before "farmer" in the surface structure. Rewrite rules cannot account for introducing auxiliaries and shifting them about in generating surface structures. The generic name for the new rules is "transformational" rules, hence the characterization "transformational generative" grammars. (In passing, it is interesting to note that De Saussure among others has proposed generative grammars that are not transformational in character, but that propose other theories explaining how sentences are generated.[13])

The formulation that expresses the generation of "Does the farmer milk the cow" from the deep structure "farmer milk" is the following:

$$\text{farmer} + \text{milk} + \text{present} \xrightarrow{\text{Q yes/no}} \text{does the farmer milk the cow}$$

or the more general form:

$$\text{NP} + \text{VP} + \text{tense} \xrightarrow{\text{Q yes/no}} \text{Aux} + \text{D} + \text{N} + \text{V} + \text{D} + \text{N}$$

The double arrow in the formulation should read "is transformed by" and the superscript over the double arrow "the rules governing questions of the 'yes/no' type." There are question transformation rules of another type since not all English questions can be answered by "yes" or "no" as is the case for the one in this surface structure.

This formulation implies other, preliminary formulations that must be understood. One of the preliminary formulations is the rewrite rule governing Aux (the auxiliary that is chosen). In generating the surface structure, two options were available: "does milk," "is milking." The choice of the second option implicitly demands the change of the verb to its participial form. The rewrite rule for the auxiliary is stated as follows:

$$\text{Aux} \rightarrow \begin{Bmatrix} \text{does} \\ \text{is} \ldots \text{ing} \end{Bmatrix}$$

Further, the semantic content of the verb "milk" implies the existence of the complement "cow." Only a few words may substitute for "cow": "goat, camel" and perhaps others. Although metaphors permit such substitutions as "lines" (the farmer milks his lines in the play), most other nouns could never appear as complements: *the farmer milks gasoline. Other deep structures prohibit noun complements: *farmer remain; while others, admitting noun complements, prohibit those implied by "milk": *farmer sing.

Of course, work with transformational rules need not begin with those governing yes/no questions. Any of the other transformations and the resulting analyses and syntheses will support the instruction. The intention is to express all the rules and to specify all the semantic content of all the deep structure inputs in the most explicit and at the same time most generally applicable statements as is possible.

Summary

This cursory and somewhat impressionistic review of the alternative grammars that are being taught in the schools today is, in large measure, gratuitous. Teachers with the appropriate training have no need of such a review, and they should have little difficulty in planning their instruction. On the other hand, since this review cannot possibly substitute for such training, the untrained person can make no use of it in instructional planning. It has been offered simply as an overview of what is involved in grammar teaching today.

Although we have examined traditional school grammar because it is used in many places, the authors state emphatically that such instruction is at present indefensible. The ill-informed assumptions that the written language is somehow superior to speech and that language change is equivalent to degradation are unsupportable. The purpose underlying the instruction, that of effecting improvement in speech and writing, has been discredited by overwhelming empirical evidence. The inconsistent formulations of the grammar itself have been discredited to the extent that ". . . it has been very hard to get traditional materials published . . ."[14]

As for structural linguistics, the transformational grammarians have shown a great many weaknesses in that view of the nature of language, in the procedures of analysis, and in the results of the analyses. Generally, transformational grammar has superseded descriptive grammar as far as academic approbation is concerned. Beyond this, there is some question as to the value of the classroom study of the material since the purpose of the study is to provide an accurate description of the language. Why should native speakers need a description of the language that they already know and use? Certainly, such study is defensible on the grounds of the humanistic argument that all human endeavors are worthy of study. This argument could admit any area, even bricklaying, for curriculum consideration. However, since all topics may be supported by reference to humanistic ideals, all are in competition for teachers' and students' time and energy. Since no assertion has been made about the consequences of achieving an accurate description of a language, should such a description be achieved, one wonders if grammar study must exist as an end in itself, essentially.

Certainly work in dialects needs some foundation from descriptive linguistics. It may be the case that stylistic analysis can be done satisfactorily in no other way since other approaches tend to result in ambiguous statements about style. However, even granting the possible use of descriptive grammar in these other areas of study, one must decide on how much time may be devoted to grammar study per se. Unless the teacher has these other goals in mind, the value of learning about descriptive linguistics in the secondary school seems questionable.

In view of the disclaimers of the use of their grammar as models of the behavior of speakers or writers that have been made by the transformational grammarians themselves, it is doubtful that this study can have much value for high school students. The purpose of the grammarian is to express a coherent theory of language. If the native speaker does not need a description of the language he uses, certainly, a theory of that language could be of little consequence to him. At best, classroom work in developing such a theory without the hope that it refers to actual human language practice must be regarded as dilletantism in secondary school classes.

Generally, the purposes of the study argue against any extensive pursual of grammar in secondary school. Additionally, most teachers are not well enough trained to handle the teaching. Beyond this, the classroom experience of students when they study grammar tends to be extraordinarily dull as well as fruitless. In view of these considerations, except for a special elective course available to those who show an inclination toward the study of grammar, that study should most certainly be minimized in secondary schools, if not eliminated altogether. As Owen Thomas, a transformational grammarian, has stated in the final chapter of his book, *Transformational Grammar and the Teacher of English:*

"A child should study language rather than grammar."[15]

NOTES

1. Squire, James R. and Roger K. Applebee. *High School English Instruction Today: The National Study of High School English Programs* (Champaign: National Council of Teachers of English, 1968), p. 144.

2. a. *The National Interest and the Teaching of English,* NCTE number 19704 (Champaign: National Council of Teachers of English, 1961).

   b. *The National Interest and the Continuing Education of the Teachers of English,* NCTE number 19606. (Champaign: National Council of Teachers of English, 1964).

3. Long, Ralph B. "English Grammar in the 1970's," *College English,* Vol. 31, No. 8, May 1970.

4. Gleason, H. A., Jr. *Linguistics and English Grammar.* (New York: Holt, Rinehart, Winston, 1965), p. 29.

5. Fries, Charles C. *The Structure of English.* (New York: Harcourt, Brace and Jovanovich, 1952), pp. 9–19.

6. Gleason, *op. cit.,* pp. 31–47.

7. Winter, Werner. "Form and Meaning in Morphological Analysis," *Linguistics,* 3, January 1964.

8. Chomsky, Noam. *Syntactic Structures.* Mouton and Company, Printers, The Hague, Netherlands, 1957.

9. De Saussure, Ferdinand. *Cours de Linguistique Generale,* Payot, Paris, 1949 (developed by Charles Bally and Albert Sechehaye).

10. Bach, Emmon. *An Introduction to Transformational Grammars.* (New York: Holt, Rinehart and Winston, 1964), p. 186.

11. Chomsky, Noam. *Aspects of a Theory of Syntax.* (Cambridge: M.I.T. Press, 1965), p. 9.

12. Wardhaugh, Ronald. *Reading: A Linguistic Perspective* (New York: Harcourt, Brace and Jovanovich, 1969), p. 50.

13. De Saussure, *op. cit.*

14. Long, *op. cit.,* p. 766.

15. Thomas, Owen. *Transformational Grammar and the Teacher of English.* (New York: Holt, Rinehart and Winston, 1965), p. 209.

SUGGESTIONS FOR FURTHER READING

1. NELSON FRANCES. *The Structure of American English.* New York: Ronald Press, 1958. A basic comprehensive text of the structural linguist's analysis of language, including a chapter by Raymond McDavid introducing the study of dialects.

2. OWEN THOMAS. *Transformational Grammar and the Teacher of English.* New York: Holt, Rinehart and Winston, 1965. An introduction to the procedures and results of transformational-generative grammar with comments on its value to the teacher of English.

3. OTTO JESPERSEN. *Growth and Structure of the English Language.* New York: Doubleday, 1955. An exemplar of the careful thorough study of language structure by earlier "traditional" grammarians.

Semantics | 19

Basic Concepts

Semantics is the study of the meanings of words. Theoretically, we could choose any verbal or written symbol to stand for anything or any group of things; the symbols of language are arbitrary in this respect. But practically, our choice of symbols is, of course, not arbitrary. Words can communicate only if we agree upon what they stand for. Language is, therefore, a social contract.

It is such an intimate part of our lives that we often treat it as if it had a life of its own, as if it did things. But it is we who do things, who "abstract," "connote," and "define." These functions are inaccurately ascribed to language because to do otherwise demands awkward circumlocutions. Therefore, whenever language is the subject of an active verb in this chapter, the device is a shortcut and not an implication of word magic.

The *denotation* of a word is that set of things that the word stands for or represents. The denotation of the word "horse," for example, includes all those animals for which the word stands. Similarly, the denotation of the word "water" includes all that substance for which the word stands.

A word is not the same as the thing it denotes, however, because it represents only some of its characteristics. The word calls our attention to, is associated with, or abstracts certain aspects of real objects. The word "horse," for example, abstracts only certain characteristics of its denotation and does not give information about the differences that exist among the things denoted—their color, size, speed, breed, length of mane, intelligence, and so on. Similarly, the word "water" includes, among other things, mud puddles, distilled water, the ocean, and rain.

Words are also indefinite in their denotations. If we tried to give the perfect, or definitive, denotative definition of a word, it would be impossible to do so because it would be impossible to agree exactly upon all the things that should be assembled to give the perfect denotative definition. What about ponies? What about those tiny ancestors of the horse? What about those things on merry-go-rounds? What about that stuffed toy horse in the baby's crib? What about mules? Do these belong in the set of things denoted by the word "horse"? If not, what set do they belong to? Are ponies a subset of the set "horses"? Are merry-go-round horses "wooden, half-sized models of horses?" Or are they models of ponies? Such considerations may seem to be splitting hairs, but the consequences are extremely important. Since words abstract only certain characteristics of things, and since we cannot define exactly the characteristics that they abstract, we are in constant danger of using words that identify different characteristics for the listener than they do for the speaker. Since we use these words that identify a variety of characteristics of a large group of objects in connection with specific objects, we are in danger of having the listener associate different characteristics with the specific object than we intended. We are thus in danger of identifying the set of objects as identical rather than identical in only certain abstracted characteristics. In short, a word is an abstraction that identifies only certain, not totally unambiguous, characteristics of a thing or set of things.

When we try to define words, we do not usually attempt a denotative definition—that is, assemble a group of things that are identified by the word. Instead, we define it by giving—in other words—a list of those characteristics that the word abstracts. This kind of definition is called the *informative connotation* of the word. Such a definition is never totally complete or totally accurate for two reasons. First, the denotative definition, as we have pointed out, is not totally accurate. Second, the informative connotation can never perfectly match the denotative characteristics for the same reason. If each of us were to be as exact as possible, language would still display these inaccuracies.

But we do not try to be as exact as possible. Each of us is limited to his own experiences and consequently a different set of characteristics that we ascribe to words, both in denotation and informative connotation. In addition, we are sloppy in our use of language, accepting the inexact match between the characteristics we abstract from a word and those that our listeners abstract from the same word. Otherwise, we would have to spend our lives qualifying for exactness and specificity. In the preface to *Semantic Analysis,* Paul Ziff says, "some years ago while working on a manuscript in aesthetics I thought it would be helpful to say at least roughly what the phrase 'good painting' means in English . . . But then I began to wonder what had led me to say what I did . . . And so I worked back and back to the beginning of this essay."[1] The result was a 247-page book.

The desire to communicate many things is in constant conflict with the desire to communicate exactly. We are constantly deciding how exact we need to be in order to communicate adequately. The abstract character of language allows us to communicate at the same time that it limits the exactness of our communication. Language simplifies through abstraction, but its simplification is both a vice and a virtue.

Some words are more abstract than others. The words used as examples thus far—horse and water—are concrete in that they refer to things that can be touched. They are names of categories and, as such, general rather than specific. The contrast between general and specific is, however, a relative matter. For example, "thoroughbred" is more specific than "horse" because it names fewer touchable objects, but it is more general than "Percheron" because it names more objects. Although the words used as examples may differ on the general-specific scale, they are all concrete because they name real things. (Although the distinction between the general-specific scale and the abstract-concrete scale seems quite clear when presented with these illustrations, it will not hold generally; their interrelations are far more complex than this discussion suggests. In general usage, the two scales are interchanged indiscriminately.) The word "justice" is more abstract than "horse" because there is no "thing" that the word denotes, although it refers to relationships among real (sometimes), perceivable events. Prepositions are abstract in the same way; they refer to relationships and are extremely difficult to define with an informative connotation. (Try to define, for example, "on" in "The book is 'on' the table," and "The light is 'on' the ceiling.") Other function words are even more difficult to define descriptively—for example, "is" in "Julius Caesar 'is' the hero of the book." The words of grammar are abstract because they refer to attributes or relational qualities of words rather than real things. In fact, words that refer to words (like "verb") or words that are used to describe language (like "semantics") have a special name—"metalanguage." The word "abstract" is yet more abstract. It refers to a lack of concreteness in qualities that have been in themselves abstracted from real things. In other words, it is a characteristic of characteristics.

Affective connotation refers to the values that people give to words because of the attitudes and values that they have toward the things that words represent. The word "policeman," for example, represents, or stands for, a group of people whose characteristics include enforcement of the law. We could add many other characteristics to identify the informative connotations of the word. If anyone disagreed with such a carefully constructed definition, we could say that he was at fault because he did not adequately understand the "meaning" of the word. But if someone were to say that a policeman is a vicious, sadistic persecutor of the poor, we cannot say that his definition of the word is wrong. We can say that the affective connotations that he associates with the word "policeman" are different from ours. Or we might more probably say that his attitude toward policemen is different from ours. Notice the shift in the previous sentence. The focus has changed from metalanguage —his association with the *word*—to language—his attitudes toward the *thing*. We constantly get our reactions and feelings toward things mixed up, tied up, or associated with our reactions to words. These feelings and reactions, attitudes toward and values given to the things that words represent are the affective connotations of words. Take any four-letter Anglo-Saxon obscenity. Its physical characteristics as black print on white page would be the same as any other word on this page, but if it were there in print, it would cause a stronger response than the other words. Those responses are the affective connotation of the word. These affective connotations may differ between individuals even more than the informative connotations they associate with words.

Differences of affective connotation are so strong that they often lead to new words. The present use of "fuzz" for "policeman" is one example. The two words are apparently synonymous in their informative connotations and apparently differ only in their affective connotations. Note that the word "synonym" in no way distinguishes between informative and affective connotation and is, consequently, ambiguous and inexact.

Differences in affective connotation are also evident in changes in meaning. In the early part of the twentieth century, the word "square" was used in sentences such as "He's a real square shooter." Informatively, the connotation is similar to that of "honest." Affectively, the connotation is one of praise and positive feeling. In the 1940s and 1950s, the word "square" meant something different. Informatively, the connotations are still close to those of the word "honest," although there is obviously some shift. Affectively, the connotations have reversed to condemnation and negative feeling. This kind of change in meaning obviously involves consideration of the metaphoric use of words; in neither case are the characteristics of the geometric shape abstracted in the word "square" associated with the people with whom the word "square" is associated. Also, this kind of change in meaning involves sarcasm, or the purposeful use of a word to represent characteristics antithetically related to its usual meaning.

Up to this point, we have indicated that words often represent some real thing or things (denotation); that they represent only certain characteristics of these things (abstraction); that they are not definite in their meanings; that they vary on a continuum of general-specific and on a continuum of abstract-concrete; that the communication made possible by words is both a vice and a virtue; that we can define words by citing either their informative connotations, their affective connotations, or both. But we have dealt with all these characteristics of words *in isolation*. Now we must consider the effect of putting words together.

If we were to come across an essay entitled "Transportation in the Glorious 1980s," we would be faced with an ambiguity created by the possibility of sarcasm in the word "glorious." The only way we would be able to determine whether the word represents positive or negative affective connotations is to read the essay. (Note that the informative connotation of "glorious" is merely a statement of its affective connotations. Incidentally, the usual informative connotation has changed from the obsolete "boastful or vainglorious" to its present "praiseworthy,"[2] a shift from negative to positive affective connotation.) The meaning of the word "glorious" in the essay's title is not determined in this case by its general usage, nor by the informative and affective connotation reflected in a dictionary, but rather by its context—the other words that surround it. Of course, the meaning of the word in this context is partly determined by our previous knowledge of its usual meaning. Many meanings could fill the slot "Transportation in the _____ 1980s." The presence of the word "glorious" in this context reduces the possibilities drastically. In fact, only from the context of the essay could we determine that the usual affective connotations of "glorious" are inappropriate. The conflict of these connotations creates a tension of apparent ambiguity. Our knowledge of sarcasm resolves the ambiguity by allowing us to take "glorious" to connote the opposite of its usual connotation.

Other verbal contexts limit the possible meanings of a word even more exactly. "Producing musical notes by means of the voice is called _____." Few words will fit the restrictions of this verbal context. This is not surprising when we consider the fact that a definition, except in those very few cases where we point to a thing, is always the supplying of verbal context. The point is that the meanings of words depend to a great extent upon their relationship to other words. Consider again the word "glorious." How do we know what it means? How would we explain to someone else what it means? We cannot point to things; the word is not denotative. We can only use other words—splendid, resplendent, delightful, magnificent, praiseworthy, brilliant, worthy of glory. If our audience doesn't know those words, we can try to define one of them: splendid—gorgeous, sublime, superb. Or we can say that it means "very, very good" or "I like it very much." But we're still caught in the same problem. How do we know what "good" and "like" mean? At this point we might be willing to say that most language is a vast tautology. We could surely support such a statement with evidence from many conversations in which we have been involved.

The problems of semantics, then, lie in the relationships of language to external reality (denotation), of language to people's attitudes and values (affective connotation), and of word meanings within the language (informative connotation; context).

Evaluation of Curricular Importance

Will an understanding of these concepts increase the students' literacy?

1. Functionally? Yes. The ability to use context to define word meaning aids students throughout their lives in the most basic aspects of word comprehension. Recognition of the use of words with powerful affective connotations will help them understand and control their responses to mass media—advertising, news, editorials, political propaganda.

2. Educationally? Yes. Varying the levels of abstraction is an important skill of good writing. The ability to build definitions will aid students in any course.

3. In terms of the English curriculum? Yes. The interactions of words as parts of a single context is basic to the study of poetry. Sensitivity to subtleties of meaning plays an important part in both composition and literature. The basic concepts of semantics are more important to the study of English than the concepts of any other approach to language study.

4. Linguistically? Yes. The major weakness of most instruction in grammar/linguistics is that it is treated as an esoteric closed system unrelated to problems that are meaningful to students. The grounding of semantics in meaning is a significant introduction to the study of language and provides a basis for later more rigorous study.

Developing Curricular Materials for Basic Semantic Concepts

First, let us deal with the idea that words are arbitrary symbols that are useful for communication only because of the social contract to which we adhere. This idea involves many concepts—arbitrary, symbol, communication, social contract—each of which the student must understand in order to grasp this basic idea of semantics. The creativity of the teacher is important in finding ways to make these concepts clear to the student. One way to introduce the concept of symbols is to ask the students about the relationships between a word, a picture, an object. The teacher puts a picture of an apple on the board. The dialogue might go like this:

Teacher: What is this?
Student: An apple.
Teacher: Can you smell it or take a bite of it?
Student: No.
Teacher: Is it really an apple?
Student: No, it's a picture of an apple.

Then the teacher writes the word "apple" on the board.

Teacher: What is this?
Student: The word "apple."
Teacher: Is it a real apple?
Student: No.
Teacher: But we use it when we want to talk about the thing it stands for. What do we call a thing that stands for something else?
Student: A symbol.
Teacher: Is the picture a symbol?

Student: Yes.
Teacher: Is the word a symbol?
Student: Yes.

Admittedly, this is a simple dialogue, but it establishes the basic concept that words are symbols and not the things they stand for. Further, by having students write out characteristics that they associate with "school," it is simple to demonstrate that words mean different things to different people.

How can we introduce the idea of the arbitrary nature of linguistic symbols? We could continue the previous dialogue by asking the students the difference between the picture symbol and the word symbol. As soon as they respond with the phrase "looks like," the dialogue easily moves to the arbitrary character of word symbols. A second approach might be the presentation of a group of words from different languages that all refer to the same set of objects, followed by the appropriate dialogue that leads very naturally into the idea of social contract. Another approach that leads to the idea of social contract is that of making up words. The teacher points to the flat surface of the table and says, "bres." The students are puzzled. The teacher points rather frantically at the table and says more urgently, "bres." Finally one of the students says, "Oh, you mean the table!" And the teacher looks pleased and relieved and says, nodding his head in agreement, "bres." Then he points to the chair and says, "bros." This time the students catch on more quickly. Then he points to one of the chairs with a writing surface that the students use and says, "brosterbres." Perhaps returning to "bres" and "bros" separately will be necessary before the students catch on. Pointing to the parts of the students' desk, the teacher says "brosterbres." Then he continues. Pen is "glick," paperclip is "sloan," pen with clip is "glicktersloan," drawer is "floss," desk with drawer is "bresterfloss." Then he puts the compounds on the board: brosterbres, glicktersloan, and bresterfloss. "Ter," he asks, and the students—again the teacher may have to backtrack—respond "with." Then he asks, "Aren't these words as good as the ones we normally use." The discussion will point out not only the arbitrary nature of language but also the need for social agreement. Another approach is the use of readings that make the point, as the following lesson plan indicates.

Lesson Plan   The Arbitrary Nature of Linguistic Symbols

TERMINAL OBJECTIVE

To write a paragraph explaining the arbitrary nature of linguistic symbols using an example.

MEDIAL OBJECTIVES

1. To use the word "arbitrary" appropriately.
2. To answer the study guide questions for the reading selection.

3. To explain orally how the reading selection illustrates the arbitrary relation of words to their denotation and informative connotation.

PROCEDURES

1. Tell the students what the word "arbitrary" means and give them examples of arbitrary decisions, for example, deciding by a flip of the coin. Write the word on the board, and give the students examples of arbitrary and rational decisions to see if they can distinguish them. Review yesterday's lesson and ask them in what sense words are arbitrary.

2. Divide the class into homogeneous groups of four or five students and give them these instructions:

"Read the selection I am distributing. When you have finished, discuss the answers to the questions. When you have discussed all the questions, select someone in your group to explain the selection to the class."

3. As they begin, circulate among the groups, giving necessary background information about the selection. As they finish their group work, distribute copies of all the selections to all the groups. Reassemble the class and have a student group explain its selection after the rest of the class has read it.

4. Write a model paragraph with the class about one of the selections. Assign the writing of a similar paragraph about one of the other selections for homework.

EVALUATION

Use the criteria established in developing the model paragraph to evaluate the homework assignment.

EVERYTHING HAS A NAME from *The Story of My Life:*[3] by Helen Keller

The morning after my teacher came she led me into her room and gave me a doll. The little blind children at the Perkins Institution had sent it and Laura Bridgman had dressed it; but I did not know this until afterward. When I had played with it a little while, Miss Sullivan slowly spelled into my hand the word "d-o-l-l." I was at once interested in this finger play and tried to imitate it. When I finally succeeded in making the letters correctly I was flushed with childish pleasure and pride. Running downstairs to my mother I held up my hands and made the letters for doll. I did not know that I was spelling a word or even that words existed; I was simply making my fingers go in monkey-like imitation. In the days that followed I learned to spell in this uncomprehending way a great many words, among them *pin, hat, cup,* and a few verbs like *sit, stand,* and *walk.* But my teacher had been with me several weeks before I understood that everything has a name.

One day, while I was playing with my new doll, Miss Sullivan put my big rag doll into my lap also, spelled "d-o-l-l" and tried to make me understand that "d-o-l-l" applied to both. Earlier in the day we had had a tussle over the words "m-u-g" and "w-a-t-e-r." Miss Sullivan had tried to impress it upon me that "m-u-g" is *mug* and "w-a-t-e-r" is *water,* but I persisted in confounding the two. In despair she had dropped the subject for the time, only to renew it at the first opportunity. I became impatient at her repeated attempts and, seizing the new doll, I dashed it upon the floor.

We walked down the path to the well-house, attracted by the fragrance of the honeysuckle with which it was covered. Some one was drawing water and my teacher placed my hand under the spout. As the cool stream gushed over one hand she spelled into the other the word *water,* first slowly, then rapidly. I stood still, my whole attention fixed upon the motions of her fingers. Suddenly I felt a misty consciousness as of something forgotten—a thrill of returning thought; and somehow the mystery of language was revealed to me. I knew then that "w-a-t-e-r" meant the wonderful cool something that was flowing over my hand. That living word awakened my soul, gave it light, hope, joy, set it free! There were barriers still, it is true, but barriers that could in time be swept away.

I remember the morning that I first asked the meaning of the word, "love." This was before I knew many words. I had found a few early violets in the garden and brought them to my teacher. She tried to kiss me; but at that time I did not like to have any one kiss me except my mother. Miss Sullivan put her arm gently around me and spelled into my hand, "I love Helen."

"What is love?" I asked.

She drew me closer to her and said, "It is here," pointing to my heart, whose beats I was conscious of for the first time. Her words puzzled me very much, because I did not then understand anything unless I touched it.

I smelt the violets in her hand and asked, half in words, half in signs, a question which meant, "Is love the sweetness of flowers?"

"No," said my teacher.

Again I thought. The warm sun was shining on us.

"Is this not love?" I asked, pointing in the direction from which the heat came, "Is this not love?"

It seemed to me that there could be nothing more beautiful than the sun, whose warmth makes all things grow. But Miss Sullivan shook her head, and I was greatly puzzled and disappointed. I thought it strange that my teacher could not show me love.

A day or two afterward I was stringing beads of different sizes in symmetrical groups—two large beads, three small ones, and so on. I had made many mistakes, and Miss Sullivan had pointed them out again and again with gentle patience. Finally I noticed a very obvious error in the sequence and for an instant I concentrated my attention on the lesson and tried to think how I should have arranged the beads. Miss Sullivan touched my forehead and spelled with decided emphasis "Think."

In a flash I knew that the word was the name of the process that was going on in my head. This was my first conscious perception of an abstract idea.

ANSWER THE FOLLOWING QUESTIONS

1. Why did the first "finger play" not mean anything to Helen. What had she failed to do?
2. What was the first word that had meaning to her? Why was it easier at the well than it had been when the water was in the mug?
3. What does "abstract" mean?
4. Why were the words "love" and "think" so hard for Helen to learn?
5. If Helen had learned the motions for "think" as meaning "love," and the motions for "love" as meaning "think," would it have changed her knowledge? Would it have changed her ability to communicate?
6. In what sense are words arbitrary? In what sense are they not arbitrary? How does this selection show this?

Mark Twain, from *The Adventures of Huckleberry Finn*[4]

"Why, Huck, doan' de French people talk de same way we does?"

"No, Jim; you couldn't understand a word they said—not a single word."

"Well, now I be ding-busted! How do dat come?"

"I don't know; but it's so. I got some of their jabber out of a book. S'pose a man was to come to you and say Polly-voo-franzy—what would you think?"

"I wouldn' think nuffin I'd take en bust him over de head . . ."

"Shucks, it ain't calling you anything. It's only saying, do you know how to talk French?"

"Well, den, why couldn't he say it?"

"Why, he is a-saying it. That's a Frenchman's way of saying it."

"Well, it's a blame ridicklous way, en I doan' want to hear no mo' 'bout it. Dey ain' no sense in it."

"Looky here, Jim; does a cat talk like we do?"

"No, a cat don't."

"Well, does a cow?"

"No, a cow don't, nuther."

"Does a cat talk like a cow, or a cow talk like a cat?"

"No, dey don't."

"It's natural and right for 'em to talk different from each other, ain't it?"

"Course."

"And ain't it natural and right for a cat and a cow to talk different from us?"

"Why, mos' sholy it is."

"Well, then, why ain't it natural and right for a *Frenchman* to talk different from us? You answer me that."

"Is a cat a man, Huck?"

"No."

"Well, den, dey ain't no sense in a cat talkin' like a man. Is a cow a man?—er is a cow a cat?"

"No, she ain't either of them."

"Well, den, she ain't got no business to talk like either one er the yuther of 'em. Is a Frenchman a man?"

"Yes."

"Well, den' Dad blame it, why doan he talk like a man? You answer me dat!"

ANSWER THE FOLLOWING QUESTIONS

1. Why is Jim's criticism of Frenchmen unfair? What has he not understood about words?
2. What important problems has Jim recognized about language that comes from the arbitrary relation of words and things?
3. Answer Jim's last question.

Lewis Carroll, from *Through the Looking Glass:*[5]

"I don't know what you mean by 'glory,'" Alice said.

Humpty Dumpty smiled contemptuously. "Of course you don't—till I tell you. I meant 'there's a nice knock-down argument for you!'"

"But 'glory' doesn't mean 'a nice knock-down argument,'" Alice objected.

"When *I* use a word," Humpty Dumpty said, in a rather scornful tone, "it means just what I choose it to mean—neither more nor less."

"The question is," said Alice, "whether you *can* make words mean so many different things."

"The question is," said Humpty Dumpty, "which is to be master—that's all."

Jean Piaget, from *The Child's Conception of the World:*[6]

[A child is being questioned.] "Could the sun have been called 'moon' and the moon 'sun'—*No*—why not?—*Because the sun shines brighter than the moon.* . . . But if everyone had called the sun 'moon,' and the moon 'sun,' would we have known it was wrong?—*Yes, because the sun is always bigger, it always stays like it is and so does the moon.*—Yes, but the sun isn't changed, only its name. Could it have been called . . . etc.? —*No* . . ."

ANSWER THE FOLLOWING QUESTIONS

1. In what situations is it important for Humpty to use the meanings that other people do?
2. In what way are Humpty's problem and the child's problem the same? In what way are they exactly opposite problems?

3. Who is the master? Is the man the master of words or are words the master of the man? Use the word "arbitrary in your answer. Use the examples of both Humpty and the child in your answer.

Another basic concept of semantics is that words abstract only certain characteristics of the things they represent. Two procedures for introducing that concept follow.

Teacher: How many of you know what the word "woman" means?

Students: (All raise their hands.)

Teacher: Then picture a woman and on a piece of scratch paper answer these questions: How old is she? How tall is she? How much does she weigh? What color is her hair? What is she wearing? What is she doing?
Do you expect your answers to agree with the other students in the class?

Students: No.
The teacher lets some of the students read their answers.

Teacher: Why did you say you knew what the word "woman" means if it means different things to each of you?

As the discussion continued, it would arrive finally at the characteristics that are included in the informative connotation of the word "woman" and would in the process indicate numerous characteristics that are not part of that informative connotation. Another approach is to play a game similar to twenty questions, in which the teacher answers only yes or no to the students' questions seeking the object he has in mind. As the game proceeds, the teacher diagrams student questions on the board:

thing
mineral
movable
bigger than a bread basket
transportation
car
station wagon
Chevrolet
Chevy II
the teacher's car

Analysis of the pattern they followed from less to more limited categories leads to conclusions about the abstract nature of words.

Given a set of planned activities, the next step is to integrate reading and writing activities when they can be an integral part of the development of the semantic concepts. Of course, it is not necessary to have language, literature, and composition activities for each classroom period. But it is appropriate to integrate these activities and build skill in each when such integration aids in fulfilling the objectives of instruction. For example, the teacher might wish to integrate these skills in the study of levels of abstraction. If he were to write out his rough plan for the lesson, it might take the form below:

LESSON ON LEVELS OF ABSTRACTION

PURPOSE:

See that different words are at different levels of generality and abstraction.
Be able to use principle in questioning reading.
Use principle to improve writing.

PREVIOUS LESSONS:

1. Arbitrary, symbolic, contractual nature of language.
2. Denotational meaning.

STEPS

1. Introduce concept.

Objectives:	To discriminate words in terms of the number of referents they have.
	To determine which words have little denotational meaning (for example, function words and abstract words).
Medial Objectives:	Understand "general," "specific," "abstract," "concrete."
	Spelling.
	Recognize that terms are relative.
Activities:	Twenty questions game, discussion.
	Building ladder of abstraction.

2. Use concept in reading.

Objectives:	To find words that are abstract/general.
	To find part of passage that makes these words more specific/concrete.
	To state possible communication failures.
Activities:	Reading and discussion.
Medial Objectives:	Vocabulary in articles.

3. Use concept in writing.

Objectives:	To make writing more specific.
	Define terms.
Activities:	Practice definitions.
	Practice specifying general/abstract statements.
	Rewriting.

Notice that the statements of purposes, objectives, and activities lead logically to the statement of additional medial objectives, which in turn require additional activities. For example, a later curricular objective of defining *per genus et differentiam* suggests that the activity of building a ladder of abstraction should not be the simple listing from general to specific as was suggested above, but should rather include branching:

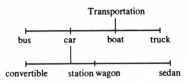

In this way the student will be better prepared to write definitions when he comes to that activity. In addition, it is necessary to repeat this and other activities often enough for the student to gain fluency.

The teacher must give students class time to practice writing under his direction both in small groups and individually. The same kind of extension of activities is necessary to have them write about their reading. In other words, those writing activities involve medial objectives, and the teacher must plan to include the activities necessary to reach these medial objectives.

The teacher must also look carefully at all the activities to see what assumptions they imply about student ability. These assumptions in turn become the bases for additional medial objectives. The most obvious problem is vocabulary, its understanding, spelling, and usage. In the readings suggested are the words "tussle," "persisted," "confounding," "consciousness," and "contemptuously," which the teacher must explain to the students before they read. More important, the teacher must introduce words for the concepts of the lessons: "symbol," "symbolic," "symbolize," "arbitrary," "denotation," "denotes," "denotative," "informative," "connotation," "abstract," "define," "definition." If the students are to know and use these words (which is certainly not as important as understanding the ideas they represent), they must be taught. If they are to work in groups, they must be given the necessary direction to be able to proceed with a minimum of disturbance. All these factors become medial objectives. The results of this kind of analysis are the specific formulation of materials and activities. For example, the selection from Helen Keller, used in the lesson on levels of abstraction, would have a study guide like the following:[7]

STUDY GUIDE: Selection from *The Story of My Life* by Helen Keller

VOCABULARY:

flushed	tusssle	symmetrical
uncomprehending	confounding	sequence
		perception

1. In paragraphs one and two, Helen Keller knows both words and things. What does she fail to do?
2. In paragraph two, does "mug" have a referent? Does "water" have a referent?
3. Why is it easier for Helen Keller to understand "water" in the situation in paragraph three than in the situation in paragraph two?
4. Why are the words "love" and "think" more difficult for Helen Keller to understand than the words "mug" and "water"?
5. What events in the story illustrate the word "think"? the word "love"?

This introduction to abstract words in a text should be followed by an analysis of abstract words in other selections, such as the one below. Again students must be taught how to work with the concept.

WORKSHEET: Abstract Words

In both design and materials, the building is a major architectural innovation and is expected to exert a lasting influence on the planning of stadiums and exhibition halls of the future. Essentially it is a tent made of plastic, open on all sides except where the supporting cables are anchored to the earth. In sunlight the skin is translucent, and both the patterns created by the exterior cables and the flowered pattern of the interior are visible.

"Major architectural innovation" is an abstract phrase. Underline the words and phrases that make this abstract phrase more specific.

Such reading activities can be extended in length and sophistication as is appropriate for the particular class or individuals within the class. The writing activities can follow the pattern established by these reading activities. Students can be asked to specify such general statements as: The plane flew; the men shook hands; the woman drove the car, and so on.

The study of affective connotation begins with the distinctions among words with positive, neutral, and negative connotations. Students can begin with such simple examples as nag, horse, thoroughbred, and work with similar examples.

These activities can easily be extended into the analysis of advertisements and letters to the editor, both excellent sources of highly connotative writing. Again, more sophisticated students can work with more sophisticated ma-

WORKSHEET: Affective Connotations[8]

Below are thirty words or phrases. The eleven that are underlined have been put in the right place in the chart. Put the other nineteen in the chart. old, discreet, influential speaker, idealist, orator, officer of the law, tolerant, decayed, warmhearted, obedient, do-gooder, immigrant, rabble-rouser, humanitarian, cautious, Indian lover, official, alien, flatfoot, mature, cowardly, musky, bureaucrat, loyal, nondiscriminating, Pilgrim, slavish, sentimental, office-holder, detective.

Good connotation	*Little connotation*	*Bad connotation*
1. _____	cautious	_____
2. loyal		_____
3. _____	sentimental	_____
4. _____	old	_____
5. _____		Indian lover
6. _____	idealist	_____
7. Pilgrim		
8. orator	influential speaker	rabble-rouser
9. _____	office holder	_____
10. _____	_____	_____

LESSON PLAN: Principles of Advertisements

TEACHER INTRODUCTION: Men can be persuaded to believe many different things. Hitler persuaded the people of Germany that they should go to war. The casualties that resulted were 8,500,000 killed, 21,220,000 wounded, and 7,700,000 missing. Christ has influenced untold millions of people over the last 1900 years. Today in America alone there are approximately 120,900,000 Christians.

Both of these men, then, had a tremendous influence over other men, one for good, the other for evil. Both had the ability to persuade—to change the way men act. Why? How is it that men can be persuaded to do things? Well, let's see: Try this for me. Put your arms straight out in front of you. Go ahead, straight out in front of you. That's right. All right, now while your arms are in front of you, fold your hands. Got them folded? All right, now keeping your hands folded, raise them over your head. Fine, now you can put your arms down, because you have just been persuaded. You just went through a bunch of silly gestures. Why did you do it? You thought there was a reason for it, didn't you? You thought something was going to result from it, didn't you? In other words, just by asking you to do it, I had promised you something. I had promised you that it was worthwhile doing. And this is one of the basic ingredients behind the power of persuasion. People are persuaded to do things because the persuader gives them a promise of results. The promises aren't always stated in so many words, but they are usually there, lurking behind the words.

terials. Also, writing exercises involving differing points of view are obviously appropriate at this point.

The use of these concepts is, of course, an important step for students. The application in advertisements demands a more thorough investigation.

WORKSHEET I: Promises

Underline the promises in the following statements:

1. "Aw, please, Mom, let me go with you. I'll be good."
2. "O.K.! O.K.! I'll carry out the trash, but let me watch the rest of this program first."
3. "It's the first dance this year, and it won't cost much money!"
4. "If you let me get a driver's license, I'll wash the car every week!"
5. "I'm sorry, Dad, but if I didn't have to do so much work around the house, I'd study more."
6. "The needle will hurt just a little, but then you won't feel a thing when I pull the tooth."
7. Double your money back if not fully satisfied.
8. I can help you lose ten pounds in just two weeks. Send twenty-five cents for my booklet "How to Lose Weight."
9. "If you don't smoke until you're twenty-one, I'll give you one hundred dollars."
10. "If you aren't home by 11:30, you won't be allowed out of this house next week."

Of course, the reason for making the promise in each of these examples is that the speaker is trying to persuade the hearer to do something. In the following blanks, explain what it is that the speaker wants the hearer to do in each of the examples.

1._____
2._____
3._____
4._____
5._____
6._____
7._____
8._____
9._____
10._____

WORSHEET II: Promises

Fill in the blanks with the promises that advertisers might offer each of the following people:

1. A fat man_____

2. A student who is getting poor grades_____

3. A girl with a poor complexion_____

4. A boy who is skinny_____

5. A man who is poor_____

6. A mother who has a sick child_____

7. A man who wants a better job_____

WORKSHEET: Needs

Name the basic needs that are suggested by the following groups of promises:

1. Do people turn away when you talk to them? Try Sweetmint Gum to get rid of bad breath.
   Be the life of the party. Buy our book of magic and watch people flock around you.
   Lose that flabby fat and become a hit with the girls. Write for our six-week muscle-building course.
2. Too many debts? Too many bills? Not enough money? Call your nearest Friendly Finance office now!
   Earn money in your spare time! Send for our course in radio repair. Get your boss's job! Learn how to manage people and watch your salary rise!
3. Feel tired? Lifeless? Need pep? Try Peter Piper's Pick-me-up for that quick energy lift!
   Bouncing Flash shoes will help you win those races! Bouncing Flash shoes will keep you on the go! Bouncing Flash shoes will help you feel healthy! Be a bouncing flash! Buy Bouncing Flash shoes!
   From football to bowling. From golf to hockey. Champions prefer PEP breakfast food.
4. Be the Joneses that everyone tries to keep up with! Subscribe to Home-maker's Magazine to make your house the most beautiful on the block.
   Everyone will watch when you step out of your Arrow convertible. Everyone will envy you in your Arrow convertible. Buy Arrow and hit the bullseye.
   Only one man in a hundred is good enough to wear a Smithe Suit. Are you one man in a hundred?
5. Do the dishes, wash the clothes, make the beds, dress the children—too much to do? Save hours every day with an automatic dishwasher.
   Take a train! It's easier than driving.
   Any job, anytime, anywhere, it's easier and quicker with a Presto Pen.

Additional analysis of ads will lead the class to develop a list of key questions that seem to be most significant for analysis. They will probably include questions like—What does this ad do to attract your attention? What does it do to hold your attention? What promises does it make? What words are most connotative? What words are informative? What does the ad do to get you to act? What audience does it appeal to? What is its purpose?

With this kind of analysis behind them, the students can select a product and develop their own ads for that product.

Extension of Basic Semantic Concepts

The first unit obviously contains in embryonic form many concepts that are open to further development later in the curriculum. Even though the further development of some of them may be rejected as inappropriate to the curriculum, they are still important for the teacher to know. An uninformed teacher cannot determine their significance to the curriculum and will consequently be handicapped in creating a good one.

The ideas about definition introduced in the first unit are obviously inadequate if the informative connotations of words are as difficult to specify as we have suggested. The unit deals, not with the difficulty of defining, but rather with the basic technique of defining. Although definition may not be a necessity for functional literacy, it is certainly an important skill in terms of other criteria. It should be developed and reinforced in nearly every unit of instruction in English, but to insure its adequate elucidation it is treated here as an isolated subject of discussion. In actual classroom practice, it would be far better to incorporate various aspects of definition into those units in which they will be used. In this way definition would be treated more realistically— as a constantly developing set of skills—than it would be if it were isolated in the curriculum.

The first unit on semantics will accomplish the first step toward the development of definition skills. On its completion, the students will have become aware of the difficulties of specifying the informative connotations of words, will have recognized the arbitrary nature of categories, will have tried their hand at *per genus et differentiam* definitions, and will have had some experience with contextual definition. The purpose of additional instruction will be to develop further skill in these areas that have been already introduced and to introduce other techniques for definition.

First, words can be defined in nonverbal ways. Pointing is the basis of denotational definition. Pictures are the next best denotational device and are often used in dictionaries. Pantomime can help define many words. Diagrams and maps can be used as definitional devices. All such nonverbal approaches to definition are particularly valuable with young students and older nonverbal students for two reasons: they involve the students, and they emphasize the real purpose of definition—the communication of meaning. The formal study of definition, on the other hand, can lead to the students' viewing it as a kind of esoteric ritual. That result is, of course, a disservice to them. It is important, consequently, that any teaching of definition be clearly focused on the real purpose—communication of meaning. Work with nonverbal definitions will help accomplish that purpose.

A second major approach to definition is the use of examples. Students normally use this approach without instruction. If the teacher asks, "What does 'angry' mean?" it is not unexpected for a student to reply, "Well, if I was told to be home by 10:00, and I didn't get home 'til 11:00, then my mom would be sitting up waiting for me and she'd be angry." Such a situational context for a word is a beginning of a definition, but it fails to be specific enough since many meanings can logically fit this situation. This weakness can be overcome by using multiple examples so that the questioner can get a feel for the similarities of situations that will more clearly define the word. There is no question that this approach to definition is far less exacting than a formal, expanded definition. But it works, and as the previous paragraph emphasized, this is a more important criteria for many students.

The same is true for the teacher's attempts to define words for students. The criterion of communication of ideas is far more important than the criterion of formal definition. Yet too often teachers teach words rather than ideas. For example, there is very little value in having the student be able to define the word "irony." The more time spent in class defining the word and the more time spent writing definitions, the more chance that the student's learning is rote. On the other hand, if the students are given illustrations in the form of stories and poems and situations, they may understand what irony is without being able to define it. Also, the teacher can test the student's understanding of irony by asking him to make up a situation that is ironic. The following situation was devised by a seventh-grade student:

A head bank executive puts some valuable diamonds in a safe and does not lock it properly. A bank clerk, known for his honesty, notices and can't resist. As the clerk is driving home, his conscience bothers him, and even for the money he cannot do it. Figuring that no one would ever know, the man drives back to the bank. He puts the diamonds in the safe and triggers the alarm, and is arrested for robbery.

Whether or not this student is able to define irony, his example illustrates an understanding of the concept. Thus, definition by example is important to both teacher and student as a device for communicating understanding.

A third approach to definition is to supply synonyms and antonyms. If the student knows which words have the same meaning as the object word, or the opposite meaning, he is beginning to understand the object word. This beginning is obviously inadequate, however. If words are really synonyms, there is no basis for choosing among them. But if they do not have precisely the same meaning, then there should be some attempt to discriminate among the apparent synonyms. Each of our synonyms helps us to define vaguely the area of meaning involved. The discrimination among these synonyms helps subdivide that area of meaning and thus make it more specific.

In fact, any attempt to define can be viewed in this light. Metaphorically, we may consider the meaning of a word as an area. Any attempt to define the word is an attempt to mark the area of meaning that the word represents. Obviously, the more exactly the definition establishes (defines) the area of meaning, the better it is. Thus, a denotational definition (pointing) becomes more and more adequate as it includes more and more items within the semantic area. Yet to be even more adequate, it must also point to those things that are "nearby" but not included in the semantic area. Definition by example suffers from the same weakness. It says in effect: "This example is in the semantic area," but it does not specify the extent of the area or the boundary lines. Definition by synonym, on the other hand, suggests vaguely very broad boundaries for the area but does not delimit the area unless the definition distinguishes among the synonyms. On the other hand, definition proceeding from the general to the specific defines the broader inclusive meaning area by describing the genus and limits the area more exactly by distinguishing among different word meanings within that area.

Thus, any of these approaches to definition can become more and more sophisticated by more exactly delimiting the area of meaning appropriate to the word. Such growing sophistication in the process of defining should be a continuing part of the English curriculum. In addition, students should become aware of the variety of approaches appropriate for different definition problems. Location, physical appearance, parts, composition, function, causes, and development are all appropriate approaches to definition with some words. However, there are two major weaknesses of genus-differentiae definition: the suggestion of rigidity it implies and the failure to deal adequately with affective connotation.

Rigidity is implied in the process of categorization. Establishing and discriminating categories, a process basic to definition, implies an either-or, yes-no discrimination that is in most cases an oversimplification. Semantic space is not so simply and exactly divided as the discussion thus far has implied. What, for example, is poetry? Or, in metalanguage, what does the word "poetry" mean? Is there a set of characteristics that are sufficient in all cases to define a given piece of language as poetry? Form would seem to be a sufficient criterion in the case of limericks. Yet we might prefer to consider limericks as, at best, marginal to our conception of poetry. If we consider a criterion such as "emotive power," we find that it is neither necessary nor sufficient since many works that are obviously poetry are not moving and many works that are obviously not poetry are extremely moving. Thus, the person who asks, "Well, is it poetry or not? It's got to be one or the other!" is rather unsophisticated in his desire to classify rigidly. We must be sure that our teaching of definition leads our students toward precision and understanding rather than rigidity and hair-splitting.

Affective connotations are an important part of meaning that create difficulty in definition. All the precision possible will not begin to encompass the emotions that are far more easily (though perhaps less exactly) conveyed by metaphoric, descriptive statements. Whitman's "When I Heard the Learn'd Astronomer" is an excellent example of the inadequacy we often feel in definitions that attempt precision at the expense of affective connotations. Obviously, we must help the students to develop skill in explicating the emotive qualities of words as well as their informative qualities.

A second area of concern that grows directly from the first unit on semantics is logic. After we have scrubbed away all the affective connotations presented in an advertisement, letter to the editor, editorial, or essay, we still have the job of deciding whether or not the argument holds. Techniques for evaluating and discovering weaknesses in arguments are the province of logic.

A third major concern suggested by the first semantics unit is the problem of the basic units of meaning. Obviously meaning is derived from endings ("ed"), word parts ("de," "tion"), words ("cat"), phrases ("after dark"), syntactic patterns ("The bear bit the man; the man bit the bear"). A fourth concern implied in the first unit is the problem of changes in meaning. These concerns are more appropriately considered as the province of linguistics in Chapter 21.

These four concerns—definition, logic, units of meaning, and change of meaning—are tangential outgrowths of the consideration of basic concepts of semantics. Another outgrowth is the further development of the central problems of semantics, the study of meaning. To reiterate, the major questions are "What does the word ———— mean?" "How can we more exactly describe the meaning of ————?" and "How do words acquire meaning?" As the disciplines of philosophy, mathematics, psychology, and linguistics are becoming more concerned with semantics as a central problem in their respective fields, more and more work is being done to refine semantic analysis. The studies of Miller,[8] Osgood,[9] Foder and Katz,[10] Joos,[11] and that reported by Minsky[12] all suggest that in the near future there may be striking developments in the field of semantics. But even at its present level of development, general semantics has high priority in the teaching of English. It introduces concepts that are of continuing value in the study of composition and literature. It introduces study that should be pursued in the fields of definition and logic. It introduces, in a way meaningful to students, concepts that are basic to further linguistic study. And in the work of writers like those cited above, it affords techniques of study that can be used by students who have a strong interest in pursuing more esoteric study in the field.

NOTES

1. Ziff, Paul, *Semantic Analysis* (Ithaca, N.Y.: Cornell University Press, 1960).
2. *Webster's New International Dictionary,* 2nd ed. (Springfield, Mass: G. C. Merriam Company).
3. Keller, Helen, *The Story of My Life* (New York: Doubleday, Doran and Co., 1933), pp. 22–24 and 29–31.
4. Clemens, Samuel, *The Adventures of Huckleberry Finn,* Chapter 14.
5. Carroll, Lewis, *Through the Looking Glass,* Chapter 6.
6. Piaget, Jean, *The Child's Conception of the World,* pp. 81–82.
7. McCrimmon, James, adapted from Raab, Earl, and G. J. Selznick, *Major Social Problems* (White Plains, N.Y.: Row Peterson and Co., 1959).
8. Miller, George A., *Language and Communication* (New York: McGraw-Hill Book Co., 1951), Chapter 9.
9. Osgood, Charles O., "The Nature and Measurement of Meaning," *The Psychological Bulletin,* Vol. 49, May 1952, p. 213.
10. Fodor, Jerald, and Gerrold Katz, *The Structure of Language: Readings in Philosophy of Language* (Englewood Cliffs, N.J., Prentice-Hall, 1964), part 5, Chapter 19.
11. Joos, Martin, "Semology: A Linguistic Theory of Meaning," *Studies in Linguistics,* Vol. 13, No. 3–4, 1958.
12. Minsky, Marvin, ed., *Semantic Information Processing* (Cambridge: MIT Press, 1968).

SUGGESTIONS FOR FURTHER READING

1. LOUIS B. SALOMON, *Semantics and Common Sense.* New York: Holt, Rinehart & Winston, 1966. A brief introduction to the principles of general semantics including an excellent (though unannotated) bibliography.
2. S. I. HAYAKAWA, *Language in Thought and Action.* New York: Harcourt, Brace, 1939. A more thorough exposition of principles of general semantics with many exercises easily adaptable for student use.
3. MARVIN MINSKY, ed., *Semantic Information Processing.* Cambridge: MIT Press, 1968. The chapters illustrate recent attempts to develop a semantic theory more precise and exacting than the field of general semantics has accomplished.

20 | Dialectology and Language Change

The study of language at a particular point in time is often referred to as synchronic linguistics whereas the study of language across time is called diachronic linguistics. But they are treated in the same chapter here because of their pedagogical similarities. The purposes of instruction in both are essentially the same. They are included in the curriculum to develop the student's general sensitivity to language. More specifically, it is hoped that the student will come to realize that language is a dynamic tool, that it is used differently by different people in different situations, and that it is flexible. These realizations may have some effect upon the way the student uses language, although their effectiveness in producing greater language sensitivity or a change in usage has not been proven.

The study of dialectology and language change are particularly interesting aspects of the study of language. This should, perhaps, not be surprising, considering the fascination we all show for "peculiarities" of other people's language and our easy adoption of neologisms. When students are given the techniques and opportunity to carry on investigations of these aspects of language study, their involvement in and enthusiasm for such investigation are in striking contrast to the antipathy and apathy that the teacher often faces when he introduces the study of grammar.

Also, the teaching structure for these two kinds of study is essentially the same. It consists of three major steps. First, the teacher presents a striking situation that focuses the students' attention on the area of study and uses this introduction to outline the major segments that the study will involve. Second, he leads the class in examining each of these major segments to help the students develop skill in using the techniques of linguistic investigation. Third, the students use these techniques to carry out their own study in one of the segments and report their findings to the class. This teaching structure is particularly adjustable to individual differences. The teacher can adapt the instruction to the particular class and to individual students in the class through his management of four major variables: the depth and rigor of each segment of the overview, the grouping of students for their individual or small-group study, the support he gives each group or individual, and the format of reporting that he allows. In these ways he can be reasonably successful in involving the students and adapting the work to their levels of proficiency. So although dialectology and language history may be in many senses totally different kinds of study, they are in many ways similar pedagogically.

Dialectology

Instruction in dialect will merely enhance and perhaps objectify knowledge that the student already has. He knows that people use language differently; in fact, he adapts his own language to many different situations. The obvious first step is to call to his attention the vast differences that exist between different people's language patterns. This can be easily accomplished by presenting him with some recorded piece of language and directing the resulting discussion toward the kinds of differences that occur in language use. The discussion will lead to an outline of many of the major kinds of language variations. The teacher can then use additional stimuli either to pursue distinctions that the students have suggested or to introduce distinctions they have overlooked. As each kind of language variation is introduced, the teacher can help the students learn how to work with the material. As a result, at the end of these introductions, the students will have enough familiarity with the main distinctions and enough skill with the procedures that they can undertake an individual or small-group project of their own in the area of their greatest interest. Or the class as a whole can plan a single project to which each student can make an important contribution. With such an organization, it is easy for the teacher to vary the depth of treatment to fit a particular class and particular students within the class.

Many records, films, and TV programs can be used to focus discussion on language usage initially. A few questions by the teacher will serve to develop the discussion. The three most basic ones are: How does the language differ from ours? (pronunciation, vocabulary, grammar) What do we learn about the speaker from his language? (where he lives, what groups he belongs to) Is he unusual, or do most people have special language patterns? The kinds of answers that the students give to such questions and the specificity they are able to accomplish in their answers will give the teacher a general diagnosis of the directions he should emphasize in the unit. He should be sure to bring out in this first introduction the distinction between pronunciation, vocabulary, and usage since these are basic categories that are useful in working with the various kinds of language variation. For example, if the teacher were to use Andy Griffith's "What it was, it was football,"[1] as an introduction, he could develop a set of guide questions for directing the discussion toward the major segments of dialect study that the unit of instruction will investigate.

DISCUSSION GUIDE QUESTIONS

A. Why is the record funny?
   1. How does the speaker's language differ from ours?
      a. What word did he lack for describing a football game?
      b. How did he pronounce "town," "here," and "right here"?
      c. How would we say "what it was that was agoin' to happen"?
   2. What do we assume about the speaker because of his language?
      a. Where does he live?
      b. What is his position in the community?
      c. What does he do for a living?
      d. How old is he?

B. Was the language effective?
   1. Was the way the speaker used language effective?
      a. What interfered with communication?
      b. Did he get the ideas across?
   2. Was it effective for Andy Griffith?
      a. What was his special purpose?
      b. Does he always talk that way?

C. Does our language reveal the same things about us in the same way?

The guide has at least one question for each of the major aspects of dialect study, and they are arranged in an outline form. It is possible that the first questions will touch off the entire discussion without the use of additional ones. It is also possible that the class will need additional questions to direct their attention. For example, if question A2d draws the unanimous opinion that his speech tells us nothing about his age, it would be necessary to ask additional questions such as "How does your speech differ from your parents?" to help them see that language does sometimes reflect age level. With this introductory lesson, the students will be ready to investigate dialect differences.

Since the rationale for this instruction is to achieve greater sensitivity to language, it would seem appropriate to begin attacking that problem early. It is important from this point of view to attack the problems that students will often display. They will make prejudiced judgments about correctness; usually the prejudice will be in terms of distance from their own language—the greater the distance, the "queerer" the speaker. Second, they will assume that language differences occur only with "foreigners" or "hillbillies," or any groups whose circumstances are considerably different from their own, but not with people they know. Both are of course the kind of language prejudice that blocks sensitivity or that is caused by a lack of sensitivity. If the unit deals only with the kind of distant case that student prejudice describes, it is much less likely to be effective than if it can make a point with language closer to home. Although this emphasis should be maintained throughout the unit, it can be started immediately as an investigation growing directly from the first lesson. Note that the last question in the discussion guide begins this emphasis.

The second step of instruction is, then, the beginning of the examination of the students' immediate linguistic environment. Again the teacher focuses the discussion with the use of appropriate questions: "Do you know anyone who uses peculiar pronunciation, vocabulary, or grammar? Can you give me an example? Who has a little brother or sister about three years old? Do they use any funny variations that your family has picked up? What do I say that sounds funny? I bet you can think of some things that I don't even know myself," and so on. Once the students are aroused, the teacher must provide a method of recording information. All that is necessary is a large stack of three-by-five cards and a brief discussion of what information the class will want when a student reports on his findings. Using one of the examples that the students have given, the class will probably conclude with a citation slip that asks for answers to four questions: (1) What is the expression? (2) Who was the speaker? What is his age, occupation and approximate educational level? (3) In what circumstances did he use the expression? Who was his audience? (4) Why did he use the expression? (To be funny? unconsciously? for emphasis?) On the citation slip itself these questions should be reduced to what, who, when, why. With such procedures established, the teacher must allow some time each day for the students to report on their new findings and continue this emphasis throughout the unit. (A bulletin board displaying cards in an outline following the unit plan is a good project for students.) After this pattern is developed, the teacher proceeds with materials that stimulate the investigation of the major areas of language diversity.

Language patterns vary according to vocational or avocational interests. This particular aspect of language variety is a good starting place for student investigation because it is easy to identify and familiar to the students. (It should be noted that this kind of investigation is not a primary interest of the dialectologist. If he deals with it at all—which is unlikely—it will be as an adjunct to "social dialects." But the interests of good secondary school teaching are not, of course, exactly the same as those of the academic profession.) The variation in language patterns according to vocational interests involves vocabulary items primarily, although pronunciation and usage may vary to some extent. As a matter of fact, most vocational and avocational interest groups have developed their own dictionaries. Consequently, such study is a reasonably simplified matter for research. In addition, students find it interesting to pursue for two reasons. First, it allows them to pursue and display knowledge of special interests that are usually not useful in school. (This is a good time to refer to the students' interest inventories and encourage their display of such interests.) Second, in the school setting itself they have built-in models of such language specialization in the curricular and extracurricular interests they are pursuing. Cooking, football, and the orchestra are all sources for the study of specialized language. Once the original discussion has introduced the concept, a few leading questions will easily focus the students' attention on their own uses of specialized vocabulary. The field is elementary enough and the students' natural interests usually well enough developed that they can work reasonably independently at a brief project in this area. Better students may also build new interests in such a project.

PROJECT DIRECTIONS: Technical Language

1. Select an occupation, hobby, or special interest that you would like to tell the class about. (Sailors, cowboys, astronauts, stamp collecting, guns, rocks, football, cooking, sewing, baseball, and so on.)
2. Select ten important words in that field that most outsiders do not understand. Make a dictionary of those ten words.
3. Write a paragraph that briefly explains what the field is about. Use the important words that you have defined in your dictionary.
4. Write a paragraph that says the same thing as the previous paragraph, but this time *do not use* any of the special words of the field.

Notice that this exercise offers a variety of possibilities for building basic English skills—use of the reference sources of the library, understanding the structure of dictionary entries, and structuring a paragraph. Notice also that it does not call for the more complex skills necessary to integrate the information into a well-structured paragraph. If weaker students are having trouble with these kinds of skills, this project is an excellent one for them to pursue at greater length as an individual project at the end of the unit. At this point, it serves only as an introduction to this segment of language difference. It will not require much discussion for the students to objectify the major point— that an individual's use of language differs due to his interests and background.

This concept can be extended by discriminating between specialized vocabulary that serves a special need by naming some thing or concept that does not have a name in everyday speech and specialized vocabulary that simply gives a big name to something that has an equally precise name in everyday language. A discussion of this distinction can point out the difference between specialized language that identifies ideas and specialized language that identifies membership in a particular group. Usually students are aware that their slang identifies them with their peer group. The introduction of this idea leads logically to a discussion of slang. (Again, this topic is of pedagogical concern but not of important concern to the dialectologist.) The investigation is very close to the students' knowledge and interests but does demand skill that the second lesson (technical language) did not demand. Although the material is at hand, it has not been systematized either by the students' prior pursuits (as in the case with hobbies) or by any available library source. (Although there are slang dictionaries, they are never up-to-date on new slang. Also, the teacher may wish to review slang dictionaries before having the class use them. They often contain expressions that the teacher may wish to avoid.) The students must develop skill in collecting and organizing their own research.

If the students have been given an opportunity to report on language peculiarities that they have noted on citation slips and their work has been displayed on the bulletin board, all of them will have developed some skill with citation slips. The teacher need only focus their attention on their own slang.

Teacher: What does the word "cob" mean as you use it?
Student 1:   It means to steal something; when you "cob" something, you steal it.
Student 2:   No, it doesn't. It's not that bad. It's not serious like stealing. You could cob somebody's pencil or book, but if you took something from a store you wouldn't say you "cobbed" it.
Student 3:   Yes, you would.

After a consensus of definition, the teacher continues the discussion.

Teacher: What do we need to put on the citation slip?
Student 3:   The word and the definition.
Student 4:   And who used it.
Student 1:   And not just who, but what kind of people use it, like just teen-agers.
Teacher: Do all teen-agers use "cob"?
Student 6:   No, just us around here.
Teacher: You mean all over town?
Student 1:   Well, maybe not. Maybe just at this school.
Teacher: Then what do we need on the citation slip?
Student 1:   Well, his name tells us that unless we don't know him, then we need to know where he goes to school.
Teacher: Good. O.K., now everybody make up a citation slip for "cob."

After students have done so and the teacher has collected them:

Teacher: O.K., let's see how many teen-age slang words we can list on the board in the next minute.

Citations on additional findings are discussed the next day, the teacher collects the citations, and after a brief discussion the students write a brief paragraph about adolescent slang.

With this background the investigation of geographic distinctions in language can perhaps be pursued with more detachment than prejudice. In fact, the teacher can evaluate his teaching up to this point by the detachment with which the students can discuss the problems of language geography. We are finally dealing with a concern of importance to dialectologists.

The sophistication of some dialectologists in determining the geographic origins and backgrounds of individuals through analysis of language is phenomenal. They are sometimes able to place individuals within miles of their homes, often placing them exactly in large cities. A major tool in making such distinctions is a phonetic alphabet that permits the accurate transcription of language samples. With the careful use of this tool, dialectologists have discovered the specific pronunciation peculiarities that distinguish areas and have formulated lists of key words that will elicit these distinctions from inhabitants of those areas. Vocabulary items and grammatical peculiarities have also been carefully classified. The results have been more specific dialect boundaries (isoglosses) than many would have imagined possible.

In addition, these investigations suggest a variety of causes for dialect distinctions, which might be classed under the general heading of influence patterns. The original language patterns of an area will be very similar to those of the area from which the original inhabitants come. These language patterns will spread along courses of migration, which are influenced by geographic barriers. The more isolated the language community, the more likely it is to reflect its origins. The more it is influenced by communication with, and migration from, other areas, the more it will absorb other patterns. If two areas are in close communication, they may become a single language community by mutual influence, or the patterns of one area may become dominant. Dominance usually flows from cultural and political centers of influence toward outlying districts.

Various recordings for the study of American dialects are available commercially. (See Chapter 14.) Some teachers have their classes send tapes along with questionnaire forms to schools in various parts of the country, asking that students in those schools record their answers to the questions and return the tapes. It is best to make arrangements with teachers in such cooperating schools in advance. Sometimes, a particular school will be fortunate in having students from various parts of the country. Such students may be willing to act as informants in a class's study of dialect. Other schools will have student populations that represent a variety of dialect patterns. In addition students enjoy seeing some of the dialect maps and questionnaire forms used in studies such as Kurath's *A Word Geography of the Eastern United States*. In short, a little effort will provide resources for students to conduct some analysis of dialects in their own immediate environment and around the country.

If the students wish to develop a questionnaire to send to other schools or to give to students from other areas, they must work out the necessary questions to elicit response. For example, they might ask, "What do you call staying out of school all day without anyone knowing it?" or "What do you call going somewhere else when you should go to school?" Kurath lists the following variants in response to such a question:

played truant
skipped school
played hookey
hooked school
hooked jack
bagged school
bagged it
lay out (of school)
laid out (of school)[2]

The next step is to have them suggest other questions that might elicit other differences. The teacher may also extend the lesson into grammar problems, but since they are minimal, he may only mention the possibility. Drake's suggestions are helpful to the teacher:

Window coverings on rollers
Devices at edges of roof to carry off rain
Small porch, often with no roof
Kind of wooden fence
Wall made of rocks or stones
Heavy metal utensil for frying
Water outlets
Playground equipment—goes up and down by balancing two people
Bread made of corn meal
Round flat confection with hole in middle
Homemade cheese
Food eaten between regular meals
Worm used for bait in fishing
Sick ———— stomach
To coast lying down flat[3]

Another extremely important lesson is to teach the students to recognize how one individual may use different language patterns in different situations. The students are, of course, aware that they "wear different language hats" at different times and in different places. The procedures for the teacher follow the same pattern: Focus attention on the problem, and provide procedures for collecting and reporting evidence. At this point in the unit, it would be difficult to avoid direct confrontation of the issue of value judgments connected with language. The issue is part of the larger issue of custom and tradition and the appropriateness of such criteria for making value judgments. Although these issues cannot be resolved, it does seem necessary to let the students face the problem: Is our adaptation of our language a reflection of good manners and consequently appropriate, or is it, on the contrary, a failure of pride in self-identity and a form of hypocrisy? The concept of appropriateness can be extended to a consideration of the differences between oral and written language and to the arbitrary, tradition-oriented requirements that various writing styles demand. Again, the purpose of the instruction up to this point is not to develop the concepts with great depth, but rather to introduce them in such a way that the students' interest will be stimulated.

With this background, the fourth major step of the instruction can begin. The students pick topics for further investigation and proceed with the investigation and preparation of reports on their discoveries. Such reports should be judged on the usual compositional criteria and can serve as an evaluation of the teacher's success in reaching his major objective—greater sensitivity to language usage.

Obviously the teacher can easily vary the individual assignments. For example, the slowest students might simply extend and synthesize the work they have already done. For the more advanced students, the problems could range in difficulty all the way up to those appropriate for graduate students in college.

There are many possible ways to supplement or extend these activities, the most important being the addition of reading assignments. Shaw's *Pygmalion* is particularly appropriate. Shuy has many suggestions for activities in his *Discovering American Dialects.*[4] Having a variety of such materials available is very helpful in providing worthwhile activity for students who finish projects first. However, the instruction can be judged successful without them if the students' projects indicate that they have a less biased and more sensitive view of dialect differences.

Language Change

The instruction on language change should begin and proceed in much the same fashion as the unit on dialectology, beginning with a startling illustration of how the language has changed and proceeding by answering the questions, "In what ways has language changed?" and "Why does language change?" Each major kind of change should be the subject of whole-class instruction so that all students can answer the questions in a general way. After such an overview, they can proceed by studying any one aspect of change in greater depth.

The history of the English language is usually segmented into four major periods. The first begins with the withdrawal of the Roman Empire from the British Isles and the invasion of the isles by Teutonic tribes. Celtic, the earliest language, had survived the invasions of the Roman Empire, and at the beginning of the Teutonic invasions in the fifth century, both Celtic and Latin were spoken in the British Isles. The Teutonic invaders included the Angles, Saxons, and Jutes, all apparently from the area of present Denmark and the Netherlands. As they settled first in the southeast corner of the isles and gradually spread inland, their Germanic language gradually replaced the earlier Celtic, which retreated with its speakers to the northern and western area. This

---

POSSIBLE RESEARCH TOPICS

1. Write a dictionary of the contemporary slang of your school.
2. What do adults know about teen-age slang?
3. Of the slang of the 1920s, 1930s, or 1940s, what words became standard English? What words have died? Do adults still use these words? Can an adult's age be determined by the slang he knows?
4. What is the slang of the fifth and sixth graders of your community? What words does it have in common with your slang? What words are different?
5. Are there differences in slang among the various schools at the same grade level?
6. What differences distinguish the language of teachers and students?
7. Are there differences in language between students of the same age in different socioeconomic levels?
8. What distinguishes the language of adults from the language of students?
9. What distinguishes the language of people who are from different areas of the country?
10. How many distinct sounds are there in the English language? Give examples of each sound.
11. What are the differences in the use of the vocal organs that create the different sounds of our language?
12. Describe the characteristics that distinguish the language of a TV personality.
13. Select a special interest group and determine what distinguishes the language of the group (plumbers, musicians, football players, and so on).
14. How have patterns of speech moved west as our country developed?
15. Develop a map of the isoglosses of your community.
16. Explain the differences in language usage that one person shows in different situations.
17. Discover the peculiarities of language that develop within a single family.
18. What gestures do people use when speaking? What do they mean?
19. What peculiarities of language can be found in the lyrics of modern popular music?
20. Develop a bulletin board of peculiar language usages that you hear on TV and radio or see in newspapers and magazines.
21. What evidence of foreign language influence can be found in your community? In individuals of your community?
22. Do people speak differently on the telephone?

---

change in the language of the British Isles was well-established by the twelfth century, and it is this period of time—from the fifth century through the twelfth —that gives our language its basic Germanic characteristics. The language of this first period is called Old English (O.E.).

The period from the twelfth century through the fifteenth century is called

Middle English (M.E.). The beginning of this period, which immediately follows the Norman conquest in 1066, is marked by the use of French as the language of the upper classes. By the end of the Middle English period, however, French had lost its influence. The steady inroads of English into the speech of the upper classes was accelerated in the fourteenth and fifteenth centuries by the Hundred Years' War, which made French the language of the enemy, so that by the fifteenth century English was a language common to all the people. During this period the language changed in many ways. The inflectional endings that were a characteristic of Old English were dropped, and word order became more important. Latin and French words replaced Old English words. The language of the beginning of the Middle English period is in most of its essentials foreign to today's speaker of English. By the end of the period, however, the language is recognizable as the precursor of our present one.

Modern English (Md.E.) begins with the sixteenth century, at the start of the Renaissance. This period shows two profound influences on the English language. The first is the spread of literacy, which was influenced by an increase in schooling and the invention of the printing press. Both of these forces had an essentially conservative effect and probably helped to stabilize both the grammar and the orthography of the language. The second major influence was the Renaissance itself, which, because of the tremendous expansion of knowledge in many fields, greatly increased and changed the vocabulary. The following centuries are ones of regularization and stardardization through such influences as the continued increase in schooling, vast improvements in communication, the development and use of dictionaries, and the study of grammar. Although the language continued to change, changes were relatively minor, and the written language of the seventeenth, eighteenth, and nineteenth centuries is very close to that of today.

As we approach the present, language history shares the problems of all historical efforts. Our lack of distance from the subject may distort our perspective, and what we think are general trends and developments may in fact be passing fancies. Nevertheless, the present language of our country is usually identified as Modern American English (M.A.E.) or Current American English and is most often discussed as a synchronic entity rather than as a diachronic extension of the past. Some generalizations about M.A.E. do, however, seem possible. The "melting pot" has had the profound effect of extending the language through borrowings from other languages. Scientific development has accounted for the inclusion of many words from Latin and Greek roots. Our gadget-oriented society has caused a vast expansion of vocabulary through neologisms. Writers such as E. E. Cummings and Madison Avenue advertising men illustrate our willingness to play with and innovate language. It seems fair to conclude that M.A.E. will in the future be considered a period of change in language, but we are too close to it to define with any certainty just how the change will affect it.

Secondary school students seem to assume that language is static. Probably the school's prescriptive emphasis on "correctness" in language reinforces this view. A recording of a passage in O.E., M.E., and Md.E. strikes most students as astonishing; some may respond with disbelief. But with this introduction, they are ready to consider two basic questions: In what ways does language change? and Why does language change? They will have no difficulty naming

---

WORKSHEET: Changes in Vocabulary

Be prepared to explain to the class what influence you would expect the following events to have on the English language:

1. As English settlers move west, they communicate with native American Indians who have names for crops, utensils, and places that the English do not have.
2. New Orleans is founded and settled by the French but eventually is absorbed by the English.
3. As the Southwest is settled, raising cattle becomes a major occupation. The workers learn many of the methods of the Spanish people who had been living in the area for many years and use many of their tools.
4. Many Oriental people settle on the West Coast. They make many contributions to the area, but they are particularly noted because they will work for low wages and because their food is very different and very good.
5. The discovery of electricity leads to a device that will carry people's voices over thousands of miles by means of wire. Finally, a new invention carries their voices without wires.
6. A device is invented that will provide the power to pull people in a carriage without a horse.
7. A man named McAdam invents a cheaper way to make roads smooth and easy to travel on.
8. A machine is invented that will actually move through the air.
9. A new game, baseball, is invented that becomes a national craze. Everybody talks about it, and the words that describe special happenings in the game become common knowledge to everyone.
10. A war occurs that not only involves many people in fighting but makes it necessary for everyone to make great changes in the way he lives.
11. The invention of the atomic bomb causes us to change our thinking about war. It also suggests that a new era is starting in which many things will change.
12. The Americans are in competition with the Russians. The Russians send up the first space capsule, which they call sputnik.

Specific questions:

What do items 1–4 have in common? _____

What name could you give these kinds of language changes? _____

What do 5–8 have in common? What name would you give them? _____

What do 9–12 have in common? What name would you give them? _____

the three major areas of language change: pronunciation, vocabulary, and grammar. Moreover, they will probably be able to mention some causes of vocabulary change, such as events and new products. But this will probably be the extent of their knowledge. The general discussion of the two questions will establish what they are able to articulate and will prepare them for instruction in these areas.

Studying the specifics of early change in the English language is a complex task. For that reason, instruction should begin with other problems. Perhaps the easiest one for students to work with is the change in vocabulary that is evident in today's culture. All they need for material is recent magazines and newspapers and a few carefully constructed worksheets from the teacher to develop their knowledge of the causes and kinds of vocabulary change that can occur in language.

This introduction will identify three major causes of language change—the influence of borrowing, the influence of major historical events, and the influence of specific new products or items that require new words to describe them. Each of these may be developed. For instance, neologisms may be explored as in the following worksheet.

WORKSHEET: Neologisms.

Neologisms are new (neo-) words (logo). There are many ways in which people coin new words.

1. The following words are called acronyms. How were they made up?
   a. AWOL   VISTA   WASP   SCUBA
      UNESCO   WAC   CORE   radar
   b. Find two acronyms other than those listed.
2. How was the word "acronym" made up?
   (*acro,* the Greek word for outermost, or the first letters + *nyma,* the Greek for name = names made up of the first letters of a group of words.)
   Look up "homonym," "synonym," and "homograph" to see how they were created by joining two forms that already meant something. Find at least one additional word created by combining Greek or Latin forms.
3. Many words are borrowed from other languages like "Volkswagen" and "sputnik." Find two more examples like these.
4. Some words are used because of their connotations—"Timex" for a wristwatch, "Heet" for an antifreeze, "Contac" for a cold medicine. Find two additional examples and explain how the original meaning is appropriate for its new use.
5. Many new words are adaptations of names of people or places—a "macadam" road, a "maverick" for an independent person. Find two more examples of this kind of neologism.
6. See if you can find neologisms that do not seem to fit any of these categories of coinage.

To investigate word borrowings requires special dictionary skills, so it is important that the teacher check to see that the available dictionaries include the necessary etymological information and that students are versed in the use of the etymological abbreviations that the dictionaries use. Looking up the derivations of words in a few passages such as the one below provides insight into the variety of sources from which English has borrowed words.

WORKSHEET: Word Borrowings

Tell when and from what languages the underlined words came into the English language:

A castle basks in the sun. A small Scottish breeze ripples across the loch. It is afternoon in the Highlands.

As you travel around Britain, sights like this may tempt you to forget your schedule and loaf. Go ahead. Britain offers umpteen ways to take it easy.

The study of the way in which major events lead to the formation of new words in English is even more demanding if it requires research. Some problems can be selected that will demand relatively simple research. Those that

---

WORKSHEET: Major events that have influenced our language.

Recent integration problems have led to many new words: The names of groups, such as CORE and the Black Muslims; the names of new events, such as sit-ins and freedom rides. We can find many other major events that have had a strong effect on our language. Research one of the following events to discover what new words it brought into our language:

1. Women's recent dress fashions
2. New schools of art in the 1960s
3. Cosmetic and beauty-aid advertisements
4. The atomic age
5. The space age
6. The automobile
7. Baseball
8. Football
9. Prohibition and the 1920s
10. World War I
11. World War II
12. Integration
13. Roman control of England
14. The French conquest of England
15. Pioneers moving west
16. The Civil War

need more research can be saved for the better students. Also, students might work in groups on these projects.

Changes in pronunciation and syntax are more difficult for students because they demand a more specialized knowledge of the history of the English language. Some general principles can be illustrated in M.A.E. For example, word shortening is apparent in the change from airplane to plane, automobile to auto, and gymnasium to gym. Analogical change can often be observed in the language of young children or in such nonsense verse as the following:

PLURALS ARE SINGULAR

Now if mouse in the plural should be,
    and is, mice,
Then house in the plural, of course,
    should be hice,
And grouse should be grice and spouse
    should be spice
And by the same token should blouse
    become blice.
Then if one thing is that, while some
    more is called those,
Then more than one hat, I assume,
    would be hose,
And gnat would be gnose and pat
    would be pose
And likewise the plural of rat would
    be rose.[5]

The analysis of unintentional lapses in language can be developed into many categories, as Muinzer shows in his excellent brief summary of the field of language history.[6] But such activity seems of relatively minimal importance to the student or to developing his understanding of how language changes. Additional lessons must draw more directly on the work of language historians. Three major kinds of activities seem basic: the relation of English to other languages, the changes of inflection and pronunciation in the history of English, and semantic change.

At the beginning of the nineteenth century, it was established that Sanskrit had many similarities to European languages. In fact the study of old Sanskrit manuscripts led to a recognition of underlying similarities among many languages including Old English, Gothic, Latin, Greek, and Sanskrit.

On the basis of this kind of comparative work, linguists have established that many present languages have grown from a single parent language, which has been named Indo-European to reflect the geographic areas whose languages can be traced to it. Charts showing the relationships among languages appear in most dictionaries.

The principles behind the comparative study that makes this analysis possible can be demonstrated to students, using language samples like those below that are from Schlauch's *The Gift of Language.*[7]

WORKSHEET: *Indo-European Languages.* All these language samples mean the same thing. Group them according to their similarities and differences.

Danish:	Ja, mor, jeg har tre.
Dutch:	Ja, moeder, ik heb drie.
French:	Oui, ma mère, j'en ai trois.
Czech:	Ano, matko, mám tři.
Icelandic:	Já, módir, ek hefi prjá.
Portuguese:	Sim, mãe, tenho tres.
Polish:	Tak, matko, mam trzy.
German:	Ja, Mutter, ich habe drei.
Italian:	Si, madre, ce n'ho tre.
Flemish:	Ja, moeder, ik heb drie.
Norwegian:	Jo, mor, jeg har tre.
Rumanian:	Da, mama mea, eu am trei.
Russian:	Da, mat^j, u men^j á tri.
Spanish:	Sí, madre, (yo) tengo tres.
Swedish:	Ja, moder, jag har tre.
English:	Yes, mother, I have three.

TEACHER DISCUSSION GUIDE: Indo-European Languages

Distribute Worksheet I on Indo-European expressions. (If possible, print each on a 3″ by 5″ card and give each student a set, so he can manipulate them more easily.) Tell the students that each foreign sentence means the same thing as the English, and ask them questions that will help them group these languages according to their similarities and differences. For brighter classes, few questions will be necessary. Slower students may have to be led step by step through the analysis of similarities and differences; for such students it is wise to use fewer languages. The following questions should be used as they are necessary in the particular class to gain an *adequate* classification. It would be far better to follow the spontaneous lead of the class than to try to use the specific questions and answers, which are presented here only to illustrate the kind of procedure involved.

1. All these languages have many similarities that suggest that they are somehow related. What characteristics do all these languages have in common? (Initial letter in *mother* and the "r" in *three*.)
2. How would you group these languages on the basis of their similarities and differences?
   a. What three groups could we make on the basis of the second letter in the word *mother*?

I	II	III
English	French	German
Dutch	Portuguese	
Norwegian	Rumanian	
Swedish	Polish	
Flemish	Spanish	
Danish	Italian	
Icelandic	Czech	
	Russian	

3. What letters in the words for "yes" suggest that our classification of Group I is correct? (the initial *y* or *j* that all in Group I have in common.)
4. On the basis of this evidence, is German closer to Group I or Group II? (Put German back into Group I.)
5. What letters of the words for "have" are similar in all Group I words? (Initial *h* in all the Group I words.)
6. Let's look further at the languages we have included in Group II. Do you see any basis for subdividing them into two or three groups?
   a. How could we divide them into two groups on the basis of the letters in the words for "yes"? (*i* versus *a;* note that this misclassifies Rumanian as Slavic rather than Romance.)

IIa	IIb
French	Rumanian
Spanish	Czech
Portuguese	Polish
	Russian

   b. How do the letters of the word for "I have" support our classification? (All IIb languages include the letter *m.*)
   c. How does Rumanian differ from the other languages in IIb? (No *t* in mother; more than four words; *e* in three.)
7. Where should we put Rumanian? (If the discussion flounders, the class could decide by vote; the decision is not important at this point.)

   If students have developed fluency in this pattern of analysis, they should be divided into small groups to follow the same pattern in subdividing the languages of Group I. If they have not developed fluency, the teacher should continue to direct the analysis until it is completed.
   When the student analysis is completed, distribute copies of the correct subdivision. Explain to the students that their analysis may differ from the linguists' because the linguists had more information to work from, including the pronunciation of these words.

An analysis of the changes in English from O.E. to M.E. to Md.E. to M.A.E. is fairly complex and relatively difficult to present to students. Recorded and transcribed comparative passages in O.E., M.E., and Md.E. are a basic tool. With these available, the teacher may lead the entire class in a brief analysis of some specific changes in vocabulary, pronounciation, orthography, and syntax. Additional study of this area should be reserved for special projects of advanced students.

The final introductory lesson is an analysis of semantic change. The work sheet below will allow students to discover changes in meaning from general to specific, specific to general, good to bad, and bad to good:

WORKSHEET: Semantic Change.

The following words illustrate four of the chief types of semantic change (changes in meaning) in English. For each word, the first meaning given in parentheses is the old or original meaning; the second is the modern one. Arrange these words into four groups according to the kind of semantic change they represent.

1. *acorn* (various kinds of nuts—the seed or nut of oak trees)
2. *bonfire* (a fire for burning bones or corpses—any large outdoor fire)
3. *boor* (a farmer—an ill-mannered person)
4. *boycott* (an Irish captain who was ostracized by his neighbors—refusal to associate with any person or group)
5. *cad* (a younger son of an aristocratic family—an ill-mannered fellow)
6. *cattle* (property or wealth—cows, bulls, and steers)
7. *champagne* (wine from a French district—any wine resembling French champagne)
8. *corn* (a hard particle—the seed of a particular cereal crop)
9. *cunning* (knowing or skillful—tricky or meanly clever)
10. *dean* (an officer in charge of ten people—a major college administrator)
11. *deer* (any small animal—a particular animal with antlers)
12. *discard* (reject a card—throw something away)
13. *ferry* (travel—travel by boat)
14. *gossip* (a godparent—a spreader of rumors)
15. *hussy* (a housewife—a woman of low morals)
16. *knave* (a boy—a villainous man)
17. *knight* (a young male servant—a titled person)
18. *lady* (a breadmaker—a woman of quality)
19. *martinet* (a French general who was a stickler for discipline—any rigid disciplinarian)
20. *minister* (a servant—a clergyman or statesman)
21. *pedagogue* (a slave—an educator)
22. *shibboleth* (a password used in the Bible—any word or phrase that identifies a particular group)
23. *shirt* (a loose outer garment worn by either sex—a garment worn by a man)
24. *skirt* (a loose outer garment worn by either sex—a garment worn by a woman)

Students who are interested in pursuing semantic change as an individual project may be offered additional suggestions for study, such as the following.

WORKSHEET: Dead Metaphors and Doublets.

Many words that once embodied sharp metaphors have been used so long that the comparison they originally conveyed has been forgotten. We call these words "dead" metaphors. Here are some words that you will find more interesting to use when you know the lost metaphor that each conceals. Look up the origin of these words in a good dictionary and be ready to explain the dead metaphor in each case.

1. aplomb	11. magazine
2. capricious	12. muscle
3. career	13. prevaricate
4. contrite	14. precipitate
5. delirium	15. result
6. easel	16. sarcasm
7. eliminate	17. subtle
8. embarrass	18. superfluous
9. eradicate	19. tribulation
10. grenade	20. urchin

The following pairs of words or doublets have similar origins. Consult an unabridged dictionary. Sometimes you will find that one of the words retains the original meaning and the other is a later development; sometimes both have left the original meaning far behind. Tell what element of meaning is common to each set of doublets, what the original meaning was, and how the other meanings appear to have developed.

If the dictionary you use gives definitions in the order of their historical development, as most dictionaries do, the order will help you see the way the meaning has changed. The explanatory notes at the beginning of your dictionary tell whether historical order or frequency of use determines the order of the definitions. Do not overlook quotations that show you how a word was used at a certain date.

1. daft, deft	11. parole, palaver
2. danger, dominion	12. poignant, pungent
3. etiquette, ticket	13. praise, price
4. genteel, jaunty	14. sergeant, servant
5. guest, hostile	15. shirt, skirt
6. jealous, zealous	16. sole, sullen
7. lap, lapel	17. soprano, sovereign
8. lace, lasso	18. tabernacle, tavern
9. mosquito, musket	19. tradition, traitor
10. onion, union	20. vast, waste

The instruction in language change has introduced students to the following ideas: (1) Language changes in pronunciation, vocabulary, and grammar. (2) Contact with other languages influences change. (3) New words are made up in a variety of ways. (4) Major events have a strong influence on language. (5) Analogy and shortening affect language. (6) English is one of the Germanic languages of the Indo-European language family. (7) The meanings of words shift in many ways. Each of these is an appropriate topic for the student to pursue as an individual project. As with dialectology, the teacher may control the difficulty of the task and should judge the success of the unit by its effectiveness in making the students more sensitive to the diversity of language.

NOTES

1. Griffith, Andy, *Just For Laughs,* Capitol Records T962.
2. Kurath, Hans, *A Word Geography of the Eastern United States* (Ann Arbor: University of Michigan Press, 1949), p. 79.
3. Drake, James A., "The Effect of Urbanization on Regional Vocabulary," *American Speech,* Vol. 36, No. 1, February 1961, pp. 17–33.
4. Shuy, Roger W., *Discovering American Dialects* (Champaign: National Council of Teachers of English, 1967).
5. Mittler, Frank, *Little Book of Word Tricks* (Mount Vernon, N.Y.: Peter Pauper Press, 1958), p. 33.
6. Muinzer, Louis A., "History: the Life of the Language" and "Historical Linguistics in the Classroom," *Illinois English Bulletin,* November 1960.
7. Schlauch, Margaret, *The Gift of Language,* formerly *The Gift of Tongues* (New York: Dover Publications, 1955), pp. 51, 53, and 55.

SUGGESTIONS FOR FURTHER READING

1. HANS KURATH, *A World Geography of the Eastern United States* (Ann Arbor, Michigan: University of Michigan Press, 1949). *The* scholarly publication resulting from the work of dialectologists.
2. ALBERT C. BAUGH, *A History of the English Language* (New York: Appleton-Century-Crofts, 1957). A standard text on the history of the English language.
3. ROGER SHUY, *Discovering American Dialects.* Champaign: National Council of Teachers of English, 1967.
4. A. L. DAVIS, ed., *American Dialects for English Teachers.* Washington: United States Office of Education, 1969. Contains checklists of items for variations in regional and social dialects as well as an extensive bibliography.

Composition

The teacher of composition should base his instruction on a systematic approach rather than on his own ad hoc intuitions. Yet he cannot rely to any great extent on research findings since the research that has been done is too limited to offer many fruitful guidelines. What he needs, then, are two theories of composition: a theory of the composing process and a theory of instruction. Both theories should result in teaching procedures that are adapted to various types of compositions as they are differentiated in terms of the writer's motivation, his purposes, and his analysis of the probable responses of the intended audience.

Before the teacher can plan instruction, he must know what his students' needs are and how he can best meet those needs. Chapter 21 presents a series of inventories related to composition skills: spelling, the mechanics of punctuation and capitalization, organization, and originality. The results of each item in the battery have implications for instruction.

The traditional approaches to teaching composition have not proven entirely satisfactory. Chapter 22 examines the various weaknesses in these traditional approaches.

Chapter 23 presents a model of the composing process. This model emphasizes the role of communication in verbal composing, demonstrating how writing is influenced by the writer's purposes, his intended audience, and his environment.

Planning is essential to effective instruction in composition. The teacher must plan the type of instruction that will be best suited to the needs of his particular students. He must also plan on how he will tie in the composition instruction with the rest of the English curriculum. Finally, he must consider how to evaluate the finished papers in a way that will contribute to the students' further progress. These subjects are discussed in Chapter 24, which presents models for composition lessons.

Several different types of compositions—and the appropriate instructional techniques—are discussed in Chapters

25 through 28. Student compositions are used as examples throughout. Chapter 25 deals with the type of writing that will best meet the students' everyday school needs—writing that is intended to convey information. Poetry, fables, and other types of form-oriented writing are discussed in Chapter 26. Writing that is intended to draw an emotional response from the reader is the subject of Chapter 27. This chapter suggests ways in which students can be taught both to analyze and to imitate such writing. Chapter 28 explores some of the introspective and environmental elements that may influence students' writing.

Finally, Chapter 29 discusses the needs of dysfunctional writers and outlines a number of techniques that will be useful in bringing such students up to a functional level.

As noted above, Chapters 24–29 contain many examples of student composition. The examples are presented in the form in which they came to the teacher's desk, before they were red-marked. Consequently, the reader can expect to find in them errors of various sorts. Although the reader will find errors in the compositions, if the writers had not had the kinds of lessons described in Chapter 24 there would have been a great many more errors of many kinds. Unless otherwise noted, most of these compositions are the work of students in the lower secondary grades, mainly eighth and ninth. Generally, the work is several cuts higher than that which is customarily produced by students of this age—in spite of the errors present. The work of younger writers has been chosen to indicate several things: first, the diversity in writing that one finds in a narrow age range; second, the capacity that younger students have; third, by extrapolation, the heights to which high school juniors and seniors (and their teachers) may aspire.

Composition Inventories

Composition instruction should start in the inventory period at the beginning of the year because before the teacher can begin to plan writing lessons, he must have a clear idea of his students' writing ability. In addition to their composing, he must assess their needs and abilities in spelling and in the mechanics of punctuation and capitalization. Since these instructional areas are important only as they relate to writing, they must be integrated with the composition curriculum.

Spelling

The spelling inventory is intended to yield two kinds of data: the general types of misspellings made by the individual students and the independent study method that should prove to be the most advantageous for them.

Probably the single most difficult aspect to learning English is its spelling. There is not a one-to-one relationship of grapheme (letter) to phoneme (significant sound). In many languages, Spanish, for example, there is very nearly such a one-to-one relationship, and even the few exceptions to the rule pattern regularly. Consequently, in many of these countries spelling is not taught at the secondary school level because it presents no problem to the students.

Since, with our language, spelling is a continuous problem, the teacher is faced with spelling instruction at all grade levels. The character of this instruction rests on a three-part analysis of the problem. (1) What are the situations in which spelling is done? (2) What are the demands made by the language itself? (3) What are the functions of the learner in terms of learning to spell? The inventory itself will reflect the results of the analysis in each of these areas.

(1) *Spelling Situations.* With the exception of such institutions peculiar to some classrooms as the spelling bee, very little occasion for the oral spelling of words is ever encountered by anyone. One such occasion is the use of spelling as a kind of code to confuse young children. Another common occasion is the oral spelling of a word to

clear up ambiguity caused by the graphemic-phonemic inconsistency in the language. There may be other occasions. Whatever the case may be, the problem of oral spelling can be regarded as so trivial as to be dismissed without further consideration as a significant conditioner of general needs (but not as a learning device! See below).

Situations involving the spelling of words in lists and in contexts analogous to lists cannot be dismissed as lightly. Much business writing (including that of school personnel) involves the listing of items; many business forms are set up in this way. Large sections on employment applications, tax forms, and college applications, for example, require responses that are essentially listings. The social importance of these situations is great.

In the schools (and colleges), however, spelling problems are more usually encountered in the broader context of extended, related sequences: sentences, paragraphs, and longer compositions. Because of the subtle shifts of pitch, stress, and juncture that occur when words are taken from lists and put into contexts, the spelling problem already significant in terms of words on lists, for many writers, is intensified. For example, even the simple word "have," when put into the context "I would have tried harder" becomes "of" on many papers: "I would of tried harder." Similarly, tests of such listed items as "all right" and "too," "to," and "two" will often display the students' apparent mastery of the words, whereas compositions from the same students will show the form "alright" and confusion in the appropriateness of "too" and "to." Consequently, the spelling inventory is developed as a context.

(2) The words used in the context of the inventory should be members of classes that have long been established in spelling research. The classes, which are determined by various considerations, are: basic writing words; words formed by following conventional orthographic rules; spelling demons; and other words.

BASIC WRITING WORDS If we were to select a number of writing passages at random and count and tabulate the words in them, we would find that certain words would recur much more frequently than others, such words as "a," "an," "the," "and," and the like. Rinsland found that only 100 of these frequently recurring words accounted for about 60 percent of all the words used in a person's writing.[1] Other researchers have shown that if a list of the 1,000 most frequently recurring words is made, the words on it account for upwards 90 percent of the total number of words used in writing.[2] If the list is further extended to include the 3,000 most frequently recurring words, these words constitute close to 95[3] percent of the total. At about this point, the extension of the word list becomes of somewhat less value. Increasing the frequency list to 10,000 words extends the percentage of the total by only a relatively small amount;[4] apparently, something analogous to the concept of diminishing returns sets in at about the 3,000 word-count level.

These 3,000 words, then, can be regarded as basic to writing. If a person has complete mastery of them, only 5 percent of his total writing can contain spelling errors. An interesting point to consider is that most of these words are the targets of spelling instruction in most schools by the end of the third grade.

ORTHOGRAPHIC RULES Spelling instruction has been plagued by "rules" of the mnemonic kind that are supposed to aid the speller. In many cases these alleged rules lack generality to the extent that following the rule may result in more misspellings than nonadherence to it. Such rules often involve learning lists of exceptions, both "regular" exceptions and "irregular" ones—or exceptions to exceptions. Consider one of the more popular such rules: "the ie-ei rule."[5] If the student remembers the mnemonic accurately—"Is it *i* after *e* or *i* before *e,* except after *c*? Or is it before *c* or when sounded 'eigh' as in neighbor or weigh?"—and even if he remembers the whole rule, what is the result of his applying it in such situations as the formation of the plurals of nouns ending in *cy* such as democracy, in such phrases as "The Great Democrac———s"?

The only significant orthographic rules are limited in number and have much broader applicability. They concern such spelling details as the conventions of plural formation, the uses of the apostrophe, and the conventions associated with adding various kinds of suffixes and similar details of spelling. Most desk dictionaries contain sections on these rules of orthography, as do the school grammar books. These sources can be used as references to develop a complete listing of these rules. Words exemplifying the usages are included in the inventory. Unhappily, even these rules are not without exception. But at least the few exceptions are themselves nearly "regular" in character.

SPELLING DEMONS If spelling errors were collected and treated in the same way as was described in the formulation of the basic writing list above, a similar phenomenon would be observed. Certain words in misspelled form would tend to appear over and over again. For some reason, certain words invite misspelling more than do others. Frequency of use is one of the factors. For example, "to," "too," and "two" are used very frequently; hence one can expect a greater number of misspellings of these words than of words like "bivalve" and "opt," which are less frequently used. Obviously, however, there are deeper reasons for such misspellings than can be accounted for by considerations of frequency. After all, "a," "an," and "the" are used with greater frequency than "to," "too," and "two" and are rarely misspelled.

To date, no one has developed a foolproof instructional attack on these words ("to," "too," and "two") nor on a great many others on the demon lists. For our purposes, the inventory will present samples of such words to see whether the students have mastered them. Mastery of them, needless to say, reduces the probability of spelling errors immensely and is theoretically second in importance only to mastery of the basic writing words. Even after intensive work, however, many writers fail to learn the proper spelling of these words.

In addition to these words that pose a general spelling problem, there will very likely be particular words that the individual writer has difficulty with, for example, new words in the writer's vocabulary and words that he persistently misspells. With some of these words, he may be aware of his uncertainty about the spelling; with others, he may not know that he has a spelling problem. Finally, words containing specific sounds or letter configurations may give him trouble.

As the year's work develops, many heretofore unknown terms will be introduced into the writer's vocabularies.* Before beginning a unit of work, the teacher should preview the new terms that the students will encounter and give specific instruction on their spelling. In other words, in addition to their importance in other aspects of the unit, the new words should be considered as "spelling words." Obviously, no such words should be included in the inventory.

Other types of words enumerated above are relevant only to individuals and their own specific problems. Although there will be little opportunity in the brief inventory for a systematic survey of the particular spelling problems of individual students, some of them will be revealed. In any case, the teacher will become aware of them as the year's work progresses.

(3) *Consideration of Learning Patterns.* Not everyone has the same learning patterns; nor is a pattern that proves efficient for one person in a given situation equally efficient for all others in comparable situations. Once the character of needs in spelling has been described, teacher and student are both faced with determining the most efficient and effectual ways to meet the needs.

One method of teaching spelling that has been employed is to have the learner locate the correct spelling (of a word he has misspelled) in some appropriate source such as the class "speller" or dictionary. Once located, the word is copied some magic number of times—three, five, seven, ten. All too familiar is the case in which the conscientious learner does the copying—and does it wrong! Thus, by using a technique that is inappropriate to his process of learning spelling, he not only fails at learning, but he learns error, an inefficient and ineffectual procedure.

The spelling inventory should help to determine how students' learning patterns differ; the teacher will be able to vary his instructional techniques accordingly. For example, some persons learn to spell primarily through visual means. In fact, some studies have indicated that visual learners make the best spellers.[6] Other studies in spelling have found that younger children learn to spell many words incidentally in connection with learning to read.[7] Most of

---

* A person has many vocabularies, and not simply a single, comprehensive one. Generally, there is a great deal of overlap in these vocabularies. But each person will have a number of words that he will find only in his reading, use only in his speech, use only in his writing, etc. A spelling problem often arises when a word from one of the vocabularies is encountered for the first time in another.

us know people who have trouble spelling words aloud but can detect misspellings in print. Some visually oriented persons may misspell a word in writing and then, on rereading, will recognize that the word is misspelled and correct it.

There is evidence that most persons acquire the greater part of their spelling learning through hearing in their earlier years and through vision in their later schooling. The transition appears to take place for most students during the middle schooling (junior high school) ages.[8]

A relatively small number of persons find neither the visual nor the auditory method initially effectual. Rather, the best way for them to learn words, both in reading and writing, is through a kinesthetic method involving tracing with their fingers.[9]

The most beneficial approach for some students may be one combining two or three of these procedures.

Spelling Inventory Procedures

The spelling inventory should reflect the foregoing aspects of analysis. The administration of the inventory should provide insight into the students' ability to spell words in context, to take dictation, to copy accurately, and to proofread. The passage itself should include basic writing words, words exemplifying orthographic rules, words from the list of demons, and others.

The context of the inventory should be developed to be interesting to the students. For example, the one in this inventory is on the subject of breaking in new cars, a subject that should be appealing to ninth and tenth graders, especially since many of them are looking forward to getting their licenses. Appropriate topics for younger students might be "developing hobbies" or "babysitting"; for older students "applying for jobs" or "applying for college admissions."

INVENTORY PROCEDURES

Distribute sheets of blank paper, size 8½″ x 11″, and have the class fold the paper in half so that a little folio leaflet, size 5½″ x 8½″, is formed. The headings should be placed on the *outside* of the leaflet. Give directions approximately as follows:

"Open your leaflets so that you see two blank pages before you. I am going to dictate a short passage that I want you to write on the left-hand page. Leave the right-hand page blank; we will use it later. I will read the passage twice. The first time, you will just sit and listen to get the sense of the whole thing. The second time, I will dictate it slowly enough for you to write everything I say. You will take down my dictation on the left-hand page only. If I am going too fast, raise your hand, and I will slow down. Are there any questions?"

After answering questions, go over the instructions again, point by point, by posing questions to the class. (Examples: "Which page will you write on?" "What do you do with the other page?")

Dictate the inventory passage slowly, aiming for as much naturalness in delivery as possible at the slower speaking rate. Use your natural dialect, and take special care not to distort pronunciation. Do not let the spelling of a word dictate an artificial or unnatural pronunciation. (One reason for misspelling is that spelling and pronunciation do not match.)

Include as part of the dictation all marks of punctuation and all capital letters. (These will be inventoried elsewhere.)

DICTATION

Breaking in new cars requires skill, care, and knowledge about machines from their owners. Frequent oil changes are important. Clutches and brakes need attention and adjustment. Avoid a lot of fast stopping. You can't be too careful about engine overheating. A careful owner babies a new car along, taking as much time as he needs to. A careless owner's car is driven too fast before its engine is ready.

When all the dictation is completed, direct the class to make an exact copy of the left-hand page on the blank, right-hand page, *including any errors they notice.*

When the copying is completed, have the students underline twice any words they know they have misspelled. If they know the correct spelling, they should write it on the back of the sheet. Direct them to underline once any word whose spelling they are unsure of. All underlining should be done on the right-hand (copied) version.

The Inventory Results and Their Implications

A two-dimensional chart such as the one described in the reading comprehension inventory (Chapter 11) will prove useful in analyzing the results of this inventory. A page in the gradebook will suffice for the chart.

The first thing to check is the students' accuracy in taking dictation. Of course, there may be misspellings, but for the present, ignore them. Has every word been accounted for? Have all the punctuation marks been included? Have words been capitalized as dictated? If the student has missed dictated items, an oral-aural study method is inadvisable. If a student cannot take this simple dictation, he will probably not be able to write down spelling words accurately from dictation.

Next, the accuracy of the copy should be checked. If inaccuracies are noted, copying as a visual study method is also inadvisable. Most students, however, will display neither type of omission, their writing from dictation will be complete as will their copying. A copying study method is therefore indicated because it can be used independently.

Now the spelling is checked. Were the words that were underlined twice indeed misspelled? Have appropriate corrections been made? A person who exhibits a good pattern here should be encouraged to proofread all his written work because he is apparently able to catch errors and correct them. Are there words underlined once? Students who make this response should be encouraged to consult dictionaries in the course of their proofreading.

The teacher should then look over the left-hand (dictation) side of the page to find initial misspellings that were not detected by the student in the copying-proofreading. The teacher should try to classify the nature of the misspellings. Has the student misspelled any of the basic writing words? Has he violated any of the orthographic rules? Which demons has he misspelled? What are his own spelling idiosyncrasies?

A person in secondary school who misspells words in the basic writing vocabulary (other than the demons) has a very serious spelling problem since these words are ordinarily mastered by the fourth grade. He is therefore in need of remedial work. His immediate task is to master these basic writing words. The earlier parts of the analysis of his inventory may suggest the appropriate study approach for him to use. The teacher can supply the list of basic writing words, and appropriate materials are available commercially in workbook form. He may require help from someone at home—perhaps his mother or an older sibling. It should be emphasized that he is in serious trouble and must work conscientiously and without delay to make corrections. If he has other spelling problems, and this is likely to be the case, more thoroughgoing inventories will be needed. The teacher should consult the reading specialist or skilled elementary teachers for advice on subsequent procedures.

Should a considerable number of students show weakness in dealing with the orthographic rules, a need for class instruction in this area is indicated. If the number of students with this problem is relatively small, instruction can be limited to a group of students. If the students demonstrate that they are capable of dealing with the special orthographic regulations, there is no point in using class time for that kind of instruction. The teacher may find that his school grammar series and its workbooks provide useful lessons in this area.

The teacher will find that many students will have trouble with the demons, but this can hardly be considered abnormal behavior. Although the teacher should utilize every available approach in dealing with these words, he should not blame himself if his methods prove ineffectual to any degree. This is a pedagogical area that invites considerable attention of the scholarly and scientific kind. The classroom teacher, even the neophyte, is in a key position to do such work. Working out a nearly foolproof method of instruction in the spelling of these problem words would be a boon to the entire English teaching fraternity.

In dealing with the student's own spelling peculiarities, the teacher should motivate him to proofread in order to catch careless errors and to use the dictionary in cases where he is uncertain about the spelling of a word. Both of these methods place the major burden on the student.

In the case of the presumed "new" word, the teacher must arrange an opportunity for discrete instruction. What form should this instruction with "new" words take? As previously indicated, the first step is a teacher preview of the content of anticipated units. The teacher should make a list of all words which will be encountered by students and can be presumed to be unfamiliar to them, including familiar words that will take on new meanings in the new instructional context. The list should be broken down into short groups of words in the order in which they will appear in the instructional context. In this way, the teacher can present a group of words immediately before the students encounter them in the instructional context, whether it be reading, discussion, or writing. The teacher should present each word separately, writing it on the board and at the same time pronouncing it. The students should copy it into their notebooks, pronouncing the word in unison when there is any doubt that students will have difficulty with pronunciation. The teacher should then indicate various appropriate contexts in which the students can expect to come across the word, including (should this serve the teacher's broader purposes) some kind of definition of the word. In other words, as many avenues as possible should be used in introducing new words.

Some new words will have associated forms that should be introduced at the same time. For example, the noun "plot" has the related participle form "plotted" that exemplifies an orthographic rule. If the class is familiar with the orthographic rules, the associated forms can be derived inductively in teacher-led discussion; otherwise, the teacher should simply present the related forms (which can be used subsequently in inductively deriving orthographic rules during the spelling lessons).

Of course, these procedures are not solely spelling procedures but relate to vocabulary learning, to which spelling is incidental. It is wise to deal with another consideration .at this time. Certain words have developed around them conventionalized usage patterns that are specific to these words. For example, the noun "symbol" has generated the verb "symbolize." As indicated above, both forms should be introduced at the same time. In most discussions, the convention used when employing the third-person singular, present tense form of the verb is the form "symbolizes" in preference to such forms as "is symbolizing." This convention must be made manifest to the students, or they may use a form not ordinarily employed, resulting in awkwardness of expression—although the form may not be "wrong" in a technical sense.

Soon after introducing each list of new words, the teacher should administer a spelling drill, dictating the new words as a list. After the dictation, the students should check their own papers and make appropriate corrections as the teacher provides the correct spelling of the words on the list.

This simple procedure represents the most efficient method for dealing with spelling that researchers have yet discovered. This assertion requires some elaboration, however. Although such dictation-correction drills may not teach the correct spelling of all the words on the list, the method is as effectual for the great majority of learners as any other and more effectual than some.*

The foregoing discussion underlines the importance of developing spelling lists as part of the overall development of the curriculum content. The lists should include technical terms used in the course (like "anapest," "semicolon," "phrase," and "novel") as well as key "general" vocabulary in the reading, and words that might be needed for specific composition lessons. (For example, a composition about T. S. Eliot's poetry might require the use of such words as "ambiguous," "vague," and "interpretations" as well as technical terms like "image" and "metaphor.") It goes without saying that demons, whether those found on one of the published lists or those noted by the teacher as words that many students frequently misspell, should find a place on any such list.

DEALING WITH STUDENTS' SPELLING PROBLEMS

The individual student should also keep a word list. As he reads a student's writing, the teacher should indicate misspellings with a red pencil as he comes across them in the work. The student should find the correct spelling of these words and record them in a section of his notebooks. A word may be written a "magic number" of times, but students who do not copy accurately should *not* use this technique. (If the teacher or student is so minded, the problem of optimum magic numbers can be explored experimentally. A not very elaborate experimental design along these lines might result in a valuable contribution to the literature on spelling; such a project is within the power of even a practice teacher.) From time to time, the conscientious student can, with a little assistance from someone, drill on these personally troublesome words.

For most students, this practice is not impossibly onerous. Usually, there will not be more than 1 or 2 such occasional misspellings in a running context of, say, 150 words. But in most classes there will be a student or two who transgresses more frequently. Let us suppose that a hypothetical student who has mastery of the basic writing words consistently produces misspellings in the neighborhood of 8 or 10 per running 100 words and seems unable to detect his errors in proofreading. Such students are, happily, not commonplace, yet they are not rare. Keeping a personal spelling notebook becomes a burdensome chore for such a student. Therefore, the teacher should look for an alternative approach.

The teacher should first work with the student to try to uncover, through various analyses, the underlying reasons for the general spelling ineptness. He may have some basic perceptual disability that prevents him from making the appropriate associations between sounds and letters. The misspellings may

---

* In this case effectuality is determined by how close student performance—the correct spelling of words in a specific set—comes to ideal performance—the correct spelling of all the words in the set.

usually involve particular vowel or consonant sounds or analogous graphemic configurations. Perhaps his difficulty is associated with the use of a foreign language at home. Or he may have a general writing dysfunction. There are many possible approaches. Consultation with the school psychologist and reading and speech specialist will be helpful. But the problem of the chronic misspeller who exhibits no other intellectual dysfunction is persistently perplexing to educators, as well as interesting to those oriented to educational psychology.

Some Final Words on Spelling

We are often editorialized on spelling deficiencies in the products of our schools, the editorializing occurring in such places as P.T.A. meetings, the popular press, and informal conversations. The editorializing is voluminous, but specific documentation in support of the grievance is not often produced. One supposes that of all the areas of language usage, punctuation, organization, style, etc., that the specific character of established spelling usage renders this area one of extreme comfort for the layman. Spotting misspellings requires attention to words taken only as individual entities and consequently, requires neither superior intellectual endowment nor extensive intellectual exercise. The man-in-the-street is, therefore, well equipped to detect spelling errors.

In addition, the obvious vagaries of English spelling make good spelling appear to be some sort of superior accomplishment. ("Isn't it obvious that somebody who can't spell is inferior—at least to I, who can spell right? Furthermore, it is the job of the schools to teach spelling. Give me the good old three r's; and never mind all this modern junk. The kids today just don't know how to spell, etc., etc.") Despite the presence of some underlying relevance in such lay speculation, the problem of spelling is complex and not susceptible to pat answers.

Nonetheless, spelling error is readily noted; and many persons will base invidious judgments on both speller and schools, however unfairly, on their observation of spelling errors. In light of this, we do what we can with spelling!

However, this enjoiner is not to be taken as carte blanche to preempting inordinate amounts of instructional time from other aspects of class study.

Spelling, when viewed in the perspective of the entire English curriculum—reading, the interpretation of literature, expression in speech, and such writing skills as organization and the techniques of persuasion—must not be a paramount consideration, or even nearly so for most students, although it may be for certain individual students. Therefore, the teacher should undertake most of his spelling instruction on an individual basis, meeting needs as they are found.

Punctuation and Capitalization

Often the most numerous red marks on compositions are those indicating errors in punctuation and capitalization. The teacher should use a proofreading inventory to check the students' familiarity with the conventions governing the use of capital letters, punctuation marks, italics, and the like.

A proofreading inventory is a relatively simple matter to construct and administer. The teacher merely itemizes the usages that he intends to have the class employ, or expects that they will employ, develops a passage of moderate length that contains these usages, omits some of the appropriate punctuation marks and capitals from the passage, and submits copies for class correction. If the students consistently fail to make certain types of corrections, the teacher should follow up the inventory with specific instruction in those areas. Many school grammars contain passages that would be appropriate for such an inventory as well as exercises for follow-up instruction. The teacher should, however, avoid some of the "inventories" presented in the grammars. Some of them are arranged as discrete sentences and otherwise contain too many cues for satisfactory utility. Insofar as possible, the proofreading inventory (like all the others) should try to duplicate actual experiences. Therefore, a passage containing a number of consecutive sentences must be used since this more nearly approximates the student's task as he handles his own work.

In constructing the instrument, it is not necessary to run the entire gamut of punctuation. It is far better to concentrate on the types of punctuation that the students will inevitably be using, for example, the conventions for punctuating and capitalizing titles. To some extent, the students' needs will change from grade to grade. Some high school seniors should be made aware of such niceties as the distinctions in usage that are observed in connection with the dash, the comma, and parentheses. Most eighth graders, on the other hand, would find this kind of information rather esoteric, if not downright exotic. Contrariwise, most senior English students are undistressed by terminal punctuation, whereas many an eighth grader shows some anxiety in distinguishing between the conventional choices that appear open to him in the matter of the command vis-à-vis the exclamation.

The scoring of the inventory can be facilitated by having students indicate the changes on a special answer sheet rather than on the passage itself. In such a case, however, the passage will have to be more carefully constructed, but the additional time used in preparation will be more than repaid by the time saved and the increased accuracy in scoring. If the teacher chooses to use an answer sheet, the students may be allowed to score one another's work.

When the teacher constructs a passage (an example appears on p. 490) for use with an answer sheet, he should observe certain procedures. For one thing, to avoid ambiguity in the order of responses, there should not be more than one error per line. There will be some instances, however, where an error will require more than one correction. For example, the passage may include a run-on sentence like "Do you notice this message is not in code is it any wonder?" If the student does not choose to use a semicolon, he will have to insert a question mark and change the *i* in "is" to upper case. Since these changes are immediately contiguous, there is no real problem either in the use of the answer sheet or the scoring of the answer.

Proofreading Inventory

1.   Curious Correspondence Years from now
2   Reader, it was early in September, 1988 that a book bearing the inter-
3   esting title, *Intelligence that conquers the World,* fell into
4   the hands of a certain friendly power. One of the chapters
5   the one called: In Cuba—This," is presented for you inspection.
6   It begins with the following letter:
    7   Office of the Chief
    8   Division of Intelligence
    9   Havana Cuba
    10   December 23, 1965
11   Operative X-13
12   Delesseps hotel
13   Ciudad Trujillo, Dominican Republic
14   Dear sir: ·
15   Do you notice this message is not in code is it any
16   wonder? What else could you expect? The last message
17   the one you received three weeks ago, was very badly mis-
18   interpreted don't you think?
19   As you recall, I wrote "Put the bomb in the Ambassador's
20   car." How could you possibly have believed that I meant our
21   *own* Ambassadors car?
22   Also how could you possibly have misread "stick bomb" as
23   stink bomb"? Do you know what the dreadful consequences
24   Are? Now, ambassador Tequila won't be able to see anyone
25   for at least three weeks it's just terrible smelling so!
26   Answer these questions in code after all, you do need the
27   practice, dont you?
28   Yes have a Merry Christmas.
29   Respectfully yours
30   Jose Z-14 Chief of Intelligence
31   We know that its hard for you to believe a letter like
32   this one reader. There follows next, another letter, written in
33   code, decoded and reproduced here. Wait until you read that one you
34   just wont believe it.
    35   Cuban Embassy building
    36   Ciudad Trujillo, Dominican Rep
    37   Dec. 29, 1965

38   Chief of Intelligence
39   Division of Intelligence
40   Havana, Cuba
41   Dear Chief
42   I received your letter of December 23 and I
43   respectfully reply. You say, why don't I learn the
44   proper code?
45   I reply, why don't you take time to work out careful
46   messages?" I followed, to the letter, the chapter, Book
47   Codes". You wrote, "Hit the Ambassador in the south." All
48   the other ambassadors were in the capitol in the North. I
49   apologize for "stink" and wish you a Happy New Years Day.
50   Your servant

                            Operative X-13

The lines of the passage should be numbered, and there should be corresponding numbers on the answer sheet. Some lines of the passage should be errorless. If the student notices an error in a line, he should record the words in the middle of which the error appears (usually two words, the one preceding the omission and the one following it) together with the appropriate changes on the answer sheet. For example:

22   Also how could you possibly have misread "stick
23   bomb" as stink bomb"?

Answer Sheet

As it appears	*Correction*
22 Also how	Also, how
23 stink bomb"	"stink bomb"

All the foregoing suggests that proofreading is a dull, mechanical process, but, unfortunately, it is one to which writers must become habituated. It makes little sense to spend a considerable period of time in planning and executing a composition and then not take a few more minutes to catch errors that tend to deprecate the value of the work, however distasteful the activity involved in those few minutes might prove to be.

We have emphasized proofreading in connection with punctuation and capitalization work. The intuition of many teachers seems to be that when the rules of mechanics are understood and learned by writers, the writers simply generate compositions that contain appropriate usages. The presumption is that punctuating can become an automatic part of the composing process. Acting on this presumption, many teachers have developed lessons in punctuation and capitalization in which they conscientiously drill their students. Most *experienced* writers and editors, however, are not confident of their ability to generate work that is free of mechanical error. Consequently, when they have finished writing, they inevitably proofread their work to detect and correct inadvertent error.

Although many people do seem to learn the appropriate usages in school as a result of lessons in the mechanics of punctuation and capitalization, there is some serious question about the usefulness of such classroom drill as a teaching technique. Educational literature is replete with studies that purport to show the futility of instruction in many aspects of usage, including punctuation and capitalizing. At any rate, the completed composition must be proofread, even if the writer has mastered the rules and punctuation has become an integral part of his writing.

Certainly, more research is needed in connection with instruction in these matters. In the absence of pertinent research, it is fair to make some assumptions about the design of instruction in this area.

First of all, it is fruitless to introduce instruction on topics for which the writer will find no use, as with the example given above about the dashes, commas, and parentheses in the eighth grade. Continuing along the same line, if a person's writing does not make use of such structures as introductory adverbial clauses, there is little point in teaching him how to punctuate them. Possibly, many of these punctuation usages and the structures requiring them can be more strongly related to the student's own development as a writer, an instance where more research is needed.

Next, it makes little sense for those who have mastered certain punctuation conventions to have to experience lessons in them. Therefore, some individualization of instruction is inescapable. Individualizing instruction and practice proves most useful here, since such a plan enables different students to work on specific problems in terms of their own needs. All students might work on punctuation exercises, but not all on the same one at the same time.

Let us suppose that the inventory reveals that one group of students in a class has trouble with the capitalization of titles, another group is unfamiliar with the conventions for handling direct discourse, and a third group handles parenthetical clauses badly. Each student should be made aware of his weakness. The teacher, using whatever resources he has—the class grammar, workbooks, programed materials, homemade materials—should plan a sequence of lessons designed to instruct in each of the three areas. During the same period of class time, each group should work only through the lessons on the weakness shown by its members. Such differentiation of instruction, in terms of time, should prove more effective than the whole-class, lock-step approach, which ignores individual needs and, worse, those students who have already mastered the material in the lesson.

Further, the sequence of work can be scheduled in terms of the relative importance of the students' apparent shortcomings. For example, terminal punctuation is generally more significant than internal punctuation. Therefore, priority should be assigned to an individual's problems with terminal marks over his problem with commas.

Finally, many punctuation usages occur in clusters. Think of the cluster of usages connected with direct discourse: Each time there is a new speaker, a new paragraph must be used; quotation marks must enclose the speaker's words; commas may be used to set off the quotation; there are special conventions for terminal punctuation; the discourse must begin with a capital, and so on. Thus, whenever the writer employs direct discourse, he must bring to mind a cluster of conventions.

Many school grammar books ignore this in their organization, however. Instead of treating all these matters in an organic way, they are organized topically. There will be a section on capital letters, for example, that will include prescriptions for using capitals at the beginnings of sentences, with proper nouns and adjectives, in abbreviations, in direct discourse, in business letters, and so on. Consequently, the student must learn a series of discrete usages that are related only in that they all employ upper-case forms. Is it any wonder that only the best students will learn the rules?

The use of these various conventions of capitalizing and punctuating is somewhat more arbitrary than many of us have been led to believe. They are not bound to the Latin alphabet; they vary from country to country and from language to language. For example, German usage prescribes the capitalization of *all* nouns; Spanish usage prescribes an inverted question mark to introduce questions, as well as a question mark at the end; the French use a special marking for direct quotations. There is even extreme variation in usage among English-speaking nations. For example, the *Encyclopaedia Britannica* employs such usages as Cedar *r*iver, Floyd *c*ounty. Various publishers are guided by their own house rules in such matters as the use of commas after introductory adverbial clauses, using the word length of the clause as the criterion in determining whether or not the comma is used at all. Finally, established authors display great latitude in their use of these conventions. For example, William Saroyan has eschewed the quotation mark.

Possibly, it is because of the essentially arbitrary nature of these conventions that many young writers do not generate them as an integral part of their writing. Certainly, more research is needed to discover the relationships of capitals and punctuation to other elements in the writing gestalt. At any rate, an increased emphasis on the role of proofreading in the whole composition process more closely approximates real writing situations than does the practice of punctuating grammar book exercises.

Organization

The purpose of devoting an inventory to an assessment of the students' organizational skill in writing is that expository writing is an inalienable feature of the English course—possibly the only kind of composition that can be so characterized—and the central feature of expository writing of the utilitarian kind is its organization. A real composition is used as the instrument in this case: the first book report of the year.

At the first or second class meeting the assignment of the first outside reading should be made. It is useful to have students select a book whose topic is generically related to the stories in the reading inventory. That is, if the stories in the reading inventory are all mysteries, the first outside reading should be a mystery. The teacher should tell the students that they are to write a book report on this book and set a tentative due date, but he should also warn them not to begin writing the report until he gives them specific instructions at a later date.

When the reading inventory has been completed, some class time should be taken to review the ways in which the stories in the inventory are related. Small-group discussion is best for this, since it is desirable for the students to arrive at their own decisions about the nature of the theme that unifies the stories. After this discussion, the teacher should give specific directions for the content of the book review and make the due date firm.

In giving the directions, the teacher should tell the students that, in addition to reviewing the book, they must tell whether its theme is the same as, or different from, that of the stories in the reading inventory. These directions are somewhat vague and pointedly so. More specific instruction would serve to cue the organizational details of the composition whereas the purpose of the inventory is to find out about the students' own organizing ability.

The Inventory Results and Their Implications

The teacher can expect to encounter five different types of responses: a very well organized paper; a paper that shows a native skill at organization but is lacking in the finer points; a paper that is generally disorganized but understandable; a truly incomprehensible paper; no paper at all.

The very well organized paper has most of the following features:

1. A general thesis statement of some kind.
2. A statement of the plan and purpose of the paper.
3. A body that follows the plan and exhibits generalizations supported by specific examples, as well as appropriate definitions of terms.
4. A general summary.

This kind of paper suggests that the student has had previous instruction in organizational skills and that further instruction along these lines is, at best, gratuitous.

The second type of paper presents a less formal organization. It rehashes the book and, to some extent, discusses the theme. These elements are, in the main, kept separate. Papers of this kind imply little previous instruction in organization. At the same time, they suggest a high degree of readiness for such instruction. Such a paper follows:*

TO SIR, WITH LOVE

For my Book report I read *"To Sir, With Love"*, by E. R. Baithwaite. This story takes place in the east end of London. A negro teacher named Richard Baithwaite is teaching Seniors in high schools. These are not normal seniors because they are rebelliouess, rude, and vulgar, and they are not allowed in ordinary public schools. Mr. Baithwaite teaches these teenagers to be courteous. He teaches them to call him "Sir", the girls Miss ———, and the boys by there last name. There takes place a big change when this teacher arrives at this school.

In the four short storys we read—"This happened to me" (rubbernose), "The first proms the hardest", "Bad influence", and "Why did this happen to me", teenages are growing up I think the authors wanted to show that each teenagers has its own problems. They have to striaghten out themselves. Today more than ever teenagers are getting more independent of parents and grownups and less confiding.

In *"To Sir, With Love"*, Its the same problem. The teenagers are rebelliouess because they have problems and don't know what to do about them. They think by being rude and vulgar there problems will vanish.

When you compare the four short story's and this book you find that they are quit similar because they all have teenagers in it.

Ninth-grade girl

The third type of paper is a rather meandering presentation built around a rehash of the book. Unless the paper is so poorly conceived that the teacher cannot understand it at all, bad organization is probably its real fault, and the writer will very likely profit from work in expository organization. The following is an example of this type of paper:

"GOING ON SIXTEEN"

"Going on Sixteen" is they story of a young girl growing up on a farm and her curious problems, and responsibilities toward school and home.

One of the first problems she encounters is about the bringing-up of four young pups whose mother had died of a blood disease. These pups were bred to be champions. One died despite her help but she raised the

* The compositions in this section are presented as they came to the teacher's desk in uncorrected form and before proofreading instruction.

others from eyedropper to saucer and finally into young dogs. Two of the dogs were taken to training kennels while the one she liked best stayed with Jody (the gril).

In school Jody wanted to become one of the crowd. Her efforts and good intentions were of no help to her, Jody had quite a talent for art. There was a contest in which a poster she made, won and was used in the high school play. Gradually she became more like herself and acted that way too.

She acquired more friends and even had a date or two.

Meanwhile she was worried sick that eventually they would come and take her dog away. Finally that day came and in the days that followed she grew lonlier by the minute. Even redoing the living room with the help of her art teacher didn't help.

One day she was sent some tickets for the dog show her dog (sonny) was going to be in. When she and her father (her mother died when she was younger) got there and saw the dog before the show, the would not perform right, after that. So, Jody showed the dog instead of the trainer and she and and the dog won first prize. After that, Jody kept sonny and showed him every so often. This made everybody happier.

I think this story was much like the ones we read in class. When Jody's poster won the prize, she at once became more popular and starting acting more like herself.

     The End

Ninth-grade girl

The next class of papers is of an entirely different order. If a paper is, in fact, incomprehensible or is so riddled with mechanical errors that comment on such things as organizational structure is obviated, then the writer should be regarded as dysfunctional.* Such writers will have to learn to write words, sentences, and single paragraphs—in other words, to become generally functional—before they are ready for expository writing. The following report exhibits some of the characteristics of the dysfunctional writer:

This Teenager story is a bout a gril Jane who though she was in love with Charles Barbour. Jane's problem was that she dont think Charles and he wont talke to her she use to have fights like made with Joe to.

He was dirty and messy boy, who only cared in machinery. Joe moved out next door Charles moved in. Jane was so exited started takeing to Charlie over the hedge. The thyme of this story is gril meets boy and likes him but its only his apertence.

Ninth-grade girl

---

* See Chapter 2 for an example of the work of a dysfunctional student.

If a student does not turn in a paper at all, the teacher should determine the reason before making any decisions about future work. It may be that the student recognizes his own dysfunction and, consequently, doesn't even try to do compositions. Or he may have failed to develop good study habits. The teacher can observe his writing in class to determine which of the two possibilities is the more reasonable.

In the case of the student with poor study habits, the teacher's first job is to determine whether his study habits are generally poor—that is, he does very little outside work for any class—or whether they are poor only for his English classes, this particular class, or this particular assignment. At this point, the teacher should utilize the cumulative folder of all the student's writing, the English department folder, and the testimony of previous teachers. In addition, a conference with the student is in order. The teacher should try to find the cause of the poor study habits and, if possible, remove it. The results of the study skills inventory can be helpful in this regard (see Chapter 2).

In summary, if the teacher does not have a pretty fair idea of what the book was about after reading the book report, the student probably lacks organizational skills. After all, the book itself was organized, and the student merely had to follow that organizational pattern—a simple task.

Originality

The final writing inventory is an optional one that attempts to assess originality in writing. Its central purpose is to determine the extent to which the teacher and the class will pursue belletristic writing in the course of the year.

Originality is a concept that is difficult to define. In assessing this nebulous quality, the teacher must rely entirely on his own judgment. He will find that originality is relative. To the beginning teacher, all the compositions of his first class will seem to be somewhat original (although even the beginner can establish situations in which he can make some reasonable assessments of originality). But as he works with more and more students, and as composition topics are repeated from class to class and from year to year, his judgment as to what is original and what is rather commonplace becomes more and more acute.

The composition to be used in the assessment of originality is the one in the interest inventory (Chapter 2) entitled "The Person I Interviewed." The rationale behind this is that a person who can display originality in treating so mundane a topic truly possesses an original flair in writing. However, if the teacher feels that another topic would be more highly conducive to original treatment, he should obviously use that one.

The teacher should give the following instructions:

"Now that you have completed your interview work up your interview notes as a composition. Try to be as original as possible in this composition. See if you can get away from strict reporting and at the same time convey all the information you have found out. If this doesn't seem possible, then a straightforward report will do. But extra credit will be given for originality."

Just as in the organization inventory, some dysfunctional compositions may be received, and some students may not turn in papers. The other compositions may be classified in three ways: straightforward accounts; deviations from these that are typical; and atypical deviations. The typical deviations retain the character of the interview but change the personae of those involved in the interview. The atypical deviations take many forms and thus represent the more original approaches. The following two student-made models, which were developed from the classroom interview, exemplify these generalizations. The first is a ninth grader's work. The second is from a seventh grader.

THE PERSON I INTERVIEWED

"This is Lynn Fargo here! I'm reporting from the scene of the riot, where, just now, police are moving in with fire hoses and billy clubs. Fire trucks are hopefully trying to douse the blaze which has quickly arisen.

"I'll try to get ahold of one of the rioters to find out what kind of background they have and if it affects their feelings towards the rioting.

"Pardon me, son, pardon me. Could you please tell us your name?"

"Jody Johnson."

"Well, Jody, tell us a little about yourself. Start with your family."

"I've got one brother, sixteen, one sister, thirteen. I'm fourteen. My father's a dentist."

"Where do you live?"

"In Dober, Mass."

"What are some of your hobbies, Jody, rioting?"

"Ha. Ha. I collect coins."

"What sports do you enjoy?"

"I sail and swim. In the winter I ski."

"Where do you sail and swim?"

"On the Cape at Wareham."

"I see. Where do you attend school?"

"I go to Jackson High School. I'm in the ninth grade."

"Do you have any subjects you like or dislike?"

"Yes. I like science, but I hate French. It bores me."

"Do you have electives?"

"I take technical drawing."

"Do you know what you'd like to be later on?"

"No. I haven't decided yet."

"Thank you very much, Jody."

"Well, folks, from what I have found here, this boy is an unrooted American who has yet to find his place in life. Things bore him, so he needs some excitement to . . ."

"Ah, excuse me, Miss Fargo."

"Yes, Jody, what is it? I'm on the air."

"Well, I don't mean to be rude, but I just arrived here ten minutes ago. I'm up here with my parents for the weekend. I'm visiting my aunt."

"Well, folks, as I was saying, we need more youngsters like Jody Johnson: kind, considerate, polite . . ."

Ninth-grade girl

The writer here has been unable to get away from the interview pattern, and although she has transposed herself into the persona of a radio interviewer and the situation into the scene of a teenage riot, the narrative is not essentially different from the straightforward classroom interview. Notice the title. The voice of the writer is the first person, perhaps suggesting limited maturity—self-centered thinking. This judgment is supported by the satirical tone employed toward adult critics of the writer's peer group. The composition shows some originality, but the presentation is a typical deviation from a straightforward account of the direct-life experience on which it is based.

Although the second writer is chronologically younger than the first, her narrative suggests greater maturity in composition:

THE LITTLE ANGEL

Once upon a time, there was a little angel up in Heaven and she was called Judy.

But Judy was the only sad angel in heaven.

All the other angels were as happy as could be. Why, there were beautiful gardens, and trees, and birds, and stars, and just everything to make an angel happy. But still she was very sad; and do you know why? It was because she was the littlest angel in heaven, and there were no other little angels for her to play with.

So one day, Judy climbed up on the "Pearly Gates of Heaven", and started to think of all the happy things she knew back on earth.

She remembered her Daddy and Mommy, her big brother Kevin and her little cat Jingles. She remembered the fun rides she had on her Daddy's bus, and how hard it was to push the big keys on her Mommy's typewriter, and sitting with Kevin while he did all the homework that he got from college.

Then she thought of going to school and iceskating in the winter, and then going to the lake and swimming all summer long. But especially she thought of all her little playmates, and all the fun they had had together.

She thought of her happy earth life all day long until it was time for evening prayers. So with a heavy heart she climbed down off the great big heavenly gates and slowly walked back over the clouds to the prayer garden. She knelt down in her place and started to pray. But soon after, she saw a little figure walking toward her. She looked up and to her great delight and surprise another little girl angel knelt down beside her.

Seventh-grade girl

The writer of this composition has abandoned the interview format entirely. She uses the omniscient viewpoint to relate the narrative, thus keeping herself out of it. The writer of the previous composition, by contrast, sees herself as "Lynn Fargo" and, for all intents and purposes uses the first person to relate the narrative. The title of this composition relates to the composition and not to the lesson assignment. The subject of the interview that led to this composition was a very little girl—even for a seventh grader—and that subject receives a far subtler treatment than does Jody in the earlier composition. The imitation of children's Sunday-school story style is in keeping with the whole approach and shows far greater internal consistency to its type than does the interview: no radio interviewer would use the questions used by Lynn. For a much older writer the piece might be considered trite; but for a seventh grader, this is an original approach. The consistency of the style, the subtlety in treatment of the subject, and the author's excluding herself from the composition are all suggestive of greater originality and maturity.

Should the teacher receive a number of compositions of the kind that deviate from the straightforward reporting type, he should consider very carefully weighting the year's work in composition in the direction of belles-lettres at the expense of utilitarian writing. A predominance of rather straightforward approaches, on the other hand, strongly suggests that utilitarian writing should be the focus of the course.

The principal function of composition in school is to communicate data, usually as part of teachers' evaluation procedures. Therefore, the immediate needs of the students are related to the techniques of clear and well-organized writing. Learning utilitarian writing will be challenge enough for most pupils. Of course, imitating belletristic forms may be helpful in learning the characteristics of those forms. But unless the students show some flair for belles-lettres, both they and their teacher will have a difficult time in a program heavily weighted toward this type of writing.

Classifying Students As Writers

We have already discussed the dysfunctional writer whose papers are of such an order that they are unable to communicate the message he intends. They are error riddled and actually (not merely pedagogically) uninterpretable. There are two additional classifications of student writers: the functional writer and the fluent writer.

Most students in secondary school are functional at writing. Of course, they make mechanical errors. The teacher often notes on their papers cryptic messages like "awkward," "ambiguous," "rethink." Nevertheless, communication has not broken down in a fundamental way; otherwise the teacher would not be able to recognize awkwardness, ambiguity, and irrationality in expression. Such shortcomings are noticed only because these items stand out against a more satisfactory tapestry.

There are a few students who write so well that the teacher looks forward to reading their papers and often can make no pertinent suggestions for improvement. The suggestions that are made are often gratuitous or certainly very tentative. Such students can be classified as fluent.

All of the writing inventories considered together provide the basis for this classification of students, which is important in molding the teacher's thinking about the general kind of instruction that is indicated for each type.

The dysfunctional student requires remediation, and his instructional needs have been sketched. Reading has priority over writing if a priority decision must be made, and the general English teacher must be guided by specialists in developing a suitable correctional program.

Helping the fluent writer may also be beyond the power of the teacher but, of course, for different reasons. The teacher's role here is to open doors. He can expand the repertoire of the fluent writer by using literary models to introduce forms and techniques heretofore unknown to the student. He can be introduced to some critical analysis so as to lead him to insights about the hidden things that can be put into writing. And beyond motivating him to clean up mechanical weaknesses (spelling, punctuation, defining techniques, and the like), the best recourse for the teacher is to accord recognition to the writer and to provide every encouragement to him.

In general, most students will be neither dysfunctional nor fluent, although anyone may attain either such classification under special circumstances, such as in writing certain forms of poetry. The students in the general category of functional writers will benefit from a careful, structured writing curriculum. An important feature of such a curriculum is the use of composition models for purposes of both analysis and imitation. But although literary models are suitable for analysis, it may be inadvisable to have the functional students attempt to imitate them. It would be better for the teacher to develop a file of good student-made models for imitation because the functional writer should be encouraged to imitate the writing of the good student; the literary model, almost by definition, is beyond his powers.

When the teacher completes the inventories and his assessments of what they reveal, he can begin his planning of composition work.

NOTES

1. H. D. Rinsland, *A Basic Vocabulary of Elementary School Children* (New York: Macmillan, 1945).
2. James A. Fitzgerald, *The Teaching of Spelling* (Milwaukee: Bruce Publishing Co., 1951).
3. *Ibid.,* p. 12.
4. E. L. Thorndike and Irving Lorge, *The Teacher's Word Book of 30,000 Words* (New York: Teachers College, Columbia University, 1944).
5. Falk S. Johnson, "New Rules for 'IE-EI' Spelling," *English Journal,* XLIX, No. 5 (May 1960).
6. D. H. Russell, "A Second Study of the Characteristics of Good and Poor Spellers," *Journal of Educational Psychology,* Vol. 46 (March 1955), pp. 129–141.
7. Thomas D. Horn, "Research in Spelling," *Children's Writing: Research in Composition and Related Skills* (Champaign: National Council of Teachers of English, 1960–1961).
8. Russell, *op. cit.*
9. Grace Fernald, *Remedial Techniques in Basic School Subjects* (New York: McGraw-Hill Book Co., 1943).

SUGGESTIONS FOR FURTHER READING

The following offer extensive bibliographies, comments and summaries on various phases of composition.

1. BRADDOCK, RICHARD, LLOYD-JONES, RICHARD, and SCHOER, LOWELL, *Research in Written Composition.* Champaign: National Council of Teachers of English, 1963.
2. BURROWS, ALVINA T. (Editor) Children's Writing: *Research in Composition and Related Skills,* Champaign: National Council of Teachers of English, 1960–1961.
3. SHANE, HAROLD G. and MULRY, JUNE GRANT, *Improving Language Arts Instruction through Research,* Washington: Association for Supervision and Curriculum Development, NEA, 1963.

Traditions in Composition Teaching   22

Composition is probably the most generally dissatisfying area in English teaching. The assignments frustrate the students; the results of the assignments frustrate their teachers. Educational literature is full of articles that report teachers' frustration and their attempts, successful and otherwise, to deal with it. What makes the whole situation particularly serious is that the bulk of a teacher's out-of-class time is spent in dealing with compositions.

How much time should a teacher spend reading and reacting to a composition? Suppose that this time is a function of the length of the composition, a logical supposition. Then, how much time should a teacher spend reading and reacting to a composition one hundred words long? Thirty seconds? Two minutes? Five minutes? Longer? Assuming that five minutes is not unreasonable, how long will it take to read a set of compositions from a class of thirty students? Then how long will it take to read the compositions of five such classes?

Assuming it takes about twelve hours to read very short compositions from the students, and assuming further that most of this grading is done outside school hours, when will the teacher find time to make tests and score them? Where will the time for lesson planning come from (including those lessons leading to the writing of other compositions)? Having vouchsafed answers to these questions, there is another facing the teacher that is even more pointed: how valuable is a composition only one hundred words long?

Although the intended ring of the foregoing is ironic, the irony derives from the situation that faces the English teacher in the work-a-day world. J. Nicholas Hook, in a study of teachers of the winners and runners-up of the National Council of Teachers of English achievement awards, found that the teachers (of classes smaller than thirty) spent seven to nine hours weekly reading compositions and that, in addition to their five classes, they spent two hours a day working in cocurricular activities.[1]

It is clear that, because of this situation, the teacher had better know what he is about in dealing with instruction in composition, but it is equally clear that too many teachers do not. One reason for this sorry state of affairs is that composition teaching has been dominated by a number of unexamined traditions, the force of whose influence has weakened the whole structure of the curriculum apparatus. Let us examine some of these traditions, which connect variously with limiting the field, purposes, objectives, procedures, and theory.

The Limited Viewpoint

A written composition exists only as an end product of the composing process. Yet, typically, teachers have restricted their thinking about the teaching of writing to the final composition products, and little attention has been given to the process of composing.

Students are asked to write on a narrow range of topics suggested by the teacher; the due date is set. Compositions are turned in. The teacher attends only to the composition products. For example, there are no discussions about *how* professional writers write, only about *what* they have written. There is no opportunity for introspection by the students, no examination of what happens to him while he is engaged in the composing process, no consideration of the personal rewards that writing brings, and no recognition of writing and composing as a way of perceiving, of coming to know.

In short, the attention of both student and teacher has traditionally been riveted to the finished piece of work, which is viewed as an artifact without any connection to the personality that produced it.

Ordinarily, the topics the students write about spring from the intuitions of the teacher. If he has strong intuitions, then the topics and the compositions that follow from them may be interesting. However, since year after year a student's writing experience is controlled by his teachers' ideas for topics, his whole curriculum experience is almost certain to be unproductive. Such topics as "What I Did Last Summer" and "My Goals in Life" may be interesting and challenging *once*. But too many students must face such writing assignments year in and year out.

Usually, after reading a number of uninspired compositions, a teacher discards the obviously poor topics from his repertoire, and over the years he adds a few "good" ideas. But there is rarely, if ever, long-range planning of a sequential composition curriculum. The student is left to his own devices in the matter of any sequential development of his writing skill.

Purpose of Teaching Composition

Why do we teach composition? Since purposes condition practices, this has been a key question in the development of composition curricula. The answer that has traditionally been put forward is that the "life needs" of the student demand a high degree of writing skill. These life needs presumably are of three different kinds:

1. Some of the students may become professional writers. There are thought to be many vocational opportunities for those skilled at writing.
2. Students who plan to attend college have an obvious need to learn to write well.
3. Normal daily social intercourse demands writing as an essential communications skill.

The limited number of vocational opportunities for professional writers refutes the first point. The Department of Commerce, in its figures for the experienced labor force 1960, has listed the number of authors, editors, and reporters (considered in one group) as 132,000. Listed in the same source are public relations men and publicity writers: 31,000. Taken together, these figures approximate half the total of plumbers and pipefitters. Of the total labor force 14 years of age and over, the 163,000 professional writers account for a little more than two-tenths of 1 percent. Of the total population, 14 years and over, professional writers represent a bit more than one-tenth of 1 percent.[2] Thus the picture seems bleak for aspiring professional writers.

It is bleaker yet for teachers whose motivation is to turn out writers. If a teacher has a load of five classes per year, and his average class size is thirty, after ten years of teaching, he can expect to have taught 1.5 future professional writers. Of course, members of professions are routinely called upon to do writing. The writing of these adults, however, will be of a highly specialized character, and the value of their output will tend to be determined by the character of their training and experience at least as much as, by their skill in belles-lettres. Much of the writing done by most professional persons consists of exposition and argument and is highly utilitarian in intent. So, despite the fact that professional writing requirements do often exist on an occupational basis, it seems safe to dismiss this life need as a central purpose in determining course content.

What are the needs of the college-bound student? Is he typical in the English course? The imminent danger faced by any teacher, and especially the English teacher, in responding to these questions, is basing the response on the needs that he himself perceives in his own experiences. Everyone tends to think of himself as rather average. But the teacher is not representative, in any way, of the average person; nor is the English teacher the average teacher. As a holder of a baccalaureate, the teacher (of English or not) has placed himself in an extremely atypical position with respect to the general population.

If we examine the statistics on education, we find that one-third of the population that begins school drops out before completing high school. Only about one-third of the pupils who are in school in the fifth grade will even *enter* college. Of those who begin college, less than 50 percent will complete their first degrees. Only about 8 percent of the general population holds academic degrees.[3] In short, it is true for only a small proportion of the population that students must learn to write in order to go to college.

If it were reasonable to assume that only the college-bound population has life needs that are oriented to composition skills, we could discount life needs as a purpose for instruction in composition for two-thirds of the students.

But this would not be entirely realistic: everyone does some writing, whether it is a business letter, social correspondence, or a letter to the editor. There are also tax forms, business forms, and employment applications, and even notes to milkmen. But in terms of the secondary school composition program, such a catalog of life needs is certainly not imposing. Most students are amply equipped to meet them (possibly excepting business letter forms) by the time they have finished the elementary grades.

Aside from the college-bound, by what rationale do we devote so much of our instruction to composition? If the assumptions about the relative irrelevance of composition skills in terms of life needs for most students do make any sense, then instruction in composition must be predicated on other considerations.

In the traditional use of the term "life needs," there has been an assumption that life is what begins when schooling has ended; yet this is a rather narrow interpretation of life. For most of us, the decade between the ages of six and sixteen is a period in which school is the central feature of our experience. Metaphorically, school *is* life during these years.

School attendance is very nearly universal in our culture. Within the educational institution—and especially in the English class—the writing of compositions is a highly valued activity. The success of a person's integration into the patterns of the educational institution is in no small measure dependent upon his writing proficiency. A recognition of these conditions results in the following formulation of purpose with respect to teaching writing beyond mere functional proficiency: We teach this kind of writing in our schools because *students must do this kind of writing in our schools.* True enough, the position is somewhat embarrassingly circular. But it states the case.

At the risk of being accused of developing a position based on truisms, let us go on to consider the nature of the objectives of the secondary school composition program. In light of the statement of purpose, the objectives can be readily formulated: to write in such a way as to insure the most effective integration with the educational institution possible; to learn how to do such writing as efficiently as possible. In this formulation "efficiently" is taken to mean rapidly and with as few errors as possible.

It is likely that many students have never entertained these objectives expressed in just these terms. But in hypothetical discussions, hypothetical students behave hypothetically.

Having established the terminal objectives of the instruction, it is necessary to determine the nature of the medial objectives upon which the attainment of those terminal objectives is contingent. This determination will rest upon a description of the kinds of writing that will be necessary for success in school, "success" here being the equivalent of effective integration. This description can be made only after an empirical survey of the kinds of writing that a person will be likely to do in secondary school and beyond.

For the purpose of this discussion, it is fair to assume that most students, by the time they enter secondary school, will have mastered, or at least have little difficulty with, the kind of writing that characterizes one- or two-sentence responses on tests as well as the skills needed in listing. If this is not the case, the immediate objective is to attain the relevant proficiencies, especially since, as noted earlier, such skills are likewise relevant for integration with the general culture after schooling has ceased. What kinds of writing are required beyond this writing, which is of a rather limited degree of sophistication?

A survey of the writing required in school reveals that a number of different kinds are needed. But the kind that is encountered most frequently and in most places is the kind that is intended to communicate information. In secondary schools—in science courses, social studies courses, and English courses, where the occasions for writing are the most frequent—the information-oriented composition is the type most frequently used. In colleges, the information-oriented composition is virtually the only kind that is encountered. The term "information" as it is used here includes the opinions of the writer when such opinions are presented as information, as, for example, in his dealing with such topics as "What I think about _____." Information-oriented papers will include such forms as have been traditionally characterized as exposition, argument, and description. The information-oriented classification also includes most business correspondence.

There are also some other forms to be found, especially in English classes: narrative, drama, poetry, and various other personalistic forms, and even occasional odd forms, such as parodies and jokes. However, the most extensively and frequently encountered kind of writing in our schools and universities is by all odds the rather utilitarian composition intended to communicate information. Therefore, in any listing of medial objectives of the composition curriculum, proficiency in the information-oriented, utilitarian forms must be assigned priority.

The reason for the occurrence of the other forms in the English classes relates to the value system peculiar to English studies in that literature is considered of even greater value than writing in English.[4] Persons working in English spend most of their time on works of literature. If the reading is not itself literary art, then it involves the criticism of literary art. Since literary art is thus highly valued, it follows that some composition work will be with forms that are aesthetically designed—belletristic—as opposed to those of utilitarian design. Of course, the categories are not necessarily mutually exclusive from the viewpoint of the audience or the writer, but, in general, they are differentiated by the central purpose of communication, as well as other conditions.

The dichotomy belletristic/utilitarian calls to mind another of the traditional notions in composition instruction, that there are two kinds of writing, "creative" writing and the other kind. The term "creative" applied to the class of compositions that includes drama, poetry, and the like is unfortunate because it somehow implies that the other kind of writing does not involve a creative process. Although it may not be as aesthetically rewarding for most readers to read a critical analysis of Shakespeare's sonnet as it is to read the sonnets themselves, it is absurd to assume that the critic was not engaged in a creative process in writing his criticism.

Teaching Procedures

Another set of questionable traditions in the teaching of composition has to do with both theory and intuition as they have governed teaching procedures. For example, every teacher notices mechanical errors in punctuation and capitalization when reading a set of compositions and wants to do something about it. Relying on his intuition, he may reach for the trusty grammar book and plan a series of lessons and drills in the areas of need that the mechanical errors indicate. Yet, innumerable studies have shown that classroom drills do not eliminate error in compositions.[5] The evidence is disheartening. Supplementary to published evidence is the experience of teachers who, after painstaking work through lessons and units on mechanics intended to correct flaws in composition, and after finding what appears to be mastery of principles in grammar book exercises, encounter the same old flaws marring subsequent compositions. Such is the folklore of the faculty room.

The folklore may be partly caused by reliance on impression rather than systematic enumeration and classification of errors. For example, one of the more frequently reported errors, the sentence fragment, is actually relatively infrequent in secondary school compositions (when compared to well-formed sentences) and seems to disappear as students mature.[6]

There does indeed seem to be undoubtedly serious question as to the efficacy of direct instruction in usage of all kinds—including punctuation, spelling, and pronoun case, among other areas. Thus, the teacher's intuitive reaction to the detection of mechanical errors—that of grammar book drill—usually does not achieve its goal, the elimination of the errors from compositions.

Another tradition that governs much of school practice is the assumption that a composition can be best described by the model in Figure 22.1. The model suggests that compositions result from combining elements that are hierarchical in character. Letters are linked together in strings to produce words; words, to produce sentences; sentences, to produce paragraphs; and paragraphs, to produce longer compositions.

Acting on the basis of this conception, a teacher may read a set of papers and notice that some papers contain run-on sentences or sentence fragments. Despite the fact that the same papers contain many more well-formed sentences, the teacher may accept the few errors as evidence that the students "cannot write sentences." All work with superordinate structures in the

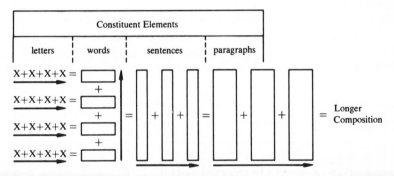

Arrows represent the strings taken as wholes. Each arrow is the equivalent of one element in the successive expression in the equation.

FIGURE 22.1

hierarchy is then delayed while the class is taught a number of lessons dealing with "sentence sense."

A similar approach is made when the teacher finds longer compositions containing paragraphs that are somehow "inadequate" in his terms. Perhaps, for example, some paragraphs may lack "topic sentences." Practice in writing paragraphs that are "built around topic sentences" ensues, and no composition longer than a single paragraph is written until the single paragraph is "mastered."

A movement downward through the hierarchy shows the weakness of this theoretical thinking. Should the teacher move below the sentence level, he might delay consideration of the sentence until no misspellings of words are encountered in his students' writing. Or if he notices badly made letters, he may delay work with spelling until letter forms are mastered. (This problem, if uncorrected in lower grades, often persists in high school students.)

It is enlightening to observe the processes employed by elementary school teachers in their work with children who are just beginning to write. Instruction in letter formation is scheduled in a sequence that is determined by the presence of analogous elements in the shapes of the various letters, the frequency of use of the letters in words, and the relationships of the words in the writing curriculum to those in the reading and speaking vocabularies of the children. Ordinarily, when the child has learned a few letters, he is taught to form words that contain only those letters. Meanwhile, he adds to his letter stock. When he has learned enough appropriate words, he is taught to write sentences. Frequently, a child can write sentences before he has learned to form all the letters in our alphabet.

This process suggests a model that is a better description of the structural elements within a composition and suggests better inferences about the generating process.

The process can be explained in this way: A person writing a particular letter is not simply producing an element of a word; rather, he produces a part of a word, a sentence, a paragraph, and a longer composition—all of these at once. This implies that the formation of even a single letter strongly

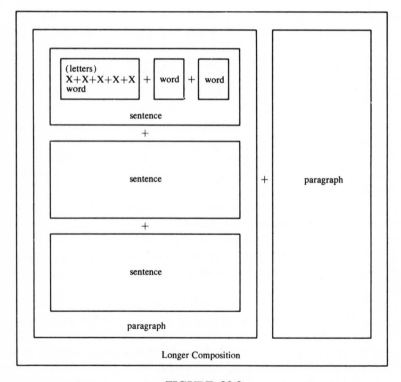

FIGURE 22.2

suggests a preliminary formulation of the whole composition as a gestalt towards which the successive production of strings of words, sentences, paragraphs, and so forth, moves.

The process hypothesis that has been thus derived from the model contains a number of interesting suggestions. Should a student exhibit such patterns as forming letters badly, misspelling words, or punctuating sentences inappropriately, his problem is not primarily one of inadequate association of part to part, but rather of an inadequately developed gestalt of the complete composition.* It follows, then, that the instructional work in composition is best developed with the longer composition units as opposed to working toward a mastery of their smaller subordinate components.[8]

The accident of the graphemic conventions of English can lead to the perceptions of composition writing in terms of a model of structures strung together. It is well to note, in passing, a more general limitation imposed on both the writer and his readers as a result of the graphemic system. Ordinarily, reading and writing are done from left to right in a linear way. Therefore, any ideas communicated must be expressed or perceived one at a time from left to right. Very often, however, it is the intent of the writer to express the sensations that he is aware of simultaneously: the feel, scent, and appearance of a rose, for example. Even by introducing such words as "simultaneously" into the context of his writing, he is unable to communicate his experiences in the way they happened. To an extent, the limitations of our normal graphemic conventions explain the departures from these conventions made by such authors as E. E. Cummings and the speculations on the graphemic system of Chinese by such critics as Ezra Pound.[9]

Another difficulty caused by the left-to-right generation is with the matter of spelling. The writer in generating a string of words may be temporarily or totally blocked by being unable to produce a word whose spelling he does not know.

The Rhetorical Tradition

Two traditions of rhetoric have significantly influenced composition teaching practices. The first is the familiar "class" concept, which holds that there are four types of composition: narration, description, exposition, and argumentation.

According to this view many pieces of writing may be characterized as

---

* In the description made by Loban of children's speech[7] the occurrence of mazes (structures in which the speaker halts his forward movement, goes backward to change what he has said, moves forward, goes back again, and so forth) strongly suggests an editing process. This in turn suggests a preliminary formulation of broad verbal patterns toward which the speaker works. This seems to support the view of the structure of composition expressed in this chapter.

one of these four types. Some compositions are predominantly one type but contain elements of any or all of the three others.

Acting on the basis of this concept—or what is more likely, using a textbook designed along lines suggested by it—the teacher limits class consideration only to those kinds of compositions that fit it. Although many pieces of literature can be included among these four types, a great many cannot because the concept lacks generality.

Many works of literature that display great power are, for various reasons, difficult, if not impossible, to classify into any of the categories named in this fourfold scheme. Is Lincoln's Gettysburg Address essentially argument, exposition, or description? Is the "Parable of the Sower" (Luke 8:5–8) a narrative, description, exposition, or argument? What is the essential nature of any allegory? Is the *Parallel Lives* by Plutarch narrative, descriptive, or expository? How does one classify any biographical or historical work? Is Harvey's discussion of the circulation of blood mainly descriptive, expository, or an argument in opposition to Galen's view?

Many contemporary authors have exploited such techniques as stream-of-consciousness and surrealism. There is no place for these in the fourfold classification. Beyond such imaginative prose, many examples of drama and poetry do not yield to classification.

If the teacher limits his work to the compass of this theory, he rejects much that is valuable from curricular consideration.

The second rhetorical view that has exerted considerable influence is the concept that a piece of writing must display the three principles of unity, coherence, and emphasis. Many teachers have used this concept as a basis for criticizing and evaluating composition work.

The unity principle indicates that all the elements of a composition must contribute to the central idea or display a consistency of viewpoint and that this singleness of effect must be maintained by a consistent style. The composition is considered to have coherence if all its elements have a logical connection or congruity arising from a common central relationship. Emphasis is the appropriate prominence given to one or more of the elements contained in the piece.

Teachers who use this concept in their work sometimes make faulty evaluations because of the internal inconsistencies in the formulation.

Although it may be possible to conceive of a work that is coherent but not unified, a unified work could not be incoherent. Yet this rhetorical scheme regards unity and coherence as conceptually parallel. Further, should elements of a work exhibit emphasis, such emphasis need not pose a threat to coherence but might readily threaten the unity of the work.

Let us consider two examples of the dream genre of writing in terms of this theory. The first will be hypothetical; the second, real.

Many teachers encounter from time to time a composition whose final paragraph reads: "And then I woke up." Their ultimate evaluation, whether or not this is conveyed to the writer, is that the piece is of low merit. Triteness aside, the evaluation is made on the basis of the unity, coherence, and emphasis theory.

The final paragraph is certainly emphatic. Without it, the whole composition, in terms of the writer's intent, is incoherent. The difficulty seems to be that in introducing "And then I woke up," the writer violates the principle of unity. By introducing the note of a dream experience, he shifts from developing one narrative to developing two, possibly, and the original unity as perceived by the reader is spoiled. Should the writer have "played fair" with his reader and "gone to sleep" before he began his inner narrative, the narrative frame would still be present. Thus, although if the "I went to sleep" device is used and emphasis shifts, the coherence is unaffected, but the disunity still exists because the dual nature of the narrative is maintained, perhaps even intensified. The composition is still devalued because of the violation of the principle of unity.

In the same way, our second example, a real composition—*Pilgrim's Progress*—suffers from a lack of unity because the writer places one narrative within another, a journey within a dream. In these terms we must reexamine much of our literature that involves the device of the narrative frame. Does *The Ancient Mariner* lack unity? Does the medieval poem *The Pearl? The Arabian Nights? The Decameron?* If these works do indeed lack unity, are they the worse for it?

Beyond these examples, some contemporary practices seem to contravene these principles. For instance, the "slice-of-life" genre often appears to avoid the emphatic image or statement. Surrealism demands incoherence. Stream-of-consciousness lacks unity. Yet there are examples in all these genres that exhibit artistic integrity and a high degree of aesthetic value.

Should we apply this second rhetorical principle to the first that states that argumentation is one of the four types of composition and ask about where the emphasis is placed in a well-made argument, on the premises or on the conclusion, we will have succeeded in embarrassing both points of view.

Both rhetorical principles suffer from a graver flaw than any suggested up to this point because their analyses and descriptions relate only to the finished composition. As such, they are more properly guides to reading compositions than to writing them. Granted, the writer must know the characteristics (criterion statements, if you will) of a good composition in order to write one, but knowing what those characteristics are is in no way the equivalent of knowing the process that generates them. At best, the information furnished by concepts such as those discussed here is only peripherally helpful to a writer when he is engaged in the actual process of composing.

All the foregoing traditions have been influential in general composition curricula in the past. Partly because of their influence, composition teaching has been, in the main, generally unsatisfactory.

The traditions do not represent a unified point of view at all. They do not support one another in any organic way and, as shown, may work against one another. Experimental research in composition also presents a patchwork picture containing many holes and many overworked areas. Nor is intuition a reliable guide for long-range planning of instruction.

As a result, composition instruction must proceed on the basis of a theory that encompasses the composing process as well as the composition products in a unified field. In addition to a general theory of composition itself, the teacher will need a theory of composition teaching. Theories of both kinds are examined in the next chapters.

NOTES

1. J. Nicholas Hook, "Characteristics of Award Winning High Schools," *English Journal* L (January 1961), pp. 9–15.
2. Based on data from U.S. Bureau of the Census, *Statistical Abstract of the United States,* 86th Edition 1965, (Washington, D. C., 1965).
3. *Ibid.*
4. For example, in the report of the Commission on English, *Freedom and Discipline in English* (New York: College Entrance Examination Board, 1965), about 75 percent of the paper discusses literature and literary criticism.
5. Ingrid M. Strom, "Research in Grammar and Usage and Its Implications for Teaching Writing," *Bulletin of the School of Education of Indiana University,* XXXVI, 5 (September 1960).
6. Kenny, Anna W., "Instruction in Remedial English: A Suggested Program Based on he Analysis of Certain English-Usage Difficulties Among Students in Chicago Public High Schools and Colleges." Unpublished Ph.D. Dissertation, University of Chicago, 1945.
7. In Walter D. Loban's description of children's speech in the monograph "The Language of Elementary School Children" (Champaign: National Council of Teachers of English NCTE, 1963).
8. Francis G. Gilchrist, "The Nature of Organic Wholeness," *The Quarterly Review of Biology,* 12 (September 1916) pp. 44–45.
9. Ezra Pound, *Letters of Ezra Pound,* ed. D. D. Paige (New York: Harcourt, Brace & World, 1954), pp. 292–293.

SUGGESTIONS FOR FURTHER READING

For some alternative views in teaching composition:

1. FOWLER, MARY ELIZABETH. *Teaching Language Composition and Literature.* New York: McGraw-Hill Book Co., 1965.
2. GORDON, EDWARD J., ed. *Writing and Literature in the Secondary School.* New York: Holt, Rinehart & Winston, 1965.
3. MOFFETT, JAMES. *A Student-Centered Language Arts Curriculum, Grades K-13; A Handbook for Teachers.* Boston: Houghton-Mifflin Co., 1968.
4. ROBERTS, HOLLAND DE WITTE, ed. *English for Social Living.* New York: McGraw-Hill Book Co., 1943.

5. SAUER, EDWIN. *English in the Secondary School.* New York: Holt, Rinehart & Winston, 1961.
6. SHERER, PAULINE and LUEBKE, NEAL. *Writing Creatively, Lessons for a High School Class.* New York: Teachers College, Columbia University, 1962.
7. STRUNK, WILLIAM JR. *The Elements of Style,* rev. by E. B. White. New York: Macmillan, 1959.

23

The Composing Process: A Theory

What can a composition teacher base his work on? Although he can get some help from educational literature, he will not find it as helpful as he may hope. Many researchers have worked over such areas as the teaching of spelling and the mechanics of punctuation, capitalization, and the like, and the literature provides many suggestions and implications for teaching them. But these areas are comparatively trivial when they are viewed against the whole tapestry of what a writer must do and what a teacher can do to help him learn to write. As a teacher gains experience, he will discover many assignments that work well for him and a number that do not work at all. In his beginning years at teaching, he has only intuition to guide him. If his intuitions are good, he is in luck.

The best plan is for the teacher to develop or adopt a general theory of composition based on his own writing experiences, his observation of his classes, work, and the reading that he does in literature, criticism, and in the education journals. A composition theory will give direction to his work by helping him to order lessons and units, to generate lessons, and to avoid pitfalls. In addition to a theory on how writing is done, he must have a theory of how writing is *taught,* what the techniques and steps are that help a student to learn to write.

Let us first consider developing a theory of composition. (Perhaps a more rigorous statement would be "a composition hypothesis.") At the outset, it seems fair to assume that not all persons write in the same way. Obviously, compositions as widely different as a dissertation about chemical compounds and a love sonnet are both produced by writers. Any theory must account for composition products as well as composing processes. Thus, it must have two parts, one dealing with the process and the other with the product.

Elements of the Writing Process

Most of us, when we write, bring our writing under conscious control—or, at least, we think we do. We usually have a clear purpose in writing, and, generally, the clearer that purpose is, the greater the control we have over the writing. Moreover, we usually have a particular audience in mind. A writer with any sophistication at all tries to vary his message to suit his purpose with his audience. For example, a lawyer writes in one way when addressing a justice, in another way when addressing a letter to his client's legal opponent, and in yet another way when writing to his sweetheart. No one can raise a question about the generality of these elements in a writing situation *where communication is the intent of the writer*. These basic elements of the writing process can be described by a communications model:

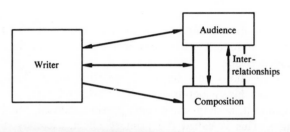

FIGURE 23.1

This model indicates that the writer analyzes his audience, thinks about the effects that alternate kinds of compositions might have on it, decides on the most appropriate composition in terms of the desired effect, and finally writes the composition. Thus, his audience influences him, and the presumed interrelationships between the audience and his composition influence him as well.

There is another, more subtle dimension involved in purposive writing. The writer may see himself included with the other elements in the model in some "situation." For example, a lawyer who writes letters on behalf of a client hoping that his letters will avoid litigation is definitely involved in the situation as he sees it. On the other hand, many writers will not see themselves included in a situation involving their audience and their compositions; biographers, historians, and advertising writers are examples. The model must be expanded to include the new element:

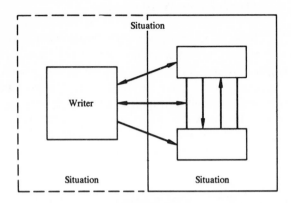

FIGURE 23.2

The extension of the situation block by *dotted* lines so as to include the author indicates that sometimes he may include himself in the situation but at other times he may not.

What specific reactions does he anticipate from his audience? Whenever he writes, he wants his reader to read his work and react to it internally, perhaps understand it, perhaps have some passion aroused, but to have some internal reaction. This is called the primary effect. He may also want his audience to take some direct action as a result of reading and reacting internally—answering a letter, voting Republican, or buying a product. This is called the secondary effect and is not always part of a writer's purpose.

Whether a writer wants his composition message to result in both effects or simply the primary one, something made him decide on writing in the first place—he had an impulse to write. This impulse may have arisen as a result of his perception of the situation, regardless of whether he saw himself involved in it. It may have arisen from some mysterious inner prompting or from a need to show some new accomplishment (as when a student "spontaneously" produces a number of compositions of a new type he has learned), or it may arise in response to something in the broader environment (even broader than the situation). Or the impulse may stem from all these elements working in concert.

How can the writer produce his composition message? Suppose he decides that the most effective composition will be a business letter in one case and a sonnet in another. He can write either one, only because he knows what the forms generally are. He knows that a business letter contains a heading, an inside address, salutation, and so on, and that a sonnet is fourteen lines of rhymed iambic pentameter. These forms are in his writing repertoire as general types of composition. Any specific composition of a particular type is

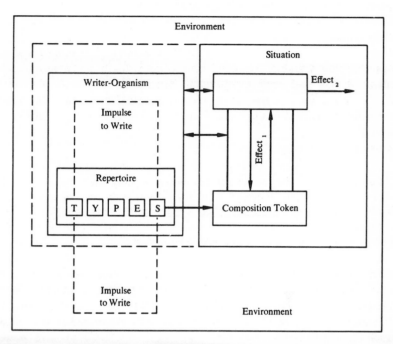

FIGURE 23.3

called a "token" of that type. The letter or sonnet he finally writes will thus be a token of that general type.

Let us expand the model so as to include all the new elements: primary and secondary effects; impulses to write; the repertoire; the types included in it; and the broader environment.

Let us analyze the model now somewhat more carefully. The arrow leading to the composition token moves from a type in the repertoire. This indicates that any token is limited to whatever general types the writer has in his repertoire. How did the types get into the repertoire? Two ways: either he learned them, whether through direct instruction or indirectly, or he invented a type (as Adelaide Crapsey invented the cinquain, basing it on other experiences).

The repertoire contains types other than conventional composition forms. For example, words and syntactic structures are also included. Writers can learn these, or they can invent them. Shakespeare, Gerard Manley Hopkins, Ogden Nash, and Walter Winchell all have invented words, as have many others. Gertrude Stein and E. E. Cummings, among others, have invented structures, syntactic and otherwise. (Perhaps these "inventions" are really discoveries or realizations of language potentials.)

The double-headed arrows entering the writer indicate that his perceptions influence him.

The writer now is seen as an organism containing a repertoire and other things, including impulses—an organism in contrast with an environment.

Many writers find their environment extremely important to their productivity. Some, for example, must have background music in order to write, whereas others need absolute quiet. Some can write only at night; others work best in the morning.

Tolstoy has written:

> I always write in the morning. I was pleased to hear lately that Rousseau too, after he got up in the morning, went for a short walk and sat down to work. In the morning one's head is particularly fresh. The best thoughts most often come in the morning after waking, while still in bed or during the walk. Many writers work at night. Dostoevsky always wrote at night.[1]

Their physical condition is highly important to some writers. Some must be well-rested, alert, or newly awake for writing, whereas others work best at the end of the day with their senses a bit dulled. Some need artificial stimulants such as coffee or tobacco. Some need to be depressed as with alcohol.

T. S. Eliot has written:

> I know, for instance, that some forms of ill health, debility or anaemia, may (if other circumstances are favorable) reproduce an efflux of poetry in a way approaching the condition of automatic writing—though, in contrast to the claims made for the latter, the material has obviously been incubating within a poet and cannot be suspected of being a present from a friendly or impertinent demon.[2]

This influence of environment or physical condition on writing is a dominant consideration for many writers. This observation introduces a new element into the composing theory: compulsion in writing. There are many elements that work to compel a writer, some of which he may not be aware of. There is abundant evidence that, with some writers, much of their work is entirely compulsive. The above quotations from Tolstoy and Eliot imply compulsion. Let us examine some of the other evidence for compulsion in writing.

The character of the language that the writer must use and the character of the culture in which both the writer and his language exist exert powerful compelling pressure on him, even though he may be unaware of the nature and extent of these influences. Benjamin Lee Whorf has indicated the power of language in limiting thought itself and thus compelling certain aspects of writing:

And yet the problem of thought and thinking in the native community is not purely and simply a psychological problem. It is quite largely cultural. It is moreover largely a matter of one especially cohesive aggregate of cultural phenomena that we call a language. We are thus able to distinguish thinking as the function which is to a large extent linguistic.[3]

Many critics, particularly of the school of Myth Criticism, have opined the existence of a "collective unconscious" (the idea deriving from the writing of C. G. Jung[4]) as a compulsive cultural force in composition. In particular, Northrop Frye has written:

The fact that revision is possible, and that the poet makes changes not because he likes them better but because they are better, means that poems, like poets, are born and not made. The poet's task is to deliver the poem in as uninjured a state as possible, and if a poem is alive, it is equally anxious to be rid of him, and screams to be cut loose from his private memories, and all the other navel strings and feeding tubes of his ego.[5]

Joseph Conrad testified to the power that the English language exerted over him:

The truth of the matter is that my faculty to write in English is as natural as any other aptitude with which I was born. I have a strange and overpowering feeling that it had always been an inherent part of myself. English was for me neither a matter of choice nor adoption. The merest idea of choice had never entered my head. And as to adoption—well, yes, there was an adoption; but it was I who was adopted by the genius of language, which directly I came out of the stammering stage made me its own so completely that its very idioms I truly believe had a direct action on my temperament and fashioned my still plastic character.

It was a very intimate action, and for that very reason it is too mysterious to explain. The task would be as impossible as trying to explain love at first sight. There was something in this conjunction of exulting, almost physical recognition, the same sort of emotional surrender and the same pride of possession, all united in the wonder of a great discovery; but there was on it none of that shadow of dreadful doubt that falls on the very flame of our perishable passions. One knew very well that this was forever.[6]

When a culture develops a written language, the writing conventions themselves add compulsive elements to the composing process, and the very act of writing introduces compulsive potentials. Writing has been seen as deriving from the spoken language. On a historical basis, in terms of the experience of a linguistic community as a whole, this is undeniably the case. However, this general view of the relationship of writing to speech tends to obscure certain phenomena involving individuals' learning and use of writing.

Notice of these phenomena can lead to valuable insights into the nature of all writing.

Many persons deaf from birth have never heard or spoken any language. Yet these persons learn writing and employ it appropriately. This observation indicates that writing, when viewed in a synchronic way, is not necessarily secondary to speech.

Some persons stricken with aphasia display the following pattern: Although unable to express themselves in speech, they are able to do so in writing.[7] This phenomenon indicates that, within some individuals, writing is dissociated from speech; metaphorically, the written language assumes a life of its own.

The failure of the written language to correspond to the spoken language has often been noted. Even as many conventions of speech are inadequately expressed in writing, many writing conventions are not reflected in speech. The colon, for example, which inevitably predicts an explanatory or specifying discourse of some kind, is a feature of English writing. Speech, however, lacks such an unambiguous, particularizing counterpart, since superfixes in speech that signal following explanatory comments also signal other things. Similarly, paragraphs are a feature of writing only, as are capital letters. E. E. Cummings was influenced by the extra emphasis suggested by the capital letter, and he varied his typography accordingly.[8]

In some cases the written language has asserted a primacy over the spoken. People sometimes mispronounce words because of the way they are spelled.[9]

In many ways writing manifests a life of its own. A peculiar occurrence, associated with various, somewhat exotic states indicates how powerful this "life" can be. There are many reports of *automatic writing* in various literatures.[10] Without doubt, some of the instances of this phenomenon are fraudulent.[11] But automatic writing has been reliably associated with forms of hysteria[12] and with induced hypnotic states.[13] The writer of automatic writing often seems oblivious to any of the writing content.[14] This phenomenon strongly indicates that some writing may be almost entirely compulsive in character.

Many professional writers have reported influences on themselves that are interpretable as elements in their experience that have compelled writing.

A. E. Housman has written:

> Having drunk a pint of beer at luncheon—beer is a sedative to the brain, and my afternoons are the least intellectual portion of my life—I would go out for a walk of two or three hours. As I went along, thinking of nothing in particular, only looking at things around me and following the progress of the seasons, there would flow into my mind, with sudden and unaccountable emotion, sometimes a line or two of verse, sometimes a whole stanza at once, accompanied, not preceded, by a vague notion of the poem which they were destined to form a

part of. Then there would usually be a lull of an hour or so, then perhaps the spring would bubble up again, I say bubble up, because, so far as I could make out, the source of the suggestions thus proffered to the brain was an abyss which I have had occasion to mention, the pit of the stomach. When I got home I wrote them down, leaving gaps, and hoping that further inspiration might be forthcoming another day. Sometimes it was, if I took my walks in a receptive and expectant frame of mind; but sometimes the poem had to be taken in hand and completed by the brain, which was apt to be a matter of trouble and anxiety, involving trial and disappointment, and sometimes ending in failure. I happen to remember distinctly the genesis of the piece which stands last in my first volume. Two of the stanzas, I do not say which, came into my head, just as they are printed, while I was crossing the corner of Hampstead Heath between the Spaniard's Inn and the Footpath to Temple Fortune. A third stanza came with a little coaxing after tea. One more was needed, but it did not come: I had to turn to and compose it myself, and that was a laborious business. I wrote it thirteen times and it was more than a twelvemonth before I got it right.[15]

Goethe has described a similar experience:

At other times it has been totally different with my poems. They have been preceded by no impressions or forebodings but have come suddenly upon me, and have insisted on being composed immediately, so that I have felt an instinctive and dreamy impulse to write them down on the spot. In such a somnambulistic condition, it has often happened that I have had a sheet of paper lying before me all on one side, and I have not discovered it till all has been written, or I have found no room to write any more. I have possessed many such sheets written crossways, but they have been lost one after another, and I regret that I can no longer show any proofs of such poetic abstraction.[16]

William Blake has written:

I have in these three years composed an immense number of verses on One Grand Theme, similar to Homer's *Iliad* or Milton's *Paradise Lost,* the Persons & Machinery entirely new to the Inhabitants of Earth (some of the persons Excepted). I have written this Poem from immediate Dictation, twelve or sometimes twenty or thirty lines at a time without Premeditation & even against My Will; the Time it has taken in writing was thus render'd Non-Existent, & an immense Poem Exists which seems to be the Labour of long Life, all produced without Labour or Study.[17]

Thus, some writing is wholly or in part the result of impulses that motivate a compulsive reaction from the writer.

Many persons keep diaries without any conscious intent that these be seen by eyes other than theirs. This practice seems open to interpretation as compulsive writing, although in some cases an intent of private historical recording may be hypothesized. Most of us know writers of letters who seem to do their writing compulsively. Perhaps such characterization is not simply in the nature of hyperbole. Certainly there is doubt as to whether letters of the billet-doux genre are executed compulsively or purposefully. Certain walls of public places bear mute testimony to the likelihood of a compulsion for writing.

Teachers have long been aware of the potential power of introducing elements that project compulsive writing into composition situations. The use of reactionnaires reflects this awareness. When a teacher plays music, or shows dramatic pictures, or the like, and asks the class to write about how they feel or what they think about these experiences, he encourages writing that is at least partially compulsive in character.

Because of a good part of the composing process and some composition products may be described as compulsive, the theoretic model must be again expanded to include these elements as part of the process theory. Notice that the arrow labeled "compulsive writing" arises from the repertoire: A person writes only what he is capable of, even if he is wholly or partially unaware of his capacity.

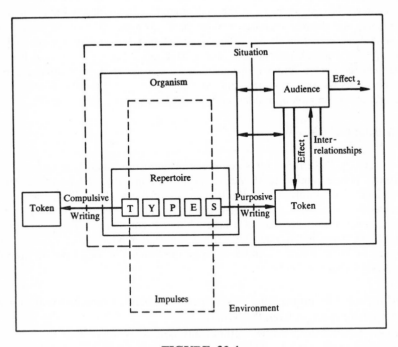

FIGURE 23.4

Let us summarize the elements of the composing process as it has been analyzed to this point:

The writer experiences an impulse to write, which may originate within his organism or may enter his experience from his environment. He may write in a compulsive way, or he may have his writing under conscious control. However, all of his writing is limited by the conventions of the language he uses and by his repertoire of linguistic and formal types. Consciously controlled writing is directed by the writer's purpose and his analysis of his audience. The composition product that results from the process is a unique token of some type that has been internalized as part of the writer's repertoire. The token becomes a real element in the communications situation.

The End Product

Thus, we arrive at the token, the end product of the composition process. Let us consider composition products in terms of a model.

The product model begins with the dichotomy, compulsive and purposive writing. Both these categories derive from the writer's repertoire and will reflect it. The category purposive writing subsequently dichotomizes into types that are differentiated on the basis of the intent of the author. (Compulsive writing may not be strictly characterized as intentional since *intent* connotes purposive control.)

The dichotomy of the second level, responses characterized by detachment vs. those characterized by involvement, indicates the general type of response that the writer intends the audience to make. Involvement, in this formulation, indicates a response of the kind in which a reader (audience) psychologically projects himself into the token, perhaps identifying himself with elements in it; ordinarily, his response is emotionally charged. A detached response is one that, in its initial stages at least, keeps the reader psychologically outside the reading, although he may experience an emotional *reaction* to it. (For example, the reader of a critical theory may become angry as a result of reading and disagreeing with the theory. The anger is possible only as a result of the evaluation he makes, which is initially as a remote viewer rather than an involved participant.) Of course, the writer may not anticipate the response of the audience accurately, but any such wrong judgment on his part is distinct from his intent.

Writing intended to elicit detached responses is of two kinds. The first expects the reader to respond to elements of data contained within the token; thus the token is *information-oriented*. For example, the writer of a business letter ordering a number of parts intends that his reader attend to the heading, inside address, the description of each part, billing directions, and any other particulars of information piece by piece. The author of a learned treatise presented as an argument intends his reader to consider his presenta-

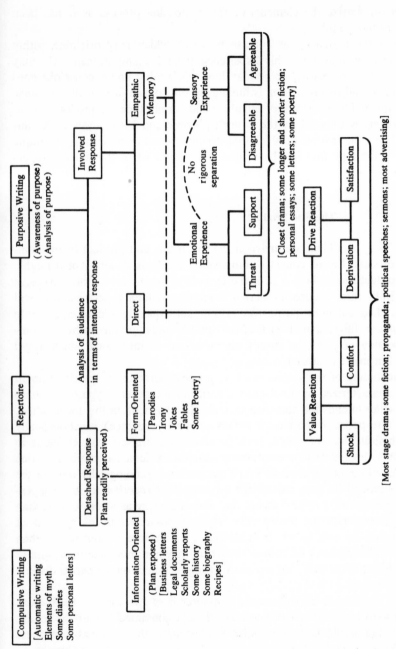

FIGURE 23.5 A General Theory of Composition, Product Model

Tokens representative of each type are bracketed. The arrangement of purposive dichotomies is from left to right. Material above the broken line equals ease of analysis.

tion point by point, examining each premise, then the conclusion. If the argument must be finally considered *in toto* because of the interrelationships of the parts, this need and the reasoning behind it will likewise be presented as specific data to the reader.

The second kind of detached response is that made to a work taken as a whole. For example, the author of a fable that includes a moral intends that the reader consider both the narrative and the moral together; either element is incomplete without the other. Although it is doubtless the intent of many writers of belles-lettres to have each of their works considered as a whole for purposes of critical aesthetic evaluation, the work is not classified as *form-oriented* unless they have intended that the reader at no point experience empathy. Thus these tokens have two intentional markers: the reader remains detached and the response must be made to the whole work.

The detached response is essentially intellectual; the reader is not emotionally pulled into the work. The involved response, on the other hand, is essentially emotional. There are two kinds of responses requiring emotional contact that the writer may intend to elicit from his audience.

The first kind is direct: The reader responds immediately to the token itself without extensive intermediate memories being evoked by it. Strictly speaking, memory of some kind must trigger the response, but ordinarily the reader is unaware of any memory mechanism. For example, if a person reads, "No Smoking. Danger. Explosive," he extinguishes his cigarette—without conscious memory of the experience implied by the message. Such direct responses are controlled by the reader's value system or his drive system. Tokens aiming at the value system will provide either shock or comfort to that system; those aimed at the drive system will suggest either deprivation or satisfaction. Much advertising copy is intended to obtain a direct emotional response.

The second kind of involved response is vicarious: The empathy is contingent upon memories of experiences that the message evokes in the readers. The memories will be of either emotional experiences (threatening or supporting) or sensory experiences (agreeable or disagreeable). Emotional and sensory experiences in a person's memory are often closely interwoven. For example, the memory of nearly drowning involves disagreeable physical sensations and concomitant emotional threats. Popular novels intend empathic responses.

Tokens that result from compulsive writing may resist any further classification. Their generation, necessarily through the repertoire, must reflect it. However, compulsive writers are motivated by some arcane need to express themselves through writing; communication is not a central conditioner of their behavior. Therefore, further classification of their work by the reader is invalid. Unless the reader *knows* the intent of the writer, he may classify writing as purposive and then further subclassify it only by inference.

Although a rigorous classification of a token by the reader is not strictly possible without knowledge of the writer's intent, the token may yet be analyzed on various bases:

1. On the basis of *presumed* intent.
2. On the extent to which the token reflects the reader's model of the type from which it apparently derives.
3. On the power of the token to compel any effect on the critic as part of the intended audience.
4. On its power to compel any effect on the audience as the critic observes this, the critic not being himself a part of the intended audience.

All of these underline the essentially subjective nature of both composition and criticism.

A perhaps apocryphal incident dramatizing the efficacy of these theoretical formulations is related about Abraham Lincoln's being introduced to Mrs. Harriet Beecher Stowe. On that occasion Lincoln remarked, "So this is the little lady who started the War."

Perhaps Lincoln, as audience, was prompted to the remark on the basis of an analysis of the process analogous to that presented here. Many writers of the period who were then, and are still, regarded as better authors (Emerson, Alcott, Bryant, and Lincoln himself, as examples) had used various tokens —essays, sermons, and political speeches—to produce the secondary effect of arousing their audiences to eliminate slavery. The most successful of all such tokens was Stowe's *Uncle Tom's Cabin,* albeit our contemporary critics would probably devalue the work. (After all, our contemporary critics were not part of Stowe's intended audience.)

In light of this, Lincoln might just as well have said, "So this is the little lady who developed the most appropriate analysis of the situation and the audience, had in her repertoire a suitable type, and produced the most effective token in terms of both primary and secondary effect." Admittedly, in terms of style, such a pronouncement could not be regarded as very Lincolnesque.

NOTES

1. Koteliansky, Samuel S. and Woolf, Virginia, translators, Goldenveizer, A. B., *Talks with Tolstoi* (New York: Horizon, 1969), p. 160.
2. Eliot, T. S., *The Use of Poetry and the Use of Criticism* (Cambridge: Harvard University Press, 1933) p. 137.
3. Benjamin Lee Whorf, *Language, Thought and Reality,* edited by John B. Carroll (Cambridge: MIT Press, 1956), p. 65.
4. Especially in Jung's *Modern Man in Search of a Soul* (New York: Harcourt, Brace & World, 1933).
5. Frye, Northrop, "My Credo," *Kenyon Review,* XII (Winter 1951), pp. 97–98.

6. Joseph Conrad, in the "Author's Note" preceding *A Personal Record/The Shadow Line* (in one volume) (Garden City: Doubleday, 1927), pp. vii–viii.

7. Miller, George A. *Language and Communication* (New York: McGraw-Hill Book Co., 1951); reprinted as a paperback in 1963, p. 239.

8. Cummings, E. E., in his introduction to *XLI* (New York: Henry Holt, 1944).

9. Mencken, H. L., *The American Language,* fourth ed., rev. by Ravin I. McDavid and David W. Maurer (New York: Alfred A. Knopf, 1963), pp. 657–658.

10. Miller, *op. cit.,* p. 190.

11. Frank Podmore, "Automatic Writing," *Encyclopaedia Britannica* (L959).

12. D. H. Rawliffe, *Illusions and Delusions of the Supernatural and Occult* (New York: Dover, 1959), pp. 140 ff.

13. Podmore, *op. cit.*

14. B. F. Skinner, "Has Gertrude Stein a Secret?", *Atlantic Monthly* (January 1934).

15. A. E. Housman, *The Name and Nature of Poetry* (Cambridge, Eng.: Cambridge University Press, 1938), pp. 48–50.

16. Johann Goethe, *Conversations of Goethe with Eckermann.* (New York: Dutton, 1930), pp. 355–356.

17. William Blake, *The Letters of William Blake, Together with a Life by Frederick Tatham,* edited by Archibald G. B. Russell (Charles Scribners, Sons, 1906), pp. 115–116.

24

Planning Instruction in Composition

Before beginning instruction in composition, the teacher must take into account many elements that will influence the instruction. First, he must consider the implications that his theory of composing brings to his teaching. Next, he must have some idea of what his students are like and what their needs are. The composition teaching must be articulated with other parts of the English curriculum. The structure of the lessons, and their sequence must be planned. Finally, he must anticipate the ways in which he will deal with the papers when they come into his hands. When he has thought through these problems and has perceived their interrelationship, he will have developed an instructional theory.

What the Curriculum Should Cover

The composing theory suggests various elements as topics for discrete instruction in the curriculum. The program must include lessons on the nature of purposive writing developed along the lines suggested by the communications model around which the theory was built. For example:

1. The students must learn how to analyze consciously the situation that gives rise to the written communication.
2. They must learn to specify their purposes in writing each composition.
3. They must learn the technique of audience analysis, with especial emphasis on the anticipation of primary effect. This implies lessons on alternative types to use in particular situations.

The most conspicuous weakness of most composition curricula, even those that pay lip service to the idea that composition is a form of communication, is the absence of lessons and writing assignments dealing with the elements that are present in communication situations. Students should learn how to analyze an audience and how to vary the same messages to suit their purposes with different audiences, in other words, how to slant their writing. In addition to preparing the "same" messages for different audiences, students ought to explain how they thought out the alternatives.

The following is an example of how a seventh-grade boy slanted his writing by using affective connotations (see pp. 434–437) in word choice and how he analyzed his technique:

The leaky, condemned barge was finally going to be sunk. It carried a cargo of rot and filth to take to the river bottom. Its companion was to be the slimy mud. There the slime would rot what was left of it and that would be the end of its smelly life.

The barge, faithful to the last, was going to its final resting place. For many cold winters, it had towed coal and oil to the townspeople to keep them warm. Now, the cargo was only the stains of service. The only one that would be company to it was the river bottom. There, it would be forgotten and would slowly cease to exist with nobody caring.

(Student self-analysis of his writing process)
These two paragraphs are two different viewpoints of the same thing, getting rid of the barge. The first one is a memo from an ex-barge captain who is now the president of the company, written to stockholders. The second is a description written to another ex-barge captain who retired. In the first one I wanted the writer to seem practical. In the second one I wanted him to be cheering up his friend. Some of the contrasts I used (in their paragraph order) to get the right slanting were "leaky, condemned" against "faithful to the last." I contrasted "cargo of rot and filth" with "cargo was only the stains of service." "The end of its smelly life" is against "cease to exist with nobody caring." I also said "slimy mud" instead of just "river bottom." The first examples are negative affective connotation, and the second examples are positive.

Seventh-grade boy

The next example written by an eighth-grade boy shows how undefined technical terms mark a message aimed at an audience experienced in a field in contrast to a message aimed at a more general audience:

The race is about to start, five four, . . . one, zero. I'm off on a starboard tack flying through the water but boats are passing me to windward and leeward as if I were standing still. I then split tacks with the fleet and got a lift in towards shore. I now could just make the marker and pulled in front of the fleet once more. As I rounded the mark, my crew took the tiller and I yanked up the spinnaker, and it set perfectly; and it seemed like I was moving right along when the second place boat caught up to me and by the time I got to the mark I was in last again. It was a beat back to the finish. I tried that same tack again and got another lift. At ten yards from the finish I was winning. All of a sudden I got a header and by the time I got over the line four boats had passed. I got a fifth with only a hope of doing better tomorrow.

The race is about to start, three, two, one, bang. I'm off with the wind coming over the right side of the boat. The boat is flying through the water but boats are passing me to the right and left as if I were standing still. I then took off in the opposite direction of the other boats and got a lot of wind in towards shore. I now could just get around the marker (the point which you have to round which makes up a sailing course) and pulled out in front of the fleet once more. As I rounded the mark my crew took the tiller (which you steer with) and I yanked up the spinnaker (a balloon like fore sail which can only be used when the wind is coming from in back of you). It set perfectly and it seemed like I was moving right along when the second place boat caught up to me and by the time I got to the marker I was in last place again. To get to the finish we had to turn back and forth against the wind. I tried the same tactics as before and got the wind again. At ten yards from the finish I was winning. All of a sudden I lost my wind and by the time I got over the finish line four boats had passed. I got a fifth with only the hope of doing better tomorrow.

(Student self-analysis of his writing process)

My audience in the first paragraph knows about sailing. The audience in the second paragraph doesn't. In the first paragraph I could just call things by their names. I had to make changes in the second. You cannot change a word like "spinnaker", so I defined it in parentheses. It's too complicated to define "leeward" so I changed "leeward and windward" to "left and right sides" because it amounts to the same thing anyway. Some of the terms stay the same because anybody knows that you "set a sail" for instance. As for abstraction, "other boats" is more abstract than "fleet" because this fleet was only the club fleet and "other boats" includes many other boats.

Eighth-grade boy

The foregoing exercises are an introduction to audience analysis. Next, specific criteria that differentiate audiences should be studied; sex, whether male, female, or mixed; age range; social status; place of residence—urban, suburban, or rural; interests and background experience, including educational level, vocation, religion, hobbies, and race. The next step is to collect advertisements that are designed to appeal to a specific audience and analyze what in an advertisement provides specific appeal.

The types of appeals in the advertisement should be classified—for example, testimonial, plain folks, bandwagon, snob appeal. Next, the appeals should be analyzed to show the probable purposes of the authors as well as the intended audience. Other kinds of propaganda such as newspaper editorials and political speeches should also be analyzed in terms of their appeals.

The final step is for the students to develop original advertisements (or other types of propaganda). The most useful technique is to have a committee of students work together on this. The group work affords give-and-take in discussion that is more effective in the learning than is individual work.

The advertisements produced should be uniform in size. Each group should have some particular problem to serve as a hidden purpose—for example, the product they are advertising costs more than competing products—and this problem should be kept confidential. When the class evaluates the finished advertisement, they should try to determine the nature of the hidden purpose. All advertisements should be displayed at the end of the unit together with analyses of the intended audience and the content. The analyses should show influences of the unit's work: connotations of words, slanting, specific appeals, and so on.

Much of the curriculum should be devoted to expanding the students' repertoire. This expansion involves not only the learning of such conventionalized forms as the business letter and the sonnet but also an extension of vocabulary, and the use of various devices ranging from puns to figures of speech and rhetorical tricks. Techniques of stylizing must also become part of the repertoire. Obviously, the curriculum for any single year will not complete the job of expanding the repertoire. The teacher must determine what has been done along this line previously and what this logically suggests for his year's work. Ideally, intergrade curriculum committees ought to deal with the scope and sequence of this phase of the program.

The teacher must decide on how to include compulsive components of the composing process in his instruction: which elements to use in his own purposing and which to bring to the direct attention of his class.

Finally, the discussion of the process hypothesis in Chapter 22 indicates that all composition work should deal with complete composition patterns since the hypothesis is that the writer visualizes a complete work before he starts writing, although he may modify his vision as he works along.

Considering the Students' Needs

The results of the inventory battery and his follow-up procedures (see Chapter 21) enable the teacher to classify his students in terms of their demonstrated skills. He may find himself faced with dysfunctional, functional, and fluent writers in the same class; or he may find that administrative grouping has segregated his students homogeneously.

Among the functional group he is sure to find students who will write only reluctantly—who will consistently deal with composition assignments in a minimal way, trying to get the work finished as quickly as possible or not doing it at all. These reluctant writers evince comparatively little mechanical difficulty with their writing; they simply seem to lack interest in most composition assignments. It is possible to use techniques with these students that will motivate compulsive writing.

In addition to classifying the students, the inventories will yield information about their deficiencies in punctuation, capitalization, and the like. Chapter 21 suggests ways in which the teacher can plan instruction in these areas.

The students' needs will give the teacher some indication of the appropriate sequencing of study. Since most of the student's writing needs, at least his most immediate ones, derive from the necessity for written communication in school, the types of composition that he will be frequently called upon to produce in school must receive first priority. These will usually involve the communication of data; therefore, the early part of the instructional sequence should concentrate on the information-oriented type of compositions. Any preliminary writing experiences must be developed only because they lead to the goal of learning to write information-oriented compositions.

Of course, in this early stage the students may also work with forms designed to give them a feeling of success and achievement with writing in a general way. This can mitigate any undesirable emotional concomitants to the perhaps more demanding kind of composition experiences involved in working up information-oriented tokens. Should a student experience frustration and undue anxiety in connection with any writing, he might avoid any experience with writing at all costs or limit such experience to the smallest possible amount.

Another consideration has to do with the maturational level of the student. In a broad way it is obvious that maturation controls many aspects of a person's writing abilities. Consequently, the teacher should ask himself such questions as, "At what age does a person write good narrative in the omniscient voice? How old will someone be before he can write sonnets? Are tenth graders really capable of writing sophisticated criticism of poetry?" It is unfortunate that educational literature has not discussed questions of this kind to any great extent. On the very crucial issue of composition type as it relates to the student's maturation, the teacher, at this point in the development of our profession, is left to his own devices of observation and analysis for many of the decisions he will have to make.

The final general consideration has to do with motivating devices. Because publication is probably the most powerful single extrinsic motivation for writing, the teacher should consider developing classroom publications as well as school-wide publications to get his students' work into print. School-wide publications, such as the school literary magazine, tend to be selective and ordinarily contain only choice pieces from the most talented writers. Classroom publications, on the other hand, can include work from all class members and can be designed to contain work from a single lesson or unit (say a limerick from each student) or selected work gathered over a long period. Students should do as much as possible of the editorial work and mechanical work on the publication. In addition to publications, bulletin board displays of compositions are useful in rewarding those whose compositions get displayed.

Resource speakers from the community can provide good motivation for writing: reporters, stringers, editors, publishers of house organs and trade papers, copywriters, teachers who have published, and parents who are authors are all sources. The teacher can obtain leads to these resource persons by including appropriate items in the interest inventory (see Chapter 2). In passing, this inventory can also locate parents who can do typing for classroom publications.

Students from previous years provide another reservoir of resource speakers. A twelfth grader who wrote especially good free verse when he was in the tenth grade or who is writing it in the twelfth grade, for example, can come into a present tenth grade class and discuss his techniques, a tremendously valuable experience for the speaker as well as his audience.

Composition and the Total English Curriculum

In what ways does composition articulate with literature and language study? At what points does the articulation occur? The most obvious points of articulation are in the evaluation procedures. Student compositions reporting on their work in literature and language form one kind of evaluative instrument in these areas. Information-oriented compositions are used in these cases. Composition may also play a part in concept development. For example, when working on a semantics unit, students may practice slanting in composition exercises as a way of learning what "slanting" means. A useful technique in teaching a literary form is to have the class imitate the form in original writing exercises. Compositions analyzing the form are likewise useful, but they will be information-oriented.

Work with style articulates all three curricular areas. Both connotations of "style"—the more mechanical aspects as well as expression—are relevant here. What is ordinarily called "style" in the handbooks—punctuation, capitalization, spelling, case agreement, and so on—is in the domain of usage and is, strictly speaking, apart from the analysis of syntax and phonology. Syntactic, semantic, and poetic analysis are all involved in the study of literary styles of professional writers as well as of school students.

"Style" in both its connotations can also feature the study of dialect and idiolect. When a student studies his own writing style, he is elevating to conscious control an otherwise compulsive element in his writing.

Lesson Structure

Like Gaul, all composition lessons are divided into three parts: preparation for writing, independent writing, and follow-up procedures.

When they make composition assignments, many teachers, especially beginners, know in only a general way the characteristics of the finished compositions they wish to receive from their students. It often happens that only after the work has been turned in and they have read it, do they know precisely what they were after in the first place. In this situation a student must rely on his intuition in doing his work. If he can "psych out" his teacher, he does "good" work. Otherwise, he works in the dark.

A certain period of such trial-and-error teaching may be necessary in a teacher's experience, but its results are of dubious value to students, who may learn considerable error. The obvious implication is that, whenever possible, the teacher should provide models of the type of writing under consideration as a part of the preparation for writing.

In addition to the practical values of using models for writing, their use has important theoretic value, which derives from the fact that the writer's repertoire develops through his conceptualization of types, and this conceptualization will turn on his experience with models.

Needless to say, the choice of the models must reflect the principles being considered during composition instruction. This is especially true in the early stages. But limiting consideration to models of a "pure" type can result in the development of a distorted view of literature. As the students show mastery of principles, they must be introduced to models that appear to deviate from the norms developed by theoretic principles.

As an example, consider the haiku, a simple poem form that originated in Japan (see pp. 109–115). Its normal structure is three unrhymed lines, the first containing five syllables; the second, seven; the third, five. Many effective haiku deviate from this pattern, however. As students master the form, they should be introduced to deviant examples and engage in appropriate discussion about the author's or translator's probable reasons for deviating.

In general, the use of models should be conditioned by the observed proficiency of the students. The models should be first analyzed and then imitated. Three kinds should be used: literary models (tokens); student-made models (tokens); theoretic models generalized by analysis of tokens that usually, but not exclusively, are student made. Ordinarily, the original analysis that leads to the development of this last-named kind of model is done by the teacher. (See Chapter 29.)

In view of the analysis of composing suggested by the theoretic model and discussion in Chapter 22, all work should be with models of complete literary forms. Because some of them will contain shorter complete forms as constituents, it is possible to develop sequences in which the shorter constituents are studied first; these, too, can be treated as complete forms. For example, information-oriented tokens often contain definitions of terms. Therefore the definition can be studied as a composition problem in itself before the study of information-oriented forms.

The beginning teacher will have no student-made models unless the department has a file of them. One source is back issues of school-wide publications. As the beginning teacher works through various lessons, he can save and make copies of good compositions for use as models in subsequent years. The writers of these compositions can be speakers to later classes.

The types of students in the class indicate which kind of models are appropriate as well as how the students should use them. Fluent writers should concentrate on literary models, and their talent may enable them to approach the quality of these models in their own writing. They should be allowed to use their own judgment in deciding whether to imitate the model directly or to base their writing on an analysis of it. Such an analysis can, in part, result from teacher-led classroom work, but very likely there will be a high degree of intuitive analysis. In dealing with these students, the teacher should select models that are appropriate to the assignment and appropriate to the natural propensities of the students as well. In other words, by virtue of his wider experience with literature, the teacher acts as a resource person or consultant for fluent writers. He can also encourage them to seek and use models from their own experience.

Functional writers may also use literary models for analysis. But it is folly to hope that they can approach the quality of the published work of professionals. They can, however, approach the work of other students. Therefore the analysis and imitation of student-made tokens should be prominent in the preparatory instruction of the functional group. In the early stages of dealing with a particular literary type, they will imitate the model closely, but when the principles become familiar, they will move away from mimicry.

Dysfunctional writers present special problems and these are discussed at length in Chapter 29. Briefly, the teacher should make special models for them to analyze and imitate.

Some students who are fluent at particular kinds of writing, but not generally fluent may present a peculiar problem for the teacher. For example, some may write only free verse fluently. Others may handle all kinds of poetry very well but be merely functional at prose. Some are fluent in information-oriented forms; others, fluent with empathic types. Consequently, the particular model to use in these cases may depend upon the individual student.

In general, the teacher should specify which models are to be used only in those lessons that are intended to expand the writer's repertoire. When the class does its writing in the broader context of analyzing the whole communications situation, selecting the best approach should be part of the analysis. Consequently, the teacher should not indicate which specific model to follow, but he might lead a discussion on the available alternatives and the advantages and disadvantages of each.

In addition to work with models, any content work in literature and language should be part of the preparation for writing that is used either in concept development or evaluation. Since information-oriented compositions are used in evaluation, the teacher must be careful to give instructions in the appropriate form *before* he makes an assignment that presumes competence in that form. Otherwise, he will find that he must comment on such things as organization, techniques of defining, and so on, when he should be commenting on the ideas that the writer is expressing. If he tries to deal with both kinds of content, he will probably experience frustration, and his students certainly will.

The next phase of the lesson is the independent writing of the students. As the year's work progresses, the students should be introduced to more and more of the compulsive elements in composition—such as under what environmental conditions they do their best work. These things can themselves be composition topics. Additionally, there must be a continuous awareness of the need for specifying purposes, analyzing the audience, and selecting the appropriate approach from the repertoire.

The final phase of the lesson has to do with follow-up procedures, editing and proofreading the completed composition.

Perhaps because spelling and mechanics are secondary, writers generate compositions that will include errors in spelling and mechanics; for many writers, an appropriate use of spelling, punctuation, and capitalization is not integral to their writing. Therefore, in order to correct such errors, they must reread what they have written and make appropriate changes. In the course of this kind of revision, they may edit the semantic and structural content of their work as well. In doing this editing, they must approach their writing from the point of view of the audience.

Any teacher will testify that such editing all too often does not get done; and when it does get done, it is not done very thoroughly. (In this connection, the teacher may recall the image suggested by Frye, which was presented earlier, of the author giving birth to his work and wanting to be rid of it.) Many find such editing of "completed" papers a disagreeable business. But one who aspires to composition must do it, disagreeable or not. The teacher who functions mainly as a proofreader, not only does a disservice to himself but hinders his students in their total development as writers. Instruction in proofreading and proofreading itself must be an integral part of instruction in composition.

A more esoteric kind of review of the finished writing is also in order. When a student has worked through the composition process, he should have an opportunity to make a critical comparison of his work against that of others. Perhaps he is aware of certain inadequacies in his analysis of the situation. The opportunity for comparing notes with his peers in this regard should serve to sharpen his self-criticism and help to develop more general critical powers at once.

The following classroom techniques can be employed after the composition writing has been completed but before papers are turned in to the teacher:

1. Time should be set aside for the students to proofread and revise their own work carefully. They should read their papers twice, the first time to detect undesirable semantic and syntactic content and the second time to check the papers for mechanical errors, reading word by word, line by line, using some pointer or marker such as a pen or finger, and silently reading so as to include "capital," "period," "comma," and the like as an integral part of the reading. Enough time should be provided so that this can be done slowly and carefully.
2. The students should be paired off in terms of their ability and rapport and treat one another's work in the manner indicated above. After reading, they should discuss their work with each other, questioning elements in the work when necessary.
3. Groups of four or five students should be formed, and each student should read his composition to the group. The paper representing the best overall approach should be chosen to be read to the class. This practice provides experience with a number of good models close to the writer's potential level of achievement.

And after the papers are turned in:

4. In marking the student's papers, the teacher should not characterize each error specifically but rather use some general device such as a marginal check mark on any line in which he sees an error and then return the papers to the students for revision. A comparison of the first paper with the revised version will indicate which areas in spelling, punctuation, and the like need attention via direct instruction, since a fair assumption is that a student's failure to correct errors indicates that he is ignorant of their nature.

Dealing with the Finished Papers

The last-described technique opens for consideration the whole topic of the teacher's red-marking of papers as well as other kinds of responses he makes.

When teachers mark mechanical errors in punctuation and the like, it is their hope that the writer willl attend to each specific error and eliminate the faulty usage from subsequent compositions. But there is some evidence that students respond otherwise.[1] Apparently, students generally believe the red marks to be deprecative of the *whole composition* rather than of the particular errors. Heavy red-marking usually results in subsequent compositions that are shorter and that contain shorter, less complex sentences and simpler word choice. Presumably, when students face a teacher who uses the red pencil excessively, they "play it safe" and the teacher's broader purpose of improving writing is frustrated.

In most cases not much is gained by marking each and every error on each and every paper. It is not in any way lazy or unethical to refrain from marking every mistake. Ordinarily, it is more useful to be discretionary and selective when using the red pencil. The guiding principle is to mark only the errors that are persistent with each individual and only those that there is some hope of remedying.

For example, a student may write a composition in which he discusses *The Odyssey*. Let us suppose that he consistently makes two mistakes in his employment of the form *"The Odyssey"*: First, he misspells "Odyssey" throughout the paper (an easy thing to do), and he misspells it the same way each time; second, he never signals through punctuation (such as quotation marks or underlining) that the term is a title. Should the teacher conscientiously mark both errors with his red pencil each time they occur throughout the paper? Certainly marking the errors *once* ought to be sufficient to point out that the usages involved are ill-advised; this marking practice must, of course, be supported by a marginal comment to the effect that the ill-advised usages have been employed throughout the paper.

Consider another hypothetical case, one in which the student, who is generally characterizable as a functional writer, nevertheless makes a number of different types of mechanical errors on his papers—but not to the extent that intended communication is interrupted by them. Suppose that among his persistently recurring errors there appear the following: (1) he confuses "to" and "too," (2) he leaves out commas after introductory adverb clauses, and (3) he uses sentence fragments. The teacher, after noting that these things (along with some others) represent recurrent patterns in his writing, develops a priority list in which items that he feels to be the most serious breaches or the most easily remedied are given first priority. He will mark these items *whenever they occur*. Other items will remain unmarked until the first-priority items show very definite signs of clearing up. In conjunction with the red marking, he will hold conferences with the student and will remind him of the error under attack during proofreading activities. Also, he will be careful to write notes of praise on papers that do not display these errors (or on papers in which many opportunities for errors are present but only very few have been forthcoming).

Praise for good work is an extremely effective practice. A high mark on a paper is, of course, a general symbol for good work and is, as such, a mark of praise. Probably more effective is a short note at the end of the paper (and, of course, appropriately placed in the margin). A useful technique in commenting in writing at the end of a student's paper is to sandwich negative comments between positive ones. Another strong technique is to use the writer's name in connection with good comments, thus:

"I enjoyed your humor very much, Tony. It shows you used a thoughtful approach. Such good work was spoiled a bit when you failed to underline your titles; keep working on this. Your papers continue to get neater. Keep this up, by all means."

The composition theory developed in the preceding chapter was formulated as a foundation that proves useful for the work of *teacher as critic.* It cannot be construed as a general theory of criticism because of the importance in the formulation of the author's intent in writing. In most literature we cannot be certain of the intention of the author of a work. When the intent of a piece of student writing is not clear, the teacher can ask about it.

Generally, when reacting critically to a composition, the teacher should base the criticism on the intent or apparent intent of the writer. This has the distinct instructional advantage of consistency of viewpoint no matter what type or specific form is under consideration. When criticizing any purposive paper the teacher should ask:

1. What was the writer's problem as he analyzed it?
2. How suitable was his approach in terms of his purpose and perceived audience?
3. Has he produced an appropriate and effective token?

Thus, the teacher can make the students aware of the evaluative criteria. These criteria relate to them and their work rather than to some rhetorical canon of which they may be entirely unaware.

To summarize, priority in composition instruction must be assigned to work leading to the mastery of information-oriented writing because the need for that form of writing is foremost in school. Since use of this type will be determined by the student's analysis of the writing situation, lessons in situation analysis must precede lessons in writing information-oriented forms. If the inventory gives evidence that students lack organizational skill, lessons in organizing must precede work with information-oriented tokens. To the extent that the type includes other complete forms, such as definitions, lessons in these forms must come first.

Work with other forms should precede work with information-oriented writing insofar as such work will support writing as an activity, that is, provide feelings of success associated with writing.

As students master information-oriented forms, the other forms should be introduced into the curriculum. The study of any form should be controlled by similar principles:

1. Easier forms should be studied before harder ones.
2. Generally, the ease of a form should be determined by the ease of analyzing it, since the first step in learning to write it is to analyze a model of it. The second element conditioning ease is its length. Obviously, the shorter ones are easier.

3. If a form is composed of, or contains within it, shorter forms, these should be studied first. And they should be studied as complete forms. For example, quatrains should be studied before sonnets.
4. As "ideal" models are mastered, effective deviants should be studied.

Many diverse elements enter into the teaching of composition. All must be accounted for in planning. Taken together, the planning and the elements represent an instructional theory. Should the teacher proceed without a guiding theory, he must rely on intuition. His instruction will probably not relate to his students' development as writers in a sequential way. Even if their writing skills were to develop well, it would not be as the result of his instruction.

NOTE

1. Gladys C. Halvorsen, "Some Effects of Emphasizing Mechanical Accuracy on Written Expression of Sixth Grade Children." Doctoral Dissertation, University of California, 1960.

Information-Oriented Compositions: Utilitarian Writing | **25**

The most important kind of writing for students is the rather utilitarian type that is intended to convey information. This is the type of writing that they are required to use in school not only in their English classes but in most other classes as well. Those who go on to college will continue to use it in their term papers.

Traditionally, writing of this kind has been called expository, a classification that would presumably include not only term papers and their secondary school progenitors—book reports, critical essays, and the like—but also such diverse works as essays appearing in "The Talk of the Town" in *The New Yorker,* UPI news stories, The Declaration of Independence, *The Spectator, Origin of Species,* real estate advertisements, Boswell's *Life of Johnson,* and Johnson's *Dictionary.* The traditional classification asserts that these are all of a piece, all exposition. Yet, it is clear that from the point of view of their author's intent, they are vastly different.

Basing instruction in this type of writing on models of one kind or another is a common enough practice in composition texts. The models are usually seen in the light of presumed (and often demonstrated) arrangements of their contents in terms of a highly specific principle such as "cause/effect," "time sequence," "size order," "internal/external," and the like. One such text offers nine analyses of ten different arrangements in the area of exposition and seven in the area of argument.

Imagine the student's problem if his writing is done along the lines suggested by such an organization. He must first decide whether his paper is to be one of exposition or argument. Then, he must remember sixteen different models and their analyses. Next, he must choose the one to follow and then follow it appropriately.

Although some students might find such an instructional approach useful, most would be better served by a single, all-purpose model that could serve for either "exposition" or "argument." Most compositions written in school course work, whether traditionally classed as exposition or argument, share many features, the most important being the intent of the writer to convey information (including his opinions) to the reader as unambiguously as possible.

Model for the Compositions

Martin Joos in his monograph "The Five Clocks" discusses a speech style that he calls "formal." His discussion serves as a basis for the all-purpose model for the utilitarian, information-oriented composition:

> Beyond its code-labels, formal style is strictly determined by the absence of participation. This absence infects the speaker also. He may speak as if he were not present, avoiding such allusions to his own existence as "I, me, mine," with the possible exception of "one"—a formal code-label—or "myself" in desperate situations. The speaker protects both the text and himself from involvement; presumably he will be absent if the roof collapses.
>
> Lacking all personal support, the text must fight its own battles. Form becomes its dominant character. Robbed of personal links to reality, it scorns such other links as the stone painfully kicked to refute an idealist philosopher; instead, it endeavors to employ only logical links, kept entirely within the text, and displays those logical links with sedulous care. The pronunciation is explicit to the point of clattering; the grammar tolerates no ellipsis and cultivates elaborateness; the semantics is fussy. Background information is woven into the text in complex sentences. Exempt from interruption, the text organizes itself into paragraphs; the paragraphs are linked explicitly: thus this is the third of a quadruplet.
>
> Formal text therefore demands advance planning . . . the formal speaker has a captive audience, and is under obligation to provide a plan for the whole sentence before he begins uttering it, an outline of the paragraph before introducing it, and a delimitation of fields for his whole discourse before he embarks on it. One who does all this currently, keeping the three levels of his planning under continuous control, is correctly said to think on his feet; for clearly it calls for something other than brains; and intelligent persons do not attempt it but instead have the text all composed and written out at leisure.
>
> The defining features of formal style are two: (1) Detachment; (2) Cohesion.[1]

Thus, the information-oriented paper will contain the following features:

1. The plan of the paper should be explicated as part of the paper. Usually, the plan will stand first. Failing a complete initial explication of plan (as this may not always suit the author's purpose), the elements of the plan are introduced appropriately before the text described by the plan appears.

2. The presentation is governed by logical considerations:
    a. possibly ambiguous terms are defined before they are employed extensively in the context;
    b. generalizations are explicit;
    c. specific illustrations support generalizations;
    d. ambiguity of any kind is generally absent.
3. The first person pronoun is avoided. In addition to tradition, such avoidance is dictated by psychological considerations: The reader should focus on the data and not be distracted by the author.

In addition to these criteria suggested by Joos' monograph are the following:

4. The second person pronoun is avoided.
5. Longer papers should feature some sort of summary.

It is clear that by expressing his plan in his paper, the writer is forced to think out any arrangement he may wish to use before he starts writing at all. Therefore, it is not necessary for him to spend time and effort in learning any number of hypothetical models purported to exemplify arrangements of various kinds.

A more or less traditional feature of school composition programs has been instruction in outlining as a corollary to instruction in composition. Doubtless, many writers have found the outline to have great utility in helping to plan papers, especially those that are information-oriented. But many, especially writers of shorter papers (of six to ten paragraphs), do not use outlines. Sometimes, well-meaning teachers have insisted on the presentation of an outline along with the finished paper, and after completing the paper the student has written his outline in order to conform to the assignment. Obviously, this order in doing the work defeats the purpose of the assignment. Just as obviously, someone who can do the work in the reverse order doesn't need an outline at all; requiring one places an unnecessary (and unrealistic) burden on him. An expression of plan serves the same purposes as an outline for the writer and increases the value of the paper to the reader at the same time.

Teaching Procedures

The character of the information-oriented composition suggests the general instructional plan that should be used in dealing with it. In the preliminary lessons, the students should make definitions of various kinds as composition exercises. Other exercises should include writing a plan for some model that is presented without a plan; outlining the contents of some essay for which a plan is presented; writing a summary for a model presented without a summary; making a generalization based on a series of specific illustrations; and writing a short series of illustrations to support a model generalization (for example, "Driving can be dangerous").

After mastering these separate elements, the class should analyze models of complete forms and then imitate appropriate ones in producing original compositions. Since a new learning is taking place during this period, the papers must be returned to the students as soon as possible. If the composition is found to be defective in meeting the criteria, it should be revised.

The feature that generally gives the greatest trouble to young writers is avoiding first and second person pronouns—for example, "I think *The Rime of the Ancient Mariner* is partly allegorical." Typically, students will avoid the objectionable pronoun usages by substituting such locutions as "This composition will show that *The Rime* . . ." Others of the same genre: "This paragraph affirms . . ." "This last sentence proves . . ." It is a good idea to place these usages on the proscription list in the initial phase of instruction.

There are times, of course, when a writer's style in expression is greatly simplified, or perhaps made less formal, by using the first person. Therefore, as these information-oriented forms are mastered, the teacher should introduce models that are not "pure" in this respect. In reading the students' papers written in the first person, however, he must consider whether the first person actually does improve the style. In any case, he must comment on the usage as part of his written appraisal.

The following two eighth-grade* examples of data-oriented compositions, the first from a functional writer and the second from a fluent writer, treat the same topic. The marginal analyses show how they meet the criteria that have been established for this type of composition:

Euphemisms

In our ever-changing language, one of the most common examples of figurative language is the euphemism. It is a very widely employed and necessary part of the English language.

"Our" is unavoidable here.

A euphemism is a word that can be used in place of another word, but

Early definition of term "euphemism."

---

* The use of eighth-grade examples here does not imply that this form has been mastered by students at higher levels. On the contrary, many college freshmen are innocent of organizational techniques. Rather, the examples from this grade level suggest that with appropriate instruction, most students can master the form. Further, the fact that later examples in this chapter are from ninth and tenth graders does not imply that the instructional sequences described here must take place over a three-year period. They can be presented at a single grade level if the students are ready. Some seventh graders will be; some twelfth graders will not be.

is considered more dignified and "better" sounding. For example, one of the more common euphemisms is the use of the word "attorney" as a substitute for "lawyer."

Euphemisms are more prevalent in the following areas: (1) Occupations, as seen in the previous example; (2) In naming a place of work; (3) In naming a room; (4) In the case that one would want to cushion a particularly sorrowful occasion; and (5) In avoiding the direct naming of the deity.

In the case of occupations, many euphemisms can be found in the yellow pages of a telephone book. Some examples of euphemisms dealing with occupations are sanitary engineers for garbagemen, beautician for one who works in a beauty shop, etc.

Also, there are many examples of euphemisms in everyday use of the employment of euphemisms to dignify a particular piece of work. A men's clothing store has become a haberdashery, a beauty shop has now become a beauty salon and so on.

In the instance of improving the degree of dignity given to a room via the use of euphemisms, a euphemism employed by some hotels is the substitution of "boudoir" for "bedroom." This euphemism is very effective in this case because French is considered such a continental and flowing language that it very naturally improves your impression of the room.

Probably the most common case in easing the pain of a particularly sorrowful or distasteful subject is death. There are a vast number of substitutes for "died." Just a sampling is "passed away" and "passed on." These are all very frequently employed.

The plan of the paper is laid out.

Following the plan, the student first discusses *occupation.* He generalizes. Then he provides specific examples to support his generalization.

In the subsequent paragraphs he follows the plan expressed earlier. Each paragraph begins with a generalization. Then the writer provides supporting specific examples.

The use of "your" should be avoided. This is noted as a marginal comment on the composition.

One of the most frequent uses of euphemisms and one of the times when people least realize they are employing them is using euphemisms in masking a cuss word or a direct naming of the deity. As an example of a masking or disguising of a direct naming of the deity, one often hears "For goodnesssake" or another phrase resembling that one. In this case, the word "goodness" is used to avoid directly naming the deity.

So, as is seen from these examples, euphemisms play a very colorful and important role in our always progressing language.

Composition ends with a brief summary. This composition was written by a functional writer.

Euphemisms in Today's World

No person has a desire to be regarded as unimportant, nor do they wish their everyday acts to be thought of as being trivial. "Ordinary" has become a dirty word in American society. For this reason the American people have developed more distinguished and high flown terms for various occupations, businesses and stores of all sorts, organizations, and even sections of the home. These terms are called Euphemisms.

A more subtle explication of plan.

As American civilization has progressed men have taken on names referring to the work they do. The men whose job it is to keep the schools in top condition were known as janitors, a term which was fairly well respected years ago but today, this same term has become a derogatory expression in the eyes of the *Building Superintendent.*

The student follows his plan but the whole effect is smoother.

Many people avoid words pertaining to certain kinds of clothing. For this reason companies no longer deal in women's underwear but rather in *Ladies' Lingerie.* The women of today would never stoop so low as to purchase underwear!

When women, excuse me, ladies, go to have their hair styled they no longer go to the Hair Dresser but rather the Beauty Salon, Beauty Parlor, or Coiffures Shoppe. Any shop owner with a sign reading "HAIR DRESSER" had better go into the construction business; he certainly has no future in *Ladies Coiffures!*

People have gone so far as to apply Euphemisms to parts of the home. Never ask where the bathroom of a friend's house is located or you will find yourself regarded as a member of the inferior class; rather, inquire as to the whereabouts of his *restroom, powder room,* or *lavatory.*

Euphemisms never leave the English language but instead continue to be added to it. A *Building Superintendent* will remain a *Building Superintendent* only until the average person realizes that he is, in truth, a janitor. When this happens a new Euphemism will be formed for janitor. In this manner euphemisms come and go until the average American is so thoroughly confused that it is impossible for him to decipher their reference, let alone understand their connotations.

This section is not predicted in the plan. Probably, it was added because of the pun in the last sentence.

The writer is inconsistent in his use of italics. This is brought to his attention with a note.

This composition is the work of a fluent writer.

Some elements of instruction have now been established. Analysis of models should be in terms of criterion statements about the structure and style of finished compositions. Additionally, some elements in the instructional sequence have been named: For example, the student learns to write definitions as complete composition exercises before learning to write compositions containing definitions. But a deeper analysis of the type is required before the whole instructional design is completed.

Up to this point, it should be clear that the teaching sequence is determined by the relative complexity of the successive forms. The general nature of the assignment should determine the structural complexity of the completed composition. For example, the above compositions were written in response to this assignment: "Write a composition explaining how some figure of speech is used." This assignment predicts a simple problem because the writer concentrates on a single controlling idea—any *one* figure of speech.

The next assignment in a sequential series should force him to deal with two ideas in some way. An assignment involving a comparison is a good one for this. The plan he expresses will demonstrate, by itself, the more complex nature of his problem. Consider the following two examples:

A Critical Comparison of the "Adams Family" and "The Munsters"

Most people would consider the "Adams Family" and "The Munsters" alike as television programs in terms of the writers' purposes. Yet, actually, both programs have different purposes. The writer's purpose in the "Adams Family" is burlesque, and the writer's purpose in "The Munsters" is parody. Burlesque is when the writer is ridiculing something through exaggeration, but he doesn't necessarily want the thing changed. A parody is when the writer's purpose is to imitate the characteristic style of some other work or of another writer. The writer does this in a humorous manner but he doesn't necessarily want the style changed.

The writer's purpose in the "Adams Family" is burlesque because the writer is making fun of people in general through exaggeration, but he doesn't want people to change. Most people want their children to be happy at play. The parents in the program are very gay and creepy. They always

The plan contains a thesis statement as well as definitions. The whole plan is laid out at the beginning.

The definitions are weak because they are introduced by "when." This defect is noted marginally.

want the children (if they are playing with a train set) to crash up the trains and make an explosion. Everything they do is abnormal compared to what modern parents do. Almost all parents allow their children to have pets. Little Wednesday's pet is a black widow spider! Many people get excited when they hear a foreign language, especially French. Everytime Gomez hears French he goes wild and starts kissing Morticia's arm. Double take is often used in the "Adams Family." An example of this is: the Adams family has a box in which a hand pops out when called for, named Thing. Every time a visitor is in the house and Thing pops out of the box, the visitor has to look twice.

The writer's purpose in "The Munsters" is a parody, because the writer is imitating the old horror movies in a humorous manner, yet he doesn't necessarily want the movies to change. Herman Munster plays the part of Frankenstein, Grandpa Munster plays the part of Dracula, Eddie Munster plays the part of the Wolfman. Herman works in a funeral parlor, and Grandpa works in his laboratory and often turns into a bat. Pratfalls are often used in "The Munsters." An example of this is: Herman Munster would fall over something and would break everything and get himself all banged up. Take and double-take are also used, an example of this is: Herman or Grandpa would be walking down the street and all the people passing would look a second time and their eyes would practically come out of their heads.

Because the organizational elements have been mastered, the teacher concentrates on stylistic weaknesses in negative comments.

As is seen from the above, the "Adams Family" and "The Munsters" are really two different types of programs.

An example of "functional" writing.

Ninth-grade girl

The composition was the result of work done in a unit similar to that outlined in Chapter 1.

In the next sample the author varies his strategy with respect to expressing his plan. The plan is broken into two parts. After demonstrating his original thesis that the two works have much in common, he goes on to show that the elements they have in common raise a question about them: Are they allegories? Then, following his original sequence in discussing the elements, he completes his argument. He has, of his own accord, moved away from the lines of the original model:

"Rhinoceros" and "Masque of the Red Death"

Both the play "Rhinoceros" by Ionesco and the short story "The Masque of the Red Death" by Poe contain many symbols, morals, and characters who represent types of people.

Brief explication of plan.

The symbols in both "Rhinoceros" and "The Masque of the Red Death" are plentiful. Of course, the most prominent feature of "Rhinoceros" is the fact that each character in the play except the supposedly stupidest of all, Berenger, turns into a rhinoceros, a symbol of stupidity. Similarly, in "The Masque of the Red Death" there is a prominent symbol, or rather symbols, these being the variously colored rooms, each symbolizing something different.

Each work contains a moral or more than one moral. These need not be discussed since they are quite clear.

A marginal note to the writer suggests that he specify the morals.

Finally, in each work the characters

represent types. In "Rhinoceros," Berenger represents a "bum," who although a drunkard, thinks rationally. Jean represents the well-dressed, well-to-do know-it-all. And the bystanders represent the common people who have one idea in most matters, perhaps only one idea. In "The Masque of the Red Death," Prince Prospero represents the high-society show-off who acts brave and really isn't. The others who attend the ball are high-society people who are followers.

Both of these works, as has been pointed out, contain three like elements. The general structure of both is also the same. But now, let us move to another problem: are both like established allegories such as *Aesop's Fables*? If they are essentially the same, we can label both allegories.

A new problem and an extension of the plan.

In all of *Aesop's Fables* there is symbolism. For instance, in "The Grasshopper and the Donkey," the dew which the donkey ate symbolizes knowledge.

Certainly, all of *Aesop's Fables* have morals. This is what they are noted for. In "The Grasshopper and the Donkey" the moral is: "Be happy with what you are."

The characters in the *Fables* represent types of people. The grasshopper is one who has some special skill, and the donkey is a status seeker.

When "Rhinoceros" and "The Masque of the Red Death" are compared to known allegories and are found to be the same, it can be safely said that both are allegories.

Ninth-grade boy

Subsequent composition problems involve dealing with more than two ideas, as with the following:

Literary Analogues

Although there are several analogous elements in "The Masque of the Red Death" by Poe, "The Seven Stages of Man" by Shakespeare and "Brahma" by Emerson, the three cannot really be considered literary analogues. For even though there are quite a few similarities in them they cannot be paralleled. The analogies are not strong enough.

In "The Masque of the Red Death," Prince Prospero and his men put themselves under quarantine to avoid catching the disease known as the Red Death. This disease consisted of bleeding and sores, especially on the face. The whole period of the disease lasted one half hour. In order to quarantine themselves the Prince and his men (and women) stayed in an old but magnificent castle. In this castle there was an apartment of seven rooms. These rooms, all except one, had stained glass windows to match the furnishings of the rooms. The colors were as follows: blue, purple, orange, green, violet, and white. The seventh room had black furnishings and red stained glass windows. In the room was a great grandfather's clock which chimed every hour, on the hour. During the time of the quarantine, the Prince and company were having a masked ball. It took place in the first six of the seven rooms of the apartment. As the dancers danced the clock would chime on the hour and momentarily the dancing would stop,

The plan.

for the noise was a very sudden and stirring sound. When the clock chimed twelve mid-night, the dancing ceased. But this time when it started up there was one more person among them. One masked as the Red Death. When the Prince, who was in the blue room, saw him he ordered him unmasked and hung at sun-up. When no one obeyed his command, the Prince himself chased him back through all the rooms. In the last room though, Prince Prospero caught the Red Death and died. The others followed immediately.

In "The Seven Ages of Man," Shakespeare talks about the world as a stage with the people playing the seven stages of life and life development. These seven stages are: the infant, school-boy, lover, soldier, the justice, pantaloon, and one dying.

The analogy in "The Masque of the Red Death" and "The Seven Stages of Man" is that in both, it talks about six things someone goes through before dying. In "The Masque of the Red Death" Prince Prospero goes from the blue room, which is the first one, straight through, to the black and red room in which he dies. In the other one, man goes through the six stages of infant to "slipper'd pantaloon" and then he also dies.

Other than this, there are not any analogous elements in the two of them, and it is not strong enough to say that the two are literary analogues.

Of course, when deciding whether or not some things are analogous or not, one must understand the different compositions. Therefore one must understand "Brahma" and to understand "Brahma" one needs to know a little about Hindu philosophy.

Is the fragment permissible here? A marginal comment to the writer on this and "hung."

Again, since organization is mastered, comments relate to stylistic lapses.

The life background of this student, child of missionaries to India, enables her to bring special critical insights to her work. This is possible only in composition.

It is the Hindu's belief that life is a dream, an illusion, that nothing in life is real. This illusion is known in Sanskrit as "Maya." The Hindu, therefore, is constantly trying to realize that life is a bad dream, for when he does, he will wake-up and find that he is Brahma. Brahma is the most divine of the Hindu gods. In fact, most Hindus don't worship him directly because they are not worthy. They worship seven gods under Brahma. In Sanskrit, this awakening and finding oneself is referred to as "TAT TUAM ASI," meaning: "That am I." Another belief of the Hindus is the cycle of history and the reincarnation of life. This means they believe that history keeps on turning and therefore repeating itself constantly. The reincarnation is the rebirth of all animals and people. When someone dies, it is believed that he has gone on to a new life, a new form of living, maybe as a fly or maybe as a Brahmin, who is the highest caste Hindu. In the first stanza of "Brahma" it says, "If the red slayer think he slays . . ." etc. referring to the reincarnation or the awakening of a Hindu. For even if one is killed one will either be reincarnated to a new form or will wake up from the dream of life. In the second stanza when it says "Far or forgot to me is near . . ." etc. it is talking about the unreality of life. Since life isn't real there is really no difference between shame and fame, shadow and sunlight, far and near. As Brahma is everything and everything centers around Brahma, people who leave him out of their philosophy (stanza 3) aren't intelligent, don't think straight and since Brahma created everything (in his dream) when people fly, he is the one who gives them power, "is the wings." In the last stanza it says, "The strong gods pine for my abode . . ." etc. This means the gods who get worshipped, the sacred seven are trying to wake-up from their dream but cannot for they are not meek or lovers of the good. For the good find Brahma (me) and respect him.

There are not really analogous elements in "Brahma" and "The Masque of the Red Death," but in "The Seven Ages of Man" there is the idea of illusion and unreality in that the world is just a stage on which the people perform. Since this is the only analogous element the two poems are definitely not literary analogues.

Tenth-grade girl

Another factor that controls the difficulty of writing—and thus the structure of the composition and the order of scheduling in the curriculum—is the difficulty of the material to which the writer must respond in solving his problem. For example, taking a problem of the simplest type (single idea), it can be readily seen that if the writer is writing about a one-act play such as *The Old Lady Shows Her Medals* by James Barrie, his job is not nearly so complex as when he writes about *All My Sons* by Arthur Miller; and again, this is not so complex as writing about *The Tempest*. (Of course, there are various elements of difficulty germane to the contents of these three plays other than their mere length, but length alone would suffice as a measure of difficulty.)

At this point, the teacher should introduce another dimension of the componential structure of the composition, that of documentation. Especially in the course of critical writing, the writer should employ various pieces of evidence, both those that are internal to the problem he is considering and those that are external to it. In both cases he will have to learn appropriate techniques for documenting his material. The problem arises very early in the production of compositions of the type under discussion here.

Because he wants to provide good definitions for his terms, the young writer will very often use the definition provided by his dictionary. Generally, this is a defensible practice (although if the teacher asks such questions as

"What is literal meaning?" the young writer who employs the dictionary—any dictionary—as a source for a solution will run into difficulty).

It is at this point that he should be taught to document his source. He should not be given the idea, however, that it is wrong to use outside help. On the contrary, he should be strongly encouraged to seek authoritative support of all kinds for positions he develops. The only caveat is that *he should develop his position first.* A well-made literature program will have him ultimately criticizing the views presented by authorities (including those presented by the editors of dictionaries). The use of documented support for a position is a feature of information-oriented articles presented by and to scholars. Rather than discouraging any such practice, the teacher should structure appropriate documentation techniques into his composition instruction. The sooner the principle of intellectual honesty is learned in this regard, the better for the learner: it ought to be second nature to any writer.

There is yet one dimension to the problem of the production of information-oriented tokens that must be dealt with before the instructional sequence can be regarded as being completed. Up to this point, the discussion has indicated that the writer writes in response *to a problem.* Very likely the reader has inferred that the problem is developed and presented by the teacher. In the initial phases of instruction, this is more or less the case. In learning the elements that are featured by these types of compositions and producing the compositions themselves, the students have quite enough to occupy them. One suggestion is in order at this point. It is a good idea for the teacher to present a variety of problems of comparable difficulty in any one lesson. This procedure has two advantages: the student can select the problem that interests him the most (perhaps a compulsive element in the writing situation), and the teacher will be able to read a variety of compositions. Imagine reading upwards of a hundred compositions on the theme of "Crossing the Bar," say. In that way lies madness.

The following are six different writing problems connected with an analysis of *A Midsummer Night's Dream.* An adequate response to any one of them will result in an analysis of the whole play.

1. One of the chief production problems of this play is casting the roles. Suppose yourself the casting director. Analyze the characters physically and psychologically. Now name stage, movie, or TV actors or personalities who would be suited to play each role and support your choices.
2. At least three forms of humor are used in the play: parody, satire, and burlesque. Where is each form used? Which is used most successfully? Which humor-producing devices have helped in its presentation?
3. Shakespeare is often inconsistent in the way in which he deals with time. Discuss the inconsistencies in this play, determining (1) if they could be changed, (2) if they *should* be changed, and (3) how they might be changed.

4. Shakespeare reveals many of the features of the superstitions of the European folk in the Elizabethan age. Develop a guidebook to help a reader interpret the references to superstitious belief and behavior encountered in the play.

5. A large part of Shakespeare's reputation rests upon the way he uses language and upon the way in which he develops character. In this play he has his characters use four different types of language: prose; blank verse (unrhymed iambic pentameter); heroic verse (rhymed iambic pentameter); and trochaic tetrameter (also other sing-song verse). Generally, characters use only one of these patterns, but occasionally a character will deviate. Why do the characters speak the way they do, and why do they deviate?

6. As does most comedy since Aristophanes, this play deals with love as an important theme. We see many developments of this theme from Pyramus and Thisbe and their "tragedy" to young love, to mature romance, to long-time "wedded bliss"—and there are other types. By examining all these relationships, show Shakespeare's attitude towards romantic love.

Although some mature writers, such as reporters and advertising copy writers, must write in response to a problem dictated by somebody else, ordinarily the mature writer uses his writing to analyze a problem that is of interest to him primarily—a problem that he has seen for himself or has developed in connection with elements peculiar to his own experience. At any rate, such is the case in ideal situations. The teacher can work toward the development of such an ideal situation in his classes. After the students have learned the formal aspects of writing information-oriented compositions, they should be taught to develop questions that can form the basis for composition topics.

Such work can be effectively integrated with the study of literature. For example, if there is a unit on poetry, the students can formulate questions that will provide a basis for analyzing the poems. The following procedure is suggested:

1. Following work with appropriate model questions and poems, each student should choose a poem for which he will construct a series of guide questions to aid another reader in the analysis of the poem.

2. A committee of students should read one another's questions and the poems they were based on and criticize the questions, which should then be revised by their authors.

3. Each student should exchange his questions with a partner who is not in his criticism group. Each of them then writes an analysis of the poem, working along the lines suggested by his partner's questions.

4. The finished papers should be read and criticized by the authors of the questions. The results are discussed by the partners.

5. Finally, each person should choose a new poem and write an analysis of it which should be read and criticized by the teacher.

The following examples from one student illustrate this sequence:

GUIDE QUESTIONS FOR "ULALUME" by E. A. Poe   Student A

1. What is/are the central meaning(s) of Ulalume? How is/are the meaning(s) represented?
2. What is/are the central image(s) of the poem?
3. Name some of the less important meanings and images.
4. Where is the poem taking place? Does it have any effect on the poem? How?
5. Why is the person or thing describing the poem? Who is Psyche? What do the two represent?
6. What or who is Ulalume?
7. What were they (Psyche and the person describing the happening) doing in the poem? What happened at the end?

Because writing guide questions of this kind is difficult, the instruction should proceed in four stages. The first is part of the teacher's instruction in the analysis of poetry. Each time he presents a poem, he should present guide questions leading toward the analysis. As far as possible, the questions from poem to poem should be parallel in structure—that is, the same types of questions asked in the same order. The next stage is a teacher-led analysis of a poem without the customary guide questions. After the discussion, committees should work together to develop a set of guide questions. When they have finished, the questions should be compared. In the next stage, which also features group work, each group should work on a different poem and, using the guide questions produced, teach the poem to the class. The class should criticize the questions when each lesson is finished. Finally, each student should work independently on his own poem. When he has finished, he should submit his questions to his fellow committee members for criticism, and then revise them.

The following compositions, which are characterized by awkwardness in organization and expression, are unrevised versions of the work. It often happens that a new kind of writing assignment produces compositions that are awkward, probably because of the general frustration involved in learning something new. As exercises with the new type of assignment are repeated, the awkwardness diminishes.

ANALYSIS OF "ULALUME"   Student B

Having an unhappy life, Poe shows it in his writing. "Ulalume" was written with a lot of this personal feeling.

Poe had a very sorrowful life which was climaxed by the death of his wife. He was very depressed about it, and took up heavy drinking, dying two years later. His morbid feelings are found in his writing. "Dim Lake of Auber," "Misty midregion of Weir," "dank tarn of Auber," and "ghoul haunted woodland of Weir" are morbid description of unreal places. This probably described the type of life he lived "in."

Then "I" (Poe is I) says he walks and talks with Psyche. This is metaphoric because Psyche is a personified soul. Therefore when it says he talked with Psyche, it meant he was thinking deeply and Psyche's responses are his conscience.

As the "journey" is taking place, there comes a great light ("crescent" moon which is personified) which is to show the way from these morbid surroundings. In other words, he would be taken from this unhappy life. Psyche, his conscience, doesn't want to follow this light. "Oh, let us not linger." But, I, (Poe) wants a way out. "With hope" "will lead us aright." Thus they follow it to the end of the "vista." (This again shows the metaphoric because vista is a mental view and Poe writes of it as a journey with his Psyche.)

The finale is the two coming across a tomb and Psyche crying "Tis the vault of thy Ulalume." This brings Poe back to his morbid state again. The tomb probably symbolizes his wife's death. I, myself, have no verification of the latter point, since there is no meaning for Ulalume, but the implication, particularly "thy lost" points to the idea of it being his wife.

To sum up, this poem tells of Poe's trying to escape from his morbid life. Any time he tries to be happy, he always feels the pang of sorrow about his wife's death.

CRITICISM OF STUDENT B'S ANALYSIS OF "ULALUME" Student A

I think that Student B's interpretation of the poem "Ulalume" is completely valid based on her reasons which are very interesting.

When I read the poem, I knew that Poe was the person relaying the happening and that Psyche was Poe's conscience. Student B agrees with me on these points but she also opened two new concepts to me, which were very important in the poem.

One was that Poe's life affected his writing quite a bit. Apparently his existence was an unhappy one, and this shows in a lot of his work. Another important relationship in the poem that Student B brought out was the tie-in between the death of Poe's wife and the grave towards the end of Ulalume which obviously affects "I" (Poe) very deeply.

The one problem which both Student B and I had was trying to find the meaning of the word Ulalume. Neither of us succeeded, so I am supposing it to be one that Poe invented.

That is the only criticism that I have of Student B's interpretation of the poem except to say that I think she did a good job. It was a difficult poem to understand but I think she handled it well.

During the course of this discussion, the examples that were given related to the explication of literary topics. Naturally, information-oriented papers can treat other kinds of topics. But certain considerations of English class culture tend to direct this kind of writing toward criticism undertaken at various levels of sophistication.

The central value of English studies is that attached to literature, and the study of literature becomes increasingly sophisticated. One measure is the critical attack made on a work. Since a reader can read anything "for enjoyment" at any time he wishes, why is such reading a feature of the instruction in English classes? The only pertinent reason for such practice concerns motivation, and this in turn relates to otherwise reluctant readers. However, this position involves a paradox: If a student is reluctant to read, it is because he has not found enjoyment in reading. Perhaps, in many cases, the intellectual problems connected with the analysis of meanings (or form) in literature can provide the motivation for readers who find no pleasure in reading.

The unreluctant reader, needless to say, does not need class-related opportunities for "enjoyment" reading. Therefore, instruction should be devoted to experiences of the kind that require the guidance of a teacher; in other words, instruction that leads to literary criticism.

Assuming, then, that a sophisticated approach to literature is the key feature of the English course, some evaluation is possible through the use of objective tests, but they fail to take into account the life experience that the critic brings to his reading, which is an important dimension of criticism at any level of sophistication. This ingredient can, however, be revealed in compositions. Therefore, information-oriented compositions, most of which will be written in connection with the critical approach being developed in the study of literature, are an inalienable feature of evaluation in a literature program.

Although there are other types of information-oriented writing that are legitimate features of an English course—business letters, for example—they present no real instructional problem. The traditions that surround them dictate the appropriate patterns of instruction, and school grammars supply numerous models and exercises. Therefore, treatment here is unnecessary.

NOTE

1. Joos, Martin, "The Five Clocks," *International Journal of American Linguistics*, Vol. 28, No. 2 (April 1962), pp. 25–26.

SUGGESTIONS FOR FURTHER READING

1. For technical background in terms, devices, definitions, and so on, in analyzing literary materials, two good general books are:
   (a) BLOOM, EDWARD A., PHILBRICK, CHARLES H., and BLISTEIN, ELMER M. *The Order of Poetry* (New York: Odyssey, 1961) and

(b) SANDERS, THOMAS E. *The Discovery of Poetry* (Glencoe: Scott, Foresman and Company, 1967).

2. For deeper analytical techniques in handling prose fiction see BOOTH, WAYNE C. *The Rhetoric of Fiction* (Chicago: University of Chicago, 1961).

3. A collection of essays that surveys many facets of rhetoric, contemporary and and historical is BAILEY, DUDLEY. *Essays on Rhetoric* (New York: Oxford, 1965).

26 | Form-Oriented Writing

One rather simple critical position held by many is that prose and poetry are polar opposites. If that is true, we move now from the minus to the plus side of the scale in considering the content of composition lessons. The previous chapter dealt with the most coldly formal kind of prose; let us now consider instruction in the writing of poetry.

The poetry under consideration falls in the form-oriented class of compositions. In addition to poetry, the category includes some prose forms.

In form-oriented writing, in contrast to the information-oriented composition, the reader is expected to respond to the work taken as a whole. A fable, for example, is form-oriented because its story and its moral cannot be dissociated if a complete meaning is to be communicated, although it may be the case that each element if presented separately might convey some meaning. The intent of the author is that in the reader's experience both elements support each other. Either part alone, however, is ambiguous, that is, liable to more than one interpretation.

Jokes often turn on ambiguity; the reader is also expected to respond to the joke taken as a whole. Much poetry, especially shorter forms—and most especially *imagiste* forms—makes the same demand of the reader, that of responding to the piece as a whole. Kenneth Pike has noted that some jokes and some poems suggest that their grouping together is rational.[1]

Irony is another example of form-oriented literature. In the case of parody, the whole piece is ironic. In some other works, such as O. Henry's "The Cop and the Anthem," the irony is interpersed throughout the piece, whereas in others, such as Maupassant's "The Necklace," it is not revealed until the end. Whatever the case, such work will require a response to the whole piece.

This type of writing displays another characteristic in that the reader does not empathize with the characters. Metaphorically, he stands away from the work. Although he may sympathize with Soapy in O. Henry's work, or with Mme. Loisel in Maupassant's, he does not feel as one with them or with any other element in the presentation. He may, however, *reflect* that some deeper meaning within the work has immediate pertinence in terms of his own experience or philosophy.

Thus, the category contains such superficially diverse types as poems, short stories, essays, fables, parables, many other kinds of allegories, parodies, and jokes. But these share many features: The reader does not become involved; the parts cannot be separated from the whole without destroying the central meaning; ambiguity will often be created by the relationship of the parts; and the works involved are usually shorter.

Poetry

By what rationale do teachers have adolescents write poetry? The discussion of purpose in the composition curriculum outlined in Chapter 22 argues that extensive instruction in composition in the secondary school is very nearly unsupportable on any pragmatic basis. If the pragmatist grudgingly yields to the necessity for learning to write rather formal prose— and this only because of its importance in the school itself and the university —he must surely throw up his hands (and possibly other things as well) at the suggestion that poetry be included in the curriculum. Many teachers— even English teachers—agree with him on this. Unbelievably, many English teachers are suspicious of poetry, nay, even afraid of it—and *not* the writing of poetry, the *reading* of it.

We hear that poetry is too "hard" for adolescents. Poetry is too delicate. Poetry should be delayed. Etc. Etc. Everyone has heard this faculty-room folklore; again not with reference to writing it, but to reading it.

Heavens! Only poets write poetry (poytreh?). When it is indicated to some teachers that the writing of poetry necessitates the analysis of poetry, one observes further throwing-up of hands. (Don't you know that analyzing poetry ruins it?)

An even worse breed of folklorist is the kind who agrees to teach poetry, but who agrees to teach it "on a developmental basis": *Casey at the Bat, The Highwayman, The Cremation of Sam McGee.* And you know what we write: Limericks.

There is certainly nothing wrong with reading works like those named, nor writing limericks. But *limiting* the consideration of poetry, even in the fifth grade, to work of this kind presents such a distorted view of the nature and value of poetic art that it would be better for everyone concerned if these reading and writing poetasters joined forces with the pragmatist and threw the whole thing up.

Why teach poetry as composition? Some forms of poetry are easy both to analyze and to produce. The haiku (see Chapter 5), for example, all but insures success in composition even for dysfunctional writers. The following were written by fluent, functional, and dysfunctional students (but not in that order):

Rain in the night time
Comes knocking at my window
Keeping me awake.

The nightingale's song
Makes the hot summer
A sweet lullaby.

Red is full of life
Like a swiftly flowing spring
On Fugi in May.

Since writing of this kind brings success at composition, it provides general support for all composition experiences. Beyond this, the writing of various forms of poetry helps the student to appraise these forms critically in the literature program.

Some teachers say that adolescents are too young for poetry. Yet Thomas Hardy was writing poetry when he was nineteen. By the age of eighteen, Longfellow, Byron, Poe, and Arnold had had poetry *published*. Schiller published at seventeen; Keats and Emerson were writing by eighteen; Milton, Pope, Coleridge, Wordsworth, and Goethe were writing verse by age sixteen. Gerard Manley Hopkins began his versifying in English grammar school. Blake, Tennyson, and both Brownings had written poetry by the age of twelve.

Beyond these considerations, adolescents are ripe for experience with poetry. In fact, it appears that students produce more work of higher quality in poetry than in any kind of prose.

The general pattern of instruction in poetry parallels that of prose. A model of the form should be analyzed inductively, with particular emphasis on its structure and meanings. Then the students should compose a poem that either imitates the model directly or is derived from the analysis of it. The following poem by an eighth-grade boy, which imitates a model closely, displays an effective, if odd, imagery:

A noisy restless cricket.
Chirping on flowers made of gold
Sometimes down depressed, head bent,

Then suddenly launching like a bullet into the unknown
Never tiring, chirping madly.

Oh, my heart beating.
Always alone in your happy way
Then sometimes down depressed like your life is broken
Always rebounding in a joyous way,
Beating wildly, happy again.

The writer has imitated the lines of his model very closely. That model is a fragment from Walt Whitman:

A NOISELESS PATIENT SPIDER

A noiseless patient spider,
I mark'd where on a little promontory it stood isolated,
Mark'd how to explore the vast surrounding,
It launched forth filament, filament, filament, filament, out of itself.
Even unreeling them, ever tirelessly speeding them.

And you I my soul where you stand,
Surrounded, detached, in measureless oceans of space,
Ceaselessly musing, venturing, throwing, seeking the
    spheres to connect them.
Till the bridge you will need be form'd, till the
    ductile anchor hold,
Till the gossamer thread you fling catch somewhere,
    O my soul.[2]

The next poem is based on the analysis of the same model, rather than being a direct imitation of it:

A fire burning
There—thriving upon wood, twigs,
Igniting, burning, consuming the fuel which strengthens it
Spreading quickly to vulnerable places
Leaving destruction behind.
And there, there is hate.
Living on hearts of men.
Catching, kindling, eating the everlasting food
Attacking and influencing the undecided ones.
To ruin and destroy goodness of mankind.

Eighth-grade girl

Because figurative language is a key component of poetry, the students must be familiar with figures of speech before they can analyze poems. Work with figures should be completed as part of an introductory unit. As a few figures are mastered, the work should begin with poems whose models employ these figures. The haiku is a good place to start.

It is difficult to make statements about the language of poetry. The principal caveat is to avoid the trite. Yet there is no way to recognize triteness other than as a result of experience with language, and younger writers, by virtue of their youth, lack such experience. The teacher as critic walks a tightrope in handling triteness and best deals with the problem in conference with individuals.

One other note on things to avoid. Traditionally, poets enjoy "poetic license" in their use of language. In the past, this license has led to the overuse of such forms as " 'tis" and " 'twas" and inversions like "thought I." Unsophisticated writers tend to imitate such usages, believing that they are a mark of poetry. Generally speaking, the teacher should warn the students to avoid poetic license of this sort.

Other experimental work with language should be encouraged, however. Very often, poets use language that is far in advance of the usage of their language community. Shakespeare, for example, borrowed and coined words as he needed them. Blake used an incredibly simple language, for his time, both in terms of his vocabulary and his syntax. Hopkins was as complex in his language as Blake was simple, coining compounds on the basis of Gaelic and Anglo-Saxon patterns and generally developing difficult rhythm and syntax. E. E. Cummings' poetry features any number of advances in the use of language and typography. Poetry in general is marked by an unrestrained employment of linguistic innovation. Students should be encouraged to experiment in this regard. Although some of their experiments may work out badly, many more will not, as in the following poem.

WITH NO REGARD FOR MY SOUL

As I walked along the ocean, the
wet, cool sand moistened my sun-
patched feet,
The winds which came off from
the ocean, refreshed my spirit and
soul
A red ball of fire hung over my
head—hot violent.
just beat-red.
The sun sucked up what moisture
I had on my body with no
regard for my soul.

Seagulls flew over the sea
occasionally driving down
to the depths of the ocean.
The sun left no prey on land,
And the bodies were strewn
over the sands.
The ocean, so vast and wide,
was a friend to all, who stayed
in motion.
The sun was heartless, the only
songs it knew were those played
by a dead band.

Eighth-grade girl

Long-Range Planning of Poetry Instruction

The work should be scheduled over the year—and longer periods—on the basis of the relative difficulty of structures. The difficulty is determined by the number of different formal components the writer has to consider in his model analysis and his production of the poem.

The first forms should be unrhymed and rather short, like the haiku. Next should come rhymed forms in which the meters are not rigid, the blues stanza, for example. After these come the shorter rhymed forms containing a fixed number of syllables with a rigid pattern, such as quatrains in iambic pentameter. Then come the longer forms containing shorter ones as structural components, like ballads and sonnets.

Free verse should be studied late in the sequence. It must be emphasized that free verse is not undisciplined verse. The students should learn the disciplinary conventions *first* as a way of emphasizing that free verse requires care, thought, and work.

Usually, as with their other writing, the students will first imitate the models closely. As they gain familiarity with the forms and confidence in writing them, they will move further and further away from the mere aping of the model.

A typical scope and sequence chart for three years' work, which might begin at any grade level or even be telescoped into a specialized advanced course in college, follows:

1. haiku	closed couplet	quatrains	ballads
2. cinquain	blues stanza	any "French" form	typographical experiments
3. tanka	terza rima	sonnets	Arnold stanza patterns

Let us first consider the types of poetry in the first vertical group:

Haiku. These are poems containing three unrhymed lines: the first is five syllables in length; the second, seven; the third, five. The poem presents a unified image that alludes to a passage of time and contains a figure of speech.

Cinquain. The cinquain form, invented by Adelaide Crapsey, is modeled on Oriental syllable-counting verse. There are five lines, two, four, six, eight, and two syllables long respectively. Ordinarily, the poem contains two images, the second either a contrast to the first or an echo of it.

Tanka. Another form derived from the Japanese, the tanka contains five lines, five, seven, five, seven, and seven syllables long, respectively. The first three lines constitute a haiku. Often, the form contains a poetic paradox.

Thus, the poems in the first vertical strand, all involving syllable counting as the central formal feature, advance in length and difficulty, from grade to grade.

In the same way, the first horizontal row develops a sequence of forms that is progressively more difficult. The haiku is followed by work with closed couplets in any convenient meter; the new element is the rhyme. Quatrains are next in sequence, and the writer may use a choice of rhyme-schemes, *abba, abab,* consecutive couplets, or four rhyming lines. Finally, the ballad is introduced. This narrative form begins the writer's experience with planning a longer form and adds the refrain to his repertoire.

In the next year, after the cinquain, the writer again encounters a verse form demanding rhyme as a discipline. The blues stanza is essentially a couplet with a repeating first line, but the meter is not rigid since only the accented syllables are significant. For example:

Where are you, baby, so far away from me;
Where are you tonight, baby, so far away from me;
Why can't they mail you, baby, across the deep blue sea?

In addition to rhyme, refrains complicate the pattern. A French form such as the triolet also uses repeating lines as well as rhyming lines. The rhyme-scheme is *ABaAabAB,* with capitals indicating lines which are either repeated or have repeated rhyme words. The form is clearly more complex and longer than the quatrain. The final experience in the sequence is the imitation of such "shape" poems as those by E. E. Cummings ("Portrait," for example) in which the typographical arrangement supports the imagery.

In the last year, the second sequential element is the terza rima series of three-line stanzas—*aba, bcb, cdc*—in iambic pentameter ending with a couplet. Next is the sonnet. (The vertical sequence is arranged so that it moves from quatrains through longer rhymed forms to a fourteen-line form.) Finally, there is the Arnold stanza, a type of free verse that is characterized by blank verse lines mingled with rhyming lines and lines of unpredictable meter.

Of course, a student's classification by the school as an eleventh or twelfth grader does not imply his readiness for writing the forms appearing at the end of this sequence. While one or two students in a senior English class might write fairly successful sonnets without experience with the earlier forms, many more will not. They will experience much frustration and irritation. Some students who have had success with the simpler forms will not be able or willing to attempt the more complex forms. Thus, although this series of forms is described as a three-year sequence, it is wise with many twelfth-grade classes to use only the forms on the first or second levels. As with the other subject matter aspects of English, the teacher must make the judgment about what is appropriate for his students as learners, a judgment which cannot be made on the basis of meaningless grade-level classifications.

Fables

In addition to poetry, the class of form-oriented writing should contain prose forms.

Fables are easy to analyze and serve as a good introduction to narrative writing. When the form has been studied, the teacher should suggest some ideas that will help the students to start writing fables, for example, a dog asking a bird to teach him how to fly. The student should then develop a complete narrative and supply a moral. The following are other typical ideas for fables:

A squirrel sees a cat near a tree where nuts are hidden.
A scarecrow and a telephone pole discuss sparrows.
A young tadpole and an old mosquito talk about their pond.
A circus horse and a plough horse consider tractors.

The following is a fable written by a dysfunctional student in a remedial writing program (only misspellings are corrected in this version, a first draft):

A dog didn't know what he wanted to be. One day he saw a bird and he said that's what I'll be a flying dog.

He said to the bird, "How did you learn to fly?" The bird said my mother taught me and the dog said how and the bird said she pushed me off a tree.

So the dog said, "That's too bad. I can't climb trees."

The bird told him there's a pretty good cliff over there, just jump.

So the dog went over to the cliff and he did but he didn't fly because it was a dog.

moral: Be satisfied the way you are but try to improve.

The didactic influence of the school guidance program that is so obvious here gives this composition added poignancy. Because the fable form is short, readily analyzed, and carries humorous undertones, it is useful even in work with the weakest students. That the resulting composition is ironic and a parody was not the intention of the writer.

Parodies

An intentional parody is form-oriented, that is, it imitates another work taken as a whole. One problem sometimes not perceived by beginning teachers in dealing with parodies in the literature program is that the work that is being ridiculed by the parodist must be familiar to the reader in order for the parody to be successful. The same is the case when teaching parodies in composition.

Work with parodies should begin by having the students analyze one and also the work, genre, or style that it is ridiculing. The whole class should then imitate the parody under study. The primer parodies of George Ade and Eugene Field and the parodies of Will Cuppy are good for this purpose, since each work is rather short. Here is a parody in imitation of Will Cuppy by an eighth-grade boy:

THE DUCK

The duck walks around on very flat feet. He sings through his nose. His song is that of a quack. The duck is ambiguous. He likes to swim in the briny deep.[1] Ducks glide through the air with the agility of an elephant. If you happen to ask a duck why he has flat feet his answer would be something like this: "All the better to stamp out Beatles with."[2] One of the duck's many worries is the hunter. The hunter always likes to have the duck as the guest of honor at the dinner table.[3] Ducks live on eelgrass which they like quite a bit (the ducks that is). All that they do is hang-around the hunters.[4] If you happen to have a pet duck at home you will know what they like to eat—quackers.

[1] Of mud puddles that is
[2] Water beatles is what I mean
[3] As the main course
[4] They are often called decoys!

The next step in working with parodies is the imitation of various writing styles. In preparation for the assignment, the class should read a number of highly stylized models: stories by Poe, poetry by Ogden Nash, articles from *Time,* essays in "The Talk of the Town" in *The New Yorker,* confession magazine stories, passages from the Bible, scenes from Shakespeare's plays, fairy tales, Howard Pyle, and so on.

After several days' reading, the class should be told that they will be imitating one of these styles and that each person should select the one that he thinks he can do best in the assignment, which will be to select a well-known story told in one style (such as Rumpelstiltskin) and rewrite it in another (such as Poe's style). When the students have decided on their styles, committees should be formed on the basis of the style they will imitate—for example, a Poe group, a Bible group, a *Time* group.

After the group discusses samples of the style to illuminate specific characteristics, each person should write his parody.

When the teacher receives the papers, he should give them a general reading, group by group, to determine which students have mastered the styles chosen. These students should then serve as editors in their groups to help weaker writers correct their stylistic shortcomings. The following composition parodies the style of primers and first grade readers.

NOAH'S ARK

God was mad. He did not like man. "Oh, oh, oh," says God. "I wish that I did not make man. Bad, bad man."

"Look," said Noah. "Look, look, look. See the funny man. Hear him talk. His name is God. God is mad. He only likes Noah. Lucky, lucky Noah."

God says, "I am very mad. I will make it rain. Rain, rain, rain. Build a boat. A big, big boat."

"Look, look," says Noah. "See me build the boat. It is a big, big boat. See the boat. It is a pretty, pretty boat. I can hit a nail. I can saw wood. It is a nice big boat."

"O Father, look, look, look," says Noah's son. "See all the animals come in our boat. See the dogs. See the cats. I see two dogs and two cats. See the other animals. Funny, funny animals."

"Yes, yes," says Noah. "See the animals. See the food. Look at all the food."

"Good, good," says God. "That is good."

Soon it rained. Noah got in his boat. The animals got in the boat. Everybody got in the boat.

"Oh, look," says Noah. "See it rain. See it pour. I am safe. The funny animals are safe. See it rain, rain, rain."

Tenth-grade girl

Obviously, while students can write successful parodies in imitation of Eugene Field's primer parodies and of Will Cuppy's or George Ade's parodies at any grade level from seventh upwards, depending on their background, most students have more difficulty writing parodies which are based on the analysis of style. At higher grade levels, functional and fluent writers can focus on more complex aspects of style and on more complex styles through their work on parody. Many twelfth graders will be incapable of making the analysis of even a style as distinctive as Poe's to produce a parody such as the example in Chapter 13 on pp. 306–307. However, functional and fluent writers can learn a good deal about the nature of style in making the analysis in preparation for writing parody. The teacher can control the difficulty of the exercise by his suggestion of materials. For instance, analyzing and parodying J. D. Salinger's style in *The Catcher in the Rye* is far simpler than doing the same thing with Milton's style in *Paradise Lost*. A good source of parodies, by the way, is Dwight MacDonald's *Parodies, An Anthology from Chaucer to Beerbohm—and After* (New York: Random House, 1965).

Irony

The most difficult kind of form-oriented composition is the piece that leads to an ironic conclusion. Many short stories and some poetry (like Shelley's "Ozymandias") have such a conclusion; their final lines or image are ironic counterpoint to the bulk of the composition. After a number of literary models of this type have been read and analyzed, the teacher should give the following assignment:

"From your own experience or knowledge of current events or history, reconstruct an incident as a narrative or a poem in such a way that the very last part of the composition makes an ironic comment on either the whole incident or the central image of the incident."

Examples of some appropriate imagery or incidents should be elicited and suggested, such as:

Scraps of paper blowing in the wash of a modern jet airliner.
Oklahoma farms of the 1920s and the Dust Bowl.
An empty stadium after a World Series game.
A military conqueror who surveys his conquest, a city he has razed in a long siege.
A school building after a severe fire or the day after summer vacation starts.

A model for this type of writing appears in Lesson 12 of the "Courage" unit in Chapter 14. The model was composed in an independent writing assignment by a very fluent ninth-grade student. While the lesson appears in a unit designed primarily for seventh and eighth graders that particular writing lesson has been used successfully, apart from the unit, with tenth- and eleventh-grade functional writers. In examining the structure of the model, which tells of a volcanic eruption, the students should particularly note the two main sections of the essay, what might be called before and after descriptions in which the writer treats the same details, first in tranquillity and then as the volcanic eruption takes place.

In addition, compositions of this type are appropriate in "The Outcast" unit which appears in Chapter 9. Students imagine themselves as outcasts telling of their own feelings from the first person point of view as they experience rejection by others. The speaker in such a story experiences some change in attitude as he discovers the attitudes of others. Students can have considerable success with such writing because they can deal directly with a change in feeling, which is usually ironic, yet do not have to work out the personalities of characters in detail, or develop dialogue or complex plots.

An assignment that is interesting to both teachers and students, and one that can provide valuable insights to both, is having the students discuss—in corollary compositions—how they did their writing. Invariably, the discussions that are turned in with the work that is form-oriented will tell about planning the composition—and *that is all*. The same emphasis is present with discussions about the writing of information-oriented compositions—to the extent that the teacher reads what is virtually a sentence outline of the composition.

Planning and analysis are necessary even with poem forms that might ordinarily suggest esoteric composing processes. The following example is from a ninth-grade girl:

Tanka and Analysis

DAWN

> The air, like a cloud
> Is from the day. Yet the owl
> Still sings his night song.
> What art thou, Dawn, day or night?
> Gray Dawn, thou art night and day.

This poem is a tanka. Tanka is Japanese poetry composed according to strict rules:

1. The first three lines must conform to the rules for haiku.
2. Two lines consisting of seven syllables each are added.
3. The tanka must contain a paradox.

I will tell you how I composed mine. First, I thought of two opposites—day and night. I then contrasted day and night to form a paradox, the resolution of this being the time when day and night meet, dawn. I then arranged my thoughts in poetical form, according to the tanka rules.

Ninth-grade girl

Apparently, with information-oriented writing, the entire organism is so focused on planning that, even with introspection, the writing experience seems to be entirely defined in terms of the content of the token and the way in which it is laid out.

With form-oriented writing, on the other hand, the work seems to be seen in two stages that are clearly separate to the writer: planning and execution. There is little resistance to writing about how the piece was written (unless the token itself is lengthy and the introspective writing imposes a real burden).

Presumably, the central feature of the writing of both types is in the planning.

This contrasts strongly with responses that are obtained from "side" assignments with other kinds of writing (to be discussed in greater detail in the next chapter). In Chapter 24, student comments on their work with slanting inevitably relate to how and why particular words and images were chosen, and usually there is a discussion of expected reader response. But there is little discussion of overall planning per se.

NOTES

1. Kenneth L. Pike, "Beyond the Sentence," *College Composition and Communication,* XV (October 1964), pp. 129–135.
2. Walt Whitman, "A Noiseless Patient Spider" in *Immortal Poems of the English Language,* ed. Oscar Williams. New York: Washington Square Press, 1960, p. 411.

SUGGESTIONS FOR FURTHER READING

1. The following books are useful as background for the analyses required in teaching form-oriented writing:
   (a) BLOOM, EDWARD A., PHILBRICK, CHARLES H., and BLISTEIN, ELMER M., *The Order of Poetry* (New York: Odyssey, 1961) and
   (b) SANDERS, THOMAS E., *The Discovery of Poetry* (Glencoe, Illinois: Scott, Foresman, 1967).

Empathic Writing | 27

The two broad subclasses of compositions characterized by emotional involvement of the reader include the *direct* and the *empathic* types. With the type eliciting *direct* response, the intent of the writer is to trigger an immediate emotional response to the writing. On the other hand, the *empathic* types evoke response that is more complex. The reader is reminded of elements in his own past experience and psychologically "enters" the work as a result of his remembered experience.

With just a little training even relatively unsophisticated readers can be made aware of the mechanisms involved in responding to tokens that elicit *direct* responses. Their awareness of the quickly triggered emotions is the touchstone of their analysis.

The analysis of *empathic* tokens is quite another thing. The writer develops his token with a great deal of subtlety since one secret of producing the desired responses is to keep the reader unaware that he is being manipulated. Consequently, the techniques used in manipulating him must themselves be hidden. Very likely, production of the most successful of these tokens is the result of the intuition of the writer as much as of any conscious planning. Supposing that much of the "planning" is intuitive—and certainly the techniques are not made obvious—then, these tokens resist analysis. In contrast, tokens eliciting *direct emotional involvement* are, ordinarily, readily analyzed.

DIRECT EMOTIONAL INVOLVEMENT The class of writing that intends to evoke a direct response will be marked, in the main, by the connotations of the words and images that the writer employs. There are, in various literatures, lists of words that have been shown to have the power to invoke rather immediate and direct responses of the type that can be empirically measured with verbal reactionnaires and even more directly with laboratory instruments such as the sphygmomanometer, the psychogalvanometer, and the like.[1] Various tests have been standardized on the basis of verbal responses made quickly to words and images of various kinds.[2]

The responses will derive from either (or both) the value or the drive systems of the audience. George Orwell, in *1984,* depicts the effect of communication intended to evoke such responses; at the same time, *1984* threatens the value system of many in Orwell's own audience.

Other writing in this category is advertising copy, political, religious, and other kinds of propaganda, such as sermons, political speeches, and safety messages. Many love letters and much poetry can be so classified, as can the greetings on many greeting cards.

Whenever one of his students chalks certain messages on his blackboard and sits in class awaiting a response, a teacher is involved as audience in a communications situation defined by the writer's (usually) threatening his value system. This is not to be confused with the compulsive writing of such messages, since in this classroom case the intent of the writer is largely purposive, although it may be colored by compulsive elements.

Most of the writing in this classification is covered in the introductory unit described in Chapter 24. The emphasis on audience analysis and the resulting care in word choice have a general carry-over value for all writing. The production of mock advertisements is fun for the class and illustrates the principles involved in this kind of writing.

One other type of assignment bears mentioning in connection with this category. When the class has finished work with parodies as discussed in the previous chapter, they can do some work that is based on the skills they have learned.

The teacher should lead a discussion on satire and the attitude of the satirist. A number of broader satires (such as some of the work of Mark Twain) should be read and discussed in terms of the probable motivations of their authors.

Next, the students should suggest some subjects from their direct experience that invite satire: current demagogues, the school staff, hypocrisy in their churches, status seeking in their neighborhoods, and the like. The next step is to describe the behavior and speech of persons involved in a typical situation that invites the satire. After a typical vignette has been described, it becomes the central element in a composition. The composition should be written in a highly stylized way, reflecting the work done with parodies.

The intent of the stylization is to burlesque the target of the satirical attack. For example, a football coach who gives especially unctuous talks in school assemblies about school spirit and the uplifting values of sports but who violates the ideals of sportsmanship in his coaching might be attacked through a composition in this vein:

> He saith unto them:
> "Bring unto me the heroes who are numbered among ye. Bring unto me the youths of an hundred weights and heroes will I make of them. Bring unto me the youths four and five cubits high and them will I make mine ends. Deliver unto

me thy youths of comely grace and surpassing speed and them will I make like unto the stars that shineth in the firmament. Stars of the night will I make them yea, verily, and stars of the day."

And he added saying:

"Unto the youths will I not give succor but labor. For from labor the spirit springeth forth; and by the spirit wilt thou be known."

And they did as he had commanded them and brought unto him the comely youths of many shekels and surpassing speed. And when they had been delivered unto him he spoke again saying:

"Behold thine enemies. Go out unto them with the talon and the tooth. Meet them with thine ears unafraid, and fire in thine eyes and evil in thy soul. Fear not for the officials and the sheriffs. For is it not written that when their heads are turned away, their eyes are blinded? Go then unto thine enemies with malice and with hate. The bones of men were made but to be broken and the faces of men but to be striped. Know ye that by their stripes are we healed. Peace be unto you."

EMPATHIC WRITING The writer of empathic tokens intended a response produced from the memory of the reader that is, as such characterized as vicarious, may, perhaps, choose the first person to involve the reader in the work.

Whatever befalls "I" or "we" happens immediately to the reader. Additionally, the writer tries to convey emotional and sensory experiences directly. Often, he will employ figurative language to intensify the reader's involvement. Burns' often-quoted "My love is like a red, red rose . . . My love is like a melody" is of different order of comparison from "the controlling mechanism of a telescope is like a watchworks." Because of their power in invoking empathic responses, symbols are often employed. The writer may even, at times, use some of the more blatant stylistic devices that are used in direct empathic writing. This class of writing includes much of both longer and shorter fiction, drama, personal essays, personal letters, and many forms of poetry.

Probably, the writing in this category that is featured most frequently in English curricula is the short story. Within the context of English classwork, the short story is considered a longer narrative form. We have already considered some types of narratives.

In teaching narrative writing, it is best to begin with form-oriented writing because it can be readily analyzed. For example, the structure of the fable is obvious. A short story with an ironic twist, presents no difficulties in analysis. Parodies are relatively simple to analyze. Because these forms do not seek to involve the reader in an empathic way, they have an additional advantage in that the writer need not concern himself with techniques for gaining reader involvement. In addition to being relatively easy to analyze, these forms are readily imitated.

This is not the case with the type of narrative under discussion here. Since such narratives involve the reader, usually from the outset, they are easy to read. For that reason, people are misled into thinking they are also easy to write. But this is hardly the case.

As an extreme example of the failure of readability to reflect "writability," consider the income tax form. Such a document is anything but easy to read. How many readers are there who aren't certain they could write a better document? Works by Hemingway, on the other hand, are not nearly so difficult to read as works by various governmental tax agencies. Yet how many of his readers think for a moment that they could improve upon him in their own writing?

Analysis of Models

The first difficulty that faces the teacher and students is that of analyzing the work, and the first analytical problem is to determine the probable purpose of the writer. However, aside from the obvious desire to obtain the primary affect of reader involvement, the author's purpose in terms of the secondary affect can be obscure, sometimes deliberately so.

Let us consider as an illustration (although it is not narrative prose) *Androcles and the Lion*. The uninitiated reader would probably assume that any secondary affect relates exclusively to the readers' reexamination of the Christian ethic in terms of Shaw's characterizations. Yet it is almost astonishing to read a commentary on the play made by the author himself:

> It was currently reported in the Berlin newspapers that when Androcles was first performed in Berlin, the Crown Prince rose and left the house unable to endure (I hope) the very clear and fair exposition of autocratic Imperialism given by the Roman captain to his Christian prisoners. No English Imperialist was intelligent and earnest enough to do the same in London. If the report is correct, I confirm the logic of the Crown Prince, and am glad to find myself so well understood. But I can assure him that the Empire which served for my model when I wrote Androcles was, as he is now finding to his cost, much nearer my home than the German one.[3]

Who but the very perceptive reader would see in this play an attack on British imperialism?

Another example where the author's purpose is possibly ambiguous is Upton Sinclair's *The Jungle*. Many readers see the book as an attack on the the meat-packing industry. According to Peter Finley Dunne in the persona of Mr. Dooley, even Theodore Roosevelt interpreted the book in this way and moved quite dramatically to change the situation. No doubt effecting such a change was part of Sinclair's purpose, but the last four chapters of the book suggest that one of his central purposes was to propagandize for socialism.

To take another example, is Conrad's *Secret Agent* mainly a close analysis of depraved and inept revolutionaries or a biting satire directed against the theory of anarchy?

If it is difficult enough to analyze purpose in fiction, it is even more difficult to analyze its structure. Traditionally, there is a general feeling that the structure of most fiction can be expressed in a diagram showing a line of "rising action," a "turning point" (crisis), and a line of "falling action:"

Many works, however, appear to be designed on other structural models. De Hartog's *The Inspector,* for example, seems cyclical or spiral in design. Picaresque works seem to be modeled on a chain. The "slice of life" genre seems to be virtually "formless."

How does one analyze the function of characters? It seems clear, for example, that Dr. Watson in Conan Doyle's stories is intended to represent the reader. In the *Gold Bug,* does the Negro slave have the same function? What is the function of Le Grande? After all, Poe might have had the protagonist find the scarab.

Thus, because the plan of this kind of writing may not be open and obvious, the teacher of composition is faced at the outset of instruction with a tremendous obstacle.

It is also difficult to analyze the technique used to obtain the desired empathy from the audience. In nonempathic works the technique is readily apparent: the summary within the information-oriented piece; the moral within the fable; the figurative image within the poem. But in empathic works the technique is not so obvious. How is empathy produced while the plan for producing it is obscured?

One means of arousing empathy is the voice the author chooses to use. For example, younger authors often write narratives in the first person, and some of them are indeed powerful in compelling empathy. But is the use of the first person the result of a deliberate stylistic choice by the authors, or is it a compulsive element in their writing?

Student Compositions

Besides being difficult to analyze, this type of narrative prose is perhaps the most challenging of all compositions. Yet, how many teachers blandly assign the writing of short stories when they themselves have never seriously attempted the form, let alone completed one? Is this question an echo of the anathematic: "Them as can't do, teach"?

Most students must be classed as functional, but not fluent, writers. If the teacher has never—or only rarely—successfully completed a short story, how can he expect them to do the work? Generally speaking, then, the composition of short stories is best delayed until later years.

A general teaching principle arises at this point. Before he decides to teach any kind of writing, a teacher should himself attempt the form. If he has a great deal of trouble with it or cannot handle it, he should not have his students try it because when he reads their papers, he will not be able to see the problem from their viewpoint. His own failure indicates that he cannot deal with the composing problem, although he may be able to deal with the problem as a critical *reader*. Even if a critic sees flaws in a work, however, that in itself is no indication that he is skilled enough as a writer to put flaws into a work of his own, let alone eliminate them from the work of others.

Let us examine the work of one ninth-grade girl in a belletristic writing program having as its terminal objective the completion of a short story.*

YOU HAVE TO GROW UP SOMETIME

The air inside the classroom was stifling hot, and moist, and although the windows were all wide open, not even the slightest breeze stirred the atmosphere. The kids sprawled, dazedly, in stiff chairs, drowsed before propped open textbooks, barely hearing the droning, disinterested voice of the teacher, who, himself, was bored and lethargic. Glazed eyes wandered to the window, mouths gaped like vast pink canyons in wide yawns. It was June, and school was nearly over; it was the time when everyone felt classes were an imposition, and school was now stealing precious summer freedom.

The shrill shouts of the gym classes below on the playing fields wafted up. Wasps and flies buzzed angrily in corners of the ceiling. A flushed, perspiring boy crushed beetles under his feet, and ground them into the floor, his heels making a rough grinding noise. Outside, the leafy green maples were motionless against a cloudless, deep azure sky.

Peter Haley was certainly not concentrating on the solving of radical equations. He was planning, in complete, intricate detail, how to ask Julie Newman to the ninth grade Prom. He phrased and re-phrased his invitation, imagined himself suavely delivering it, and Julie graciously, delightedly, accepting.

"All right, you can start on your homework now," the teacher raised his voice and broke in on Peter's reverie. "Page 327, Part B and C, and Page 328. Part One—odd numbers. I'll put the assignment on the board. Get a good start now, and it'll only take a few minutes to finish tonight. Steve, Barry, pass out papers please. No talking."

Absently, Peter flipped to page 327 of his math book and wrote his

---

* She was a student of a gifted teacher of composition, Mr. Gary Eliot, of Warren Junior High School, Newton, Massachusetts.

name and class, and the date at the top of his paper. He numbered the examples, and the page number, put down his pencil and yawned. Glancing at the clock, he saw that there were 15 minutes left in the period. Then he'd have to face Julia and ask her. But he wasn't ready yet. A pang of fear and apprehension caught at his throat. Just relax, he told himself.

Over and over, on the page intended for his math homework, Peter traced Julie's name. He printed it in block letters, decorated it with curlicues and designs, wrote it in flowing script, backwards, forwards, every variation he could dream up.

"Hey, Pete!" someone hissed.

Hastily, he covered the paper, and looked up. He caught a flying folded square of composition paper, and the tall, freckled red-head three seats away grinned and made a "V" victory sign.

Peter opened it and read the scribbled contents:

"Pete,

Have you asked Julie to the Prom yet? Are you *going* to? I asked Susan and she accepted. Naturally. Michael and Audrey are going, and Roger and Pamela. We can all go out before the dance. Okay?? Hurry up and invite someone. Good luck, Romeo.

Write back.

Joe"

Peter tore off a strip of notebook paper and addressed it. Just then, the student bell clanged the end of classes. Thirty chairs slammed against thirty desks, thirty voices rose in a noisy chorus, and thirty students surged eagerly toward the door.

Peter and Joe met at the door.

"I guess I'll go ask her now," Peter said casually.

"Good, man" Joe slapped him across the shoulders. "Give her a sexy smile and promise her orchids."

"Cut it out, wise guy. See you after school in the breezeway."

Joe turned into his homeroom but Peter cut through the crowding, jostling mob in the third-floor corridor, making slow but steady progress toward the lockers across from the Music Room. At the water fountain he paused and shoved his books on the top of the row of lockers. He gulped a long icy drink, then dipped his fingers under the spray and splashed cold water on the damp, sticky hair plasted to his forehead. He then carefully combed his hair, to the side and a little forwards, and tucked his wrinkled blue shirt into his trousers. Stretching his sixty four and a half inches as far as he could he assumed an expression of nonchalance and friendly aloofness.

"What the hell are you primpin' for, Princess?" taunted a tall athletic boy, with mocking eyes and long blond hair.

Peter blushed self-consciously, and noticed the blond boy, and several friends regarding him with scornfully amused eyes.

"This *ain't* a beauty parlor, y'know," the boy jeered.

The others laughed, adding to Peter's embarrassment. Instantly, Peter felt dull and plain, and very young and unpopular. Compared to the slender blond athlete, with sharp, good looks and carefree easy manner typical of the "in crowd," he felt like Porky Pig. Peter grabbed his books and hurried away from his tormenters, from the cool green eyes that made fun of his masculinity.

He found Julie easily, standing by her open locker, unloading a pile of books. He steeled himself, and sauntered up.

"Hi, Julie," he began.

"Oh, hi Peter. How are you?" she seemed mildly surprised to find him coming right up to her.

"Okay." He couldn't remember how he had planned to broach the dance. Panicky, he sought for conversation topics. She rescued him unknowingly.

"Have we got French homework tonight?" she asked.

"Uh, just to, uh, study for the v-verb t-test tom-tomorrow," he stuttered. Ashamed and angry at himself for stuttering, he plunged in.

"Um, Julie—uh, would you, uh, go to the Prom with me?" he gulped.

She faced him then. Was that surprise, amazement in her expression?

"Oh, Peter, I'm sorry. I'll be away that weekend, with my family. I put up a fuss—of course—I didn't want to miss the Prom—but I couldn't get out of it, and I still can't. The arrangements are made, of course, and can't be broken . . ."

"Are you sure?" he tried desperately.

"I'm afraid so," she shut the green metal door firmly, and locked it. It clanged, and echoed hollowly, and Peter was surprised to find the hall nearly vacant.

He shifted his books to his other arm.

"I'm sorry, Peter, really. I would've loved to go with you . . ."

Well, those were the breaks, Peter thought.

"It's all right," he said, pretending not to care. "I'll see you around."

"Good-bye."

He rushed to his homeroom, just in time for the dismissal bell. The hordes of kids tore for the outdoors, and liberty, but Peter loitered, hoping to avoid the curious, probing questions of his friends. Somehow he didn't like to admit the refusal, even though there was a plausible, truthful reason. It wasn't as if she didn't want to go with him, but, still . . .

Peter slowly strolled towards the end of the corridor. Just as he reached the drinking fountain, near the corner where the two halls intersected, he was stopped by a high, giggly voice.

"*Who* asked you?" shrieked one girl.

"Peter Haley!" giggled another. "Can you believe it? That *baby,* that utter *child.* I'll bet he's never even made out, or smoked, or anything!"

A third girl burst into wild laughter.

"I don't believe it! As if you'd *go* with him. He must've had a crush on you, Julie, he must've worshipped you from afar, and then got the nerve up to invite you—"

She broke off in a gust of merriment.

The second girl spoke again. "He stuttered and blushed and everything. He was *so* serious, *so* embarrassed. It was *funny!* Too bad you missed it."

Dully, he recognized the voice as Julie's. A hotness rose to his cheeks and spread all over his body, a thick aching lump lodged itself in his throat. He groped for the wall, and leaned, dizzily, against its coolness, hidden from view in a little nook. His heart beat rapidly, and he could not move from the spot.

"I told him I was going away for the weekend. The dumb little thing naturally believed me."

The girl snorted.

"Anyway, Dennis will be asking me soon, probably. If he doesn't I'll go with Jerry or Buck. I'm not desperate enough to go with Peter Haley."

The laughter burned his ears again. He had made a gross error, he realized, a dreadful mistake. Everything between Julie and himself had been in his imagination. The time they walked home together—he saw it now not as a show of affection for him, but just something she couldn't avoid, and didn't really care much about.

And Dennis, he knew Dennis. A cool, popular blond boy—an athlete. A boy who made him feel like Porky Pig, who taunted him and shamed him. By tomorrow, Dennis would have material for more jokes, new taunts.

He couldn't stand it any more. Desperately he wheeled and raced down the hall, away from the girls' voices. Blindly, he bounded down the stairs, and burst out into the sweltering afternoon.

He avoided all people, and kept running, although it was so hot. Sweat poured down his cheeks, and glistened on his neck, but the physical discomfort was nothing compared to the emotional pain.

He climbed the brick steps and pulled opened the screen door, letting it swing back and slam jarringly against the house. He stood in the cool vestibule, waiting.

"Mom?" he yelled hoarsely.

"I'm upstairs, Petey."

Petey, she called him. He went upstairs anyway.

"How was your day, son?"

"Oh, okay."

"Everything go all right?"

"Yeah."

"Get an A on your history quiz?"

"A—"

"That's good. Want any lemonade?"

"Later, maybe."

"Are you sure you're all right, Pete?"

"Yes, I'm all right," he raised his voice angrily. "I told you, I'm fine."

"All right, all right. You'd better go make your bed now."

He went to his room. It was cool and dim and sheltering; the curtains were drawn. He gazed in the mirror, seeing for the first time the pimples on his chin, the pale, dull eyes, mousy brown hair, the plump cheeks. Before, he had always looked all right; only girls worried about being good-looking and boys just had to look decent.

But—he was short and unattractive. It *did* matter. Julie's cruel phrases still rang clearly in the chambers of his mind. He saw again her amused, pitying face, Dennis' knowing scornful sneer. He could even picture his own red, chubby, naïvely hopeful face as he stammered out the invitation. His cheeks burned.

He leaned his elbows on the window sill. Peering through the curtains, he could feel the hot, relentless sun. He could feel the humid warmth. He pressed his face against the screen, still and silent, turbulent, disjointed thoughts tumbling in his mind.

A rude awakening to life and truth, he thought grimly.

But it was too soon. Peter knew that if he were a girl, he would cry.

A story of this quality is unusual among high school students, but it certainly did not come as the result of the sort of assignment that far too many teachers make: "Now that we have read several short stories, you write one of your own for next Friday." Such an assignment produces little except frustration for students and disgust for the teacher when he reads the papers. Stories such as the one above are likely to be produced only after very careful preparation extending over several days.

First, the student chooses a story idea that he thinks he would like to write about. The teacher should encourage simple plot lines, since complex plots in student stories frequently result in terribly unconvincing resolutions. The teacher should consult with students about the initial story idea and at each step during the preparation leading to the final product. However, at this point the student idea need be only a story germ.

Next, the student selects a story which he will study as a general model. His selection should be made after thinking about the probable general content of his own story and after reading a number of short stories by established writers. But the choice is largely intuitive. The students should analyze their models by writing an outline of the story elements. The elements represent a list of the minimal components of narrative fiction: character, point-of-view, structure, and theme.

A short story will contain characters, which the author may develop in many ways: introspectively, through the use of the first person and/or stream-of-consciousness techniques; objective description from the omniscient point of view; the objective (reader) point of view; or from the viewpoint of one or more of the other characters. Thus, the development of character relates strongly to another element: the point of view of the author.

Dialogue is another aspect of character development that is technically very important in connection with reader involvement. Because of this, it should be considered as a separate element in the analysis. Good dialogue helps engage the reader; inadequate dialogue may keep him distant. A fineness of perception for dialects of various kinds and for idiolect is required for the production of good dialogue. This implies the need for both student and teacher to have some linguistic background.

Of course, the story structure must be analyzed. If the narrative turns on conflict, as most will, all conflicts must be explicated as must their interrelationships. Often, key symbolic and thematic motives are placed at critical structural points in the narrative: in the title itself, at the inception of the action, at the crisis, at the climax, or at the conclusion. Therefore, pertinent imagery at key points must be discussed in the analysis.

Finally, the theme or underlying philosophical generalization must be uncovered since it is the theme that gives substance to serious literature.

These are minimal elements. The pattern for the independent analyses by the students should be set in a preliminary lesson by a teacher-led analysis of some story. After the oral analysis, the teacher should present a duplicated version of that analysis—and this in turn should be analyzed. A student analysis in outline form of "Paul's Case" by Willa Cather follows:

Short Story Outline

PAUL'S CASE by Willa Cather

  I. Significance of title
- A. General idea of the story—it is a brief but poignant study of a boy.
- B. The word "case" is apt, used to give the idea that the story is a study almost like a write-up of "cases" of delinquent, mentally retarded children, or student, like a psychiatrist or social worker or teacher might write—concise, brief but thorough.
- C. Resembles a counselor's report on an abnormal character

 II. Point of View
- A. Consistent—objective
- B. Paul's thoughts are especially emphasized and open yet there is a deep part of Paul that is left closed and hidden for the reader to find himself.
- C. The thoughts of the other characters are generally exposed, although not in detail.
- D. An example:
  "He felt grimy and uncomfortable"
  "As he fell, the folly of his haste occurred to him with merciless clearness, the vastness of what he had left undone."

III. Character and Characterization
- A. Paul
  1. Misunderstood
  2. Dreams, his fantasies
  3. Unsure in common life
  4. Worships music and drama, loses himself in it
  5. Cannot stand (is truly repelled) by people, school life, home, family and neighborhood
  6. Puts on false arrogance, cannot communicate, nervously jaunty and seemingly brash and merry to cover up feelings of hurt, anxiety, misery, loneliness, confusion

B. Minor Characters
  1. Father
    a. Doesn't understand him
    b. Criticizes him for lack of down-to-earth spirit and normal behavior
    c. Does not sympathize with boy's fantasies and love of music
  2. School teachers and principal
    a. Same attitude as father
    b. Are puzzled, chagrined and angered by Paul
    c. Cannot stand his queer traits
C. All minor characters seen *only in relationship* to Paul.
D. His conflicts are the focal point of story
E. Paul is characterized *almost* totally in the round, all the characters enter only briefly with description only in regard to their actions towards Paul. His father and several neighbors and teachers are characterized in profile.

IV. Plot
  A. Conflicts: Paul in conflict with society (school, home), Paul conflicting in his mind
  B. Paul is a high school boy living in Pittsburgh
  C. Called before teachers who are considering Paul's case—as he is abnormal and irritating
  D. Paul does not care for petty troubles and runs to his job as usher in an open theatre. He quits school, gets a job.
  E. Cannot tolerate coming home, being scolded, Sunday school; the ugliness of his house and neighborhood—his life—hit him harshly
  F. Runs away to New York, goes on a spree, lives like a gentleman
  G. When his father comes in pursuit and his stolen money runs out, Paul jumps onto the track in front of a train and is instantly killed
  H. Climax: His suicide

V. Theme
  A. Paul represents the extreme case of people who do not fit in with society and cannot be understood, are somehow repulsive and pathetic. He is wild, reckless, deranged, but is somehow still like more normal individuals who have difficulty adjusting.

VI. Dialogue
  A. *No* dialogue employed
  B. Everything is defined as narrative
  C. Author will say what so-and-so said but a character will not speak directly

---

The next step is an exercise, a character sketch. The sketch should be developed so that the subject bears some characteristics parallel to those in the incubating final short story.

CHARACTERIZATION

I immediately noticed the man getting on the subway at the third stop. He stumbled on, limping heavily, and fumbled with his wallet and cane. He was a tall, gaunt man, very thin and with a premature, old, worn out look. He stooped, and bent his head like a man of eighty though he was probably only in his early thirties. Perhaps he was trying to hide the black pirate patch covering his left eye, or the puckered reddish scars—like ridged caterpillars—that disfigured his skin. His face was creased and leathery, weatherbeaten to a dull tan. I noticed his expression, the mouth drawn in a painful grimace of strain and the eyes wild and hard with frustration.

As he tapped his way up the aisle, hesitant and embarrassed, I saw that his right arm ended in a hook, a dull iron hook which he constantly pushed into a fold of his coat. Several times, he poked his bad leg with the hook.

He groped at a seat and found it vacant. Sliding creakily and slowly into a corner of the seat, he turned his eye upon me and I saw the glassy stare of the partially blind. Conscious of the stares and feelings of pity and revulsion, the man turned from the passengers to the window, to escape from reality as best he could.

The obvious parallel element here is the self-consciousness about physical appearance. Not so obvious is the importance of the element of containment or entrapment: the character is forced to be inside something and seeks escape, symbolically, by looking out the window. The window detail occurring in this sketch (and twice in the short story) emerges as an important symbol. In both, it has been placed at conspicuously important structural junctures. A notable weakness in the sketch results from the choice of point of view. The writer deliberately chooses the first person voice and in the last sentence attributes motives to "the man" in a way that is impossible to her narrator, even though she has successfully avoided this earlier.

The next exercise is the development of a dialogue through which a conflict is presented. Once again the exercise must embody elements that will parallel elements in the anticipated story. The obvious element here is the parent-child conflict. Not so obvious is the sense of alienation of the daughter.

DIALOGUE

"Joanne, I don't want any more of your insolent backtalk at the dinner table. You are rude and cruel, and to your *father;* you should respect him. I won't stand for your fresh remarks any longer and I am demanding just a peaceful evening meal!"

"I was simply stating the fact, mother. You and he are so antiquated— *so medieval* and his phoniness and preaching makes me ill. Why should I stand for that? Maybe you forget that I'm a person too!"

"Don't talk to me that way, young lady. You know it's your attitude and your impudence. You *deliberately* misinterpret me."

"Mother, I'll talk to you the way I want to and have any attitude I please. You and he aren't going to boss *me* around!"

"After all I did for you, sacrificing and guiding, you repel me and hate me. Your father would die for you, he does whatever you wish, gets you things without being asked. I get a job to provide you with luxuries. We all cater to you. And what happens? You treat us like dirt."

"Listen, if I just had freedom and no responsibility to "the family" I wouldn't care about material things. Don't work if you don't want to. *Don't* cater to me. Just let me be."

"You're not ready to cope with independence. You'll thank me someday. You'll realize I was right—you're strewing roses on my grave. It'll be too late then. At least when I was young, I was more tolerant, and I would never dream of—"

"Okay, okay. So you were an angel, I'm human."

"You must have no feelings! You abuse your father, you hurt your sister and you stab my heart with your chatting tongue. People have feelings, Joanne, haven't you? Can't you understand? Oh, you're so hard, so heartless . . . you don't love anyone."

"You sound like Billy Graham hollering about sin. But I've got—"

"Listen to me. We could have such a warm relationship. You and your sister, too, she wants to look up to you. And you should love your father!"

"The less I see of this family, the better. You're always yelling at me to help or clean or set the table or practice the piano. My dear sister tattle-tales on me at every chance, the little two-faced rat. My father never ceases blaming me for something and complaining. A loving family! Hah! That's a laugh!"

"You make me sad."

"You make me sick."

"Just leave me alone now, please—go!"

"Gladly."

"You always have to have the last word."

The final exercise, before writing the short story, combines the elements of description, dialogue, and conflict and introduces some minor related conflicts. In this exercise, the window image is a central detail, probably a symbolic one since inside the building are the constricting rules of the adult world, while outside is freedom. The major weakness is an uncomfortableness of dialogue. "Okay, just a moment. I hafta get a book." The "moment" doesn't fit well. However, the idiolect "Okay" is very strong as is the ear for adolescent speech generally. The obvious parallels are the plotting between the girls and the lack of communication between the girls and their parents.

LIBRARY VISIT

At six-forty, Shara and Laurie pushed open the heavy wooden door of the Westwood Free Library and entered the musty, quiet building. In a distant back office, a single typewriter clacked rapidly. Two old men hunched in the chairs studying the newspaper. Near them, several high-school boys conversed in rough, hoarse whispers and shuffled through a pile of papers spread out on their table. It was only mid-April—just before daylight savings—but outdoors the setting sun still provided much light, and sunlight poured inside through the windows on the west of the building.

Shara and Laurie walked over to a table in the corner furthest from the librarian's desk. The chairs squeaked across the scuffed floors as they sat down.

"Did your mother give you any trouble?" Laurie asked.

"No," replied Shara. "I told her I had to do a social studies project and had to use a lot of research books. And I said I'd be home by eight-thirty. Of course, she hated to let me go but she couldn't think of a reason to keep me in."

"Yeah . . . my old lady's not home so I got out easy. I have till nine o'clock if I want."

"What time are they coming down?" Shara asked.

Laurie grinned. "Impatient, huh? Well, Jerry has to babysit while his parents go shopping. Then he's picking up John and they'll be down by seven-fifteen or so."

The librarian threw them a disapproving look. Shara sighed and nodded her head. "Laurie, we've got twenty minutes to waste. What are we supposed to do here? We can't even talk."

"Want to read?" Laura giggled.

"You kidding?" croaked Shara. "Let's go to the drugstore for a coke."

"Jerry and John are meeting us at the bridge. I know—I know it's near your house, but we won't stay there."

"Okay. Now I can say I went to the library with a straight face," Shara said. "Hey, how about that coke?"

Laurie stood up.

"Okay, just a moment. I hafta get a book or else my father'll get suspicious. Just let me grab one and we can go."

Shara followed Laurie to the book shelf. She moved into the sunlight by the window and leaned against the radiator, her eyes closed.

"Tell me about John again," she murmured.

"Again? I've described him fifty times. Well, all right. He's got dark hair, see, kind of reddish brown and long, of course, as long as his parents will allow. And he has freckles and light blue eyes with really long eyelashes. His nose is kind of wide, though. John's kind of quiet except when he's mad. Then, he yells his head off. Oh, here's a new tip—Jerry told me last night. He hates to be tickled because he goes absolutely hysterical with laughter."

"Will he understand that I have to watch out for my parents and be careful about being seen?"

"Probably. Just don't make too much of sneaking around and avoiding your parents, okay?"

"Okay." Shara agreed.

They padded over to the librarian's desk and lounged against the desk as the stiff, grey haired librarian expertly stamped Laurie's book and slipped the card out.

Shara shoved open the heavy, squeaky door and the girls emerged into the dusky twilight. Neon signs dotted the shopping center and bright vividly colored lights lined the turnpike. A cool wind chilled the mild air and ruffled the leaves of tall elms and maples standing like sentries around the library. The sky was a cloudy dark blue-grey, spattered with tiny blinking diamonds already, although the horizon was still a blinding streak of crimson.

The two girls sauntered down the sidewalk, tingling with delicious fear and a sense of impending action. They were ready to live.

Generally, the short story, "You Have To Grow Up Sometime," does not sustain its quality as well as the shorter exercises, and in some places the influence of the phrasing of adolescent fiction is evident. But short story writing is by all odds the most difficult of all the potential assignments in secondary school composition. This one was worth the effort. In most classrooms the effort is better directed elsewhere.

NOTES

1. Vance Packard, *The Hidden Persuaders*. (New York: David McKay Co., 1957), p. 8.
2. *Ibid.*, p. 23.
3. George Bernard Shaw, *Nine Plays by Bernard Shaw* (New York: Dodd, Mead & Co., 1935), p. 980.

SUGGESTION FOR FURTHER READING

1. A good background source for the analysis of narrative is BOOTH, WAYNE C., *The Rhetoric of Fiction* (Chicago: University of Chicago, 1961).

Introspective Elements in Writing

An interesting part of our literary tradition is the introspective view that writers have provided on their creative experiences. There is an imposing literature of the kind quoted in Chapter 23 in which writers report on how they write. Much of the reportage deals with elements in the personality that influence writing in ways that appear to lack volitional direction.

It is natural that professional writers should be interested in their own composing and writing mechanisms. Presumably, they sense that introspection along these lines helps to bring their writing under conscious control; hence, they are less at the mercy of the muse. Certainly, if a writer finds that he works best at night, he can spare himself both energy and frustration that he might otherwise waste in trying to work by daylight. Even if his beliefs about his work are self-delusions, they may serve as conditioners in helping him work, or at least as mnemonics having the same function. Anyway, writers do write about how they write, and perhaps this kind of writing is itself compulsive.

Introspection about writing is a valuable part of the composition program, as valuable to the teachers to whom the introspection is communicated as it is to the students. One purpose in this self-analysis is to bring as much of the composing process under volitional control as possible.

Assignments in Introspective Writing

Two kinds of assignments are appropriate. The first is to have the students write about the process involved in working up specific compositions. This assignment should be given only when the target of instruction is a relatively short piece (as with the samples on pp. 531, 533, and 575). If they have to do this extra work in connection with longer writing assignments, they may resent it and treat the self-analysis in a superficial way. Moreover, many students schedule work on longer assignments over several days and, as a result, may forget important details of the composing process.

The second kind of introspective writing is on a general topic, such as "The Way I Write." If this assignment is given late in the course as a regular or "extra credit" composition assignment, the students are highly motivated to take it seriously. The areas that can be readily blocked off for such consideration are the environment and the condition of the organism as compulsive components of the composing process. Another area for consideration, especially for the mature student, is style.

The series of examples below were written as "extra credit" work (that is, optional assignments). They were submitted without the follow-up proof-reading, criticism, and revision indicated as part of the routine process in Chapter 24 so that the teacher could get at the informational content when the form was pristine. All the writers were eighth graders. All of these papers were written by members of the same class. The diversity of the self-analyses suggests strongly that students have different needs in terms of their composing processes. The implication, then, is that a teacher in developing his composition program must provide for these differences at every stage of the program.

1

As I sit at my desk in my room crazy thoughts go through my head. If I get an inspiration from them. I pick up my pen and write.

Very few things I write are really my own. I am usually given an assignment to write about a subject, use or copy someone else's style, or analyze another's work. My mind, being restricted to these various areas, is usually trapped without words to write. I need an inspiration to start me, and sometimes one does not come. My surroundings, mood, and appetite affect my thoughts and inspirations greatly.

My favorite surroundings are in my room. It looks basically average, messy but comfortable. In one corner there is a pile of clothes on a chair and junk all over my bed. On the other side of the room I keep my mice. Next to the table that they are on is a sloppy thing I call my desk. This is usually covered with papers, dirty nylons, books, etc. Also on it is my radio which I always have on when I do my homework. These are the conditions I work under. If they were different I wouldn't be able to stand it.

My mood also affects my writing. If I'm angry at someone or something I can't concentrate. When I'm depressed I don't think straight and if I don't like the subject I am writing the composition for, I probably won't bother to do a good job.

Strange as it may seem my appetite affects my work too. I can't work unless on a full stomach. Usually I can only be satisfied with certain foods. One time it was raspberry jello. Another time it was two glasses of lemonade. (If this composition doesn't seem very good, it's because I'm on a diet and I didn't have a snack at all!)

All these things set my mind whirling with thoughts as I write. After I get ideas the only problem I have is putting them down with words. Somehow I seem to manage. Sometimes in better ways than others.

2

When I write I make sure everything around me is in order. One will often find me cleaning my room before I write. I can't conceive why, but it seems that when I write I can't have my conscience bothering me. The space around me is neat but my paper is unreadable by anyone other than myself. I always have an extra sheet of paper beside me where I will write all the words I don't know how to spell. By the time I'm finished just about all 27 lines are taken up with one word a piece. I also drink 2–3 glasses of water because my mind gets dried up from talking so much.

3

I have to write on impulse and think about my assignment first for a long time. Sometimes I talk about my assignment with friends just to have some ideas. When I do the final writing I have to be completely alone, being in my room with the door shut and the window blinds closed. I also have to have an empty stomach. I sort of keep myself going by having a goal of food and can't eat until I have finished my English.

I usually work best under pressure. Many times I put off my homework till the morning it is due and I make myself get up at 6:00. Even then I put off the homework till 7:00 and then I have only a half an hour to work because I have to get dressed by about 7:45 and then eat breakfast, which takes about twenty minutes because I am a very slow eater. Then I have to catch the bus. Some of my best compositions have been finished up in the morning before I got to school. That way I really have to rack my brain. I write everything I need in the composition. At times I have leisure time to write my compositions but then it takes a longer time because I don't really concentrate. When I write a paper the morning it's due I usually take most of the night to think about what to write.

4

Anyone who writes any sort of materials such as compositions, books, poems, plays, etc. probably has special conditions under which they write. This is true of myself. Someone would think that most people require silence. Under my circumstances this is not true. I have to write my compositions where there is activity, or where it is noisy. This usually takes place in our kitchen. If there is no one around me to make noise I turn the radio on. But before I can do any of this I have to have something to eat so I can concentrate on what I'm doing.

Once I settle down and turn on the radio I start to think of possibilities for my composition. Once I get the main idea I turn off the radio and start writing down my information before I forget it. If I should think of something that would fit well in the middle or end of the composition before I think of the beginning, I take a few notes on it so I won't forget to put it in. This is the plan I follow for compositions that require no facts from books.

When I write a composition that requires information from books I write it in a little different fashion. First I look over the facts from the book and jot down important features on a piece of paper, then I arrange them in their best order, and then go to work writing up my composition and see places where improvements can be made, then I fix them.

5

When I am going to write something, whether it is a composition or just a letter, I must first be inspired. Unless I've got an inspiration I cannot write. I cannot write if I am hungry, either. Often I will go and eat or drink something before starting to write. Another thing I need is moderate quiet. If there is a lot of noise and confusion I cannot concentrate. I think I write best in the evening, in a room by myself, with a low murmur of noises. I can't write with a lot but there must be some noise. If there is no noise my mind starts to wander and if there's a lot I can't concentrate.

Before I start writing I will develop the whole plan for whatever it is in my mind. I don't usually bother to write it down but I don't just sit down and write. Even a letter, I organize mentally. I do not have any habits, though, such as sharpening pencils, going for walks, or eating something before I write.

6

When I finally settle down to write a poem, book report or whatever, I am definitely under pressure. One of the reasons for this may be the time at which I prefer to attempt a composition, at night. Settled in a quiet room with perhaps a radio playing softly in the background. I sit or lounge on my bed and begin.

If a particular piece of work may be due in two days, it has a habit of slipping to the last night. But this does not, in any way seem that I have forgotten about it. Why at any time walking down halls, getting on a bus, etc., when my mind is not in constant demand, I may suddenly find myself thinking of ideas that may form into sentences, into paragraphs which may fit into the work itself. Even if the assignment is a long one, I can take notes if necessary, gather ideas but for sure I can only feel fully capable working quite near due date. An example of this is the exam of *A Midsummer Night's Dream*. This may be because of laziness or I'm inclined to believe that I'm afraid I may leave something out and not be able to put it in the paper.

Last, I have a thing about revision, and unless this is absolutely a must, I prefer to leave my work in its first form, of course this does not include first drafts.

7

When I write, my conditions, and environment are very important for my concentration. To start out, I have to have a radio on, usually loud. If I haven't been sleeping lately, and I try to force my mind to focus, and pay attention, I get a headache. I just can't do it. The other things that distract me most, besides a quiet room, is a hard chair, that I can't move around in, people talking (not on the radio), and being hungry or thirsty. I do my best writing after meals (preferably supper) and in a rocking chair. The reason I say supper is because during the morning or afternoon, the light in my room from the windows distracts my mind to things outdoors.

When I am assigned to do things with my opinions in them, it is harder for me than explaining things. The reason is: When I write my words change my mind, often in the middle of the writing, to an opposite side. My brain is influenced quite easily.

My first draft is done quickly and easily. I leave my punctuation at the end of sentences out sometimes. When I go over it, I change the whole thing, but it helps me to get my first thoughts about the subject down first. Teachers in previous years had the class pass in their rough drafts along with their final copy. If the two papers weren't alike word to word, we would get marked off. This always presented a problem, because when ever I wrote a copy, I would find better or more adequate words to put in. I finally ended up changing my rough draft to fit the first.

When I'm assigned a subject, my ideas either come right away or in a long time, never inbetween. If I have a general idea of what I'm going to do, I can write easily, and words will come to me: or, I have to think every word and then place it, spell it, and see if it makes sense. My styles of writing change a lot. It depends on nothing. Just my mind.

8

My best ability is shown when I use poetry. I feel this is because I enjoy it quite a bit more than prose. In my opinion surrealism has the best qualities because for one you're not writing for anyone else but yourself. I don't believe in the narcotic taking type of poetry when you're writing mainly what you don't understand. I think the complications of the world where we don't need narcotics is the best.

My year in eighth grade so far has given me freedom with my writing. My interest in expression with prose and poetry has risen one-hundred percent since my entering eighth grade. For further training I plan on going on into Latin.

When I start to write I jot down my most precious ideas to try and work them into my piece. Revising and more revising in the process. Once the various paragraphs and phrases are, in my opinion, coherent and flowing I then make my final copy with a little revision here and there. This procedure applies to both prose and poetry.

Although my results to me have been satisfactory I should look for a better procedure, but first things first. I must perfect this one.

The conditions required for me to do my best is very faint mood music and to have the piece of paper not on a desk but on my lap. When sitting on my bed I get best results. I don't like to use a desk because it makes me edgy and uncomfortable.

9

There isn't too much unusual about my writing habits and the kind of writing that I do best. Mostly I just write!

The times when I write best are Sunday afternoons. I sit on the second from top stair on the staircase leading from the downstairs to the upstairs hall. Most of the time my brothers are play fighting in front of me just to annoy me. Sometimes this helps me to work and sometimes it hinders me (especially when one of them lands on top of me).

Another time during which I write well is after supper. I sit at my desk and I must have a "Peter, Paul, and Mary" album on the record player, turned down so I can hardly hear it.

I have to stop every once in a while because my mind tires easily because of the way in which I hold a pencil, so this gives me some time to think about what I want to say.

It is difficult to write on an empty stomach so I usually write after Sunday dinner or on a week day after supper. I can't write well during the day or if I'm comfortable.

Now about the kind of compositions that I write best. First, I think, is expository. It is easiest to express myself, mostly because the first thing that I do is to make a plan by gathering my ideas together so all I have to do is follow the plan.

Next comes poetry. Sometimes it is easier for me to use poetry, but it is usually more difficult because it is hard for me to find the right words to express myself well. (form-oriented work)

These are my two favorite types of compositions, and I don't think there is too much unusual about my writing habits.

10

The way in which people begin to write a composition is interesting and sometimes unusual, although I can not say this for my particular habits. With many people the environment affects them in the style and quality of their work. Many people use references in other works to get started. Others make an outline for the subject to have something to refer to. My personal preference to this will be shown in this composition.

The environment I need when I write is definitely away from school. I am never able to think or concentrate in school well enough to compose as essay, etc. The reason for this is probably because of the other students talking and moving about. At home, in the kitchen with a lot of books around (whether they pertain to the subject or not) and a dictionary is the environment I want to work in. I should have piles of paper and a pen whose color ink I like—cobalt blue. Then, at 7:00 to 7:30 I begin.

The way I go about it is to first think about the subject on which I am to write. If it is, say, literary analogues, I must write on a piece of scrap paper what I think literary analogues are. Then I think about the pieces of work, if there are any, I have to work with. I reread the pieces and let my mind absorb the information.

The next plan is to look at the assignment—whether it is to compare the compositions or to explain them, etc. I *always* then look up in the dictionary word(s), literary analogues, in this case, and compare the two definitions. If they agree I keep in mind, throughout the composition the previous definition because it is usually easier to understand.

If the composition is to be long, my next step is to write an outline.

Here is an example:

1. Explanation of Work
   A. Plan
   B. Definition
      1. Dictionary's
      2. Mine
   C. Introduction to works

Then, on scrap paper, I begin the first copy. I try to state my plan, give the definitions, the introduction to other works, the comparison, and summary, with a few additions in between, I usually follow this fairly closely.

I, at this point, take a break. After a few minutes I start rewriting the second copy. I perk up the language and fix it in a few places, and take another break. And for the last time, I begin the *second* final copy—cutting out a few things that are unnecessary and again fixing the language.

I clear the table, throw away every other copy and begin to read the composition I have just written aloud. After I am finished, I sit down and read it to myself and criticize it aloud again and put it in my notebook and start on a new subject.

Use of Reactionnaires

The most common classroom technique that takes advantage of compulsive elements in writing is the use of reactionnaires. The teacher shows a painting or plays a piece of music and directs the class to write "whatever they think of." Another variation is to show a painting, photograph, or magazine cover and ask these questions:

"What happened just before the scene?"
"What happened just after the scene?"
"What is this person thinking of?"

From time to time, a teacher may encounter a class that is largely composed of writers who are functional but seem uninterested in writing or in anything else connected with school. One way to activate these students to write is by using a kind of verbal reactionnaire, a number of statements written on the chalkboard.

Before the class enters the room, the teacher writes several statements on the board that are calculated to threaten the class's value system. The intent here is to obtain a direct emotional response from the students. The statements should be something like these:

1. The black-jacketed youths hanging around street corners, smoking and drinking, are typical of the teenagers in today's world.
2. People below their junior year of high school are simply too young for dancing. They should not be permitted to dance until they are mature enough. There are plenty of other activities available that are more suited to their age.
3. We need a curfew in this town. All children under the age of sixteen should be off the streets by eight o'clock unless accompanied by an adult. On weekends the time can be extended to nine. Growing youngsters need their rest.
4. The reason for so much failure in school is that school-age children spend too much time listening to the poor current songs that clutter up radio waves and record stores. The noise should be completely eliminated.
5. Teenagers are natural fall-guys for every fad and all the junk merchandise that comes along. They should be allowed about fifty cents a week to spend so they can learn the value of money. Everything above this amount should be turned over to their parents who know how to use it better. Many P.T.A.'s recommend this.
6. Because teenagers have more accidents than any other age groups, the age for driver's licenses should be raised to twenty-one.

When the class enters and gets started, the teacher should indicate that these statements have been made by responsible members of the community. After the students have read them and start talking about them among themselves, the teacher should ask if anyone would like to comment. He will get a few comments. When the same points are being made for the second time, he should indicate that he wants the students to organize their thoughts better. Each student should then be asked to comment on at least one statement in writing. A number of emotionally charged compositions, like the following from tenth graders, will result:

I would like to comment about number 2. Most of our lives we have looked upon the opposite sex as being almost an enemy. Nobody told us not to, and we never go along. But all of a sudden we get attrackted to each other as we mature physically and mentally. No one told us to, but we wanted to dance. All of a sudden we wanted to dance, and make out and all the rest, and their trying to tell use that we are too young for something nature tells us that we are not too young for. Times have changed. Its the twentieth century and not the 17th. We do our dancing and they do theirs. There is nothing wrong with dancing; just let us entertain ourselves the way we like, not the way they think we should. Dancing keeps us out of trouble. If they told about half the good things that we did instead of all the bad things we do then there wouldn't be enough hours in the day to tell you about it.

Tenth-grade boy

I think the statement depends on the parents. If a parent wants their teen to stay out until midnight it's up to the parent. If a parent wants a teenage kid around the house all night with a blasting radio, dancing, talking on the phone it's up to the parent. I'm sure the parent would get pretty darn sick of their kid acting up at home. Whereas if the teenager is out the parents have some peace and quiet. So if a parent wants their child out and in a half decent place all night long they should agree to a certain point. If a parent doesn't care about their children they can let the kid out on the street.

Maybe their behavior isn't like an angel but who's going to sit at home talking to parents, to grandparents, when you learn all the things parents say about when I was a boy or girl I didn't act like you. My mother didn't let me out till 10:30. Times have changed, I don't think they'll turn back to early 1900's.

Tenth-grade girl

Surrealistic Writing

Another lesson that exploits compulsive writing is an assignment in surrealistic writing. As preparation, the teacher asks the students to describe the structural characteristics of dreams. If this question proves puzzling, he expands it by saying, "I don't mean 'What do you dream about?' I'm asking about such things as whether people dream in technicolor or black and white."

An active discussion is likely to ensue. As characteristics of dreams are elicited, they should be written on the chalkboard: the distortion of time and space relationships; the double viewpoint of the actor and observer; the abrupt changes, and so on. The discussion should be allowed to run its course. In the course of the discussion, the subject of dream interpretation will arise. The teacher should explain that many attempts to interpret dreams in various ways, have had a place in history, and he should sketch some of them: Joseph in the Bible and prophetic dreams, Freud and dream imagery as symbols, and the like.

Next, he should relate the interest in dreams to the Surrealist movement in the arts, showing some surrealist prints and pointing out their dream-like characteristics. Following this, the class should read and analyze some Surrealist prose and poetry in terms of their dream-like characteristics.

As an assignment, the class should be asked to write a composition that conveys dream-like imagery and structure. To maintain the dream-like tone, the students should be told that the composition should not reveal that it is about a dream (unless such a realization is part of the dream itself), nor should they write about going to sleep or waking up.

When the prose compositions are finished, the class should rewrite them as free verse, each taking his own composition *in toto* or selecting a section of it. The following are examples of this type of work:

A force beckoned me to come forward. With a pulling jerk I could feel myself transformed into a long bony creature with a bent beak that looked of an enemy's curse and felt of the burden I knew it became by the minute. Blood was dripping from my fang-like feet. My scanty carcass felt as does a sausage skin, too small for its contents, and my body reeked of the innocent smell of death, a smell permanently transplanted onto my nostrils as though the deity had commanded its presence. At last I had discovered my wings, the right as pure white as those of the beings who lived far above me, and my left as dark and unknown black as those of the fearful ones far below me.

My entire being is shrouded in a mist that allows me only to see glimpses of myself of what is below or around me. I have only my sense to guide me, through cold of mist, heat of sun, and scenery below. I am flying on an endless course, as a puppet left behind to hang on a string. I feel my existence resting on that one thread.

Only now do I realize the others on the mirrored waters below. They are not equipped with my lovely wings. Perhaps it is justice for them to be drowning. I dare not risk my safety for them. Have I not my own string to worry about, its strength lessening and leaving me every minute?

While I through the mist
Only glimpsed my winged self
And below in the mirrored water
They scream without wings
Or even strings, threads to hold
And pull them through the mist

With the strength of pull on the thread
Through the mist where I fly
With my wings.

Ninth-grade girl

Suddenly there was a little clicking noise at the front door. I felt a chill run through my body. I nearly screamed, but I was too scared to do anything. (Then the door opened slowly and he walked in. He smiled and started toward me. He didn't say a word, but just kept on walking. His smile turned into an evilish grin and as he walked I saw something in his hand. It was a black silk scarf. He sat down beside me, and gently placed the cloth around my neck. Then gradually he pulled the noose together tighter and tighter. I screamed and I screamed and screamed and wouldn't stop, until finally she ran in. She looked at me and smiled and then her smile changed into an evilish grin and she laughed and laughed and laughed . . .)

The Smile of Life and Death

And the door opened slowly
And he walked in and smiled
He moved nearer and nearer
And didn't stop, and he smiled.
And he smiled an overcoming smile.
And his smile was death.
His smile of Death surrounded me,
And it trapped me, and blackened my spirit
I screamed for Life until she appeared
And she smiled.
And she smiled a dying smile.
And soon her smile faded away.
And it would never return,
For her smile was Life.
But he stayed and never wandered.
For his smile was Death.

Tenth-grade girl

It is interesting to note one of the comments about how this assignment was written:

I could rightly say that I chose to eat grapefruits while doing surrealistic writing, for I can recall in the last assignment, to compose or recall a dream, the first thing I did was to eat grapefruit, something I felt I had to do. Whether this influenced my work I can't say.

Journal Writing

Many teachers believe that requiring their students to keep journals in which the students report their responses to various experiences—both in and out of class—is a useful procedure. Some teachers may make weekly suggestions for entries. For instance, they might suggest that the student describe something he has never before observed, write down his feelings of anger over some experience, or describe his feelings about someone he likes (or hates) very much. The teacher's suggestions may be ignored if the student has some special entry he would like to make. Some teachers set aside special class time for journal entries. Others have students make their entries as part of homework assignments. Usually, students are free to make any entries they like, from descriptions of scientific experiments to poems and short stories.

The teacher should check the journals at regular intervals, but if he has 130 or more students per day, he can hardly check each of them every week. An energy-conserving plan is to stagger the checking points for classes, checking the journals of two or three classes per week. His comments on journal entries should not be punitive and need not be extensive; they should be encouraging wherever possible. He should concentrate on noting strengths in expression, suggesting how the writer might improve his entries, and suggesting journal entries that might be worked into longer compositions as part of the regular writing program.

Style and Stylization

A final consideration in writing is the way in which the writer uses language. In this regard it is useful to distinguish between style and stylization. A stylization is the conscious reshaping of a piece of work so that a characteristic kind of expression emerges as its feature. *The New Yorker* and *Time* feature highly stylized materials.

Many professionals continually revise their work both during the writing and on completion. The focus of their revision is usually the style in their expression: word choice and syntactic structuring.

Much of the work of professionals is done on the finished piece:

I can't understand how anyone can write without re-writing everything over and over again.[1]

—TOLSTOY

Looking at the work of the professional as a corpus, his conscious styling becomes a matter of deep concern after he has passed through his formative period:

. . . but then comes the question of achieving a popular—in other words, I may say, a good and lucid style. . . . Without much labour, no writer will achieve such a style. He has very much to learn; and, when he has learned that much, he has to acquire the habit of using what he has learned with ease. But all this must be learned and acquired,—not while he is writing that which shall please, but long before.[2]

—Anthony Trollope

Probably, some writers aim at a characteristic stylization; certainly, the dialect writers such as Damon Runyon and Joel Chandler Harris must have done this.

Should adolescent writers be concerned with conscious stylization? One danger is that the young writer may develop preciosity in his writing, an objectionable artificiality that he cannot recognize or evaluate adequately by himself, because of his lack of sophistication.

Another problem has to do with maturation. Most young writers have enough trouble dealing with the main problems in their writing: planning adequately, then carrying out the plan.

If styling problems are essayed in the course of instruction, they should be dealt with as part of polishing the finished work in follow-up procedures.

The writing of parodies as described in Chapter 27 will serve to indicate which students can do styling. Those who do not show signal success in their stylization parodies are probably unable to attack their own style problems in any depth. If writing results indicate that some students are ready to study style, two avenues are open: a systematic, unambiguous self-analysis, using the tools provided by the linguist, and the introspective technique indicated above.

Using the first approach, the writer should select from his writing a sample or two that he feels is typical and subject it to rigorous analysis. In this way, he can determine what the style characteristics of his syntax are. He can then perform the same operations on any style he admires and consciously adjust his writing, or revise it, to approach that style. Following are two tenth-grade examples of such work:

STRUCTURE ANALYSIS

This composition, analyzing my style of structuring compositions, is entirely based on "Comparison of Richard III and Cyrano de Bergerac." All statistics actually refer to that composition only.

My compositions average about 500–550 words. They are composed of approximately 45 sentences, which range in length from 6 to 28 words. The sentences have a mean of 12 or 13 words. My compositions are composed of only 14% adjectives and adverbs, thus they are not especially descriptive. They do not include too much action (15% verbs) and ¼ of all the words are nouns. The highest percent of words falls in the function word category. Function words, having no referent, add a touch of complexity to the composition. Also adding a touch of complexity is the fact that over half of the words are poly-syllables. A purpose and plan of the composition is included in each composition. The average length of my paragraphs is 69 words. The first and last paragraphs are usully the shortest, as they contain only the purpose, plan or summary. For example, at the beginning of "Comparison of Richard III and Cyrano de Bergerac" I said, as a plan and purpose of the composition, "Although both Richard and Cyrano have physical deformities they react differently to the rather disillusioning situation (one paragraph). As a summary or conclusion at the end I said, "Thus in all fields Cyrano de Bergerac is more acceptable to the reader."

Thus, when analyzing one of my compositions, the structural construction becomes apparent.

It would be hard to find two people who wrote in the same exact style. This essay will try to show you my style of writing and what makes it different.

First of all we will look at words. In my composition I have used 288 words. 28% of the words used are nouns and 25% of the words are verbs. This is a close ratio and shows good noun-verb relationship. There were 17% adverbs and 15% adjectives or adverbs but a fair amount is employed. There were 20% function words which show I'm certainly not afraid of them. A great use of function words might indicate that the author is not writing an essay for a young person or is a young person. This is so because function words can not adequately be explained and would be hard to grasp for a young reader. There are no immediate recursives in my composition. 30% of the words used are pronouns. This shows that I use quite a few pronouns.

Sentences are the next important step in the analysis of style. There are twenty-five sentences and an average of twenty words per sentence. If you try to write twenty words you will find that it is a good amount of words. 40% of the sentences are compound-complex, 25% are complex, 20% are compound and 15% are simple. There is not really a great difference but it does show very few sentences are simple as far as compound and complex go but compound-complex have a much greater percent than the others. There are no commands, questions, or exclamations. These things will usually tell the difference between a story and an essay. In statement patterns there are two; clause then subject then predicate, and prepositional phrase then subject then predicate. I use a more than average number of recursive sentences and clauses. It seems that I like to dwell on a subject and not leave it.

The next important step in analysis is the paragraph. I use an average of six sentences to a paragraph and an average of 73 words per paragraph. This is not a great number of sentences but a good number of words to a paragraph. I use a pattern of a few short sentences and then a burst of long sentences. Usually after my longest sentence I will follow up with a short sentence such as "But just wait a minute". I do have topic sentences and they are all at the very beginning.

I have covered all three main subjects. Before ending I would like to say that I try to use a personalizing or editorial approach in my writing.

In closing this composition I hope you have seen the various characteristics of my essay and will be able to compare it with accurate results.

Obviously, such a project demands a preliminary study of the appropriate analytic techniques.

The second method is a more subjective analysis of style through introspection. The following work of another tenth grader is an example:

As for my style of writing, I really don't think I have one particular style. I don't think that a writer should have one definite style because then he (she) feels that he has to keep up that way of writing. When I write something and I have good ideas, I don't think that a certain way of writing was going to stop me from writing that. When an author or writer has to think of work which will follow his style I think that his writing is what you might call "forced".

I think that anyone who is writing a piece of work should write what he thinks suits the paper, and what comes easily and naturally to him.

A good note on which to close the discussion of style!

NOTES

1. Goldenveizer, A. B., *Talks with Tolstoi*, Koteliansky, Samuel S. and Woolf, Virginia, translators (New York: Horizon, 1969), p. 50.
2. Anthony Trollope, *An Autobiography* (Berkeley: University of California Press, 1947), p. 148.

29 | Working with Dysfunctional Writers

The best instructional situation for working with dysfunctional writers is made possible by administrative grouping practices; it is the situation in which a class is composed exclusively of dysfunctional writers. Relatively few schools, however, provide such special classes.

Skill at reading, which is prerequisite to skill at writing, is by far the more important of the two from the point of view of pupil needs. Reading problems must therefore be attacked first. Of course, some writing activities should be used as part of the remediation, but any extensive writing serves only to distract from the problem of clearing up reading dysfunction. Most teachers who have to deal with verbal dysfunction, hopefully can, however, bring constant pressure to bear on the administration to form separate classes. The ticket for admission to the remedial composition class is functional skill at reading.

Although this chapter has been written in terms of a special class for dysfunctional writers, some of the techniques suggested may be used by a teacher with only one or two students whose writing is dysfunctional.

The first step in designing a correctional program in writing skills is to analyze the student's writing problem to see where the blocks are occurring and what their character might be. In making this analysis, the teacher must first evaluate the student's fundamental verbal ability. The characteristic division of tests of mental abilities is into verbal and nonverbal processes. Verbal processes are those that have to do with language; that is, the use of language is the central feature of verbal processes. There is evidence that the presumed dichotomy of verbal-nonverbal is not so neat and clear as we would like to have it.[1] However, operationally, it is useful as well as convenient to consider verbal processes as a distinct type of intellectual function. The verbal processes may be further divided into those that have to do with receiving and interpreting language information and those that have to do with composing and expressing language information. It is at this stage that the function of the writer may be breaking down: he may be unable to handle words, morphology and syntax at all in composing and expressing. The verbal block may result from difficulty with all language generally, the English language, or it may be related to specific dialect problems.

Dialect differences are far more likely to cause trouble in writing than in reading. No mater what dialect a student uses when he speaks, his writing must conform to standard English spelling patterns, whereas when he reads, he can translate the printed symbols into his own speech patterns. A real dialect problem can occur in connection with the writing of Negro children, one that is partly phonological and partly morphological.* Many tend to omit the *s* when they form noun plurals, possessives, and third-person singular verbs and to omit the marker *ed* of the past tense and participial forms of weak verbs. Another pattern is the omission of auxiliaries in forming verb phrases. Spanish-speaking students who are learning English often confuse *b* and *v* and also *n* and *ng* and the various spelling configurations of the high front vowels. Anyone learning a new language will have a great many problems with its syntax, which ordinarily presents very few problems across dialect lines.

Another kind of writing difficulty is connected with sentence patterns. Perception of sentences in English is in large part dependent upon perception of the English superfixes: stress, pitch, and juncture. Probably, pitch patterns give dysfunctional writers the greatest problem. The great difficulty is that in oral expression we frequently use patterns that are acceptable as complete sentences to our listeners, but if these patterns are reduced to writing, they are not ordinarily read with the superfix patterns that signal sentences. For example, the answer "When I get my homework done" can be made to *sound* like a sentence easily; but it does not *read* like a sentence. Run-on sentences also relate to superfix patterns. Such locutions as "Hurry, hurry, hurry" and "I came, I saw, I conquered" testify to the disparities that exist between the spoken language and analogous written forms. On occasion, even a functional writer uses problematic locutions: "He's on time so regularly, he's a clock." The argument that the locution is made possible as a result of the phenomenon of ellipsis is questionable since the clauses are readily reversible: "He's a clock he's on time so regularly."

The second cause, then, for composing difficulty is syntax problems.

Spelling may also create writing difficulties because of the failure of English sounds to correspond with letters in any consistent way. Thus, a student may be blocked in his writing because although he knows what he wants to say, he cannot spell the words.

The final item to consider in writing dysfunction is handwriting. Illegible

---

* Similar dialect-related problems have been noted in those persons, blacks or whites, who use plantation speech and other Southern dialects.

handwriting may be in part a deliberate attempt to conceal spelling deficiency, or it may reflect general frustration at writing. It may also be a cue to immaturity since the small muscle control necessary in handwriting develops after control of large muscles develops. Such handwriting difficulty could itself frustrate a student in writing a composition.

The teacher must consider all four of these factors—general verbal ability, sentence perception and formation, spelling deficiencies, and handwriting—in planning the instructional program for dysfunctional writers.

Empirical Exploration

When dealing with dysfunctional writers, the teacher should extend the inventory period to encompass a considerable amount of exploratory work. He should try out many different writing situations in an attempt to discover the specific ones in which these students do their best work. He should, for example, give them dictation, have them give dictation to one another, and have them write on the chalkboard.

The spelling inventory (Chapter 21) will provide initial evidence of the students' ability to handle dictation of sentences and to copy what they have written. In addition to noting any spelling weaknesses and ascertaining whether some study methods are indicated or contraindicated, the teacher should note whether the handwriting on the copied material is significantly better than that on the dictated material. Students who have a great deal of trouble taking dictation of verbal material *presented as a context* should be grouped together and receive dictation of individual words. The teacher should make clear that the purpose of this dictation of a word list is not to test spelling but rather to test the ability to take dictation. Therefore, when dictating, the teacher should spell out any words the students have difficulty with. It may be the case that some students are generally inefficient at writing from dictation. On the other hand, some students who make mistakes in taking dictation even of single words at their desks may do much better work taking dictation at the chalkboard because chalkboard writing makes greater use of large muscles than does writing on paper.

The students who have had difficulty with copying their own work should try copying printed material. Both kinds of copying should be tried at the chalkboard as well as at their desks. They should also work at their desks copying material written on the chalkboard.

The early emphasis on copying and dictating is an effort to exclude from the complete writing gestalt those factors that are related to composing and the internal handling of language generally. The dictating and copying provide an opportunity for writing that is freed from the immediate frustrations that may attend verbal composing. Many students will be able to perform these mechanical tasks adequately yet will not be able to do any extensive writing that must be based on their own ability to compose, thus suggesting the possible nature of their blocks. The dictating, copying and chalkboard activities that characterize this early exploration are similar to the activities of the elementary school, especially in the lower grades. It is useful for the teacher of the dysfunctional writer (and reader) to conceptualize his students as being extremely immature in their skills. For this reason, the methods that work with pupils who are actually chronologically younger may very well work with them. The content of the material that is dictated and copied, however, should reflect the interests of older age groups. Adolescents, who will be all too aware of their deficiencies in skills, are insulted and humiliated when they are forced to work with "baby" materials.

When instruction in handwriting begins in the lower elementary grades, the typical pattern is to teach the students to print letters first. (This is called "manuscript" writing; ordinary handwriting is called "cursive" writing.)

The typical procedure in teaching young children to write is to delay their writing until after they have had some success with reading. The handwriting instruction itself is carefully preplanned. The children learn to form letters on the basis of the structure of the letters, their frequency of occurrence, and similar considerations. The writing of words and the correct spelling of these words is achieved without discrete attention to the spelling per se. The sequence in which the words are learned interrelates with the letter learning sequences. Additional factors that help to determine learning sequences are the familiarity with the words in preliminary reading experience, speaking vocabulary, and usefulness in generating sentences. Ordinarily, initial instruction, as was noted above, is with manuscript writing—a kind of printing. Ideally, when students are able to use manuscript writing with ease, they are gradually shifted over into cursive writing.

One of the cleavages in elementary school procedural philosophy has to do with manuscript writing as opposed to cursive writing. In some school systems it is believed that since the function of handwriting is legibility and manuscript is generally more legible than cursive, it is unnecessary for people to learn cursive writing at all. Staying with only one system has the additional advantage of not burdening the learner with two systems; and the time that might be used in teaching cursive writing can be put to other uses in the elementary school teacher's total instructional program. Because manuscript writing more nearly resembles printing than cursive writing does, it is felt that practice in manuscript alone provides support in reading.

On the other hand, in other school systems it is believed that since the general adult population employs cursive writing, and not manuscript, it behooves the schools to teach cursive writing. Some schools, aware of the possible difficulties that might arise as a result of learning two systems, do not teach manuscript at all, but begin instruction directly and immediately with cursive writing. However, it is more usually the case that, a youngster first learns manuscript, and then is taught cursive.

Whatever the relative values of the differing viewpoints may be, it is best for the secondary school teacher not to take sides in the issue. But the teacher of the dysfunctional writer in the secondary school must be aware of the varying practices. One kind of problem that the secondary school teacher frequently encounters with dysfunctional writers is that of the student whose initial writing experience was in a school system committed to one form of writing and who later transferred to another school that taught the other form. He may thus find himself "behind" in writing and never catch up.

The secondary school teacher must be aware of all the alternatives in dealing with the problem of handwriting. If under all the conditions of dictating and copying named above the student exhibits uniformly poor handwriting, the teacher and student should explore together the possibility of his using a completely different style, that is, if he is a cursive writer who writes badly, he should try manuscript; if he uses only manuscript and his manuscript is poor, he should try cursive. If he has both manuscript and cursive and they are both poor, or if he cannot learn the form that he does not use, then he should explore typewriting.

Dysfunctional writers in general, should have the opportunity to do typing since the neuromuscular patterns involved in typing are much different from those involved in handwriting. Certainly, from the point of view of legibility, typing is vastly superior to either of the handwriting forms. For some students typing may be the answer to their writing problems.

If typewriters and typing instruction are not available, and handwriting is a major problem, the teacher will have to do some work in improving the student's handwriting. Since secondary school teachers are not trained in this area, the first move is to secure help. Help may be obtained from the reading specialist, or skilled teachers in the lower elementary school. Handwriting manuals and workbooks are available. In addition, there are some unsophisticated techniques that can be tried in an effort to improve legibility.

The first of these is to have the students skip lines in their writing. Another is to have them try writing on *unlined* paper. Another avenue is simply recopying. For many students recopying results in vastly improved papers. For some writers a kinesthetic approach may be indicated. It is beyond the scope of this chapter, even of this book, to detail all the kinesthetic procedures. Since there are a number of people who seem to be able to learn in no other way, the teacher must familiarize himself with kinesthetic techniques. Unfortunately, working with the kinesthetic approach demands much one-to-one relationship between teacher and pupil. It is essential for the teacher to observe the various phases of pupil behavior attentively. Because the kinesthetic approach teaches reading, spelling and handwriting at once, it is extremely valuable for working with the severely disabled student. The writing of Grace Fernald is recommended for insights into kinesthetic methodology.[2]

After the early exploration has indicated which students take dictation adequately, the teacher should pair students, with at least one member of each pair a student who can write from dictation fairly well. That student should then receive dictation from the other, or if both members can take dictation, they should alternate. The dictation should start with original sentences. Through this procedure, the student is able to separate the act of creating original sentences from the physical act of writing. In other words, the student who does the composing does not have to write, and the student who writes is not faced with the problems of composing; this is a way to involve students in original composition while minimizing their frustrations. If the pairs experience success at single sentences, they should go on to longer structures such as short personal narratives, directions on how to do something, or descriptions of simple scenes or procedures.

The next writing situation that should be explored is one in which the students are provided support in their composing efforts. Groups of four should be formed, with each including at least one member who is adequate at taking dictation. The class should be given a writing problem or series of problems structured in this way:

1. "You are going to have a party. *Step one:* You plan the party. Decide when and where it will be held, which people you will invite, what games you will play, whether or not you will dance, what records you will play, and finally what kinds of goodies you will eat. *Step two:* Invite all the people that you plan to ask and make all the arrangements, such as buying the food and collecting the phonograph records. *Step three:* Describe the party itself.

2. "You are planning a trip to another planet. *Step one:* Decide all the preparations you will make, what the different crew members will have to do and who they will be, what things you are going to take with you, the date and place you are leaving from, and the characteristics your space ship will have to have. *Step two:* Assemble the crew, set up the space ship for takeoff, and get together all the necessary equipment, food, and so on, that you will need. *Step three:* Describe the trip itself.

3. "You are planning a game of baseball (or any other game). *Step one:* Decide who will play on the team, what equipment will be necessary, where you will obtain this equipment, and when and where the game will take place; it may also be necessary to decide on who your opponents will be and who the umpire will be. *Step two:* Assemble the players and the umpire and all the necessary equipment at the right place and at the right time. *Step three:* Describe the game itself."

The writing should be done in three stages corresponding to the three steps in each problem. The writing of the first step should be a group effort; the second step should be written by pairs of students; and the third by individual students. The writing of the first two steps will involve a great deal of repetition. The third step will result in writing that is somewhat different in content but yet closely related to the content of the first two. Each group of four students should make a selection from the problem series.

In the first stage of the writing procedure, each group should thoroughly discuss each of the three steps of its writing problem—that is, what they will probably say in each. When all three steps have been discussed, the group should go back and discuss the first one in detail. (While the groups are working, especially during the discussion period, the teacher should move from group to group giving help as it is needed.) When all the ideas have been worked out orally, then the group should dictate its version of the first step to the group secretary, the person who is best in the group at taking dictation. If necessary, the secretary should make a neat copy of the dictation to be signed by all group members. The papers should then be turned in to the teacher.

When the teacher reads these compositions covering the first step in the assignment, he should first of all note whether the content is adequate—have enough specific details been included? The next item to consider is the sequencing of the details: Is it reasonable? The next is sentence structure. Are the sentences adequate? Finally, the teacher should consider mechanics: Are words spelled properly? Are capitalization and punctuation adequate?

Instead of just marking errors, the teacher should indicate appropriate forms, especially in connection with spelling. This activity is designed, not to give instruction in these areas, but to reduce frustration.

At the next meeting the papers should be returned to be revised along the lines indicated by the teacher's marking and comments. If it is clear that some group or groups have had considerable difficulty, the teacher should visit them to give them more specific help. When the revisions have been made in each group, each individual member should make his own copy of the group composition, making additions if he wishes to.

In the second stage of the writing procedure, each group should be divided into partnerships. Each member of the partnership now has a copy of step one of the assignment as completed by his group (probably a paragraph). The partners should now thoroughly discuss the content of the next two steps of the composition. When they have finished their discussion, they should go back and discuss in detail the content of the second step, and then, working together, they compose it. This second step will be almost identical in content with the first one, varying only slightly. When a good copy of this step of the composition is made, both partners should sign it and turn it in. The teacher reads these in the same way that he read those that came from the groups of four. Using the same follow-up procedure, he works with the partners who seem to need help the most. Next, each partner makes a finished copy of his work and adds this to the part that resulted from working with the group of four. The composition is now two-thirds finished.

The last stage of the work begins when the partnership separates. Now each student is working as an individual, and his problem is to develop the third step of the composition. He has had a good deal of preparation for this: first of all, he was a member of a group of four, and he discussed all three parts of the composition with the others in the group. Next, he was a member of a partnership, and he discussed the final two parts of the composition with his partner. By this time, he should have a pretty good idea of what he wants to say. Now his problem is to say it.

When the teacher reads the final section, he will be able to determine which students can perform adequately when they have been given thorough preparation and which students cannot write even with such preparation.

The next type of writing situation to be tried is the individual writing of a short composition that has been structured in a general way. The students should first be given a short reading assignment—a short story, an essay, a magazine article such as one from *The Reader's Digest,* or an article in the encyclopedia. They should tell about what they read, in the first part of the composition and in the second part, they tell about something new they found out in their reading (or something they especially liked in it). Very little original thinking is involved here. The specific organization of the first part of the student's composition has been done for the student by the author of the material, and the student merely has to repeat what he has read. The general organization of the composition has been taken care of by the teacher. The student's only real problem is responding to the second part of the writing problem—that is, deciding what he learned that was new (or what he liked best)—a formulation he must make on his own. When the teacher reads the finished composition, he can decide the extent to which the prestructuring has aided the student in his composing—both the prestructuring the teacher himself has given, and the more careful prestructuring that has been given by the author of the material in the reading assignment.

The next prestructured writing is somewhat longer and follows after a longer reading experience, a book report. The teacher should tell the students to devote the first paragraph to what the story is about; the second to a description of the character that they thought was the most important, and the third to what they especially liked or did not like about the book. Once again the first paragraph is merely repetition of what they read, requiring very little original work from the student other than condensing the organization that the author of the book used. The second paragraph requires a bit more original work, that is, extracting specific items that occur throughout the story and developing a brief characterization based on this extraction process. The third part of the book report involves the greatest amount of original thinking.

This last assignment brings to a close the exploratory period of the year's work. This period will be rather long, but at the end of it the teacher will have a good idea of the various strengths and limits both mechanical and intellectual, of each student's writing performance.

The Instructional Program

After the teacher has completed the exploratory activities, the content of his instructional program should be conditioned by the immediate and eventual needs of the students.

Because the students find writing frustrating, the first part of the year should be devoted to finding out what specific elements in the writing gestalt frustrates them and which phases of writing they seem to be able to deal with. When instruction begins, the teacher should design the program so that the students can avoid the activities that are frustrating to them and concentrate on those that they can do rather easily. As the year goes on, however, they should be gradually introduced to those activities they had found to be frustrating. If they were to avoid them, they would not become functional at writing.

In addition to the type of activity, the frustration can derive from the length of time that a student spends in doing it. Obviously it is more difficult to write thirty paragraphs than one paragraph. Therefore, the teacher should observe behaviors in the exploratory period very carefully with an eye to determining how long his class can work at a given task. As he notes symptoms of frustration—looking up from the work, gazing around the room, pounding on the desk, distracting others, breaking pencils, dropping pens, sharpening pencils, excessive erasing, requests to go to the lavatory, and so on—the teacher will have an idea of how long he can spend on an activity. As the year goes on, he can gradually lengthen the time spent. At the beginning of the year, it is not impossible that a class may be able to stand only two or three minutes at an activity. Therefore, the teacher must have a variety of different activities in his program, planning them so that the different types alternate with one another. For example, if the class is doing copying at their seats, the next activity should involve something that contrasts with it strongly, such as group discussion. After that could come chalkboard work and then a listening activity. Then the cycle might be repeated, starting with more work at their seats.

The class is likely to be made up of very immature persons who are hostile to authority in general and teachers in particular. Having had little success in school work, they are likely to have a defeatist attitude toward their own potential. They will display a great many negative behaviors, which the teacher should accept insofar as possible, recognizing that such a display is, in part, a means of testing him. In order to build up the students' confidence and self-esteem, the teacher must be alert at all times to find ways of rewarding them with praise for their efforts as well as their actual achievement. He schedules his work so that very easy things are encountered before things of even slight difficulty are encountered. He gives copious praise for successful completion of the easiest tasks. He must never indicate that any task is easy. Nor must he indicate that it is unusually hard. Some of the tasks will be obviously simple, and if the teacher indicates otherwise, the students will suspect his integrity. The teacher must make it clear that the easy tasks are foundations and that they will not be able to do the harder ones unless they have mastered the easy things. In this respect, writing skills can be compared to such other skills as weight lifting, track practice, and swimming practice— that is, a person starts with things that he can do and gradually increases his tasks and efforts until eventually he can do things that he could not possibly have done in the first place.

The teacher should watch for students who are not making an effort. Although he should not chide these students because that would interfere with rapport, he should not pretend that they are making an effort when it is obvious that they are not. He must consciously encourage and support them. Often the simple act of standing near a student who has never learned to work or has forgotten how encourages that student to work. A high value should be placed on work. The students should never be asked to do the best they can since the conscientious ones are probably already doing it and it is almost impossible for a person to give the best that is in him consistently. Rather, they should be encouraged to work reasonably hard. Also, the teacher should make it plain that he understands that reasonably hard work *is* hard. He must also make it clear that he understands that what is easy for one person may be quite hard for another.

Routines are important for dysfunctional students. If the same kinds of activities are done in the same order each day, the instructional pattern itself will support their learning. Another advantage is that this will save time that might otherwise be spent in giving directions. Moreover, the student does not have to learn new directions and new procedures each day.

A good procedure is to start each lesson with a spelling drill. The results of the spelling inventory will indicate whether there is a widespread need for attention to basic writing words. If there is, the basic writing vocabulary should receive first attention. The teacher should next drill the students on words that are not in the basic writing vocabulary but that will be encountered on forms of various kinds: school forms, business forms, tax forms, and the like. Much of the writing that is done by adults in daily life has to do with filling out lists, and such items as days of the week, months of the year, addresses, and so on will be found on all these lists. Mastery of these items is essential.

When the spelling lists have been developed, they should be scheduled for daily drills with some convenient number of new words being introduced each week—ten is a good number. A set of words written on the blackboard should be copied by the students into their spelling notebooks; they can be studied by the methods discussed in Chapter 21. Each day a quick spelling quiz should be given by a student. Papers can sometimes be exchanged for correction and at other times be corrected by their writers. The student who administers the test should choose the next day's administrator from those whose words are all correct. After the first week, the test should be divided into two parts—the first containing all the words for that week presented in a different order each day and the second made up of selections from the words of all the previous weeks. In this way there can be a continual review of all the words. As the year goes on and work with pluralizing, the use of the apostrophe, and other orthographic rules is introduced, the weekly spelling list can contain general words that exemplify the rules that have been considered. Additionally, other words that the class as a whole or various members have found troublesome can be introduced onto the list.

Another kind of spelling drill, and one that has a high degree of motivation inherent in it, is based on the use of a flashing device. The teacher should make a series of slides or obtains slides or film strips from commercial sources. Such devices as the tachistoscope and speedioscope, which are available commercially, can be attached to overhead projectors or filmstrip projectors; they govern the speed at which words can be flashed on a screen, from a few seconds to fractions of a second. After the teacher flashes a word on the screen for a moment, the class writes it down. After a series of such presentations—say ten words—the teacher returns to the first word, opens the shutter, and lets the class check their responses to that word, and so forth down the whole list.

Another way to provide motivation in spelling is with various spelling games. One such game is Hangman, in which the sketch of a gallows is drawn on the board and a series of dashes is put beneath it, each dash representing a letter of a word. The students should try to guess the word by guessing each of the letters. As a letter is guessed correctly, it should be written into each of the spaces in which it occurs. For example, suppose the word is *school.* The spaces should be written on the board, one for each letter as follows: − − − − − −. If a student guesses *o,* the two *o*'s should be filled in. As wrong guesses are made, the stick figure of a man should be gradually built under the gallows. For example, if the student guesses *e,* the head of the man should be drawn in. If another student guesses *a,* the neck should be added. If another guesses *i,* the shoulders should be added, and so forth. The students may guess at the word, as well as the letters; whenever a wrong word is guessed, another part should be added. If the stick figure is completed and the word has not been guessed, the teacher should supply it, and the stick figure should be erased and the game begun again. If a student guesses the word, he becomes the game leader and supplies dashes for his own word. (It is a good idea for the teacher to check the spelling of the student's word before the dashes are put on the board.)

Another good spelling game is Ghost. The class is divided into teams, and a member of the first team suggests a letter, which is written on the board. The first member of the second team adds a letter to it; the second player on the first team adds another letter; and the second player on the second team adds another, and so on. The object of the game is not to add the last letter of a word. Proper nouns are not used, and only words three letters in length or longer are counted. Should a student, in order to avoid putting the last letter on a word, suggest a letter that is patently absurd, the next player on the other team can say "I challenge you." If the previous player cannot supply a word spelled in that way, his team loses a point. Whenever any player adds the last letter to a word, his team loses a point, and the teacher scores the loss, by writing a letter of the word "ghost" on the blackboard. The first time a player adds the last letter to a word or loses a challenge, his team gets the *g.* The next time the player on that team loses a point, his team gets an *h,* and so on until the team loses five points and "ghost" is spelled.

Other word games, such as Scrabble and crossword puzzles, also add interest to spelling lessons.

Because it is an important and frequently encountered writing experience, filling out forms should be a frequent activity of the remedial writing class. In the course of the school year, it is necessary to have many school forms made out. The teacher of the dysfunctional writing class should therefore make every effort to have these forms delegated to him for work in class. (This is in contrast to the attitude of the teacher of the regular English class who avoids this sort of scut work at all costs.) In addition to school forms, the teacher can obtain business forms, especially employment forms, from such sources in the community as grocery chains, filling station chains, factories, and utility companies—in short, from employers who hire a great many unskilled, non-professional, noncollege-trained persons. In addition to these forms, the teacher can construct a great many forms for evaluating compositions. (An example of such a form is given below in the evaluation of business letters.)

Another feature of instruction in classes for dysfunctional writers has to do with training in the perception of sentences. One of the rules for whole-class discussion should be that all answers must be made in the form of sentences, no matter how inefficient, clumsy, or silly this practice may seem. Insisting on sentences in oral work not only provides practice in the formation of sentences but also keeps the students' attention riveted on sentence patterns. The teacher can give extra credit to those who detect answers that are not in the form of complete sentences, and double extra credit can be given for detection of teacher locutions that are not sentences. If a student characteristically writes run-on sentences or incomplete sentences, the teacher should have a conference with him and ask him to read his composition aloud. If his voice makes the appropriate superfix patterns, the teacher should alert him to these patterns and ask that he be guided by the patterns in reconstructing or repunctuating his writing. If he does not produce the patterns appropriately in his oral reading, he will have to do a great deal of oral work and oral analysis of sentence patterns and forms until he can recognize and produce the appropriate superfixes. Students who use the superfix patterns appropriately in their oral work should be encouraged to read their written work aloud in their proofreading.

If the analysis of the exploratory period has indicted the need, many of the class activities should be oriented toward oral work, which can take the form of interviews (as described in Chapter 2), mock interviews of different kinds —such as employment interviews—mock telephone conversations, and work with drama.

The inventories, the exploratory period, and the permanent records of the school will indicate which students are dysfunctional writers because English is not their native language or because they speak a nonstandard dialect. Each language presents unique syntactic and phonological characteristics. Therefore, unless a teacher is familiar with the native language of his student, he will be unable to provide contrasts between the patterns of that language and English. Only acutely perceptive persons can infer pattern differences on the basis of an analysis of the writing that a nonnative speaker does. If the linguistic literature that deals with analysis of the language in question is unavailable to him, the best help for a teacher will be the foreign language teachers in his school system. They may be able to provide a good deal of help on the phonological, spelling, and syntactic problems of some students. In the absence of such help, the teacher will be forced to rely on oral work. He may find that work with a language laboratory, if one is available in his school, will be instrumental in solving the problems of those who are not native to English or not native to a standard dialect of English.

Probably a great deal of work in the year will involve copying and analyzing short passages of writing. Most school grammars are good sources for this sort of material because their exercises are composed of relatively short sentences that are introduced separately and are usually carefully constructed on some principle that the lesson is built around. The lesson on parallel construction, for example, is very helpful in sentence analysis. Because the sentences can be dealt with as single entities, not much time is required in dealing with an individual sentence, thus reducing the student's frustration. Another advantage of the grammar is that the student will be copying printed material, and any incidental learning he acquires, such as how to spell certain words, will be of the correct rather than the erroneous forms. Another advantage is that these grammar book drills concentrate on sentence analysis rather than vocabulary development. Consequently, the vocabulary that the student encounters is rather easy. Of course, the teacher's primary purpose in assigning the grammar book drills is not to have the students learn rules or analysis but to support their work in writing—that is, to provide practice material for copying, simple composing, and so on. At the same time, because the students are using grade level textbooks, the work tends to support the development of a healthy self-image. The traditional school grammar book, then, is a useful tool to the teacher of dysfunctional writers.

Because their structure is so important, the study of business letters is useful in working with dysfunctional writers. Although most of these students will, in fact, probably never write a business letter, they are aware that this is a "real life" kind of writing and are thus more easily motivated to practice business letter exercises than many other kinds of exercises. Practicing the writing is the important consideration here.

The letters should be analyzed part by part, with the students mastering one part at a time. When they finally write complete letters, they can criticize their own work and that of the other class members. The use of a form for this criticism can provide additional practice in using forms. Each student should put his finished letter on a duplicator stencil, and after the stencils are run, each member of the class should be given one to be analyzed according to the following form:

Name: Date in Full:
Class: Author of letter:

Comment on the letter in general:
Neatness: Margins
Placement of parts   top:
   heading: bottom:
   inside address: l. side:
   greeting: r. side:
   body:
   closing:
   signature:

Comment on contents of parts, punctuation, abbreviation, completeness:
   heading
   inside address
   greeting
   body
   closing
   signature

Is the message clear? If not, what is unclear:

Suggestions for improvement:

A new letter should be criticized each day. This criticism not only helps the class to learn the characteristics of business letters but gives them practice in filling out forms.

Another kind of composition that is useful to the teacher of dysfunctional writers is the Japanese poem form haiku. Because the form is short, it is challenging but not frustrating. Even the very weakest students can have a measure of success in writing it. The first step in the lesson is to analyze models of the haiku. When the analysis has been completed, the students should write their own haiku. Booklets of the haiku composed by the class are useful in motivating the students and increasing their self-confidence (see Chapter 5 for a detailed presentation of the haiku lesson).

The All-Purpose Model Paragraph

There will be some students who, according to the inventories and the teacher's subsequent investigation, will not be able to do very much writing unless it is carefully prestructured for them.

The student's most pressing writing need—beyond simple lists such as those used for filling out forms—is to transmit information. Therefore, the writing problems of these students can be drastically reduced through the use of an all-purpose model paragraph structure into which information can easily be fitted. All the student has to do is to memorize the paragraph structure and order the information within that structure.

The following is a model paragraph, the structure of which was empirically established after a study of several hundred paragraphs written by functional writers:[3]

> The Siamese is the most interesting cat as a pet. When a cat owner brags about his blue-eyed friend, he usually has a Siamese in mind. Because of its unusual coloring, its fondness for killing rodents, and its love of a good swim, it is always the subject of some interesting doings. Its love of swimming is probably its most interesting feature, since cats usually dislike water. Its many unusual characteristics make its owner the object of envy of other catkeepers, and this is despite the fact that the bathroom is out of bounds when someone is taking a bath.

Let us first abstract the structure from the paragraph. The paragraph contains five sentences, and the structure of each of them is as follows:

1. The first sentence is short and is the topic sentence of the paragraph. If blanks are substituted for the parts of speech, a model sentence structure is derived. "The Siamese is the most interesting cat as a pet" becomes "The _____ is the (most) _____ _____ (preposition) _____." This model can generate any number of sentences: "The center is the most important player on the basketball team." "Gauze is the most difficult fabric to work with." "Candy is the most dangerous food for the dieter."

2. The second is a complex sentence of the "if-then" form. Other introductory words can be substituted for "if": "when," "whenever," "as," "since," and so on. The "then" in the second clause can be inserted, or it can be omitted completely as it is in the Siamese cat model. "If the center wins the tap, then his team has the advantage." "Since gauze has little body, working with it on a sewing machine presents very special problems." "When you go to the movies, you are tempted to eat candy."

3. The third sentence is a catalog of characteristics of the subject that is introduced in the topic sentence. "The best centers are fast rugged players, have good vision, and are very tall." "Gauze is used in making bandages and dressing for wounds, inexpensive displays of various kinds, and theatrical costumes." "Candy haunts you not only in the movies but also at parties, in the cafeteria, and in snack dishes around the house."

4. The fourth sentence expands on one of these catalog items. "Height is not only important in controlling the tap, but it helps him control the backboards." "Although gauze is used in inexpensive costumes, the difficulties in sewing it require a lot of time and planning." "The most dangerous of these temptations is having the candy around the house because it is always there."

5. The last sentence summarizes all that has gone before and then provides a contrast in ideas; it is a compound sentence. "Tall boys are usually chosen as centers, but often they are clumsy and will handicap their team in its play." "You can get nice effects inexpensively by using gauze, but it tears easily so you have to be careful with it." "Candy is always around to tempt the dieter, but it tastes pretty good when you yield to temptation."

Thus, the model can generate a number of paragraphs.

The teacher should begin his instruction with this model by initiating a discussion of cats, leading this to Siamese cats, and developing all the points that are made in the model itself. Next he distributes duplicated copies of the Siamese cat paragraph. While these are being distributed, he writes the first sentence on the chalkboard.

He then asks his students which words can be changed without changing the meaning of the sentence. When the answer " 'cat' can be changed to 'animal' " is given, he erases the word "cat," draws in a blank space, and writes the word "animal" over the empty space. He then reads the sentence, "The Siamese cat is the most interesting animal as a pet," and asks the class whether they agree with the statement. The dog lovers and horse lovers will disagree. He next asks which word in the sentence on the board could be eliminated and another substituted. When someone says "Siamese," he erases it and draws a line. Above the empty space he writes the word "horse." Then he reads the sentence: "The horse is the most interesting animal as pet." Next, he asks whether the horse is really a pet. Many in the class will declare that it is not. He erases "pet," draws in the blank, and writes "farm animal" over the space. He reads the new sentence: "The horse is the most interesting animal as a farm animal."

Next, he asks whether "interesting" really fits well in the new sentence. "Of course, it doesn't." "What would fit?" "Oh, something like 'hardest working.' " "Interesting" should be erased and "hardest working" substituted. Now the

model structure is complete. "The _____ is the (most) _____
_____ as a_____."

He asks whether the same sentence could be used in talking about something other than animals. Probably the response will be in the realm of automobiles. "The Mustang is the most stylish car as an automobile." The teacher
should point out that the word "as" might be changed so that the last phrase
could be something like "on the road."

Next, the teacher distributes paper and asks the class to think of a subject that they know a great deal about. It can be something around the
house, a hobby, an animal, but it must be something that they have a lot of
information on. This subject should become the title for their composition,
and they should write it on the top line. Next, everyone in the class should indicate what his topic is. The next step is to write the first sentence in a paragraph on this topic. The sentence will follow the form "The _____
is the (most) _____ (as) a _____." When these sentences are
completed they should be read aloud. No more work is done that day on that
activity.

The teacher collects the papers and checks on their fidelity to the model.
The papers should be returned the next day, when the class should go through
a similar procedure in adding the second sentence to the paragraph.

On the third day, sentences three and four should be worked on together.
The catalog of items must be so arranged that the item that will be expanded
in the fourth sentence appears last in the catalog in the third sentence. Students should be warned that the thing they think of first in this list of items
will probably be the one they want to expand on in the fourth sentence.
Therefore, when they think of it they should jot it down, and then think of
some other things to mention. Developing these two sentences requires a
good deal of thought in composition. After the two sentences are developed,
the whole paragraph should be rewritten to this point, so that it contains the
first four sentences. After they are collected, the teacher checks them for
fidelity to the model. On the fourth day of instruction, the last sentence
should be composed and added to the paragraph. Each time something new is
added to the paragraph, all that has gone before should be copied over, a process that helps the student to learn the model. Byt the end of the fourth day,
he should have fairly good control of the model.

The next step is to practice new writing with the model as a guide. Each
student should be assigned to one volume of an encyclopedia to look for an
article on an animal he knows something about but would like to learn more
about. After marking his place, he then goes on to look for an article about
an animal that he has never heard of before. He should take notes on both
these animals and then write a composition on each of them, following the
lines of the model paragraph. Again, the teacher should check to see whether
these paragraphs are faithful to the model.

Once it is clear that the students have learned the model and it is helping them to generate paragraphs, they should begin work with longer compositions. Longer compositions are essentially strings of paragraphs having the same structure. The first step in producing them is to have the students think of two subjects that they might easily compare, such as two breeds of dog, a dog and a cat, or two persons.

When the subjects have been chosen, the students should write a paragraph on each. If a student has demonstrated competence in handling the model, the teacher should be lenient if he moves away from its precise lines. By this time, most students will do this on their own initiative. When the two separate paragraphs have been finished, the teacher should indicate that the student must think of original sentences to join them together, to introduce them, and to summarize the whole composition. Such a completed composition follows:

The battery is the most important part of baseball defense. You need a pitcher and a catcher in a battery. I will tell you about the pitcher first.

The pitcher is the most interesting player on the team. When a team wants to win, then it needs a good pitcher. A pitcher needs a strong arm, a good pickoff motion and a cool head. The most important thing is a cool head because in tight spots everybody's on you. Although a pitcher looks like a star, he looks bad when he throws too many homer balls.

You know about pitchers. Now I will tell about catchers.

The catcher is the key player on the team. When a pitcher starts to crack up, the catcher has to calm him down. The catcher needs a good throw from a crouch, speed with his hands to pick up bad ones and guts. Guts are the most important to cut off runners from third. Even if he can't hit, he is important because he does everything else.

You can't have a winning team without a good battery. But you might win a few games without one.

Ninth-grade boy

In the course of this discussion on dealing with dysfunctional writers, a great many reading activities have been indicated. However, if the class is composed of students who are dysfunctional at both reading and writing, it follows that reading activities cannot play a large part in writing instruction. It is better to concentrate on eliminating the reading dysfunction first.

Although a great many of the reading and writing problems of students will be cleared up within a year of exposure to carefully structured, thoughtfully worked out remediational programs, one cannot expect all the problems of students to be cleared up within that time. Some of them may have persisted over six or seven years of the elementary grades, when these students were under the direction of teachers who were specifically trained to deal with instruction in reading and writing. Therefore, it is not reasonable to expect instant correction in the secondary class. In any case, the objective in instruction is not perfection in either reading or writing skill. Rather, the objective for the student is to attain enough proficiency at the skill in question to become functional with it.

The teacher working with dysfunctional students must be primarily concerned with their cognitive responses because, once they are in and by the secondary years, they have little time left. Students must learn the skills. However, a teacher who is deeply concerned about his students' real needs may run the risk of so loading his program with skill-developing activities and drills that the program becomes tedious, dull, and generally unmotivating to his students. Although cognitive responses are paramount in importance, affective responses cannot be ignored.

To some extent, students are rewarded as they see their skills improve, but such results are often visible only over long stretches of time. Although student-kept progress charts will help them to see long-term growth, the teacher must be always alert to short-term procedures that will evoke positive affective responses. Some useful procedures have been indicated: games, copious praise, and a choice of composition topics related to adolescent interest (planning parties, baseball, science fiction, fantasy). If the students are functional readers, the reading program can center on highly interesting stories. Movies should be used as often as possible. Field trips add excitement and interest to the program. Briefly, whenever possible, the teacher should use activities that will help the students to *like* the class.

The teacher must always be conscious, however, that interesting activities do not in themselves result in cognitive learning but rather promote a generally good atmosphere for that learning.

Recently, it has become faddish for teachers of ghetto students to exploit the poorly spelled and punctuated writing of their students to show that they have been able to motivate these students to write. The writing of such students, however, is not really dysfunctional; it can be understood with little trouble on the part of the reader. Yet these teachers give the impression that to teach writing one must merely motivate: let students write about the things that are really important to them, that they feel strongly about. The incoherent writing of dysfunctional writers is interesting, but pathetically interesting, *because of its defects.* The same passages made coherent and correctly spelled, although expressing the same ideas and emotions, would not excite the same attention. Certainly such motivational techniques must be part of the teacher's repertoire, and he must capitalize on whatever is honest and striking in his students' writing. But he also has the ultimate responsibility of helping his students to learn the skills that will allow their writing to stand on its own merit and not simply as an example of what a potential dropout can do when motivated. Writing characterized by gross errors might be acceptable to school teachers who are sympathetic to the writer. But outside of school such writing, no matter how expressive, is not likely to have a sympathetic audience. On the contrary, it might simply support undesirable stereotypes.

NOTES

1. Grace Fernald, *Remedial Techniques in Basic School Subjects* (McGraw-Hill Book Co., 1943).
2. *Ibid.*
3. Bernard J. McCabe, "Teaching Composition to Pupils of Low Academic Ability," *Classroom Practices in Teaching English—'65–'66* (Champaign: National Council of Teachers of English, 1965).

SUGGESTIONS FOR FURTHER READING

Although dysfunctional writers may not be physiologically disordered, the insights offered by teachers of aphasics are useful to the classroom teacher. The following books are especially practical.

1. AGRANOWITZ, ALEEN, and MILFRED RIDDLE MCKEOWN. *Aphasia Handbook for Adults and Children.* Springfield, Ill.: C. C. Thomas, 1964.
2. GRANICH, LOUIS. *A Guide to Retraining.* New York: Grune and Stratton, 1947.

Because information about and approaches to teaching non-English speakers must differ as their native languages differ, no one source will suffice for all the possible teaching problems. However, the two following offer suggestions and leads to appropriate materials:

1. J. VERNON JENSON. *Research on Childhood Bilingualism and Procedures to Follow in Educating the Bilingual Child.* Champaign, Ill.: National Council of Teachers of English, 1963.
2. Center for Applied Linguistics. *Reference List of Materials for English as a Second Language.* Available from Champaign, Illinois NCTE (Stock No. 12701).

The following sources give a general background in social and regional dialects, and implications for teaching:

1. EVERTTS, ELDONNA L., ed. *Dimensions of Dialect.* Champaign: NCTE, 1965.
2. SHUY, ROGER W. *Discovering American Dialects.* Champain: NCTE, 1964.

A Note on the Type

The text of this book was set on the Linotype in a face called TIMES ROMAN, designed by Stanley Morison for the Times (London), and first introduced by that newspaper in 1932.

Among typographers and designers of the twentieth century, Stanley Morison has been a strong forming influence, as typographical advisor to the English Monotype Corporation, as a director of two distinguished English publishing houses, and as a writer of sensibility, erudition, and keen practical sense.